LLEBG	Local Law Enforcement Block Grants	OJJDP	Office of Juvenile Justice and Delinquency Prevention	QUOD	Quantified Organizational Decision Making
MBO	Management By Objective	OJP	Office of Justice Programs	RBT	Reality-Based Training
MBWA	Management By Walking Around	OJT	On-the-Job Training	RCPI	Regional Community Policing Institute
MIS	Management Information System	ORM	Operational Risk Management	RISS	Regional Intelligence Sharing System
MMPI	Minnesota Multiphasic Personality Inventory	OVC	Office for Victims of Crime	RMS	Records Management System
MPFS	Mandatory Physical Fitness Standards	PDA	Personal Digital Assistant	ROI	Return On Investment
MPO	Master Patrol Officer	PDM	Participatory Decision Making	SAC	Special Agent in Charge
NAFTO	National Association of Field Training Officers	PERF	Police Executive Research Forum (Foundation)	SBC	Suicide By Cop
NAPO	National Association of Police Organizations	PFI	Police Futurists International	SCA	Sudden Cardiac Arrest
NASA	National Aeronautics and Space Administration	PIO	Public Information Officer	SHARK	Skim, Highlight, Assess, Reread, Keep
NCJOSI	National Criminal Justice Officer Selection Inventory	PMO	Police Motorcycle Officer	SHSG	State Homeland Security Grant
NCJRS	National Criminal Justice Reference Service	POP	Problem-Oriented Policing	SMILE	Stress Management In Law Enforcement
NCLB	No Child Left Behind	POST	Peace Officer Standards and Training	SRO	School Resource Officer
NGT	Nominal Group Technique	PPBS	Planning-Programming-Budgeting System	TQM	Total Quality Management
NIJ	National Institute of Justice	PSOEA	Public Safety Officer's Educational Assistance (Program)	TSC	Terrorist Screening Center
NIMS	National Incident Management System	PTSD	Posttraumatic Stress Disorder	UASI	Urban Area Security Initiative
NLRB	National Labor Relations Board	PWC	Personal Watercraft	UCR	Uniform Crime Reports
OCFAF	Open Case Fired Ammunition Files	Q & A	Question and Answer	UDT	Unarmed Defensive Tactics
		QID	Qualified Individual with a Disability	USERRA	Uniformed Services Employment and Reemployment Rights Act
OIC	Office for Interoperability and Compatibility	QUID	Quantified Interpersonal Decision Making	VIPS	Volunteers In Police Service
				ZBB	Zero-Based Budgeting

Management and Supervision in Law Enforcement

Fifth Edition

Wayne W. Bennett, LL.B.
Former Chief of Police
Boulder City, Nevada, and
Edina, Minnesota

Kären M. Hess, Ph.D.
President, Institute for Professional Development
Instructor, Normandale Community College
Bloomington, Minnesota

with contributions by Christine Hess Orthmann, M.S.

THOMSON ™
WADSWORTH

Australia • Brazil • Canada • Mexico • Singapore
Spain • United Kingdom • United States

THOMSON

WADSWORTH

Management and Supervision in Law Enforcement, Fifth Edition
Wayne W. Bennett and Kären M. Hess

Acquisitions Editor: *Carolyn Henderson Meier*
Assistant Editor: *Rebecca Johnson*
Technology Project Manager: *Amanda Kaufmann*
Marketing Manager: *Terra Schultz*
Marketing Assistant: *Jaren Boland*
Marketing Communications Manager: *Tami Strang*
Project Manager, Editorial Production: *Matt Ballantyne*
Creative Director: *Rob Hugel*
Art Director: *Vernon Boes*

Print Buyer: *Rebecca Cross*
Permissions Editor: *Joohee Lee*
Production Service: *Graphic World Inc.*
Photo Researcher: *Terri Wright*
Copy Editor: *Graphic World Inc.*
Cover Designer: *Yvo*
Cover Image: *©IndexStock/Stewart Cohen*
Compositor: *Graphic World Inc.*
Text and Cover Printer: *Transcontinental Printing*

Printed in Canada

2 3 4 5 6 7   10 09 08 07

Library of Congress Control Number: 2006932069

ISBN13: 978-0-495-09341-1
ISBN10: 0-495-09341-6

Wadsworth/Thomson Learning
10 Davis Drive
Belmont, CA 94002-3098
USA

For more information about our products,
contact us at:
Thomson Learning Academic Resource Center
1-800-423-0563
For permission to use material from this text or product,
submit a request online at **http://www.thomsonrights.com.**
Any additional questions about permissions can be
submitted by e-mail to **thomsonrights@thomson.com.**

Brief Contents

Contents

SECTION II

 BASIC MANAGEMENT/PERSONAL SKILLS

SECTION III

 MANAGERS AND THE SKILLS OF OTHERS

SECTION IV

 MANAGING PROBLEMS

SECTION V

 GETTING THE JOB DONE . . . THROUGH OTHERS

Preface

Welcome to the fifth edition of *Management and Supervision in Law Enforcement.* Based on feedback from students and instructors, we have made several changes in this edition, but we have retained our focus on writing a reader-friendly text that provides a comprehensive, up-to-date overview of management and supervision in law enforcement, blending theory and practice. The content applies to agencies of all sizes at all levels: local, county, state and federal.

Key Themes

Although significant changes have been made, three themes continue from previous editions. First, managers and supervisors need to move from an authoritative style to a participative leadership style—empowering all personnel to become contributing team members. Second, community policing and problem solving are key to preserving the peace and fighting crime. Citizens can become allies in both. Law enforcement cannot go it alone any longer. How community policing and problem solving affect management is illustrated throughout the text.

Third, change must be viewed as an opportunity rather than a threat. Not only must managers help their people grow and develop, but also they must continuously grow and develop, looking for new and better ways to accomplish their mission. As futurist Alvin Toffler asserts: "The illiterate of the 21st century will not be those who cannot read and write, but those who cannot learn, unlearn and relearn." This text is a beginning toward opening your mind to new ways of thinking and doing.

Organization of the Text

Section I, Management and Supervision: An Overview, takes a broad look at management, beginning with the law enforcement organization itself and the challenges this organization presents (Chapter 1). Next the role of the manager and the various levels of management and leadership in law enforcement are discussed, including the challenge of participatory management (Chapter 2). The section concludes with an in-depth look at community policing and how it affects management (Chapter 3).

Section II, Basic Management/Personal Skills, focuses on basic skills that affect everything done by law enforcement managers at all levels. A critical basic skill that can make or break a law enforcement manager is skill in communication. Effective communication is at the core of effective management (Chapter 4). The manager's role, by definition, includes decision making and problem solving (Chapter 5). How decisions are made and by whom are vital management questions. Among the most important decisions are those involving how time will be spent—the time of individual managers, officers and the agency as a whole (Chapter 6).

Section III, Managers and the Skills of Others, focuses on how managers can develop the numerous talents of their subordinates through participatory leadership. It first explains the importance of training (Chapter 7) and then suggests ways managers can go beyond training to fully develop the potential of all personnel (Chapter 8). Managers must not only build on the strengths of their people and accommodate their weaknesses but also motivate their officers to be as effective as possible. Research has shown that tangible rewards such as pay raises and fringe benefits are not necessarily the most successful motivators. In fact, they are often taken for granted, making managing much more challenging. Managers who can develop and motivate their team members will make a tremendous contribution to the department and to the accomplishment of its goals, objectives and mission. In addition, many concepts basic to motivation are directly related to keeping morale high. Attending to employees' motivation and morale is critical to being an effective manager (Chapter 9).

Section IV, Managing Problems, discusses difficulties to be anticipated in any law enforcement organization. They are an inevitable part of the challenge of accomplishing work through others. Managers must recognize problem behaviors and use an appropriate combination of constructive criticism, discipline and incentives to correct the problems (Chapter 10). In addition, supervisors and managers will be faced with numerous complaints and grievances from their subordinates, their superiors and the public they serve. They or their officers may, in fact, be the objects of civil lawsuits. Effectively handling such matters requires great knowledge as well as skilled communication. Conflicts, disagreements, differences of opinions and outright confrontations may also occur and must be dealt with diplomatically by law enforcement managers (Chapter 11). Finally, all the preceding, plus the challenges inherent in law enforcement work itself, can result in extreme stress for supervisors, managers and subordinates. Reducing such stress and the hazards related to it are critical tasks for administrators (Chapter 12).

Section V, Getting the Job Done . . . Through Others, focuses on meeting responsibilities through effective leadership. People would rather be led than managed. Personnel must be effectively deployed and their productivity enhanced (Chapter 13). Other important decisions involve how resources other than time can be most effectively managed—that is, the ongoing task of budgeting, which has a direct effect on what individual managers, their officers and ultimately the agency can accomplish (Chapter 14). The section then discusses the selection process and dealing with unions (Chapter 15). A final management responsibility is evaluating the efforts of the officers, managers and the entire department. Evaluation should be continuous and should include both formal and informal evaluation. The results should be used to help employees continue to grow and develop and to make the department more effective as well (Chapter 16). The section concludes with a discussion of the need for managers to be forward looking, considering what the future of law enforcement and the entire criminal justice system may hold (Chapter 17).

New to This Edition

- The chapters on financial management (Chapter 6 in the previous edition) and on hiring and labor relations (Chapter 7 in the previous edition) have been moved to the last section on the text in response to reviewers' comments.
- A new chapter on community policing has been added (Chapter 3).
- "Challenges" at the end of each chapter challenge the reader to react to real-life scenarios.
- The entire text has been completely updated, with over 600 references from 2003 or later. The impact of the 9/11 attack on America in many areas of management and supervision is included.

- A mini-index of areas of civil liability managers face in performing their roles is included.

Among the numerous additions to this edition are the following:

- Chapter 1, The Law Enforcement Organization—unified command and incident command; the effect of Prohibition on the evolution of law enforcement; more in-depth coverage of August Vollmer and O.W. Wilson; the blue ribbon commissions of the 1960s and 1980s; the Omnibus Crime Control and Safe Streets Act; the Equal Employment Opportunity Act; challenges to the professional model; current models of policing; and the influence of technology on management and the law enforcement organization.
- Chapter 2, The Role of Management and Leadership in Law Enforcement—dispersed leadership and the International Association of Chiefs of Police Leadership Development Model; expanded discussion of delegation; leading from the front; the 2003 National Institute of Justice study on how management style influences patrol officer performance; the influence of politics on law enforcement management, including being political without playing politics; common-sense leadership; 20 fundamentals of leadership; Colin Powell's rules for leadership; and the importance of multiagency teams.
- Chapter 3, Community Policing—new chapter in response to reviewers' request and the changing face of law enforcement; thorough discussion that progresses from the theoretical to the practical; definitions; goals; dimensions; understanding community; how citizens can be involved with law enforcement; the two critical components of partnerships and problem solving; implementing community policing and the changes required; analyzing the community; strategic planning; selecting and developing strategies; making time for partnerships and problem solving; challenges to implementing community policing; and the benefits that might be received.
- Chapter 4, Communication: A Critical Management Skill (previously Chapter 3)—types of written communication required of supervisors and managers; the hazards of e-mail; a new listening quiz; four key obstacles to sharing information, deconfliction, the National Criminal Intelligence Sharing Plan (NCISP), interoperability; expanded discussion of working with the media, including how to create sound bites, handling bad press, leaks and publicity as a means to prevent crime.
- Chapter 5, Decision Making and Problem Solving (previously Chapter 4)—the decision-making, problem-solving environment; data mining; operational risk management (ORM); the distinction between problem solving and problem-oriented policing; the six required elements of a problem in problem-oriented policing; potential sources of information for identifying problems; the problem-analysis triangle; using CompStat in problem solving; the magnet phenomenon; federal assistance in problem-solving efforts; the problem-solving process and evaluation; qualitative and quantitative data; process and impact evaluation; handling a call versus solving a problem; creative approaches to problem solving.
- Chapter 6, Time Management: Minute by Minute (previously Chapter 5)—leveraging time; putting first things first.
- Chapter 7, Training and Beyond (previously Chapter 8)—civil liability; keys to avoiding civil liability related to training; civil liability for injuries sustained

during training; four generations of officers and how they influence training needs; the learning curve; ineffective and unsafe teaching styles and practices; digital game-based learning; four modes of policing and core competencies; training, community policing and terrorism; the Firefighter's Rule; the Institute for Operational Readiness and Continuous Education in Security.

- Chapter 8, Promoting Growth and Development (previously Chapter 9)—unconditional backup; grooming standards; *Whren v. United States* and pretext stops; racial profiling after 9/11; behavior pattern recognition; the FBI's Terrorist Screening Center (TSC); the US-VISIT program; results of the *Police-Public Contacts Survey 2002*; developing "career currency."

- Chapter 9, Motivation and Morale (previously Chapter 10)—the Hawthorne Effect; McDonald's Rule of Four; the effect of officer resignations.

- Chapter 10, Discipline and Problem Behaviors (previously Chapter 11)—decoupling; general orders; passive resistance; abuse of sick leave; force continuums; change from Early Warning Systems (EWS) to Early Intervention Systems (EIS); five guiding principles of EIS; expanded discussion of sexual harassment and possible forms of retaliation for officers who complain of being harassed.

- Chapter 11, Complaints, Grievances and Conflict (previously Chapters 12 and 13)—potential benefits of mediation; disability discrimination; intergenerational diversity in the workplace; reframing.

- Chapter 12, Stress and Related Hazards of the Job (previously Chapter 14)—the split-second syndrome; negative effects of caffeine; stressors of rural and small-town patrol officers; expanded discussion of stress caused by administration; expanded discussion of the effects of stress, including alcohol and substance abuse, domestic abuse, divorce, and depression and suicide; stress-exposure management training; programs to reduce stress in the police family.

- Chapter 13, Deploying Law Enforcement Resources and Improving Productivity (previously Chapter 15)—the organizational contradiction of patrol officers being the backbone of the department but having the least status and lowest pay; take-home patrol car programs; Segway patrol; expanded discussion of emergencies, including lessons learned from Hurricanes Katrina and Rita; mapping crime; geographic information systems (GIS); CompStat; the criminal event perspective; mutual-aid agreements; deploying personnel for homeland security, including an expanded discussion of the Department of Homeland Security (DHS); the five-level, color-coded security system; renewal of the USA PATRIOT Act; the critical role of local law enforcement; collaboration with private security; best practices, terrorism and crime; intelligence-led policing.

- Chapter 14, Budgeting and Managing Costs Creatively (previously Chapter 6)—communication and budget support; determining personnel costs; importance of facts and emotions (winning minds and hearts) when making budget presentations; expanded discussion of asset forfeiture, appropriateness of donations to law enforcement agencies; Department of Homeland Security grants; No Child Left Behind grants.

- Chapter 15, Hiring Personnel and Dealing with Unions (previously Chapter 7)—the shrinking applicant pool; use of illegal drugs and smoking policies; bachelor of arts versus bachelor of science degree; expanded discussion of the Americans with Disabilities Act; expanded discussion of the Fair Labor

Standards Act and its provisions on overtime, comp time and covered activities; expanded discussion of collective bargaining to cover key clauses in the contract and midterm bargaining.

- Chapter 16, Measuring Performance: Assessment and Evaluation (retitled)— inspections; quotas; mandatory physical fitness standards and legal liability; internal surveys; evaluating integrity; cybernetics; PER Center for Survey Research; the need for practical research that can be applied now.

- Chapter 17, Challenges in Managing for the Future—current and emerging trends in law enforcement; issues facing law enforcement; wearable computers; augmented reality; development of eXtensive Markup Language (XML); further expanded discussion of homeland security; fusion centers, the Futures Working Group; distributed intelligence; resistance to change; the change-capable organization; long-term change.

Learning Aids

Management and Supervision in Law Enforcement, fifth edition, is a planned learning experience. It uses triple-strength learning, presenting all key concepts at least three times within a chapter. The more actively you participate, the better your learning will be. You will learn and remember more if you first familiarize yourself with the total scope of the subject. Read and think about the table of contents; it provides an outline of the many facets of law enforcement management and supervision. Then follow these steps as you study each chapter.

1. Read the objectives at the beginning of the chapter. These are stated as "Do you Know?" questions. Assess your current knowledge of each question. Examine any preconceptions you may hold.
2. Read the list of key terms and think about their possible meanings.
3. Read the chapter, underlining, highlighting or taking notes if that is your preferred study style. Pay special attention to all information that is highlighted. Also pay special attention to all words in bold print—these are the key terms for the chapter.
4. When you have finished reading the chapter, reread the "Do You Know?" questions to make sure you can give an educated response to each. If you find yourself stumped by one, find the appropriate section in the chapter and review it. Also define each key term. Again, if you find yourself stumped, either find the term in the chapter or look it up in the glossary.
5. Read the discussion questions and be prepared to contribute to a class discussion of the ideas presented in the chapter.
6. Periodically review the "Do You Know?" questions, key terms and chapter summaries.

By following these steps, you will learn more, understand better and remember longer.

Note: The material selected to highlight using the triple-strength learning instructional design includes only the chapter's key concepts. While this information is certainly important because it provides a structural foundation for understanding the topics discussed, you cannot simply glance over the "Do You Know?" questions, highlighted boxes and summaries and expect to master the chapter. You are also responsible for reading and understanding the material that surrounds these basics—the "meat" around the bones, so to speak.

Exploring Further

The text also provides an opportunity for you to apply what you have learned or to go into greater depth in specific areas through discussions, InfoTrac® College Edition assignments and Internet assignments. Complete each of these areas as directed by the text or by your instructor. Be prepared to share your findings with the class. Good learning!

Ancillaries

To further enhance your study of management and supervision, these supplements are available:

- Instructor's Manual—Completely revised and updated by Deborah Laufersweiler-Dwyer of the University of Alabama at Little Rock, the Instructor's Manual for the Fifth Edition includes learning objectives, a chapter outline, a chapter summary, key terms and definitions, classroom discussion questions, student activities, and suggested answers to the Challenge questions featured in the text for each chapter. Additionally, the test bank portion of the Instructor's Manual contains approximately 60 questions for each chapter in multiple choice, true/false, fill-in, and essay format.

- ExamView® Computerized Testing—Create, deliver and customize tests and study guides (both print and online) in minutes with this easy-to-use assessment and tutorial system. ExamView offers both a Quick Test Wizard and an Online Test Wizard that guide you step by step through the process of creating tests, while its WYSIWYG capability allows you to see the test you are creating on the screen exactly as it will print or display online. You can build tests of up to 250 questions using up to 12 question types. Using ExamView's complete word-processing capabilities, you can enter an unlimited number of new questions or edit existing questions.

Acknowledgments

We would like to thank Christine Hess Orthmann for her thorough research and writing for this new edition. We would also like to thank Tim Hess for his review of and contributions to the manuscript, Bobbi Peacock for her assistance on the photo program and Richard Gautsch for developing the Challenges for the text.

In addition, a heartfelt thanks to the reviewers of the past editions of the text and their valuable suggestions: Timothy Apolito, University of Dayton; Tom Barker, Jacksonville State University; A. J. Bartok, Regional Law Enforcement Academy, Colorado; Bill Bourns, California State University–Stanislaus; Lloyd Bratz, Cuyahoga Community College; Gib H. Bruns, Arizona State University; Michael Buckley, Texas A&M University; David Carter, Michigan State University; Dana Dewitt, Cadron State College; Bill Formby, University of Alabama–Tuscaloosa; Larry Gould, Northern Arizona University; Lori Guevara, University of Texas–Arlington; Joseph J. Hanrahan, Westfield State College; Robert G. Huckabee, Indiana State University; Alan Lawson, Ferris State University, Michigan; Muriel Lembright, Wichita State University; Stan Malm, University of Maryland; William McCamey, Western Illinois University; Robert L. Marsh, Boise State University; John Maxwell, Community College of Philadelphia; Robert G. May, Waubonsee Community College; Dennis M. Payne, Michigan State University; Carroll S. Price, Penn Valley

Community College; Lawrence G. Stephens, Columbus State Community College; W. Fred Wegener, Indiana University of Pennsylvania; Stanley W. Wisnoski, Jr., Broward Community College; and Solomon Zhao, University of Nebraska, Omaha.

We would like to thank the following reviewers for their insightful suggestions for this fifth edition: Chris Carmean, Houston Community College–Northeast; Samuel L. Dameron, Marshall University; Hank DiMatteo, New Mexico State University; and Joseph J. Hanrahan, Westfield State College. We are deeply indebted to them for their work. Any errors, however, are the sole responsibility of the authors.

Finally, a special thanks to our executive editor, Carolyn Henderson Meier; assistant editor, Rebecca Johnson; and project manager, Matt Ballantyne, at Thomson/Wadsworth; photo researchers Terri Wright and Austin MacRae at Terri Wright Design; and our production editor, Mike Ederer, at Graphic World Publishing Services.

About the Authors

The content of this text is based on the practical experience of the late Wayne W. Bennett, who spent 45 years in law enforcement and taught various aspects of management and supervision over 30 years, as well as the research and experience of Kären M. Hess, Ph.D., who has been developing instructional programs for over 30 years. The text itself has been reviewed by several experts in management and supervision in law enforcement. Any errors, however, are the sole responsibility of the authors.

Wayne W. Bennett (d. 2004) was a graduate of the FBI National Police Academy, held an LL.B. degree in law and served as the Director of Public Safety for the Edina (Minnesota) Police Department as well as Chief of Police of the Boulder City (Nevada) Police Department. He was also co-author of *Criminal Investigation*, Seventh Edition.

Kären M. Hess holds a Ph.D. in English from the University of Minnesota and a Ph.D. in criminal justice from Pacific Western University. Other Wadsworth texts Dr. Hess has co-authored are *Corrections in the 21st Century: A Practical Approach, Criminal Investigation* (Eighth Edition), *Criminal Procedure, Introduction to Law Enforcement and Criminal Justice* (Eighth Edition), *Introduction to Private Security* (Fourth Edition), *Juvenile Justice* (Third Edition), *Community Policing: Partnerships for Problem Solving* (Third Edition), *Police Operations* (Fourth Edition), and *Careers in Criminal Justice and Related Fields: From Internship to Promotion* (Fifth Edition).

Dr. Hess is a member of the Academy of Criminal Justice Sciences (ACJS), the American Society for Law Enforcement Trainers (ASLET), the International Association of Chiefs of Police (IACP), the Police Executive Research Forum (PERF) and the Text and Academic Author's Association (TAA), in which she is a fellow.

CHAPTER 1

The Law Enforcement Organization

Good organizations are living bodies that grow new muscles to meet challenges.

Robert Townsend, corporate consultant

Do You Know?

- How law enforcement agencies were traditionally organized?
- What three eras of policing have been identified?
- What should drive an organization?
- How goals differ from objectives and work plans? From policies and procedures?
- What line and staff personnel are?
- What advantages and disadvantages are associated with specialization?
- What the chain of command does?
- What authority should be coupled with?
- What type of organization law enforcement managers should recognize?
- What management tools help coordination?
- What the emerging law enforcement agency looks like?
- What needs to be reexamined in light of the challenges facing law enforcement and our country?

Can You Define?

accountability	empowered	line personnel	responsibility
administrative	field services	mission	scuttlebutt
services	flat organization	mission statement	span of control
authority	formal organization	objectives	specialists
bifurcated society	generalists	organization	spoils system
chain of command	goals	organizational chart	staff personnel
channels of	guiding philosophy	paradigm	stakeholders
communication	hierarchy	paradigm shift	unified command
community era	incident command	political era	unity of command
coordination	informal	professional model	values
decentralization	organization	pyramid of authority	work plans
delegation	key result areas	reform era	

Introduction

An **organization** is an artificial structure created to coordinate either people or groups and resources to achieve a mission or goal. Organizations exist for many different reasons. One important reason is that a group can accomplish things an individual could never do alone. For example, no single individual could have put a person on the moon, but an organization—NASA—was successful.

The need for organizing has been recognized for centuries. Since recorded time people have banded together into societies. Within these societies they have sought ways to protect themselves from nature and from those who would harm them or their possessions. They made rules, set up ways to enforce these rules, and provided swift punishment to those who did not obey. Modern-day law enforcement agencies are an outgrowth of this need for "law and order."

To understand the present, it is often helpful to look at the past—where traditions and the status quo originated. Therefore, this chapter begins with a brief history of the development of law enforcement agencies and the typical military, pyramid-style structure that evolved during the three eras of policing. This is followed by a description of the models of policing that have developed, individual influences on the development of police management, and the influence of technology on management and supervision.

The chapter next looks at the mission of law enforcement agencies and the functions they serve. The effect of this mission on an organization's goals, objectives, work plans, and policies and procedures is then described. Then the discussion focuses on the formal and informal organization within a department and the importance of coordination. The chapter concludes with a discussion of the emerging law enforcement organization and the importance of unified and incident command.

The Evolution of Law Enforcement Organizations

Most agencies have a rich tradition dating back to seventeenth-century England, when the Industrial Revolution changed that country from a rural to an urban society. Accompanying this urbanization were the problems of unemployment, poverty, and crime, conditions that ultimately led to the formation of the London Metropolitan Police in 1829. The fundamental principles on which this police force rested were set forth by Sir Robert Peel, often called the "Father of Modern Policing," and included the following:

- Police must be stable, efficient, and organized militarily.
- Police must be under governmental control.
- The deployment of police strength by both time and area is essential.
- Public security demands that every police officer be given a number.
- Police headquarters should be centrally located and easily accessible.
- The duty of the police is to prevent crime and disorder.
- The power of the police to fulfill these duties is dependent on public approval and on their ability to secure and maintain public respect.
- The police should strive to maintain a relationship with the public that gives reality to the tradition that *the police are the public and the public are the police.*
- The test of police effectiveness is the absence of crime and disorder, not the visible evidence of police activity in dealing with these problems.

The first five principles were embraced almost immediately in the United States, and its cities developed police departments modeled after the London Metropolitan Police. The last four principles, however, were not fully accepted until the advent of community policing, discussed in Chapter 3.

New York City established the first modern American city police force in 1844, modeled after London's Metropolitan Police Department.

In 1874 the Texas Rangers were commissioned as police officers and became the first agency similar to our present-day state police. Federal agencies were also established; the Federal Bureau of Investigation (FBI) was created in 1908. In addition to these, many jurisdictions established county law enforcement agencies. These early organizations were modeled after the military, with ranks, levels of command, and uniforms. Just as the military has a commander in chief, law enforcement agencies also have chiefs (or sheriffs). Likewise, just as the commander in chief is ultimately responsible to the citizens of the United States, law enforcement chiefs are ultimately responsible to the citizens of the political entity their department serves.

© Bettmann/CORBIS

New York City police officers pose in front of the 20th Precinct Station during the 1880s.

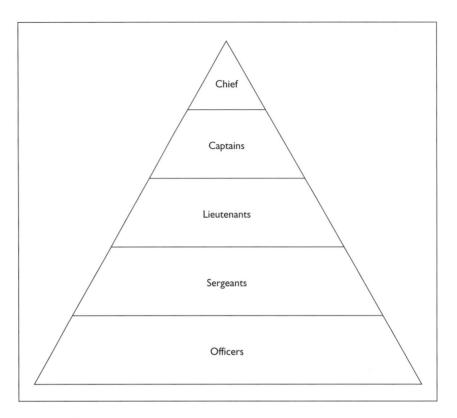

Figure 1.1   The Pyramid of Authority—Organizational Hierarchy

The Traditional Law Enforcement Organization

 The traditional law enforcement organizational design is that of a pyramid-shaped hierarchy based on a military model.

Law enforcement agencies provide their services to the political entity from which they derive their authority and responsibility. Providing services is their sole reason for existence. It is highly likely that newly created municipalities would expect *someone* to respond to their needs for the many services provided by police. Americans have come to expect and demand reasonably safe communities, so they demand law enforcement organizations. As such organizations develop, they resemble those already in existence in other communities because tradition and experience are enduring.

Further, most present-day law enforcement managers inherited their organizations when they assumed their positions. Many have perpetuated the traditional organization, diagrammed in Figure 1.1, because it has worked.

Pre–World War II law enforcement agencies followed the industry pattern by placing maximum emphasis on the job and minimum attention on the human interrelationships of people filling the positions. Rigid rules and regulations were used excessively, along with frequent use and abuse of the threat of job loss. Individual needs were almost totally ignored. Early law enforcement management was characterized by the general attitude of, "If you don't like the job, plenty of others want it."

Law enforcement organizations were simple. The typical **pyramid of authority** predominated with its **hierarchy** of authoritative management. Command officers and supervisors had complete authority over subordinates, and there was little opportunity for departmental appeal except through the courts. Communication flowed downward. Little or no specialization existed, and training was nonexistent or minimal. Selection was based largely on physical qualifications, and most applicants had military experience.

The majority of personnel were assigned to foot patrol. Police radio communications systems and other technology were virtually nonexistent. University- or college-level training, training programs, and even courses were unheard of. Ten-hour days and six-day weeks were common, accompanied by extremely low salaries. Flexibility was nonexistent, and fringe benefits were few.

The Three Eras of Policing

Policing has evolved in the way it views itself, its responsibilities, and the most effective means of meeting those responsibilities. Some writers look at the changes by decade. Kelling (2003), for example, describes scientific policing of the 1930s, consolidation of reforms from 1940 to 1960, shocks and change during the 1960s, the implementation of research during the 1970s and 1980s, and contemporary policing. Another way to view the evolution of policing is to consider three distinct eras.

 Three distinct eras of policing have been identified: the political era, the reform era and the community era.

The Political Era (1840–1930)

In the **political era**, policing was characterized by police authority coming from politicians and the law, a broad social service function, decentralized organization, an intimate relationship with the community, and extensive use of foot patrol. Because of the close tie between police authority and politics during this era, corruption was common. One factor underlying this corruption was the prevalent **spoils system**, whose motto, "To the victor go the spoils," resulted in political interference with policing. The prevailing party believed its members should be immune from arrest and receive other special privileges. Furthermore, the spoils system enabled politicians to give their friends key positions in police departments. A major step toward reducing corruption within police departments occurred when, in 1883, Congress passed the Pendleton Act, creating the civil service system by which job applicants were tested and awarded employment based on their test scores. Promotions were to be based on merit, not politics. The act also made it unlawful to fire or demote a government employee for political reasons.

During the political era police served a broad social service function, with some even running soup lines. Police were also close to their community, with foot patrol bringing beat officers into contact with the people. However, Prohibition changed this relationship.

Prohibition The Prohibition movement (1920–1933) resulted from passage of the Eighteenth Amendment in 1919; this amendment outlawed the manufacture, sale, or transportation, including importing and exporting, of intoxicating liquor

pyramid of authority • the shape of the typical law enforcement hierarchy, with the chief at the peak and having full authority, down through managers (captains and lieutenants) and supervisors (sergeants), to those who accomplish most of the tasks (officers).

hierarchy • a group of people organized or classified by rank and authority. In law enforcement, typically pyramid shaped with a single "authority" at the top expanding down and out through the ranks to the broad base of "workers."

political era • characterized by police authority coming from politicians and the law, a broad social service function, decentralized organization, an intimate relationship with the community, and extensive use of foot patrol.

spoils system • motto, "To the victor go the spoils," resulted in political interference with policing.

beverages within the United States and its territories. Prohibition placed the police organization in opposition to large segments of respectable citizens in their communities. The enforcement of Prohibition laws created hostility toward the police and made contacts between the police and the public increasingly adversarial.

Prohibition ended in 1933 with ratification of the Twenty-First Amendment repealing the Eighteenth Amendment. The inability of the police to control consumption of alcoholic beverages might be likened to the contemporary challenge of controlling use of illegal drugs. The rise of crime during this period resulted in the formation of the Wickersham Commission.

The Wickersham Commission In 1929 President Herbert Hoover appointed the National Commission on Law Observance and Enforcement to examine the American criminal justice system. The commission, named after chairman George Wickersham, devoted two reports to the police. Report 11, *Lawlessness in Law Enforcement*, described the problem of police brutality, concluding that "the third degree—the inflicting of pain, physical or mental, to extract confessions or statements—is extensively practiced." Report 14, *The Police*, focused on police administration and called for expert leadership, centralized administrative control, and higher personnel standards. In other words, Report 14 called for police professionalism, which led to the second era.

The Reform Era (1930–1980)

reform era • characterized by police authority coming from the law and professionalism, crime control as the primary function, a centralized and efficient organization, a professional remoteness from the community and an emphasis on preventive motorized patrol and rapid response to crime.

The reform era developed in reaction to the political era. The **reform era** was characterized by police authority coming from the law and professionalism, crime control as the primary function, a centralized and efficient organization, a professional remoteness from the community, and an emphasis on preventive motorized patrol and rapid response to crime. J. Edgar Hoover (1895–1972) was director of the FBI from 1924 to 1972 and placed the agency's emphasis on catching criminals.

As early as the 1920s, August Vollmer, often called the father or dean of modern police administration, was calling for reforms in policing. Vollmer was first town marshal and then police chief for Berkeley, California, from 1905 until 1932. Vollmer introduced the latest advancements in criminalistics, the first juvenile unit, and psychological screening for police applicants and was first to emphasize the importance of college education for police officers.

His department was the first in the nation to use automobiles for patrol and the first to hire a full-time forensic scientist. Vollmer developed the first degree-granting program in law enforcement at San Jose State College. He also advocated that police officers serve as social service workers and that police act to prevent crime by intervening in the lives of potential criminals, especially juveniles.

During the 1930s use of the radio and motorized patrol and the collection of crime statistics through the FBI's Uniform Crime Reports added to the professionalism of the police. As stated by the National Commission of Law Observance and Enforcement (1931): "With the advent of the radio-equipped car a new era has come."

professional model • crime control as the primary function, a centralized and efficient organization, a professional remoteness from the community and an emphasis on preventive motorized patrol and rapid response to crime.

A Vollmer protégé, O. W. Wilson, became the main architect of this new era and the style of policing known as the **professional model**. Wilson accepted a professorship at the University of California, Berkeley, and in 1947 he founded the first professional school of criminology. Like his mentor, Wilson advocated efficiency within the police bureaucracy through scientific techniques. He became police chief in Wichita, Kansas, and conducted the first systematic study of the effectiveness of using one-officer squad cars. Wilson's classic text, *Police Administration*, set forth specific ways to use one-officer patrol cars to deploy personnel and to discipline officers.

Wilson (1950, pp.17–18) decried political influence on the police: "When the police department is controlled by the machine, political influence begins with the appointment of the recruit, rallies to save him from discipline, helps him to secure unearned wages or disability benefits, grants him unusual leaves of absence, secures an unwarranted promotion for him, or gives him a soft job. In countless ways the creeping paralysis of political favoritism spreads and fastens itself upon the force to sap its vitality and destroy its morale for the benefit of the party, at the expense of both the public and of the police force itself."

Wilson (p.388) also called for cooperation with the public: "Public cooperation is essential to the successful accomplishment of the police purpose. Public support assists in many ways; it is necessary in the enforcement of major laws as well as of minor regulations, and with it arrests are made and convictions obtained that otherwise would not be possible."

The reformers sought to disassociate policing from politics. They were to become professionals whose charge was to enforce the law, fairly and impartially. The social service function became of lesser importance or even nonexistent in some departments as police mounted an all-out war on crime. Two keys to this war were preventive patrol in automobiles and rapid response to calls. This is the style of policing with which most Americans are familiar and have come to expect.

Unfortunately, the war on crime was being lost. Crime escalated, and other problems arose as well. In the 1960s violent ghetto riots, most triggered by incidents in which white officers were policing in black ghetto areas, caused millions of dollars in damages, thousands of injuries, and many deaths. In addition, civil rights and anti–Vietnam War demonstrations and riots began to pit the police against middle- and upper-class Americans, similar to the situation during Prohibition. During these confrontations police often used force—sometimes excessive—and became viewed as an armed force who maintained order at the expense of justice.

Kerlikowske (2004, p.7) points out:

> "The [professional] model was neat and orderly, especially internally, and completely unprepared to deal with the social change, upheaval and the overwhelming demographic challenge of the 1960s. The thin blue line that had won wars abroad could not win peace or even calm in the neighborhoods wracked by exploding crime rates and deep social unrest. Forgotten in the professional model was the familiarity that existed between officers and the community in the earlier era, when residents saw officers as neighborhood problem solvers and when their efforts attracted some level of community support. Instead, professional officers were viewed as an occupying army."

As a result, several blue-ribbon commissions were established.

Blue-Ribbon Commissions Kelling (p.14) describes five national commissions that resulted from the turmoil in U.S. cities and controversy surrounding police practices in the 1960s and early 1970s:

- The President's Commission on Law Enforcement and Administration of Justice, which published its reports in 1967 and 1968, was influenced by urban racial turmoil. Among the outgrowths of its work were the Safe Streets Act of 1968 and the Law Enforcement Assistance Administration, which provided significant funding for police-related programs.

- The National Advisory Commission on Civil Disorders (popularly known as the Kerner Commission) was similarly inspired by riots and other disorders occurring in many U.S. cities during the summer of 1967. Its report (1968) examined patterns of disorder and prescribed responses by the federal government, the criminal justice system, and local governments. The comprehensive, scathing report placed much of the blame on racism in society and severe underrepresentation of blacks in police departments.

- The National Commission on the Causes and Prevention of Violence was established after the 1968 assassinations of Martin Luther King, Jr., and Robert Kennedy. Its report, *To Establish Justice, To Insure Domestic Tranquility*, was published in 1969.

- The President's Commission on Campus Unrest was established following student deaths related to protests at Kent State and Jackson State universities in 1970.

- The National Advisory Commission on Criminal Justice Standards and Goals issued six reports in 1973 in an attempt to develop standards and recommendations for police crime control efforts.

The National Institute of Justice (NIJ) The Omnibus Crime Control and Safe Streets Act (1968) established the National Institute of Justice as a research and development agency to prevent and reduce crime and to improve the criminal justice system. Among the institute's mandates were that it sponsor special projects and research and development programs to improve and strengthen the criminal justice system, conduct national demonstration projects that employed innovative or promising approaches for improving criminal justice, develop new technologies to fight crime and improve criminal justice, evaluate the effectiveness of criminal justice programs, and identify those that promised to be successful if continued or repeated.

The Equal Employment Opportunity Act Directly influencing police hiring practices was passage of the Equal Employment Opportunity Act (EEOA) in 1973. The Equal Employment Opportunity Act prohibits discrimination on the basis of sex, race, color, religion, or national origin in employment of any kind, public or private, local, state, or federal.

The effect of this act on police departments today is discussed in Chapter 15. Despite the commissions and legislation, reforms that had begun during the 1930s and thrived during the 1950s and 1960s began to erode during the 1970s. Once again the professional model began to be challenged.

Increasing Challenges to the Professional Model One event in 1972 had a great impact on eroding the reform strategy. The classic Kansas City Preventive Patrol Experiment called into question the effectiveness of preventive patrol and rapid response—the two central strategies of the reform era.

Other challenges facing the professional model include the breakdown of the family unit, the inability of "traditional" police approaches to decrease crime; the rapidly escalating drug problem; the pressing problems associated with the deinstitutionalization of thousands of mentally ill people, many of whom became homeless; and dealing with thousands of immigrants, some legal, some illegal, many speaking no English.

Table 1.1 The Three Eras of Policing

	Political Era 1840 to 1930	Reform Era 1930 to 1980	Community Era 1980 to Present
Authorization	Politicians and law	Law and professionalism	Community support (political), law, and professionalism
Function	Broad social services	Crime control	Broad provision of services
Organizational Design	Decentralized	Centralized, classical	Decentralized, task forces
Relationship to Community	Intimate	Professional, remote	Intimate
Tactics and Technology	Foot patrol	Preventive patrol and rapid response to calls	Foot patrol, problem solving, public relations
Outcome	Citizen, political satisfaction	Crime control	Quality of life and citizen satisfaction

Source: Linda S. Miller and Kären M. Hess. *Community Policing: Partnerships for Problem Solving,* 4th ed. Belmont, CA: West/Wadsworth Publishing, 2005, p.17. (Summarized from George L. Kelling and Mark H. Moore. "From Political to Reform to Community: The Evolving Strategy of Police." In *Community Policing: Rhetoric or Reality,* edited by Jack R. Green and Stephen D. Mastrofski. New York: Praeger Publishers, 1991, pp.6, 14–15, 22–23.)

Many began asserting that the police and the criminal justice system could not control crime and violence alone because they have no control over the factors contributing to crime such as inequality, poverty, lack of opportunity and the like. This realization made the time ripe for the current era, the community era.

The Community Era (1980–Present)

Following changes occurring in corporate America, many police departments became customer-oriented, viewing citizens as consumers of police services. Policing during the **community era** is characterized by police authority coming from community support, law, and professionalism; provision of a broad range of services, including crime control; decentralized organization with greater authority given to patrol officers; an intimate relationship with the community; and the use of foot patrol and a problem-solving approach.

Community policing is discussed in depth in Chapter 3 and throughout the remainder of the text, because it affects all aspects of the contemporary police organization and function in most departments throughout the country. Table 1.1 summarizes the distinguishing characteristics of the three eras of policing.

community era • characterized by police authority coming from community support, law, and professionalism; provision of a broad range of services, including crime control; decentralized organization with greater authority given to patrol officers; an intimate relationship with the community; and the use of foot patrol and a problem-solving approach.

Current Models of Policing

Sharp (2005, p.88) describes four models of policing that have evolved: professional (also known as paramilitary), community, CompStat, and a hybrid model. His study found that law enforcement agency administrators are constantly assessing the models in place in their jurisdictions and changing the model if they see a need. He reports that 51 percent had switched from one model to another recently. His survey did find "an escalating trend from traditional models to community policing."

Sharp (p.89) reports that of his respondents, 56 percent used the COP model, 26 percent used a hybrid model, 12 percent used the professional model and 6 percent used CompStat. According to Sharp (p.89), the model selected was not only based on the top administrator's preference but also was influenced by civilian administrators and rank-and-file preferences; the community's diversity; recommendations from professional organizations; the agency's history, mission, goals, and objectives; and the opinions of the citizens.

Sharp (p.97) stresses: "A resounding 84% of the respondents said they believe that the efficient delivery of customer service is more important than which model a police department operates under." Whichever model a department uses, other influences have also affected how policing has evolved.

Individual Influences on the Evolution of Police Management

Management principles evolving in the business world have directly influenced how police executives have managed their forces. Such changes have taken police management and leadership philosophies from a strict control approach to an approach that delegates increased responsibility to the line officer.

Max Weber

Max Weber (1864–1920), a German sociologist and economist, helped establish the foundations of modern sociology. He considered bureaucracy to be the most important feature of modern society. Weber believed that business was conducted from a desk or office by preparing and dispatching written documents through an elaborate hierarchical division of labor directed by explicit rules impersonally applied. These rules were meant to design and regulate the whole organization on the basis of technical knowledge with the aim of achieving maximum efficiency.

According to Weber: "Bureaucratic administration means fundamentally the exercise of control on the basis of knowledge" ("Bureaucracy," 2005). One of the most fundamental features of bureaucracy according to Weber was a highly developed division of labor and specialization of tasks. This was achieved by a precise, detailed definition of the duties and responsibilities of each position. Bureaucracy was (and is) important in the organization of police departments.

Frederick W. Taylor

Also influential and living in the same time period was Frederick W. Taylor (1865–1915), an American industrial engineer, sometimes referred to as the father of scientific management. Taylor suggested that production efficiency in a shop or factory could be greatly enhanced by observing individual workers and eliminating wasted time and motion. The impact of his time and motion studies on mass production was immense, but they fostered resentment and opposition from labor ("Taylor, Frederick W.," 2005).

Taylor's book *The Principles of Scientific Management* (1911) called for a small span of control, a clear chain of command, a tall organizational hierarchy, and centralized decision making modeled after the military. This method of management style became standard in police organizations during the reform era.

Peter Drucker

During the 1940s, American economist, management specialist, and consultant Peter Drucker (1909–2005) became influential, asserting that productivity was the result of self-starting, self-directed workers who accepted responsibility. He advocated a shift from traditional production lines to flexible production methods. Among his most quoted statements are the following:

- Efficiency is doing better what is already being done.
- There is nothing so useless as doing efficiently that which should not be done at all.
- Today knowledge has power. It controls access to opportunity and advancement.

- Management is doing things right; leadership is doing the right things.
- The individual is the central, rarest, most precious capital resource of our society.

Drucker's ideas were influential in the shift in management styles discussed in the next chapter.

The Influence of Technology on Management

As noted, the introduction of the police radio and motorized patrol revolutionized how policing was done. This was just the beginning. Consider establishment of the National Crime Information Center (1967), automated fingerprint systems, DNA analysis, computer-aided dispatch, computerized records management systems, bar codes in evidence rooms, digitized photographic lineups, CompStat—the list goes on and on. Most of the technologic advances have greatly improved the delivery of police services and helped managers and supervisors be more efficient, but they have also posed challenges as police administrators struggle to implement the latest technology with shrinking budgets.

As Cowper observes: "Policing is a human endeavor and people are the most important aspect of what we do. Human relationships and interactions are what solve problems between and among people, not technology" (Stephens, 2005, p.15). The impact of advances in technology, particularly information technology (IT), are described throughout the text.

Although police departments have changed substantially since their early beginnings in this country, from their very beginnings police departments have had a mission, stated or unstated.

The Law Enforcement Mission

Stephens (2003, p.33) contends: "Rather than beginning with externally mandated objectives and then figuring out how to achieve them, police executives are beginning with the question of mission." The primary purpose of most law enforcement agencies has become less clear over the past decades. Traditionally, as the name implies, the mission was to enforce the law, that is, to fight crime. In the twenty-first century, however, many departments have changed their focus to providing services while other departments seek a combination of the two. It is important for departments to clearly articulate their **mission** or overriding purpose in writing.

mission • the reason an organization exists.

mission statement • a written explanation of why an organization exists.

 A **mission statement** is the driving force of an organization, including a law enforcement agency, and provides a focus for its energy.

Mission statements articulate the rationale for an organization's existence. A mission statement can be the most powerful underlying influence in law enforcement, affecting organizational and individual attitudes, conduct, and performance. Mission statements are best developed by an appointed committee, representative of but not too large for individual participation. Developing the statement is only the first step. It must then be distributed, explained, understood, and accepted by all department members. A mission statement is not automatically implemented or effective. It must be practiced in everyday actions and decision making by management and field personnel.

stakeholders • those affected by an organization and those in a position to affect it.

The mission statement of a law enforcement agency should be believable, worthy of support, widely known, shared, and exciting to key stakeholders. **Stakeholders** are those *affected by* the organization and those in a position to *affect it*. In a law enforcement organization, stakeholders include everyone in the jurisdiction. Two key questions to answer are (1) what do the stakeholders *want*? and (2) what do the stakeholders *need*? What people want and what they need are *not* necessarily the same. Stakeholders should, however, have input into what is provided for them.

An example of an effective mission statement is that of the Charlotte (North Carolina) Police Department:

> The Charlotte Police Department is committed to fairness, compassion and excellence while providing police services in accordance with the law and sensitive to the priorities and needs of the people.

A mission statement such as this can both guide and drive an organization. Mission statements are usually part of an organization's overall guiding philosophy.

An Organization's Guiding Philosophy and Values

guiding philosophy • the organization's mission statement and the basic values honored by the organization.

values • the beliefs, principles or standards considered worthwhile or desirable.

A **guiding philosophy** consists of an organization's mission statement *and* its basic **values**, the beliefs, principles, or standards considered worthwhile or desirable. Consider, for example, the values set forth by the International Association of Chiefs of Police (IACP):*

> The members of IACP are committed to the values that are reflected in the association's constitution, member Code of Ethics and Strategic Plan. These include: A commitment to fair and impartial enforcement of laws and ordinances and respect for fundamental human rights.
>
> A commitment to advancing the principles of respect for individual dignity and respect for constitutional rights of all persons with whom their departments come into contact.
>
> A commitment to the highest ideals of honor and integrity to maintain the respect and confidence of their governmental officials, subordinates, the public and their fellow police executives.
>
> A dedication to innovative and participative management, at all times seeking to improve their departments, increase productivity and remain responsive to the needs of their jurisdiction.
>
> A commitment to friendly and courteous service by striving to improve communications with all members of the public, at all times seeking improvement in the quality and image of public service.
>
> A dedication to improve their personal knowledge and abilities and those of their colleagues through independent study, courses, meetings and seminars.
>
> A reverence for the value of human life and commitment to conduct themselves so as to maintain public confidence in their profession, the department and their performance of the public trust.

*Reprinted from *The Police Chief*, Vol. LXI, No. 11, November 1993, p.14. Copyright held by The International Association of Chiefs of Police, Inc., 515 N. Washington St., Alexandria, Virginia, 22314. Further reproduction without express written permission from IACP is strictly prohibited.

Some readers may be thinking that mission statements and value statements are fine, but that they are simply words. How do such words get translated into action?

Our Declaration of Independence was a statement of the guiding philosophy of our country, but it did not establish how the United States should be structured or governed. This was accomplished through our Constitution and Bill of Rights. A statement of philosophy is meaningless without a plan or blueprint for accomplishing it. Goals, objectives, work plans and policies and procedures provide this blueprint.

Goals, Objectives, Work Plans and Policies and Procedures

Goals, objectives and work plans are interdependent. All three are needed to carry out an organization's mission.

 Goals are broad, general, desired outcomes. **Objectives** are specific, measurable ways to accomplish the goals. **Work plans** are the precise activities that contribute to accomplishing objectives. Policies and procedures specify how the activities are to be carried out.

Goals

Goals are visionary, projected achievements. They provide guidelines for planning efforts. They are what in business would be called the **key result areas**. Goals provide the foundation for objectives and ultimately for work plans. Among the commonly agreed-upon goals of most law enforcement agencies are to enforce laws, prevent crime, preserve the peace, protect civil rights and civil liberties, provide services, and solve problems.

Few people would argue about the value of these goals. The disagreements arise over which are most important and how resources should be apportioned. For example, providing how much service and of what kind, compared with how much enforcing of laws? It is also often difficult to determine which objectives might accomplish the goals.

Objectives

Objectives are needed before work plans can be developed. They are much more specific than goals and usually have a timeline. Objectives are critical to planning, assigning tasks, and evaluating performance. For example, one objective might be to reduce traffic accidents by 20 percent by the end of the year.

Good objectives are clear and understandable, especially to those who will be responsible for carrying them out. They are also practical; that is, they are realistic and achievable. Personnel must have the knowledge, skill, and resources to accomplish their objectives. Effective objectives deal with important matters. They should motivate and energize each person to perform not only at a high level individually but also as a team member. Good objectives provide the basis for a department's work plans.

Work Plans

Work plans, sometimes called *tactical and strategic plans*, are the detailed steps needed to accomplish objectives. They are tied to a timeline and are an effective

goals • broad, general, desired outcomes; visionary, projected achievements. What business calls key result areas.

objectives • specific, measurable ways to accomplish goals. They are more specific than goals and usually have a timeline.

work plans • the precise activities that contribute to accomplishing objectives. Detailed steps or tasks to be accomplished.

key result areas • the goals of an organization.

way to evaluate an organization's performance. To accomplish the objective of reducing traffic accidents, a department might establish the following work plans (in January):

- Analyze where accidents are happening to determine their cause by July 1.
- Based on this analysis, take steps to correct identified problems by December 1.
- Conduct ten educational meetings regarding traffic safety for the public by June 1.
- Design and display five educational billboards regarding drinking and driving by April 1.

Policies and Procedures

Policies and procedures are usually contained in a manual distributed to all personnel within the department. Sharp (2004, p.75) contends that the true test of a policies and procedures manual is not how professional it looks but how up-to-date it is. He suggests that while such manuals may have been low priority in the past, that can no longer be the case: "Currently, they are the first thing that opposing counsel asks for when something bad happens." Sharp (p.74) suggests that the primary emphasis in the policies and procedures manuals should be on legal and liability issues.

In addition to addressing these issues, Delattre and Behan (2003, p.612) state that policies and procedures need to incorporate the values of the department: "To successfully incorporate worthwhile values into the policies and practices of their departments, police managers must simultaneously be both realists and idealists." Realistic idealism recognizes what is possible given the existing situation while aspiring to high principles and a worthwhile mission. The importance of policies and procedures is discussed further in Chapter 10.

After a law enforcement agency has determined its goals and objectives, developed work plans, and established policies and procedures, these must be put into action by people organized to do so.

The Formal Organization

The **formal organization** is put together by design and rational plan. The essential elements of a formal organization are:

- A clear statement of mission, goals, objectives, and values (as discussed previously).
- A division of labor among specialists.
- A rational organization or design.
- A hierarchy of authority and responsibility.

Typical Divisions in Law Enforcement Agencies

Law enforcement agencies typically are divided into field and administrative services, with personnel designated as line and staff personnel.

 Field services using **line personnel** *directly* help accomplish the goals of the department. **Administrative services** using **staff personnel** *support* the line organization.

Field services' main division is the uniformed patrol. Larger agencies may have other divisions as well, such as investigations, narcotics, vice and juvenile. Line personnel fulfill the goals and objectives of the organization. This is what most people think of as law enforcement—the uniformed police officer on the street.

formal organization • how a group of people is structured on paper, often in the form of an organizational chart.

field services • directly help accomplish the goals of the department using line personnel. Main division is uniformed patrol. Also includes investigations, narcotics, vice, juvenile and the like.

line personnel • those who actually perform most of the tasks outlined in the work plan.

administrative services • supports those performing field services. Includes recruitment and training, records and communication, planning and research and technical services.

staff personnel • those who support line personnel.

Field service divisions are typically further broken into shifts to provide service within a framework of geographical space and extended time. Continuity of service must be provided between areas and shifts. Larger departments may divide the political entity they serve into distinct *precincts* or *district stations*, the geographical areas served by a given portion of the officers, essentially forming a number of smaller organizations subject to overall administration and operational command. Time is typically divided into three eight-hour shifts so that service can be provided continuously. Officers frequently rotate through these shifts. Personnel assigned to specific divisions and shifts vary depending on the community's size and service needs.

Administrative services, which are usually centralized, include recruitment and training, records and communications, planning and research, and technical services. Staff personnel assist line personnel, including supervisors. The laboratory staff, for example, assists line personnel, acting as liaisons, specialists, or advisory personnel. They are technical experts who provide specialized information. Legal staff (city, county, or district attorneys) act as legal advisors to all members of the agency.

Conflicts can and do arise between line and staff, particularly when staff attempts to act in a capacity beyond advisory or informational. Both line and staff are necessary components of the law enforcement organization. They must, however, be coordinated and controlled to achieve department goals.

Stephens (2003, p.52) describes a frequent problem that occurs when support functions are placed in a line division that does not serve the entire department. For example, the records section (a support function) often reports to the head of investigations (a line function). But officers in other divisions and the public may also need access to these records, and in this scenario the records are more difficult for them to obtain than if records and other support functions were in the same area.

Division of Labor: Generalists and Specialists Law enforcement agencies, despite their organizational hierarchy, are basically decentralized units, with most decisions made at the level of the patrol, detective, juvenile, and narcotics officers and that of the first-line supervisor. Even the authority to arrest is made at the lowest level of the organization. Most arrests are made by patrol officers, detectives, and juvenile officers.

Law enforcement agencies cannot function without division of work and, often, specialization. Neither can they function without maximum coordination of these **generalists** and **specialists**. As the organization grows in size, specialization develops to meet the community's needs. The extent of specialization is a management decision.

generalists • officers who perform most functions, including patrol.
specialists • those who work in a specific area: investigators, juvenile officers, SWAT officers and the like.

Specialization occurs when the organizational structure is divided into units with specific tasks to perform. The patrol unit is assigned the majority of personnel and provides the greatest variety of tasks and services. Even though specialized units are formed, the patrol division often still performs some of these units' tasks.

For example, patrol officers may investigate a crime scene up to the point at which they must leave their shift or area to continue the investigation. Or they may investigate only to the point of protecting the scene and keeping witnesses present or immediately arresting a suspect. At this point they may complete their report on tasks performed relating to the specific crime and either turn it over to another shift of patrol officers or to the investigative unit. Regardless of the division of tasks performed by generalist or specialist units, close communication about cases must occur or problems develop.

Specialization creates a potential for substantially increased levels of expertise, creativity, and innovation. The more completely an employee can perform a task or set of tasks, the more job satisfaction the employee will experience. When specialization is not practical, people must understand why the division of labor is necessary. It must also be clear where patrol's responsibility ends and that of the investigative unit begins.

The greater the specialization, necessary as it is, the greater the difficulties of coordination, communication, control, and employee relationships. Conflicts and jealousies may arise, including an attitude of "Let the expert do it if he or she is going to get the credit."

Officers in a small agency must perform all tasks. They cannot afford the luxury of specialization. However, with more standardized training requirements and accreditation, all officers have similar backgrounds for performing tasks, regardless of the size of the agency. The major difference is the frequency of opportunity.

 Specialization can enhance a department's effectiveness and efficiency, but overspecialization can impede the organizational purpose.

Overspecialization fragments the opportunity to achieve the organizational purpose of providing courteous, competent, expeditious law enforcement services. The more specialized an agency becomes, the more attention must be paid to interrelationships and coordination.

Rational Organization and Hierarchy of Authority

The structure of most police departments, as noted, has traditionally been a semi-military, pyramid-shaped hierarchy with authority flowing from the narrow apex down to the broad base. This hierarchical pyramid is often graphically represented in an organizational chart.

organizational chart • visually depicts how personnel are organized within the department. Might also depict how the department fits into the community's political structure.

The Organizational Chart An **organizational chart** visually depicts how personnel are organized within an agency and might also illustrate how the agency fits into the community's political structure. Figure 1.2 shows the organization of the Boulder City (Nevada) Police Department. This is typical of how police departments are organized in smaller cities. The figure also shows how the police department fits into the city's organizational structure.

This formal organization is generally supported in writing by rules and regulations, department operational manuals, and job descriptions. All provide control and a foundation from which actions can be taken.

The larger the agency and the jurisdiction it serves, the more complex the organization and the chart depicting it. Figure 1.3, a chart of the Minneapolis Police Department, shows how a large police department is organized.

chain of command • the order of authority; begins at the top of the pyramid and flows down to the base.

Chain of Command The **chain of command** is the order of authority. It begins at the top of the pyramid with the chief or sheriff and flows downward through the commissioned ranks in the agency—from deputy chief to captain to lieutenant to sergeant and finally to the patrol officer.

 The chain of command establishes definite lines of authority and channels of communication.

channels of communication • how messages are conveyed; usually follow the chain of command.

Each level must forward communications to the next higher or lower level. **Channels of communication** are the official paths through which orders flow

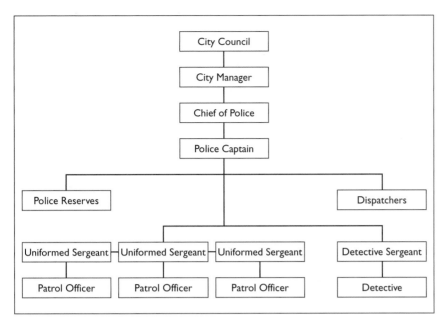

Figure 1.2 A Typical Small Police Department Organizational Chart
Source: Courtesy of the Boulder City Police Department, Boulder City, Nevada.

from management to workers. Most companies set up these channels carefully and for good reasons. They are the "highways" for orders and communications to follow and keep everyone aware of events. They coordinate the organization into a whole unit instead of a series of parts. When an individual leaves these channels and takes a shortcut, he or she is apt to run into problems. For example, a patrol officer who takes a complaint directly to the chief rather than to the sergeant would probably fall out of favor in the department.

Sometimes in law enforcement work, however, emergencies exist that cannot wait for information to be sent through the expected channels. This is one of the challenges of police work.

Another important part of the organizational design is unity of command. **Unity of command** means that every individual in the organization has only one immediate superior or supervisor. Unity of command is extremely important and needs to be ensured in most instances. Each individual, unit, and situation should be under the control of one—and only one—person.

Yet another factor in most law enforcement organizations is the number of people one individual manages or supervises. The **span of control** refers to the number of people or units supervised by one manager. The span of control depends on the department's size, the supervisors' and subordinates' abilities, crime rates, community expectations, and the political environment. Often the greater the span of control, the less effective the management or supervision.

However, technological advances involving communications with personnel in the field, higher levels of education and training, and the extent of the empowerment and flattening of the organization may allow managers to increase their span of control and remain effective. Do not confuse span of control with how many people one person has authority over. The chief, for example, has authority over everyone in the department, but the chief's span of control extends to only those who report directly to him or her.

unity of command • means that every individual in the organization has only one immediate superior or supervisor.

span of control • how many people one individual manages or supervises.

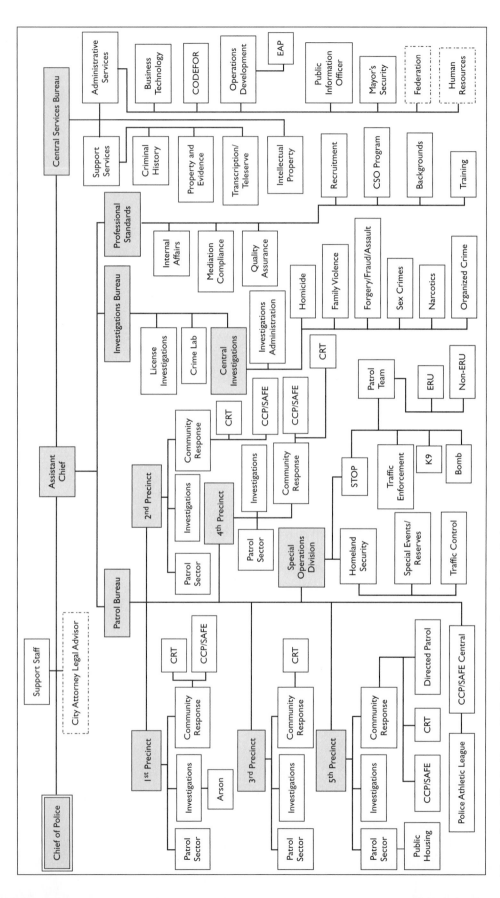

Figure 1.3 A Typical Large Police Department Organizational Chart

Source: Courtesy of the Minneapolis (Minnesota) Police Department.

The span of control must be realistic. If too few people report to a manager, that manager is not earning his or her salary. If too many people report to a manager, that manager cannot do a good job with all of them. Within a law enforcement agency, the more levels in the pyramid, the smaller the span of control. A number of factors must be considered:

- Distance in space and time between manager and subordinate
- Difficulty of tasks performed
- Types of assistance available to the manager
- Amount of direction subordinates need
- Extent of subordinates' skill and experience

Each factor must be considered as personnel are assigned. Other important considerations are who has authority, who has responsibility, and what can be delegated.

Authority, Responsibility and Delegation

Authority, responsibility and delegation are key factors in any organization. Without them organizations could not exist.

Authority is the power to enforce laws, exact obedience, and command. **Responsibility** means being answerable, liable, or accountable. Thus, managers have the authority to give commands, and subordinates have the responsibility of carrying out the commands. This is very much in keeping with the militaristic model.

authority • the power to enforce laws, exact obedience, and command.
responsibility • answerable, liable, accountable for.
delegation • assigning tasks to others.

The third concept, **delegation**, is also crucial in any organization. Organizations exist because they can accomplish what no one person can accomplish. That single person, the chief, must be able to assign (delegate) tasks to others, who may, in turn, further delegate.

 When authority is delegated, it should be coupled with responsibility.

Delegation is discussed in Chapter 2. The concept is key for all managers, at whatever their level within the police organization, for this is how **accountability** can be ensured. Accountability makes people responsible for tasks assigned to them. Accountability is needed because all tasks specified in the agency's work plans must be accomplished by someone if the organization is to fulfill its mission. As important as the formal organization of a police department is, as in any group, an informal structure also exists.

accountability • makes people responsible for tasks assigned to them.

The formal organization groups people by task and responsibility and clearly delineates the chain of command and channels of communication. The informal organization exists side-by-side with this formal organization and may in fact be a truer representation of the way the department actually functions.

The Informal Organization

Within any organization some people may emerge as leaders, regardless of whether they are in a leadership position. In addition, within any organization people will form their own groups—people who enjoy being together and perhaps working together.

 Managers should recognize the informal organization that exists within any law enforcement agency.

informal organization • groups that operate without official sanction but influence department performance.

The **informal organization** operates without official sanctions, but it influences the agency's performance. It may help or harm the agency's goals, and it may support the organization or cause dissention.

Inasmuch as informal organizations are going to exist regardless of whether the supervisor likes them, it might be wise to view them as a positive force and use them to facilitate the department's work. This can be done by thinking of the informal leader not as a ringleader but as a person "in on things," one whose talents can benefit the whole group.

scuttlebutt • one employee complaining to another, uninvolved employee, who cannot remedy the situation, about an adverse action taken by upper management.

One aspect of the informal organization is **scuttlebutt**, that is, gossip or rumors. Scuttlebutt can undermine morale and reduce productivity. This important aspect of internal communication is discussed in Chapter 4. Successful managers are able to coordinate the efforts of both the formal and the informal organization.

Coordination

coordination • ensuring that all members of the department perform their assigned tasks and that, together, the department's mission is accomplished.

Coordination ensures that each individual unit performs harmoniously with the total effort to achieve the department's mission.

 Management tools for coordination include:

- A clear chain of command and unity of command.
- Clear channels of communication and strict adherence to them.
- Clear, specific job descriptions.
- Clear, specific goals, objectives, and work plans.
- Standard operating procedures for routine tasks.
- An agency regulation guidebook.
- Meetings and roll calls.
- Informational bulletins, newsletters, and memos.

Coordinating efforts should be a part of an agency's work plan. Coordination is especially important in departments that are changing their focus from crime fighting to community policing and problem solving.

The Emerging Law Enforcement Organization

Business and industry are undergoing sweeping changes in organization and management styles to remain competitive. Law enforcement agencies are also facing the need for change to meet the competition of private policing. Harr and Hess (2005, p.72) report that private security has become a "major player" in safeguarding Americans and their property. They suggest that as our elderly and business populations continue to occupy high-rise condominiums and office buildings, the reliance on private security will also increase. Law enforcement cannot practically be expected to patrol such structures.

Police departments and other law enforcement agencies not only must compete with private police but also must compete for the bright, young college graduates entering the work force. No longer will law enforcement agencies be recruiting a majority of candidates with a military background. Instead they will be recruiting college graduates who will not accept authority blindly. Other changes are also evident in police departments across the country.

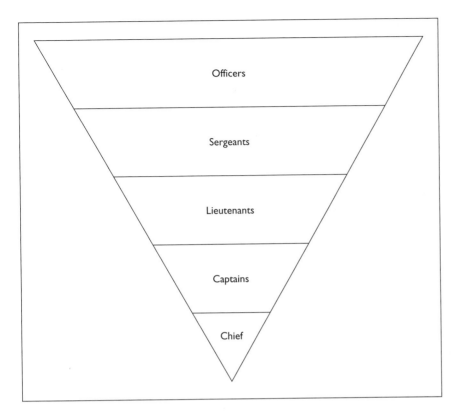

Figure 1.4 The Inverted Pyramid of Authority—Organizational Hierarchy

 The emerging law enforcement agency has a flattened organization, is decentralized, and empowers its employees.

A Flattened Organization

Like businesses, for the sake of efficiency, many police departments are turning to a **flat organization**, one with fewer lieutenants and captains, fewer staff departments, fewer staff assistants, more sergeants, and more patrol officers. Typical pyramid organization charts will have the top pushed down and the sides expanded at the base. Some police departments are beginning to experiment with alternative organization designs. One example of such experimentation places the patrol officers at the top with everyone under them playing a supporting role (Figure 1.4).

Top-heavy organizational structures are no longer tolerated in business. Progressive firms are flattening their structure, restructuring top-heavy organizations, and pushing authority and decision making as low as possible. Accompanying this change in organizational structure is decentralization.

flat organization • one with fewer lieutenants and captains, fewer staff departments, fewer staff assistants, more sergeants, and more patrol officers.

A Decentralized Organization

Decentralization generally refers to a department's organizational structure and operations: It encourages flattening of the organization and places decision making at the level where information is plentiful, usually at the level of the patrol officer. Flattened, decentralized organizations empower line personnel.

Successful businesses concentrate on soliciting ideas from everyone in their organizations about every facet of their operations. This approach should be applied to policing, especially in larger departments.

decentralization • encourages flattening of the organization and places decision-making authority and autonomy at the level where information is plentiful; in police organizations, this is usually at the level of the patrol officer.

Stephens (2003, p.52) says departments with centralized control tend to create very steep vertical organizations with many levels of middle managers. Centralized control requires officers to look to higher levels of the organization to act. Stephens (p.53) states: "In a decentralized organization, individuals have much greater freedom to make decisions about what work should be done to contribute to the overall objectives of the organization and about how it should be done."

Stephens cites three advantages of decentralization: (1) It frees managers from having to spend all their time and intellectual energy on day-to-day operational matters, allowing them to concentrate more time on strategies that will improve the organization's capabilities to perform; (2) it improves operational decisions because they are made by those closest to the facts of a situation; and (3) it challenges more people to be creative and take responsibility for the problems in their area. A likely result of decentralization is that officers will feel empowered.

Empowered Officers

"Empowerment," according to Weiss and Davis (2004, p.70), "is the act of giving line supervisors and officers the power to take the initiative, make decisions, and take appropriate action during incidents and times of crisis without waiting for administrative approval—and without finger pointing or blame." They (p.72) stress that, when empowered, people will make mistakes but that this comes with freedom to problem solve and be creative.

empowered • given legal authority to act on one's own discretion.

Empowered officers are given legal authority to act on their own discretion. According to Weiss and Davis (p.71): "Empowerment is not a specific program; it is a departmental philosophy. Department heads must believe in it and trust their staff. Above all, they must remember not to expect perfection; mistakes will be made; everyone should learn from mistakes." They (p.73) conclude: "The goal of the philosophy of empowerment is to give the police staff the authority to take the appropriate action to solve a problem with confidence. . . . Empowerment shows that police administrators believe in those they command."

If officer retention is to be maintained and loyalty and morale preserved and heightened, officers should be empowered. This change is discussed in detail in Chapter 2.

Why the Need to Change?

Some readers may be thinking, "If it ain't broke, don't fix it. What's wrong with the way the law enforcement agencies are organized? They have worked fine for the past 200 years."

However, law enforcement must now deal with disruptive social, demographic, and technological changes. America is becoming increasingly diverse, with more minorities and more elderly people. Immigrants, legal and illegal, are streaming into our country. People with disabilities are entering into mainstream America after the passage of the Americans with Disabilities Act, and thousands of mentally ill people have been released from institutions, often becoming homeless. In addition, America is becoming a **bifurcated society** with more wealth, more poverty, and a shrinking middle class. The gap between the "haves" and the "have nots" is widening. Other social and cultural changes include the weakening influence of family, church, and school.

bifurcated society • a society in which the gap between the "haves" and the "have nots" is wide—that is, there are many poor people, many wealthy people, and a shrinking middle class.

Technology is also forcing policing to change. Technology has revolutionized law enforcement, affecting everything from crime scene investigations to law enforcement gear, weapons, and police vehicles.

In addition, as Morreale and Ortmeier (2004, p.89) note: "Since the Vietnam War era, even the military model has changed dramatically and many departments have failed to keep pace, electing to retain an antiquated, hierarchical structure in which all decision making is reserved for command staff."

Finally, the inability of law enforcement to win the "wars" on drugs and terrorism has shown that the police cannot fight crime and disorder by themselves. They need the help of the citizens within their jurisdiction. This need has become even greater after the tragic events of September 11, 2001. The fear of terrorism affects all Americans. Combating this heightened threat to our national security requires a combined effort.

 The challenges facing not only law enforcement but also our entire country necessitate reexamining our public organizations, including law enforcement.

These changes may require a **paradigm shift**, a dramatic change in how some basic structure is viewed. A **paradigm** is a model, theory or frame of reference.

For example, in the early beginnings of our country, we were an agricultural society. The Industrial Revolution dramatically changed how we viewed our society. We have since shifted to an information-based society. Likewise, law enforcement appears to be undergoing a paradigm shift from an emphasis on crime fighting to an emphasis on order maintenance and peace keeping.

It is important that law enforcement managers at all levels re-examine past assumptions, consider future projections, and think very carefully about the future of policing, law enforcement, and the entire criminal justice system, including the move toward community involvement in every aspect of policing, courts, and corrections.

Thus far, the discussion has focused on the organization of local law enforcement. However, local agencies do not operate in a vacuum. They need to communicate and corroborate with other local jurisdictions; county, state and federal agencies; and other stakeholders, depending on the situation. To effectively do so, it is important to understand the concepts of unified and incident command.

Incident and Unified Command

Incident and unified command are related yet distinct concepts. **Incident command** is an organizational structure designed to aid in managing resources during incidents. The Incident Command System (ICS) is a standardized on-scene emergency management construct that integrates facilities, equipment, personnel, procedures, and communications operations. ICS reflects the complexity and demands of single or multiple incidents, without being hindered by jurisdictional boundaries. It is used for all kinds of emergencies and applies to small as well as large, complex incidents (*National Incident Management System*, 2004, p.130).

Several states have adopted ICS as their standard for emergency management, and others are considering adopting ICS. As ICS gains wider use, there is a need to provide training for those who are not first responders (i.e., law enforcement, fire, or emergency medical services personnel) who may be called upon to function in an ICS environment.

To ensure coordination during incidents involving multiple jurisdictions or agencies, a single jurisdiction with multiagency involvement, or multiple jurisdictions with multiagency involvement, the principle of unified command applies. **Unified command** allows agencies with different legal, geographic and

paradigm shift • a dramatic change in how some basic structure is viewed.

paradigm • a model, theory or frame of reference.

incident command • an organizational structure designed to aid in managing resources during incidents.

unified command • allows agencies with different legal, geographic and functional authorities and responsibilities to work together effectively without affecting individual agency authority, responsibility or accountability.

functional authorities and responsibilities to work together effectively without affecting individual agency authority, responsibility or accountability (*National Incident Management System*, pp.11–12). Unified command not only coordinates the efforts of many jurisdictions, but provides for and assures joint decisions on objectives, strategies, plans, priorities, and public communications.

 ## SUMMARY

Managers need to understand the organizational structure within which most law enforcement agencies function. The traditional organizational design is that of a pyramid-shaped hierarchy based on a military model. This model has evolved through three distinct eras of policing: the political era, the reform era, and the community era.

The mission statement should be the driving force of any organization, including law enforcement agencies. This mission statement can direct the development of meaningful goals and objectives and realistic work plans. Goals are broad, general, desired outcomes. Objectives are specific, measurable ways to accomplish the goals. Work plans are the precise activities that contribute to accomplishing objectives. Along with a mission statement, goals, objectives, and work plans, a formal organization of personnel is mandatory to accomplish the tasks.

One aspect of an agency's organizational structure is division into field services with line personnel and administrative services with staff personnel. Line personnel directly help accomplish the goals of the department. Staff personnel support the line organization.

An organization typically relies on a chain of command and set channels of communication. The chain of command establishes definite lines of authority and channels of communication. These organizational features are necessary to ensure the efficient delegation of tasks. The delegation of authority should go hand-in-hand with responsibility.

As agencies become larger, they often become specialized. Specialization can enhance an agency's effectiveness and efficiency, but overspecialization can impede the organizational purpose. Specialization also requires a higher degree of coordination, although coordination is critical for any department, large or small, specialized or not. In addition to the formal organization depicted in an organizational chart, any law enforcement agency also has an informal organization that managers should recognize. The informal organization can help or hinder accomplishment of the agency's mission.

Management tools for coordination include a clear chain of command and unity of command; clear channels of communication and strict adherence to them; clear, specific job descriptions; clear, specific goals, objectives, and work plans; standard operating procedures for routine tasks; an agency regulation guidebook; meetings and roll calls; and informational bulletins, newsletters, and memos. The emerging law enforcement agency has a flattened organization, is decentralized, and empowers its employees.

 ## CHALLENGE ONE

You are the new chief of the Greenfield Police Department. After 30 years of iron-fisted control, Chief Slaughter has retired. Slaughter believed in the military model of police management and a traditional crime-fighting policing strategy. He was fully entrenched in the war on crime and ran his department like an army unit. His book of rules and regulations was a foot thick, and he demanded absolute compliance. Decisions were made in the chief's office and passed down to the officers through layers of captains, lieutenants and sergeants. At Chief Slaughter's retirement ceremony, the mayor slaps you on the back and says, "You've got some big shoes to fill, son. That guy knew how to fight crime, and his officers never stepped out of line. Our crime rate was below the national average every year he was here." The City Council presents Slaughter the Meritorious Service Award for 30 years of crime fighting.

As a student of police history you realize that most police departments battle complex social problems and seldom march off to war. You know that crime rates are minimally influenced by crime fighting and are a poor indication of policing success. You also know that traditional organizational structures and policing strategies are slow to change and often are out of sync with one another. Most of your questions to the captains about department operations have generated the same response: "Because that's the way we've always done it. If it ain't broke, why fix it?"

You decide to visit with members of the community. A homeowner tells you that Chief Slaughter's officers do a great job of patrolling her neighborhood, but she's worried about the future impact of the deteriorating apartment complex across the street. She realizes it's not a police problem. The manager of a senior citizens' residence tells you that there hasn't been a crime reported in their neighborhood in over a year, but the residents are afraid to go out at night. He thinks it's the rumors that spread from crime reports on the television news. The business owners in the shopping center complain that customers are being driven away by kids skateboarding in the parking lot. They understand that the police have more urgent crime problems to fight. The high school principal praises the police department's stringent traffic enforcement before and after school. He wishes he could resolve the growing truancy problem as efficiently as the police handle traffic. None of the people you talk to is personally acquainted with a Greenfield police officer.

It appears the Greenfield Police Department is trapped in the reform era. They rely on preventive patrolling and rapid response as their primary policing strategies and seldom interact with the community. You review their mission statement and find it emphasizes the professional model of crime fighting.

1. Suggest a mission statement that emphasizes the community era rather than the reform era.

2. What process would you use to develop a new mission statement? Who would you include in the process? Is it wise to order officers to accept a mission statement?

3. What changes would you introduce in policing strategies?

4. What changes would you make in the organizational structure to enable the new strategy?

5. Identify some quality-of-life issues that are not being addressed by the crime-fighting strategy of Chief Slaughter.

DISCUSSION QUESTIONS

1. Who is a law enforcement manager?

2. Is there a difference between the terms *pyramidal structure* and *hierarchy*?

3. What is the difference between unity of command and chain of command?

4. What are staff positions in a typical police department?

5. What is the purpose of law enforcement management?

6. What does delegation mean? Can you delegate authority? Responsibility?

7. What does an organizational chart indicate?

8. How could you reorganize to force decision making downward? Is this desirable?

9. What is an informal organization?

10. What changes do you foresee in law enforcement agencies in the twenty-first century?

REFERENCES

"Bureaucracy." *Encyclopedia Britannica*, 2005. Online. Accessed October 3, 2005.

Delattre, Edwin J. and Behan, Cornelius J. "Practical Ideals for Managing in the New Millennium." In *Local Government Police Management*, 4th ed., edited by William

A. Geller and Darrel W. Stephens. Washington, DC: International City/County Management Association, 2003, pp.500–614.

Harr, J. Scott and Hess, Kären. *Careers in Criminal Justice and Related Fields: From Internship to Promotion*, 5th ed. Belmont, CA: Wadsworth Publishing Company, 2005.

Kelling, George. "The Evolution of Contemporary Policing." In *Local Government Police Management*, 4th ed., edited by William A. Geller and Darrel W. Stephens. Washington, DC: International City/County Management Association, 2003, pp.3–26.

Kerlikowske, R. Gil. "The End of Community Policing: Remembering the Lessons Learned." *FBI Law Enforcement Bulletin*, April 2004, pp.6–10.

Morreale, Stephen A. and Ortmeier, P. J. "Preparing Leaders for Law Enforcement." *The Police Chief*, October 2004, pp.89–97.

National Incident Management System. Washington, DC: Department of Homeland Security, March 1, 2004.

Sharp, Arthur. "Keep Policies and Procedures Updated." *Law and Order*, June 2004, pp.72–75.

Sharp, Arthur. "There Is No Model Administrative Model." *Law and Order*, June 2005, pp.88–98.

Stephens, Darrel W. "Organization and Management." In *Local Government Police Management*, 4th ed., edited by William A. Geller and Darrel W. Stephens. Washington, DC: International City/County Management Association, 2003, pp.27–66.

Stephens, Darrel W. "IT Changes in Law Enforcement." In *Issues in IT: A Reader for Busy Executives*. Washington, DC: Police Executive Research Forum, February 2005, pp.7–28.

"Taylor, Frederick W." *Encyclopedia Britannica*, 2005. Online. Accessed October 3, 2005.

Weiss, Jim and Davis, Mickey. "Empowerment or Finger-pointing." *Law and Order*, October 2004, pp.70–73.

Wilson, O. W. *Police Administration*. New York: McGraw-Hill, 1950.

BOOK-SPECIFIC WEB SITE

Go to the Management and Supervision in Law Enforcement Web site at www.thomsonedu.com/criminaljustice/bennett for student and instructor resources, including Internet Assignments and Case Studies.

CHAPTER 2

The Role of Management and Leadership in Law Enforcement

The watchwords of the new leadership paradigm are coach, inspire, gain commitment, empower, affirm, flexibility, responsibility, self-management, shared power, autonomous teams and entrepreneurial units.

Donald C. Witham, Chief, FBI Strategic Planning Unit

DO YOU KNOW?

- How authority and power are alike? How they differ?
- What basic management skills are important?
- What four tools successful managers use?
- What management by objectives (MBO) involves?
- What management style is best suited for law enforcement work?
- What typical levels of management exist in law enforcement?
- What essential functions chief executives perform?
- How strategic and tactical planning differ?
- With whom law enforcement chief executives typically interact?
- What basic difference exists between managers and leaders?
- What theories of leadership have been researched?
- What leadership styles have been identified and their main characteristics?
- What constitutes effective leadership training?
- What the attributes of a high-performing team are?

CAN YOU DEFINE?

autocratic leadership	free-rein leadership	management by objectives (MBO)	strategic planning
consideration structure	holistic management/ leadership	mechanistic model	supervision
consultative leadership	initiating structure	organic model	synergism
democratic leadership	interactors	participative leadership	tactical planning
dispersed leadership	interfacers	seagull management	total quality management (TQM)
facilitators	laissez-faire leadership	situational leadership	trait theorists
	leadership	SMART goals and objectives	transformational leadership
	management		Wallenda Effect

Introduction

The organizational chart discussed in the preceding chapter is inanimate, like a house without people. The form and foundation exist and are necessary, but the structure is in no sense vital or exciting. Vitality and excitement come when the boxes in the chart are filled with people, men and women patrol officers, investigators, sergeants, lieutenants, captains and chiefs, interacting and working together to accomplish their mission—"to serve and protect." The organization accomplishes its mission through management directing and guiding employees and resources, both internal and external to the organization.

Managers in law enforcement face unique problems because of the continuous need for service, 24/7, 365 days a year. The chief executive officer (CEO) of the law enforcement agency obviously cannot be physically present for this extended period and must therefore rely on the organizational structure to permit other members to perform administrative and operational functions. In addition, challenges facing today's law enforcement administrators are enormous, including strained budgets and cutbacks, greater citizen demands and expectations for service and an increasingly diverse society.

This chapter examines the complex role of the law enforcement manager, the challenges presented by management and the relationship between authority and power. This is followed by an overview of the basic skills and tools required of an effective manager. Contributions to management from the business world, including management by objectives and total quality management, are the next area of discussion, followed by an analysis of the various management styles. The chapter then examines the levels of management typically found within law enforcement agencies, responsibilities at each level, management challenges most commonly encountered and law enforcement management as a career. Next is a discussion of the differences between managing and leading and a review of key characteristics of leaders. This is followed by a review of research on and theories related to leadership, the various leadership styles and the apparent need for change within law enforcement agencies. Next is a discussion of leadership training and development, the new skills required and guidelines for effective leadership. The chapter concludes with a discussion of holistic management and a team approach to law enforcement.

Managers and Management

management • the process of combining resources to accomplish organizational goals.

Manage means to control and direct, to administer, to take charge of. **Management** is the process of using resources to achieve organizational goals. Law enforcement management is a process of deciding goals and objectives, adopting a work plan to accomplish them, obtaining and wisely using resources and making decisions that result in a high level of performance and productivity. Those who undertake these activities are called managers.

Managers and supervisors control and direct people and operations to achieve organizational objectives. Managers and supervisors are also jointly involved in planning, organizing, staffing and budgeting. In fact, many gray areas exist in the duties of managers and supervisors. This is increasingly true in organizations that have been "flattened" by eliminating some middle-management positions and empowering employees at the lowest level.

Managers must also support the development of *individual* responsibility, permitting all employees to achieve maximum potential while simultaneously supporting organizational needs. The sum total of individual member energy is transferred to the organizational energy needed for success.

Authority and Power

Authority, responsibility and accountability were discussed in the preceding chapter. Consider now the relationship between the authority and the power of police managers.

Authority is the legal right to get things done through others by influencing behavior. Just as an agency has a formal and an informal organization, it also relies on formal and informal authority. Formal authority comes from rank or credentials. Informal authority comes from friendships or alignments with others.

Power is the ability to get things done with or without a legal right. Authority is generally granted by law or an order. Power is the influence of a person or group without benefit of law or order. U.S. National Security Advisor Condoleezza Rice has said of the goal of power: "Power is nothing unless you can turn it into influence" (Aldrich, 2003, p.35).

 Authority and power both imply the ability to coerce compliance, that is, to *make* subordinates carry out orders. Both are important to managers at all levels. However, authority relies on a law or order, whereas power relies on persuasion.

In a democracy authority and power are not always regarded as desirable. Even though managers may use both, and employees recognize management's right to use both, a limitation exists in the employees' mindset as to how much is acceptable. They expect some freedom of choice.

Managers should never manipulate employees and should avoid **seagull management**. According to management guru Ken Blanchard: "[Seagull managers] hear something's wrong, so they fly in, make a lot of noise, crap on everybody and fly away."

Managers need authority and power, but they should also share this authority and power. Aldrich (p.36) suggests that power grabbers do not realize that each time they miss a chance to help a group complete the right work, their power actually ebbs: "Power grabbers may grow increasingly manipulative trying to overcompensate for a lack of results." To share authority and power, managers must learn to delegate effectively.

seagull management • manager hears something's wrong, flies in, makes a lot of noise, craps on everybody and flies away.

Delegation

Transferring authority, or delegating, is a necessary and often difficult aspect of management, because it requires placing trust in others to do the job as well as, or better than, the manager would do it. As discussed in Chapter 1, it is also a form of empowerment. Theodore Roosevelt once said: "The best executive is the one who has enough sense to pick good people to do what he wants done, and self-restraint enough to keep from meddling with them while they do it." Yet many managers fail to delegate effectively because they believe "If you want something done right, you have to do it yourself."

Delegation is *not* passing the buck, shirking personal responsibility, or dumping on someone. It is the way managers and supervisors free up time to get their work done while avoiding getting tied up in "administrivia." Managers can put their minds at ease when they delegate important tasks by carefully selecting the right person, thoroughly defining the task and specifying the qualifications for doing it well. The results, standards and deadlines should be clearly defined. Managers should also decide how much authority, support and time the officer will need ("Prepare before You Delegate," 2003, p.10).

Managers who find themselves wondering why their officers cannot take more responsibility or who feel they must drop every detail of every project into their officers' laps may not be delegating effectively ("Management by Delegation," 2003, p.4). Key points to remember are:

1. Stress results, not details. What is important is the final outcome, not the day-to-day details.
2. Do not be drawn in by giving solutions to employees' problems. Help them learn to solve their own problems, which will save managers time in the long run.
3. Turn the questions around; ask for possible answers.
4. Establish measurable and concrete objectives.
5. Develop reporting systems.
6. Set strict and realistic deadlines.
7. Keep a delegation log to monitor progress of tasks that have been delegated.
8. Recognize employees' talents and personalities.

It is not enough to delegate a task. The employee also needs the necessary authority to get the task done ("Delegate with the Right Level of Authority," 2003, p.1). To avoid problems, managers need to match tasks with one of three levels of authority:

1. Recommending: When facing a decision a manager must make because of its importance, the manager might assign an employee to research the available options and present them with a recommendation of the best choice.
2. Informing and implementing: When facing an important decision that an employee assisting a manager can make, the manager should be able to assign the employee to research and choose the best option, inform him or her and be ready to implement it.
3. Acting: If a manager is confident an employee can handle a task independently, the authority to act should be given.

In addition to knowing how to delegate effectively, managers need several other basic management skills and tools.

Basic Management Skills and Tools

To be effective, managers at all levels must be skilled at planning, organizing, coordinating, reporting and budgeting. Equally critical, however, are people skills such as communicating, motivating and leading, as will be discussed throughout the text.

 Basic management skills include technical skills, administrative skills, conceptual skills and people skills.

Technical skills include all the procedures necessary to be a "good cop": interviewing and interrogating, searching, arresting, gathering evidence and so on. Police officers often become sergeants because of their technical skills.

Administrative skills include organizing, delegating and directing the work of others. They also include writing proposals, formulating work plans, establishing policies and procedures and developing budgets.

Conceptual skills include the ability to problem solve, plan and see the big picture and how all the pieces within it fit. Managers must be able to think in terms of the future; synthesize great amounts of data; make decisions on complex matters; and have broad, even national, perspectives. They must see the organization as a whole, yet existing within society. They must also have a sensitivity to the spirit—not just the letter—of the law.

People skills include being able to communicate clearly, to motivate, to discipline appropriately and to inspire. People skills also include working effectively with managers up the chain of command, as well as with the general public. The higher the management position, the more important people skills become.

Basic Tools

According to Blanchard (1988, p.14): "Successful managers use four tools to accomplish their goals."

 Successful managers have:

- Clear goals.
- A commitment to excellence.
- Feedback.
- Support.

"Good performance," says Blanchard, "starts with clear goals." The importance of goals cannot be overemphasized. Just as important, however, are the objectives developed to meet the goals. According to Blanchard, **SMART goals and objectives** are *s*pecific, *m*easurable, *a*ttainable, *r*elevant and *t*rackable.

SMART goals and objectives • objectives that are specific, measurable, attainable, relevant and trackable.

The Role of Self-Confidence

Most police supervisors and managers have been promoted into their positions because they possessed or had learned the necessary skills and tools. But with the excitement and pride of promotion often comes an instinctive tinge of self-doubt. Taking on a new level of management is a major challenge and involves risk. Though initially daunting, change can serve as a catalyst for growth.

Change often requires that a person use already acquired skills in a new context, which can be threatening. Asking a person to walk across a six-inch wide board on the ground poses no threat. Put it 40 feet in the air, and the person is unlikely to take even the first step. To maintain self-confidence, seek the support of your peers, set goals for yourself in mastering the skills you need and get feedback.

A lack of self-confidence can lead to failure and other dire consequences, a situation sometimes referred to as the **Wallenda Effect**. In 1968 tightrope aerialist Karl Wallenda said: "Being on the tightrope is living; everything else is waiting." He loved his work and had total confidence in himself. Ten years later he fell to his death. His wife, also an aerialist, said that he had recently been worried about falling. This was in total contrast to his earlier years, when all his energy was focused on succeeding.

Wallenda Effect • the negative consequences of fear of failure.

Lessons Learned from Business

Just as the development of the law enforcement organization has been influenced by business, law enforcement management has followed the lead of business in some important ways, including management by objectives (MBO) and Total Quality Management (TQM).

Management by Objectives

Management theorist Peter Drucker, introduced in Chapter 1, is credited with first using the term *management by objectives (MBO)* in the early 1950s. It has been popular for over 50 years.

management by objectives (MBO) • involves managers and subordinates setting goals and objectives together and then tracking performance to ensure that the objectives are met.

Management by objectives (MBO) involves managers and subordinates setting goals and objectives together and then tracking performance to ensure that the objectives are met.

Drucker's theory can be summed up as "Expect to get the right things done." Drucker also says: "Intelligence, imagination, and knowledge are essential resources, but only effectiveness converts them into results." The key to the MBO system is to get workers to participate in deciding and setting goals, both individually and in work groups. The performance achieved is then compared to these agreed-upon goals.

Total Quality Management

total quality management (TQM) • Deming's theory that managers should create constancy of purpose for improvement of product and service, adopt the new philosophy, improve constantly, institute modern methods of training on the job, institute modern methods of supervision, drive fear from the workplace, break down barriers between staff areas, eliminate numerical goals for the work force, remove barriers that rob people of pride of workmanship and institute a vigorous program of education and training.

The pioneer in **total quality management (TQM)** was W. Edwards Deming (1900–1993), a management expert who assisted Japanese businesses in recovering and prospering following the end of World War II. In the 1980s Deming's ideas were taken up by American corporations as they sought to compete more effectively against foreign manufacturers. His quality-control methods focused on systematically tallying product defects, analyzing their causes, correcting those causes and then recording the effects of the corrections on subsequent product quality ("Deming, W. Edwards," 2005). The watchword of TQM is *zero defects*.

Although Deming's famous "14 Points" were originally aimed at business, several are applicable to the public sector as well—including law enforcement:

■ Create constancy of purpose for improvement of product and service.
■ Adopt the new philosophy.
■ Improve constantly.
■ Institute modern methods of training on the job.
■ Institute modern methods of supervision.
■ Drive fear from the workplace.
■ Break down barriers between staff areas.
■ Eliminate numerical goals for the work force.
■ Remove barriers that rob people of pride of workmanship.
■ Institute a vigorous program of education and training (Deming, 1982, p.17).

Dahl (2004, p.16) questions the effectiveness of TQM, suggesting that "zero defects" may stifle innovation: "Innovation, change and experimentation are all loaded with potential defects." Yet as has been noted previously, progress often demands risk taking and mistakes. Dahl suggests: "Most of us would like to strive for a positive number—but that would be 'on the other side' of zero. That's where you find innovation, change and good ol' Yankee ingenuity." TQM may work well in manufacturing, but its value to those in the service industries may not be as great.

Management Styles

Just as different managers use different types of authority and power, they also have varied personalities and management styles. Managers at any level may be sociable and friendly, firm and hard driving, or analytical and detail oriented. Several theories regarding management style have been developed, including those of McGregor, Likert, Argyris and Blake and Mouton. Within each theory "pure" or ideal types are described, but in reality management style should be viewed as a continuum, with "pure" types at the opposing ends. Table 2.1 summarizes the four theories about management style.

Which Management Style to Select?

It was once thought that fist-pounding, authoritarian managers were the greatest achievers. People now believe that many styles of management or combinations of several can be effective. The management style selected depends on the individuals involved, the tasks to be accomplished and any emergency the organization is facing, such as a hostage incident, a multiple-alarm fire, or an officer down.

Management styles might be depicted as falling along a continuum, with the task on one end, the people on the other end, and the time available to accomplish a goal determining where on that continuum the management style falls. If the task requires a great deal of time and will involve working with the same group of people throughout the duration, it is important to cater to group morale and manage more from the people side of the continuum. Take care of the people, and they will take care of the task/goal. In contrast, if time is short and the task will be over before morale becomes a factor, manage more from the task side of the continuum. Battles are won by task-oriented managers; wars are won by people-oriented managers.

 No one management style is more apt than another to achieve the agency's mission. The selected style must match individual personalities and situations.

Next consider some specific functions performed at the three basic levels of management, beginning with the first-line, supervisory level.

Levels of Managers

 Management typically has three levels:

- The top level or CEO (chief, sheriff)
- The middle level (captains, lieutenants)
- The first-line level (sergeants)

First-Line Supervisors

Most first-line managers or supervisors are sergeants, who are responsible to the next highest rank in the organization unless their positions are specialized. Management consultant Drucker says: "Supervisors are, so to speak, the ligaments, the tendons and sinews of an organization. They provide the articulation. Without them, no joint can move."

The transition to first-line supervisor is one of the most difficult in law enforcement, for it is here that they begin to make decisions that separate them from their

Table 2.1   Four Theories about Management Style

Theory and Originator	Basic Premise
Theory X/Theory Y—Douglas McGregor	Managers act toward subordinates in relation to the views they have of them.
	Theory X views employees as lazy and motivated by pay. The average worker has an aversion to work and does not want responsibility. Management's responsibility is to provide constant employee supervision and control workers through coercion, threats and punishment. Management makes all decisions and directs employees to carry them out. Theory X might have worked in the past, but with better-educated workers, it could create hostility.
	Theory Y views employees as committed and motivated by growth and development. They are willing workers who can be trusted to do a good job and given reasonable goals to accomplish. Employees should share in decision making. The humanistic approach reflected in Theory Y is more effective in today's work world. Management should encourage self-motivation and fewer outside controls. Decisions could be delegated. Employees would be responsive to management's goals if management set the proper environment for work.
Four-System Approach— Rensis Likert	System 1, similar to McGregor's Theory X, is the *traditional*, dictatorial approach to managing people. This system generally exploits employees and uses coercion and a few economic rewards. Communication flows downward from the top, and there is little to no feedback.
	System 2 is similar to System 1, except that economic rewards replace coercion. Some information on organizational development is permitted but not in opposition to management's control.
	System 3 is more liberal, uses employee initiative and gives employees more responsibility.
	System 4 is participative management (the complete opposite of System 1). Final decisions are made by management but only after employees have added their input. Communication flows back freely through the organization, and there is much feedback. Also includes team management, which is widely used today.
Mature Employee Theory— Chris Argyris	Organizations and individuals exist for a purpose. Both are *interdependent:* Organizations provide jobs and people perform them.
	As individuals develop, they mature from passive to active and from dependent to interdependent. Individuals and organizations need to develop together in much the same way. They need to grow and mature together to be of mutual benefit.
	The work force has energy to be released if management recognizes it. An organization that restricts individuals and keeps employees dependent, subordinate and restrained will engender a work climate of frustration, failure, short-term perspective and conflict and will hinder employees from achieving the organization's mission.
Managerial/Leadership Grid Theory— Dr. Robert R. Blake and Dr. Jane S. Mouton	Describes five management styles as falling on a grid—the vertical (Y) axis measures "concern for people (low to high) and the horizontal (X) axis measures "concern for results" (low to high).
	Lower right corner (high concern for results; low concern for people): *Authority–Compliance Management* style, the early autocratic, authoritarian approach. The manager is a no-nonsense taskmaster. Concern is for manager authority, status and operation of the organization. Employees have little say and less influence, and production is the only concern. This is also known as *Task Management*.
	Upper left corner (low concern for results; high concern for people): *Country Club Management* style. Managers are overly concerned with keeping employees happy at the expense of reasonable productivity. The work atmosphere is friendly and comfortable. Concern for employees is utmost; concern for productivity is limited.
	Lower left corner (low concern for results; low concern for people): the *Impoverished Management* style, which permits workers to do just enough to get by. Managers and employees put in their time and look ahead to retirement. Little real concern exists for employees or management. Little is expected and little is given. Minimal effort is made. The prevailing attitude: ignore problems and they will go away.
	In the center (moderate concern for results; moderate concern for people): *Middle-of-the-Road Management* style, with the manager showing some concern for both employees and management but in a low-key manner that is not really productive. The manager is a fence straddler, appeasing both sides, avoiding conflict and satisfying no one.
	Upper right corner (high concern for results; high concern for people): *Team Management* approach, suggested as the ideal. The manager works with employees as a team, providing information, caring about their feelings and concern, assisting, advising and coaching. Managers encourage employees to be creative and share suggestions for improvement. Employees are committed to their jobs and organization through a mutual relationship of trust and respect. Goals are achieved as a team.

fellow officers (Hale, 2005, p.34). The conversion from law enforcement functions to supervisor functions is difficult. Supervisors may not have the same camaraderie they enjoyed with members of the rank and file. They are now management and will not always be liked, as they may have to make unpopular decisions (Johnson, 2005, p.24).

Supervisors' fundamental responsibility is to ensure that what needs to be accomplished during any given shift is accomplished effectively and legally. They are concerned with **supervision** of the day-to-day concerns of law enforcement officers—that is, overseeing the activities of all nonranking employees in the agency. Among their functions are:

supervision • overseeing the actual work being done.

- Managing line personnel in the field.
- Supervising patrol activities.
- Conducting inspections.
- Maintaining discipline.
- Enforcing rules and regulations.
- Conducting roll call.
- Managing field operations.

New supervisors soon learn they are only as good as their officers and that their officers' performance often directly reflects on the supervisor's abilities (Hale, p.33). Weak supervisors spend a lot of time trying to cover up anything negative that happened on their watch; strong supervisors, in contrast, spend their energy finding out what went wrong and making sure it doesn't happen again (Weiss and Davis, 2004, p.73).

The sergeant is the first stop in line for almost everything in police work: the first supervisor to most scenes, the first one to know when an officer needs something, the first to yell when an officer makes a mistake, the first to talk to angry citizens who have been stopped for speeding, the first one officers run to when they are in trouble and the first one to jump to his or her officers' defense against the "brass" (Oldham, 2005c, p.30). It is "absolutely crucial" for sergeants to know their officers so that they can spot those who are in trouble and those who are teetering on the edge of self-destructive behavior (Oldham, 2005a, p.28). Sometimes all that is needed is to listen.

A sergeant's first priority is to bring his or her officers home alive at the end of their shift. Sergeants must therefore strictly enforce officer safety practices and follow them themselves. If they teach that backup guns and body armor save lives, they should be wearing theirs: "Let them see you out there doing the same job they do in the way you are telling them it should be done. No one has more impact than someone who is leading from the front" (Oldham, 2005e, p.16). There is a good reason it is called leading from the front: "A sergeant who is in the trenches and on the calls with his or her officers, enduring the same hardships and same long hours, it is relatively easy for that sergeant to pull the officers forward" (Oldham, 2005b, p.32). Officers would much rather hear "follow me" than "go do such and such."

As noted, a sergeant is likely to be the first commander on the scene to deal with any incident. In chaotic situations, sergeants need to command, but calmly: "One lone, calm voice is capable of staving off chaos" (Oldham, 2005d, p.26). Sergeants are expected to step up and take charge when the shift needs it and to step back and allow their officers to run the show and grow in their capabilities when they do not need that firm, calming hand.

A National Institute of Justice (NIJ) study, "Identifying Characteristics of Exemplary Baltimore Police Department First Line Supervisors," identified sergeants considered exemplary and those considered less so. Among the vital traits identified by the focus group were character and integrity, knowledge of the job, management skills, communication skills, interpersonal skills, ability to develop entry-level officers, problem-solving and critical-thinking skills, effectiveness as a role model and as a disciplinarian and the ability to be proactive. The greatest difference between the exemplary sergeants and their less exemplary peers was in moral reasoning: "They could solve police-related moral issues far better than their peers. . . . They came up with more solutions and solutions that were more complete and of better quality." Interestingly, exemplary sergeants, on top of other attributes, took less sick leave ("Good, Better, Best," 2003, pp.1, 6).

Another NIJ study identified four distinct supervisory styles—traditional, innovative, supportive and active—and found the *quality*, or style, of field supervision more significantly influenced patrol officer behavior than did the *quantity* of supervision (*How Police Supervisory Styles Influence Patrol Officers' Behavior*, 2003, p.1). According to the study, *traditional supervisors* expect aggressive enforcement from officers, are highly task oriented and expect officers to produce measurable outcomes, especially arrests and citations. *Innovative supervisors* tend to form relationships with their officers, to have a low level of task orientation and to hold more positive views of subordinates. They embrace community policing and problem solving and encourage their officers to embrace new philosophies and methods of policing.

Supportive supervisors protect subordinates from discipline or punishment perceived as "unfair" and provide "inspirational motivation." They are less concerned with enforcing rules and regulations and paperwork. They encourage officers through praise and recognition. *Active supervisors* embrace a philosophy of leading by example. They are heavily involved in the field alongside subordinates while controlling patrol officer behavior. In effect, they perform the dual function of street officer and supervisor. Officers with active supervisors spent more time on self-initiated activities, community policing activities and problem solving. The study concluded: "An 'active' supervisory style—involving leading by example—seems to be the most influential despite potential drawbacks. Indeed, active supervisors appear to be crucial to the implementation of organizational goals."

Supervisors frequently are not trained in the new skills they need. Initial training should concentrate on the "people activities" performed by supervisors, with particular emphasis on motivating others. As General George Patton wrote in his battle journal: "Don't tell people what to do. Tell them what you want done and let them surprise you with their ingenuity." Training is discussed later in the chapter.

Middle Management

Middle management usually includes captains and lieutenants. Captains have authority over all officers of the agency below the chief or sheriff and are responsible only to the chief or sheriff. Lieutenants are second in rank to captains. They are in charge of sergeants and all officers within their assigned responsibility, and they report to captains. Captains and lieutenants may perform the following functions:

- Inspecting assigned operations
- Reviewing and making recommendations on reports
- Helping develop plans
- Preparing work schedules
- Overseeing records and equipment

Mulder (2003, p.94) asserts: "Middle managers are the elite corps of an organization. They can either make or break a leader's agenda and career. It is the middle manager who should have a finger on the pulse of the organization and who can offer consultative advice to the leader on how his initiates are being implemented and responded to by the department." According to Mulder, the middle manager champions the leader's agenda to the troops. It is also middle management that bears the responsibility of developing newly promoted sergeants.

In larger departments one of the most demanding middle management positions is that of patrol district commander, which Fuller (2003, p.113) describes as a "killer management responsibility." He notes that in effect such a manager is essentially the chief of police in their own geographic area of operations. Fuller (pp.113–115) offers three basic boilerplate axioms as managerial guideposts:

1. You have to keep crime down. This is the bottom line.
2. You have to control your officers.
3. You have to get along with the political and community leadership in your district.

The Top Level—The Executive Manager

The executive manager, or the chief executive officer (CEO), is the top official in any law enforcement agency. The title may be chief of police, director, superintendent, or sheriff, but the authority and responsibility of the position are similar. The executive manager is either elected or appointed by the city council, the county commission or the city manager, subject to approval of the city council.

Executive managers have full authority and responsibility as provided by the charter provisions of their local jurisdictions. People appointed to this position are to enforce the applicable laws of the United States as well as state and local jurisdiction and all rules and regulations established by local government or the civil service commission.

Executive managers are responsible for planning, organizing and managing the agency's resources, including its employees. They are responsible for preserving the peace and enforcing laws and ordinances. The duties and responsibilities of executive managers often include:

- Developing a mission statement.
- Formulating goals and objectives.
- Preparing an annual budget.
- Preparing and periodically reviewing agency rules and regulations and general and specific agency orders.
- Developing strategic long-term and tactical short-term plans for organizational operations.
- Attending designated meetings of the city council or other organizations.
- Preparing required reports for the governing authority or person.
- Coordinating with other law enforcement agencies.
- Participating in emergency preparedness plans and operations.
- Developing public relations liaisons with the press.
- Administering ongoing, operational financial processes.
- Developing training programs to meet local needs.
- Acting as a liaison with community agencies.

Texts on management often convey the image of an executive working at an uncluttered desk in a spacious office. The executive is rationally planning, organizing, coordinating and controlling the organization. After careful analysis the executive makes critical decisions and has competent, motivated subordinates readily available to offer insightful input. The executive has a full schedule but no unexpected interruptions. Timelines are met without problem.

Several studies, however, indicate that this is *not* a realistic portrayal. In fact, most executives work at an unrelenting pace, are frequently interrupted and are often more oriented to reacting to crises than to planning and executing.

In *The Effective Executive (1993)*, Drucker describes Sune Carlson's 1951 study on executive behavior, which Drucker says is the one study of top management in large corporations that actually recorded the time use of senior executives. In this study, even the most effective executives found most of their time tied up with the demands of others and for purposes that added little if anything to their effectiveness.

The study concluded that the executive's time seemed to belong to everyone but the executive. If one were to define an executive operationally, that is, through his activities, one would have to define him as a captive of the organization. Everybody can move in on his time and everybody does. According to Drucker: "Executives might well be defined as people who normally have no time of their own because their time is always pre-empted by matters of importance to someone else." As one top level manager said in 2005 of this situation: "Ironically, that is how I feel. I dread any time I hear someone say, 'Sir, do you have a minute?' Inevitably that means they need at least half an hour. Some things haven't changed in 50 years for some chief executives." This challenge is discussed in Chapter 6.

The executive manager's roles in law enforcement may differ from other levels of managers. Executive managers are responsible for the big picture, for not only accomplishing the department's mission through goals and objectives but also for interacting with the community, its leaders, organizations and individual citizens, as well as the entire criminal justice system.

Essential Functions of Law Enforcement Executives

 Acting in a *managerial* capacity, law enforcement executives serve as:

- Planners.
- Facilitators.
- Interfacers.
- Interactors.

Planners Law enforcement managers must possess basic skills for planning—that is, the ability to set goals and objectives and to develop work plans to meet them. Whether managers personally formulate these goals and objectives or seek assistance from their staff, plans are essential. As Garrett (2005, p.6) says, goals are like New Year's Resolutions. We all set them, but few of us accomplish them. Why? We fail to plan how to accomplish them. As the saying goes: Most people don't plan to fail, they fail to plan. Law enforcement organizations cannot function efficiently without tactical and strategic planning.

tactical planning • short-term planning.

strategic planning • long-term planning.

 Tactical planning is short-term planning. **Strategic planning** is long-term planning.

Tactical planning includes the year's work plans. Strategic planning, on the other hand, is futuristic planning.

Some people may use the term *tactical* in an operational or military sense to refer to unusual situations in which combat might be expected. In law enforcement this might include serving warrants, conducting drug raids, dealing with hostage situations and the like. In this context tactical planning would mean planning designed to carry out a tactical operation.

Tactical planning is most often necessary to provide the flexibility needed for change; determine personnel needs; determine objectives and provide organizational control; and handle large incidents such as drug raids and special events such as sports competitions, popular concerts, large conventions and parades.

A meeting of line and staff personnel can determine the events for which tactical planning is necessary. Special problems can then be resolved and personnel needs assessed and assigned. A review of similar past events may require assistance from other police agencies in the area or state or federal aid. Tactical planning should be flexible because of changing conditions such as the number of people involved. Tactical plans are sometimes cast in the form of an action plan such as that shown in Figure 2.1.

OBJECTIVE: _____

_____

_____

STRATEGY: _____

_____

_____

WHAT IS KNOWN ABOUT THE SITUATION (+'s and –'s): _____

_____

_____

What will be done (Tasks)	Who will do it (People)	When it will be done	Resources needed	Evidence of accomplishment

Figure 2.1 Action Plan Sample Worksheet

Strategic plans, in contrast, focus on the future and on setting priorities. Strategic planning is important because, as Drucker says: "Long-range planning does not deal with future decisions, but with the future of present decisions."

A department might decide to place more emphasis on the use of technological advances, including communications and technology training. It might decide to continue the same emphasis on the level of recruitment and in-service training for sworn personnel and to place less emphasis on the use of sworn personnel for nonsworn duties. In addition it might identify new activities such as developing accurate job descriptions and career paths for all employees and eliminating other activities such as free services that most agencies charge for (e.g., fingerprinting, alarms and computer entry).

Glensor and Peak (2005, p.31) suggest that strategic planning provides several benefits, including clarifying future directions, establishing priorities, making decisions in light of their future consequences, developing a coherent and defensible basis for decision-making, solving major organizational problems, improving organizational performance and building teamwork and expertise. In addition to planning, managers must be facilitators of those plans.

facilitators • assist others in performing their duties to meet mutual goals and objectives.

Facilitators Facilitators assist others in performing their duties. Law enforcement managers at any level do not personally bring the agency goals, objectives and work plans to fruition. This is accomplished through a joint agency effort, as well as with the assistance of others external to the agency.

Rules, regulations, personal rapport, communications, standards, guidelines, logic, basic principles and direction all assist others in performing their duties. After managers have directed subordinates on what to do and how, they should let people carry out their duties independently. Trust, honesty and integrity are important in the manager-subordinate work relationship.

Operating within this environment is constant change. All levels of management must recognize change and be flexible enough to adapt to its demands.

interfacers • coordinate law enforcement agency's goals with those of other agencies within the jurisdiction.

Interfacers Law enforcement executive managers must be **interfacers** who communicate with all segments of the agency, from chief deputy to patrol officer. They must have knowledge of communications and specialized staff activities and relationships and must understand the division of labor and the allocations of personnel.

Managers must set agency goals and work plans with input from all agency members. They are the interfacers between all actions of agency personnel and all other people and agencies in contact with these personnel. Like good drivers, they can look toward the horizon without losing sight of immediate concerns.

interactors • communicate with other groups and agencies: the press, other local government departments, the business community, schools and numerous community committees and organizations.

Interactors Law enforcement managers also must be **interactors** who work effectively with a number of groups. They act as the department's official representative to the press, other local government departments, the business community, schools and numerous community committees and organizations.

Figure 2.2 illustrates the interactions of a typical law enforcement executive and, to some extent, all law enforcement managers. This diagram shows that only one-fifth of the executive manager's role is with the law enforcement organization. Executive managers have political, community, interorganizational and media roles as well.

Each organization with whom the executive interacts sees the importance and conduct of the position from different viewpoints. Law enforcement managers

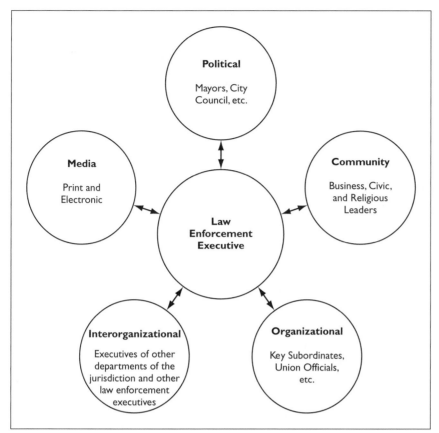

Figure 2.2   Typical Role Set of a Law Enforcement Executive

Source: Donald Witham and Paul Watson. *The Role of the Law Enforcement Executive.* FBI Management
Science Unit, 1983.

must determine these varied expectations and develop goals and work plans to
meet them effectively.

 Law enforcement executives typically interact with politicians, community groups, the
media, and executives of other law enforcement organizations, as well as individuals
and groups within the agency itself.

Attendance at intergovernmental staff meetings is mandatory. Law enforcement agencies need services and information exchange from engineering, finance,
planning, building inspections and other departments, just as other departments
need the police department's services.

Although media communications have some undesirable aspects, if reporters
and law enforcement personnel establish honest, forthright rapport, they can establish generally good working relationships. Law enforcement needs the media as
much as the media need it. (Dealing effectively with the media is discussed in
Chapter 4.) Personal contact with representatives of all groups develops an atmosphere of trust, integrity and respect for each other's duties and responsibilities.

On Becoming an Executive Manager Robert Frost once said: "By working
faithfully eight hours a day, you may eventually get to be boss and work twelve
hours a day!" Benson (2004, p.92) comments: "Police chiefs have the only position without a peer group within their organizations; they are truly alone at the

top of the organization. Often they hold the only position in the organization without job protections, yet they are asked to lead, to discipline, to take professional risks, and to create positive change."

When a person first becomes a chief of police, whether selected from within the department or as an outsider, many rumors concerning the appointment will precede the new chief's first day on the job. New chiefs should call a department meeting as soon as possible. At this meeting they should openly state that they understand the officers' concerns and past loyalties but expect to earn their respect. They should also describe the working relationships they seek. Such an open meeting will help allay fears, squelch rumors, decrease suspicions and establish an early rapport with the staff and line personnel.

A chief's management style should be adjusted to the department's needs. Some important changes should be made as soon as possible, but lesser changes should be instituted slowly. Change is stressful for an organization as well as individuals. People will have different opinions about the need for change. A participative approach that invites input from all employees usually works best, as discussed later in the chapter. Decisions should be based on what is good for the community and the department, not on what pleases specific individuals or interest groups.

Whether the department is small or large, the chief of police holds a powerful position in the governmental structure and in the community. The position is also challenging, exciting and filled with barriers and pitfalls. Chiefs should allow time for contemplation, innovation and creative thinking. They must be both managers and leaders. Their responsibilities are heavy, but their rewards are great.

If chiefs adopt a coequal management approach with the department's formal and informal leaders, they may find that their organizational philosophy will be accepted more readily, thus enabling the organizational changes to occur with less resistance.

A major goal of chief executive officers should be to establish an environment in which success is expected and excellence is desired. Ideally, the chief of police is also a leader within the community, particularly in interactions with the city council and the city manager.

Politics Benson (p.93) surveyed police chiefs from 50 larger municipal police departments and reported that the chiefs listed their most discouraging, dissatisfying aspect of their job as the frustration of working in the political environment and dealing with politicians.

With a clear mission, goals and objectives, a department's day-to-day operations should *not* be influenced by politics. However, chiefs must recognize that politics can influence how much funding the department receives. In addition, Stucky (2005, p.140) reports: "Research both old and new suggests that local politics can influence criminal justice outcomes generally and policing specifically."

Trautman (2003, p.104) points out that political interference is a major cause of corruption in law enforcement. He describes six different types of interference: interference with hiring standards, promotions and transfers, discipline, adequate budget, fair enforcement of laws and work environment.

Gray (2005, p.132) advises: "Be political but do not play politics. Being responsive to the community, the council and the mayor is part of chief's political reality because the chief works for them." He contends that effective politics means effective relationships: "Chiefs who are not political do not last long and those who play political games have even shorter careers."

The political nature of police administrative positions also requires chiefs to keep abreast of changes in legislation. Police administrators must become proactive in the legislative process to effectively serve their departments and communities. Police chiefs have a duty to ensure that the laws enacted are sensible and allow law enforcement agencies to successfully overcome the challenges confronting them and to effectively protect the citizens and communities they serve (Polisar, 2004a, p.6).

Law Enforcement Management as a Career

Deciding to become a law enforcement officer is an exciting career choice, but becoming a manager in law enforcement is even more challenging. It is an opportunity to develop personally and a responsibility to develop others. You can become a successful law enforcement manager in many ways.

Prepare and develop yourself for promotion. Study, attend training programs, take correspondence courses, read trade journals, attend academic courses, use the public library and the law enforcement agency's library and listen to contemporaries. Be ready when opportunity arises.

Be available. Once prepared, you become a valuable resource to the law enforcement organization. Assert yourself at appropriate times. Support your organization's goals and objectives. Participate in work programs. Volunteer to do more than others. Become so valuable to the organization's future that it cannot do without you. Become an information source who is willing to selflessly share information.

Support your manager. An old adage advises: "If you want your manager's job, praise and support him or her because soon that person will move up the ladder. Be derogatory to your manager and he or she will be there forever." Complaining, continually finding fault and being negative or nonsupportive are fast tracks to organizational oblivion. You may accomplish a short-term goal, but in the long run you will destroy your career. Be supportive; if you criticize, make it constructive criticism. Be positive. Praise the good things happening.

Select an advisor or mentor. These are people within or outside the police organization who can assist and counsel you. Advisors can point you in the right direction. They can be a sounding board.

Be positive at and toward work. Either like what you do or change to another job. Rarely can you excel at something you hate. Work longer, more diligently and more competently than anyone else in the organization. Before you know it, you will be an expert.

Nurture interpersonal relationships. Management is getting things done through others. This is impossible to do without treating others as important. Working with others is one of the keys to success. Working alone is a long, hard road. Develop your interpersonal relationships. Combine their strengths with your weaknesses and their weaknesses with your strengths.

Leadership

Leadership has been defined as "working with and through individuals and groups to accomplish organizational goals" (Hersey and Blanchard, 1977). Reintzell (2003, p.36) says, "Leadership is inspiration, backed by perspiration and intellect. It is a potent force that overcomes inertia and begets action." Leadership generates an emotional connection between the leader and the led.

leadership • influencing, working with and through individuals and groups to accomplish a common goal.

Effective leaders develop strong interpersonal relationships, working with and through other individulas and groups to accomplish the organization's goals.

Centuries ago, Lao Tzu observed: "The good leader is he who the people revere. The great leader is he whose people say, 'We did it ourselves.'" President and World War II Commanding General Dwight Eisenhower defined leadership like this: "Leadership: The art of getting someone else to do something you want done, because he wants to do it."

Collins, author of the bestselling *Good to Great (2001)*, contends: "Good is the enemy of great." To make the transition to great, good leaders recognize that complacency can set in when things are going well. Great leaders have what Collins calls BHAGs, Big Hairy Audacious Goals. He gives as examples Abraham Lincoln's goal of ending slavery and John F. Kennedy's goal of putting a man on the moon (Edelson, 2004, p.3).

Characteristics of Leaders

A leader in the purest sense influences others by example. This characteristic of leadership was recognized in the sixth century B.C. by Chinese philosopher Lao Tzu when he wrote:

The superior leader gets things done
With very little motion.
He imparts instruction not through many words
But through a few deeds.
He keeps informed about everything
But interferes hardly at all.
He is a catalyst,
And although things wouldn't get done as well
If he weren't there,
When they succeed he takes no credit.

And because he takes no credit

Credit never leaves him.

Right Management Consultants asked 570 white-collar workers what they considered to be the most important trait or attribute for a leader to possess. The top five traits were honesty, integrity/morals/ethics, caring/compassion, fairness and good relationships with employees (including approachability and listening skills) ("In Search of an Honest Manager," 2003, p.6).

Vernon (2004, pp.60–61) defines leaders with five statements: (1) the ability to clearly understand and articulate the goal, (2) the confidence to be out in front and show the way to the goal, (3) the ability to convince people to follow as an act of their free choice, (4) the desire and ability to help people develop and pursue excellence and (5) the capability to inspire people to achieve their full potential. Research conducted over the past 10 years has identified four highly valued traits in leaders: (1) being a good listener, (2) admitting when they're wrong, (3) giving recognition and (4) keeping commitments (Vernon, 2005, p.57).

Other desired attributes of leaders are (1) a lively, intellectual curiosity—an interest in everything; (2) a genuine interest in what other people think and why they think the way they do; (3) a feeling of responsibility for envisioning a future that's different from a straight-line projection of the present; (4) the attitude that risks are not to be avoided, but to be taken; (5) the feeling that crisis is normal, tensions can be promising, and complexity is fun; (6) the realization that paranoia and self-pity are reserved for people who don't want to take the lead; (7) the quality of unwarranted optimism; and (7) a sense of personal responsibility for the general outcome of his or her efforts (Zemke, 2003, p.10).

One of the most important qualities a leader possesses is being visionary: "A leader sees more than others see (quantity); farther than others see (distance); before others see (timing); and helps others see what the leader sees" (Sokolove and Field, 2003, p.75). The only way leaders can ever make their vision clear and concise is by spending a great deal of time with the vision. Lack of vision results in poor focus, little coordination and haphazard planning (Sokolove and Field, p.75).

Leadership creates a special bond that has to be earned. To build and maintain credibility, it is necessary to clarify values, identify the wishes of the community and employees, build a consensus, communicate shared values, stand up for beliefs and lead by example.

A good leader knows being the boss does not mean bossing. Rather it means giving employees the resources, training and coaching they need and providing them with information so they can see their organization's mission.

It is apparent that authorities on leadership vary in what they perceive to be the most important characteristics of leaders. George (2003, p.78) offers the following for consideration: "[Leadership is] *not* about your style, your persona, your characteristics or your skills. Authentic leadership is about being yourself, developing your character and becoming the kind of person who people want to follow." Parachin (2003, p.112) likewise stresses the importance of character and integrity, quoting Ralph Waldo Emerson's statement: "What lies behind us and what lies before us are tiny matters compared to what lies within us." He (p.114) advises that leaders pay attention to the "small stuff," despite many experts' advice to the contrary, citing the wisdom of Lao Tzu: "Deal with the difficult while it is still easy. Solve large problems when they are still small."

Table 2.2   Management versus Leadership

Management	Leadership
Does the thing right	Does the right thing
Tangible	Intangible
Referee	Cheerleader
Directs	Coaches
What you do	How you do it
Pronounces	Facilitates
Responsible	Responsive
Has a view of the mission	Has vision of mission
Views world from inside	Views world from outside
Chateau leadership	Front-line leadership
What you say	How you say it
No gut stake in enterprise	Gut stake in enterprise
Preserving life	Passion for life
Driven by constraints	Driven by goals
Looks for things done wrong	Looks for things done right
Runs a cost center	Runs an effort center
Quantitative	Qualitative
Initiates programs	Initiates an ongoing process
Develops programs	Develops people
Concerned with programs	Concerned with people
Concerned with efficiency	Concerned with efficacy
Sometimes plays the hero	Plays the hero no more

Source: Bill Westfall. "Leadership: Caring for the Organizational Spirit." *Knight Line USA*, May–June 1993, p.9. Reprinted with permission of Executive Excellence, Provo, Utah. September 1992, p.11.

Leading versus Managing

More than 20 years ago Drucker conducted a study of the Los Angeles Police Department requested by the chief. Among Drucker's findings was: "You police are so concerned with doing things right that you fail to do the right things." In other words, the administration was so concerned with managing that they failed to lead. He also said: "Police are so concerned with doing things right [that] you promote for the absence of wrongdoing rather than for the presence of initiative, innovation and leadership." Recall Drucker's quote: "Managers do things right; leaders do the right thing." Table 2.2 highlights several other differences between managers and leaders.

 A basic difference between managers and leaders is that managers focus on tasks, whereas leaders focus on people. Manage things; lead people.

A manager operates in the status quo, but a leader takes risks. Police administrators must be both skilled managers and effective leaders. Leaders solve problems, maximize potential with competent associates, take safe risks, take responsibility, move forward, lead by example and have vision. Managers may or may not be leaders, and leaders do not have to be managers. A true leader has the potential to influence from any position in the organization, formal or informal.

In the twenty-first century, most people resist being managed. They seek leadership. However, if management is defined as the administrative ordering of things—with written plans, clear organization charts, well-documented objectives, detailed and precise job descriptions, and regular evaluation of performance—few would deny that competent management is essential to any law enforcement agency. To be truly effective, those in positions of authority combine managerial and leadership skills. All leadership and no management would be as serious a problem as the current imbalance in the other direction in many organizations.

Research on and Theories Related to Leadership

Leadership has been studied over the past several decades from many different perspectives.

 Theories about leadership include the study of traits, the classic studies conducted at Michigan State and Ohio State Universities, the Managerial/Leadership Grid and situational leadership.

Trait Theorists

The first group of leadership researchers, the **trait theorists**, examined the individual. They looked at leaders in industry and government to determine what special characteristics or traits these people possessed. According to Haberfeld (2006, p.211), early trait theory, also called the "Great Man" theory, leadership characteristics were "innate, fixed, and relative to all situations." He notes that in the nineteenth century leadership traits included physical characteristics such as height.

trait theorists • those who research special characteristics that leaders possess.

Bennis and Nanus (1985, p.27) identified four leadership traits that can be learned:

1. Attention through vision: Leaders have an agenda and are result oriented.
2. Meaning through communication: Leaders have the capacity to project/articulate meaning.
3. Trust through positioning: Leaders operate with integrity and buy into their own ideals.
4. Deployment of self through positive self-regard: Leaders project acceptance, respect and trust.

Kirkpatrick and Locke (1991) modernized trait theory by stating that certain leadership traits—drive, the desire to lead, honesty and integrity, self-confidence, cognitive ability, and knowledge of the business—are simply preconditions and do not guarantee success, but without them, a person is unlikely to become an effective leader. With these traits, however, all that is needed is skills, vision and implementation.

Although many leadership traits have been identified, none dominate. Leadership trait theory was highly popular because it simplified the process of selecting leaders. Guaranteed leadership through possession of specific traits, however, was never fully realized because of the number of traits identified and the fact that no single person possessed them all. No criteria determined which traits were more desirable than others. Even possession of all the traits did not guarantee leadership success.

After many studies and experiments, trait theorists could not empirically document leadership characteristics. Researchers in the 1940s and 1950s turned their attention to the situations in which leaders actually functioned.

The Michigan State and Ohio State Universities Studies

Research conducted at Michigan State University and Ohio State University also provides insights into effective leadership. These studies determined that leaders must provide an environment that motivates employees to accomplish organizational goals.

The Michigan State study looked at how leaders motivated individuals or groups to achieve organizational goals. It determined that leaders must have a sense of the task to be accomplished and the most favorable work environment. Three principles of leadership behavior emerged from the Michigan State study:

- Leaders must give task direction to their followers.
- Closeness of supervision directly affects employee production. High-producing units had less direct supervision; highly supervised units had lower production. Conclusion: Employees need some freedom to make choices. Given this, they produce at a higher rate.
- Leaders must be employee oriented. It is the leader's responsibility to facilitate employees' accomplishment of goals.

The Ohio State study on leadership behavior used similar methods. This research focused on two dimensions: initiating structure and consideration structure.

initiating structure • looks at how leaders assign tasks.

consideration structure • looks at establishing the relationship between the group and the leader.

Initiating structure looked at the leader's behavior in assigning *tasks*. It focused on leaders who assigned employees to specific tasks and asked them to follow standard rules and regulations. **Consideration structure** looked at establishing the *relationship* between the group and the leader. It focused on leaders who found time to listen to employees, were willing to make changes and were friendly and approachable.

The Ohio study used these two variables—focus on task and focus on relationships—to develop a management quadrant describing leadership behavior.

The Managerial Grid from a Leadership Perspective

Blake and Mouton developed their Managerial Grid from the studies done at Ohio State University and the Group Dynamics Leadership studies. Their classic Managerial Grid has been further developed into the Management/Leadership Grid, as summarized in Table 2.1. Hersey and Blanchard (p.96) summarized the attitudinal preferences of each management style in several areas, including their basic production/people beliefs, guiding slogans, decision making, conflict with superiors and peers, conflict with subordinates, creativity and promotion of creative effort (Table 2.3).

Situational Leadership

situational leadership • leadership viewed as an interplay between the amount of direction (task behavior) a leader gives, combined with the amount of relationship behavior a leader provides and the maturity level that followers exhibit on a specific task the leader is attempting to accomplish through the individual or group (Hersey and Blanchard).

Hersey and Blanchard took existing leadership theory a step further. They viewed leadership as an interplay between the amount of direction (task behavior) a leader gives, combined with the amount of relationship behavior a leader provides (the Managerial/Leadership Grid) *and* the readiness level that followers exhibit on a specific task the leader is attempting to accomplish through the individual or group.

Situational leadership specifies that initially workers need support and direction. As they become more task-ready, they need less direction and more support, up to the point where even support can be reduced. The basic premise of situational leadership theory is that as the followers' readiness level in relation to task increases, leaders should begin to lessen their direction or task behavior

Table 2.3   Attitudinal Preferences of Various Management Styles

	Authority–Compliance Management	Country Club Management	Middle-of-the-Road Management	Impoverished Management	Team Management
Basic Production–People Beliefs	Sees good relationships as incidental to high production. Supervisors achieve production goals by planning, directing and controlling all work.	Sees production as incidental to good relations. Supervisors establish a pleasant work atmosphere and harmonious relationship between people.	Sees high production and sound relations in conflict. Supervisors stay neutral and carry out established procedures.	Seeks a balance between high production and good human relations. Supervisors find middle ground so a reasonable degree of production can be achieved without destroying morale.	Sees production resulting from integrating task and human requirements. Good relationships and high production are both attainable. Supervisors get effective production through participation and involvement of people and their ideas.
Guiding Slogans	Produce or perish.	Try to win friends and influence people.	Don't rock the boat.	Be firm but fair.	People support what they help create.
Decision Making	Inner-directed, depending on own skills, knowledge, attitudes and beliefs in approaching problems and making decisions.	Other-directed, eager to find solutions that reflect the ideas and opinions of others so that solutions are accepted.	Avoids problems or defers them to others.	Samples opinions, manipulates participation, compromises, and then sells the final solution.	Seeks emergent solutions as the result of debate, deliberation, and experimentation by those with relevant facts and knowledge.
Conflict with Superiors and Peers	Takes a win-lose approach, fighting to win its own points as often as possible.	Avoids conflict by conforming to the thinking of the boss or peers.	Keeps its mouth shut and does not express dissent.	Expresses opinions and then tries to find reasonable compromises.	Confronts conflict directly, communicating feelings and facts as a basis to work through conflict.
Conflict with Subordinates	Suppresses conflict through authority.	Smooths over and tries to release tension by appeals to the "goodness of people."	Does not get involved with conflict. It usually avoids issues that might give rise to conflict by simply not discussing them with subordinates.	Deals with surface tensions and symptoms only, letting conflict situations "cool off" for a while, working for a blending of different positions so a somewhat acceptable solution is reached.	Confronts conflict directly and works through it at the time it arises. Conflict is accepted so the clash of ideas and people can generate creative solutions to problems. Those involved are brought together to work through differences.
Creativity	Considers ideas the responsibility of the few, not expected of the majority.	Expects no one to be creative, but a creative person is congratulated.	Sometimes has good ideas "pop up," but ideas are usually unrelated to company goals or morale.	Values creativity and seeks it from everyone, usually under nonthreatening conditions that will not disturb staff or the authority structure.	Expects those interested in and able to tackle a problem to do so. A high degree of interplay of ideas exists. Experimentation is the rule rather than the exception. Innovations further shared goals and solve important problems.
Promotion of Creative Effort	Promotes innovation by rewards and promotions. When a conflict of ideas arises, it is "survival of the fittest."	Encourages innovations by accepting all ideas uncritically. Ideas that will generate conflicts are side-stepped.	Discourages creativity. Ideas are not discussed on the job, so conflicts are unlikely.	Encourages innovation under controlled conditions. Brainstorming and "idea of the month" campaigns are used.	Uses feedback of results of experiments as a basis for further development and thinking. Open expression of differences and mature conflict are accepted. Everyone encourages innovations by defining and communicating problems.

Source: Adapted from Hersey and Blanchard (1977).

and simultaneously increase their relationship behavior. This would be the leaders' strategy until individuals or groups reach a moderate level of task-readiness.

As followers or groups move into an above-average level of readiness, leaders would decrease both their task behavior and their relationship behavior. At this point followers would be ready not only from the task point of view but also from the amount of relationship behavior they need. Once a follower or group reaches this level of readiness, close supervision is reduced and delegation is increased, indicating the leader's trust and confidence.

Transformational Leadership

transformational leadership • treats employees as the organization's most valuable assets. Is employee centered and focuses on empowerment.

The most recent form of leadership to be recognized is **transformational leadership**, which treats employees as the organization's most valuable asset. It is employee-centered and focused on empowerment.

An important aspect of transformational leadership is its employee orientation. Transformational leadership seeks to empower people to make the fullest possible contribution to the organization. What is often lacking, however, is a model for effective *followership*. A leader cannot simply tell people they are empowered and expect them to instantly know how to perform. Employees need training, resources and authority if they are to be empowered.

According to the Center for Leadership Studies (CLS): "Transformational leaders set high standards of conduct and become role models, gaining trust, respect, and confidence from others; articulate the future desired state and a plan to achieve it; question the status quo and [are] continuously innovative, even at the peak of success; and energize people to achieve their full potential and performance" (Morreale and Ortmeier, 2004, p.89).

The focus on leadership rather than management complements the move toward community-oriented, problem-solving policing because it stresses resolving problems and not simply reacting to incidents. It encourages experimenting with new ways and allows honest mistakes to encourage creativity.

Leadership Styles

Management literature has identified many leadership styles, several of which can be found in police organizations.

Leadership styles include autocratic, democratic or participative and laissez-faire.

autocratic leadership • managers make decisions without participant input. Completely authoritative, showing little or no concern for subordinates.

Autocratic leadership is most frequently mentioned in connection with the past. Many early leaders inherited their positions. They were members of the aristocracy, and through the centuries positions of leadership were passed down to family members.

In early industrial production efforts, the boss was often a domineering figure. He (bosses were invariably men) was specifically chosen because he displayed traits associated with autocratic leadership. His authority was uncontested, and employees did what they were told out of fear. This style of management emerged in response to the demands of the Industrial Revolution, when masses of illiterate workers used expensive machinery and needed to follow explicit orders.

mechanistic model • divides tasks into highly specialized jobs where job holders become experts in their fields, demonstrating the "one best way" to perform their cog in the wheel (Taylorism). The opposite of the *organic model*.

Managers who used autocratic leadership made decisions without participant input. They were completely authoritative and showed little or no concern for subordinates. Rules were rules, without exception. This **mechanistic model** of management derived from the theories of Frederick Taylor, introduced in Chapter 1, divides jobs into highly specialized tasks where employees can become experts in their task. Certain circumstances may call for autocratic leadership.

Consultative, Democratic or Participative Leadership

Consultative, **democratic** or **participative leadership** has been evolving since the 1930s and 1940s. Democratic leadership does not mean that every decision is made only after discussion and a vote. It means rather that management welcomes employees' ideas and input. Employees are encouraged to be innovative. Management development of a strong sense of individual achievement and responsibility is a necessary ingredient of participative or consultative leadership.

Democratic or participative managers are interested in their subordinates and their problems and welfare. Management still makes the final decisions but takes into account the input from employees. This leadership style is a good fit with the **organic model** of management: The model is flexible, participatory, democratic and science-based, and accommodates change. In contrast to the mechanistic model, which focuses on efficiency and productivity, the organic model focuses on worker satisfaction, flexibility and personal growth.

Laissez-Faire Leadership

Laissez-faire leadership implies nonintervention and is almost a contradiction in terms. The idea is to let everything run itself without direction from the leader, who exerts little or no control. This style arises from the concept that employees are adults, should know as well as the manager what is right and wrong and will automatically do what is right for themselves and the organization.

Laissez-faire leaders want employees to be happy and believe that if employees are happy, they will be more productive. Employees *should* feel comfortable and good about their work, but this should be because they participate. Even when they participate, employees must still do the job and meet the organization's goals and objectives. Leaderless management, sometimes called **free-rein leadership**, may result in low morale, inefficiency, lack of discipline and low productivity. Figure 2.3 shows the continuum of leadership styles.

Common Sense Leadership

Another style that has been advocated, though not as frequently discussed, is common sense leadership. Cottringer (2005, p.164), author of *You Can Have Your Cheese and Eat It Too*, says that leaders need to return to "sweating the small stuff" that they have been "prematurely" advised to dismiss and to refocus on using common sense as the best way to handle the current information overload. "Common sense always represents the action that gets the best results, with the least cost or side-effects" (Cottringer, 2004, p.110).

Implications

Research on leaders and leadership is abundant. Each theory offers something to the law enforcement manager. However, no one type of leader or leadership style will suffice in all situations.

Leaders must often be autocratic in one situation and democratic or participatory in another. They must know when to make an immediate decision and when to make a decision only after input, discussion and consideration.

consultative leadership • employees' ideas and input are welcomed, but the manager makes the final decision.

democratic leadership • does not mean every decision is made by a vote, but rather that decisions are made only after discussion and input of employees.

participative leadership • managers build a team and view themselves as a part of this team.

organic model • a flexible, participatory, science-based structure that will accommodate change. Designed for effectiveness in serving the needs of citizens rather than the autocratic rationality of operation. The opposite of the *mechanistic model*.

laissez-faire leadership • involves nonintervention; lets everything run itself without direction from the leader; there is little or no control.

free-rein leadership • leaderless, laissez-faire management.

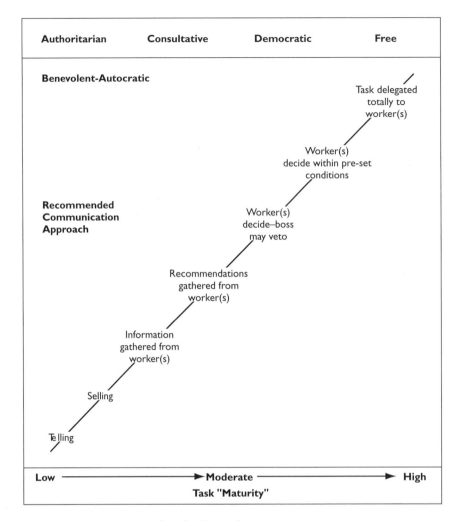

Figure 2.3   Continuum of Leadership Styles

Source: Paul R. Timm. *Supervision*, 2nd ed. St. Paul, MN: West Publishing Company, 1992, p.269.

Emergency situations rarely permit the opportunity for democratic or partici-patory decision making. Employees in nonemergency situations rarely respond well to autocratic leadership for routine task performance over the long term.

Leaders know what to do, how to do it, when to do it and with what type of employee, according to the demands of the individual situation. Internationally, leaders have been recognized because of the leadership abilities they displayed for a particular time, place and need. Put into another situation and time, they might not have become leaders. Regardless of the situation or time, most leaders have adhered to several adages, listed in Table 2.4.

Section II of this text presents many of these adages in the context of manage-ment and supervision.

Leadership—A Call for Change

Managers must pay attention to the new ideas and trends emerging from America's businesses: a commitment to people, the development of a people-oriented work-place and the belief that leadership can and does make a difference. Leadership in

Table 2.4 Leadership Adages

1. **Move your organization up the "wisdom pyramid."** If you can assist your organization in moving from a focus on data and information to a concentration on knowledge, understanding and wisdom, better decisions for both the short term and the long term will be reached.

2. **Don't postpone joy.** If there is something to celebrate do it now. Don't wait until next week, next month or next year to publicly congratulate those who have just accomplished something extraordinary.

3. **Use your wit to amuse not abuse.** Laughing at others is hurtful. On the other hand, laughing at yourself is healing for you and others. Humor used well is wonderful for you and those around you. He who laughs, lasts.

4. **Polish your negotiation skills.** People often ask me, "What is Colin Powell's greatest talent?" I explain how he brings together people, often who are very angry with each other. By using humor and the spirit of cooperation and compromise, he finds workable solutions that everyone can support.

5. **Beware of clever, manipulative subordinates**. This was the major leadership failure at CNN during the nerve gas debacle in 1998. The CEO of CNN not only got snookered by some clever subordinates, but it also took him much too long to hold a few top people accountable for their unethical behavior in the production of CNN's "Valley of Death"" special.

6. **Don't neglect the intangibles.** Too many leaders focus all their attention on what they can measure—sales numbers, quarterly reports, cash flow, stock price, etc. These leaders often neglect such vital intangibles as morale and *esprit de corps.*

7. **Practice forgiveness.** Be willing to forgive those who make honest mistakes. Also, be sure to forgive yourself after you acknowledge the fact that you have made an error. Self-flagellation is not a good quality for a leader.

8. **Scan the environment widely.** Too many bosses are unwilling to look outside their own organization for fresh ideas. For instance, I have learned in the fifteen years since I retired from the military that there is much that corporations can learn from the military and vice versa.

9. **Don't spend too much time with malcontents.** It only encourages them. Spend most of your time with those who are seriously contributing to the accomplishment of the mission.

10. **Enjoy your work and your people.** Working for a boss with a furrowed brow or an angry scowl is no fun, nor does it inspire people to do their very best. If you are obviously enjoying your work, most people will be captured by your enthusiasm and joy and will enjoy their work also.

11. **Acknowledge mistakes quickly and completely.** Be willing to fully air your dirty linen. The best leaders acknowledge their mistakes quickly, and take corrective actions to reduce the possibility of a similar mistake in the future. Good news may improve with age, bad news does not.

12. **Don't overconcentrate on the details.** No amount of genius can overcome a preoccupation with detail. This was the fundamental mistake of the Carter presidency. A man of compassion and intellect failed because he was unable to empower subordinates and to think and act strategically.

13. **Never roll the ball over.** Leaders should remind themselves often that when they play sports, the object is not to win but to compete with total integrity. Many people play fast and loose with the game of golf—they cheat—yet they somehow justify their conduct (Bill Clinton uses the term "a do over" to explain the 30 or so Mulligans he uses during his golf rounds).

14. **Anticipate impending crises.** The best leaders have the ability to look around corners and anticipate problems and impending crises. When you see a crisis headed your way, take some quick actions to end the crisis and to minimize the damage.

15. **Don't use "I don't trust you" phrases.** Be very careful about using the following phrases: "I never want to be surprised," "Before you start anything, check with me first," and"When I am on the road, I will call in every morning for an update." All of these phrases send strong messages to subordinates that you want to keep them on a close leash and, even worse, that you do not trust them.

16. **Welcome criticism.** All leaders should fully understand that criticism and loyalty are mutually supporting. When subordinates quit complaining, that can be very bad news. It means that they are either afraid to complain or have given up on making things better within the organization. Both are deadly.

17. **Don't set unreasonable deadlines.** There is an expression in the Pentagon, "If you want it bad you will get it bad." Try to give your folks enough time to put together a solution that you can be proud of.

18. **Expect exceptional performance.** Although perfectionism in a leader can be deadly in any organization, leaders must not let the pendulum swing too far in the other direction. If leaders don't ask for exceptional performance from their associates, they are not likely to get it.

19. **Don't allow yourself to become a wind chime.** If your primary skill is blowing with the wind by being politically agile, you will not be respected by those you lead. Have a backbone and exercise your strength of character by taking strong positions on important issues.

20. **Fight the temptations to get even.** If someone does something to you that is mean spirited, think of it as his or her problem—not your problem.

21. **Focus on goals, not process.** It is important to be clear about the job to be done but to be very flexible about the way you do the job.

22. **Be a blame acceptor.** If something goes wrong within the organization you lead, you must be willing to accept the blame even though you personally may be only a tiny part of the failure. Too many bosses try to blame others, especially their subordinates. By doing so they often lose the respect of their people and their bosses.

continued

Table 2.4—continued

23. **Establish self-reinforcing relationships.** Praise and support those who can move smoothly from competition to cooperation. Encourage those who find solutions that reconcile the opposites. The French have it right in their national motto: liberty, equality and *fraternity*.

24. **Be a leader developer.** A big part of leadership is mentorship. Helping people to develop their leadership skills can be immensely rewarding. Also, leaders should help subordinates think like them and like their bosses. When these subordinates get promoted they will then be ready to take on the big job.

25. **Never try to get even.** Trying to get even seldom works, lacks dignity and makes you look petty and mean-spirited. You can never get ahead by getting even.

26. **Find an anchor and hold on to it in the tough times.** I have been blessed with a number of wonderful anchors. My wife of more than 42 years has lifted me up when I was down and eased me down when I was sky high. My two adult children have been very helpful, especially when I was dealing with issues of integrity. A few other close friends have helped so many times when I was in great need of advice, comfort, solace or support.

27. **Leverage opportunities.** The best leaders leverage their time, their talents, their technology and their friends. In fact, if you use leverage, many things you do will become easier and quicker. Let me give two personal examples. I am a terrible typist but I have a fast computer with an excellent spelling checker that allows me to crank out written material quickly. Also, I am blessed with the talent of speed reading. It has allowed me to get through my "in box" quickly and get out with the troops as well as maintain a regular reading program of about four books per month.

28. **Be a servant leader.** Too many leaders serve their ambitions or their egos rather than their people. As I reflect on the marvelous leadership opportunities I have enjoyed, I realize that I spent most of my time serving the people who worked for me. Whenever they reached out to me for assistance, I tried to help them.

Source: Perry M. Smith is the author of *Rules and Tools for Leaders, Assignment Pentagon* and *A Hero Among Heroes: Jimmie Dyess and the 4th Marine Division*. In June 1998, he resigned his position as military analyst to CNN. He now serves as military correspondent for CBS radio.

law enforcement historically depended on a strong, authoritarian chief. However, this style of leadership neglects everything known about people and their behavior. Coercion discourages creativity and risk taking and often causes people to rebel. President Eisenhower used to demonstrate this aspect of leadership with a simple piece of string. He would put the string on a table and say, "Pull it and it'll follow wherever you wish. Push it and it'll go nowhere at all." It is the same with people.

Managers must shift from telling and controlling the people they work with to developing and enhancing them. They must ask for their input before making critical decisions that affect them. They must also listen to their customers—the citizens—in new and more open ways. Managers must stop reacting to incidents and begin solving problems. They must permit risk taking and tolerate honest mistakes to encourage creativity and achieve innovation. To better understand this change in leadership style, compare the key concepts from each, summarized in Table 2.5.

Changing from autocratic management to any other style is a slow, evolutionary process. Developing a new corporate culture for an organization can take years. Part of the challenge is the bureaucracy within most law enforcement agencies, as discussed previously.

Leadership Training and Development

An appointment to fill a position on an organizational chart does not automatically make one a leader. By the same token, relatively few leaders are able to simply step into the role without needing to develop and refine their leadership skills and abilities. Covey (2003, p.128) observes: "The challenge before today's police administrators is not how to manage and control their people more effectively, but how to develop all their people as principle-centered leaders who embody the character that the profession demands."

Table 2.5 Authoritarian and Participatory Leadership Styles Compared

Authoritarian (Mechanistic) Style	Participatory (Organic) Style
Response to incidents	Problem solving
Individual effort and competitiveness	Teamwork
Professional expertise	Community orientation; ask customers what they want
Go by the "book"; decisions by emotion	Use data-based decision making
Tell subordinates	Ask and listen to employees
Boss as patriarch and order giver	Boss as coach and teacher
Maintain status quo	Create, innovate, experiment
Control and watch employees	Trust employees
Reliance on scientific investigation and technology rather than people	Reliance on skilled employees—a better resource than machines
When things go wrong, blame employees	Errors mean failed systems/processes—improve them
Organization is closed to outsiders	Organization is open

The trend in the twenty-first century is to not tie leadership to rank, but rather to instill leadership qualities through the department, referred to as **dispersed leadership.** The International Association of Chiefs of Police (IACP), through a grant from the Office of Community Oriented Policing Services (COPS), has developed two leadership bulletins. "Leadership in Police Organizations Training Bulletin 1" (2005, p.3) states: "The bottom line is that today's police leaders cannot do their jobs alone. They must develop leaders at all levels of their department by practicing dispersed leadership." "Leadership in Police Organizations Training Bulletin 2" (2005, p.1) describes the essentials of dispersed leadership:

dispersed leadership • the twenty-first century trend to not tie leadership to rank, but rather to instill leadership qualities throughout the department.

- Shared understanding of what leadership means
- Commitment to shared goals and values
- Leaders at all levels of the organization
- Leaders leading differently at different organizational levels
- A way to develop leadership knowledge and skills throughout the organization
- A way to determine where you are as an organization and as individual leaders

According to the second training bulletin (p.2): "It is paramount to understand that there is no silver bullet or vaccination for leadership. All leaders are developed; they are not born." The leader is developed through learned professional values, training, and job experience over time. This leadership development perpetuates the mission, values and goals of the agency. The bulletin cites as a quick answer to leader development the simplicity of the U.S. Army's "Be, Know, Do." In other words, leadership training must develop character, technical skills and leadership knowledge and provide the chance to express this knowledge in ethically sound leadership behaviors. Figure 2.4 illustrates this leadership development system. Polisar (2004b, p.6) says of the IACP model: "The IACP model reflects documented best practices in the public and private sectors, the military, and the justice system. It is rooted in community oriented policing theory and addresses leadership as an agency-wide concept reaching all ranks and positions."

Vernon (2005, p.54) observes: "When you become a police officer, you must accept the mantle of leadership that comes with the job, regardless of rank." In other words, all officers at all ranks are leaders at one time or another and need to

Figure 2.4   Leadership Development Series
Source: Reprinted from Leadership in Police Organizations Training
Bulletin, 2, p.2. Copyright held by the International Association of
Chiefs of Police, 515 North Washington Street, Alexandria, VA 22314
USA. Further reproduction without express written permission from
IACP is strictly prohibited.

have the appropriate skills. As the most visible form of government, people look
to police for leadership. Every time a police officer puts on a uniform and goes
into the field, people look to him or her for leadership (Stainbrook, 2004, p.8).
Moreover, line-level officers need leadership skills to address the community-
based policing challenges they face (Morreale and Ortmeier, p.89).

Also of importance is developing new sergeants into leaders: "Guiding that
neophyte supervisor through the transition to the rank of sergeant is a crucial responsibility" (Johnson, p.24). They must be guided through the conversion from
a law enforcement function to the role of supervisor and must learn to command
as well as to delegate.

Leaders who have adopted a specific leadership style can change that style
through training. They can turn their weaknesses into strengths through studying,
working with mentors or observing other leaders in action. Leaders are not born;
they are developed. Task-oriented leaders can become people-oriented leaders.

Leadership training before appointment is highly desirable. If that is not possible, it should happen soon after appointment. Each leader must be an individual,
not a mirror image of the predecessor.

 Leadership can be developed through comprehensive training programs, including
participative management and team-building theory, motivational theory, communications and decision making.

Table 2.6 summarizes the skill layers for law enforcement managers/leaders.

Guidelines for Effective Management/Leadership

Several guidelines have been developed for effective management and leadership:
- Know your work and those you manage.
- Know how to get and maintain cooperation.
- Learn as much as possible about decision making.
- Learn as much as possible about how to be a leader.

Table 2.6 Skill Layers for Managers/Leaders

A	B	C
When used alone, these skills are suited to a rigidly traditional workplace.	Combined with the skills in column A, the skills below are needed in today's progressive workplace.	Combined with columns A and B, these skills are needed to build and maintain a team environment.
Direct people.	Involve people.	Develop self-motivated people.
Get people to understand ideas.	Get people to generate ideas.	Get groups of diverse people to generate and implement their own best ideas.
Manage one-to-one.	Encourage teamwork.	Build teams that manage more of their own day-to-day work.
Maximize the department's performance.	Build relationships with other departments.	Champion cross-functional efforts to improve quality, service and productivity.
Implement changes from above.	Initiate changes within the department.	Anticipate, initiate and respond to changes dictated by forces outside the organization.

© 1991 Achieve Global (formerly Zenger-Miller)
Source: John H. Zenger et al. "Leadership in a Team Environment." *Security Management*, September 1992, p.29. Reprinted with permission from Achieve Global. Copyright © MCMXCI Achieve Global, Inc. All rights reserved. Not for resale.

- Learn how to give praise and constructive criticism.
- Learn to think positively; create rather than destroy.
- Learn to handle bad situations as well as good ones.
- Know when to discipline and when to be authoritarian or democratic/participatory.
- Help your employees improve themselves. Doing so will in turn improve you. Give them responsibility, tell them your expectations and provide instructions.
- Be honest with yourself and your officers. Expect honesty from them. Maintain integrity in yourself and demand it in others.
- Use your employees' abilities. They can provide new approaches to problems. Establish two-way communication to capture the vast amount of information contained within the group. Use participation to achieve more acceptance of decisions.
- Do not oversupervise. Employees do not like managers constantly breathing down their necks.
- Remember that you are part of management, and never downgrade management or managers. If a problem exists, help solve it rather than creating a worse one.
- Keep your perception of your leadership abilities in line with subordinates' perceptions. Ask them what you can do better for them.
- If you call a meeting, make it worthwhile. Excessive meetings that provide a façade of participation are worse than no meetings. Every meeting should produce a result.
- Treat employees' mistakes as a teaching responsibility, not a punitive opportunity.
- Develop officers who differ with you, rather than clones. Develop officers who can compensate for your weaknesses. The tendency is to do the opposite.
- Be consistent. Be direct. Be honest. Be fair.
- Listen. Lead by example.
- Develop people skills.
- Be a risk taker.

When considering what it takes to be a great manager and leader, it is also important to remember that every officer is also an individual and should be treated as such. This principle is at the heart of holistic management.

Holistic Management/Leadership

holistic management/leadership • views personnel as total individuals who make up their team.

The **holistic management/leadership** approach recognizes that both management and leadership skills are required for an agency to accomplish its mission. It recognizes the importance of teamwork, but it also recognizes that all those within the organization are individuals who have answered a special calling. Police officers feel a high sense of peer identification—no call has higher priority than a fellow officer in danger. Police officers also receive an ego boost by the fact that they are readily identified by their uniforms and have certain powers above and beyond those of the average citizen.

The police manager/leader is responsible for ensuring that the officer does not lose this feeling of ego satisfaction (e.g., after a citizen has flashed an obscene gesture to the officer) and continues to develop this sense of belonging to a unique profession geared toward helping one's fellow human beings. The holistic management/leadership approach views law enforcement officers and support personnel as total individuals who make up a *team.*

The Team Approach

Sanow (2004, p.4) contends: "Team building is critical for the success of any endeavor, even policing." He believes team building is the ultimate act of leadership. A team consists of two or more people who must coordinate their activities regularly to accomplish a common task. The team approach builds on the concept of **synergism**, that the group can channel individual energies to accomplish together what no individual could possibly accomplish alone—that the whole is greater than the sum of its parts.

synergism • synergism occurs when the whole is greater than the sum of its parts; the team achieves more than each could accomplish as individuals.

Synergism is all around. Athletics provides countless examples of how a team, working together, can defeat a "superstar." Examples of synergism also come from the music world. Consider the power and energy produced by a top-notch marching band or symphony orchestra. Every musician must know his or her part. Individual players may have solos, but ultimately what is important is how it all sounds together. Anthropologist Margaret Mead has said of the value of collective efforts: "Never doubt that a small group of thoughtful, committed citizens can change the world. Indeed, it is the only thing that ever has" (Delinger, 2004, p.110).

The Wilson Learning Corporation has identified eight attributes of high-performing teams (Buchholz and Roth, 1987, p.14).

Attributes of high-performing teams are:

- *Participative leadership*—creating interdependency by empowering, freeing up and serving others.
- *Shared responsibility*—establishing an environment in which all team members feel as responsible as the manager for the work unit's performance.
- *Aligned on purpose*—having a sense of common purpose about why the team exists and the function it serves.

- *High communication*—creating a climate of trust and open, honest communication.
- *Future focused*—seeing change as an opportunity for growth.
- *Focused on task*—keeping meetings focused on results.
- *Creative talents*—applying individual talents and creativity.
- *Rapid response*—identifying and acting on opportunities.

Although Buchholz and Roth were speaking of teams in the business world, the same eight attributes are likely to be present in a high-performing law enforcement agency.

True leaders are not intimidated by outstanding team members. They do not fear for their jobs. They develop followers who will surpass them. Athletes, for example, will become coaches and train other athletes who will break their records.

One way to initiate action is to encourage employees at the lowest level to work together to solve their problems, with or without manager involvement. These are not highly organized, trained teams but rather groups of employees with a common problem who band together. They are organized informally from anywhere in the organization to focus on a specific problem or project. They are usually self-formed, self-managed and highly productive. When they have met the need, the group dissolves.

Multiagency Teams and Task Forces

Multiagency teams are an important element of current-day policing. Gehl (2004, p.145) describes the leadership challenges in multiagency teams: "The cultural norms that define police organizations and influence organizational behavior generally do not support the process of forming teams for interagency partnerships." Among the cultural norms that impede interagency teams are case ownership, secrecy, organizational isolation, and valuing individuals above the team (pp.147–148).

Seven systemic issues interfering with multiagency teams, in order of significance, are (1) lack of common database systems, (2) paramilitary structuring, (3) politics and regionalization, (4) organized labor issues, (5) lack of common case management systems, (6) resource issues and (7) policy differences (Gehl, pp.148–149). Despite these barriers, Gehl (p.150) contends: "There is no question that multiagency teams are essential to the future of policing."

He suggests communication protocols are the first necessity to overcome the barriers. What is needed is communications that drive timely decision making to form the team, communications that ensure the team can function as an independent unit, and communications that satisfy the contributing organizations' need to be kept informed at appropriate levels. According to Gehl (p.153): "The leadership challenge to create effective multiagency teams will no doubt continue to be a concern for police agencies."

Domash (2004, p.42) describes four task forces established by the U.S. Marshals Service to assist local law enforcement with tracking and apprehending fugitives, including terrorists. Each task force is operated by marshals and local, state and federal authorities. The four task forces are the New York/New Jersey Task Force, the California Task Force, the Chicago Task Force and the Georgia Task Force.

One of the most analyzed and publicized is the multijurisdictional DC sniper investigation, a case that involved more than twenty local, two state and at least ten federal law enforcement agencies. During the three-week investigation, law enforcement executives as well as government leaders at the local, state and national levels grappled with questions about leadership and its role in solving crimes and addressing community fear (Murphy and Wexler, 2004, p.19).

The Sniper Task Force vested leadership with three individuals: Montgomery County Police Chief Charles Moose, Federal Bureau of Investigation (FBI) Special Agent in Charge (SAC) Gary Bald and Bureau of Alcohol, Tobacco, Firearms and Explosives (ATF) SAC Michael Bouchard. These leaders were responsible not only for leading the main task force but also for five task forces within the jurisdictions affected as the case unfolded—the counties of Montgomery, Spotsylvania, Prince William, Fairfax and Central Virginia (Murphy and Wexler, pp.21–22). Chief Ramsey of the Metropolitan Police Department (p.24) recommends: "Don't manage the other task forces. Rather, make certain that every task force leader knows his or her obligations, which are to manage information, keep chiefs informed and follow up on leads." He (p.29) also observes: "Chiefs have to be willing to give up some control. Admittedly, this is difficult for chiefs, sheriffs and SACs, but unless it is done, the investigation won't succeed."

Murphy and Wexler (pp.31–33) report several lessons learned regarding leadership in a multijurisdictional task force, including the following:

- Executives should clearly establish who is in charge as well as the scope and nature of their authority.
- Multi-agency task force leaders should always speak with one voice.
- Task force leaders have to ensure that communication and meaningful information flow both into and out of the task force. Executives must swiftly determine their roles and responsibilities and focus on addressing six immediate tasks: (1) Make order out of chaos, (2) remain flexible and help others to be adaptable, (3) focus on the entire agency, (4) let a competent workforce do its job, (5) provide personnel with the resources they need and (6) work with external stakeholders.
- Executives should push responsibilities down and give personnel the resources they need to do their job.

The importance of cooperation and collaboration among local, state and federal agencies is discussed further in the next chapter.

 SUMMARY

Managers have authority and power, which both imply the ability to coerce compliance—that is, to make subordinates carry out orders. Both are important to managers at all levels. However, authority relies on force or on some law or order, whereas power relies on persuasion and lacks the support of law and rule.

Basic management skills include technical skills, administrative skills, conceptual skills and people skills. Successful managers have clear goals and a commitment to excellence, feedback and support. Management by objectives (MBO) involves managers and subordinates setting goals and objectives together and then tracking performance to ensure that the objectives are met. Several management theories have evolved over time, yet no one style is more apt to achieve the department's mission than another. The selected style must be matched to individual personalities.

Management typically has three levels: the top level (chief, sheriff), the middle level (captains, lieutenants) and the first-line level (sergeants).

Law enforcement executives are planners, facilitators, interfacers and interactors. They are responsible for both tactical and strategic planning. *Tactical planning* is short-term planning. *Strategic planning* is long-term planning. In addition to these roles and responsibilities, law enforcement executives typically interact with politicians, community groups, the media and executives of other law enforcement organizations and individuals and groups within the law enforcement agency itself.

Three important management challenges for law enforcement are administering the budget; maintaining effective community relations; and establishing and administering personnel systems and procedures, including recruitment, selection, training and discipline of key employees.

The basic difference between managers and leaders is that managers focus on tasks, whereas leaders focus on people. A leader in the purest sense influences others by example. Theories about leadership include the study of traits, the classic studies conducted at Michigan State and Ohio State universities, the Managerial Grid, situational leadership and transformational leadership.

Trait theorists identified characteristics leaders possessed. The Michigan and Ohio studies determined that leaders must provide an environment that motivates employees to accomplish organizational goals. Situational leadership specifies that initially workers need support and direction. As they mature they need less direction and more support, up to the point where even support can be reduced. Transformational leadership treats employees as the organization's most valuable asset. It is employee centered and focused on empowerment. Research has also identified several leadership styles, including autocratic, consultative, democratic or participative and laissez-faire.

Leadership can be developed through comprehensive training programs, including participative management and team-building theory, communications and decision making.

Attributes of high-performing teams are participative leadership, shared responsibility, aligned on purpose, high communication, future focused, focused on task, creative talents and rapid response. Leaders must balance the need for synergism and the need for survival of the organization.

 CHALLENGE TWO

After five years as an officer, you were recently promoted to the rank of patrol sergeant by the new chief of the Greenfield Police Department. The chief tells you he is expanding the authority and responsibility of sergeants and is looking for strong leadership at the supervisor level. Many of the officers you are now supervising, including your old partner, have considerably more experience than you. Your old partner is a 20-year veteran and trained you as a rookie. You consider him a mentor and a good friend. You confided in each other when you had problems.

You were a popular officer and often attended social gatherings after your shift. You've declined several invitations since your promotion. Some officers are greeting you less cordially, and you hear talk that your promotion has changed you. Others openly wonder why your old partner was passed by for the promotion. Your old partner seems less friendly and sometimes questions your decisions at roll call. He often brings up things you did in the past and openly criticizes management.

1. The transition from officer to supervisor is difficult and sometimes isolating. Discuss some issues that complicate the transition.

2. What should you do as a new sergeant to prove to your officers that you haven't changed? Should you use your new authority to demand compliance and establish your position of authority over your old peers?

3. What is the best style of leadership for a new sergeant?

4. Do different situations require different leadership approaches?

5. Do different officers need different levels of direction and support?

DISCUSSION QUESTIONS

1. Who should be responsible for law enforcement planning? How should it be accomplished?

2. Why is coordination important? What are some examples?

3. What are the main problem areas of the different levels of law enforcement managers?

4. How do you develop yourself to be a law enforcement manager?

5. What is your definition of leadership?

6. What traits do you attribute to successful law enforcement leaders? If you had to select one most important characteristic of a law enforcement leader, which would you select?

7. Which style of leadership do you prefer? Which style do you perceive you use most of the time?

8. What are the merits of the holistic approach to leadership?

9. What direction should law enforcement leaders take for the future?

10. What leadership traits do you possess? What leadership traits do you need to develop?

REFERENCES

Aldrich, Clark. "The New Core of Leadership." *Training and Development*, March 2003, pp.32–38.

Blanchard, Ken. "Getting Back to Basics." *Today's Office*, January 1988, pp.14, 19.

Bennis, G. and Nanus, B. *Leaders: The Strategies for Taking Charge*. New York: Harper and Row, 1985.

Benson, Bruce L. "The Frustrations of Police Chiefs and How to Solve Them." *The Police Chief*, August 2004, pp.92–94.

Buchholz, Steve and Roth, Thomas. *Creating the High-Performance Team*. New York: John Wiley and Sons, 1987.

Cottringer, William. "Common Sense Leadership." *Law and Order*, September 2004, p.110.

Cottringer, William. "Are You Practicing Common Sense Leadership?" *The Police Chief*, April 2005, pp.104–170.

Covey, Stephen R. "Enhancing Public Trust: It's an Issue of Character and Leadership." *The Police Chief*, April 2003, pp.128–134.

Dahl, Tor. "The Other Side of Zero." *Minnesota Business*, August 2004, p.16.

"Delegate with the Right Level of Authority." *The Manager's Intelligence Report*, November 2003, p.1.

Delinger, David. "Flexibility and Teamwork." *Law and Order*, May 2004, p.110.

Deming, W. Edwards. *Quality, Productivity, and Competitive Position*. Cambridge, MA: Institute of Technology, Center for Advanced Engineering Study, 1982.

"Deming, W. Edwards." *Encyclopedia Britannica*, 2005. Accessed September 29, 2005.

Domash, Shelly Feuer. "Federal Aid." *Police*, May 2004, pp.40–46.

Drucker, Peter. *The Effective Executive*. New York: Harper Collins Publishers, Inc., 1993.

Edelson, David. "Jim Collins Delivers Keynote Address on 'Good to Great.'" *Subject to Debate*, May 2004, pp.1, 3.

Fuller, John. "The Patrol Commander's Primer." *Law and Order*, June 2003, pp.113–115.

Garrett, Ronnie. "Set Goals, Then Plan." *Law Enforcement Technology*, January 2005, p.6.

Gehl, A.R. "Multiagency Teams: A Leadership Challenge." *The Police Chief*, October 2004, pp.142–153.

George, Bill. "Secrets of Leadership." *Minnesota Business*, October 2003, p.78.

Glensor, Ronald W. and Peak, Kenneth J. "Strategic IT Planning." *Issues in IT: A Reader for the Busy Police Chief Executive*. Washington, DC: Police Executive Research Forum, February 2005, pp.29–38.

"Good, Better, Best." *Law Enforcement Technology*, March 14/31, 2003, pp.1, 6.

Gray, John L. "Tips on Police Leadership." *The Police Chief*, September 2005, pp.126–132.

Haberfeld, M. R. *Police Leadership*. Upper Saddle River, NJ: Pearson, Prentice Hall, 2006.

Hale, Charles. "The Employee Interview Exercise." *Law and Order*, August 2005, pp.33–35.

Hersey, Paul and Blanchard, Kenneth H. *Management of Organizational Behavior*, 3rd ed. Englewood Cliffs, NJ: Prentice–Hall, 1977.

How Police Supervisory Styles Influence Patrol Officer Behavior. Washington, DC: National Institute of Justice, June 2003. (NCJ 194078)

"In Search of an Honest Manager." *The Manager's Intelligence Report*, April 2003, p.6.

Johnson, Roy. "Developing the New Sergeant." *Law and Order*, August 2005, p.24.

Kirkpatrick, S. A. and Locke, E. A. "Leadership: Do Traits Matter?" *The Executive*, May 1991, pp.48–60.

"Leadership in Police Organizations Training Bulletin 1." Alexandria, VA: International Association of Chiefs of Police, 2005.

"Leadership in Police Organizations Training Bulletin 2." Alexandria, VA: International Association of Chiefs of Police, 2005.

"Management by Delegation." *The Manager's Intelligence Report*, January 2003, p.4.

Morreale, Stephen A. and Ortmeier, P. J. "Preparing Leaders for Law Enforcement." *The Police Chief*, October 2004, pp.89–97.

Mulder, Armand. "Leadership and Destructive Criticism." *Law and Order*, October 2003, pp.92–94.

Murphy, Gerald R. and Wexler, Chuck. *Managing a Multi-jurisdictional Case: Identifying the Lessons Learned from the Sniper Investigation*, Washington, DC: Police Executive Research Forum, October 2004.

Oldham, Scott. "Control Your Emotions." *Law and Order*, September 2005a, p.28.

Oldham, Scott. "First Line Supervisors." *Law and Order*, April 2005b, p.32.

Oldham, Scott. "The Sergeant." *Law and Order*, January 2005c, p.30.

Oldham, Scott. "Take Command, Calmly." *Law and Order*, July 2005d, p.26.

Oldham, Scott. "What Are You Prepared to Do?" *Law and Order*, May 2005e, p.16.

Parachin, Victor. "The ABCs of Great Leadership." *Law and Order*, October 2003, pp.112–115.

Polisar, Joseph M. "Do Your Elected Officials Know Your Agency's Concerns?" *The Police Chief*, February 2004a, p.6.

Polisar, Joseph M. "The IACP Center for Police Leadership." *The Police Chief*, April 2004b, p.6.

"Prepare before You Delegate." *The Manager's Intelligence Report*, September 2003, p.10.

Reintzell, John F. "Leadership Lessons from History." *The Law Enforcement Trainer*, July/August 2003, pp.36–38.

Sanow, Ed. "Team Building." *Law and Order*, April 2004, p.4.

Sokolove, Bruce and Field, Mark. "How to Fail as a Leader." *Law and Order*, October 2003, pp.74–80.

Stainbrook, Mark G. "Make Yourself a Leader." *Police*, March 2004, p.8.

Stucky, Thomas D. "Local Politics and Police Strength." *Justice Quarterly*, June 2005, pp.139–168.

Trautman, Neal. "Stopping Political Interference." *Law and Order*, October 2003, pp.104–110.

Vernon, Robert. "The Character of Leadership." *Law and Order*, January 2004, pp.60–63.

Vernon, Bob. "It's About Character." *Law Officer Magazine*, July/August 2005, pp.54–57.

Weiss, Jim and Davis, Mickey. "Empowerment or Finger Pointing." *Law and Order*, October 2004, pp.70–73.

Zemke, Ron. "The Leader's Mindset." *Training*, October 2003, p.10.

BOOK-SPECIFIC WEB SITE

Go to the Management and Supervision in Law Enforcement Web site at www.thomsonedu.com/criminaljustice/bennett for student and instructor resources, including Internet Assignments and Case Studies.

CHAPTER 3

Community Policing

The police are the public and the public are the police.

Sir Robert Peel

DO YOU KNOW?

- What community policing is?
- What four essential dimensions of community policing are?
- What three generations of community policing have been identified?
- How traditional and community policing differ?
- What the majority of police actions have to do with?
- What demographics includes?
- What role organizations and institutions play within a community?
- What the broken window phenomenon refers to?
- How citizens have become involved in and educated about what police do?
- What the two critical key elements of community policing are?
- What the core components of a successful partnership are?
- Who might be key collaborators in community policing?
- What problem solving requires of the police?
- What changes implementing community policing requires of a department?
- Which may be more important, targeting a "critical mass" of individuals or mobilizing the community at large?
- How implementing community policing may affect the core functions of law enforcement?
- What benefits of implementing community policing might be expected?

CAN YOU DEFINE?

bifurcated society	critical mass	911 policing
broken-window phenomenon	demographics	proactive
	heterogeneous	problem-oriented policing
call management	homogeneous	
call reduction	incident	reactive
call stacking	incivilities	social capital
community policing	integrated patrol	working in "silos"

Introduction

Rosenthal et al. (2003, p.34) assert: "Community policing is one of the most significant trends in policing history." Police departments, and to a lesser extent, sheriff's offices, throughout the United States report that they are involved in community policing. Sixty-eight percent of local police departments and 55 percent of sheriff's offices had a community policing plan in 2000. Two thirds of all police departments (Hickman and Reaves, 2003a, pp.14–15) and nearly two thirds (62 percent) of sheriff's offices were using full-time community policing officers (Hickman and Reaves, 2003b, pp.14–15).

Wuestewald (2004, p.22) points out: "Certainly, our communities expect much more from a police officer today than when I first pinned on the badge. It's not as simple as putting the bad guys in jail anymore. Citizens expect us to communicate and collaborate. They expect openness and access. They expect us to solve problems and form partnerships. Police work always has involved much more than enforcing the law. But, today, the social aspects of policing are center stage."

This chapter on community policing has been added because the ramifications of the change from a professional model to a community-oriented model affect all aspects of police operations. The chapter begins with an overview of community policing and a comparison of traditional and community policing. Next is a discussion of the importance of community and how citizens can be involved and educated. This is followed by a discussion of the importance of partnerships as well as problem-oriented policing. Then a discussion of implementing community policing and its effects is provided. The chapter concludes with a discussion of the challenges to community policing and the benefits that might be expected.

Community Policing—An Overview

Community policing is viewed in many different ways. A starting point is to look at the varying definitions of community policing.

Community Policing Defined

Although numerous definitions of community policing exist, watch for the common thread that runs through them as you consider the following definitions of **community policing**:

- "Community policing is a philosophy or orientation that emphasizes working with citizens to solve crime-related problems and prevent crime" (Miller and Hess, 2005, p.483).
- "Community policing is a philosophy of full-service, personalized policing where the same officer patrols and works in the area on a permanent basis from a decentralized place, working in a proactive partnership with citizens to identify and solve problems" (Allendar, 2004, pp.18–19).
- "Four general principles define community policing: community engagement, problem solving, organizational transformation and crime prevention by citizens and police working together" (Skogan, 2004, p.160).

> **community policing** • decentralized model of policing in which individual officers exercise their own initiatives and citizens become actively involved in making their neighborhoods safer. This proactive approach usually includes increased emphasis on foot patrol.

 Community policing is an organization-wide philosophy and management approach that promotes (1) community, government and police partnerships; (2) proactive problem solving to prevent prime; and (3) community engagement to address the causes of crime, fear of crime and other community issues.

Kelling (2003, p.17) notes that although definitions of community policing vary, a "broad consensus" exists that it includes common elements.

Common Elements of Community Policing

Among the common elements of community policing are the following:

- A focus on problems
- A recognition of citizen and neighborhood concerns
- Increased focus on crime prevention compared with reactive case processing
- Increased emphasis on collaboration with criminal justice and other governmental agencies, private sector agencies and services, the faith community, and citizen and community groups
- An understanding that in a democratic society citizens must, at minimum, obey police and, at best, be partners with them (Kelling, p.17)

These basic elements will be discussed in different contexts within this chapter and throughout the text. Also consider what many believe to be the goals of community policing.

The Goals of Community Policing

Fridell (2004a, p.4) states: "The goals of community policing are to reduce crime and disorder, promote citizens' quality of life in communities, reduce fear of crime and improve police-citizen relations." Three essential efforts are required to achieve these goals: (1) community engagement, (2) problem solving, and (3) organizational transformation (Fridell, 2004a, p.4).

Rosenbaum (2004, p.96) expands on these three efforts. *Community engagement* should be designed to stimulate and empower community residents in preventing crime and disorder. *Problem solving* should be based on the real concerns and problems expressed by neighborhood residents rather than police priorities. *Organizational changes* should encourage a closer relationship between police officers and the neighborhoods they service such as decentralization of authority, attendance at community meetings, and foot and bike patrols. Each of these efforts is discussed in this chapter.

The Dimensions of Community Policing

Cordner (1999, p.137) provides a framework consisting of four dimensions for viewing community policing and determining whether the essential elements are in place.

 Four dimensions of community policing are the philosophical dimension, the strategic dimension, the tactical dimension and the organizational dimension.

The Philosophical Dimension Many advocates of community policing stress that it is a philosophy rather than a program. And it does have that important dimension. The three important elements within this dimension are citizen input, a broadened function and personalized service. Cordner (p.138) contends that citizen input meshes well with an agency that "is part of a government 'of the people, for the people, and by the people.'" A broadened police function means expanding responsibility into areas such as order maintenance and social services, as well as protecting and enhancing the lives of our most vulnerable citizens: juveniles, the elderly, minorities, the disabled, the poor and the homeless. The personal service element supports tailored policing based on local norms and values as well as on individual needs.

The Strategic Dimension A philosophy without means of putting it into practice is an empty shell. This is where the strategic dimension comes in. This dimension "includes the key operational concepts that translate philosophy into action" (p.139). The three strategic elements of community policing are reoriented operations, a geographic focus and a prevention emphasis.

The reorientation in operations shifts reliance on the squad car to emphasis on face-to-face interactions. It may also include differential calls for service. The geographic focus changes patrol officers' basic unit of accountability from time of day to location. Officers are given permanent assignments so they can get to know the citizens within their area. Finally, the prevention emphasis is proactive, seeking to raise the status of prevention/patrol officers to the level traditionally enjoyed by detectives.

The Tactical Dimension The tactical dimension translates the philosophical and strategic dimensions into concrete programs and practices. The most important tactical elements, according to Cordner, are positive interactions, partnerships and problem solving. Officers are encouraged to get out of their vehicles and initiate positive interactions with the citizens within their beat. They are also encouraged to seek out opportunities to partner with organizations and agencies and to mediate between those with conflicting interests—for example, landlords and tenants, adults and juveniles. The third essential element, problem solving rather than responding to isolated incidents, is the focus of Chapter 5.

The Organizational Dimension Cordner's fourth dimension, the organizational dimension, was discussed in Chapter 1.

The Three Generations of Community Policing

Oliver (2000, p.367) contends that community policing has become the "paradigm of contemporary policing, evolving significantly over the past 20 years." He (p.367) notes: "That which was called community policing in the late 1970s and early 1980s only somewhat resembles community policing as it is practiced today." Oliver describes three generations of community policing.

 The three generations of community policing are innovation, diffusion and institutionalization.

First Generation: Innovation (1979–1986) The innovation generation also marked the beginning of the community era previously described. Influences on this first generation were Goldstein's focus on problem solving coupled with Wilson and Kelling's "broken window" theory. Says Oliver (p.375): "The innovation stage of community policing was primarily characterized by a few isolated experiments in a small number of major metropolitan areas across the United States that were testing specific methods of community policing, generally in a small number of urban neighborhoods."

Second Generation: Diffusion (1987–1994) As the experiments in community policing showed indications of success, the concepts and philosophy of community policing began to spread among American police departments. According to Oliver (p.376): "Community policing during the diffusion generation was largely organized through various programs that consisted of newly created units or extensions of previously existing organizational units." A good example of such programs was the COPE (Citizen Oriented Police Enforcement) program in Baltimore County, Maryland.

Third Generation: Institutionalization (1995 to Present) Says Oliver (p.378): "This specific term [institutionalization] is used to denote the fact that community policing has seen widespread implementation across the United States and has become the most common form of organizing police services." In September 1994, President Clinton signed into law the Violent Crime Control and Law Enforcement Act, allocating almost $9 billion to hire, equip and train 100,000 police officers in community policing. The Office of Community Oriented Policing Services (COPS) was created and began funneling grant money to state and local law enforcement agencies. The COPS Web site, http://www.usdoj.gov/cops, houses information on COPS initiatives plus details about training and technical assistance, as well as resources to implement community policing. Through the already existing community Policing Consortium and newly created Regional Community Policing Institutes (RCPIs), training on community policing became available for agencies throughout the country.

Traditional and Community Policing Compared

Traditional police departments are insular organizations that respond to calls for service from behind the blue curtain. This insular, professional approach began to change in many agencies in the late 1970s and early 1980s. According to Allendar (p.19): "Law enforcement professionals, equipped with lessons learned during the problem-laden traditional policing period and the failed team policing initiative, realized the need to work with the various communities they served to identify issues viewed by each neighborhood as significant." This is a basic difference between traditional and community policing. Table 3.1 summarizes the differences between these two approaches to policing.

 Traditional policing is reactive; community policing is proactive. Traditional policing focuses on fighting crime and measures effectiveness by arrest rates; community policing focuses on community problems and measures effectiveness on the absence of crime and disorder. Traditional policing believes crime is a police problem; community policing believes crime is everyone's problem.

Reactive versus Proactive

reactive • simply responding to calls for service.

proactive • recognizing problems and seeking the underlying cause(s) of the problems.

Where traditionally policing has been **reactive**, responding to calls for service, community policing is **proactive**, identifying problems and seeking solutions to them. The term *proactive* is taking on an expanded definition. Not only is it taking on the meaning of identifying problems, but it also means choosing a response rather than reacting the same way each time a similar situation occurs. Police are learning that they do not obtain different results by applying the same methods. In other words, to get different results, different tactics are needed.

Reactive policing has a long-standing tradition. Hoover (2005, p.19) points to the guiding principle of O. W. Wilson: "When the phone rings, we will come." He notes: "Bashing O. W. Wilson has become a rite of passage into the inner circle of

Table 3.1 Comparison of Traditional Policing and Community Policing

Question	Traditional Policing	Community Policing
Who are the police?	A government agency principally responsible for law enforcement.	Police are the public and the public are the police; the police officers are those who are paid to give full-time attention to the duties of every citizen.
What is the relationship of the police force to public service departments?	Priorities often conflict.	The police are one department among many responsible for improving the quality of life.
What is the role of the police?	Focusing on solving crimes.	A broader problem-solving approach.
How is police efficiency measured?	By detection and arrest rates.	By the absence of crime and disorder.
What are the highest priorities?	Crimes that are high value (e.g., bank robberies) and those involving violence.	Whatever problems disturb the community most.
What, specifically, do police deal with?	Incidents.	Citizens' problems and concerns.
What determines the effectiveness of police?	Response times.	Public cooperation.
What view do police take of of service calls?	Deal with them only if there is no real police work to do.	Vital function and great opportunity.
What is police professionalism?	Swift, effective response to serious crime.	Keeping close to the community.
What kind of intelligence is most important?	Crime intelligence (study of particular crimes or series of crimes).	Criminal intelligence (information about the activities of individuals or groups).
What is the essential nature of police accountability?	Highly centralized; governed by rules, regulations and policy directives; accountable to the law.	Emphasis on local accountability to community needs.
What is the role of headquarters?	To provide the necessary rules and policy directives.	To preach organizational values.
What is the role of the press liaison department?	To keep the "heat" off operational officers so they can get on with the job.	To coordinate an essential channel of communication with the community.
How do the police regard prosecutions?	As an important goal.	As one tool among many.

Source: Malcolm K. Sparrow. *Implementing Community Policing.* U.S. Department of Justice, National Institute of Justice, November 1988, pp.8–9.

community policing." Hoover suggests that such bashing is "misplaced at best and just plain ignorant at worst." He contends that this guiding principle is the ultimate democratic process in policing premised on the equality of the citizens and equal protection of the law. Community policing does *not* imply that officers will not respond to calls, just that they may respond differently.

Crime Fighting versus Service and Problem Solving

Police departments are often divided on whether their emphasis should be proactive or reactive. Every department will have officers who are incident oriented (reactive) and believe their mission is to do **911 policing.** As noted, they are incident driven—reactive—and may speak disparagingly of the community-policing officers as social workers.

911 policing • incident-oriented (reactive) policing.

Is the best police officer the one who catches the most "bad guys"? Certainly police departments will continue to apprehend the "bad guys." The crimes they target may, however, contribute to negative police-community relations. The police usually focus on certain kinds of crime, particularly common crimes such as burglary, robbery, assault and auto theft. The police expect that offenders who commit these crimes might flee or try to avoid arrest in some other way. Police may need to use force to bring offenders to justice.

The majority of police work involves nonenforcement activities, including the provision of services such as giving information, working with neglected and abused children, and providing community education programs on crime prevention, drug abuse, safety and the like. Here, an Austin, Texas, police officer distributes anti-drug literature to kids.

As Klockars (1985, p.57) notes, since the police officers' domain is the streets, "Those people who spend their time on the street will receive a disproportionate amount of police attention . . . particularly people who are too poor to have back-yards, country clubs, summer homes, automobiles, air conditioning, or other advantages that are likely to take them out of the patrolman's sight."

These facts contribute to the impression that the police are focused solely on the kind of crime poor people and minorities commit—hence the impression that they are hostile to those who are poor or members of minority groups. This negative impression does little to foster good community relations.

Police work involves much more than catching criminals. It is a complex, demanding job requiring a wide range of abilities. Studies suggest that 80 percent of police officers' time is spent on nonenforcement activities. The vast majority of the problems police attend to are in response to citizen requests for service.

 The majority of police actions have nothing to do with criminal law enforcement but involve service to the community.

A key strategy of community policing is linking policing to the delivery of city services. Community service translates into customer service. If policing is viewed as a business, its product is service, and its customers are the citizens, businesses, organizations and agencies within its jurisdiction.

Taking a page from the business world, "customer oriented" means providing the best service possible; being courteous, honest, open and fair; treating each person as an individual, not as an inconvenience; listening and being responsive to what each person wants; keeping promises; knowing who to refer people to; and thanking people when they are helpful. Police officers should be "consumer friendly" as they serve and protect.

Police departments may provide a wide variety of services, including giving information, directions and advice; counseling and referring; licensing and registering vehicles; intervening in domestic arguments; working with neglected and abused children; rendering emergency medical or rescue services; dealing with alcoholics and the mentally ill; finding lost children; dealing with stray animals; controlling crowds; and providing community education programs on crime prevention, drug abuse, safety and the like.

Community-policing officers are frequently advised to treat citizens as customers because these officers have both protector and servant roles.

Responsibility for Crime

One distinguishing element of community policing is its emphasis on partnerships. As Stephens (2003, p.42) contends: "The police cannot succeed in their efforts without an effective partnership with the communities they serve. Indeed, the community itself is in the best position to control both crime and fear." Partnerships are discussed later in the chapter. Consider first the importance of the community as a whole.

The Importance of Community

Community has many definitions. It has been defined as a group of people living in an area under the same government. It can refer to a social group or class having common interests. Community may even refer to society as a whole—the public. This text uses a specific, admittedly simplistic, meaning for community. *Community* refers to the specific geographic area served by a police department or law enforcement agency and the individuals, organizations and agencies within that area.

Police officers must understand and be a part of this defined community if they are to fulfill their mission. The community may cover a very small area with a limited number of citizens, organizations and agencies, perhaps policed by a single officer. Or the community may cover a vast area and have thousands of individuals and hundreds of organizations and agencies and be policed by several hundred officers. And while police jurisdiction and delivery of services are based on geographic boundaries, a community is much more than a group of neighborhoods administered by a local government. The schools, businesses, public and private agencies, churches and social groups are vital community elements. Also of importance are the individual values, concerns and cultural principles of the people living and working in the community and the common interests they share with neighbors.

Community also refers to a feeling of belonging—a sense of integration, shared values and "we-ness." Where integrated communities exist, people share a sense of ownership and pride in their environment. They also have a sense of what is acceptable behavior, which makes policing in such a community much easier. Research strongly suggests that a sense of community is the "glue" that binds communities to maintain order and provides the foundation for effective community action. Bucqueroux (2004, p.81) notes that a sense of community can be developed by providing people a chance to *create* something new, to *relate* with one another and to *donate* to something bigger than themselves. Whether this sense of community can be developed often depends on the community's demographics.

demographics • the characteristics of the individuals who live in a community; includes a population's size; distribution; growth; density; employment rate; ethnic makeup; and vital statistics such as average age, education and income.

Community Demographics

Demographics refer to the characteristics of the individuals who live in a community.

Demographics include a population's size; distribution; growth; density; employment rate; ethnic makeup; and vital statistics such as average age, education and income.

Although people generally assume that the smaller the population of a community, the easier policing becomes, this is not necessarily true. Small communities generally have fewer resources. It is also difficult to be the sole law enforcement person and therefore being, in effect, on call 24 hours a day. A major advantage of a smaller community is that people know each other. A sense of community is likely to be greater in such communities than in large cities such as Chicago or New York.

When assessing law enforcement's ability to police an area, density of population is an important variable. Studies have shown that as population becomes denser, people become more aggressive. In densely populated areas, people become more territorial and argue more frequently about "turf." Rapid population growth can invigorate a community, or it can drain its limited resources.

The community's vital statistics are extremely important from a police–community partnership perspective. What is the average age of individuals within the community? Are there more young or elderly individuals? How many single-parent families are there? What is the divorce rate? What is the common level of education? What is the school dropout rate? Are there gangs operating in the community? How does the education of those in law enforcement compare? What is the percentage of latchkey children? Such children may pose a significant challenge for police.

Income and income distribution are also important. Do great disparities exist? Would the community be described as affluent, moderately well-off or poor? How does the income of those in law enforcement compare? Closely related to income is the level of employment. What is the ratio of blue-collar to professional workers? How much unemployment exists? How do those who are unemployed support themselves and their families? Are they on welfare? Do they commit crimes to survive? Are they homeless?

homogeneous • a community in which people are all of a similar ethnicity.

heterogeneous • a community in which individuals are of different ethnicities.

The ethnic makeup of the community is another consideration. Is the community basically homogeneous? A **homogeneous** community is one in which people are all quite similar. A **heterogeneous** community, in contrast, is one in which individuals are quite different from each other. Most communities are heterogeneous. Establishing and maintaining good relations among the various subgroups making up the community is a challenge. Usually one ethnic subgroup will have the most power and control. Consider the consequences if a majority of police officers are also members of this ethnic subgroup.

A Rapidly Changing Population Communities have been undergoing tremendous changes in the past half century. In 1950 the white population made up 87 percent of the population. The white population declined from 80 percent in 1980 to 69 percent in 2000.

The greatest growth has been in the Hispanic population, growing from 6 percent in 1980 to double that in 2000. The black population grew by 1 percent.

bifurcated society • a society in which the gap between the "haves" and the "have nots" is wide—that is, there are many poor people, many wealthy people and a shrinking middle class.

In addition to a change in ethnic makeup, the United States is also experiencing a widening of the gap between those with wealth and those living in poverty. The middle class is shrinking, and the gap between the "haves" and the "have nots" is widening, resulting in a **bifurcated society.**

The following trends in the United States are likely to continue: The minority population will increase, and white dominance will end; the number of legal and illegal immigrants will increase; and the elderly population will increase.

Organizations and Institutions

In addition to understanding the demographics of the community and being able to relate to a great variety of individuals, community policing officers must also be familiar with the various organizations and institutions within the community and establish effective relationships with them. A strong network of community organizations and institutions fosters cohesiveness and shared intolerance of criminal behavior and encourages citizens to cooperate in controlling crime, thereby increasing the likelihood that illegal acts will be detected and reported. These networks and partnerships are essential, for no single organization or group is able to address all the problems and concerns of a community alone. And all the organizations and groups working beyond their individual capacity are unable to do more than apply localized, specific band-aid solutions to the total community problems.

 Organizations and institutions play a key role in enhancing community safety and quality of life.

Operating within each community is a power structure that can enhance or endanger police–community relations. The formal power structure includes those with wealth and political influence: federal, state and local agencies and governments; commissions; regulatory agencies; and power groups. The informal power structure includes religious groups, wealthy subgroups, ethnic groups, political groups and public-interest groups.

Organizations and institutions police officers should interact effectively with include the Department of Human Services, health care providers, emergency services providers and any agencies working with youths. Communities may also have libraries, museums and zoos that would welcome a good relationship with the police. Such cooperation often poses problems, however, as Wilson and Kelling (1989, p.52) note:

> The problem of interagency cooperation may, in the long run, be the most difficult of all. The police can bring problems to the attention of other city agencies, but the system is not always organized to respond. In his book Neighborhood Services, John Mudd calls it the "rat problem": "If a rat is found in an apartment, it is a housing inspection responsibility; if it runs into a restaurant, the health department has jurisdiction; if it goes outside and dies in an alley, public works takes over." A police officer who takes public complaints about rats seriously will go crazy trying to figure out what agency in the city has responsibility for rat control and then inducing it to kill the rats.

In other words, if responsibility is fragmented, little gets accomplished. This is a part of the concept of social capital.

Social Capital

Communities might also be looked at in terms of their **social capital**, which Coleman (1990, p.302), who developed this concept, defined as: "A variety of different

social capital • a concept to describe the level or degree of social structure within a community and the extent to which individuals within the community feel bonded to each other. Exists at two levels (local and public), and can be measured in terms of *trustworthiness*, or citizens' trust of each other and their public institutions and *obligations*, or the expectation that service to each other will be reciprocated.

entities having two characteristics in common: They all consist of some aspect of a social structure, and they facilitate certain actions of individuals who are within the structure." Coleman saw the two most important elements in social capital as being (1) trustworthiness, that is, citizens' trust of each other and their public institutions and (2) obligations, that is, expectation that service to each other will be reciprocated.

Social capital exists at two levels: local and public. *Local social capital* is the bond among family members and their immediate, informal groups. *Public social capital* refers to the networks tying individuals to broader community institutions such as schools, civic organizations, churches and the like, as well as to networks linking individuals to various levels of government—including the police.

Community Factors Affecting Social Capital If citizens perceive low levels of physical disorder, they will feel safer. If citizens feel safe and trust one another, social capital is heightened. The higher levels of public social capital, the higher the levels of collective action will be. It is likely that adequate levels of social capital are required for community policing to work. Unfortunately, the communities that most need community policing are often the ones with the lowest levels of social capital.

Sociologists have been describing for decades either the loss or the breakdown of "community" in modern, technological, industrial, urban societies such as ours. Proponents of community policing in some areas may be missing a major sociological reality—the absence of "community"—in the midst of all the optimism about police playing a greater role in encouraging it.

Lack of Community

Community implies a group of people with a common history and understandings, a sense of themselves as "us" and outsiders as "them." In reality, many communities lack this "we-ness." In such areas, the police and public have a "them-versus-us" relationship. Areas requiring the most police attention are usually those with the least shared values and limited sense of community. When citizens cannot maintain social control, the result is social disorganization.

All entities within a community—individuals as well as organizations and agencies—must work together to keep that community healthy. Such partnerships are vital, for a community cannot be healthy if unemployment and poverty are widespread; people are hungry; health care is inadequate; prejudice separates people; preschool children lack proper care and nutrition; senior citizens are allowed to atrophy; schools remain isolated and remote; social services are fragmented and disproportionate; and government lacks responsibility and accountability.

Broken Windows In unhealthy communities, disorder and crime may flourish. In a classic article, "Broken Windows," Wilson and Kelling (1982, p.31) contend:

> Social psychologists and police officers tend to agree that if a window in a building is broken and is left unrepaired, all the rest of the windows will soon be broken. This is as true in nice neighborhoods as in run-down ones. Window-breaking does not necessarily occur on a large scale because some areas are inhabited by determined window-breakers whereas others are populated by window-lovers; rather, one unrepaired broken window is a signal that no one cares, and so breaking more windows costs nothing. (It has always been fun.)

The **broken-window phenomenon** suggests that if it appears "no one cares," disorder and crime will thrive.

broken-window phenomenon • suggests that if it appears "no one cares," disorder and crime will thrive.

Broken windows and smashed cars are very visible signs of people not caring about their community. Other more subtle signs include unmowed lawns, piles of accumulated trash, litter, graffiti, abandoned buildings, rowdiness, drunkenness, fighting and prostitution, often referred to as **incivilities.** Incivilities and social disorder occur when social control mechanisms have eroded. Increases in incivilities may increase the fear of crime and reduce citizens' sense of safety. They may physically or psychologically withdraw, isolating themselves from their neighbors. Or increased incivilities and disorder may bring people together to "take back the neighborhood."

incivilities • signs of disorder.

One way to promote community policing is by involving citizens and educating them about what police do.

Involving and Educating Citizens

O. W. Wilson wrote in *Police Administration* (1950, p.420): "The active interest and participation of individual citizens and groups is so vital to the success of most police programs that the police should deliberately seek to arouse, promote and maintain an active public concern in their affairs."

Community members often have great interest in their local police departments and have been involved in a variety of ways for many years. This involvement, while it accomplishes important contacts, should not be mistaken for community policing. It usually does not involve the partnerships and problem solving activities of community policing.

 Citizen involvement in the law enforcement community and in understanding policing has taken the form of civilian review boards, citizen patrols, citizen police academies, ride-alongs and similar programs.

Civilian Review Boards

The movement for citizen review has been a major political struggle for more than 40 years and remains one of the most controversial issues in police work today. As Farrow (2003, p.22) explains: "Basically, the concept is defined as a procedure under which law enforcement conduct is reviewed at some point by persons who are not sworn officers." He (p.24) reports that three fourths of the largest cities in the United States have established some form of citizen review.

Supporters of civilian review boards believe it is impossible for the police to objectively review actions of their colleagues and emphasize that the police culture demands police officers support each other, even if they know something illegal has occurred. Opponents of civilian review boards stress that civilians cannot possibly understand the complexities of the policing profession and that it is demeaning to be reviewed by an external source.

Successful resolution of this issue requires that the concerns of both the community and the police be addressed. The desired outcome would be that the police maintain the ability to perform their duties without the fear that they will be second-guessed, disciplined or sued by those who do not understand the difficulties of their job. Farrow (p.26) suggests that no perfect review system exists, so jurisdictions should pick and choose from among a wide range of alternatives to design their own review system.

Citizen Patrols

Community policing is rooted in law enforcement's dependence on the public's eyes, ears, information and influence to exert social control.

Citizen patrols are not new. The sheriffs' posses that handled law enforcement in America's Wild West have evolved to present-day citizen patrols, reserve police programs and neighborhood watch groups. Many of the citizen patrols established throughout the country focus on the drug problem. Some citizen groups have exchange programs to reduce the chance of retribution by local drug retailers. Such exchange programs provide nearby neighborhoods with additional patrols while reducing the danger. Local dealers were less likely to recognize a vigil-keeper who lived in another neighborhood.

Citizen Police Academies

Another type of community involvement is through citizens' police academies designed to familiarize citizens with law enforcement and to keep the department in touch with the community.

The first recorded U.S. citizen police academy (CPA) began in 1985 in Orlando, Florida. This program was modeled after a citizen police academy in England, which began in 1977.

Weiss and Davis (2004, p.60) describe current police academies as a series of classes where the general public can learn more about its local police department and how it operates. The goals are fairly universal: to give citizens a better understanding and appreciation of police work through education, to encourage greater cooperation between residents and the police and to acquaint citizens with law enforcement's role in the criminal justice system. They (p.62) cite as favorite classes the K-9 and SWAT demonstrations, the hands-on discussion of the weapons of the Emergency Response team, the FATS Demonstration (Firearms Training System—a video-operated shoot/don't shoot scenario that puts them in the shoes of an officer) and the uniform demonstration.

Rahtz (2005, p.51) states: "Properly structured and targeted programs can become a powerful teaching tool increasing community understanding of force issues and helping to bridge the racial divide between police and minority citizens. The time and effort spent in a well-designed CPA may be one of the best investments police leaders may make."

Citizen police academies are not without limitations. First, even if attendees sign hold-harmless waivers, the agency may still be sued if a participant is injured or killed while attending the academy. Second, officers and administrators may resist an academy, feeling law enforcement activities should not be open to the public. Third, an agency may feel its resources could be better used.

Ride-Along Programs

Ride-along programs are a popular, yet controversial, means to improve police–community relations and get citizens involved in the efforts of the department and its officers. These programs are designed to give local citizens a close-up look at the realities of policing and what police work entails while giving officers a chance to connect with citizens in a positive way.

Many ride-along programs permit any responsible juvenile or adult to participate, but other programs have restrictions and may limit ridership. Participation by officers in a ride-along program is usually voluntary. Whether riders are allowed to use still or video cameras during a ride-along varies from department to department. Many departments also require their riders to dress appropriately.

Despite the numerous benefits of ride-along programs, some departments do not get involved for legitimate reasons such as insurance costs, liability and concerns about the public's safety. Some departments ask participants to sign a waiver exempting the officer, the department and the city from liability.

CAUTION: Citizen involvement in understanding and helping to police their communities is very important, but it, in itself, is NOT community policy. At the heart of the community policing philosophy is an emphasis on partnerships and on problem solving.

 The two critical key elements of community policing are partnerships and problem solving.

Partnerships

Partnerships are a cornerstone of community policing. Sprafka (2004, p.25) stresses that partnerships are essential to a community's well-being. Officers and their departments may team up with citizens, businesses, private policing enterprises and other law enforcement agencies to achieve their community policing objectives.

Police/public partnerships exist on two levels. On a more passive level, the community assumes a compliant role and shows support for law and order by what they *don't* do—they don't interfere with routine police activities and they don't, themselves, engage in conduct that disrupts the public peace.

On an active level, citizens step beyond their daily law-abiding lives and get directly involved in projects, programs and other specific efforts to enhance their community's safety. Such participation may include neighborhood block watches, citizen crime patrols and youth-oriented educational and recreational programs. Citizens may respond independently or form groups, perhaps collaborating with the local police department.

Traditional policing expected the community members to remain in the background. Crime and disorder were viewed as police matters, best left to professionals. That meant most citizen–police interactions were *negative contacts.* After all, people do not call the police when things are going well. Their only opportunity to interact with officers was either when they were victims of crime or were involved in some other emergency situation or were the subject of some enforcement action, such as receiving traffic tickets.

Some people wonder why the police would consult the public about setting police priorities and why they would ask them to work with them to solve neighborhood problems. Some feel that the police are paid to deal with crime and disorder and should not expect communities to take any responsibility or do their job for them. Others feel that until something is done about the "whole laundry list of community woes that social scientists tell us are the causes of crime (poverty, teen pregnancy, racism, homelessness, single-parent families, lousy schools, no jobs) the crime problem will never go away" (Rahtz, 2001, pp.35–36).

To this Rahtz says: "They are flat-out wrong. Beat cops, working with the people in their neighborhoods, have proven that crime and community disorder can be reduced without waiting for the underlying problems to be solved. I am not saying that poverty, teen pregnancy, etc., are not important issues and do not deserve attention. But if we, as police officers and citizens, sit back in the belief that we are impotent in the face of crime until the problems are solved, we are doing a grave disservice to ourselves and our neighborhoods." Rahtz (p.35) calls partnerships "the glue of community policing."

Partnerships are often referred to as collaboration. Rinehart et al. (2001, p.7) explain: "Collaboration occurs when a number of agencies and individuals make a commitment to work together and contribute resources to obtain a common, long-term goal." When it works correctly, a successful problem-solving collaboration that results in a workable solution tends to be a positive experience for everyone involved.

Rinehart et al. (p.7) suggest: "Not all law enforcement relationships must be collaborative, nor should they strive to be. Under some circumstances it may be appropriate for law enforcement personnel just to establish a good communication plan. Under other circumstances cooperation between two individuals may be sufficient. Perhaps coordination between two agencies to avoid duplication of effort is all that is required. Collaboration is, however, critical for many community policing endeavors." They (p.6) cite the following reasons for developing law enforcement/community partnerships:

- Accomplishing what individuals alone cannot
- Preventing duplicating of individual or organizational efforts
- Enhancing the power of advocacy and resource development for the initiative
- Creating more public recognition and visibility for the community policing initiative
- Providing a more systematic, comprehensive approach to addressing community or school-based crime and disorder problems
- Providing more opportunities for new community policing projects

To accomplish these results, several components of a partnership or collaboration are necessary.

 The core components of effective community partnerships are:

- Stakeholders with a vested interest in the collaboration.
- Trusting relationships among and between the partners.
- A shared vision and common goals for the collaboration.
- Expertise.
- Teamwork strategies.
- Open communication.
- Motivated partners.
- Means to implement and sustain the collaborative effort.
- An action plan (Rinehart et al., p.6).

Figure 3.1 illustrates these core components.

Partnerships with Local Businesses

Grogan and Belsky (2004, pp.83–84) contend that for departments seeking meaningful, productive alliances with their communities, highly capable neighborhood

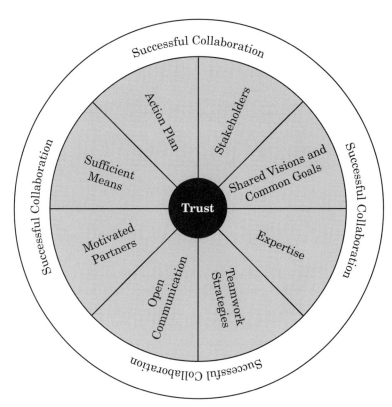

Figure 3.1 Core Components of a Successful Collaboration/
Partnership

Source: Tammy A. Rinehart, Anna T. Laszlo and Gwen O. Briscoe. *Collaboration Toolkit: How to Build, Fix and Sustain Productive Partnerships.* Washington, DC: U.S. Department of Justice, Office of Community Oriented Policing Services, 2001, p.7.

partners in the form of community development corporations (CDCs) are ready to transform philosophy into reality. They (p.85) suggest that enduring, stable partnerships between CDCs and the police are central to community policing. They (p.90) also report that most major cities now have "thriving networks of CDCs."

The community benefits from partnerships by a commitment to crime prevention, public scrutiny of police operations, accountability to the public, customized police service and involvement of community organizations. The police benefit by greater citizen support and increased respect, shared responsibility and greater job satisfaction.

In addition to partnerships with a community's citizenry and private sector businesses, police departments are increasingly partnering with the schools.

School/Law Enforcement/Community Partnerships

Deane et al. (2005, p.130) observe: "Safety in our nation's schools is an issue of paramount importance. With school violence examples such as Columbine, more recently Red Lake High School in Minnesota and the tragedy in Beslan, Russia, cooperation between schools and law enforcement agencies are at an all time high." One popular approach to enhancing school safety is to have a school resource officer (SRO) assigned to a school.

Table 3.2 Comparison between Traditional and Community Policing in Schools

Traditional Policing in Schools	Community Policing in Schools
Reactive response to 911 calls	Law enforcement officer assigned to the school "community"
Incident driven	Problem oriented
Minimum school–law enforcement interaction, often characterized by an "us vs. them" mentality	Ongoing school–law enforcement partnership to address problems of concern to educators, students, and parents
Police role limited to law enforcement	Police role extended beyond law enforcement to include prevention and early intervention activities
Police viewed as source of the solution	Educators, students, and parents are active partners in developing solutions
Educators and law enforcement officers reluctant to share information	Partners value information sharing as an important problem-solving tool
Criminal incidents subject to inadequate response; criminal consequences imposed only when incidents reported to police	Consistent responses to incidents is ensured—administrative and criminal, as appropriate
Law enforcement presence viewed as indicator failure	Law enforcement presence viewed as taking a positive, proactive step to create orderly, safe, and secure schools
Police effectiveness measured by arrest rates, response times, calls for service, etc.	Policing effectiveness measured by the absence of crime and disorder.

Source: Anne J. Atkinson. *Fostering School–Law Enforcement Partnerships.* Portland, OR: Northwest Regional Educational Laboratory, September 2002, p.7. Reprinted by permission.

The Omnibus Crime Control and Safe Streets Act of 1968 defines a school resource officer as "a career law enforcement officer, with sworn authority, deployed in community-oriented policing, and assigned by the employing police department or agency to work in collaboration with school and community-based organizations." As public safety specialists, SROs contribute daily to the safety and security of the schools in which they work. Experience has taught that the presence of an SRO can deter illegal and disruptive behavior.

The COPS Office has awarded over $715 million to more than 2,600 law enforcement agencies to fund more than 6,000 school resource officers through their COPS in Schools (CIS) Program. In addition, COPS has dedicated approximately $21 million to training COPS-funded SROs and the school administrator in the partnering school(s) or school district(s) to work more collaboratively through the CIS Program (*Cops in Schools,* 2003, p.1). The differences between traditional policing in the schools and community policing in the schools is summarized in Table 3.2.

Other Key Partnerships/Collaborators

 In addition to local businesses and schools, other key partnerships/collaborators include prosecutors, the courts, corrections, other government agencies, private security professionals and the media.

Prosecutors As community policing evolves, new collaborations continue to emerge. Just as the police are the gatekeepers to the criminal justice process, prosecutors are the gatekeepers to the judicial system. Without their assistance, cases seldom move forward. Including the prosecutor as a partner is one collaboration gaining popularity, and for good reason.

Community members' concerns are often not murder or robbery but the types of things that contribute to neighborhood decline and fear of crime; things like abandoned buildings, heavy neighborhood traffic or street drug dealing. These neighborhood stability issues are frequently addressed by police, but prosecutors tend to see them as low priority or not important.

Goldkamp et al. (2003, p.xi) state: "Community prosecution strategies signal a major milestone in changing the culture and role of the prosecutor by developing partnerships and collaborative, problem-solving approaches with the community to improve the quality of life and safety of citizens."

When prosecutors become involved as partners in community policing, they attend neighborhood meetings, ride with officers on their beats and get a completely different view of the kinds of things that devastate communities and that breed more crime and disorder. Community prosecution is gaining in popularity throughout the country. This trend can also be seen in the judicial system.

The Courts A recent alternative to the traditional courtroom is the community court. Most community courts are specialized, for example, domestic violence courts, gun courts, drug courts and youth courts. Such courts focus on identifying underlying causes of criminal behavior and treatment for the offenders. A discussion of such courts is beyond the scope of this text, but the community is usually frequently involved in the dispositions handed down. The third component of the criminal justice system, corrections, also is an often overlooked partner in the community policing effort.

Corrections As noted by Wrobleski and Hess (2006, p.445): "Community corrections includes any activities in the community aimed at helping offenders become law-abiding citizens and request a complicated interplay among judicial and correctional personnel from related public and private agencies, citizen volunteers and civic groups."

One important partnership that has proven successful is that between a patrol officer and a probation officer in the same neighborhood. Probation officers who ride along with patrol officers can often spot probationees violating a condition of their probation, and the officer can make an immediate arrest. Or the probation officer can talk with the offending probationee, letting him or her know that the illegal activities will no longer go unnoticed.

Other Government Agencies Criminal justice agencies are not the only local government agencies responsible for responding to community problems. Partnering with other city and county departments and agencies is important to problem-solving success. Sometimes described as **working in "silos,"** local government agencies and departments have traditionally worked quite independently of each other. Under community policing, appropriate government departments and agencies are called on and recognized for their abilities to respond to and address crime and social disorder issues. Fire departments, building inspections, health departments, street departments, parks and recreation departments and child welfare frequently are appropriate and necessary stakeholders in problem-solving initiatives.

working in "silos" • when local government agencies and departments work quite independently of each other. This lack of partnering with other city and county agencies hinders problem-solving success.

State and federal agencies may also be of assistance, including the FBI, the DEA, the U.S. Attorney in the region, the state's attorney, the state criminal investigative agency, the state highway department, and so forth. Another important collaborator is private security providers.

Private Security Providers Interestingly, one of the private-sector businesses that public law enforcement has begun forging partnerships with is private security. In years past, much competition and animosity existed between public and private police. Public law enforcement officers regarded private security personnel as police "wanna-be's," and those in the private sector considered public police officers trigger-happy, ego-inflated crime fighters who often held themselves to be above the law. Recently, however, these two groups have put aside their differences to focus on their common goal of ensuring public safety.

One such partnership is the Private Sector Liaison Committee (PSLC), founded by the International Association of Chiefs of Police (IACP) in 1986. The committee's stated mission is to "develop and implement cooperative strategies for the enhancement of public law enforcement and private sector relationships in the interest of the public good."

Studies on private security force staffing indicate there may be as many as 10,000 private security agencies employing slightly less than 2 million private security officers in the United States. Clearly, if these numbers are accurate, then private security officers are a vast potential resource that can assist law enforcement agencies in fulfilling their mission.

Partnerships with the Media

The media can be a powerful ally or a formidable opponent in implementing the community policing philosophy. Positive publicity can enhance both the image and the efforts of a department. Conversely, negative publicity can be extremely damaging. Therefore, police agencies can and should make every effort to build positive working partnerships with the media. The police and members of the media share the common goal of serving the public. They also have a symbiotic relationship in that they are mutually dependent on each other.

Rosenthal (2003, p.3) suggests that the media can be law enforcement's "single biggest force multiplier, and a genuine asset in time of need." Says Rosenthal: "Cops can truly win with the media if they only had the will to win and a little training on how to make that happen."

However, conflict often exists. While such conflict may arise from a variety of sources, perhaps the most basic are competing objectives and contradictory approaches to dangerous situations. A fundamental source of conflict is the competing objectives of the press and the police. The First Amendment guarantee of freedom of the press is often incompatible with the Sixth Amendment guarantee of the right to a fair trial and protection of the defendant's rights. This leads to a basic conflict between the public's right to know and the individual's right to privacy and a fair trial. Police may need to withhold information from the media until next of kin are notified, in the interest of public safety or to protect the integrity of an investigation.

Another source of conflict between law enforcement and the media is the danger members of the media may expose themselves to in getting a story and the police's obligation to protect them. While most reporters and photographers will not cross yellow police tape lines, many are willing to risk a degree of personal safety to get close to the action.

Having looked at the first of the essential components of community policing—partnerships—consider next the other essential component—problem solving.

Community Policing and Problem Solving

Problem-oriented policing and community-oriented policing are sometimes equated. In fact, however, problem solving is an essential component of community policing. Its focus is on determining the underlying causes of problems, including crime, and identifying solutions.

Community policing or variations of it that rely on problem solving are known by several names: Community Oriented Policing and Problem Solving (COPPS), Neighborhood Oriented Policing (NOP), Problem Oriented Policing (POP), Community Based Policing and the like. Eck and Spelman's classic, *Problem-Solving: Problem Oriented Policing in Newport News* (1987) defines **problem-oriented policing** as "a departmental-wide strategy aimed at solving persistent community problems. Police identify, analyze and respond to the underlying circumstances that create incidents." Regardless of differences in name, all of these use a problem-solving approach to crime and disorder. Throughout this text references to community policing infer that problem solving is involved.

Many practitioners equate community policing and problem solving. As Wilson and Kelling (1989, p.49) note: "Community-oriented policing means changing the daily work of the police to include investigating problems as well as incidents. It means defining as a problem whatever a significant body of public opinion regards as a threat to community order. It means working with the good guys, and not just against the bad guys." Wilson and Kelling suggest that community policing requires the police mission to be redefined "to help the police become accustomed to fixing broken windows as well as arresting window-breakers."

Goldstein (1990, p.20), who is credited with originating problem-oriented policing (POP) and coined the term, was among the first to criticize the professional model of policing as being incident driven: "In the vast majority of police departments, the telephone, more than any policy decision by the community or by management, continues to dictate how police resources will be used." The primary work unit in the professional model is the **incident**, that is, an isolated event that requires a police response. The institution of 911 has greatly increased the demand for police services and the public's expectation that the police will respond quickly.

Goldstein (p.33) also asserts: "Most policing is limited to ameliorating the overt, offensive symptoms of a problem." He suggests that police are more productive if they respond to incidents as symptoms of underlying community problems. He (p. 66) defines a problem as "a cluster of similar, related, or recurring incidents rather than a single incident, a substantive community concern, and a unit of police business." Once the problems in a community are identified, police efforts can focus on addressing the possible causes of such problems.

 Problem solving requires police to group incidents and, thereby, identify underlying causes of problems in the community.

Although problem solving may be the ideal, law enforcement cannot ignore specific incidents. When calls come in, most police departments respond as soon as possible. Problem solving has a dual focus. First, it requires that incidents be linked to problems. Second, time devoted to "preventive" patrol must be spent proactively, determining community problems and their underlying causes.

problem-oriented policing ● management ascertains what problems exist and tries to solve them, redefining the role of law enforcement from incident driven and reactive to problem oriented and proactive.

incident ● an isolated event that requires a police response.

Eck and Spelman (p.2) explain that problem-oriented policing is the result of 20 years of research into police operations converging on three main themes:

1. *Increased effectiveness* by attacking underlying problems that give rise to incidents that consume patrol and detective time.
2. *Reliance on the expertise and creativity of line officers* to study problems carefully and develop innovative solutions.
3. *Closer involvement with the public* to make sure that the police are addressing the needs of citizens.

Specific skills needed for effective problem solving are discussed in Chapter 5.

Implementing Community Policing

Rosenthal et al. (2003) report on a National Institute of Justice survey that listed a number of lessons learned while implementing community policing. The most frequently mentioned lesson is that it takes time to prepare for adopting community policing as well as time to implement it. Respondents recommend that community policing be adopted agency-wide rather than by special units only. These same recommendations are made by Aragon (2004, pp.67–68), who says that community policing should be implemented incrementally and slowly and that it should evolve into a department-wide and city-wide approach, with all officers being guided by the community policing philosophy.

Factors Supporting Implementing Community Policing

Aragon (p.67) describes the crime problem and why police are "behind the power curve." Two thirds of crime occurs inside, out of view of the police. Most serious crimes are perpetrated in a short time; for example, the average armed robbery takes about 90 seconds. Patrol officers intercept fewer than 1 percent of street crimes, and fewer than 4 percent of offenders are caught when police are notified of an on-going criminal activity. In addition, 6 percent of criminals commit 70 percent of all crime; the same 10 percent of locations within a jurisdiction generate about 65 percent of that jurisdiction's total calls for service.

Aragon concludes that law enforcement must work on preventing crime, stating: "Less successful agencies shoot where the target was. Average agencies shoot where the target is at now. Successful agencies shoot where the target is going."

Required Changes

 In addition to focusing on community engagement, partnerships and problem solving, implementing community policing will require a change in management/leadership style and departmental organization.

The focus on community engagement, partnerships and problem solving has been described. The other two basic changes, change in management/leadership style and in departmental organization, were introduced in Chapters 1 and 2 and are briefly reviewed here.

Changes in Management/Leadership Style Community policing usually requires a different management style. The traditional autocratic style effective during the industrial age will not have the same effect in the twenty-first century. One viable alternative to the autocratic style of management is participatory leadership, introduced in Chapter 2. A roadmap for making the change to community policing and the leadership qualities required is provided in Table 3.3.

Organizational Changes He et al. (2005, p.295) report: "Community-oriented policing has become a dominant force impelling organizational change in U.S. policing since the early 1980s." Changes in the organization usually include the following:

- The bureaucracy is flattened and decentralized.
- Roles of those in management positions take on the additional roles of leaders and mentors.
- Patrol officers are given new responsibilities and empowered to make decisions and problem solve with their community partners.
- Permanent shifts and areas are assigned.
- Despecialization reduces the number of specialized units, channeling more resources toward the direct delivery of police services to the public.
- Teams improve efficiency and effectiveness by pooling officer resources in groups.
- Civilianization replaces sworn personnel with nonsworn personnel to maximize cost effectiveness; sworn personnel are then reassigned to where they are most needed.

In addition to these organizational changes, the needs of the community must be assessed.

Analyzing the Community

At the heart of the community policing philosophy is the recognition that the police can no longer go it alone—if they ever could. They must use the eyes, ears and voices of law-abiding citizens. A starting point is to analyze the community's demographics as described earlier in the chapter. How much social capital is available for community policing efforts?

Police must develop a comprehensive picture of their community. They can do this by surveys and direct interaction with citizens. How community members respond when asked what problems they think the police should focus on and what solutions they would suggest can help the department meet the community's needs. Surveys ask for input from everyone instead of just the few citizens who are the most involved. A survey sends a message to community stakeholders that their opinions matter.

Weiss and Davis (2005, p.46) suggest that a survey can act as a citizen's report card, giving the public a chance to accurately acknowledge the value of the police department. Police managers can use survey responses to set departmental goals and objectives, guiding the agency to return maximum value to the citizens who invest in them.

While conducting needs assessments, attention should be paid to who might be community leaders to enlist in the community policing initiative. The number of citizens actively engaged in community policing activities may not be as important as the character of those participating. A given number of individuals with high levels of participation may be more effective in problem solving than many people with low levels of participation. In physics, the smallest amount of a fissionable material that will sustain a nuclear chain reaction is called a critical mass.

Table 3.3 Community Policing: A Road Map for Change

		TIME LINE			
Exploration	**Commitment**	**Planning**	**Implementation**	**Monitoring and Revision**	**Institutionalization**
	Concept	**Action Items/ Bench Marking Recommendations**	**New Knowledge and Implementation**	**Movement and Impact Data**	**Examples of Practices**
Organizational Structure	Roles and Responsibilities	Blend specialist Community Policing Organizations into overall patrol units. Define those task areas requiring specialization department-wide and train accordingly. Develop teams utilizing a combination of specialists whenever possible. Review other best practices.	■ Redo job descriptions ■ Redefine relationships across functions and work groups ■ Reduce reporting lines	■ Identify key "generalist" roles and evaluate the number of personnel who participate in this role ■ Track the efficiency of services/systems likely to be affected by a more generalist role and evaluate whether improvements are made as a result of new rules ■ Evaluate the amount of extra work that is avoided through generalist approach (fewer call backs, fewer referrals, etc.)	*Baltimore, MD*—Over the past decade, the agency has evolved from specialized community policing units with a rather narrow focus to a department-wide community policing mandate. Every facet of the agency is geared toward meeting the goals of community policing. Relationships throughout the department have been restructured to allow information, guidance, and authority to flow through the organization without supervisory barriers or traditional "chain-of-command" restraints.
	Divisional Alignment	Geographic subdivisions developed, with internal and external input for assignment of personnel. Reporting lines tailored to activity and geographic area of accountability, rather than function. Review other best practices.	■ Assign areas of geographic responsibility for all personnel ■ Study feasibility of organization for better accountability ■ Decentralize organization into geographic areas as appropriate ■ Assign cross functional teams to areas	■ Evaluate departmental effectiveness in key roles/geographical areas and note improvements as well as areas of weakness ■ Identify key problems unique to each area and track improvements over time (e.g. , less crime, fewer complaints, quality of life issues)	*Grand Rapids, MI*—One centralized agency is in the process of moving into five district areas. Officers are responsible for a geographical area within their district. *Lansing, MI*—Decentralized the department in top problem solving areas and made officers accountable for a specific area. Two new precincts were created to decentralize services. *St. Petersburg, FL*—The city was divided into geographic regions and all employees are accountable for activities in the area to which they are assigned.
	Organizational Accountability to Community	Expand measures beyond crime statistics and response times to include citizen perceptions of safety and security (quality of life). Review other best practices.	■ Create atmosphere soliciting public input ■ Survey community ■ Add citizens to internal planning processes	■ Send customer satisfaction survey following interaction with department to obtain feedback ■ Survey citizen perceptions of safety and quality of life in neighborhood ■ Develop systems for community input, suggestions, and feed-back (e.g., toll-free line, Web page, surveys, suggestion box)	*Sagamore Hills, OH*—An agency serving a rural community initiated their change to community policing by surveying residents. Based on survey, strategies for decreasing residents' fear of crime were developed.

Source: Reprinted from *The Police Chief*, Vol. LXVI, No. 12, p.19, 1999. Copyright held by The International Association of Chiefs of Police, 515 North Washington Street, Alexandria, VA 22314 USA. Further reproduction without express written permission from IACP is strictly prohibited.

In the context of community policing efforts, a **critical mass** is the smallest number of citizens/organizations needed to support and sustain the community policing initiative.

 It may be more important for COP-oriented police agencies to target this "critical mass" of individuals than to try to mobilize the community at large.

Once the needs assessment has been conducted, the next step is to develop a blueprint—that is, to do some strategic planning.

critical mass • in the context of community policing efforts, the smallest number of citizens/organizations needed to support and sustain the community policing initiative.

Strategic Planning

Recall that strategic planning is long-term, large-scale, future-oriented planning. It begins with the vision and mission statement already discussed. It is grounded in those statements and guided by the findings of the needs assessment. From here, specific goals and objectives and an accompanying implementation strategy and timeline are developed. What looks like a straightforward process can turn extremely difficult as dilemmas arise and threaten the plan.

Departments don't successfully implement community policing in a year or two. It takes time—years for most departments—to fully implement it. Again, all interested parties should be allowed input into the strategic plan, and it should be realistic.

In addition to having a realistic timeline, the strategic plan must also be tied to the agency's budget. Without the resources to implement the activities outlined in the long-range plan, they are not likely to be accomplished. Again, the transition will take time and, in some instances, additional resources. The Community Policing Consortium cautions:

> Don't get lost in the process. . . . The plan can become an end in itself. The project manager, the planning group, draft papers, lengthy dialogue, revised drafts, additional papers, circulated memoranda, further discussion, establishing working groups or sub-committees—this is the stuff that bureaucracies are made of. Some people actually enjoy it. The strategic plan and the planning process are only a means to an end—delivering the future organization built on core values, agreed goals and an effective implementation process.

The strategic plan lays the foundation for the strategies that are to be used in implementing the community policing philosophy.

Developing Strategies Hundreds of strategies have been developed to implement community policing. Among the most common are use of foot, bike and horse patrol; block watches; newsletters; community surveys; citizen volunteer programs; storefronts; special task units; and educational programs. Another common strategy is to assign officers to permanent beats and teach them community organizing and problem-solving skills. Some communities help train landlords in how to keep their properties crime free. Many communities encourage the development of neighborhood organizations, and some have formed teams (partnerships); for example, code and safety violations might be corrected by a team consisting of police, code enforcers, fire officials and building code officers. Other communities have turned to the Internet to connect with their citizens.

One of the most common strategies used in implementing community policing involves getting neighborhood residents to organize for a common purpose. Here, concerned Neighborhood Watch citizens in Austin, Texas, meet with police regarding crime, drugs and gangs in their community.

Cordner (2004, p.61) provides the following snapshot of the most frequently used community policing strategies, used by at least 75 percent of the responding agencies:

- *Citizens* attend police-community meetings, participate in neighborhood watch, help police identify and resolve problems, serve as volunteers within the police agency, and attend citizen police-academies.
- *Police* hold regularly scheduled meetings with community groups, have interagency involvement in problem solving, have youth programs, have victim assistance programs, use regulatory codes in problem solving, and work with building code enforcement.
- *Agencies* use fixed assignments to specific beats or areas, give special recognition for good community policing work by employees, classify and prioritize calls, do geographically based crime analysis, and use permanent neighborhood-based offices or stations.

The most important consideration in selecting strategies to implement community policing is to ensure that the strategies fit a community's unique needs and resources. Wycoff (2004, p.20) contends that strategies or programs that are "best for a particular community" have three common characteristics. They will be (1) responsive to community needs; (2) capable of implementation with available (or accessible) resources; and (3) supported by citizens, police and other partnering agencies. Implementing community policing also affects hiring and promoting policies of a department.

Training The Community Policing Consortium recommends that departments embark on a training program for all personnel at all levels to explain the change process and reduce fear and resistance. Training should also explore the community policing philosophy and the planning process and encourage all stakeholders

Table 3.4   Call Prioritizing Scheme

Priority	Designation	Response	Number of Units
1	Emergency	Immediate; lights and siren; exceed speed limit	2
2	Immediate	Immediate; lights and siren; maintain speed limit	2, if requested
3	Routine	Routine	1
4	Delayed	Delay up to one hour; routine	1
5	TRU	Delay up to two hours	TRU

Source: Tom McEwen, Deborah Spencer, Russell Wolff, Julie Wartell and Barbara Webster. *Call Management in Community Policing: A Guidebook for Law Enforcement.* Washington DC: U.S. Department of Justice, Policing Services, February 2003, p.50.

to participate. The consortium advises, however, "DON'T make training the spearhead of change."

The consortium says that many efforts have been made to place training at the leading edge of change in both the public and private sector. Much time and energy are expended in such efforts, but, no matter how effective the training, they will be neutralized if what is learned is at variance with practices and procedures occurring in the department. The consortium stresses: "Unless the culture, structure and management of the organization are in harmony with the training, then the impact of the latter will be minimized. . . . What is needed is the agreed vision, values, goals, and objectives to drive the organization and affect every aspect of policing—not expecting a training program to be a short cut to acceptance." Training is discussed in Chapter 7.

It should be clear from the preceding discussions that community policing is labor intensive. Without time to participate in community policing strategies and problem-solving endeavors, implementation is unlikely to succeed.

Making Time for Partnering and Problem Solving: Call Management

In most departments, calls for service determine what police officers do from minute to minute on a shift. People call the police to report crime, ask for assistance, ask questions, get advice and many other often unrelated requests. Police departments try to respond as quickly as possible, and most have a policy of sending an officer whenever it is requested. Departments might free up time for partnerships without expense through effective call management or call reduction.

In **call management** or **call reduction,** departments look at which calls for service must have an officer(s) respond and, regardless of past practice, which do not. In call management calls are prioritized based on the department's judgment about the emergency nature of the call (e.g., imminent harm to a person or a crime in progress), response time, need for back up and other local factors. Priority schemes vary across the country, but many have four or five levels. Table 3.4 presents a typical call priority scheme.

McEwen et al. (2003, p.50) stress: "In a police organization committed to community policing, the community should play a role in setting and reviewing

call management or **call reduction** • calls are prioritized based on the department's judgment about the emergency nature of the call.

INTAKE   RESPONSE

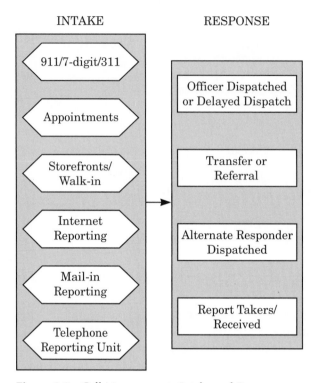

Figure 3.2 Call Management: Intake and Response
Source: Tom McEwen, Deborah Spencer, Russell Wolff, Julie Wartell and Barbara Webster. *Call Management in Community Policing: A Guidebook for Law Enforcement.* U.S. Department of Justice, Office of Community Oriented Policing Services, February 2003, p.12.

police call priorities and response policies. The community has a vested interest in how quickly officers are dispatched, the extent to which police expedite through neighborhoods, the extent to which multiple units are dispatched or stay at the scene, whether calls are handled by alternative means and related issues.

call stacking • a process performed by a computer-aided dispatch system in which nonemergency, lower priority calls are ranked and held or "stacked" so the higher priorities are continually dispatched first.

Call management usually involves **call stacking,** a process a computer-aided dispatch system performs in which nonemergency, lower priority calls are ranked and held or "stacked" so the higher priorities are continually dispatched first. According to McEwen et al. (p.35): "The objective of call stacking is to reduce cross-beat dispatches and allow the unit in the area of responsibility to handle as many calls in that area as possible. This has significant advantages for community policing, which in the majority of departments involves assigning patrol officers to specific geographic areas such as beats or neighborhoods. As officers spend more time in their beats, they gain opportunities to become familiar with conditions, problems and resources in those areas. Cross-beat dispatches reduce those opportunities by taking officers out of their assigned areas, as well as adding to the time required to respond to calls." Using an officer to take telephone reports of nonemergency, low priority calls is one change that has helped.

Similar results can be obtained by taking reports by appointment. Many people find this agreeable. Certain kinds of reports can be made on an agency's Web page, by mail or by fax. Figure 3.2 illustrates the type of intake and response common in call management. Call management may also involve having civilians handle certain calls such as calls not involving dangerous situations, suspects, or follow-up; traffic accidents (no injury), traffic control, parking issues, and abandoned vehicles; vehicle lockouts; building checks; burglary, theft and lost and found property; vandalism and criminal mischief; runaways; paperwork relays and services, subpoena service and funeral escorts; animal complaints; bicycle stops; and part patrol (McEwen et al., p.39). However, police unions may take issue with such an approach unless reserve officers are used.

Call management may also involve dealing with the 911 system. The 911 system was set up for emergency calls for assistance. But, as noted by McEwen et al. (p.7): "In one sense, 911 became too successful. It resulted in a dramatic increase in the number of non-emergency calls coming in to the police." Large numbers of callers use 911 to ask for information or to report nonemergency situations. Most agencies field hundreds or even thousands of phone calls a year from citizens seeking information, often unrelated to police services. Keeping the public informed in other ways such as on a Web site or through newspapers and newsletters with information about city policies, services, procedures and when and when not to call police can reduce the volume of calls.

People call the police for nonpolice matters for a variety of reasons, including because they don't know who can help; because they believe the police know or should know the answers to all questions; because they know the phone number (911); and because, no matter what day of week or time of day it is, they know the phones will be answered. Large cities have begun to implement 311 lines to divert nonemergency calls from 911.

Police nonemergency lines are nothing new, but since the advent of 911, most callers use it for all calls to the police because they don't have to look up a non-emergency phone number. The hope is with an easy-to-remember number for nonemergency matters, people will reserve 911 for emergencies.

The 311 number also has the potential to benefit community policing in other ways. For example, it can alert other agencies to citizen problems for which they, rather than the police, have mandates to assume primary responsibility. It can also improve accountability for follow-up by providing callers with a "tracking number" so they can check on the status of their service request. It might also coordinate city services.

Managers/leaders should be aware of other challenges facing implementing community policing as well.

Challenges to Community Policing

Despite the many advantages and benefits of community policing, its implementation is not without challenges. Critics and skeptics exist both internally, among officers and police managers, and externally, in the community at large. Furthermore, even when the community policing philosophy has the support of the department and the public, our increasingly diverse population presents an ever-expanding challenge to community policing efforts.

Many officers have difficulty accepting or appreciating the community-oriented policing philosophy. Some wonder whether officers will or should readily accept the increased accountability that accompanies greater decision-making responsibilities. Others question the willingness of police administrators to embrace decentralization, to "loosen the reins" and empower officers with greater authority, responsibility and decision-making capabilities. These organizational impediments are some of the chief barriers to implementation.

Other challenges to implementation include community resistance, a concern that community policing is "soft" on crime and structural impediments involved with making the change from a reactive to a proactive policing mission. The impediment of limited resources is also a reality: how to simultaneously respond to calls for service, solve crimes and conduct activities involved with community policing. Another large obstacle is the difficulty of changing the police culture. Hill (2005, p.46) cautions: "Community policing isn't static, it's an ongoing process. The work of building a community police culture doesn't end and requires continual rededication."

The perception that community policing goes against aggressive law enforcement practices is perhaps one of the most difficult impediments to overcome. No agency wishes to be perceived as "softies," and no community wants to place crime control and safety in the hands of "pushovers." However, the goals of community policing and aggressive enforcement are not mutually exclusive. The combination of these two elements has been termed **integrated patrol.** As has been stressed, law enforcement agencies are expected to continue their efforts to combat crime but are also being asked to look at causes for problems existing within communities and address them as well. In doing so, many impediments must be faced.

integrated patrol • the end goal resulting from the combination of the two elements of community policing and aggressive enforcement.

Miller and Hess (2005, p.128) list the following impediments to COP:

- Organizational impediments—resistance from middle management, line officers and unions; confusion about what COP is; problems in line-level accountability; officers' concern that COP is "soft" on crime; and lack of COP training
- Union impediments—resistance to change, fear of losing control to community, resistance to increased officer responsibility and accountability, fear that COP will lead to civilian review boards
- Community impediments—community resistance, community's concern that COP is "soft" on crime, civil service rules, pressure to demonstrate COP reduces crime and lack of support from local government
- Transition impediments—balancing increased foot patrol activities while maintaining emergency response time

A Change in Core Functions?

Researchers Zhao et al. (2003) examined changes in law enforcement organizational priorities related to three core functions of policing—crime control, the maintenance of order and the provision of services—during the era of community policing. They analyzed the changes by using data from three national surveys of more than 200 municipal police departments conducted in 1993, 1996 and 2000. They found that police core-function priorities remained largely unchanged, but that the systematic implementation of COP programs reflects an all-out effort to address all three core functions at a higher level of achievement. They (p.716) conclude: "Our analysis showed that the extent of implementation of COP is a statistically significant predictor of all core functions of policing. On the basis of the analysis presented here, we argue that COP can be characterized as a comprehensive effort by local police simultaneously to control crime, to reduce social disorder and to provide services to the citizenry." A basic difference, however, is that they no longer seek to do it alone, but rather through partnerships and problem solving.

In most departments implementing community policing, the core functions remain, with the difference being that police no longer seek to accomplish these functions alone.

The Benefits of Implementing Community Policing

Flynn (2004, p.25) states the benefits of community succinctly: "Community policing reduces crimes, helps minimize fear of crime and enhances the quality of life in communities nationwide." An independent study by the Government Accountability Office (GAO) found that COPS grants have consistently contributed between 10 and 13 percent to the yearly reductions in violent crime at the height of their funding ("GAO Reports," 2005, p.1). Fridell (2004b, p.45) looked at survey results conducted by the Police Executive Research Forum (PERF) in 1992, 1997 and 2002. In all three surveys more than 90 percent reported:

- Improved cooperation between citizens and police.
- Increased involvement of citizens.
- Increased information from citizens to police.
- Improved citizens' attitudes toward police.
- Reduced citizens' fear of crime.

 Community policing may result in decreases in crime and fear of crime as well as citizen involvement in preventing crime.

To help overcome doubts and misperceptions about the strength and virtue of the community policing philosophy, it is valuable to note studies that demonstrate that community policing benefits not only the community, but the participating officers as well.

Benefits of Community Policing to Officers

Hanson (2004, p.155) references the PERF 2002 survey and notes that one effect of implementing community policing is officers' increased job satisfaction. The data show that more than 80 percent of respondents reported that officers had increased job satisfaction to some extent; just over 10 percent reported a great increase in job satisfaction and only about 5 percent indicated no increase in officer job satisfaction.

 Implementing community policing is likely to increase officers' job satisfaction.

Officers engaging in community policing have job enrichment, get to know the citizens with whom they work, have greater responsibility and authority, and can build their problem-solving skills. Such benefits are vitally important for community policing officers faced with serving and protecting an increasingly diverse population.

Beyond Community

Although the focus in this chapter is on community efforts and partnerships, such efforts and partnerships can greatly benefit by going beyond community to partner with state and federal agencies. Delattre (2003, p.87) observes: "The question of effective partnerships has *deserved* our attention for at least half a century, and it *demands* our attention now." As a member of the Long Island (New York) gang task force put it: "We decide back and forth, whether it is the U.S. Attorney or the district attorney's office, what charges will get the bigger bang. We want to put the bad people away in jail for a long time. So if they will get more time on the state or the federal charges that's the way it will go" (Domash, 2004, p.25).

Russell-Einhorn (2003) suggests that collaborations between federal and local law enforcement agencies, rare until the 1980s, are now common, are generally considered successful, and are likely to expand. For local police, collaboration with federal agencies can provide greater access to national criminal information, more powerful investigative techniques and tougher penalties under federal laws. He (p.3) lists the following "powerful advantages" of prosecution under federal criminal statutes:

- Federal grand jury. This jury can be called at any time, can be kept in action for as long as three years, can hear hearsay evidence and is armed with national subpoena power. State grand juries have a shorter duration, "no hearsay" rules and limited subpoena power.
- Immunity. Limited immunity for a grand jury witness conferred by federal prosecutors does not impede later prosecution of the witness for perjury, obstruction of justice, or contempt.
- Search warrants. Federal standards for obtaining a search warrant are generally lower than those of most states.
- Preventive detention. The federal bail statute provides for preventive detention in a range of circumstances. State laws do not have such provisions.
- Electronic surveillance. Most states require a higher burden of proof for wiretaps than the federal government.
- Witness protection. In contrast to the well-developed Federal Witness Protection Program, most states do not have such a program.
- Accomplice testimony. Federal rules permit conviction on the basis of an accomplice's uncorroborated testimony. State rules generally do not.
- Discovery. Federal rules provide that a statement by a government witness need not be made available to the defense until the witness has testified at trial. Also, the defense has no entitlement to a witness list before trial or to interview government witnesses prior to trial. Most state rules provide otherwise.

Russell-Einhorn's study concludes that federal–local collaborations to combat drugs, illegal weapons and gangs have been largely successful and mutually beneficial to both parties involved. Such collaborations have become even more important since 9-11.

The September 11, 2001, terrorist attacks on America, while unquestionably horrific and devastating, had a positive effect by bringing even the most diverse, fragmented communities together in ways rarely seen before. The government's appeal to the nation's public to become "soldiers" in the effort to preserve our American way of life and to be increasingly vigilant about activities occurring in their neighborhoods is a direct application of the community policing philosophy. Everyone is made to feel they have a part to play, an implicit responsibility, in keeping themselves, their communities and their country safe from harm.

McPherson (2004, pp.127–128) believes: "Community policing is more relevant than ever in a profession that was unable to fire a single shot to stop the events of 9-11." Although terrorists may "think globally," they "act locally" (Flynn, 2004, p.33). Savelli (2004, p.40) contends that community policing has a big advantage over other aspects of policing in uncovering terrorists: "A community police officer, when deploying correctly, becomes very familiar with local citizens and merchants." These citizens know what is going on and can provide an abundance of information to police. He (p.41) points out that terrorists live and operate in communities and that, no matter how much they try to blend in, they are likely to be noticed by someone: "Block watchers, busybodies, alert citizens, retired law enforcement, military personnel, or regular citizens, are monitoring each other, purposely or inadvertently."

Giannone and Wilson (2003, p.37) describe one community policing effort in the fight against terrorism, the Community Anti-Terrorism Training Initiative, or CAT Eyes, program: "The CAT Eyes program was designed to help local communities combat terrorism by enhancing neighborhood security, heightening the community's powers of observation and encouraging mutual assistance and concern among neighbors. It has the following purposes:

- Watch for terrorist indicators, not peoples' race or religion.
- Teach average citizens about terrorism.
- Educate and empower citizens.
- Set up a national neighborhood block watch program.
- Educate school children."

Scrivner (2004, p.185) questions whether law enforcement can maintain the advance in community policing in light of the post 9-11 demands to secure the homeland. She (pp.188–189) suggests the following to maintain the balance between community policing and combating terrorism:

- Keep the core business of policing—crime control—front and center. The primary mission of law enforcement is maintaining public safety, not going to war.
- Reinforce that gathering and sharing timely information depends on strong partnerships between residents and police. Defeating criminals *and* terrorists is not an either-or situation.
- Apply the lessons learned from history related to citizens' rights.
- Enlist rank-and-file officers and middle managers in decision making on how to maintain the balance between community policing and homeland security.

Partnerships at the local, state and federal level are crucial to successful community policing efforts, not only to combat crime and disorder, but also in the fight against terrorism. In effect, homeland security begins with hometown security.

 ## SUMMARY

Community policing is an organization-wide philosophy and management approach that promotes (1) community, government and police partnerships; (2) proactive problem solving to prevent crime; and (3) community engagement to address the causes of crime, fear of crime, and other community issues. Four dimensions of community policing have been identified: the philosophical dimension, the strategic dimension, the tactical dimension and the organizational dimension. Three generations of community policing have also been described: innovation, diffusion and institutionalization.

Community policing differs from community policing in several important ways. Traditional policing is reactive; community policing is proactive; traditional policing focuses on fighting crime and measures effectiveness by arrest rates; community policing focuses on community problems and measures effectiveness on the absence of crime and disorder; traditional policing believes crime is a police problem; community policing believes crime is everyone's problem. The majority of police actions have nothing to do with criminal law enforcement but involve service to the community.

An understanding of community is essential to successfully implementing community policing. Such understanding begins with demographics. Demographics include a population's size; distribution; growth; density; employment rate; ethnic makeup; and vital statistics such as average age, education and income. Organizations and institutions also can play a key role in enhancing community safety and quality of life. The broken-window phenomenon suggests that if it appears no one cares, disorder and crime will thrive.

Citizen involvement in the law enforcement community and in understanding policing has taken the form of civilian review boards, citizen patrols, citizen police academies, ride-alongs and similar programs. Such involvement is important, but community policing requires more. Two critical elements of community policing are partnerships and problem solving.

The core components of effective community partnerships are stakeholders with a vested interest in the collaboration, trusting relationships among and between the partners, a shared vision and common goals for the collaboration, expertise, teamwork strategies, open communication, motivated partners, means to implement and sustain the collaborative effort and an action plan. In addition to local businesses and schools, other key partnerships/collaborators include prosecutors, the courts, corrections, other government agencies, private security professionals and the media.

Problem-oriented policing requires that police move beyond a law enforcement perspective in seeking solutions to problems. Implementing community policing will require a change in management style, mission statement and departmental organization. It may be more important for COP-oriented police agencies to target this "critical mass" of individuals than to try to mobilize the community at large.

In most departments implementing community policing, the core functions remain, with the difference being that police no longer seek to accomplish these functions alone.

Community policing may result in decreases in crime and fear of crime as well as citizen involvement in preventing crime. Implementing community policing also is likely to increase officers' job satisfaction.

CHALLENGE THREE

The Greenfield Police Department's new mission statement emphasizes a community policing philosophy. The new chief has increased the authority and the responsibility of sergeants to identify and solve problems affecting the quality of life in Greenfield. You are the evening shift supervisor and have learned that the residents of the Senior Citizens' Center are reluctant to venture out after dark. The Center is located in a low-crime neighborhood adjacent to a public park with walking paths. Evening walks in the park used to be a popular activity for the seniors, but no one uses the park now. The Center's owner tells you the residents are worried about all the crime they see on the news and read about in the paper. They are also concerned about thefts from their cars in the parking lot. He says rumors of criminal activity spread quickly through the Center. The owner provides classes every month on how to avoid being a crime victim. He also installed new security doors and cameras. Nothing seems to work.

You gather the officers on your shift to discuss the situation. They tell you there is no crime problem in the area of the Center. The crime statistics support the officers. There has been one car window broken in the Center's parking lot during the last year, and a few kids have been told not to skateboard through the lot on their way to the park. An officer remarks that the kids dress rather oddly and sport some strange haircuts, but they're good kids who stay out of trouble. Officers state that they patrol the area constantly and conduct frequent traffic enforcement on the street in front of the Center. They flash their red lights to make sure the residents see them in the area. The officers tell you the residents have exaggerated the problem.

1. Is there a crime problem at the Senior Citizens' Center?

2. Is fear reduction a police problem?

3. What are some possible causes of fear of crime at the Center?

4. What is missing in the current community–police relationship between the Greenfield Police department and the senior citizens?

5. Suggest a community policing strategy to reduce the fear of crime at the seniors' residence center.

DISCUSSION QUESTIONS

1. What community services are available in your community? Which are most important? Which might be frivolous? Are any necessary services not provided?

2. What do you feel are the greatest strengths of community policing?

3. What is the relationship of problem-oriented policing to community policing?

4. Might community policing dilute the power and authority of the police?

5. Are community policing and problem solving important in your police department?

6. What do you see as the greatest impediment to implementing community policing?

7. What do you see as the greatest benefit of community policing?

8. If you had to prioritize the changes needed to convert to community policing, what would your priorities be?

9. Why might citizens not want to become involved in community policing efforts?

10. Select a community problem you feel is important and describe the partners who might collaborate to address the problem.

REFERENCES

Allendar, David M. "Community Policing: Exploring the Philosophy." *FBI Law Enforcement Bulletin*, March 2004, pp.18–22.

Aragon, Randall. "Excellence in Community Policing." *Law and Order*, April 2004, pp.66–68.

Bucqueroux, Bonnie. "Community Policing in the Years Ahead: And Now for the Really Hard Part." In *Community Policing: The Past, Present and Future*, edited by Lorie Fridell and Mary Ann Wycoff. Washington, DC: The Annie E. Casey Foundation and Police Executive Research Forum, 2004, pp.73–81.

Coleman, J. *Foundations of Social Theory.* Cambridge, MA: Harvard University Press, 1990.

Cops in Schools: The COPS Commitment to School Safety. COPS Fact Sheet. Washington, DC: Office of Community Oriented Policing Services, April 8, 2003.

Cordner, Gary W. "The Elements of Community Policing." In *Policing Perspectives: An Anthology*, edited by Larry K. Gaines and Gary W. Cordner. Los Angeles: Roxbury Publishing Company, 1999, pp.137–149.

Cordner, Gary. "The Survey Data: What They Say and Don't Say about Community Policing." In *Community Policing: The Past, Present, and Future*, edited by Lorie Fridell and Mary Ann Wycoff. Washington, DC: The Annie E. Casey Foundation and Police Executive Research Forum, 2004, pp.59–72.

Deane, Marty; Holohan, Renise; and Bennett, Wayne. "NYSP School Resource Officer Program." *Law and Order*, September 2005, pp.130–133.

Delattre, Edwin. "Reflection on Successful Partnerships." In *Protecting Your Community from Terrorism: Strategies for Local Law Enforcement. Volume 1: Local–Federal Partnerships* by Gerald R. Murphy and Martha R. Plotkin with Edward A. Flynn, Jane Perlov, Kevin Stafford and Darrel W. Stephens. Washington, DC: Office of Community Oriented Policing Services and the Police Executive Research Forum, 2003, pp.87–92.

Domash, Shelly Feuer. "How to Crack Down on Gangs." *Police*, 2004, pp.25–31.

Eck, John E. and Spelman, William. *Problem-Solving: Problem-Oriented Policing in Newport News*. Washington, DC: The Police Executive Research Forum, 1987.

Farrow, Joe. "Citizen Oversight of Law Enforcement: Challenge and Opportunity." *The Police Chief*, October 2003, pp.22–29.

Flynn, Edward A. "Community Policing Is Good Policing, Both Today and Tomorrow." In *Community Policing: The Past, Present, and Future*, edited by Lorie Fridell and Mary Ann Wycoff. Washington, DC: The Annie E. Casey Foundation and Police Executive Research Forum, 2004, pp.25–38.

Fridell, Lorie. "The Defining Characteristics of Community Policing." In *Community Policing: The Past, Present, and Future*, edited by Lorie Fridell and Mary Ann Wycoff. Washington, DC: The Annie E. Casey Foundation and Police Executive Research Forum, 2004a, pp.3–12.

Fridell, Lorie. "The Results of Three National Surveys on Community Policing." In *Community Policing: The Past, Present, and Future*, edited by Lorie Fridell and Mary Ann Wycoff. Washington, DC: The Annie E. Casey Foundation and Police Executive Research Forum, 2004b, pp.39–48.

"GAO Reports that COPS Office Grants Significantly Reduce Crime." *Subject to Debate*, July 2005, pp.1, 3.

Giannone, Donald and Wilson, Robert A. "The CAT Eyes Program: Enlisting Community Members in the Fight against Terrorism." *The Police Chief*, March 2003, pp.37–38.

Goldkamp, John S.; Irons-Guynn, Cheryl; and Weiland, Doris. *Community Prosecution Strategies*. Washington, DC: Bureau of Justice Statistics, 2003.

Goldstein, Herman. *Problem-Oriented Policing*. New York: McGraw-Hill, 1990.

Grogan, Paul and Belsky, Lisa. "The Promise of Community Development Corporations." In *Community Policing: The Past, Present, and Future*, edited by Lorie Fridell and Mary Ann Wycoff. Washington, DC: The Annie E. Casey Foundation and Police Executive Research Forum, 2004, pp.83–92.

Hanson, Ellen T. "Community Policing during a Budget Crisis: The Need for Interdisciplinary Cooperation, Not Competition." In *Community Policing: The Past, Present, and Future*, edited by Lorie Fridell and Mary Ann Wycoff. Washington, DC: The Annie E. Casey Foundation and Police Executive Research Forum, 2004, pp.151–158.

He, Ni (Phil); Zhao, Jihong (Solomon); and Lovrich, Nicholas P. "Community Policing: A Preliminary Assessment of Environmental Impact with Panel Data on Program Implementation in U.S. Cities." *Crime & Delinquency*, July 2005, pp.295–317.

Hickman, Matthew J. and Reaves, Brian A. *Local Police Departments, 2000*. Washington, DC: Bureau of Justice Statistics, January 2003a. (NCJ 196002)

Hickman, Matthew J. and Reaves, Brian A. *Sheriffs' Offices, 2000*. Washington, DC: Bureau of Justice Statistics, January 2003b. (NCJ 196534)

Hill, C. Ellen. "How to Build a Culture." *Law and Order*, September 2005, pp.142–146.

Hoover, Larry T. "From Police Administration to Police Science: The Development of a Police Academic Establishment in the United States." *Police Quarterly*, March 2005, pp.8–22.

Kelling, George. "The Evolution of Contemporary Policing." In *Local Government Police Management*, 4th ed., edited by William A. Geller and Darrel W. Stephens. Washington, DC: International City/County Management Association, 2003, pp.3–26.

Klockars, Carl B. *The Idea of Police*. Newbury Park, CA: Sage Publishing Company, 1985.

McEwen, Tom; Spencer, Deborah; Wolff, Russell; Wartell, Julie; and Webster, Barbara. *Call Management and Community Policing: A Guidebook for Law Enforcement*. Washington, DC: Community Oriented Policing Services, February 2003.

McPherson, Nancy. "Reflections from the Field on Needed Changes in Community Policing." In *Community Policing: The Past, Present, and Future*, edited by Lorie Fridell and Mary Ann Wycoff. Washington, DC: The Annie E. Casey Foundation and Police Executive Research Forum, 2004, pp.127–140.

Miller, Linda S. and Hess, Kären M. *Community Policing: Partnerships for Problem Solving*, 4th ed. Belmont, CA: Wadsworth Publishing Company, 2005.

Oliver, Willard M. "The Third Generation of Community Policing: Moving through Innovation, Diffusion and Institutionalization." *Police Quarterly*, December 2000, pp.367–388.

Rahtz, Howard. *Community-Oriented Policing: A Handbook for Beat Cops and Supervisors*. Monsey, NY: Criminal Justice Press, 2001.

Rahtz, Howard. "Citizen Police Academy: Teaching the Public about Use of Force." *Law and Order*, April 2005, pp.47–51.

Rinehart, Tammy A.; Laszlo, Anna T.; and Briscoe, Gwen O. *Collaboration Toolkit to Build, Fix, and Sustain Productive Partnerships*. Washington, DC: U.S. Department of Justice, Office of Community Oriented Policing Services, 2001.

Rosenbaum, Dennis P. "Community Policing and Web-Based Communication: Addressing the New Information Imperative." In *Community Policing: The Past, Present, and Future*, edited by Lorie Fridell and Mary Ann Wycoff. Washington, DC: The Annie E. Casey Foundation and Police Executive Research Forum, 2004, pp.93–114.

Rosenthal, Arlen M.; Fridell, Lorie A.; Dantzker, Mark L.; Fisher-Stewart, Gayle; Saavedra, Pedro J.; Makaryan, Tigran; and Bennett, Sadie. "Community Policing: Then and Now." *NIJ Journal*, Issue 249, 2003, p.34. (NCJ 187693)

Rosenthal, Rick. "Training the Media." *ILEETA Digest*, October/December 2003, p.3.

Russell-Einhorn, Malcolm L. *Fighting Urban Crime: The Evolution of Federal-Local Collaboration*, Washington, DC: National Institute of Justice, December 2003. (NCJ 197040)

Savelli, Lou. *A Proactive Guide for the War on Terror*. Flushing, NY: Looseleaf Law Publication, Inc., 2004.

Scrivner, Ellen. "The Impact of September 11 on Community Policing." In *Community Policing: The Past, Present, and Future*, edited by Lorie Fridell and Mary Ann Wycoff. Washington, DC: The Annie E. Casey Foundation and Police Executive Research Forum, 2004, pp.183–192.

Skogan, Wesley G. "Community Policing: Common Impediments to Success." In *Community Policing: The Past, Present, and Future*, edited by Lorie Fridell and

Mary Ann Wycoff. Washington, DC: The Annie E. Casey Foundation and Police Executive Research Forum, 2004, pp.159–168.

Sprafka, Harvey E. "Marketing the Smaller Agency." *The Police Chief*, September 2004, pp.20–25.

Stephens, Darrel W. "Organization and Management." In *Local Government Police Management*, 4th ed., edited by William A. Geller and Darrel W. Stephens. Washington, DC: International City/County Management Association, 2003, pp.27–66.

Weiss, Jim and Davis, Mickey. "Citizen Police Academy." *Law and Order*, April 2004, pp.60–64.

Weiss, Jim and Davis, Mickey. "Citizen Survey Protocol." *Law and Order*, April 2005, pp.40–46.

Wilson, James Q. and Kelling, George L. "The Police and Neighborhood Safety: Broken Windows." *The Atlantic Monthly*, March 1982, pp.29-38.

Wilson, James Q. and Kelling, George L. "Making Neighborhoods Safe." *The Atlantic Monthly*, February 1989, pp.46-52.

Wilson, O. W. *Police Administration*. New York: McGraw-Hill, 1950.

Wrobleski, Henry M. and Hess, Kären M. *An Introduction to Law Enforcement and Criminal Justice*, 8th ed. Belmont, CA: Wadsworth Publishing Company, 2006.

Wuestewald, Todd. "The X-Factor in Policing." *FBI Law Enforcement Bulletin*, June 2004, pp.22–23.

Wycoff, Mary Ann. "The Best Community Policing Practice May Be Invisible." In *Community Policing: The Past, Present, and Future*, edited by Lorie Fridell and Mary Ann Wycoff. Washington, DC: The Annie E. Casey Foundation and Police Executive Research Forum, 2004, pp.13–24.

Zhao, Jhong (Solomon); He, Ni; and Lovrich, Nicholas P. "Community Policing: Did It Change the Basic Functions of Policing in the 1990s? A National Follow-Up Study." *Justice Quarterly*, December 2003, pp.697–724.

BOOK-SPECIFIC WEB SITE

Go to the Management and Supervision in Law Enforcement Web site at www.thomsonedu.com/criminaljustice/bennett for student and instructor resources, including Internet Assignments and Case Studies.

CHAPTER 4

Communication: A Critical Management Skill

Language is the picture and counterpart of thought.

Mark Hopkins, builder of Central Pacific and Southern Pacific Railroads

 Do You Know?

- What the communication process involves?
- What the KISS principle is?
- How much of a message is conveyed by body language and tone of voice rather than words?
- What the critical factors in selecting a communication channel are?
- What the weakest link in the communication process is?
- How much faster people can think and listen than they can talk?
- What barriers can hinder communication?
- What directions communication can flow?
- What four kinds of meetings are typically held?
- How to make meetings efficient and productive?
- What five common interview failures are?
- Whether police managers should ever lie to the media?
- What four obstacles to sharing information among local, state and federal agencies are?
- What a key to combating terrorism is?

Can You Define?

abstract words	communication	grapevine
active listening	process	horizontal
agenda	decode	communication
anticipatory benefit	deconfliction	interoperability
body language	downward	jargon
channels of	communication	KISS principle
communication	encode	lateral
communication	feedback	communication
communication	gender barrier	lines of
barriers	geographical	communication
communication	diffusion of	news media echo
enhancers	benefit	effect

continued

Introduction

Administrators are in the communication business. Of all the skills a manager/ leader/supervisor needs to be effective, skill in communicating is *the* most vital. Estimates vary, but all studies emphasize the importance of communication in everyday law enforcement operations. Greenberg and Flynn (2003, p.83) stress: "Effective communication is the basis for articulating vision, developing shared values, appreciating human resources and gaining commitment to and involvement in change strategies."

Consider how much of a person's day is occupied with communication. Conversations, television, radio, memos, letters, e-mails, faxes, phone calls, meetings, newspapers—the list is long. Even private thoughts are communication. Every waking hour, people's minds are filled with ideas and thoughts even when they do not outwardly communicate them.

Although technological advances have greatly expanded communication capabilities, the communication process has not changed. This chapter begins with a definition of communication and its importance to managers at all levels. This is followed by an examination of the communication process and its components. Next, barriers and obstacles to communication are discussed, followed by a discussion of communication enhancers. Then the lines of communication are described, including both downward and upward communication. Next is a discussion of internal communication, including meetings and newsletters, followed by a discussion of external communication, including dealing with the media and communicating with outside agencies and the public. The chapter concludes with a discussion of communication and homeland security.

Communication: An Overview

Communication is the complex process through which information *and understanding* are transferred from one person to another. This process may involve written or spoken words or signs and gestures. Communication involves more than sending an idea. Successful communication occurs when the receiver's understanding of the message is the same as the sender's intent. This sounds simple, but often it just does not happen.

communication • the complex process through which information is transferred from one person to another through common symbols.

Lack of communication is often an obstacle to correcting problems. Without effective communication, people do not know what is expected of them or how well they are doing. Managers and subordinates may not be able to agree on the quality of services they provide. Equipment needs may not be revealed. Animosities may fester. Consequences of not communicating well include low morale, increased union disputes, reduced work quality and quantity, rumors and gossip and sometimes even lawsuits. The list is long. To understand how messages can become so muddled, consider the process of communication.

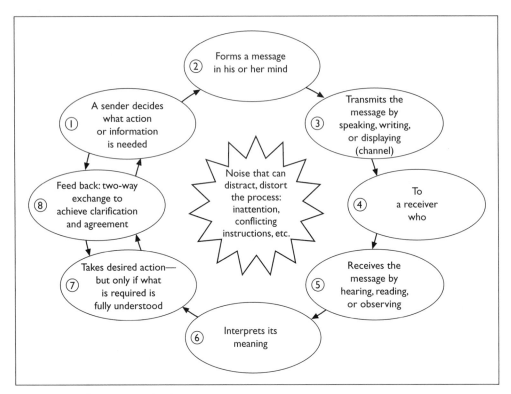

Figure 4.1   The Communication Process

The Communication Process

The basic parts of the communication process are the message, sender and receiver. The process, however, is much more complex than this, as illustrated in Figure 4.1.

A message originates in a sender's mind. The sender, having a unique knowledge base and set of values, must **encode** the message into words or gestures. The code is sent through some channel (which may distort the code). A receiver, also having a unique knowledge base and set of values, must **decode,** or translate, the message. The receiver may or may not provide **feedback** to the sender, that is, an indication that the message is or is not understood.

Successful communication occurs only if (1) the sender can correctly encode the message, (2) the channel is free of distortion and (3) the receiver can correctly decode the message.

encode • place a message into a form to be transmitted.

decode • decipher a message.

feedback • the process by which the sender knows the receiver has understood the message.

The **communication process** involves a message, a sender, a channel and a receiver. It may include feedback.

communication process • involves a message, a sender, a channel and a receiver; it may also include feedback.

Often the sender is unaware that the encoding of the message may be inappropriate. For example, a physician might refer to a person using the abbreviation "S.O.B." To medical people this quite naturally means "short of breath." Laypeople, however, would likely decode it to mean something far different.

Problems that arise from encoding and decoding from one language to another can, at times, prove quite humorous. For example, the English-to-Russian computer translation of the familiar phrase "out of sight, out of mind" is "invisible idiot."

Other times, however, the effects of miscommunication or misinterpretation can be devastating. Consider the circumstances surrounding the bombings of Hiroshima and Nagasaki. Evidence suggests that these first atom bombs might never have been dropped were it not for a Japanese translator's mistranslation of a single word—*mokusatsu*. In 1945, the Emperor of Japan and his cabinet were almost ready to accept the Allies' Potsdam ultimatum to give up or be crushed. However, the Japanese wanted more time to discuss the specific terms, so they sent a message saying they were following a "mokusatsu" policy, meaning "no comment" yet. The translation, however, said that they had *ignored* the surrender demand. This miscommunication led the Allies to proceed with nuclear bombardment (Grittner, 1969, p.32).

Messages do often get lost in translation. Imagine that thoughts could be color coded. You color code your thoughts blue, and the person you are talking to color codes his or her thoughts yellow. What will happen to the message? It may be a mixture of sender *and* receiver preconceptions and a totally different color—green. In other words, effective communication takes into consideration not only the message and channel but also the sender and receiver. How effectively messages are conveyed depends on the following:

- Communication skills of the sender
- Clarity of purpose
- Effectiveness of the message itself
- Appropriateness of the channel used
- Receptivity of the receiver
- Communication skills of the receiver
- Feedback

Shared frames of reference such as language, experience and cultural heritage are extremely important in communication. The smaller the shared frames of reference, the more likely miscommunication and misunderstanding will occur.

Turn your attention now to the specific components making up the communication process.

The Sender of the Message

Communication begins with a person or group with a message to relay. The sender of the message will have characteristics such as age, gender, educational level and past experience that may affect the message. The purpose of the message should be clearly understood. Communication usually has one or more of the following purposes: to inform, entertain, persuade or be understood.

Once the purpose is clear, the message itself must be put into language, which may be verbal (spoken or written) or nonverbal. An effective communicator has developed the basic message "sending" skills of speaking and writing, as well as the message "receiving" skills of listening and reading. The most effective communication is a two-way exchange.

The Message

The message should be in simple, **standard English**—that is, it follows the grammatical rules of American English. Whether spoken or written, the message should avoid **jargon** (the specialized language of a field) and evasive or "impressive" language. Consider the phrase "manually operated impact device"—military jargon for a hammer. In the business world, employee theft is referred to as "inventory

standard English • language that follows the grammatical rules of American English.

jargon • nonsense or meaningless language, often called legalese, for example, party of the first part, hereafter referred to as . . . . Also, specialized language of a field, for example, perpetrator.

shrinkage" and losing money as having a "net profit revenue deficiency." Law enforcement, too, has its share of jargon: aforesaid, alleged perpetrator, a party later
identified as John Doe and said officer proceeded to exit his squad.

All too often message senders attempt to avoid an issue or to *impress* rather
than *express*. The general rule is to keep the message conversational and follow the
KISS principle.

KISS principle • axiom in
communication: "Keep It Short
and Simple."

 The **KISS principle** means: Keep It Short and Simple.

Use familiar words with only one or two syllables when possible. For example,
use *find out* rather than *ascertain;* use *end* rather than *terminate;* and use *use* rather
than *utilize.*

Use prepositional phrases sparingly. For example, use *because* rather than *due
to the fact that;* use *if* rather than *in the event that;* and use *now* rather than *at the
present time.*

Omit all empty words and redundancies. For example, use *asked* rather than
asked the question; use *blue* rather than *blue in color;* use *February* rather than *month
of February;* and use *experience* rather than *past experience.*

Be especially careful in using modifiers. They can result in embarrassing statements such as the following:

> Three cars were reported stolen by our police department yesterday. (The de-
> partment did not steal the cars.) This memo offers suggestions for handling ob-
> scene phone calls from the chief. (The chief did not make obscene phone
> calls.) Stress and anxiety can be emotionally destructive to line personnel. We
> must get rid of them. (Who does *them* refer to?)

Avoid words that are ambiguous or confusing. One very ambiguous word is
subsequently. This word means "after" and also means "as a result of." This is a critical difference, especially in law enforcement, and only the sender of the message
knows which meaning is intended. Therefore, use "after" or "as a result of." Other
confusing terms are *bi-monthly* and *semi-monthly.* Ask a group of people what these
words mean and you will see that about half will come up with the correct meaning. Much better to use *every two months* or *twice a month.*

tone • emotional effect of language, for example, an angry
tone of voice.

Tone, or the emotional effect of certain words, is another factor that greatly influences the message. Some words carry negative connotations, for example, *dirt
bag, snitch, soused* and *slammer.* Be aware of such words and avoid using them
when communicating professionally.

abstract words • theoretical,
not concrete, for example, tall
rather than 6'10".

Abstract words and generalities may blur messages and result in miscommunication. A department policy that prohibits *long hair,* for example, is subject to
misinterpretation because it is not sufficiently specific. The sender needs to be precise. What does *at your earliest convenience* mean? It would be clearer to give the
date by which you would like something done. What does *contact me* suggest? That
the person write, telephone, come in for a visit, physically bump into you or perhaps try to reach you through ESP? Be as specific as possible to ensure that your
meaning is communicated clearly.

Among the critical components of a manager's communication style are coherence, clarity, receiver analysis and conciseness (Glensor and Murphy, 2005, p.84).

nonverbal communication •
messages conveyed by body
language as well as tone of
voice.

Nonverbal Messages and Body Language **Nonverbal communication** is
how messages may be transferred without words. Entire books are written about

body language and interpreting the mannerisms of other people, including eye contact or lack of it, facial expressions, leg and arm movements and so on.

 The majority of communication between two people comes from body language and tone of voice.

body language • messages conveyed by gestures, facial expressions, stance and physical appearance.

Research by Ray Birdwhistell showed 10 percent of the message delivered is verbal and 90 percent is nonverbal. If officers can correctly interpret what they see, they are arming themselves with a powerful tool. Interpreting eye contact, for example, is considered by many communication experts to be one of the most important skills a person can develop.

Many nonverbal messages are obvious: a frown, a smile, a shrug, a yawn, tapping fingers, rolling eyes and so forth. Consider what the following nonverbal cues tell about a person:

- Walking—fast, slow, stomping
- Posture—rigid, relaxed
- Facial expression—wink, smile, frown
- Eye contact—direct, indirect, shifting
- Gestures—nod, shrug, finger point
- Physical spacing—close, distant
- Appearance—well groomed, unkempt

Use caution, however, when interpreting body language.

Channels of Communication

Technology has expanded the **channels of communication,** or the means by which messages are conveyed.

 Critical factors to consider in selecting a channel include speed and opportunity for feedback. Expense is also important.

channels of communication • how messages are conveyed; usually follows the chain of command.

Verbal Channels Among the most common *two-way* verbal channels of communication are one-on-one conversations, telephone conversations, radio dispatch, interviews, meetings, news conferences and speeches. Verbal channels are often selected because they are fast, allow for feedback and are relatively inexpensive. A disadvantage of verbal channels is that they are temporary: There is no permanent record of them. This disadvantage can be negated by taping the communication. In fact, most law enforcement agencies record all calls that come in to the dispatcher.

One-way verbal communication includes audiocassettes, videos and television.

Such channels are well suited to conveying information—training, for example— but are limited in that they do not allow feedback.

Written Channels Written communication includes notes, memos, letters, e-mails, faxes, reports, manuals, bulletins and policies. The writing skills needed by managers are different from those used when writing incident reports. Supervisors are likely to be involved in writing performance reports. Middle and upper managers become involved in writing progress reports, proposals and grants. To excel in this area, supervisors and managers should browse through a bookstore's reference section and select a business writing book they can relate to. At minimum the book should cover the various forms of writing used in business and how to analyze the intended audience.

Written communication has the advantage of being permanent but the disadvantage of being slower and usually more expensive. The primary disadvantage of written communication, however, is lack of immediate feedback.

Be cautious when using faxes, because they are less secure than other forms of communication. You don't know who is on the other end receiving the fax; consequently, sensitive information may end up in the wrong hands. In addition, some organizations do not recognize a faxed signature as being legal.

E-mail is quickly becoming the most popular form of communication because it enhances the lines of communication between managers and employees and between co-workers of all levels. E-mail is not without its perils, however. E-mail can lead to virtual human relations, distancing people from one another unless organizations assume control with specific policies and procedures. Vernon (2005, p.62) points out that when the technology explosion began, the phrase "high tech, low touch" came into vogue, meaning that technology's high efficiency reduces human interaction. When managers depend on e-mail, face-to-face interaction diminishes and personal relationships built on trust and teamwork suffer: "Nothing can replace good interpersonal relations in our profession. We depend on one another on the 'thin blue line.'" Organizations that fail to preserve traditional internal communications risk losing critical organizational dynamics.

Another problem with e-mail messages is that people often do not proofread them. The quality of an e-mail reflects the professionalism of the sender. Take time to read through your replies and messages before hitting the send button. Another peril is hitting the "reply to all" and forwarding messages to unintended people. In addition, many managers are too quick to click the *reply* button. If you find yourself engaged in an online back-and-forth dialogue, pick up the phone and have a real conversation. Finally, when using the global address book, people may click on the wrong name and send information to the wrong person.

The Receiver of the Message

A key factor in any communication is the receiver of the message. Like the sender, the receiver has certain characteristics that influence how the message is interpreted, including age, gender, educational level and experiences.

First, consider the receiver from the sender's perspective. Who is the message for? How receptive is the receiver likely to be? What distractions might have to be overcome? Does the receiver have the necessary background and ability to understand or act on the message? What prejudices or values might hinder or enhance the communication?

Next, consider the receiver from the receiver's perspective. The most important responsibility of the receiver of a verbal message is to *listen*. Unfortunately, listening is one of the most neglected yet most important skills in communication.

Listening

"Listening effectively to those you manage can be the most fundamental and powerful communication tool of all and will result in a much improved working environment" (Johnson, 2005a, p.61). Johnson points out that police officers have learned to "cut to the chase," which may be effective in street situations but can be disastrous when subordinates want to be heard: "New supervisors need to be mindful of the difficult transition from street cop to caring, interested, empowering leader. Honing listening skills is essential to achieving this ideal."

Supervisors need to control the reaction to intervene in a problem. A supervisor who is formulating a response or developing a solution while a subordinate is talking is not hearing what is being said (Johnson, p.62).

Listening is also vital for middle managers, as it lets them become privy to important information otherwise known only to the rank and file. Johnson (p.63) concludes: "Police work, first and foremost, will always be about people. Personal interaction is one constant for police managers. Developing listening skills ensures these interactions are positive, constructive, and, most of all, empowering."

Of the many mistakes managers make, failure to listen is at the top of the list (Cook, 2003, p.14). According to Vernon (p.62): "Those who interact well with partners, the public and even criminals share one thing in common. They listen well." Law enforcement officers need to receive information more than they need to give it. A major portion of their time is spent receiving information for forms and reports, taking action in arrests, eliciting information in interviews and interrogations and many other duties requiring careful listening. As important as listening is, many people lack good listening skills.

 The weakest link in the communication process is *listening*.

Few people have taken courses in listening. We were taught to speak, read and write, but we simply *assume* we know how to listen. Yet most people are *not* good listeners. One of the main reasons is the gap between speaking and listening rates. The average person speaks at approximately 125 words per minute but listens at about 400 words per minute. This gap lets people daydream or begin to think about other topics.

 People listen and think four times faster than they talk.

Preoccupation is another common problem. People often "hear" the sounds but do not "listen" to the message; instead, they evaluate what they are hearing and concentrate on how they are going to respond. It is almost impossible to think, speak and listen at the same time. Poor listening habits are practiced and become entrenched. Other factors that affect listening include the person's attitude toward the speaker and/or the topic, the location, the time available, noise and other distractions and lack of interest or boredom.

Vernon (p.63) offers five tips to improve listening:
1. Make direct eye contact with the person talking.
2. Eliminate distractions.
3. Ensure you understand what's said.
4. Keep your eyes off your watch.
5. Don't get angry at the messenger for bad news. A negative or defensive reaction will usually cut off communication.

A Test of Listening Skills To determine how well you listen, take a few minutes to complete the following listening test created by Fritz.

When participating in an interview, discussion or group conference, do you:

	Usually	Sometimes	Seldom
1. Prepare yourself physically by facing the speaker and making sure that you can hear?	_____	_____	_____
2. Watch the speaker as well as listen to him or her?	_____	_____	_____
3. Decide from the speaker's appearance and delivery whether what he or she has to say is worthwhile?	_____	_____	_____
4. Listen primarily for ideas and underlying feelings?	_____	_____	_____
5. Determine your own bias, if any, and try to allow for it?	_____	_____	_____
6. Keep your mind on what the speaker is saying?	_____	_____	_____
7. Interrupt immediately if you hear a statement you feel is wrong?	_____	_____	_____
8. Make sure before answering that you've taken in the other person's point of view?	_____	_____	_____
9. Try to have the last word?	_____	_____	_____
10. Make a conscious effort to evaluate the logic and credibility of what you hear?	_____	_____	_____

Scoring

On questions 1, 2, 4, 5, 6, 8 and 10, give yourself: 10 points for each answer of *Usually*; 5 points for each answer of *Sometimes*; 0 points for each answer of *Seldom*. On questions 3, 7 and 9, give yourself: 10 points for each answer of *Seldom*; 5 points for each answer of *Sometimes*; 0 points for each answer of *Usually*. If your score is:

90 or more	You're a very good listener.
75–89	Not bad, but you could improve.
74 or less	You definitely need to work on your listening skills.

Source: *Think Like a Manager*, by Roger Fritz, PhD, president of Organization Development Consultants, 500 Technology Drive, Naperville, IL 60563. (708) 420-7673. © 2003. Reprinted by permission.

active listening • includes concentration, full attention and thought.

Active Listening Active listening includes concentration, full attention and thought. To be an effective listener, look at the speaker. Think about the words and the implied message. Ask questions to clarify, but do not interrupt, and remain objective. In addition, as Drucker is fond of saying: "The most important thing in communication is to hear what isn't being said." It is often said that everyone talks, but few listen. The results when people do *not* listen can be disastrous.

Listening skills *can* be improved. Opportunities for practice occur daily. Pay attention to those with whom you are speaking, show appropriate responses to what they are saying, listen for feelings as well as the content, look at and listen to body language and respond directly to what is being said. Active listening is hard work, but it pays off.

Recognize that in communication, receivers and senders of messages constantly switch roles. The effective communicator is skilled not only at speaking (or writing) but also at listening (and reading).

Feedback

I know that you believe that you understand what you think I said, BUT I am not sure you realize that what you heard is not what I meant!

Without feedback, communication is one way. Feedback is the process by which the sender knows whether the receiver has understood the message.

Two people may talk and yet neither may understand what the other is saying. Most feedback is direct and oral. Two people discuss something, one makes a statement, and the other responds. Head nodding or shaking, smiling, grimacing, raised eyebrows, yawns—all are forms of feedback. The better the feedback, the better the communication.

Barriers to Communication

 Communication barriers include:

- Time.
- Volume of information.
- Tendency to say what we think others want to hear.
- Certainty.
- Failure to select the best word.
- Prejudices (sender and/or receiver).
- Strained sender-receiver relationships.

communication barriers • obstacles to clear to achieve effective communication, including time, volume of information, tendency to say what we think others want to hear, failure to select the best word, prejudices and strained relationships, judging, superiority, certainty, controlling, manipulation and indifference.

Time is important to everyone, especially law enforcement officers and managers. Communication systems have greatly enhanced the ability to pass information from one person or organization to another. On the other hand, e-mails, faxes and other devices have deluged subordinates and managers alike with information. To cope, managers must be selective in what they personally take action on and what they delegate.

Another obstacle to communication is the tendency to say what we think others want to hear. This is especially true when the information is negative. This tendency can be dangerous because the person may form opinions or act on insufficient information. State all the facts about a situation so the receiver can correctly interpret them.

A fourth obstacle is certainty, the unwavering belief that the information a person has is accurate: "My mind's made up; don't confuse me with the facts." This is illustrated by the young man who went to see a psychiatrist to learn to cope with being dead. This young man was certain he was dead, but no one would believe him. The psychiatrist, eager to help the man, asked him, "Do dead people bleed?" When the young man answered, "Of course not," the psychiatrist asked for the young man's hand and permission to stick his finger with a pin. The young man consented, and, as the psychiatrist expected, the finger bled. Amazed, the young man exclaimed, "I'll be darned. Dead people do bleed!"

Logic seldom works on those who are certain of the "facts." Vernon calls this obstacle "allness," an attitude that hinders good communication based on two false assumptions: (1) It's possible to know and say everything about something and (2) what one says (or writes or thinks) includes all that's important about the subject. Both assumptions show lack of humility and prevent good interpersonal relationships.

Yet another obstacle is the varied meanings words may have. For example, the word *victim* may arouse concern and empathy, but it may also arouse annoyance and pity. Select your words carefully to convey precisely what you mean. In one department a police chief sent a memo to all officers asking for suggestions on how to improve retention. He received numerous ideas on how to help officers improve their memories. What he wanted, however, was thoughts on how to keep officers from quitting the department.

Another important obstacle to communication is prejudice. Bias against a certain race, religion, nationality, gender, sexual preference or disability can create tremendous communication barriers. Usually such biases are based on stereotypes, overgeneralizations about a certain group of people. Simons (2004, p.4) suggests that stereotypes can be helpful if used correctly: "The trick to using stereotypes intelligently is extracting the kernel of truth without digesting the husk of exaggeration." He uses this as an introduction to a discussion of generalizations about men and women in the workplace, noting there are some very real differences worth exploring.

The Gender Barrier

Zielinski (2004, p.23) contends that despite decades of being conditioned to overlook differences between men and women, most gender-communication experts agree there are very real differences in the ways men and women communicate. These differences may create a **gender barrier.**

gender barrier • differences between men and women that can result in miscommunication.

Zielinski suggests that credibility and authority are the two primary qualities men want most to project in their own communication. Another male trait is the desire to use fewer words, to "get to the point." Women, in contrast, often use qualifiers and are more likely to downplay their certainty, whereas men downplay their doubts. Zielinski (p.27) believes that each gender has areas of natural advantage and that people can learn to use the strengths of both genders in their communications.

Men can learn from women to temper the talking head, replacing a monologue with dialogue. Use inclusive language. Women tend to use words such as *we, our* and *us,* whereas men tend to say *I, me* and *mine* more often. He suggests men need to leave their ego at the door. Men should also emote now and then; a display of honest emotions is now associated more with inner strength than with weakness.

Women can learn from men to "quash the qualifiers," for example, "in my opinion" or "this might be better if." Don't personalize. Consider the difference between "I have a problem with your lack of initiative" and "The lack of initiative you have shown is troublesome." The first sentence inadvertently makes the problem about the speaker. Finally, grab authority and keep it: "Women who want to be perceived as more authoritative should minimize the factors that undermine authority—digression, indecisiveness, equivocation—and learn to be assertive in a way that radiates confidence." Table 4.1 summarizes other gender differences in communication.

Of special note is that, when communicating, men tend to not pause and to interrupt, whereas women tend to pause, allowing the male interruption. Such interruptions, even though unintentional, may create anger and tension. In addition, because men tend to speak until interrupted, they likely will dominate a conversation.

The Cultural Barrier

The most obvious barrier for individuals interacting with people from different cultures is often a language barrier. Executive Order 13166, "Improving Access to

Table 4.1   Conversational Styles: Gender Tendencies

Listening	
Male	**Female**
Irregular eye contact	Uninterrupted eye contact
Infrequent nodding	Frequent nodding
Infrequent humming sounds	Frequent humming sounds
May continue another activity while speaking	Usually stops other activities while speaking
Interrupts in order to speak	Waits for pauses in order to speak
Questions are designed to analyze speaker's information	Questions are designed to elicit more information

Speaking	
Male	**Female**
Few pauses	Frequent pauses
May abruptly change topic	Connects information to previous speaker's information
Speaks until interrupted	Stops speaking when information delivered
Speaks louder than previous speaker	Uses same volume as previous speaker
Frequent use of "I" and "me"	Frequent use of "us" and "we"
Personal self-disclosure rarely included	Personal self-disclosure often included
Humor delivered as separate jokes or anecdotes	Humor interwoven into discussion content
Humor often based on kidding or making fun of others	Humor rarely based on kidding or making fun of others

Source: Peg Meier and Ellen Foley. "War of the Words." (Minneapolis/St. Paul) *Star Tribune, First Sunday,* January 6, 1991. Reprinted with permission of the *Star Tribune.*

Services for Persons with Limited English Proficiency," requires the federal government and grant recipients to take "reasonable steps to ensure that people with limited English proficiency (LEP) have meaningful access to the programs, services and information they provide." This is important because of the nation's changing demographics. The U.S. Census Bureau projects that by 2010, people of Hispanic origin will make up 15 percent of the population, with the Asian community also expected to steadily increase (*Supporting Limited English Communities,* 2005, p.3). Aside from English, Spanish is the predominant language spoken at most federal grant sites, although Vietnamese, Pacific Island dialects, Chinese dialects, Korean and Russian are also becoming common.

The spoken language is not the only barrier. Gestures can also be misinterpreted. For example, making the "A-Okay" sign (a circle with the thumb and forefinger) is friendly in the United States, but it means "you're worth zero" in France, Belgium and many Latin American countries. The thumbs-up gesture meaning "good going" in the United States is the equivalent of an upraised middle finger in some Islamic countries. The amount of eye contact also varies with different racial and ethnic groups. For example, in the United States, Caucasians maintain eye contact while speaking about 45 percent of the time, African-Americans about 30 percent, Hispanics about 25 percent and Asians about 18 percent.

Moy and Archibald (2005, p.55) note that an even greater problem than lack of English skills is immigrants' lack of understanding of law enforcement practices and their fear of police. Among the misunderstandings they describe are recognizing law enforcement officers (some immigrants do not know the difference between police officers, security guards and firefighters), using the emergency 911 system, and responding to a traffic stop (some people stop right in the middle of the road and others refuse to sign the traffic citation). In addition, domestic calls are complicated not only by families' limited English, but even more so by their lack of understanding American laws and the legal ramifications of domestic violence.

Beyond the obvious problems of a language barrier and some immigrants' ignorance of the laws, new immigrants are unable to open bank accounts or obtain driver's licenses because they have no social security number. Immigrant parents cannot accompany their children on school field trips because the required background check cannot be completed without a social security number. Further, some immigrants are scammed by thieves who threaten them with deportation (Kathman and Chesser, 2005, p.63).

Chalmers and Tiffin (2005, p.59) describe North Carolina's first Spanish-speaking citizens' police academy. Typically academy sessions have police commanders discussing the department's mission and explaining how police efforts support the community. Extensive interaction, discussions and questions occur during the sessions, with translators assisting in the communication. The initiative has strengthened the Durham Police Department's community policing philosophy as well as the level of trust between law enforcement and the Latino community (Chalmers and Tiffin, p.59).

Obstacles within the Process

Recall that the communication process consists of a sender, a channel, a receiver and, ideally, feedback. Problems can arise within any aspect of this process.

The *message* may be *improperly encoded*. The sender must translate or *encode* the message accurately, unambiguously and precisely, avoiding complex language. It must get past the sender's prejudices, limitations and values. Nonverbal cues must support, not contradict, the message.

Further, the sender must not *misuse communication channels*. An obvious example is the department bulletin board, a potentially powerful communication channel. All too often, however, material is posted and left long past its effective life. Cluttered bulletin boards lose their communicating power. Other examples are dull, one-way meetings and department newsletters that do little more than report sports news and social events.

A more critical example is one-on-one communication between managers and subordinates that becomes one way and primarily negative or disciplinary. Most one-on-one communication should be *positive*. It should not be limited to official business but also should include more personal or casual topics to let subordinates know they are important as both individuals and employees.

"Noise in the channel" may seriously interfere with communication. This may be actual physical noise, such as an airplane flying overhead, a phone ringing or more than one person talking at once. An uncomfortable room—too hot, too cold, unpleasant odors—can also detract from communication.

Written communication can be hindered by poor copy quality, messy copy with lots of cross-throughs and write-overs, illegible handwriting, faint print and so on. Such "noise" in the channel not only interferes physically with the message, but it often annoys the receiver, further hindering effective communication.

Poor timing is another common obstacle. If the receiver is upset, angry, rushed, tired, hurt, preoccupied or unprepared, the message may not be communicated.

The *message* may be *improperly decoded*. The receiver must translate or *decode* the message accurately and precisely. The encoded message must pass through not only the personality screen of the sender but also the perception screen of the receiver.

Poor *listening* habits are a prime factor in improperly decoding messages. The criticality of listening in communication has already been discussed. It bears repeating. Poor listening habits are a *major* cause of communication breakdowns. Listeners may be defensive, too emotionally involved or distracted.

Closely related to poor listening habits are *lack of trust, credibility* and *candor.* If people think they cannot believe what someone tells them, they may misinterpret or ignore messages. For example, if a manager tells subordinates that they will be getting new uniforms and they do not, the subordinates will be less likely to believe the next "promise" and question the motive behind the promise as well. Another common example is some politicians' lack of credibility. What candidates say to get elected and what they actually do are often quite different.

Communication Enhancers

Communication enhancers are often the opposite of actions that cause communication obstructions. To overcome the obstacle of communication overload, managers must establish priorities. Not all communications need to be available to all employees. The main criteria should be whether the employees need the information to perform assigned tasks and whether it would improve morale. Overloading employees with immaterial communications will restrict their performance and productivity.

> **communication enhancers •** techniques for reducing or eliminating barriers to communication, including properly encoding messages, selecting the best channel, describing, equality, openness, problem orientation, positive intent and empathy.

If a message promises further information, follow through. Use and encourage free and open two-way communication whenever possible. Emphasize brevity and accuracy.

Obstacles to communication are difficult to eliminate, but many can be minimized by concentrating on what you say and write. Communicating openly and clearly reduces informal communications such as the grapevine and rumor mill. When you look at the barriers within the communication process itself, certain guidelines become obvious.

Properly encode messages. Say what you mean and mean what you say. Watch word choices. Consider the receiver of the message. Match nonverbal communication with the verbal message. Make sure messages are accurate and timely. Always be open, candid, honest and sincere. Such information can do much to eliminate rumors.

Select the best communication channel. Focus on one-on-one, face-to-face communication, which is the most powerful channel available. Although this takes more time than a bulletin or memo, it is decidedly more effective.

Be open. Investigate options rather than steadfastly clinging to *the* solution. Effective managers work together toward solutions rather than choosing up sides. In effect people agree to disagree without being disagreeable.

Internal Communication

Lines of communication are inherent in an organizational structure. Just as authority flows downward and outward, so can communication. However, communication should also flow upward.

> **lines of communication •** similar to channels of communication. May be downward, upward (vertical) or lateral (horizontal) and internal or external.

 Communication may be downward, upward (vertical) or lateral (horizontal). It may also be internal or external. Most effective communication is two way.

downward communication • messages from managers and supervisors to subordinates.

Downward communication includes directives from managers and supervisors, either spoken or written. When time is limited and an emergency exists, communication often *must* flow downward and one way. In such cases, subordinates must listen and act on the communication.

Top-level law enforcement managers issue orders, policies, rules and regulations, memos, orders of the day and so on. These communications are delivered primarily downward and sometimes laterally. Communication from this level filters down and is understood by receivers according to personal knowledge, training, competence and experience.

Middle-level management and the on-line supervisors also issue directives, roll-call information, explanations of directives from higher-level managers, information for department newsletters or roll-call bulletins, letters, memos and instructions. Again, such communication is distributed downward and laterally.

upward (vertical) communication • messages conveyed from subordinates to supervisors and managers or from supervisors to managers.

Upward communication includes requests from subordinates to their superiors. It should also include input on important decisions affecting subordinates. Effective managers give all subordinates a chance to contribute ideas, opinions and values as decisions are made.

Another critical form of upward communication is found in operational reports. The major portion of law enforcement operations is in the field at the lowest level of the hierarchy. Most investigations, traffic citations, arrests, form completion and other activities are at this basic level. These actions eventually travel both from the bottom up and laterally throughout the organization. Communication may take the form of reports, charts, statistics, daily summaries or logs. All are extremely important.

lateral (horizontal) communication • messages sent between managers or supervisors on the same level of the hierarchy and between subordinates on the same level.

Downward and upward communication are also called **vertical communication.** **Lateral** or **horizontal communication** includes communication among managers on the same level and among subordinates on the same level. Internal communication includes all of the preceding as well as messages from dispatch to officers in the field—among the most important communication of any law enforcement agency.

Subordinate Communication

Communicating with subordinates is an essential managerial responsibility. Managers and supervisors accomplish organizational goals through their subordinates. Employees want to know what is going on in the organization, to be "in the know." If employees do not know what the administration expects, they cannot support organizational goals and objectives.

Johnson (2005b, p.105) recommends that supervisors and managers address people by their first names: "Being addressed by your first name by a supervisor, especially one removed by several ranks, often has an exhilarating effect on an officer." He suggests that if a manager or supervisor knows he or she will be communicating with a subordinate later in the day, he or she should find out that person's first name before the meeting.

The Grapevine

grapevine • informal channel of communication within the agency or department. Also called the *rumor mill.*

In addition to the formal channels of communication established by an organization, informal channels also exist. Commonly referred to as the **grapevine,** these informal channels frequently hinder cooperation and teamwork.

Managers and supervisors must realize that even if they *wanted* to stop the grapevine, they could not. In fact, directing people to not talk about an issue often ensures that the word will spread more quickly. Thus it is important that managers make the grapevine work for them rather than against them.

The term **rumor mill,** commonly applied to the grapevine, suggests some of the problems associated with informal channels of communication. The grapevine is strongest in organizations in which information is not openly shared. Employees begin to guess and speculate when they do not know—hence the rumors. One way to positively influence the grapevine is to provide staff with *all* information needed to function efficiently, effectively and happily. This includes letting people know the bad as well as the good. Do not let the grapevine beat you to informing people of bad news that affects them.

The grapevine is also sometimes referred to as gossip. According to Moore (2004, p.110): "Gossip is like crabgrass—even a small amount allowed to grow unchecked can overtake an otherwise well-cared-for lawn. You might not be able to uproot all of it, but can make its spread less damaging." Moore suggests that gossip does not have to be negative and that it might be turned into a management tool: "If you want to know what's really on the minds of the work force, tap the power of the grapevine."

rumor mill • informal channels of communication within a department or agency. Also called the *grapevine.*

Newsletters

Newsletters can address the personal side of policing. For instance, it can focus on achievements of people within the department, sworn and civilian; acknowledge and welcome new employees; and cover topics such as weddings, births, deaths and community activities and contributions. They can also be educational. For example, each issue could contain a column on tips for effective report writing.

Communication at Meetings

It has been said that meetings are gatherings where minutes are kept and hours are lost. Too many meetings are held simply because they are part of the weekly routine or because other options (such as sending e-mails or memos) are ignored.

Meetings serve important functions and need not be time wasters. The keys to successful, productive meetings are planning and effective communication.

 Departments typically have four types of meetings: informational, opinion seeking, problem solving and new-idea seeking.

Knowing what type of meeting to plan helps to set appropriate goals for the meeting. Every meeting should have a clearly defined purpose and anticipated outcome. Some meetings serve two or more purposes. Before scheduling a meeting, however, explore alternatives: Is group action needed? Could the desired results be accomplished by one-on-one interactions? A phone call? A memo? An e-mail?

Meeting Preparation One key to successful meetings is a carefully prepared **agenda** or outline, usually given to participants *before* the meeting. The agenda should have a time frame, including beginning and ending. Ideally, the ending time will make it difficult to stay beyond what is scheduled, for example, the end of a shift. Schedule the most important agenda items first in case time runs out.

agenda • a plan, usually referring to a meeting outline or program; a list of things to be accomplished.

In addition to creating an agenda, do the following to ensure a smooth, efficient meeting:

- Schedule the meeting room.
- Prepare handouts and visual aids.
- Make name tents and arrange seating if appropriate.
- Check the room arrangement and temperature.
- Check audiovisual equipment to be used.

The meeting room should be large enough, well lit and free of distractions. Handouts and visual aids should look professional. Seating is usually most effective in a U- or an O-shape. Do not overlook the potential value of assigning seats. Name tents are especially helpful if not all participants know each other. Be sure audiovisual equipment is functioning properly. Focus the overhead projector, and be sure there is a spare bulb. Make certain flipcharts have ample paper and that colored pens are available.

Conducting the Meeting *Start on time. End on time.* Starting on time is a must. People quickly learn when a manager does not begin meetings promptly and will tend to come late as a result. To counteract lateness, close the door so those arriving late will be obvious. Some managers go so far as to lock the door.

Assign someone to take minutes or tape the meeting. At the beginning of the meeting, ask whether the agenda and schedule are acceptable. Make adjustments if necessary and then stick to the agenda and time schedule. Agree on whether to allow interruptions, including cell phone or beeper alerts, and whether to take a break.

To facilitate open communication and group participation, be aware of bad habits people may display at meetings, including speechifying, repeating the same points, interrupting, speaking without being recognized by the chair, never contributing, acting as a know-it-all or as the "we tried it and it didn't work" historian each time an idea is presented, sidetracking and changing issues.

Both the chair and participants can change such counterproductive behavior in several ways. Determine norms about how meetings will proceed. Require recognition from the chair. Outlaw personal attacks. Read the preceding list of counterproductive behaviors, and ask everyone to refrain from them. Talk to the worst disrupters before the meeting, and ask for their cooperation. Give disrupters special tasks or roles, such as taking minutes.

To facilitate discussion, comment only on behavior, never personalities. Ask the "Yes, but . . ." disrupter to give positive answers and solutions rather than objections. Stop the meeting and ask people who are engaged in side conversations to share their discussions with the entire group. Try to draw out those who do not voluntarily contribute to discussions. Smile and be reassuring.

Group-process theorists have created many models to explain group dynamics. The models explain the roles that different individuals play in making a meeting work. In these models titles are attached to the roles, such as the *initiator* who gets things started, the *harmonizer* who smoothes disputes and the *summarizer* who pulls together the pieces.

Ending the Meeting One part of meetings that is often overlooked is the windup. Before closing a meeting, summarize the main points discussed. Review new ideas, assign tasks and set deadlines. After the meeting, prepare the minutes and distribute them as soon as practical.

Keys for effective meetings:

- Prepare in advance—have an agenda.
- Start and stop on time.
- Stick to the agenda.
- Facilitate open communication and participation.

External Communication

External communication includes all interactions with agencies and people outside the department, including the news media and citizen contacts. Law enforcement agencies must effectively interact with other components of the criminal justice system—that is, the courts and correctional services. Law enforcement agencies must also interface with other social services, as well as with other departments of the jurisdiction they serve, as noted in Chapter 2.

Communicating with Other Agencies

"If we do not communicate regularly with our colleagues in neighboring jurisdictions, we will be unable to establish an effective partnership between our agencies, and as a result the capabilities of all of our departments will be reduced" (Estey, 2005, p.6). Whitehead (2005, p.138) contends: "In a disaster situation police and fire agencies have to work together to bring a quick and safe resolution. But when agencies can't communicate and work together, the result is disaster and sometimes death."

Griffith (2004, p.52) points out that public safety agencies throughout the United States have arrived at the "startling conclusion" that their wireless communications systems are "woefully inadequate" and that most were painfully aware of the problem before the 9-11 attacks. He notes that public safety agencies operate on a "spaghetti tangle of frequencies and frequency bands." The solution: interoperability.

Boyd (2005b, p.77) explains: "In the broadest sense, **interoperability** refers to the ability of public safety emergency responders to work seamlessly with other systems or products without special efforts" (emphasis added). In 2004 the Department of Homeland Security (DHS) announced the establishment of the Office for Interoperability and Compatibility (OIC) to oversee interoperability research and development, testing and evaluation, standards, technical assistance and grant guidance. One OIC program, SAFECOM, coordinates the efforts of more than 50,000 local, state, federal and tribal public safety agencies across the country working on communications interoperability. According to Boyd (p.79), what sets SAFECOM apart from other federal initiatives is its commitment to a bottom-up approach: "Interoperability needs should be defined locally, by users on the grounds, and these very same practitioners should guide the development and implementation of interoperability solutions." This makes sense given that more than 90 percent of the U.S. public safety communications infrastructure is owned and operated by localities and states with distinct needs.

The importance of interoperability in the DC sniper case is described by Careless (2004, p.36), who says it took hundreds of local, state and federal police officers working together to track down the suspects. The cooperation was possible because of interoperable radio communications: "In a very real sense, interoperability saved lives when the suspects were apprehended on October 25, 2003."

interoperability • the ability of public safety emergency responders to work seamlessly with other systems or products without special efforts.

Interoperability Continuum

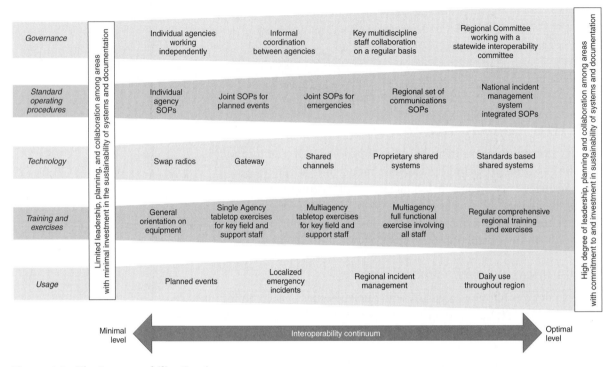

Figure 4.2   The Interoperability Continuum
Source: David Boyd. "The 5 Elements to Achieve Interoperability." *Law and Order,* August 2005, pp.70-74. Reprinted by permission.

Although interoperability depends on technology, that is only one part of the interoperability problem. Facella (2005, p.46) believes the answer to solving interoperability problems has three parts—technology, management and regulatory—and that all three must be present. Only 20 percent of the interoperability solution lies in technical and regulatory issues, whereas 80 percent of the problem is in policy and management issues (Facella). Management issues involve getting departments and chiefs to agree on procedures to share channels and resources, terminology, response scenarios and mutual aid agreements. After the plans and agreements are developed, they need to be communicated to every level of the agencies and practiced regularly.

Boyd (2005a, p.71), likewise, notes that interoperability begins with technology, but that technology is only part of the solution. He describes the Interoperability Continuum developed by SAFECOM for policy makers and public safety leaders to use in addressing five critical success factors: (1) governance, (2) standard operating procedures, (3) technology, (4) training and exercises and (5) use of interoperable communications. This Interoperability Continuum is illustrated in Figure 4.2. Boyd (p.72) stresses: "To reach the optimal level of interoperability, a region must progress along all five elements of the continuum."

Communicating with the Media

The media can be friend or foe, depending on the effectiveness of the channels of communication. As noted in Chapter 2, difficulties in dealing with the press usually arise from the need to balance the public's right to know, the First Amendment right to freedom of the press and the need of law enforcement agencies to protect the Sixth Amendment rights of those accused of crimes, as well as the privacy of crime victims, while maintaining the integrity of an investigation.

Some law enforcement agencies have a policy that line officers and supervisors are not allowed to issue statements or opinions about any activities or conditions related to their duties to newspaper reporters or radio or television stations. Such requests are referred to middle management, who may in turn refer them to a public relations department or to a public information officer (PIO). Rosenthal (2005b, pp.6–7) contends: "The PIO function is an essential element of best-practices law enforcement." He recommends that a PIO be recruited rather than appointed because public information is too important. The person should be motivated, enthusiastic and want to do the job. As to whether the PIO should be a civilian or someone from law enforcement, Rosenthal believes the best chance of success is picking someone from law enforcement: "They've walked the walk and can now talk the talk." He believes it is easier to teach a cop to be a PIO than to teach a former newsperson the "insides" of law enforcement.

Some law enforcement executives claim that every officer is a "public information officer." Whatever approach to dealing with the media a department chooses, it should have clearly defined policies and procedures.

Policies and Procedures for Dealing with the Media Procedures should address basic considerations such as who will be authorized to speak to the press as well as where and how frequently press briefings will be held. Whether a department is small or large, it must have clearly defined policies and procedures, such as those the New York City Police Department uses (Table 4.2).

Clearly formulated policies and procedures for communicating with the media are necessary to effectively conduct agency business as well as for a sound public relations/community relations program. Building partnerships with the media was discussed in Chapter 2.

News Releases Rosenthal (2005a, pp.5–6) contends that news releases are a great way to get important law enforcement messages to the public and offers the following recommendations:

- Call it a "news" release, not a "press" release. Radio and TV newspeople don't use presses and prefer the more accurate term "news release."
- Draft an outline by answering the six basic questions: What? Who? How? When? Where? and Why?
- Put a brief headline at the top of your news release.
- Put the most important, newest information in the first paragraph.
- Keep it short and simple.

A news release should be written as a **sound bite,** which, simply put, is good information stated briefly. A sound bite has two essential elements (1) it must contain good, solid nuggets of information, not speculation or your opinion, and (2) it must be short (Rosenthal, 2003, p.3).

sound bite • good information stated briefly. Two essential elements are (1) that it contain good, solid nuggets of information, not speculation or opinion, and (2) that it is short.

Table 4.2   New York City Police Department's Press Release Policy

Guidelines in Criminal Cases

The following information should be made available for publication, when and after an arrest is made:

(a)   The accused's name, age, residence, employment, marital status, and similar background information.

(b)   The substance or text of the charge such as a complaint, indictment, information, and, when appropriate, the identity of the complainant.

(c)   The identity of the investigating and arresting agency and length of the investigation.

(d)   The circumstances immediately surrounding the arrest, including the time and place of arrest, resistance, pursuit, possession and use of weapons, and a description of items seized at the time of arrest.

NOTE: P.G. 116-22 prohibits disclosure of identity of children under 16 who are arrested or complainants. Victims of sex crimes should likewise not be identified to the press.

Pretrial disclosure of the following information may cause substantial risk of prejudice to a defendant and thereby adversely affect a case. For that reason, the following information SHOULD NOT be released without first clearing with the Public Information Division.

(a)   Statements as to the character or reputation of an accused person or prospective witness.

(b)   Admissions, confessions, or the contents of a statement or alibi attributable to an accused person.

(c)   The performance or results of tests or the refusal of the accused to take a test.

(d)   Statements concerning the credibility or anticipated testimony of prospective witnesses.

(e)   The possibility of a plea of guilty to the offense charged or to a lesser offense, or other disposition.

(f)   Opinions concerning evidence or argument in the case, whether or not it is anticipated that such evidence or argument will be used at trial.

Source: Courtesy of the New York City Police Department.

News Conferences and Interviews Garner (2005, p.28) notes that what law enforcement does—good and bad—is *big* news. He explains that a news or press conference is a planned calling together of news media representatives to share information on a topic, event or incident believed to be of wide interest. He recommends that agencies hold a news conference when a high-profile crime or other incident of great media interest occurs. Agencies might also consider calling a conference when (1) the agency needs help from the public on a major case, (2) there is an ongoing danger of which the public should be made aware, (3) there are major personnel or organizational changes within the department, (4) there are important new crime prevention or other programs being launched, (5) administrators are honoring employees or citizens with significant awards and (6) administrators feel responsible for answering serious allegations of law enforcement misconduct.

Further suggestions for giving a news conference include limiting your opening statement to 10 minutes or less and then opening the floor for questions. Repeat each question after it is asked to help those in the audience who may not have heard it. Also make sure you understand the question before attempting to answer it. Keep your responses short and to the point, avoiding legalese and jargon. Do not allow questions that stray from the subject of the news conference; explain that you will answer extraneous questions later. Furthermore, let the audience know whether copies of your prepared statement are available. From start to finish, treat every microphone as "live" and every camera as "on." Finally, to better prepare for the next time, critique your news conferences objectively.

Covello, who teaches media at Columbia University, suggests the five biggest interview failures (Buice, 2003a, p.26).

 Five interview failures are failing to (1) take charge, (2) anticipate questions, (3) develop key messages, (4) stick to the facts and (5) keep calm.

*Montgomery County (Maryland) Chief Charles Moose
answers questions from reporters at a briefing at police
headquarters. In 2002, Montgomery County was the site of
five shootings attributed to the Washington-area snipers.*

It is especially important to avoid these failures when responding to the media during a crisis situation.

Media Management in a Crisis Buice (2003b, pp.24, 26) offers the following observations on dealing with a major story.

1. "Make neither threats nor promises you cannot keep." He notes that to ask the media to ignore specific information is akin to asking a fielder to drop a pop fly that might happen to land in his glove.
2. "Communication is both art and science." Perception is as important as reality and sometimes more so.
3. "Good news conferences don't happen by accident. They must be finessed."
4. "Expect the unexpected and no matter what the question is, stay on message." To continue his baseball analogy, Buice notes that instead of a knuckleball, you might face a knucklehead, so be ready. Some questions you will have to take a swing at or be penalized for inaction. Like baseball, practice and confidence can make the difference.

The nature of police business often requires the delicate handling and release (or retention) of information, and it is often difficult and time-consuming, particularly for larger agencies, to keep all officers equally informed about which details of a case may be provided to the media. On the very rare occasions where it becomes necessary to lie to the media, it must be followed at the earliest opportunity with an explanation for the deception.

 If lying to the media might save a life or protect the public safety, after the need to lie has passed, the department should explain why lying was necessary and, perhaps, apologize.

Leaks As Parrish (2003) points out: "Police officers need to be aware that they are not the only source of information and that a good reporter will often dig up non-public information." Of special concern are information leaks from within the department. Gary (2003, p.28) notes: "Inevitably, there are going to be at least a few unauthorized anonymous spokespersons in every high-profile case. At their worst, these leakers will put their own agendas ahead of the investigation." Sometimes leakers are showing off how much they know. But the results can be devastating to an investigation. Gary (pp.28–29) gives the following example that occurred in the 2003 DC area sniper crisis:

> A week after the sniper incidents began, police found a note presumably left by the killers near the school where a 13-year-old boy had been shot. Written on a Tarot card known as the "death" card, it read: "Dear policeman. I am God." Hoping to coax more communication, Moose went on live national television to deliver a thinly veiled response, alluding to God in his statement. But by the next day the Tarot card's message had been leaked. Pundits and psychics had taken their own 15 minutes to comment on its significance. Moose was outraged.
>
> Why? Because that leak sent a message to the shooters that law enforcement was not to be trusted.

Murphy and Wexler (2004, p.18), in analyzing the DC sniper case, comment: "Communication was clearly the most compelling concern in the sniper case. Investigations of this kind succeed or fail based on executives' ability to effectively manage and communicate information in a timely manner." Among the lessons learned from the case were the following:

- Agencies need a mechanism for providing a daily briefing to staff. In the absence of official information, rumors can circulate unchecked (p.87).
- Agencies should have a plan (preferably before an incident) to manage the media and, to the extent possible, stick to it throughout the event (p.100).
- Agencies should identify one point of contact for the media and the means for that law enforcement official to communicate quickly with them.
- Agencies should recognize that by providing reporters with information, they can minimize the likelihood that reporters will see the need to conduct their own independent investigations.

Sometimes media involvement alters the way law enforcement performs. For example, intense media coverage of high-profile cases may have far-reaching effects on other, more low-profile incidents and, consequently, affect how the entire criminal justice system handles such matters. This is known as the **news media echo effect,** which occurs when a highly publicized criminal case results in a shift in handling similarly charged but nonpublicized cases.

news media echo effect • occurs when a highly publicized criminal case results in a shift in processing for similarly charged but nonpublicized cases.

Handling Bad Press Garner (2004, p.22) cautions that doing the wrong thing in response to bad news will only make things worse and lengthen the time it takes for the department to recover. He suggests several failed responses to avoid. The most tempting, and almost certainly the worst, is to lie about what happened, perhaps denying the event ever occurred. When the truth comes out, that will be even worse news. As the Danish proverb states: "Bad is never good until worse happens." A second inappropriate response is to put off the media. Not talking or saying "no comment" will not make the reporters go away; it will probably goad them into working even harder to get the facts. A third problematic response is "dribbling out the story," releasing tiny bits of information over a drawn-out time. Another failed response is attacking the press.

Rather than committing the preceding mistakes, Garner (p.25) suggests the following for surviving a media shelling: tell the truth; don't play games with the media; don't try to unfairly shift the blame; keep things in perspective; keep all promises; speak with one voice; and emphasize the positive.

Using the Media The media and law enforcement may both benefit through co-operation. In fact, in some instances, law enforcement and media collaboration is quite deliberate. Consider, for example, the **perp walk,** where suspects are paraded before the news media. However, recent criticism has fallen on this practice, and several courts across the country are considering whether perp walks may violate suspects' rights to privacy. A federal court judge in New York has already handed down a ruling forcing the NYPD to suspend its perp walks after a burglary suspect was led out of the station house in handcuffs, placed in a squad car, driven around the block and then brought back into the station, all at the request of a local news station who wanted footage of the man for their newscast.

perp walk • suspects paraded before the news media.

 Some police departments are using the media in a more direct way by hosting their own television programs on the cable company's local-access channel.

Publicity as a Means to Prevent Crime Johnson and Bowers (2003, p.497) report: "The effectiveness of crime reduction schemes may be significantly enhanced by publicity. . . . Carefully planned publicity campaigns may represent a powerful yet cost-effective tool in crime prevention." Their research suggests that publicizing crime prevention efforts increases the offenders' perceptions of the risks involved in perpetrating crime. In fact, publicizing such efforts before they go into effect can have an **anticipatory benefit**—that is, criminals may be deterred even before the efforts are implemented. According to their findings, the most frequently used publicity was newspaper articles (90 percent), followed by leaflets, letters and cards (62 percent). The strategies used by participants in their research are summarized in Table 4.3.

anticipatory benefit • criminals may be deterred even before the efforts are implemented.

Their research (p.515) found that: "Of all the other variables analyzed, only the number of partner agencies involved in the implementation of the scheme, and publicity in terms of the number of press articles and radio interviews conducted, were significantly related to scheme success. In comparison to the other variables for which quarterly data were available, publicity was the most significant predictor of decreases in the burglary rate."

Another interesting finding of this research was that of a **geographical diffusion of benefit.** Properties immediately adjacent to that where the intervention was implemented also experienced a reduction in burglary. They (p.518) note: "To capitalize on this finding, we suggest that a cost-effective way of targeting resources may be to employ a kind of bull's-eye resource targeting approach, whereby an area would be divided into concentric zones, and resources targeted into every other zone," as shown in Figure 4.3. These researchers (p.519) also suggest that advertising may be more effective if done in bursts rather than over continuous periods and that the effects of advertising campaigns extend beyond the period during which they are active.

geographical diffusion of benefit • properties immediately adjacent to the intervention implemented also experienced a reduction in burglary.

Table 4.3   Number of Schemes Undertaking Different Forms of Publicity

Publicity Type	Specific Item	% of schemes (n)
General publicity	Radio interviews (local/national)	33% (7)
	Newspaper articles (local/national)	90% (19)
	Television appearances (local/national)	24% (5)
	Leaflets/letters/cards	62% (13)
	Posters	38% (8)
	Publicity directed at offenders (e.g., Christmas cards)	14% (3)
	Stickers (e.g., neighborhood watch or smartwater)	19% (4)
	Significant community meetings explaining the scheme	43% (9)
	Informal information or scheme to community offenders	14% (3)
Stand alone publicity campaigns		57% (12)
Surveys (including fear of crime, alleygating, target hardening)		33% (7)
Other (any other form of publicity)		43% (9)

Source: Shane D. Johnson and Kate J. Bowers. "Opportunity Is in the Eye of the Beholder: The Role of Publicity in Crime Prevention." *Crime and Justice*, Vol. 2, No. 3, 2003, p.505. Reprinted by permission.

Communication and Community Policing

Every contact with the public is a public relations contact. It is critical that all members of the agency, especially those in positions of authority, present a positive image and communicate effectively. This is true whether officers are giving directions or answering a call from citizens with a raccoon in their chimney. It is true whether traffic officers are issuing a ticket or the chief of police is addressing a Rotary Club or the local PTA.

As Chermak and Weiss (2003, p.1) suggest: "In community policing, it's essential to gain citizen support and involvement. The news media can play a key role in this effort through their wide dissemination of information. The police know that most people form their impressions of crime and the justice system from newspapers, television and radio rather than from direct exposure (as crime victims, for example). For the police, the media convey their message to the public; for the media, the police are an indispensable information source."

Fazzini (2003, p.6) stresses: "Police agencies easily can adapt the concepts of business marketing to help them reach their customers (citizens) and educate them about the many services they provide." He notes a reality long known in businesses regarding their customers: "Various researchers have indicated that satisfied people tell their stories of police contact to at least three other people, whereas dissatisfied individuals will tell, on average, ten others about a negative experience with the police." (p.6)

Fazzini suggests: "Today, the single most significant marketing doctrine is the marketing mix, which encompasses all of the agency's tools that it uses to influence a market segment to accomplish its objectives." (p. 7) Among the options

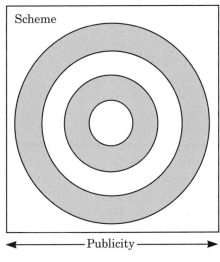

Resources targeted into this area

Diffusion zones, no resources

Figure 4.3 Bull's-Eye Resource Budgeting Strategy and Publicity
Source: Shane D. Johnson and Kate J. Bowers. "Opportunity Is in the Eye of
the Beholder: The Role of Publicity in Crime Prevention." *Crime and Justice,*
Vol. 2, No. 3, 2003, p.519. Reprinted by permission.

available to police departments are positive media stories (free advertising), a Web
site sharing department information, marketing alliances such as formation of a
citizen police academy, a media academy, joining committees and participating in
community groups, poster campaigns, public service announcements and addresses to community groups—all of these can help raise awareness of and interest in community policing.

Annual Reports

One effective way to keep the public informed about the operations of a police
department is to publish an annual report. Long recognized as effective business
communication tools, annual reports can also serve law enforcement agencies.
They might include the department's mission statement; a brief biographical
overview of department members with names, photos, academic degrees, dates of
hire, dates of most recent promotion and special duties; departmental information and statistics; a summary of projects and projected programs; a budget statement; an outline of ongoing interaction with the fire service, emergency medical
care providers, scuba and rescue units, or any emergency support group in your
community; and a closing, which may include statements of appreciation and remarks about the "state of the department."

The Internet

To provide criminal activity information to citizens, no tool is currently more efficient than the Internet. This type of external communication can be extremely
beneficial to departments that are willing to invest the time and minimal expense
to develop a Web site.

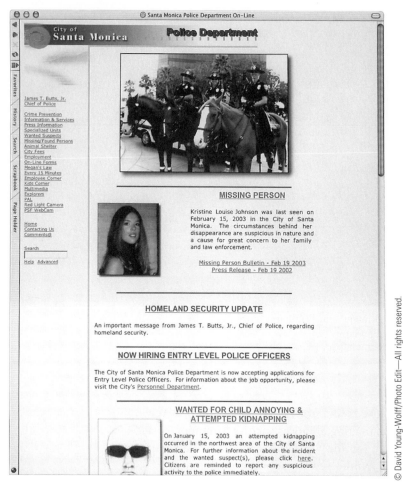

Several police departments now have their own Web sites like this one for Santa Monica, California. Internet communications help link law enforcement agencies with each other and the public.

The Internet can also help law enforcement agencies communicate more effectively with each other. Valuable information may be accessed and shared on department Web sites. Cisar (2003, p.45) reports that police Web sites around the world have several common features, including most wanted lists, crime statistics and employment information. Additional services may include press releases, links, copies of crime reports and permits.

Rosenbaum (2004, p.103) suggests that departments move beyond simply posting information to embracing the Internet as a proactive tool for obtaining new information about neighborhood conditions, solving problems, building partnerships, evaluating programs and assessing unit performance.

Communication and Homeland Security

Rubinson (2003, p.68) notes: "Since 9/11, the landscape of law enforcement has changed dramatically as emergency workers have taken on the responsibility of protecting Americans against the new threat of terrorism." The chaos during 9-11 illustrated the devastating effects of a lack of communications at Ground Zero on September 11 in the two-hour time frame before the World Trade Center towers collapsed. In one instance, an emergency official, who did not have a fire department radio to broadcast an alert that the north tower was in danger of collapsing, had to send a subordinate racing across the World Trade Center plaza to hand deliver the message to a fire chief inside. On that tragic day, up to 1,000 firefighters, rather than the usual 20 or so, were attempting to communicate with each other on one congested channel.

Garrett (2004, p.8) warns: "Our first responders need better tools than the terrorists. And that begins with the ability to communicate. We can't wait for another 9/11 to further the push for interoperable communications." Nislow (2005, p.1) describes one step toward accomplishing this by phasing out the "10-codes" used for more than 50 years by law enforcement and other first responders to communicate in shorthand over the radio and replacing it with plain talk. This is being done under a directive from the Department of Homeland Security in an effort to have all public safety agencies speaking the same language.

Carter and Holden (2003, p.299) point out: "Good communications increase awareness of security issues by the police and public alike and may improve the chance of an early warning of a terrorist attack."

Lack of interoperability is not the only obstacle to sharing information among local, state and federal agencies.

Obstacles to Information Sharing

 Four obstacles to sharing information among local, state and federal agencies are technical, logistic, political and ethical.

The technological obstacle of lack of interoperability has just been discussed. Logistic obstacles include data entry. If intelligence officers spend all their time entering data, they have no time for anything else. Political obstacles include finances and roles and relationships with the FBI and with the state police. Probably the most serious impediment to establishing a national interconnected antiterrorism database is the issue of "who pays for this?" The ethical obstacles include the issue of profiling and open records legislation. Another major obstacle to information sharing is withholding of information.

Withholding Information As Pilant (2004, p.34) explains: "Counter-terrorism and anti-terrorism are difficult tasks made even harder by the operational style that exists at almost every level of policing and in nearly every agency—that of withholding, rather than sharing, intelligence." A report by the Senate Governmental Affairs Committee (Lieberman, 2003, pp.38–41) states:

> The frontline "first preventers" in the war against terrorism lack simple, streamlined access to the federal databases that are most valuable in the effort to identify and apprehend terrorists. . . .
>
> States and localities still operate far too much as information islands, in relative isolation from their neighbors. Cities, counties and states also have few resources to learn what their counterparts around the country are doing to effectively protect their localities. . . .
>
> Many state and local officials who need high-level information access lack the necessary federal security clearances to do what their job—and our safety—demands. . . .

States lack a single point of contact for both receiving "downstream" information needs and pushing intelligence and other information "upstream."

According to White (2004, p.17): "On the surface it seems simple: Defense and intelligence communities gather information concerning possible terrorist activities in the United States. . . . Under the surface, however, a complex network of interagency rivalries, laws, security clearance issues and turf protection reduces the possibility of shared information." Polisar (2004, p.8) also asserts: "For far too long efforts to combat crime and terrorism have been handicapped by jurisdictional squabbles and archaic rules that prevented us from forging cooperative working relationships with our counterparts in local, regional, tribal and federal law enforcement. This must end."

Some information received by an agency such as the FBI is classified. Rules of federal procedure and grand jury classified material are two other limitations to what or how much information can be shared. Voegtlin (2002, p.9) reports: "In response to these concerns, the FBI has launched the State and Local Law Enforcement Executive Clearance Initiative. This initiative, which is based on a long-running FBI program, is designed to help state and local law enforcement executives obtain security clearances that will allow them to receive classified information." This initiative might help prevent local law enforcement officers from interfering with a terrorism investigation.

Savelli (2004, p.43) observes: "The last thing any law enforcement officer wants to do is compromise a terrorism investigation. The best way to avoid compromising an existing investigation, or conducting conflicting cases, is to develop a local networking module with local, state and federal law enforcement agencies to discuss investigative and enforcement endeavors to combat terrorism. . . . These networking modules should have built-in deconfliction protocol. **Deconfliction,** in essence, means avoiding conflict. Deconfliction can be deployed with declassified and confidential investigations" (emphasis added).

deconfliction • avoiding conflict when working with other agencies during an investigation; deployed with declassified and confidential investigations.

The National Criminal Intelligence Sharing Plan (NCISP)

A subtitle of the Homeland Security Act of 2002, called the Homeland Security Information Sharing Act, required the president to develop new procedures for sharing classified information as well as unclassified but otherwise sensitive information with state and local police. This charge was fulfilled in May 2002 when the International Association of Chiefs of Police (IACP); the Department of Justice; the FBI; the Department of Homeland Security; and other representatives of the federal, state, tribal and local law enforcement communities endorsed the National Criminal Intelligence Sharing Plan (NCISP). In releasing the plan, Attorney General John Ashcroft said: "The NCISP is the first of its kind in the nation, uniting law enforcement agencies of all sizes and geographic locations in a truly national effort to prevent terrorism and criminal activity. By raising cooperation and communication among local, state and federal partners to an unprecedented level, this groundbreaking effort will strengthen the abilities of the justice community to detect threats and protect American lives and liberties" ("Justice Dept. Announces Plan for Local Police Intelligence Sharing," 2004, p.5).

The importance of partnerships between law enforcement agencies at all levels cannot be overstated as it applies to the war on terrorism.

A key to combating terrorism lies with the local police and the intelligence they can provide to federal authorities.

As stressed earlier, communication should be the number one priority in any preparedness plan, and it is also number one in collaboration among local, state and federal law enforcement agencies.

 SUMMARY

Effective communication is the lifeblood of a law enforcement agency. Communication is the complex process through which information is transferred from one person to another. The communication process involves a message, a sender, a channel and a receiver, and it may include feedback. Effective communication should follow the KISS principle—that is, Keep It Short and Simple. Words themselves, however, are only a small part of the message. Ninety-three percent of communication between two people comes from body language and tone of voice.

Critical factors to consider in selecting a channel include speed, opportunity for feedback and expense. The weakest link in the communication process is *listening*. People listen and think four times faster than they talk.

Communication may be downward, upward (vertical) or lateral (horizontal). It may also be internal or external. Most effective communication is two way. Communication barriers include time, volume of information, tendency to say what we think others want to hear, certainty, failure to select the best words, prejudices (of the sender and/or receiver) and strained sender-receiver relationships.

Communication is an important part of the law enforcement job and includes meetings. Meetings may be informational, opinion seeking, problem solving or new-idea seeking. For more effective meetings: (1) prepare in advance—have an agenda, (2) start and stop on time, (3) stick to the agenda and (4) facilitate open communication and participation.

Five interview failures are failing to (1) take charge, (2) anticipate questions, (3) develop key messages, (4) stick to the facts and (5) keep calm. If lying to the media might save a life or protect the public safety, after the need to lie has passed, the department should explain why lying was necessary and, perhaps, apologize.

Four obstacles to sharing information among local, state and federal agencies are technical, logistic, political and ethical. A key to combating terrorism lies with the local police and the intelligence they can provide to federal authorities.

 CHALLENGE FOUR

Chief Slaughter loses his temper at a contemptuous labor meeting with the patrol officers' union. As Slaughter cools off in his office, he realizes some of his comments were out of line. He's actually a good-hearted guy who backs his cops. Chief Slaughter recently attended a conference where a vender was selling hats with special reflective pink brims. The vender quoted impressive statistics concerning the added safety the hats provide to officers. Chief Slaughter knows he's going to have to squeeze his tight budget to buy the hats, but it's his way of demonstrating his concern for his officers and their safety. After his outburst at the labor meeting, he thinks this will be a good time to show them he cares.

Chief Slaughter dictates a memo and has his secretary post it in the glass case outside the roll call room. He leaves for the weekend.

"New hats with reflective pink safety brims will be distributed to the entire department next week. The hats will be worn by all officers. By order of Chief Slaughter."

On Monday morning Chief Slaughter was greeted by disgruntled cops and a grievance.

1. Is there a problem in the communication process between Chief Slaughter and his officers?
2. Do you think Chief Slaughter used the most effective channel of communications for his message?
3. Was timing important?
4. Are there some inherent problems in communications between unions and administrations?
5. Suggest a better channel for communicating the Chief's message.

DISCUSSION QUESTIONS

1. Why is communication ability important to law enforcement managers?
2. How would you compare and contrast the various channels of communication?
3. Which is more difficult, written or spoken communication? Why? Which do you prefer?
4. What are the main obstacles to communication in your law enforcement agency?
5. What types of communication exist in your agency? What is the value of each?
6. What types of feedback are available in a typical law enforcement agency?
7. How is nonverbal communication used in law enforcement? How is such nonverbal communication depicted on television programs about law enforcement?
8. What methods do you use as an active listener?
9. What is the key role of the first-line supervisor as a communicator in a law enforcement agency?
10. What public figures do you consider to be effective communicators? What characteristics make them so?

REFERENCES

Boyd, David G. "The Five Elements to Achieve Interoperability." *Law and Order*, August 2005a, pp.70–74.

Boyd, David G. "Improving Wireless Communications Interoperability." *Law and Order*, June 2005b, pp.76–82.

Buice, Ed. "Keys to Successful Media Interviews." *Law and Order*, September 2003a, p.26.

Buice, Ed. "When the World Is Watching." *Law and Order*, January 2003b, pp.24–26.

Careless, James. "DC Sniper Report Highlights Importance of Interoperability." *Tactical Response*, Fall 2004, pp.36–40.

Carter, David L. and Holden, Richard N. "Terrorism and Community Security." In *Local Government Police Management*, 4th ed., edited by William S. Geller and Darrell W. Stephens, Washington, DC: International City/County Management Association, 2003, pp.291–314.

Chalmers, Steven W. and Tiffin, Charles. "Hispanic Outreach and Intervention Team." *The Police Chief*, June 2005, pp.58–61.

Chermak, Steven and Weiss, Alexander. *Marketing Community Policing in the News: A Missed Opportunity?* Washington, DC: National Institute of Justice Research for Practice, July 2003. (NCJ 200473)

Cisar, Jim. "Enhancing the Police Department Web Site." *The Police Chief*, May 2003, pp.45–48.

Cook, Jim. "Changing Management's Ways." *Training*, February 2003, pp.14–15.

Estey, Joseph G. "Communications Critical to Law Enforcement." *The Police Chief*, April 2005, p.6.

Facella, John. "Communications Interoperability: What a Chief Needs to Know." *Law and Order*, August 2005, pp.42–52.

Fazzini, Mark. "Marketing Available Police Services: The MAPS Program." *FBI Law Enforcement Bulletin*, May 2003, pp.6–9.

Fritz, Roger. "How Well Do You Listen?" *Think Like a Manager*, Naperville, IL: Organization Development Consultants.

Garner, Gerald W. "Handling Bad Press." *Law and Order*, September 2004, pp.22–25.

Garner, Gerald W. "Putting on an Effective News Conference." *Law and Order*, June 2005, pp.28–34.

Garrett, Ronnie. "Can We Talk?" *Law Enforcement Technology*, August 2004, p.8.

Gary, Charles. "How To . . . Cope with the Press." *Police*, December 2003, pp.24–29.

Glensor, Ronald W. and Murphy, Gerard R., editors. *Issues in Information Technology: A Reader for the Busy Police Executive*. Washington, DC: The Police Executive Research Forum, 2005.

Greenberg, Sheldon and Flynn, Edward A. "Leadership and Managing Change." In *Local Government Police Management*, 4th ed., edited by William S. Geller and Darrell W. Stephens, Washington, DC: International City/County Management Association, 2003, pp.67–88.

Griffith, David. "Sorting Out Communications Chaos." *Police*, November 2004, pp.50–59.

Grittner, Frank. *Teaching Foreign Languages*. New York: Harper and Row, 1969.

Johnson, Robert Ray. "Listening Skills for Supervisors." *Police and Security News*, July/August 2005a, pp.61–63.

Johnson, Robert Roy. "Personal Relationships with Subordinates." *Law and Order*, March 2005b, pp.104–106.

Johnson, Shane D. and Bowers, Kate J. "Opportunity Is in the Eye of the Beholder: The Role of Publicity in Crime Prevention." *Crime and Justice*, Vol. 2, No.3, 2003, pp.497–524.

"Justice Dept. Announces Plan for Local Police Intelligence Sharing." *Criminal Justice Newsletter*, June 1, 2004, p.5.

Kathman, Thomas E. and Chesser, Tim. "Latino Academy." *The Police Chief*, June 2005, pp.62–63.

Lieberman, Senator Joseph I. *State and Local Officials: Still Kept in the Dark about Homeland Security*. Washington, DC: A Report by the Senate Governmental Affairs Committee, August 13, 2003.

Moore, Carole. "If There Must Be Gossip, Use It for Good." *Law Enforcement Technology*, May 2004, p.110.

Moy, Jones and Archibald, Brent. "Talking with the Police." *The Police Chief*, June 2005, pp.54–57.

Murphy, Gerard R. and Wexler, Chuck with Davies, Heather J. and Plotkin, Martha. *Managing a Multijurisdictional Case: Lessons Learned from the Sniper Investigation*. Washington, DC: Police Executive Research Forum, October 2004.

Nislow, Jennifer. "10 Codes' Days May Be Numbered." *Law Enforcement News*, July 2005, pp.1, 10.

Parrish, Penny. Media relations instructor at the FBI Academy. Personal conversation, 2003.

Pilant, Lois. "Strategic Modeling." *Police*, May 2004, pp.34–38.

Polisar, Joseph M. "The National Criminal Intelligence Sharing Plan." *The Police Chief*, June 2004, p.8.

Rosenbaum, Dennis P. "Community Policing and Web-Based Communication: Addressing the New Information Imperative." In *Community Policing: The Past,* *Present, and Future*, edited by Lorie Fridell and Mary Ann Wycoff. Washington, DC: The Annie E. Casey Foundation and Police Executive Research Forum, 2004, pp.93–114.

Rosenthal, Rick. "Training the Media." *ILEETA Digest*, October–December 2003, p.3.

Rosenthal, Rick. "Training the Media—A Rapport with Reporters." *ILEETA Digest*, Jan/Feb/March 2005a, pp.5–6.

Rosenthal, Rick. "Yes, You Do Need a P.I.O." *ILEETA Digest*, July/Aug/Sept 2005b, pp.6–7.

Rubinson, Adam. "DC Emergency Web Site Keeps Citizens Informed." *Law Enforcement Technology*, August 2003, pp.68–72.

Savelli, Lou. *A Proactive Law Enforcement Guide for the War on Terrorism*, Flushing, NY: LooseLeaf Law Publications, Inc. 2004.

Simons, Tad. "Stereotypes Aren't All Bad, If You Know What to Do with Them." *Presentations*, May 2004, p.4.

Supporting Limited English Communities. Washington, DC: National Institute of Justice, July 2005. (NCJ 210506)

Vernon, Bob. "Some Things Don't Change." *Law Officer Magazine*, September/October 2005, pp.62–63.

Voegtlin, Gene. "FBI Offers Security Clearances to State and Local Law Enforcement Executives." *The Police Chief*, March 2002, p.9.

White, Jonathan R. *Defending the Homeland: Domestic Intelligence, Law Enforcement and Security*. Belmont, CA: Wadsworth Publishing Company, 2004.

Whitehead, Christy. "Emergency Deployable Interoperable Communications Systems." *Law and Order*, September 2005, pp.128–141.

Zielinski, Dave. "What Men and Women Can Learn from Each Other." *Presentations*, May 2004, pp.23–30.

BOOK-SPECIFIC WEB SITE

Go to the *Management and Supervision in Law Enforcement* Web site at www.thomsonedu.com/criminaljustice/bennett for student and instructor resources, including Internet Assignments and Case Studies.

CHAPTER 5

Decision Making and Problem Solving

Imagination is more important than knowledge. For knowledge is limited, whereas imagination embraces the entire world.

Albert Einstein

Do You Know?

■ What fosters a decision-making, problem-solving environment?

■ What levels of decision making exist?

■ What kinds of decisions managers must make?

■ What functions may be served by the brain's left and right sides?

■ What basic methods are commonly used to make decisions or solve problems?

■ What levels of the agency benefit from group participation in decision making?

■ How brainstorming can be most effective?

■ What the steps are in the seven-step problem-solving/decision-making process?

■ What force-field analysis is? The nominal group technique? The Delphi technique?

■ What the SARA Model problem-solving process includes?

■ What the six required elements of a problem in problem-oriented policing are?

■ What common thinking traps exist? Mental locks?

■ What "killer phrases" are and how to deal with them?

■ What other considerations decision making and problem solving include?

Can You Define?

Abilene Paradox
administrative
    decision
brainstorming
convergent thinking
CompStat
creative
    procrastination
cross flow
cross tell
data mining
Delphi technique
divergent thinking
driving forces

equilibrium
focus groups
force-field
    analysis (FFA)
GIGO
groupthink
impact evaluation
killer phrases
left-brain thinking
magnet
    phenomenon
management
    information
    systems (MIS)

mental locks
modified Delphi
    technique
nominal group
    technique (NGT)
operational decision
participatory
    decision making
    (PDM)
problem-oriented
    policing (POP)
process evaluation
qualitative data
quantitative data

continued

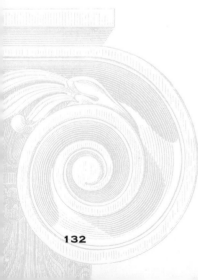

Introduction

Decision making and problem solving are primary responsibilities of law enforcement managers at all levels. Most law enforcement managers developed their decision-making skills in the field as patrol officers. They made important decisions constantly, but their decisions were usually based on clear department policies and procedures. The decision to arrest someone, for example, was made many times. If something new occurred, the first-line supervisor might be directed to the scene for a decision. Even this decision was comparatively easy because standards existed and the supervisor had to consider only alternatives to the established procedure.

Because of the discretion they had as patrol officers, most law enforcement managers are comfortable making decisions as long as guidelines exist. There is little time to problem solve if someone is shooting at you. Often, however, law enforcement managers encounter unique problems that call for problem-solving decision-making skills.

Research by Engel and Worden (2003, p.137) found that officers who adopt community policing and problem solving as their most important goals tend to see these as their supervisors' goals also and spend more time engaged in problem-solving activities. Organizations must provide time, information and rewards for problem solving by its officers.

This chapter begins by describing a decision-making, problem-solving environment and the kinds of decisions managers must make. Next, research on how the human brain processes information and modes of thinking is explored. Then basic methods for making decisions or solving problems are described, including participatory decision making, brainstorming, focus groups and groupthink. This is followed by descriptions of several more complex approaches to decision making, including a seven-step decision-making process, force-field analysis, the nominal group technique and the Delphi technique. Next is a discussion of problem-oriented policing (POP) and the decisions made in this process. Then a discussion of creativity and innovation and how they help in solving problems is presented, followed by a discussion of how creativity can be hindered by thinking traps, mental locks and killer phrases and common mistakes in decision making/problem solving. The chapter concludes with a brief discussion of ethics and risk taking in decision making and problem solving and criteria for evaluating the decisions reached.

A Decision-Making, Problem-Solving Environment

The environment that promotes decision making and problem solving must encourage diversity and disagreement. Martin (2005, p.161) suggests that managers seek out those of a different mindset to foster debate: "Debate is healthy for problem solving and should be sought after rather than avoided." He stresses that care must be taken to prevent a debate from rising to the level of an argument and emphasizes that an environment conducive to problem solving begins with a strong leader who surrounds himself with strong leaders. In such an environment, decision making and problem solving should be creative and innovative.

 Diversity, disagreement and risk taking help foster a decision-making, problem-solving environment.

Managers must make decisions and take risks. It comes with the job. It has been said "Daring ideas are like chessmen; moved forward; they may be beaten, but they may start a winning game" (Goethe). Dahl (2005, p.16) asserts: "Taking risks can bring tremendous rewards. Not taking risks can bring life-long regrets." As emphasized previously, risk taking can be of great benefit. Consider the following exchange:

A new supervisor asked his captain what the secret of his success was.

The captain replied, "I can sum it up in two words: right decisions."

"How do you make those right decisions?" the sergeant asked.

"I can sum that up in one word: experience," replied the captain.

"And how does someone get that experience?" the sergeant asked.

To which the captain replied, "Two words: wrong decisions."

Kinds of Decisions

Decisions may deal with problems that are trivial or critical, short term or long term, personal or organizational. They may also be categorized by the level in the organizational hierarchy at which they are made. The executive level mainly deals with conceptual problems and alternatives, middle management most frequently makes administrative decisions, and first-line supervisors most frequently make operational decisions.

strategic decision • executive-level decision involving long-range plans.

administrative decision • middle-management level decision.

operational decision • first-line supervisor level decision.

 Decisions may be **strategic**—executive level; **administrative**—middle-management level; or **operational**—first-line level.

Decisions at all levels involve individual skills, organizational policies, different managerial styles and a certain amount of risk taking. Decisions may also be categorized by who carries them out.

 Decisions may be command, consultative or consensual.

A *command decision* is one managers make on their own, with little or no input from others. For example, the chief of police decides to give an award to an officer.

A *consultative decision*, in contrast, uses input and opinions from others. The final decision is still made by the one in charge but only after considering others' input. For example, a lieutenant in charge of organizing a Neighborhood Watch program might ask for ideas from other officers and citizens, and he may consult other agencies that already have such a program. The lieutenant then makes decisions about the program based on this input. Managers will gain greater acceptance of and support for their decisions if they seek input from all levels and weigh that input before making their final decisions.

A *consensus decision* is made democratically by a group. It is a joint decision often made by committee members. For example, training priorities for the year might be decided by a committee established for this purpose. This committee might operate independently or seek input from others in the organization.

Law enforcement organizations regularly make all three kinds of decisions. One key to effectiveness is that the individuals involved know what kind of decision they are making. For example, a situation in which a manager makes it very clear that he or she alone is going to decide an issue is quite different from a situation in which the manager *appears* to seek input from others but is only making a gesture. Likewise, if employees believe they are to decide an issue, but the final decision is *not* what they recommended, the entire decision-making process may be undermined.

Before looking at specific methods of decision making and problem solving, you should understand the thinking process and how it functions. Managers are expected to use their heads—their brains. Most managers have attained their present positions because of this ability, which is equated with intelligence or mental ability. They also have traditionally relied upon logic and reason to solve problems, but whole-brain research suggests that this may not always be the most appropriate approach.

Whole-Brain Research

Two thousand five hundred years ago Hippocrates suggested that our emotions come from the head, not the heart. Twenty-five years ago another physician, Roger Sperry, reported on significant brain research establishing that the right and the left sides of the brain each have their own thoughts and memories and *process information differently*.

 Left-brain thinking processes *language* and is primarily *logical*. **Right-brain thinking** processes *images* and is primarily *emotional*.

left-brain thinking • primarily using language and logic.

right-brain thinking • primarily using images and emotions.

According to Dr. Sperry's research, the two sides of the brain are connected by the *corpus callosum*. In brief, his research identified the division of labor between the two sides of the brain and the critical role of the corpus callosum. He received the 1981 Nobel Prize in medicine for these remarkable findings.

Brain research also indicates differences in the way each side of the brain processes information. The left side usually processes information sequentially, logically and rationally in linear fashion. The right side usually processes information spatially, intuitively, holistically and emotionally. The left side uses reasoning; the right side, imagination and creativity. Researchers have discovered that:

1. Right-hemisphere processes add emotional and humorous overtones important for understanding the full meaning of oral and written communication.
2. Both hemispheres are involved in thinking, logic and reasoning.
3. The right hemisphere seems to play a special role in emotion. If students are emotionally engaged, both sides of the brain will participate in the educational process, regardless of subject matter.

When dealing with problem-solving, decision-making situations, our educational system and our culture tend to place more value on those factors associated with the left brain: logical, rational, objective, sequential and so forth.

Our organizations, public and private, also rely heavily on rational, logical and analytical approaches to problems. Further, most effective law enforcement managers are precise, methodical and conservative. They seek to preserve the status quo—to keep things on an even keel.

The logical approach was perhaps more appropriate when organizations were less complex and change was less frequent. Our complex, rapidly changing modern society, however, requires the ability to use *both* logic and creativity in problem solving and decision making—that is, **whole-brain thinking.** There is no "better" side. Effective decision making and problem solving rely on both logic and creativity. Because most managers are more familiar with and reliant on logic, it will be addressed first.

whole-brain thinking • using both the logical left side and the emotional right side of the brain together for best results.

Basic Methods for Making Decisions or Problem Solving

An important management tool is a decision-making process, that is, a systematic approach to solving a problem. This chapter describes several decision-making processes that can be tailored to fit specific law enforcement department problems.

 Basic methods for making decisions range from using intuition and snap decisions to using a computer, with a systematic individual or group approach falling in between.

Intuition

Intuition is insight. It is knowing without using any rational thought process. The subconscious makes decisions based on intuition. Intuition crosses the left and right hemispheres, integrating facts and feelings. There are two kinds of decisions: the slow, rational, analytic result of deliberate reasoning and the rapid, seemingly effortless, emotionally based result of intuition (Simpson, 2003, p.56).

Pinizzotto et al. (2004, p.5) point out that intuitive policing is a decision-making process officers frequently use but cannot explain; they intuitively read and react to danger signals based on training and experience. "Whether explained as an uneasy feeling, a gut reaction, a cop's sixth-sense or overlapping neural networks, the result is the same; law enforcement officers perceive danger signals that trigger alarms in their brains that set their bodies in motion" (Pinizzotto et al., p.4).

Such intuition in the field has been recognized, but what of using intuition in an administrative situation? Simpson (p.59) contends that recent research proves that intuition is an information-processing style that must be respected when making decisions in any setting: "Intuition is the outcome of well-developed neural pathways that allow intuitive thinkers to see relationships and possibilities that are not immediately obvious to others." She (p.59) concludes: "There is no right or wrong about whether decisions are made by using a structured, logical or random intuitive strategy—they're just different approaches that lead to different outcomes."

Snap Decisions

Closely related to intuition are snap decisions. Neither takes much of a manager's time. Be decisive. It is not always possible to obtain all the available information. Do not expect every decision to be perfect. Perfectionists find it difficult to make decisions because they never have sufficient information.

General Colin Powell uses what he calls the P-40-70 Rule whenever he has to be decisive. P stands for the probability of success, and the numbers indicate the percentage of information acquired. He goes with his gut feeling when he has acquired information in the 40 to 70 percent range. If time is critical, he makes the decision with only 40 percent of the information needed. According to Powell, if he waited until he had all the information, he would never make a decision; he'd always be waiting for another piece of information. It has been said that it is better to be boldly decisive and risk being wrong than to agonize at length and be right too late.

Learning to make snap decisions prudently can be extremely beneficial. A not-so-great snap decision may have better results than a good decision made slowly. This is because any kind of movement often brings a new perspective that makes the right decision more obvious.

Being decisive often inspires support from subordinates and superiors. It also lets you feel in control. Having a list of ten unsolved problems sitting on your desk can cause anxiety and stress. Many problems and decisions should be made quickly and decisively. Others can be delegated or not even made. Know when to slow down and proceed with caution, and remember that you can change your mind.

Delegating

Delegation sends the decision-making process to a subordinate. The manager is removed from the process at this point until it is time to report the results. Delegation is an excellent motivating technique and gets the job done at the level of those with firsthand knowledge of the problem.

When you delegate, establish a timeline. Delegated tasks should be concise and clear. You must also give authority along with a level of responsibility. Effective managers make sure decisions are made at the lowest level possible. They offer assistance but encourage independence. The skills needed to delegate effectively were discussed in Chapter 2.

Not Deciding

Not to decide *is* to decide. In some instances, any decision is better than none. But in other instances, such as a life-threatening situation, a wrong decision may have disastrous results. Effective managers know when they do not have to make a decision. They use **creative procrastination**—providing time for a minor difficulty to work itself out. In other instances, the "if it isn't broken, don't fix it" thinking trap works to keep managers from getting bogged down in trivia.

creative procrastination • delaying decisions, allowing time for minor difficulties to work themselves out.

Using Computers for Decision Making

A few decades ago law enforcement had limited technological assistance. Managers were truly independent decision makers with little support. The advent of computers has greatly changed this situation. A vast array of software programs is available to assist decision making at all levels.

At the operational or line level, squad cars now have computers that give patrol officers instant access to information. By tracing a license number directly from the patrol car, officers may know the history of the vehicle they are stopping before they approach it. The driver's identification and past record can also be instantly checked. This is important to personal safety and decisions about whether to arrest.

At the management level, administrative programs help with allocating personnel, budgeting, processing reports and many other functions. Computers also provide statistical information as well as analysis of this information and may even suggest implications and alternatives. Sargent (2003, p.89) suggests that the

management information systems (MIS) • software programs that organize data to assist in decision making.

"heart and soul" of any records management system (RMS) is the software program. Also called **management information systems (MIS)**, these software programs organize data to assist in decision making. They often use "what-if" analysis to project the effects of various solutions.

Among the computer files being maintained are arrests, traffic citations, stolen property/vehicles records, crash reports, calls for service, uniform crime report (UCR) summary data, alarms, personnel, criminal histories, inventory, evidence, warrants, field interviews, payroll, driver's license information, summonses, linked files for crime analysis and vehicle registration. These files are often used for data mining.

data mining • an automated tool that uses advanced computational techniques to explore and characterize large data sets.

McCue et al. (2003, p.2) describe **data mining** as an automated tool that uses advanced computational techniques to explore and characterize large data sets. They (p.3) suggest that data-mining applications include crime analysis, deployment, risk assessment, behavioral analysis, homeland security and Internet/infrastructure protection. Computers help transform information into knowledge.

Even with computer support, however, managers must adapt the information/knowledge to current circumstances and arrive at independent decisions. Computers cannot replace experience and expertise, but they can enhance them. Anyone who works with management information systems must remember the watchword of computer users: "garbage in/garbage out," or **GIGO**.

GIGO • computer acronym for "garbage in, garbage out."

Computer programs can also help review goals and objectives. Based on the experience of other organizations, they can project alternatives, one or more of which may apply to a situation. From these alternatives, managers can make more informed choices. Regional information systems, or those that give more than one agency or entity access, are becoming more common. Using information systems in problem-oriented policing is discussed later in the chapter.

Participatory Decision Making (PDM)

A participatory management environment often leads to increased and better decision making. In **participatory decision making (PDM)**, employees of the organization have a say in the decision-making process. Employees prefer PDM largely because decisions often directly affect them. They also bring a diversity of backgrounds and experiences to the decision making.

participatory decision making (PDM) • employees have a say in the decision-making process.

PDM provides more input about the number and content of alternatives because of the participants' varied experience and background. Opportunity for innovative ideas also increases. Shared input fosters better acceptance of and commitment to the final decision. Upward and downward organizational communication also increases, as does teamwork.

The participative manager outlines the problems and leaves the development of alternatives to subordinates. This encourages creativity by the participants and improves the quality and quantity of the decisions they send to the manager. The group may obtain synergistic results when the process of working together enhances sharing and functional competition. With PDM, conflict is considered an asset, and individuals who do not "go along" are viewed as catalysts for innovative ideas and solutions.

Although obtaining consensus may be more difficult with PDM, it can be achieved if participants avoid arguing to win as individuals and keep their focus on reaching the best judgment of the whole group. Group members must also accept responsibility for both hearing and being heard, so that everyone's input receives a hearing. Finally, group members should remember that the best results stem from a combination of information, logic and emotion—including participants' feelings about the information and decision-making process. Such participation will positively affect value judgments as well as the final decision.

An entirely participative decision-making process, however, may be difficult to establish because of lack of training on how to work together. It is difficult for officers to include themselves in the process if it has not been past practice to do so. It is even more difficult for autocratic managers to give up their decision-making authority.

If people are used to being told what to do, they may feel awkward when given a chance to participate. A certain amount of confusion and hesitancy may exist initially.

In addition, discussion and agreement are time consuming. Further, not all decisions *should* be democratic or participatory. Some decisions must be immediate, and others cannot be resolved by agreement. Sometimes, a final decision can be made only after top management considers the alternatives.

Nonetheless, if possible, decisions should involve those who will be affected by them. The synergism of the group can often produce results that a single person or even many people working independently would be unable to produce. Further, implementing the selected alternative will be easier because it is more likely to be accepted. *People tend to support what they help create.* Morale is improved, and participants feel commitment and loyalty.

 All levels of the organization benefit from group participation in the decision-making process.

In any law enforcement organization, newer officers can bring fresh approaches and ideas, but these must be balanced by experience.

Although full department meetings are difficult to schedule because of multiple shifts, input from all officers can be obtained through shift discussions and a joint meeting of first-line supervisors with middle and executive management. Full department meetings should be called only for critical matters or to communicate a decision.

Although participatory leadership styles support group decision making, disadvantages might also arise, such as wasted time, shirked responsibilities, a tendency toward indecisiveness and costly delays. One very common type of participatory decision making is brainstorming.

Brainstorming

Most people are familiar with the concept of brainstorming, but the practice is often not as effective as it might be. **Brainstorming** is a method of shared problem solving in which members of a group spontaneously contribute ideas, no matter how wild, without criticism or critique. It is creative, uninhibited thinking designed to produce ideas, generate alternatives, suggest solutions and create plans. Alex Osborn, the originator of the brainstorming technique, established four rules:

1. No one is permitted to criticize an idea.
2. The wilder the idea, the better.
3. The group should concentrate on the quantity of ideas and not concern itself with the quality.
4. Participants should combine suggested ideas or build on others whenever possible.

brainstorming • a method of shared problem solving in which members of a group spontaneously contribute ideas, no matter how wild, without any criticism or critique.

© Spencer Grant/PhotoEdit

As these officers brainstorm, they generate many creative solutions to a problem. Their ideas are as broad and radical as possible and are developed rapidly. Creativity has free rein.

Although brainstorming must be unfettered, it is not unstructured, as many believe. Participants should be prepared. They should know in advance the problem they will address. A leader should keep the ideas flowing and make sure no criticism or evaluation of ideas occurs. Group size should be limited to no more than 15 participants, and they should sit at a round or U-shaped table.

One key to an effective brainstorming session is to write all ideas on a flipchart. As pages become filled, tape them to the walls so the group will see the flow of ideas and be motivated to continue. All brainstorming sessions should have a definite ending time so a sense of urgency prevails. Most sessions should be limited to 20 to 40 minutes. Time is *not* unlimited.

divergent thinking • free, uninhibited thinking. Includes imagining, fantasizing, free associating and combining and juxtaposing dissimilar elements. Opposite of *convergent thinking.*

During brainstorming it is critical that **divergent thinking** (right brain) occur before **convergent thinking** (left brain). Divergent thinking is free flowing, creative, imaginative and uninhibited. Convergent thinking, in contrast, is evaluative, rational and objective.

convergent thinking • focused, evaluative thinking. Includes decision making, choosing, testing, judging and rating. Opposite of *divergent thinking.*

 To make brainstorming sessions effective:

1. Ensure that participants are prepared.
2. Write down *all* ideas.
3. Allow *no* criticizing of ideas.
4. Have a definite ending time.

After the brainstorming session, move to the critical judgment phase, where ideas are reviewed, synthesized, added and subtracted, evaluated and prioritized. Brainstorming can be a powerful decision-making, problem-solving tool. Another participatory approach is to use focus groups.

Focus Groups

The police/community collaboration emphasized in COPS can be facilitated by using focus groups to help in decision making and problem solving. **Focus groups** usually consist of people from the educational community, the religious community, Neighborhood Watch groups, business groups and professional groups, as well as ordinary citizens, who express their opinions about certain issues. The groups are directed by a moderator or facilitator and are meant to collect broad information on a focused topic in an open, personal environment.

Although involving co-workers, citizens and outside agencies is a cornerstone of community policing, hazards do exist, one of which is *groupthink*.

focus groups • usually consist of people from the educational community, the religious community, Neighborhood Watch groups and the like.

Groupthink

Groupthink is the negative tendency for members of a group to submit to peer pressure and endorse the majority opinion even if it is individually unacceptable. Groupthink is more concerned with team play and unanimity than with reaching the best solution. Group members suppress individual concerns to avoid rocking the group's boat. Groupthink is especially hazardous to law enforcement organizations because of the feeling of "family" that exists. Officers support one another, and sometimes a feeling of "them versus us" exists between law enforcement organizations and those they are hired to "serve and protect."

Even life-and-death decisions can be affected by groupthink. It can be difficult to speak up and say that safety concerns indicate that a tactical operation should be delayed, to refuse to go into a barricaded suspect incident with insufficient personnel, or wait for a back-up unit on a domestic call.

Smith and Brantner (2001, p.197) use the **Abilene Paradox** as an illustration of groupthink. Author Jerry Harvey coined the expressions *Abilene Paradox* and *a trip to Abilene* after visiting his in-laws in a small town in west Texas in the 1950s:

groupthink • the negative tendency for members of a group to submit to peer pressure and endorse the majority opinion even if it individually is unacceptable.

> On a hot afternoon during the visit, Harvey and his wife and her family decided to take a trip to Abilene, 53 miles away. They drove for an hour in a car with no air conditioning to a restaurant they didn't like, ate a meal that wasn't very good and returned home late that afternoon, arguing about who had suggested such a bad idea in the first place.
>
> Harvey realized that while everyone had agreed to take the trip, no one had really wanted to go; they simply went along with the idea and kept their reservations to themselves. In fact, they had done the opposite of what they wanted to do, which involved sitting in the shade, drinking iced tea and playing dominoes. Each family member felt he or she was a victim of someone else's poor decision to travel to Abilene, even though any of them could have prevented the trip by expressing an objection. The group had just experienced what he would later call the Abilene Paradox. . . .
>
> An Abilene Paradox begins innocently enough: At first, everyone in the group agrees that a particular problem exists. Later, when it comes time to discuss solutions, no one expresses a viewpoint that differs from what appears to be the group's consensus, even though many secretly disagree with it. Finally, after the solution has been implemented, group members complain privately about the plan and look for someone to blame for its development.

Abilene Paradox • begins innocently, with everyone in a group agreeing that a particular problem exists. Later, when it comes time to discuss solutions, no one expresses a viewpoint that differs from what appears to be the group's consensus, even though many secretly disagree with it. Finally, after the solution has been implemented, group members complain privately about the plan and look for someone to blame for its development.

Smith and Brantner (p.198) give a hypothetical example of a police chief concerned about racial profiling within the department. He calls a meeting, and nearly every supervisor present agrees there is a problem, and each knows how he or she would handle it. The chief, however, upon receiving agreement that the problem exists, declares that the only way to deal with racial profiling is to systematically scrutinize every officer's traffic stops and other citizen contacts. Any officer detaining a disproportionate number of nonwhites, regardless of the stops' validity, would automatically be subject to an internal investigation. When the chief asks for comments, no one speaks up. Each takes the others' silence to indicate approval. When the chief hears no dissenting opinions, he announces the department's new policy. The result: "Months later, many internal investigations have been opened and concluded. Citations and arrests are down. Retail theft, DUI and residential burglary are up, as are traffic crashes and citizen complaints about officer rudeness. Morale is low, line officers, supervisors, managers and commanders all express their anger and hostility about the chief's racial profiling policy—but only to one another. No one complains to the chief." This is a classic Abilene Paradox, or example of groupthink. The power of positive conflict is discussed in detail in Chapter 11.

How can groupthink be avoided? It should be stressed during meetings that individual problems and concerns about a decision should be made known. Create a heterogeneous group representing a broad range of interests. Have the chief or upper management hold back opinions until others have a chance to present their ideas. Brainstorm. Beware of premature decisions—have separate meetings for identifying alternatives and making the final decision.

More Complex Decision-Making/Problem-Solving Processes

Whether decisions are made by a group or an individual, often a more complex process is used, including the seven-step decision-making/problem-solving approach, force-field analysis, the nominal group technique, the Delphi technique or a modified form of the Delphi technique. These approaches often include brainstorming.

The Seven-Step Decision-Making/Problem-Solving Process

Many decisions can be effectively made and many problems effectively solved through a seven-step process.

 Decision making often follows these seven steps:

1. Define the specific problem.
2. Gather all facts concerning the problem.
3. Generate alternatives.
4. Analyze the alternatives.
5. Select the best alternative.
6. Implement the alternative.
7. Evaluate the decision.

Define the Problem The logical first step is to identify the problem. It must be located, defined and limited before you can seek solutions. Those involved need to agree it is a priority problem that needs to be solved. Take care not to confuse a problem with its *symptoms*. For example, patrol officers may be coming to work late or calling in sick more often. These could be symptoms of a deeper problem—low morale. The problem, not the symptoms, must be addressed.

Another important determination is whether the decision to be made is a large, organizational decision or a small, departmental one. If it is only a small problem, perhaps a command decision is most appropriate. All too often myriad small decisions rob managers' time that should be spent on more pressing problems.

Gather the Facts *All* relevant data must be obtained and reviewed, including facts that may not support existing policies. Determine existing standards, policies and rules that may affect the problem. If possible, consult everyone involved. Experience in dealing with identical or similar problems helps greatly. Sometimes experts are needed. Other times a problem may fall within department guidelines and require very little research. Take the time needed to be thorough. Avoid snap decisions for critical or recurring problems. Avoid crisis decisions.

Generate Alternatives Put the alternatives on a flipchart or white board. The following questions can generate alternatives: Is there a new way to do it? Can you give it a new twist? Do you need more of the same? Less of the same? Is there a substitute? Can you rearrange the parts? What if you do just the opposite? Can you combine the ideas? Can you borrow or adapt?

The military uses the phrases *cross tell* and *cross flow* when talking about borrowing or adapting ideas. If one unit goes through an inspection, they **cross tell** what they learned to all the other units so those units do not make the same mistake. If they encounter a problem they have never seen before, they send out a **cross flow** message stating the problem and asking the other units if they have encountered the same thing and, if so, what they did about it. This helps in two ways. If other units have not seen the problem, they can have a heads up that the problem exists. If they have encountered the problem, they can share what worked—or did not work. There is no need to reinvent the wheel.

cross tell • one department alerts other departments about a mistake revealed during inspection.

cross flow • message stating a problem and asking other units if they have encountered the same thing and, if so, what they did about it.

Analyze the Alternatives What are the likely consequences of each alternative? Among the many factors to consider in analyzing the alternatives are how they fit with the agency mission statement and goals, cost, personnel required, resources available, staff reaction, long-range consequences, union contract provisions, ethical considerations and problems that may arise as a result of the decision. Time and resources may limit the alternatives.

What are the risks involved in deciding? In not deciding? In selecting a different alternative? In being wrong? Edison was quoted as saying he did not fail to make a storage battery 25,000 times. He simply knew 25,000 ways not to make one. The U.S. Air Force's *Operational Risk Management* (ORM) (2005) involves a "continuous process designed to detect, assess and control risk while enhancing performance." It is a command policy for leaders in all functional areas and at all levels. ORM is designed as a complete decision-making tool that strives to ensure that every leader consistently and systematically evaluates the best course of action for any given situation. It recognizes that all actions involve some degree of risk. Decisions need to be made in relation to exactly how much risk is acceptable. The formal ORM process has six steps: (1) identify hazards, (2) assess risks, (3) analyze controls, (4) make decisions, (5) implement controls and (6) supervise and review.

Select the Most Appropriate Alternative Choosing the right alternative is the heart of decision making. For normal problem-solving situations, one alternative eventually appears as the best solution. For situations in which all look equal, the choice is more difficult. Most alternatives have advantages and disadvantages. Make a chart with two columns. List each alternative and its advantages and disadvantages. They may be equal in number, but assign a weight to each point. Use the total points as part of your final decision.

Determining alternatives and evaluating them is often difficult. It may require experience, knowledge, training, creativity, intuition, advice from others and even computer assistance. The more input available, the better the decision.

Implement the Alternative Implementation is usually the most time-consuming phase of the decision-making process. It involves several steps and should be carefully planned. Who will do the implementing? What resources are needed? When will implementation occur?

A critical first step is communicating the decision to everyone involved. Ideally, those involved will have taken part in the decision-making process itself and will already be quite familiar with the options and the reasons a particular option was selected.

If a decision is a command or a consultative decision, such communication is vital. Effective managers keep their people in on what is happening and enlist their support from the earliest possible minute. Support those implementing the solution. Follow up to see that needed support is continually provided. Seek feedback at all stages of the implementation.

Evaluate the Decision How effective is the alternative selected? Did it accomplish the expected result? Solve the problem? Evaluation provides information for future decisions. If the solution does not prove effective, learn from the experience. It does little good to brood over solutions that do not work. It does even less good to attempt to place blame.

The primary purpose of evaluation is to improve—to learn what alternatives work and maintain and strengthen them and to learn what alternatives do not work and to change them. Evaluation is discussed in greater depth later in this chapter.

The Steps Applied Assume that an organizational goal is to reduce vehicle crashes by 10 percent. The *problem* is increased traffic crashes. The major *cause* of the problem is motorist driving behavior. How can police action resolve the problem by reducing crashes 10 percent?

Once the problem is clearly stated, the next step is to use crash records to obtain data concerning frequency, location, day of week, time of day and causes. Computer software programs can provide data analysis and instant information.

After information is compiled, alternatives are identified. Alternative A might be to increase radar enforcement to reduce the speed of vehicles because crashes are increasing not only in frequency but also in severity. Increased speed of vehicles involved in crashes results in increased severity. Alternative B might be to station a squad car at high-crash intersections as a deterrent during the day of the week and time of day that crash occurrence is highest. Alternative C might be to add road signs to warn drivers of the crash problem. Alternative D might be to provide additional traffic patrol officers to increase enforcement of traffic violations and increase deterrent visibility. Alternative E might be to station officers in high-crash locations and have them hand out cards to motorists stopping at stop signs. The cards inform the drivers of the crash problem, locations and things they can do to help. Alternative F might be to do nothing.

Next, the alternatives must be analyzed so the best ones can be selected and implemented. Alternative A is accepted, and radar enforcement is increased in selected areas of high crash frequency. Alternative B is eliminated because of time consumption and lack of sufficient vehicles. Alternative C is accepted, and engineering is directed to install signs at the proper locations. Alternative D is eliminated because it requires funds that are not available. Alternative E is eliminated because it would take time to develop and print the card, and the officers do not think this is good use of their time. Alternative F is ruled out because measures *are* needed to reduce crashes.

The final step is evaluation, which is done six months later. It was determined that crashes were reduced by 5 percent, half the original goal. The results were disseminated to all police department members and the engineering department. A team of volunteers met to determine why the goal was not achieved, what worked and what didn't work.

Force-Field Analysis (FFA)

Force-field analysis (FFA) is a problem-solving technique that identifies forces that impede and others that foster goal achievement. Forces that impede goal achievement are called **restraining forces**; those that foster it are called **driving forces**. The problem itself is called **equilibrium**. In a problem situation, the equilibrium is not where you want it to be. Force-field analysis is illustrated in Figure 5.1.

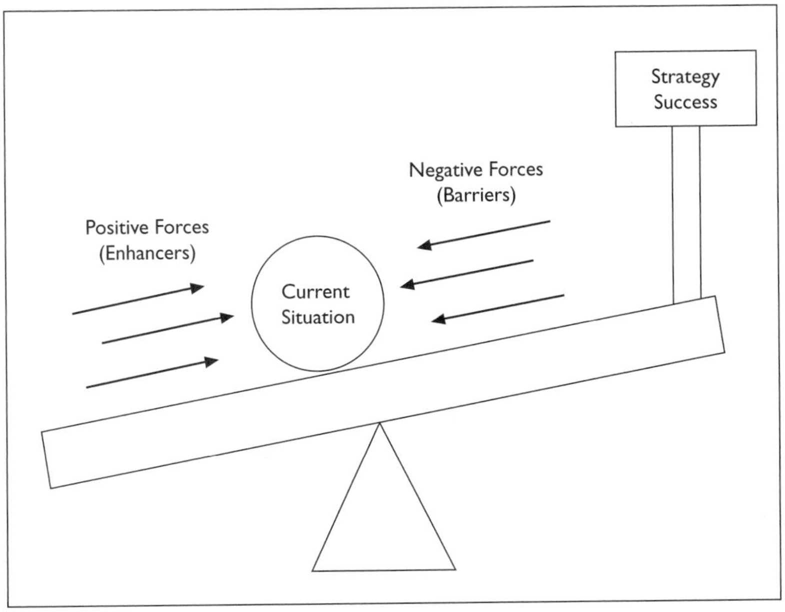

force-field analysis • identifies forces that impede and enhance goal attainment. A problem exists when the equilibrium is such that more forces are impeding goal attainment than enhancing it.

restraining forces • forces that impede goal achievement.

driving forces • forces that foster goal achievement.

equilibrium • the problem in force-field analysis—the equilibrium is not where you want it to be.

Figure 5.1 Force-Field Analysis

Source: Michael J. Evers and George Heenan. "Balancing Act: Optimizing Strategies and Projects for Success." *Minnesota Business*, March 2002, p.16.

Force-field analysis identifies factors that impede and enhance goal attainment. A problem exists when the equilibrium is upset because more factors are impeding goal attainment than enhancing it.

In force-field analysis, you can state the problem as an undesirable situation, then list and label each force as high, medium or low (H-M-L) to indicate the strength. The final step is to devise a plan to change the equilibrium. Select specific ways to reduce the restraining forces and other ways to increase the driving forces. The entire analysis can be put into a chart, as shown in Table 5.1.

The Nominal Group Technique (NGT)

Researchers Andre Delbecq and Andrew Van de Ven found that some people work better by themselves than in a group. To take advantage of this yet capture the synergism of a team approach, they developed the nominal group technique (NGT) to produce more and better ideas.

nominal group technique (NGT) • an objective way to achieve consensus on the most effective alternatives by using an objective ranking of alternatives.

 The **nominal group technique (NGT)** is an objective way to achieve consensus on the most effective alternatives by ranking them.

It works like this:
1. Divide the staff or people involved into groups of six to nine.
2. Have each person write down as many ideas for solving the problem at hand as they can—without talking to anyone. Allow 5 to 15 minutes for this step.

Table 5.1   Sample Force-Field Analysis

Problem: Increasing Drug Abuse in Our Community

Restraining Forces	Driving Forces
Lack of finances	Increase in drug arrests
Lack of organization/coordination	Church groups
Lack of school cooperation	Parental concerns
Lack of church cooperation	Suicide rate
Lack of available personnel	Increase in drug use
Public apathy	Teen pregnancies
Parental drug use	Fatal accidents
Drug sales profits	

Recommended Action Plan

Create a specialized narcotics unit.

Initiate a 24-hour "hotline."

Pass an ordinance creating a drug-free zone of 1,000 feet around any school.

Conduct educational programs such as DARE in the schools.

Conduct parenting classes.

Conduct drug-free workplace programs.

Start a newsletter to be sent to all residents in the community.

Confiscate all property involved in drug arrests.

Create an Anti-Drug Abuse Council.

Hire a drug counselor for those who cannot afford one.

Source: Stan Kossen. *Supervision.* West Publishing Company, 1991.

3. Go around the group and have each person, including the leader, read one item from his or her list while the leader writes the ideas on a flipchart. No evaluation of the ideas is allowed.
4. Continue going around the room until all ideas are posted. If more than one person gives the same idea, place a tally mark behind it.
5. After all the ideas are posted, allow questions to clarify the ideas, but no evaluation.
6. Hand out note cards and have everyone rank the five best ideas, with "1" being the best.
7. Collect the cards and take a break. Total the rankings for each idea and divide by the number of people in the meeting. Then write on the flipchart the five ideas with the highest scores.
8. Reconvene the group and have them discuss the five ideas. Usually one best idea will emerge from this discussion.

This technique works well to obtain input from everyone, but it is also very time consuming. It should be reserved for important problems that truly require a consensus decision.

The Delphi Technique

The **Delphi technique** was developed in the 1960s at the Rand Corporation. Like the nominal group process, the Delphi Technique is a way to have individual input result in a group effort. Rather than calling a meeting, management sends questionnaires to those who are to be involved in the decision making. Figure 5.2 illustrates a typical Delphi questionnaire.

Delphi technique • a way to have individual input; uses open-ended questionnaires completed by individuals. Answers are shared, and the questionnaires are again completed until consensus is achieved.

Survey on Options for Combatting the Drug Problem

As an officer on the street, you are closest to the drug problem our agency is battling. We would appreciate your suggestions on possible approaches to this problem. Please take a few minutes to answer the questions that follow. Your answers will be confidential, but all answers will be shared with all other members of the patrol division.

1. How can we increase community drug education?

_____
_____
_____

2. What are the three main drug abuse problem areas?

_____
_____
_____
_____

3. What should we do to reduce the drug problem in our community?

_____
_____
_____
_____

Figure 5.2   Typical Delphi Questionnaire

1. For each statement below, check the column that best reflects your position:
   A Agree with.
   B Not certain but willing to try for a year and evaluate.
   C Disagree with.
2. For each column where you check C, indicate in the space below the statement how you would like it amended. You may also comment if you checked A or B.

Suggested Action	A	B	C

To increase community drug education we should:
1. Start a school DARE program.
   Comment:
2. Publish in local papers a series of articles by community leaders.
   Comment:
3. Highlight drug abuse literature at the library.
   Comment:
 	
To reduce the drug problem in our community we should:
4. Increase the number of police.
   Comment:
5. Begin a community-wide Anti-Drug Abuse Council.
   Comment:
6. Provide stiffer penalties to drug dealers and users.
   Comment:			

Figure 5.3   Phase 1 of the Modified Delphi Technique

Management then circulates the answers to all participants, who are asked to again complete the questionnaire considering the various answers. This continues until a consensus is reached. Usually, three or four cycles are enough.

 The Delphi technique uses questionnaires completed by individuals. Answers are shared and the questionnaires are again completed until consensus is reached.

Delphi is actually a thoughtful conversation in which everyone gets a chance to *listen*. Groups often debate rather than problem solve. The Delphi technique removes the need for winning points or besting the opposition.

A Modified Delphi Technique

modified Delphi technique • uses objective rather than open-ended questions.

The Delphi technique can be modified to take away the open-endedness. This **modified Delphi technique** presents a questionnaire that contains policy statements representing key issues to be decided and a response column with three choices: Agree with, not certain but willing to try, and disagree with. Those who do not agree are asked to indicate the changes they would recommend that would make the statement acceptable. This is Phase 1. Figure 5.3 shows an example of how this might look.

Phase 2 shows the number replying with each option for each statement and the choice each respondent circled. Respondents are then asked to reconsider their original responses and make any changes they want based on the responses of others. Figure 5.4 shows how this might look.

Following is a tally of responses to the drug questionnaire and suggested changes that we would like you to respond to. As before, for each statement and change, check the column that best reflects your position:

A   Agree with.
B   Not certain, but willing to try for a year and evaluate.
C   Disagree with.

Suggested Action	A	B	C
To increase community drug education we should:			
1. Start a school DARE program.	5	3	3
Change: Also have parenting classes.			
2. Publish in local papers a series of articles by community leaders.	4	4	3
Change: Also articles by victims and cops.			
3. Highlight drug abuse literature at the library.	3	3	5
Change: Distribute literature through civic groups and the schools as well.			
To reduce the drug problem in our community we should:			
4. Increase the number of police.	6	5	0
Change: Increase in areas known to have high rates of drug dealing.			
5. Begin a community-wide Anti-Drug Abuse Council.	4	4	3
Change: Members appointed by chief of police.			
6. Provide stiffer penalties to drug dealers and users.	5	1	5
Change: For dealers only. Counseling for users.			

Figure 5.4   Phase 2 of the Modified Delphi Technique

Phase 3 is a tally of the responses in Phase 2 and a summary of the actions to be taken for each item, based on those responses. Any of these decision-making methods are also appropriate for a department using problem-oriented policing.

Problem-Oriented Policing

Problem-oriented policing (POP) has become extremely popular in many departments and goes hand-in-hand with community-oriented policing. The theoretical basis for problem-oriented policing was described in Chapter 3. However, the distinction between problem solving and problem-oriented policing is important. Table 5.2 summarizes some key distinctions between the two approaches.

Falk (2005, p.10) notes that in most departments using POP, problem solving is both formal and informal: "Many patrol officers use very informal methods of problem solving to quickly and efficiently resolve minor problems. Other problems require much more in-depth scrutiny and time-consuming responses." Cordner and Biebel (2005, p.155) believe that POP is a targeted, analytical, in-depth approach that results in "working smarter, not harder." Goldstein (1990, p.33), says of problem-oriented policing: "Focusing on the substantive, community problems that the police must handle is a much more radical step than it initially appears to be, for it requires the police to go beyond taking satisfaction in the smooth operation of their organization; it requires that they extend their concern to dealing effectively with the problems that justify creating a police agency in the first instance." The approach used in problem-oriented policing is typically the SARA Model.

problem-oriented policing (POP) • management ascertains what problems exist and tries to solve them, redefining the role of law enforcement from incident driven and reactive to problem oriented and proactive.

Table 5.2   Selected Comparisons between Problem-Oriented Policing and Community Policing Principles

Principle	Problem-Oriented Policing	Community Policing
Primary emphasis	Substantive social problems within police mandate	Engaging the community in the policing
When police and community collaborate	Determined on a problem-by-problem basis	Always or nearly always
Emphasis on problem analysis	Highest priority given to thorough analysis	Encouraged, but less important than community collaboration
Preference for responses	Strong preference that alternatives to criminal law enforcement be explored	Preference for collaborative response with community
Role for police in organizing and mobilizing community	Advocated only if warranted within the context of the specific problem being addressed	Emphasizes strong role for police
Importance of geographic decentralization of police and continuity of officer assignment to community	Preferred but not essential	Essential
Degree to which police share decision-making authority with community	Strongly encourages input from community while preserving ultimate decision-making authority to police	Emphasizes sharing decision-making authority with community
Emphasis on officers' skills	Emphasizes intellectual and analytical skills	Emphasizes interpersonal skills
View of the role or mandate of police	Encourages broad, but not unlimited, role for police, stresses limited capabilities of police, and guards against creating unrealistic expectations of police	Encourages expansive role for police to achieve ambitious social objectives

Source: Michael S. Scott. *Problem-Oriented Policing: Reflection of the First 20 Years.* Washington, DC: U.S. Department of Justice, Office of Community Oriented Policing Services, 2000, p.99.

 The SARA Model problem-solving process involves four steps (Eck and Spelman, 1987):

1. Scanning (identifying the problem)
2. Analysis (looking at alternatives)
3. Response (implementing an alternative)
4. Assessment (evaluating the results)

Scanning

Scanning refers to identifying recurring problems and prioritizing them to select one problem to address. The scanning step incorporates the first two steps in the seven-step decision making, problem-solving process: define the specific problem and gather all facts concerning the problem.

Clarke and Eck (2005) describe a problem as "a recurring set of related harmful events in a community that members of the public expect the police to address." The definition calls attention to what they describe as the six required elements of a problem:

 The six required elements of a problem are community, harm, expectation, events, recurring and similarity, captured by the acronym CHEERS.

Community includes individuals, businesses, government agencies and other groups.

Harmful includes property loss or damage, injury or death, serious mental anguish, or undermining the police's capacity (repeat fraudulent calls for service). Illegality is *not* a defining characteristic of problems.

Table 5.3 Potential Sources of Information for Identifying Problems
Crime Analysis Unit–Time trends and patterns (time of day, day of week, monthly, seasonal, and other cyclical events), and patterns of similar events (offender descriptions, victim characteristics, locations, physical settings and other circumstances).
Patrol–Recurring calls, bad areas, active offenders, victim types, complaints from citizens.
Investigations–Recurring crimes, active offenders, victim difficulties, complaints from citizens.
Crime Prevention–Physical conditions, potential victims, complaints from citizens.
Vice–Drug dealing, illegal alcohol sales, gambling, prostitution, organized crime.
Communications–Call types, repeat calls from same location, temporal peaks in calls for service.
Chief's Office–Letters and calls from citizens, concerns of elected officials, concerns from city manager's office.
Other Law Enforcement Agencies–Multi-jurisdictional concerns.
Elected Officials–Concerns and complaints.
Local Government Agencies–Plans that could influence crimes, common difficulties, complaints from citizens.
Schools–Juvenile concerns, vandalism, employee safety.
Community Leaders–Problems of constituents.
Business Groups–Problems of commerce and development.
Neighborhood Watch–Local problems regarding disorder, crime and other complaints.
Newspapers and Other News Media–Indications of problems not detected from other sources, problems in other jurisdictions that could occur in any city.
Community Surveys–Problems of citizens in general.

Source: John E. Eck and William Spelman. *Problem Solving: Problem-Oriented Policing in Newport News.* Washington, DC: Police Executive Research Forum, 1987, p.46. ©1987 Police Executive Research Forum. Reprinted with permission by PERF.

Expectation must never be presumed but be evident by such things as citizen calls, press reports and the like. *Events* must be describable, for example, a burglary.

Recurring events may be symptomatic of acute or chronic problems. Some acute problems dissipate quickly even without intervention. Others may become chronic if not addressed.

Similarity means the recurring events have something in common, some sort of pattern. Common crime classifications are not helpful.

CHEERS suggests six basic questions to answer at the scanning stage:

- Who in the community is affected by the problem?
- What are the harms created by the problem? What are the expectations for the police response?
- What types of events contribute to the problem?
- How often do these events recur?
- How are the events similar?

Table 5.3 illustrates potential sources of information for identifying problems obtained through scanning.

Analysis

Analysis examines the identified problem's causes, scope and effects. It includes determining how often the problem occurs and how long it has been occurring, as well as conditions that appear to create the problem. Analysis also should include potential resources and partners who might assist in understanding and addressing the problem.

Boba (2003, p.2) describes problem analysis as: "An approach/method/process conducted within the police agency in which formal criminal justice theory, research methods and comprehensive data collection and analysis procedures are used in a systematic way to conduct in-depth examination of, develop informed responses to, and evaluate crime and disorder problems."

The analysis phase incorporates the third, fourth and fifth steps of the seven-step process: generate alternatives; analyze the alternatives; select the best alternative. Goldstein's (p.ix) range of possible alternatives includes:

- Concentrating attention on those who account for a disproportionate share of a problem.
- Connecting with other government and private services.
- Using mediation and negotiation skills.
- Conveying information.
- Mobilizing the community.
- Using existing forms of social control in addition to the community.
- Altering the physical environment to reduce opportunities for problems to recur.
- Increasing regulation, through statutes or ordinances, of conditions that contribute to problems.
- Developing new forms of limited authority to intervene and detain.
- Using the criminal justice system more discriminately.
- Using civil law to control public nuisances, offensive behavior and conditions contributing to crime.

Boba (p.3) notes that problem analysis is interpretive, creative and innovative, open-ended and inclusive. It can be based on common sense or research. It is proactive and demands partnerships. Most importantly, it is fundamental to strategic policing because it focuses on formulating long-term solutions to community problems. However, research by Cordner and Biebel (p.155) found that more than 80 percent of their survey respondents indicated that time limitations hampered their ability to perform in-depth analysis. Their research found that the most common methods/resources in analysis were personal experience (62 percent) and brainstorming (26 percent).

The Problem Analysis Triangle The COPS Center for Problem Solving Web site provides a problem analysis triangle that is useful when thinking about recurring problems of crime and disorder. The triangle assumes crime or disorder results when (1) likely offenders and (2) suitable targets come together in (3) time and space in the absence of capable guardians for the target, as illustrated in Figure 5.5 (sometimes referred to as the crime triangle).

Using CompStat in Problem Solving Another resource for analyzing problems is CompStat, meaning computer comparison statistics or simply compare stats. **CompStat,** according to Shane (2004, p.13), is a strategic crime-control technique centered around four principles: (1) accurate and timely intelligence, (2) effective tactics, (3) rapid deployment of personnel and resources, and (4) relentless follow-up and assessment. Dodge (2005, p.84) notes: "The goals of CompStat coincide with the community policing practices of increased central information sharing and internal problem solving."

According to McDonald (2004, p.37), "CompStat will provide accountability for community policing activities, will ensure that all community activities have

CompStat • a strategic crime-control technique centered around four principles: (1) accurate and timely intelligence, (2) effective tactics, (3) rapid deployment of personnel and resources and (4) relentless follow-up and assessment.

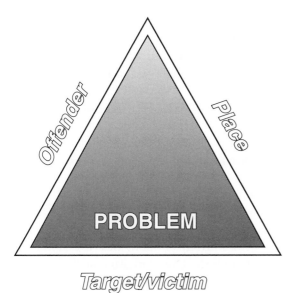

Figure 5.5 The Problem Analysis Triangle
Source: Reprinted with permission of Center for Problem-
Oriented Policing.

direction and application to solving problems and will reinforce the need for
commanders to complete their strategies by involving the community in their
problem solving."

Recognizing the Magnet Phenomenon When identifying problems, it is important to be aware of the magnet phenomenon. The **magnet phenomenon** occurs when a phone number or address is associated with a crime simply because
it was a convenient number or address to use.

A magnet telephone is one that is available when no other telephones are, for
example, a telephone in a convenience store that is open all night and on weekends. Victims of or witnesses to a crime in the area may use that telephone to report the crime, even though the store was not the scene of the crime. Similarly, a
magnet address is one that is easy for people to give, for example, a high school
or a theater. High numbers of calls from one location can give skewed results, as
the assumption is often made, for record-keeping purposes, that the location of
the call is also the location of the incident.

magnet phenomenon ● occurs
when a phone number or address is associated with a
crime simply because it was a
convenient number or address
to use.

Federal Assistance in Problem-Solving Efforts Several federal agencies can
assist in problem analysis, including the Office of Community Oriented Policing
(COPS), the National Institute of Justice (NIJ), the Bureau of Justice Statistics
(BJS) and the National Criminal Justice Reference Service (NCJRS) (Boba, p.36).
These agencies can provide funding and training as well as publishing case stud-
ies and providing examples of innovation.

Response

Response is acting to alleviate the problem, that is, selecting the alternative solution or solutions to try. The response step parallels the sixth step in the seven-
step process: implement the alternative. This may include finding out what
other communities with similar problems have tried and with what success as

well as looking at whether any research on the problem exists. Focus groups might be used to brainstorm possible interventions. Experts might be enlisted. Several alternatives might be ranked and prioritized according to difficulty, expense and the like. At this point goals are usually refined and the interventions are implemented.

Research by Bichler and Gaines (2005, pp.68–69) found that the most prevalent response to complex issues of disorder involved increased use of conventional law enforcement strategies such as enforcement. They (p.71) found that responses "conspicuously contained few tactics that involved community policing." The officers felt the partnerships were not viable or that they found other governmental agencies generally uncooperative in their problem-solving efforts. Bichler and Gaines (p.71) stress that police administrators must pave the way for partnerships: "Police officers acting alone or even through the chain of command cannot develop meaningful cooperative relationships with other agencies or citizen groups without the active support of the agency leadership. The groundwork must be laid by administration."

Assessment

Assessment refers to evaluating how effective the intervention was. Was the problem solved? If not, why? The assessment phase in the SARA Model parallels the seventh step of the seven-step process: evaluate the decision.

According to Eck (2002, p.6): "You begin planning for an evaluation when you take on a problem. The evaluation builds throughout the SARA process, culminates during the assessment and provides findings that help you determine if you should revisit earlier stages to improve the response." Figure 5.6 illustrates the problem-solving process and evaluation.

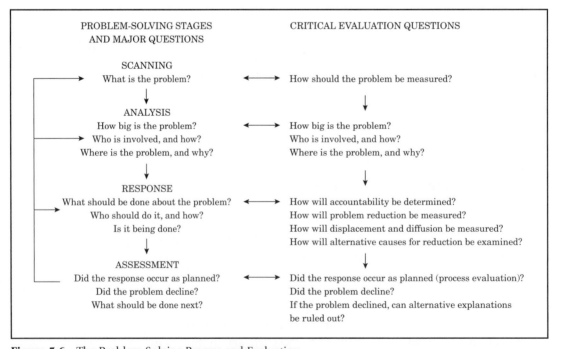

Figure 5.6   The Problem-Solving Process and Evaluation

Source: John E. Eck. *Assessing Responses to Problems: An Introductory Guide for Police Problem-Solvers.* Washington, DC: Office of Community Oriented Policing Services, 2002, p.6.

Table 5.4 Interpreting Results of Process and Impact Evaluations

		Process Evaluation Results	
		Response implemented as planned, or nearly so	Response not implemented, or implemented in a radically different manner than planned
Impact Evaluation Results	Problem declined	A. Evidence that the response caused the decline	C. Suggests that other factors may have caused the decline or that the response was accidentally effective
	Problem did not decline	B. Evidence that the response was ineffective, and that a different response should be tried	D. Little is learned. Perhaps if the response had been implemented as planned, the problem would have declined, but this is speculative

Source: John E. Eck. *Assessing Responses to Problems: An Introductory Guide for Police Problem Solvers.* Washington, DC. Office of Community Oriented Policing Services, 2002, p.10.

Assessment should include both qualitative and quantitative data. **Qualitative data** examines the excellence (quality) of the response—that is, how satisfied were the officers and the citizens. This is most frequently determined by surveys, focus groups, or tracking of complaints and compliments. **Quantitative data** examines the amount of change (quantity) as a result of the response. This is most frequently measured by pre/post data.

Eck (p.10) describes two types of evaluations to conduct: **process evaluation** that determines whether the response was implemented as planned and **impact evaluation** that determines whether the problem declined. Table 5.4 provides guidance in interpreting the results of process and impact evaluation.

Eck (p.27) suggests several nontraditional measures that will indicate if a problem has been affected by the interventions:

- Reduced instances of repeat victimization
- Decreases in related crimes or incidents
- Neighborhood indicators: increased profits for legitimate businesses in target area; increased use of area/increased (or reduced) foot and vehicular traffic; increased property values; improved neighborhood appearance; increased occupancy in problem buildings; less loitering; fewer abandoned cars; less truancy
- Increased citizen satisfaction regarding the handling of the problem, which can be determined through surveys, interviews, focus groups, electronic bulletin boards and the like
- Reduced citizen fear related to the problem

The SARA Model of problem solving stresses that there are no failures, only responses that do not provide the desired goal. When a response does not give the desired results, the partners involved in problem solving can examine the results and try a different response. Other communities might benefit from what was learned. The difference between simply handling a call and solving a problem is illustrated in Table 5.5.

The SARA Model in Action

An example of problem-oriented policing in action and implementing the SARA Model is seen in the 2001 winner of the Herman Goldstein Excellence in

qualitative data • examines the excellence (quality) of the response—that is, how satisfied were the officers and the citizens. This is most frequently determined by surveys, focus groups or tracking of complaints and compliments.

quantitative data • examines the amount of change (quantity) as a result of the response. This is most frequently measured by pre/post data.

process evaluation • an assessment to determine whether the response was implemented as planned.

impact evaluation • an assessment to determine whether a problem declined.

Table 5.5 Handling a Call versus Solving a Problem

Handling a Call	versus	Solving a Problem
Call-/case-driven response		Problem-driven response
Temporary/transient result		Longer lasting/permanent result
Less effort/energy required/expended		More effort/energy required/expended
Less imagination applied		More imagination applied
Limited results expected by officers		Less limited results expected by officers
Little collaboration with others		Much collaboration with others
Response driven by limited information		Response driven by much information

Source: Terry Eisenberg and Bruce Glasscock. "Looking Inward with Problem-Oriented Policing." *FBI Law Enforcement Bulletin,* July 2001, p.4.

Problem-Oriented Policing Award, the California Highway Patrol (CHP), for its Corridor Safety Program. The program used the SARA Model to address a high rate of fatal accidents on an infamous stretch of rural highway in California, the roadway where actor James Dean was killed in the late 1950s, dubbed "Blood Alley."

Scanning Scanning was rigorous, with 550 qualifying roadway segments examined. Three years of collision and victim data were reviewed to minimize any statistical anomalies. To be included in the selection pool, potential corridors had to pass through or be adjacent to an urban area and fall under the jurisdiction of the CHP. Segments with fewer than five deaths in three years were also eliminated. Based on statistical rankings and input from local experts, State Routes 41/46 were selected.

Analysis The CHP formed a multi-disciplinary task force. The task force found that much of the corridor was quite remote, largely without cellular phone service and having too few call boxes. Call response times for emergency services depended on the EMS unit with jurisdiction over the area, sometimes not the closest unit. The roadway lacked adequate shoulders and medians, and existing signage was confusing and inadequate, as were existing passing and merging lanes. Being an east-west route, glare was a problem during sunrise and sunset. Various roadway curves also contributed to poor visibility.

The task force also found that the primary collision factors spoke to the presence of aggressive driving and of impatient drivers behind large, slow-moving vehicles who made unwise passing decisions. The top five collision factors were unsafe turning, driving on the wrong side of the road, improper passing, driving under the influence and unsafe speed. It also suggested that many involved in collisions were local farm workers with limited English skills who were unfamiliar with California rules-of-the-road.

Response Proposed solutions fell into four categories: enforcement, emergency services, engineering and education. Special *enforcement* operations were implemented and funded through federal traffic safety grants. Ultimately officers worked 2,922 overtime hours, offered assistance and services to motorists 2,837 times and issued 14,606 citations.

Additional *emergency* roadside call boxes were installed. A CHP helicopter was permanently assigned to the roadway, and agreements were reached with emergency service providers that the closest units should respond to collision scenes without regard to jurisdictional boundaries.

Several *engineering* changes were made in the roadway. Raised-profile thermoplastic striping was installed where passing was allowed in one direction. In no-passing zones, a widened center median with rumble strips and thermoplastic striping was installed. Outside shoulders were treated with rumble strips. Several signing, striping and maintenance projects were completed. "Stop Ahead" warning signs were posted at key intersections, and chevron signs were installed to warn of impending curves.

A variety of *educational programs* and materials involved the local media, businesses, government and residents in reminding motorists to drive safely.

Assessment The efforts were quite successful, with fatal collisions reduced by 10 percent and injury collisions reduced by 32 percent. Over the five years of available data, it is estimated that the safety initiatives have saved 21 lives and prevented 55 injuries. The CHP response was not only logical, it also evidenced creativity and innovation.

Creativity and Innovation

Creativity is a process of breaking old connections and making useful new ones. It often is synonymous with innovation and involves originality. One strategy for law enforcement managers to develop more creativity is to increase interaction with corporate leaders and other administrators outside criminal justice. Police management has been evolving for decades and has been described as conservative and traditional. Techniques such as participatory management, team approaches and quality circles are foreign to many police managers, who need to be alert to management changes in the corporate world. Some corporate techniques cannot be adapted to the police environment, but others can. Exposure to new ideas and thoughts stimulates the mind.

Some police administrators reject new programs or ideas because they did not originate with them or because the idea came from the rank-and-file. Many newspapers regularly publish excellent columns by management experts, and much of this information is adaptable to police management. In fact, many of the concepts presented in this text came from corporate America.

We are all born as potentially creative people. By the time we are adults only a very few of us have overcome all the messages our society sends that stifle individuality and creativity. Think about school and what you were taught: Dogs cannot be colored purple; give the "right" answer; do not make a mess; do not be different; stay in line; be quiet; raise your hand if you want to talk; and so on. In other words, conform. Our own habits can also stifle creativity.

A Creative Approach to Problem Solving

Saltzman (2003, p.41) offers several suggestions for creative problem solving. Start by being optimistic. The more you believe you can solve the problem, the more likely you'll keep at it. Then be clear by writing down the problem as a precise question. Next write down everything about the situation you know (or think) to be true and question each assumption.

As you attempt to solve the problem, allow yourself to think of "pie-in-the-sky" solutions. It is important to refuse to accept "either/or" thinking. Always look for a third, fourth and fifth alternative. If no solution comes, walk away from it, allow it to incubate and come back to it when you are fresh. In addition to these ideas, be aware of and avoid thinking traps and mental locks.

Thinking Traps and Mental Locks

thinking traps • habits people fall into without recognizing what they are doing, including either/or thinking, deciding too quickly, deciding based on personality rather than facts, being a victim of personal habits and prejudices and being unimaginative. Also called *mental locks*.

Thinking traps are habits people fall into without recognizing what they are doing.

 Common thinking traps include:

1. Being stuck in black/white, either/or thinking.
2. Being too quick in deciding.
3. Making decisions based on personal feelings about the proposer of an idea.
4. Being a victim of personal habits and prejudices.
5. Not using imagination.

Being stuck in black/white, either/or thinking. People caught in this trap think that if one answer is bad, the other must be good. This kind of thinking causes people to miss intermediate solutions. Brainstorming many alternatives will help overcome this trap.

Being too quick in deciding. People in this trap jump to conclusions before they hear all the facts or have all the evidence. Avoid this trap by listing all possibilities and delaying decisions until each has been discussed.

Making decisions based on personal feelings about the proposer of an idea. Some people tend to support only what their friends propose. To overcome this, decide that you will listen for the facts and keep your feelings out of your decision.

Being a victim of personal habits and prejudices. "We've always done it that way" thinking can keep programs from moving forward. You can avoid this trap by asking questions such as: Who else can we serve? How can we do it differently? What more might we do?

Not using imagination. People who fall into this trap are too tied to data and statistics. They do not risk using their intuition. To bypass this trap, practice brainstorming and creative thinking—think laterally, horizontally and vertically. Take the risk of going with your hunches.

To illustrate the tendency to get stuck in a thinking rut, try the "Scottish Names" game on a colleague. (Note: It is more effective if done orally because the solution is obvious when written like this.) Ask a colleague to pronounce M-A-C-T-A-V-I-S-H; then M-A-C-D-O-U-G-A-L; then M-A-C-C-A-R-T-H-Y. Finally, ask them to pronounce M-A-C-H-I-N-E-S. If they respond "MacHines," they have become a victim of preconditioned thinking, a common thinking trap.

The mind easily gets stuck in patterns. Creativity consultant von Oech (1983) calls such thinking traps *mental locks*. He suggests that sometimes we need a "whack on the side of the head" to jar ourselves out of ways of thinking that keep us from being innovative.

mental locks • thinking patterns that prevent innovative thinking. Also called *thinking traps*.

 Mental locks that prevent innovative thinking include:

1. The right answer.
2. Play is frivolous.
3. That's not my area.
4. Don't be foolish.
5. I'm not creative.
6. To err is wrong.
7. That's not logical.

8. Follow the rules.
9. Be practical.
10. Avoid ambiguity.

The right answer. Most people will have taken in excess of 26,000 tests before they complete their education. Such tests usually focus on "right" answers. According to von Oech (p.22): "Children enter elementary school as question marks and leave as periods."

That's not logical. People need to learn to dream, create and fantasize. Both "soft" and "hard" thinking are needed. It is like making a clay pot. Clay that is not soft enough is difficult to work with. Once the pot is shaped, however, it must be fired and made hard before it will hold water. Metaphors such as this can help in problem solving as well.

Follow the rules. Parents teach their children to stay inside the lines when they color. People do rely on patterns to analyze problems, but this can be a hindrance.

Be practical. As von Oech (p.54) notes:

Because we have the ability to symbolize our experience, our thinking is not limited to the real and the present. This capability empowers our thinking in two major ways. First, it enables us to anticipate the future. . . .

Second, since our thinking is not bound by real world constraints, we can generate ideas which have no correlate in the world of experience. . . .

I call the realm of the possible our "germinal seedbed." . . . Asking "what-if" is an easy way to get your imagination going.

Avoid ambiguity. A story told by von Oech involves former FBI director J. Edgar Hoover. Hoover wrote a letter to his agents, and as he was proofreading it, he decided he did not like the way it was laid out. He wrote a note on the bottom to his secretary, "Watch the borders," and asked her to retype it. She did and then sent it to all the agents. For the next few weeks, FBI agents were put on special alert along our Canadian and Mexican borders. Ambiguity should usually be avoided. When thinking creatively, however, ambiguity can help. Ask: How else might this be interpreted?

To err is wrong. This is similar to the first mental lock—that there is a "right" answer. View mistakes as learning opportunities and as a part of risk taking. If you are made of the right material, a hard fall will result in a high bounce. Mistakes or failures can be positive. Henry Ford viewed failure positively: "Failure is the opportunity to begin again more intelligently."

Play is frivolous. According to von Oech (p.97): "Necessity may be the mother of invention, but play is certainly the father." He urges that people not take themselves too seriously, especially when engaged in innovative thinking.

That's not my area. In our complex society, specialization is a fact of life. Sometimes, however, a person outside the area in which a problem exists is better able to generate possible solutions. It is not always the "experts" who come up with the best ideas.

Don't be foolish. In the Middle Ages, kings often had "fools" as part of their court. A major role these fools played was to ridicule the advice the king's counselors gave him, a forerunner of the devil's advocate role in today's society.

I'm not creative. This can become a self-fulfilling prophecy. If you think you cannot do something, you probably will not be able to. Conversely, the power of positive thinking has been proven time after time.

Killer Phrases

Closely related to thinking traps and mental locks are certain "killer phrases" people tend to use that limit the creative participation of *others* in the group.

 Killer phrases are judgmental and critical and serve as put-downs. They stifle others' creativity.

killer phrases • judgmental, critical statements that serve as put-downs and stifle others' creativity.

Among the more common killer phrases are the following: It's not our policy. It's not our area. We don't have the time. We'll never get help. It's too much hassle. That's too radical. It won't work. Be practical. It costs too much. We've never done it that way before. Be realistic. Where did you come up with that idea? This isn't the time to try something like that. It's okay in theory, but I don't think we're ready for it yet. You don't really think that would work, do you? Get serious.

 To handle killer phrases, recognize them, describe to the group what is happening and then challenge the group to discuss whether the killer phrases are true. Encourage the group to remain open to all ideas.

Organizations that promote creativity and innovation provide more freedom to think and act, recognize ideas and provide ample opportunities for communication as well as for private creative thinking. They also invest in research and experimentation and permit ideas from outside the organization.

Common Mistakes

Common mistakes in problem solving and decision making include spending too much energy on unimportant details, failing to resolve important issues, being secretive about true feelings, having a closed mind, making decisions while angry or excited and not expressing ideas. Managers who reject information, suggestions and alternatives that do not fit into their comfortable past patterns can severely limit their decision-making capabilities. Inability to decide, putting decisions off to the last minute, failing to set deadlines, making decisions under pressure and using unreliable sources of information are other common errors in problem solving and decision making. Without the willingness to change, to reach out or to go farther, you cannot be creative or innovative.

Each of these common errors has an alternative, positive approach. For example, rather than making multiple decisions about the same problem, that is, reinventing the wheel, managers should establish standard operating procedures for recurring problems.

Ethical Decisions

 Ethical considerations are important in decision making.

A decision may be logical, creative and legal, but is it ethical—morally right? Many problems facing law enforcement decision makers involve ethical issues. For example, are issues of fairness or morality involved? Who is affected? Will there be victims? What are the alternatives? Is there a law against some behavior, or does it clearly violate a moral rule? Does the decision accurately reflect the kind of person/department you are or want to be? How does it make you and your department look to the public? To other law enforcement agencies? Ethics in law enforcement is discussed in Chapter 8.

Evaluating Decisions

When decisions have been made, they can be evaluated against the following checklist. Is the decision:
1. Consistent with the agency's mission? Goals? Objectives?
2. A long-term solution?
3. Cost effective?
4. Legal?
5. Ethical?
6. Practical?
7. Acceptable to those responsible for implementing it?

 SUMMARY

Diversity, disagreement and risk taking help foster a decision-making, problem-solving environment. Decisions may be strategic—executive level; administrative—middle management level; or operational—first-line level. Decisions may also be classified as command, consultative or consensual.

Decision making and problem solving involve thinking. Whole-brain research suggests that left-brain thinking processes *language* and is primarily *logical*. Right-brain thinking processes *images* and is primarily *emotional*. Both processes (that is, whole-brain thinking) are needed.

Basic methods for making decisions range from using intuition and snap decisions to using a computer, with a systematic individual or group approach in between.

Participatory decision making has been growing in popularity. All levels of the police department benefit from group participation in the decision-making process. Many approaches to problem solving seek solutions through brainstorming. To make brainstorming sessions effective, ensure that participants are prepared, write down *all* ideas, allow *no* criticizing of ideas and have a definite ending time.

Whether decisions are made by a group or an individual, a more complex process is often used. Among the most common systematic approaches are the seven-step approach, force-field analysis, the nominal group technique, the Delphi technique and a modified form of the Delphi technique.

The seven-step approach involves defining the problem, gathering the facts, generating alternatives, analyzing the alternatives, selecting the best alternative, implementing the alternative and evaluating the decision. Force-field analysis identifies forces that impede and enhance goal attainment. A problem exists when the equilibrium is upset because more forces are impeding goal attainment than enhancing it. The nominal group technique is an objective way to achieve consensus on the most effective alternatives by ranking them. The Delphi technique uses individually completed questionnaires. Answers are shared, and the questionnaires are again completed until consensus is reached.

One popular approach to problem solving is problem-oriented policing (POP), which uses the SARA approach: scan, analyze, respond and assess. The six required elements of a problem are community, harm, expectation, events, recurring and similarity, captured by the acronym CHEERS. Problem solving also stresses creativity.

Often synonymous with innovation, creativity can be hindered by thinking traps, mental locks and killer phrases. Common thinking traps include being stuck in black/white, either/or thinking; being too quick in deciding; making decisions based on personal feelings about the proposer of an idea; being a victim of personal habits and prejudices; and not using imagination. Mental locks that prevent innovative thinking include insisting on the "right" answer and the following opinions/statements: that's not logical; follow the rules; be practical; avoid ambiguity; to err is wrong; play is frivolous; that's not my area; don't be foolish; and I'm not creative.

Killer phrases are judgmental and critical and serve as put-downs. They stifle creativity. To handle killer phrases, recognize them, describe to the group what is happening and then challenge the phrases. In addition to seeking logical yet creative solutions, managers must be concerned with ethical considerations.

 CHALLENGE FIVE

Lt. Johnson is in charge of the patrol division of the Greenfield Police Department. While reviewing activity logs and police reports, he detects an increase in residential burglaries during the previous month. The burglaries are being reported on the afternoon shift when residents return home from work. Most of burglaries are occurring in one neighborhood. Lt. Johnson calls the afternoon patrol supervisor to inquire about the burglaries. The supervisor tells him he is aware of the problem and has been assigning officers to patrol the neighborhood. The supervisor notes that the burglaries are all on Thursdays and Fridays, but adds, "It's like trying to find a needle in a hay stack."

Lt. Johnson contacts the investigations supervisor and learns that he is also aware of the increase in burglaries. The supervisor tells Johnson that they have fingerprints from several of the burglaries, but no suspects. He speculates it might be kids because most of the losses are cigarettes, liquor and small amounts of cash.

When Lt. Johnson talks to the day patrol supervisor, he learns that the supervisor isn't aware of an increase in burglaries because none have been reported during his shift. The supervisor says they have been dealing with loitering and disorderly conduct problems at the shopping center. He says high school kids are hanging around the video arcade during the day, and he plans to meet with the high school principal to figure out why these kids aren't in school.

Lt. Johnson realizes that patrolling and reactive investigations usually have a minimal effect on preventing burglaries. He decides on a new approach.

1. How might Lt. Johnson address the burglary problem more effectively?
2. If Lt. Johnson decides on a problem-solving approach, who should he include in his group of problem solvers? Be creative.
3. Can you suggest how inviting the high school principal, the owner of the local arcade and residents from the neighborhood where the burglaries are occurring might be helpful?
4. Suggest a single problem that may be causing other problems in the community.
5. How could this problem-solving group be used is the future?

DISCUSSION QUESTIONS

1. Compare and contrast command, consultative and consensual decisions. Which do you prefer?

2. Do you support the findings of whole-brain research? If not, what problems do you see?

3. Can you give an example of when intuition has been important in a decision you have made?

4. Are you comfortable making snap decisions? If so, about what? If not, why not?

5. What would your model of decision making look like?

6. Who would you involve in the decision-making process?

7. How important do you think creativity and innovation are in dealing with typical problems facing law enforcement?

8. How might you engage in "creative procrastination"?

9. Of the systematic approaches to problem solving, which seems the most practical to you?

10. What is the greatest problem you think law enforcement is facing today? What approaches would you use to attack it?

REFERENCES

Bichler, Gisela and Gaines, Larry. "An Examination of Police Officers' Insights into Problem Identification and Problem Solving." *Crime & Delinquency*, January 2005, pp.53–74.

Boba, Rachel. *Problem Analysis in Policing*. Washington, DC: The Police Foundation, March 2003.

Clarke, Ronald V. and Eck, John E. *Crime Analysis for Problem Solvers in 60 Small Steps.* Washington, DC: Center for Problem Oriented Policing, 2005. (NCJ 211301)

Cordner, Gary and Biebel, Elizabeth Perkins. "Problem-Oriented Policing in Practice." *Criminology and Public Policy*, Vol. 4, No. 2, 2005, p.155.

Dahl, Tor. "Hazardophobic? The Risks of Avoiding Risk." *Minnesota Business*, October 2005, p.16.

Dodge, Mary. "Reviewing the Year in Police, Law Enforcement, Crime Prevention." *Criminal Justice Research Reports*, July/August 2005, p.84.

Eck, John E. *Assessing Responses to Problems: An Introductory Guide for Police Problem-Solvers*. Washington, DC: Office of Community Oriented Policing Services, 2002.

Eck, John E. and Spelman, William. *Problem-Solving: Problem-Oriented Policing in Newport News*. Washington, DC: Police Executive Research Forum, 1987.

Engel, Robin Shepard and Worden, Robert E. "Police Officers' Attitudes, Behavior and Supervisory Influences: An Analysis of Problem Solving." *Criminology*, February 2003, pp.131–166.

Excellence in Problem-Oriented Policing: The 2001 Herman Goldstein Award Winners, Washington, DC: National Institute of Justice, Community Oriented Policing Services and the Police Executive Research Forum, 2001, pp.5–14.

Falk, Kay. "Nothing New Under the Sun." *Law Enforcement Technology*, September 2005, pp.10–20.

Goldstein, Herman. *Problem-Oriented Policing*. New York: McGraw-Hill Publishing Company, 1990.

Martin, Richard V. "Problem-Solving Environment" *Law and Order*, September 2005, pp.161–162.

McCue, Colleen; Stone, Emily S.; and Gooch, Teresa P. "Data Mining and Value-Added Analysis." *FBI Law Enforcement Bulletin*, November 2003, pp.1–6.

McDonald, Phyllis P. "Implementing CompStat: Critical Points to Consider." *The Police Chief*, January 2004, pp.33–37.

Operational Risk Management. AFPAM36-2241V2. July 1, 2005.

Pinizzotto, Anthony J.; Davis, Edward F.; and Miller, Charles E., III. "Intuitive Policing: Emotional/Rational Decision Marking in Law Enforcement." *FBI Law Enforcement Bulletin*, February 2004, pp.1–6.

Saltzman, Joe. "Shake that Brain!" *Successful Meetings*, August 2003, p.41.

Sargent, Eric. "Records Management for Small Departments." *Law and Order*, August 2003, pp.88–91.

Shane, Jon M. "CompStat Process." *FBI Law Enforcement Bulletin*, August 2004, pp.12–21.

Simpson, Liz. "Basic Instincts." *Training*, January 2003, pp.56–59.

Smith, Dave and Brantner, Elizabeth. "Police Leadership and the Abilene Paradox." *The Police Chief*, April 2001, pp.196–200.

von Oech, Roger. *A Whack on the Side of the Head: How to Unlock Your Mind for Innovation*. New York: Warner Books, 1983.

BOOK-SPECIFIC WEB SITE

Go to the Management and Supervision in Law Enforcement Web site at www.thomsonedu.com/criminaljustice/bennett for student and instructor resources, including Internet Assignments and Case Studies.

CHAPTER 6

Time Management: Minute by Minute

*Time management is a question not of managing the clock
but of managing ourselves with respect to the clock.*

Alec MacKenzie, time management expert

 DO YOU KNOW?

- What time management is?
- What the greatest management resource is?
- What is at the heart of time management?
- How the Pareto Principle applies to time management?
- How to learn where your time is actually going?
- What helps you manage time minute by minute?
- What the most common external time wasters are?
- What the learning curve principle is and how it relates to time management?
- What three words can prompt you and others to use time effectively?
- What the most common internal time wasters are?
- What an effective time manager concentrates on?
- What priorities and posteriorities are?
- What the 5P Principle is?
- How to control the paper flood?
- How paperwork can be handled most efficiently?
- What the results of overdoing it might be?
- How to physically make time more productive?

CAN YOU DEFINE?

face time	Parkinson's Law	skimming
5P Principle	posteriorities	subvocalization
highlighting	priorities	tickler file system
learning curve	procrastination	time abusers
principle	regression	time log
narrow eye span	scanning	time management
Pareto Principle	single handling	

Introduction

Voltaire, an eighteenth-century French philosopher, posed the following riddle (*Zadig: A Mystery of Fate*):

> What of all things in the world is the longest and the shortest, the swiftest and the slowest, the most divisible and the most extended, the most neglected and the most regretted, without which nothing can be done, which devours all that is little and enlivens all that is great? *The answer—time.*

> Nothing is longer, since it is the measure of eternity.
> Nothing is shorter, since it is insufficient for the accomplishment of our projects.
> Nothing is more slow to him that expects; nothing more rapid to him that enjoys.
> In greatness, it extends to infinity; in smallness, it is infinitely divisible.
> All men neglect it; all regret the loss of it; nothing can be done without it.
> It consigns to oblivion whatever is unworthy of being transmitted to posterity, and it immortalizes such actions as are truly great.

With each promotion you receive comes an increase in your duties and responsibilities, with no increase in the number of hours in a day or extra days in the week.

This chapter begins with definitions of time and time management, as well as the value of time. It then discusses the importance of goals in effective time management and ways to organize your time to meet these goals. To identify how you might use time more efficiently, you should know how you are currently spending your time, so the function of time logs is described in detail. Next, the chapter discusses the importance of controlling time through use of a to-do list to make certain that priorities are set and then met through scheduling. This is followed by a look at common time abusers or unproductive time and how you might control this. One important step in managing time is controlling the paper flood and information load so common in law enforcement management. Also important is retaining what you need to remember. The chapter concludes with a discussion of how you can be most productive without overdoing—the ultimate goal of effective time management—including the physiology of productivity.

Time Defined

Time is nature's way of keeping everything from happening all at once. On a more serious note, *time* can be defined as the period between two events or during which something exists, happens or acts; it is thought of in terms of measurable intervals. Time is most often used in the legal sense to identify specific events. For example, "The crash occurred on January 26, 2003, at 1304 hours."

In the everyday, practical sense we measure time in years, months, weeks, days, hours, minutes and seconds. We also use many devices to measure time, the most popular of which are clocks, watches and calendars.

Despite much philosophizing and debate about time, it remains elusive, mysterious and difficult to define. Einstein determined that time is one dimension of the universe and that it is relative. (Two weeks on vacation is not the same as two weeks on a diet.) It is finite, instant, constant and, in a sense, an illusion. Your time belongs to you and no one else. How you spend your time is your decision. Once used, it can never be regained. Once you have read this paragraph, the time you took to read it is lost forever.

To realize the value of one minute, ask a person who just missed a train. To realize the value of one second, ask a person who just avoided a crash. To realize the value of one millisecond, ask the person who won a silver medal in the Olympics.

Imagine for a moment that you have a special bank account and that every morning it is credited with $1,440. Whatever amount you do not use each day, however, is taken out of the account. No balance can be carried over. Naturally you would try to use every bit of that $1,440 each day and to get the most out of it. You *do* have such a bank—a time bank. Every morning when you get up you have a 1,440-minute deposit that you can either invest wisely or squander. You cannot save it for tomorrow. Sleep does count as a wise investment.

Time Management: Planning and Organizing Time

Personal growth guru Stephen R. Covey contends: "Time management is really a misnomer; the challenge is not to manage time, but to manage ourselves." Likewise, *Time Management* (2005, p.xvii) says: "Time management is the discipline of controlling your life through your use of the 168 hours that are available to you every week." Time management is a primary responsibility of law enforcement managers to use both their own time and employees' time productively, best accomplished through organization, planning and review. Most law enforcement managers and their subordinates work 40-hour weeks. Some departments schedule five 8-hour days, others four 10-hour days. Each officer has approximately 2,000 working hours annually (allowing for two weeks of vacation). A 20-year law enforcement career has 40,000 assigned working hours, without overtime. Organizing and planning these assigned work hours determines both personal and public benefit: "Do not count time, but make time count." Although this chapter focuses on work time, the suggestions apply to time away from the job as well.

Successful law enforcement managers at all levels get more done in less time when they develop and follow efficient techniques for using assigned time. They have a sense of time importance and a sense of timing. Managing time involves managing yourself and your daily life. It does not necessarily mean working longer or faster. Trying to do everything is not managing. Time management is committing yourself to making quality use of your time to accomplish what is important.

time management • dividing and organizing time to accomplish the most tasks in the most efficient way.

 Time management is planning and organizing time to accomplish your most important goals in the shortest time possible.

Time management is a tool to move people from where they are to where they want to be. This means planning ahead. Do not think day by day but rather think in terms of the current year. Similar to setting New Year's resolutions, effective managers determine what are the most important objectives to accomplish in the year ahead. They then divide these objectives into months, then the months into days.

Time Management in a Service Organization

Effective time management often is evaluated based on the amount of tangible product produced—this much time spent produced these results. However, service organizations such as law enforcement agencies have inherent responsibilities that are time consuming yet not explicitly action-oriented and that yield few tangible results. Nonetheless, these responsibilities are vital to effective customer service, citizen satisfaction and community protection. Such tasks include consoling victims, talking with citizens, having a physical presence in high crash locations, following leads in a criminal investigation in which the actual monetary loss was low and so forth. To reiterate, effective managers/leaders focus more on people than on tasks. This may appear incongruous with the focus on "tasks to be accomplished" in this chapter, but to have time for their people, managers need to *make* the time. This chapter focuses on ways to do so.

Value of Time

What is your time worth to you? Have you ever determined in dollars how much your time is worth? Divide your annual salary by the number of annual work hours, usually 2,080 hours. For example, if your annual salary was $50,000, your hourly rate would be $24. If you add in your fringe benefits, your total annual compensation would be much more than that. Your time is valuable and should not be squandered.

When law enforcement managers were asked if they felt they had enough time to do what their jobs demanded, the majority said they could use more hours in the workday. This is *not* a viable solution to time problems.

It is ironic that managers who exercise good time management and complete their duties are often given extra responsibilities. In this situation managers who fail to use time wisely are, in effect, rewarded.

 Time is the greatest management resource.

All other resources can be increased, but time is fixed. If a person could gain 2 more productive hours a day, times 5 days per week, times 50 working weeks, that would be 500 hours or 3 extra *months* for each person in the department.

Returning to the definition of time management as "planning and organizing time to accomplish your most important goals in the shortest time possible," the logical place to begin developing good time management is with *goals*.

Goals and Time Management

The importance of goals to an organization has already been stressed. Goals are at the heart of efficiency and time management. It is a waste of time to do very well what you do not need to do at all.

 At the heart of time management are *goals*.

Time Management (p.15) stresses: "Goals are the starting point of effective time management. Everything else should follow from them." To effectively guide action, goals should be written in specific terms; be given a time frame; be measurable, important and aligned with the department's organizational goals; and be challenging yet achievable.

Ask yourself: "What is the most valuable use of my time right now?" You can answer this only by looking at the department's goals and objectives and what you must do to accomplish them. Time management needs to be both short and long range. Think in terms of the year, the month, the week, the day and the precise moment.

Segmenting Tasks

tickler file system • a set of file folders, organized by year, month and day, into which lists of tasks to be accomplished are placed.

Some time-management consultants advocate setting up a **tickler file system** consisting of the following 45 files:

- 2 files, one each for the next 2 years beyond the current year
- 12 files, one for each month of the current year
- 31 files, one for each day of the current month

One reason time management is so difficult is the human tendency to want to accomplish everything at once. Time management requires that time be managed—that is, organized and divided.

Some important activities may be best set aside until the following year. Simply knowing they are in the upcoming year's file clears your mind of worrying about them for the present. You may put off many activities one or more months. Put them into the appropriate monthly file.

At the end of the month, take the next month's file and divide the activities into the days available. At the end of each day—and this is a key to time management—take the next day's file and plan how to accomplish the activities slated for that day.

Goals, Objectives and the Pareto Principle

Pareto Principle • 20 percent of what a person does accounts for 80 percent of the results.

As you consider goals and objectives, the **Pareto Principle** comes into play. Alfredo Pareto was an Italian economist who observed that 20 percent of the Italian population owned 80 percent of the wealth. This and similar observations led Pareto to the conclusion that results and their causes are unequally distributed. The percentage is not always 20/80, but it is usually close. Consider the following:

- Twenty percent of your activities may produce eighty percent of your accomplishments.
- Twenty percent of your officers may constitute "problem" officers who account for eighty percent of the department's problems.
- Twenty percent of your officers may be considered "outstanding" officers who account for eighty percent of your department's successes.
- Effective leaders pay attention to the 20 percent and concentrate on improvement in those areas.

Effective time management uses the Pareto Principle to identify the 20 percent (*few*) *vital tasks* that will account for 80 percent of the desired results. It also identifies and places as low priority the 80 percent (*many*) *trivial tasks* clamoring for attention.

Figure 6.1 illustrates the Pareto Principle.

Time management expert Jeffrey Mayer (2004, p.24) calls this leveraging time: "A little bit of work generates a great deal of results. You leverage your time by working on, and completing, work, tasks, projects and activities that generate big

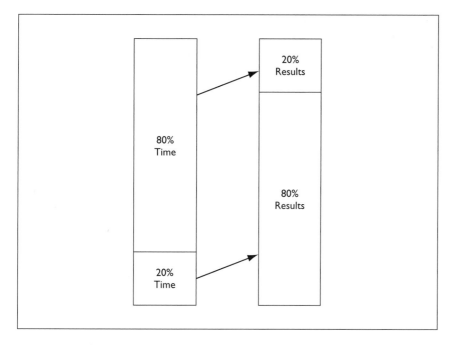

Figure 6.1   The Pareto Principle

results." He suggests three ways to make the 80/20 rule work: (1) do more of the things that work; (2) do less of the things that don't work; and (3) stop doing things that don't have a payoff—the concept of elimination.

Setting Priorities

Time is very important to police departments. In fact, response time presents an interesting time-management situation. Although research shows that response time has limited effect on arrest rates, it is important for citizen satisfaction and citizens' perceptions of police performance. *Most* departments have to prioritize calls. In some cities, during certain days of the week or times of the day, there may be a backlog of five to ten calls. Field officers have to prioritize calls for service according to severity and importance. Investigators set priorities for cases to follow up, based on the information furnished by the preliminary investigation report. Field officers' and investigators' responses are reactive. They have little or no control over the types of services required on any specific shift; they have only data based on experience. As departments become more proactive, time management will become more relevant.

Habit number 3 of Covey's *The 7 Habits of Highly Effective People* is "Put first things first. . . .Putting first things first is about time and life balance. It demands that individuals organize and execute around their most important priorities. Whatever the circumstance, it is living and being driven by the principles you value most, by the sense of purpose one pursues and by the responsibilities that our key roles demand of us" (Covey, 2003, p.132). Setting priorities requires that the urgent is differentiated from the important.

Urgent versus Important

Lyndon Johnson once noted: "The trouble with our country is that we constantly put second things first." This, unfortunately, is often true of managers as well.

Managers often spend too much time on urgent things and not enough time on the important things. Gresham's Law of Time Management says: "The urgent drives out the important." The little stuff, phones, meetings, interruptions and the like, keep managers from getting to the long-term tasks that need doing.

The importance of prioritizing is well illustrated by the story of the time management expert who was speaking to a group of high-powered overachievers. He set a 1-gallon Mason jar on a table along with a dozen fist-sized rocks and carefully began placing the rocks into the jar one at a time until it was filled to the top. At this point he asked, "Is the jar full?"

Everyone in the group shouted, "Yes."

The time management expert replied, "Really?" and reached under the table. He pulled out a bucket of gravel and dumped it in, shaking the jar to cause the pieces of gravel to work themselves down into the spaces between the big rocks. He asked the group once more, "Is the jar full?"

"Probably not," one of the group answered.

"Good," the expert replied, reaching under the table for a bucket of sand. He dumped the sand into the jar, and it went into all the spaces left between the rocks and gravel. Once more he asked, "Is the jar full?"

"No," the group shouted.

Again he said, "Good." Then he took a pitcher of water and began to pour it in until the jar was filled to the brim. Then he asked the group, "What is the point?"

One eager young man raised his hand and said, "No matter how full your schedule is, if you try really hard, you can always fit some more things in it."

"Sorry," the speaker replied. "That's not the point. This illustration teaches us that if you don't put the 'big rocks' in first, you'll never get them all in."

So tonight, or in the morning, when you are reflecting on this short story, ask yourself, "What are the 'big rocks' in my life?" Then put those in your jar first.

Organizing Time

Law enforcement officers can easily visualize the time available for each workday and may also plan for the week, but few officers at any level plan beyond a month. Seldom do people think of their law enforcement careers as 40,000 hours. After a career is over, it is a rare law enforcement officer who would not look back and say: "I could have accomplished a lot more."

This chapter presents several ways to organize and plan time. Select the method you like best or devise your own. The system you use does not matter, only that you do something to make your time more productive. The first step is to know how you are actually spending your time.

Time Logs and Lists

time log • a detailed list of how time is spent each day, usually broken into 10- to 15-minute segments.

A **time log** is a detailed list of how you spend your time each day. Keeping time logs and lists will show you how you actually use your time. Maintain such logs and lists only until you see which activities actually fill your work time.

> Keeping a daily log or time list tells you how you really spend your time, as opposed to how you perceive you spend it.

Until goals are established and can be adjusted to the actual daily use of time, a great disparity often exists between what people *think* they do and what

```
                        DAILY USE OF TIME
  DATE _____   RANK OR POSITION _____
  ARRIVAL TIME AT WORK _____
  END TIME _____ TASK PERFORMED _____ EVALUATION
  _____
  _____
  _____
  _____
  _____
  _____
  _____
  _____
  _____
  _____
  _____
  _____
  _____
  _____
  _____

  This is a task chart, not a goals chart.
  List each task in detail.
  Mark down time task ended.
  Continue listing tasks and end time for entire day.
  At end of day, review and evaluate each task as either acceptable or to be delegated,
  lengthened, shortened or eliminated. Notice at the end of the day the time spent on
  tasks that were acceptable or to be delegated.
```

Figure 6.2   Sample Log for Daily Use of Time

they *actually* do. Some time experts suggest that a time log be made once a year for several days to a week. When your job changes, make a new time log.

Four Sample Time-Use Logs The chart in Figure 6.2 asks you to list your starting time for the workday and the ending time of each task you perform. For example, if you start at 8:00 a.m. and your first task is to make a to-do list, which takes 10 minutes, your task ends at 8:10 and you are ready for the next task, which may be returning telephone calls. The difference between the times is the total task time. Figure 6.3 lists goals and objectives without regard to actual time use.

Approximately 50 percent of your time should be spent on priority 1 goals, 40 percent on priority 2 goals and 10 percent on priority 3 goals. Variations of these percentages will occur with levels of manager responsibility. The executive manager may spend 60 to 65 percent of time on priority 1 goals; command or middle-level managers, 40 percent; and first-line supervisors, 30 percent.

Determine actual time use for a designated period (perhaps a week). Then review the list and make decisions regarding delegating, shortening time devoted to certain tasks or eliminating a task. If the manager position should change, keep a new time log.

Later compare the actual time logs with the lists of goals and objectives for the position, and make adjustments to bring both lists into one actual time plan. You will need to make adjustments, but once you have learned to make a time-use plan, making changes will be easy. Figure 6.4 lists time in 15-minute periods. Otherwise, it is the same as Figure 6.2.

DAILY PRIORITIES AND GOAL LIST

A. Most important—Priority 1

1 _____   2 _____
3 _____   4 _____
5 _____   6 _____
7 _____   8 _____

B. Necessary, but less important—Priority 2

1 _____   2 _____
3 _____   4 _____
5 _____   6 _____
7 _____   8 _____

C. Least important—Priority 3

1 _____   2 _____
3 _____   4 _____
5 _____   6 _____
7 _____   8 _____

At the end of the day, compare this list with the time-use log. Think about what you actually did and what your priorities were. Eventually bring the two into one daily work plan.

Figure 6.3   Sample Daily Priorities and Goals List

Figure 6.5 lists only what is considered *unproductive* time, focusing on bad habits. Most people have at least one bad work habit. Many have several. Analyze time logs to identify time wasters.

Law enforcement managers should list their five to ten top time wasters and then make a plan to overcome them. In fact, time wasters could be a training focus or the topic of a staff meeting. Changing bad time habits requires a desire to

---

DAILY USE OF TIME

Time	Activity	Yes	No	Del	Elim
0800–0815	_____	___	___	___	___
0815–0830	_____	___	___	___	___
0830–0845	_____	___	___	___	___
0845–0900	_____	___	___	___	___
0900–0915	_____	___	___	___	___
0915–0930	_____	___	___	___	___
0945–1000	_____	___	___	___	___
1000–1015	_____	___	___	___	___
1015–1030	_____	___	___	___	___
1030–1045	_____	___	___	___	___
1045–1100	_____	___	___	___	___

Continue to record times for your entire workday schedule. Make a chart for your workday using whatever time intervals you desire: 5 minutes, 15 minutes, $1/2$ hour or 1 hour. At the end of the day, decide what tasks were necessary or could be delegated or eliminated. Check the applicable column on the right side of the page for the action you took.

Figure 6.4   Sample Log for Daily Use of Time (in 15-Minute Increments)

```
┌─────────────────────────────────────────────────────────────────┐
│                    UNPRODUCTIVE TIME LOG                          │
│                         Date _____      │
│                                                                   │
│  Task                        Approximate time spent on task       │
│  _____  _____    │
│  _____  _____    │
│  _____  _____    │
│  _____  _____    │
│  _____  _____    │
│  _____  _____    │
│  _____  _____    │
│  _____  _____    │
│  _____  _____    │
│  _____  _____    │
│  _____  _____    │
│  _____  _____    │
│  _____  _____    │
│                                                                   │
│  At the end of the day, determine whether a task should be: (1)   │
│  eliminated from schedule or (2) retained even though             │
│  unproductive because your position requires it to meet public    │
│  demand.                                                          │
│                                                                   │
│  After several weeks review this chart with other charts for the  │
│  2-week period and determine how often the same task occurs. Is   │
│  it daily, weekly, monthly or seasonal, or is there some other    │
│  reason the task falls to your position when perhaps it could     │
│  be performed at another level? Make the necessary adjustments.   │
└─────────────────────────────────────────────────────────────────┘
```

Figure 6.5   Sample Log for Unproductive Time

change. You must put the new habits into daily practice until they are firmly a part of your work routine and continue to practice them until the old habits disappear.

Using the Time Logs A time log gives you an idea of what you do at work, but you do not always know if you make the most productive use of your time. This is especially true of management positions.

Patrol officers promoted to sergeant do not continue to perform the same duties; in departments where sergeants have eight or more patrol officers to manage, sergeants will find that managing the officers is a full-time occupation. In some larger departments sergeants may have up to 25 officers to manage, a severe test for the first-line supervisor. Sergeants need to know how time is actually being used.

Moving up the ladder of command, lieutenants and captains will not perform the same functions they performed as sergeants. Likewise, police executives (chiefs, superintendents or sheriffs) will not perform the same duties as the command level. Each level will find the time log a valuable tool for providing an accurate picture of time use.

Without a time log you do not know where time goes, how much time is spent on what duties and how frequently activities occur. Usually only a small portion of the day is uncommitted, but how is it used? A time log shows where it actually goes. After you make revisions, the time log should match the desired time allotted for specific goals and objectives. You have then achieved effective time management.

After logging your time, ask: What am I doing that I don't really have to do? What am I doing that someone else could do? What am I doing that I could do more efficiently? What activities or events are the biggest time wasters for me? How can I eliminate them? What am I doing that wastes others' time? How can I change? When are my productivity peaks and valleys throughout each day? When do I tackle high-priority projects? How often am I interrupted? Why? Can I control or reduce the number of interruptions?

Your daily log should help you determine when you are at your peak. You can then schedule high-priority work during your peak working hours, and use your low-energy periods for low-priority work such as filing, catching up on reading and returning nonemergency phone calls.

Objections to Time Logs The most common objection to keeping time logs is: "I don't have time." It does take time, but the payoff is worth it. Others claim that time use varies from day to day. Again true, yet patterns do exist. Some say their days are already full.

Some object to putting what they do on paper. In some instances these objections are only excuses to continue with time-wasting habits.

The time log is a tool to help you determine whether a workday is full of the right tasks. If the tasks are wrong for the position, you can delegate, eliminate or otherwise change them. If all the tasks are right and the assigned work schedule is full, you have achieved good time management.

Every manager's time is broken up by diversions, unexpected distractions and interruptions of all types. It is realistic to allocate time for these. Knowing when and how frequently interruptions occur helps you reduce the time you spend on them. Also plan some time during the day for creative thinking about your job.

Controlling Time

The first step in controlling time is to ensure that you are accomplishing the tasks that must get done.

The Daily To-Do List

Although it is not necessary to continuously keep a daily log, it *is* critical to plan each day's time. This is best done the night before. Simply write down everything you should accomplish the following day. Then prioritize the items as follows:

A   Acute or critical—must be done.

B   Big or important—should do when A is finished.

C   Can wait—nice to do if time allows.

D   Delegate.

E   Eliminate.

The military uses a similar approach with the following designations: ! = do ASAP; A = do within the next few days; B = do within the next week; C = do within the next month; and L = long term (anything over a month to complete).

 The daily to-do list may be the single most important time management tool. It helps you manage minute by minute.

If you make a to-do list the night before, you have a jump on the next day. Sleep will come easier, and this in itself can reduce stress and tension. Do not make the list too full. Leave some time for planning and for those unexpected things that inevitably arise.

MacKenzie (1972) also describes five categories for activities:

- Important and urgent (for example, budget due next week)
- Important but not urgent (getting physically fit)
- Urgent but not important (a meeting you are expected to attend—politically important, but not task related)
- Busy work (cleaning files rather than starting on a project)
- Wasted time (sitting in traffic with no audiocassettes or cellular phone)

Of these five categories, the biggest problem is usually the important but not urgent task. Such tasks tend to be put off indefinitely. To integrate long-term tasks into your daily schedule without adding overtime, break it down into small, manageable steps and set interim deadlines on your calendar. Build in a set amount of time each day to work on the project.

Consistently write out your to-do list in one place each day. It does little good to make a list and then to lose it on a cluttered desk.

Scheduling

Morgenstern (2000/2001, pp.94–96) has a somewhat more detailed approach to the to-do list that not only prioritizes the items in the list but also specifies when tasks will be completed and how much time they will take. She uses a SPACE formula for each item on the to-do list: "Space is an acronym that stands for Sort tasks, Purge whatever you can, Assign a time, Containerize the time needed to do the task and Equalize."

To *sort* the tasks, estimate the amount of time each will take. When doing so, keep in mind the "Times Three" rule; that is, it generally takes three times longer to do something than you think. Be realistic. With a realistic time for each task, *purge* the list by determining whether someone else might be able to do the task faster or better. Noncreative, repetitive tasks and special projects can usually be easily delegated. Next *assign a time*; for example, work on a major project from 10:00 am until noon. The trick is to *containerize* the time needed; that is, start and end when you scheduled. Don't procrastinate; don't allow interruptions; and don't let it drag on. Containerizing also helps conquer the need for perfection.

The last step is to *equalize*, refine, maintain and adapt the schedule as needed. As Morgenstern (p.96) notes: "Time management is not a stagnant process. It is a constant interaction between your goals and the changing rhythms and tempos of life."

Time Management (pp.31-32) offers these suggestions for scheduling your time:

- Schedule only part of your day. This is crucial for managers and becomes more important as you move into the higher management echelons. Leave some time open to deal with crises, opportunities, the unexpected and that tried-and-true approach to management, walking around.
- Schedule your highest-priority work first.
- Consolidate tasks such as e-mail, paperwork and phone calls when possible.
- As the week progresses, move uncompleted priority tasks to future open times.

Time Management (p.54) suggests as a rule of thumb to include half the number of things you think you can do in a day and to be exceptionally diligent to keep urgent but unimportant and low-priority tasks off your schedule unless someone in authority requires you to perform them.

The Time Map

Morgenstern (p.92) also suggests that managers make use of time maps: "To make sure you leave enough time for the activities that support your personal big picture, you will need to draw up what I call a time map—a visual diagram of your daily, weekly and monthly schedule. It's a powerful tool. Instead of feeling that you have to act on every request the minute it crosses your path, you can glance at your time map, determine when you have time and schedule it or skip it."

Other Methods of Organizing Time

The Franklin Day Planner is a time-management notebook used by people all over the world and an option for busy law enforcement managers. Another option is to turn your car into a training center and use your driving time to listing to training cassettes or CDs. If you live to be 77 and drive 10,000 miles a year, you'll spend *three years* of your life in your vehicle. Yet another option is to do the least-liked tasks first. It is natural to avoid things you do not want to do. The trouble is, when you waste energy avoiding the bad things, you may lose your ability to get anything else done. One suggestion for predominantly right-brained managers is to jot each task to be accomplished on color-coded notes and stick them around the desk.

Time Management (p.37) cautions: "Schedules and day-planners work well for people whose jobs are highly structured, and less well for people, particularly higher-level managers, whose work is fragmented. People with less structured jobs can make the most of time-management tools by building more free time and flexibility into their schedules."

After you have identified, prioritized and scheduled the necessary tasks, the next step is to find the time to do them by identifying unproductive time.

Time Abusers: Combating Unproductive Time

Managers in law enforcement experience the same unproductive time problems found in other professions. Time abusers tend to develop into time-use monsters if not controlled.

Develop an image of time respect. Managers often contribute to their own demise by trying to solve too many problems for others when they should be solving their own. Some of this time abuse is normal and must be accepted as part of a manager's job. Generally, **time abusers** can be divided into external—generated from outside—and self-generated, or internal.

> **time abusers** • activities or tasks that waste time, for example, socializing, drop-in visitors and telephone tag.

External Time Wasters

Among the most common outside or external time wasters are *interruptions*. Managers are interrupted approximately every eight to ten minutes. Controlling and reducing these interruptions is important not only to save time but also to maintain continuity of thought.

 Among the most common external time abusers are the telephone; the e-mail chime; people who "drop in"; nonessential meetings; socializing; and "firefighting," or handling crises.

The Telephone The telephone offers several advantages. You save time when you make a call instead of traveling. You also have more control over the timing of a telephone conversation than you do over a personal visit.

However, the telephone also heads the list of time wasters. Allowing too many calls, permitting conversations to last too long, failing to screen incoming calls, failing to keep conversations purposeful and allowing calls to interrupt quality creative time can be devastating to productivity. Keep a telephone time log if you find the telephone to be a problem.

Avoid getting caught playing telephone tag. Leave a time to receive calls and find out when individuals you are trying to call will be available. Consider leaving your e-mail address on your voice mail message. This gives you greater control of your time and eliminates small talk. In addition, you can print out your e-mail messages. When making calls, plan what you are going to talk about and stick to the subject. Eliminate as much small talk as possible, using a timer if necessary.

Screen your calls through a secretary, a receptionist, Caller ID or an answering machine that can be monitored. Always answer the phone with paper and pencil in hand. Write down the name of the person who is calling and take careful notes. This will save time later.

Always have your calls held during your most productive, creative times and during important meetings, whether they are one-on-one or in a larger group. One effective time saver is to "batch" your calls. This relates directly to what is known as the learning curve principle.

 The **learning curve principle** states that grouping similar tasks together can reduce the amount of time each takes, sometimes by as much as 80 percent.

learning curve principle • states that grouping similar tasks together can reduce the amount of time each takes, sometimes by as much as 80 percent.

According to the learning curve, each time you repeat the same task, you become more efficient. Telephone calls are one responsibility for which the learning curve can help manage time.

Voice mail can compound the problem, however. Some managers arrive in the morning, check their voice mail, and are greeted with: "You have 37 messages." Not a good way to start the day, but a reality in many departments.

The secret is to reduce the disadvantages of telephones and multiply the advantages. Telephone companies have films you can use or trainers who can meet with your staff and point out the most efficient use of telephones.

The E-Mail Chime The e-mail chime or the message "You've got mail" can also be a distraction. Most type-A personalities cannot hear the chime or message without checking to see who just e-mailed them. *Time Management* (p.52) calls this the Pavlovian e-mail response and suggests that the chime or message be turned off to eliminate this distraction.

Drop-In Visitors Put limits on the visits of people who just stop in without an appointment. Be polite but firm. At times you may need to simply close your door when priorities demand that you have time alone.

Hang a "Privacy, Please" sign on your door during periods when you need uninterrupted time. Arrange specific times when others know your door is "open." Communication is, after all, critical to good management, but it also needs to be managed. Be available to others outside your own office. Then you have greater control over ending a conversation.

Stand up when someone enters your office, and conduct the conversation with both of you standing. Such conversations tend to be brief. Keep socializing to a minimum. Get to the topic that brought the drop-in visitor to your office and stick with that topic. If the person who stops by for a business reason asks, "Got a minute?" consider looking at your watch and saying, "Actually I have exactly five minutes. What can I do for you?" The drop-in will assume you have something important to attend to and will probably respect your time.

If a drop-in visitor stays on, you might try saying, "One more thing before you go . . ." Or you might take the person out in the hall to show him or her something—anything. Of course, you may arrange for a co-worker to interrupt you with an "emergency" if a drop-in visitor stays longer than a specified time.

Be honest. You might simply say, "I've enjoyed our talk, but I really must get *back to work.*" That simple phrase will not only be a clue to the visitor to leave but also will serve as a prompt to you.

 The words *back to work* will prompt you and others to keep on task.

Meetings As much as 50 percent of managers' time may be spent in meetings, and of this, 50 percent of the time is often wasted. Think about the hourly rate of each person attending and be sure the department is getting its money's worth. Wasted time includes not only the time in the meeting but also the time spent winding up a particular task before the meeting, traveling to and from the meeting and then getting back on task.

Organizations might consider designating someone to be a "meeting attender," to go to meetings and make brief written reports. This would create more paperwork but take less time than you attending the meeting. This practice could be useful for informational meetings that do not require the manager's personal participation. Avoid nonessential meetings, and do not call them yourself.

If your sole purpose for attending a meeting is to make a presentation, find out what time the presentation is expected, arrive a few minutes before that time, make the presentation and then excuse yourself. If you find yourself at a nonproductive meeting, it can be most efficient to simply excuse yourself and leave. Use common sense, however, especially if the meeting was called by and is being chaired by your superior.

Socializing Socializing is a factor in inefficient phone calls, encounters with drop-in visitors and meetings. Relationships are very important, and socializing is an important part of relationships. However, socializing should be confined to coffee breaks, lunch, or before and after work. The phrase mentioned earlier, "I've got to get *back to work,*" reminds co-workers that you are not getting paid to socialize.

Political Game Playing Although most managers seek to avoid politics, you cannot avoid a certain amount of political game playing. If the chief wants to talk about the grandchildren, subordinates would be wise to listen. Seek ways, however, to keep such time to a minimum.

"Firefighting": Dealing with Crises Law enforcement managers can expect to confront the unexpected daily. It comes with the job. Allow time in each day for these crises so you can deal with them calmly and rationally. Anticipate what might occur and have policies developed. Is the department likely to receive a bomb threat? To undergo a natural disaster? To be overrun by gang members?

If a crisis occurs for which no policy exists, get the facts, remain objective and think before acting. Then, when time permits, develop a policy for the situation should it arise again.

Internal Time Wasters

Not all time wasters come from the outside. Many are self-imposed or the fault of colleagues.

 Among the most common internal time wasters are drop-in employees, procrastination, failure to set goals and objectives, failure to prioritize, failure to delegate, personal errands, indecision, failure to plan and lack of organization.

Drop-In Employees Being available to employees is an important part of being a supervisor or manager. However, just as drop-in visitors can disrupt a manager's day, so can drop-in employees. Henry Ford, automobile pioneer, made a practice of conferring with managers and employees in their office rather than his own. As he explained: "I've found that I can leave the other fellow's office a lot quicker than I can get him to leave mine" (Fadiman and Bernard, 2000).

Procrastination Procrastination is putting off until tomorrow what has already been put off until today. For some people the greatest labor-saving device is tomorrow. Do not delay things. Get them done. Get right to work on priorities.

procrastination • putting things off.

One reason for procrastination is fear that if you do it, it will be wrong. Set a goal and think only of the goal. So what if you make a mistake? The person who makes no mistakes usually makes nothing at all! Think, "I can do it, and do it now." Motivational speaker Zig Ziglar, author of *See You at the Top*, gives members of his audiences a round piece of wood bearing the word *tuit*. He chides them that they can no longer say they will do something when they get "around to it" because they already have one.

The following techniques might help combat procrastination:

- Start with your most unpleasant task to get it out of the way.
- Set aside half an hour a day to work on a given project—schedule the time to do it.
- Do not worry about doing a task perfectly the first time through.
- Work briskly. Speed up your actions.

Another effective way to avoid procrastination is to set deadlines and let others know about them. If others are counting on you to have a task completed by a specific date, chances are you will do it. Accept 100 percent responsibility for completing tasks on time. Help others to do likewise. Finish tasks. Procrastination is one of your worst enemies.

Although you want to overcome the human tendency to procrastinate, you should learn to practice creative procrastination. Creative procrastination, as discussed in Chapter 5, is putting off those things that do not really matter. If you can put tasks off long enough, they probably will not have to be done. A simple example of this is sending holiday greeting cards. If you really do not feel an urgent need to send them and if you can procrastinate long enough, the holiday will pass and so will the need to send them—at least this year.

Failure to Set Goals and Objectives and to Prioritize Too much of each day is spent by people, managers included, doing very well things they do not need to do at all.

 Effective time managers concentrate on doing the right thing, rather than on doing things right.

The temptation is to clear up all the small things first so the mind is clear for the "big stuff." What often happens is that the whole day is taken up with the small stuff. Or doing the small stuff saps so much energy that little is left for the big stuff. Too many managers become bogged down in routine activities.

How do you differentiate between the trivial many and the significant few—those 20 percent described in the Pareto Principle? Consider how combat triage officers divide the wounded into three groups:

- Those who will die no matter what—make comfortable.
- Those who will live no matter what—give minimal medical attention.
- Those who will survive only with medical attention—focus attention here.

The same can be done within law enforcement agencies. Think of the consequences of what you do. Will accomplishing a given task have a positive payoff? Prevent a negative consequence? What will happen if you *do not* get a specific task done? Clearing away the trivial tasks to leave room for single-minded concentration simply does not work. It has no payoff. *You never get to the bottom of the stack.*

 Effective managers set **priorities**—tasks that they must do, have a big payoff and prevent negative consequences. They also set **posteriorities**—tasks that they do *not* have to do, have a minimal payoff and have very limited negative consequences.

Many managers excel at setting priorities but have no grasp of setting posteriorities. A day has only so many hours. For each new task a manager takes on, one task should be cut out. To continue to take on new responsibilities without delegating or eliminating others is courting disaster—often in the form of burnout.

Effective managers know how to say no. In fact, one of the most potent time management tools is the simple word no. When they cannot say no, effective managers know how to ask for help and to delegate.

Failure to Delegate Many managers think that the only way something will get done right is to do it themselves. Such managers need to ask who did it before me and who will do it after me? The effective manager is one who can be gone for a few days or even weeks and everything continues smoothly during the absence. If you do not learn to delegate, there will never be another person trained to perform the work in times of crisis.

As recommended in Chapter 2, delegate whenever possible. Train subordinates, trust them, set limited and clear expectations, provide the necessary authority for delegated tasks, and give credit when they have completed the task. Delegation gives strength to the delegator and the person delegated to. It is not an abdication of responsibility.

Delegation moves organizational communication downward. Delegation must be based on mutual trust, acceptance and a spirit of cooperation between all parties. In addition, subordinates must be empowered to do the delegated tasks.

Put delegated tasks in writing with set time limits. Keep records and follow through. Do not overdelegate to the same few workers. Delegation helps people develop and spreads responsibility throughout the organization so goals and objectives are more easily attained.

Personal Errands Only in emergencies should personal errands be attended to during on-duty time. It does not leave a good impression to see law enforcement managers on personal errands during working hours.

priorities • tasks that must be done, have a big payoff and prevent negative consequences.

posteriorities • tasks that do not have to be done, have a minimal payoff and have very limited negative consequences.

Indecision Subordinates have a reasonable expectation that managers will make final decisions, especially on high-priority issues. Indecisiveness indicates a lack of self-confidence and is most frequently caused by fear of making a mistake. Approach mistakes as learning experiences; the biggest mistake may be never making a mistake. Understanding the decision-making processes described in Chapter 5 can make this managerial responsibility less threatening.

Failure to Plan The saying goes: "Most people don't plan to fail; they simply fail to plan." Managers must learn to recognize problems and determine their causes, or time will be lost. Working the hardest or doing the most work is not necessarily the best answer if the work you choose is not of value. The average person will spend more time planning a vacation than planning a career.

 The **5P Principle** states: Proper planning prevents poor performance.

5P Principle • proper planning prevents poor performance.

Planning the use of time may save time threefold, perhaps more. If you do not take time to plan to do it right, you may have to find time to do it over.

Lack of Organization Desk signs may *incorrectly* proclaim: "A cluttered desk is the sign of genius." If you cannot see the top of your desk, it is cluttered. Do not get rid of the clutter by putting it in the drawer. Take some action to get rid of it. Out of sight does *not* necessarily mean out of mind. Set aside time once a week to eliminate clutter. Of course, the right-brained reader might be thinking: "If a cluttered desk reflects a cluttered mind, what is an empty desk a sign of?" The following suggestions may help your office organization:

- Keep on your desk only the project you are currently working on.
- Keep reference books organized and in easy reach but off your desk.
- Keep office supplies such as paper clips in your desk.
- Set aside a certain time each day for reading.

In addition to keeping your desk and office organized and neat, keep your projects organized. Use organization charts and flowcharts to graphically portray your goals and objectives, work plans and schedules. Use tickler files to find information faster. Know where and how to find needed information.

A Caution

Remember that people are more important than schedules and plans. Put a priority on people, not on going through that pile on your desk and checking things off a to-do list.

Controlling the Paper Flood and Information Load

Knowledge is doubling every two and one-half years. One issue of the *New York Times* conveys as much information as a person living in the sixteenth century would obtain in a lifetime. The information age places tremendous demands on everyone, especially managers. Managers cannot ignore the paper flood because much of it is information vital to doing an effective job.

 Control the paper flood by using single handling for most items, improving reading skills, delegating or sharing some reading tasks and adding less to the paper flood yourself.

© Shepherd Sherbell/CORBIS SABA

Police administrators must control paperwork or it will control them. Here, a police officer from Fairfax, Virginia, fills out booking paperwork on an arrest.

Managers must control paperwork or it will control them. Law enforcement tasks generate extensive paperwork because of the legal requirement to document information. Reports are a large time problem. The sheer volume of reports makes them not only time consuming to read but also difficult to absorb.

In addition to service and offense-related reports, managers deal with mountains of other printed information. Effective managers have a system for handling everything that lands in their "in" baskets, whether from an internal or external source. One system that works for many includes four categories:

1. Throw it away—opened or unopened depending on the return address.
2. Route it to someone else (delegate).
3. Take action on it.
4. File it for later action or reference.

single handling • not picking up a piece of paper until you are ready to do something with it. Applies particularly to the daily stack of mail.

This system incorporates **single handling,** that is, not picking up a piece of paper until you are ready to *do* something with it.

 Handle paperwork only once—single handling increases efficiency tremendously.

Once printed information is picked up, take action: toss it, pass it on, file it or act on it. The system works best when a specific time is allotted to handle paperwork. Remember the learning curve and the efficiency in "batching" tasks, that is, doing similar tasks at the same time. Single handling also applies to emails. In addition, color coding e-mails helps to visually prioritize what needs to be looked at immediately. E-mails from superiors might be in red. Subfolders might be created to store e-mails relating to the same subject. E-mails can also be grouped by open issues and closed issues. Managers who receive 20, 30 or more e-mails a day need some system to keep their e-mails organized.

Organize the printed information you refer to often. Information that you use every day can be condensed on file cards; put into a Rolodex; added to personal directories, address books and calendars; written on to-do lists; or placed in action files or reference files. Use computer files or microfilm to retain information for long periods in an easily accessible, retrievable form. Prepare master indexes to locate such stored information.

Controlling the paper flood increases your decision-making capabilities, permits planning and lessens the sense of guilt when you do not complete all tasks on schedule. Have a specific place to put everything that comes into your office. Have a working file for frequently used files where they can be reached without leaving your chair.

Another way to control the paper flood is to improve reading efficiency. Learn the difference between **scanning**—reading material rapidly for specific information; **skimming**—reading information rapidly for the main ideas—and actually reading. Scan or skim most reports and publications; read only those of interest and importance. Go through your business reading pile at a quick, even pace, scanning for any time-sensitive material. Assess what you can take in quickly, what you don't need to know and what you need to read in more detail. Read in greater detail the items that are truly worth your attention. Keep and label only the clippings you want filed. Or copy them to read during downtime.

Three behaviors that slow down the reading process are subvocalization, regression and narrow eye span. **Subvocalization** is moving the lips and/or the tongue to form the words being read. Talking speed is 120–180 words per minute, which is also the speed of readers who subvocalize. Such reading needs to be speeded up. Normal reading is about 250 words per minute. Managers need to read 300–500 words per minute. Subvocalization can be stopped by keeping the lips together and placing the tongue against the back of the teeth when reading. This trains the brain to read and understand words without physically forming them.

Regression is looking back over previously read material, which slows normal reading. To eliminate regression, use the hand or finger sweep. As you read left to right, use the finger as a target to follow.

Narrow eye span occurs when a person focuses on one word at a time rather than taking in groups of words and phrases in one look. Adult eye span is between two and three words. To eliminate narrow eye span, search for your name in a magazine or a newspaper. Practice taking two lines at a time as fast as you can and searching back and forth. This is what you do when you look for a name in the phone book. It is necessary to increase not only reading speed but also reading comprehension. This comes only with practice.

Time spent taking a speed-reading course pays huge dividends, because it will enhance your ability to scan information with greater comprehension. As you improve your reading skills, also improve your writing and speaking skills. Use fewer, more precise words.

Delegate reading or divide it among those who are good readers and interested in participating. It is inefficient for several people in the organization to be reading the same outside sources of information. Try having people volunteer to be responsible for a given source, such as *The Police Chief, Law and Order, Law Enforcement News, Police*, national news sources such as *Time* and *Newsweek and* local publications. The person who does the reading can highlight specific items of interest and route them to others within the department. Another way to share the information is to give brief updates at roll call or during regularly scheduled meetings.

scanning • reading material rapidly for specific information.

skimming • reading information rapidly for the main ideas, usually the first and last paragraph, the first sentence of all other paragraphs and the captions of any charts or figures.

subvocalization • the contraction of the tongue and other speech-related organs made during learning to pronounce each letter of the alphabet. Becomes ingrained and can slow down adult readers.

regression • tendency to look back over previously read material.

narrow eye span • occurs when a reader focuses on one word at a time rather than taking in groups of words or phrases in one look.

Increase your computer skills, also. Many books and training sessions on using computers are available. Computers tremendously increase the ability to retrieve and coordinate information.

Use a Palm handheld device, and carry it with you at all times so you can record your thoughts. This is an advantage at meetings, when talking to others (including the media) and in other impromptu situations. It saves time as well as ideas.

Finally, do not add to the problem yourself. Some managers like to create paperwork because it gives a sense of personal power and fulfills a desire to influence others. Resist that impulse. Before you add to the paper flood, consider: Might a phone call work as well as a letter or memo? If you must write, is it as brief as possible? Who *really* needs copies? Can it be routed instead? Do you need copies of reports you are receiving? If not, ask to be taken off the distribution list. When you receive written material, if you foresee no further use for it or it will be available somewhere else, do not file it. Have a good reason for every contribution to the paper flood created, circulated, or filed.

Retaining What You Need to Remember

Some information can be filed and retrieved when needed. Other information, however, should be retained in your mind. Forgetting has been called the relentless foe. Forgetting takes its greatest toll during the first day after learning something. To slow forgetting you must transfer the information from your short-term memory to long-term memory by *doing* something with it. This might include mentally asking yourself a question about something you have read and answering it, verbally summarizing an important concept to a colleague, highlighting the concept or taking notes on an article.

highlighting • using a special pen to graphically mark important written information. Should be done after the initial reading of the information.

Highlighting is the memory method of choice for most college students, and it is an effective way to transfer information from short-term to long-term memory *if* it is done correctly. Unfortunately, most people simply highlight what they want to remember as they read. This is very ineffective and often results in almost the entire article being highlighted. To highlight effectively, read the entire article (or chapter) first. Then ask: "What is most important about what I have just read?" Then go back and highlight *after* you have finished thinking about what you have read. This is a highly effective way to improve retention.

Productivity—The Bottom Line

Effective managers use their time wisely to boost their productivity. Time management and productivity are integrally related. "Work smarter, not harder" is a truism. Simply putting in your time will not make you productive. In fact, the term **face time** has come into vogue in describing the time a person spends coming in early or staying late to impress their superiors. It is the classroom equivalent of "seat time." Sometimes the longer people work, the more tired and unproductive they become.

face time • time spent in the agency or department long after a shift ends and on weekends when not on duty to make sure you are seen putting in extra time by those with the power to promote you.

Overdoing it is not only harmful to your health but often hazardous to the quality of your work.

The most frequent complaint of law enforcement managers is that there are too many interruptions and too many duties and tasks to be performed to accomplish the higher-priority goals of the position. They are unable to control their time to the extent necessary and are constantly operating in a crisis management environment. It is mandatory, however, to establish control not only to accomplish priority tasks but also to make time for creativity, long-term planning and short-term goal innovation; to try new ideas; to accept increased responsibilities; and to make better decisions.

Time is the most important and the scarcest resource managers possess. The organized use of your and all your personnel's time creates a productive department. Control time as you would budget dollars. How you spend time relates to how you can provide more or better law enforcement service. A capable time manager is easily recognized. Time management is one factor that moves employees up the organizational ladder.

With the future probability of fewer rather than more budget dollars, time will become even more important. Because each member of the law enforcement department is interrelated with total department time, the possibility of decreased personnel in ratio to workload will make time an even scarcer resource. This increased demand can be met only by efficient use of available time.

You cannot make time, but you *can* use available time better. Cyril Northcote Parkinson, a British humorist, summed it up neatly in his famous **Parkinson's Law:** "Work expands so as to fill the time available for its completion." Consider posting Parkinson's Law on the bulletin board for a week.

Parkinson's Law • the principle that work expands to fill the time available for its completion.

One simple way to boost your productivity (and that of your people) is to *defragment* your computer. Just as office filing cabinets get out of order from time to time, so do computer filing systems. If your computer seems sluggish, you might want to have your hard drive "defragged." Another simple time-saving method is to pack a lunch rather than going out for lunch every day. (This also saves money.) You might also consider positioning your office out of the traffic flow, reducing the chance of people poking their heads in just to say "hi."

The Physiology of Productivity

Although this chapter has focused on working smarter, not harder, that does not preclude the option to work *faster.* Pacing is a matter of habit. Many people walk slowly, talk slowly, think slowly and write slowly. You can physically take control of time and accomplish tasks within the time you have.

 Speed yourself up. Walk briskly. Talk crisply. Write rapidly.

You can actually save several minutes each day by simply walking, talking, reading and writing faster. Break out of old habits. Show that time is important by making the most of it. High performance has much more to do with perspiration than with inspiration. Speeding up physically will carry over to your mental state. You will be constantly reminded that you have a finite amount of time to accomplish your goals and objectives. However, do not let time rule your life.

 SUMMARY

Time management means planning and organizing time to accomplish your most important goals in the shortest time possible. In fact, time is the greatest management resource available. At the heart of time management are goals—what you want to accomplish. Effective time management uses the Pareto Principle to identify the 20 percent (few) vital tasks that will account for 80 percent of the desired results. It also identifies and places as low priority the 80 percent (many) trivial tasks clamoring for attention.

Keeping a daily schedule tells you what you really do, as opposed to how you perceive that you spend your time. The daily to-do list may be the single most important time-management tool. It helps you manage minute by minute and control time abusers.

Among the most common external time abusers are the telephone; people who "drop in"; nonessential meetings; socializing; and "firefighting," or handling crises. When possible, *batch* tasks that are similar, such as making phone calls, because the learning curve principle states that if you do a group of similar tasks together, you can reduce the time they take, sometimes by as much as 80 percent. In addition, the words *back to work* can prompt you and others to keep on task.

Among the most common internal time wasters are drop-in employees, procrastination, failure to set goals and objectives, failure to prioritize, failure to delegate, personal errands, indecision, failure to plan and lack of organization. Effective time managers concentrate on doing the right thing rather than on doing things right.

Effective managers set priorities—tasks that they must do, have a big payoff and prevent negative consequences. They also set posteriorities—tasks that they do *not* have to do, have a minimal payoff and have very limited negative consequences. The 5P Principle states: Proper planning prevents poor performance. An important part of planning is devising a system to control the paper flood. Practices that you might use are single handling for most items, improving reading skills, delegating or sharing some reading tasks and adding less to the paper flood yourself. Handle paperwork only once—single handling increases efficiency tremendously.

Failure to manage time and ending up overdoing is not only harmful to your health but often is hazardous to the quality of your work. Ways to accomplish more without overdoing include speeding yourself up, walking briskly, talking crisply and reading and writing rapidly. Minute by minute, you *can* manage your time.

 ## CHALLENGE SIX

Sgt. Kelly supervises the Greenfield Police Department's investigative division. Ten investigators report to her. Sgt. Kelly starts each day assigning cases to investigators and reviewing completed cases that investigators have placed in her in-basket. She has high standards of performance and expects high-quality investigations and reports from her detectives. Sgt. Kelly meticulously reads each completed case file and enters the disposition into the department's computerized records system. She returns to the assigned investigator cases not meeting her expectations. She spends several hours each day assigning and reviewing cases and reading reports.

Sgt. Kelly spends a disproportionate amount of time dealing with the reports of two of her investigators. One investigator is new on the job and very inexperienced. His reports are poorly organized and difficult to read. He usually has completed the necessary work but does not communicate it clearly in his reports. The other investigator is experienced but tends to take investigative shortcuts. His reports are well written but very brief and incomplete. Sgt. Kelly suspects he is not making all the contacts necessary to conduct a thorough investigation. The other investigators do an excellent job with their cases, including their reports.

Sgt. Kelly is frustrated that she spends so much time in her office reading cases and does not have time to supervise in the field. She feels bogged down and detached from the community. She inherited the practice of reading all the completed cases and entering the dispositions from her predecessor.

1. Is Sgt. Kelly making best use of her time?

2. How can Sgt. Kelly address the specific needs of the problem investigators?

3. Should Sgt. Kelly stop reviewing cases and trust that her investigators are doing a good job?

4. Is there a more efficient method to review cases that would take less time?

5. Should Sgt. Kelly be entering disposition data into the department's computerized records systems?

6. Sgt. Kelly learned to manage her time from the previous detective supervisor. She respected his supervisory skills and appreciated his mentoring, but she is questioning whether the way he used his time is effective for her. Is it acceptable for her to change the way she uses her time?

DISCUSSION QUESTIONS

1. Do you personally use some type of time list or log? A to-do list? Compare yours with those of others in the class.

2. What is the most unproductive time of your workday?

3. What are your greatest time wasters? Compare yours with those of others in the class.

4. What time-management ideas presented in this chapter seem most workable to you? Least workable? Why?

5. How do you determine whether a meeting is necessary? Plan the agenda of a meeting? Control a meeting?

6. What examples of Parkinson's Law can you cite in your life or experience?

7. How much of your time is used for paperwork, including correspondence, planning, analysis, reading in-house publications and improving yourself?

8. How would you prioritize your work time?

9. How does the discretionary time of police officers working in departments using the community policing philosophy differ from those using a more traditional approach?

10. What examples of the Pareto Principle have you experienced?

REFERENCES

Covey, Stephen R. *The 7 Habits of Highly Effective People.* New York: Simon & Schuster, 1989.

Fadiman, Clifton and Bernard, Andre. *Bartlett's Book of Anecdotes.* New York: Little, Brown and Company, 2000.

MacKenzie, R. Alec. *The Time Trap.* New York: AMACOM, 1972.

Mayer, Jeffrey. "Need to Leverage Your Time?" *Executive Travel*, Autumn 2004, p.24.

Morgenstern, Julie. "Taming the Time Monster." From *Time Management from the Inside Out.* New York: Henry Holt and Company, 2000. Book excerpt in *Forbes Small Business*, December 2000/January 2001, pp.87–96. *Time Management: Increase Your Personal Productivity and Effectiveness.* Boston, MA: Harvard Business School Press, 2005.

BOOK-SPECIFIC WEB SITE

Go to the Management and Supervision in Law Enforcement Web site at www.thomsonedu.com/criminaljustice/bennett for student and instructor resources, including Internet Assignments and Case Studies.

CHAPTER 7

Training and Beyond

The mediocre teacher tells. The good teacher explains.
The superior teacher demonstrates. The great teacher inspires.

William Arthur Ward

DO YOU KNOW?

- How training and educating differ?
- What the manager's single most important objective should be?
- What two areas related to training are most commonly involved in civil lawsuits?
- What are keys to avoid civil liability related to training?
- What three variables affect learning?
- What the three general categories of learners or learning styles are?
- What the key to determining the material to teach and test is? What this is called?
- What three areas training can focus on?
- What principles of learning are important?
- What instructional methods you can use?
- What instructional materials are available?
- What LETN is?
- Who else can assist with training?
- What a POST commission is and what it does?
- Of the training models typically used for recruits, which appears most effective?
- Where on-the-job training can occur?
- What the most common type of on-the-job training for new recruits is?
- What forms of external training there are?
- When training should be done?
- What the training cycle consists of?
- Who benefits from training?
- How the Violent Crime Control and Law Enforcement Act of 1994 affects training?

CAN YOU DEFINE?

andragogy	field training	interval
asynchronous	field training officer	reinforcement
learning	(FTO)	on-the-job training
content validity	Firefighter's Rule	(OJT)
eclecticism	hands-on learning	pedagogy
educating	in-service training	continued

CAN YOU DEFINE? (CONTINUED)

prerequisites	rote learning	training
Q & A	simulation	videoconferencing
rhetorical questions	synchronous	
roll call	learning	

Introduction

In the first three decades of the twentieth century, law enforcement was simple. A cop often relied on physical brawn to keep the peace and political connections to keep the job. Little formal training was required. However, the days of handing officers a badge and a gun and putting them on the street are long gone. The individual most responsible for this change was August Vollmer, who entered law enforcement by accident in 1905 when, at the age of 29, he was elected town marshal in Berkeley, California. He soon moved to the position of chief and inherited a department that was in shambles.

Although Vollmer had little formal education, in 1908 he founded the Berkeley Police School, and by 1930 recruits were receiving more than 300 hours of training. This later became the University of California–Berkeley School of Criminology, providing specialized training and orientation for officers hired to be police officers. He motivated them to train others. Vollmer reached more audiences than any other officer in history. One of his protégés, O. W. Wilson, carried on his efforts to make training a priority for police officers.

Today the importance of training is recognized as a fundamental responsibility of law enforcement managers: "The training function is a critical and significant function of any agency that is concerned about quality, productivity, liability and morale" (Scott, 2005, p.40). Among the benefits of a quality police training program are increased productivity, greater commitment from personnel, reduced lawsuits, more efficient use of resources and better delivery of services (Scott, p.40).

This chapter stresses the need for continuous improvement in police professionalism. It begins by examining the differences between training and educating and then turns to a discussion on the importance of training as a management function, including a look at training philosophy and the two areas related to training most commonly involved in civil lawsuits. This is followed by a description of the learning process, including variables that affect learning and principles of learning, particularly as applied to adults. Next the chapter explores instructional methods and materials and looks at levels of training standards and on-the-job training. The chapter then examines training at the various levels, including how external training is used. In addition to basic certification instruction, a manager must determine ongoing training needs and prioritize subjects to be included. The next discussion emphasizes the importance of ongoing training, the ideal training cycle, evaluation and the benefits of effective training programs. The chapter concludes with a look at the Crime Bill and training, community policing and homeland security.

Training versus Educating

Learning theorists make a distinction between training and educating. Training is often viewed as a lower form of learning, dealing with physical skills, the type of instruction that takes place in vocational schools and on the job in law enforcement agencies. After completing a training session, participants may be awarded a certificate or a license.

Education, in contrast, concerns knowledge and *understanding,* the kind of instruction that occurs in colleges and universities. After completing a specific educational program, participants may be awarded a degree. Some law enforcement agencies pay employees higher salaries if they have attained specific levels of education. Some require a two-year degree, and some states, such as Minnesota and Texas, are considering legislation that would require officers to hold a four-year degree before being hired.

training • generally refers to vocational instruction that takes place on the job and deals with physical skills.

educating • generally refers to academic instruction that takes place in a college, university or seminar-type setting and deals with knowledge and mental skills.

 Training generally refers to vocational instruction that takes place on the job and deals with physical skills. **Educating** generally refers to academic instruction that takes place in a college, university or seminar-type setting and deals with knowledge and understanding.

Using this distinction, a law enforcement agency might train its personnel to shoot firearms and educate them on the laws of deadly force. It might train personnel in high-speed pursuit techniques and educate them on when high-speed pursuit is to be conducted. Usually both training and education are needed, and they often overlap.

Some have suggested that officers should first receive a comprehensive law enforcement education and then be trained in police work, often under the watchful guidance of a field training officer (FTO). This text does not concern itself further with the distinction between training and education. Because the term *training* is most commonly used in law enforcement—for example, organizations have training departments and a budget line item for training—this term is used throughout this text to refer to both training and education.

Training as a Management Function

Training is a major management function. A department's efficiency and effectiveness are directly related to the amount and quality of training it provides. Training ensures that subordinates have the necessary skills to perform well, making the manager's job that much easier. For new recruits, training reduces the time they need to reach an acceptable performance level. Training also tells subordinates that the agency and the manager are interested in their welfare and development.

Training Philosophy

A written statement of training *philosophy* should articulate management's attitude toward training, the extent of resources to devote to it and the training's purpose and expectations. The training philosophy should reflect that managers are essentially assigned to develop personnel, the most expensive portion of the law enforcement budget.

 Developing human resources should be managers' single most important objective.

Included in the training should be a thorough understanding of a department's policies, because everything an officer does is dictated by these policies. Furthermore, the philosophy must be consistent with the state's training requirements and with state and federal law (Nowicki, 2003b, p.40).

Managers must be directly involved in training from determining needs through evaluating the program. The role of law enforcement managers in training depends on the level of the manager. Executive-level managers make the final decisions as to the kind of training program needed and the groups to be involved. Middle-level management usually prepares the training program and helps determine training needs. First-line supervisors determine the needs of their officers and specialized personnel because they are closest to everyday operations.

Training not only improves productivity but also reduces liability. Harvey (2003, p.43) cites the maxim "training is the last item considered on the budget, and the first one that is cut or pillaged." He suggests that with this mindset, the stark reality is that lurking around the corner is a lawsuit for failure to train: "Training is like the old automotive oil filter commercial about preventive maintenance, and paying for it now or later. Often, later is far more expensive when decided in the courtroom."

Training and Civil Liability

Griffith (2005, p.42) cautions: "Being sued is one of the greatest hazards of police work."

 Two areas often involved in civil lawsuits are failure to train and for trainees' injuries sustained during training.

A consequence of inadequate training is seen in *Davis v. Mason County* (1991), a case in which several deputies were found guilty of using unlawful force against several plaintiffs and in which their force training was deemed inadequate. The jury verdict was a judgment of $780,000 for excessive force and the failure to train (Rutledge, 2003, p.96).

Failure-to-Train Litigation The landmark case in failure-to-train suits is *City of Canton, Ohio v. Harris* (1989). Geraldine Harris was arrested by the Canton police and taken to the police station. When they arrived at the station, the officers found her on the floor of the patrol wagon and asked if she needed medical attention. Her reply was incoherent. While inside the station, she fell to the floor twice, so the officers left her there to prevent her from falling again. No medical assistance was provided. She was released to her family, who called an ambulance. She was hospitalized for a week with severe emotional illness and received treatment for a year. She sued the city for failure to provide adequate medical attention while she was in custody. She won, with the Supreme Court ruling that a municipality might be held liable for deliberate indifference for failure to train.

The Supreme Court in *Board of County Commissioners v. Brown* (1997) suggests liability for failure to train *a single officer*. A plaintiff's attorneys may search an individual defendant officer's training records to find some deficiency related to their client's claimed injury and hire an expert to identify these training deficiencies. Lawyers routinely begin their investigation by requesting the training records and evaluations of an officer being civilly sued (Pivetta, 2003, p.28).

Scott (p.42) stresses: "Every police executive should be knowledgeable with regard to the major areas of liability for his or her agency." Undoubtedly, police departments should review high-risk liability incidents and provide adequate training to avoid liability claims being upheld. Among the most common actions and incidents leading to a lawsuit against an officer and agency are officer-involved shootings, any use of force, pursuits, police vehicle accidents, detentions, arrests, searches, SWAT operations and K-9 operations (Griffith, p.46). Other areas of liability concern sexual harassment and discrimination. An area less frequently mentioned in failure-to-train lawsuits is civil rights litigation. Federal courts have found individual liability can attach when a supervisor directs subordinates to violate a person's constitutional rights, if the supervisor knew of and allowed the subordinate's unconstitutional behavior or if the supervisor tolerated past and ongoing misbehavior (Unkelbach, 2005, p.10).

 Keys to avoiding civil liability related to training are to provide first-rate training, to thoroughly document such training and to require thorough reports on any incident that could lead to a lawsuit.

Civil Liability for Injuries Sustained during Training Stone and Berger (2004, p.24) state clearly: "Police trainers cannot be held civilly liable for trainees' injuries during training." This exemption is based on "well-settled and familiar" legal defenses known as the *Firefighter's Rule* and *assumption of risk* (p.25). In essence, the **Firefighter's Rule** states that a person who negligently starts a fire is not liable to a firefighter injured while responding to the fire. Stone and Berger (p.26) point out that this rule has long been fully applicable to police officers if an officer is injured confronting a risk or conduct that occasioned his or her response or presence. The *assumption of risk* defense bars liability if a person is injured as a result of the normal dangers associated with an activity a person voluntarily engages in, for example, extreme sports.

> **Firefighter's Rule** • states that a person who negligently starts a fire is not liable to a firefighter injured while responding to the fire.

Martinelli (2004) describes an experience in which he and his associates prevailed as defendants in a lawsuit alleging "negligence in training" and "assault" for injuries incurred while attending an Unarmed Defensive Tactics (UDT) training course. "The 'Martinelli Decision' gives training providers, agencies and insurance carriers with important legal confirmation that law enforcement is a risky business and those who chose public safety as careers are enjoined in the ancillary and associated risks" (*Hamilton v. Martinelli & Associates* [2003]).

That training is essential for the safe and effective dispatch of police services is clear and uncomplicated. What is less explicit, however, is how such training should be structured and presented so as to be of most benefit to those seeking to learn from it.

Variables Affecting Learning

Research on how people learn most effectively suggests that three variables are critical.

 Three variables affect learning:

- Individual variables
- Task or information variables
- Environmental/instructional variables

Individual Variables

The first consideration is who the learner is. Among the important individual variables are the learner's age, sex, maturation, readiness, innate ability, level of

Table 7.1   Four Generations Compared

Generation	When Born	AKA	Defining Characteristics	Learning Preferences	Why Attracted to Career in Law Enforcement?
Generation Y	Between 1979/1980 and the late 20th century	Nexters, Echo Boomers, Net Generation	Used to being connected to the world by the Internet. Talk shows are a staple. Multiculturalism is expected. Self-confident, friendly, optimistic. Strong sense of civic duty and morality and are high achievers. Have seen first-hand horrors of school violence, Oklahoma City bombing.	Prefer group activities and use of technology in learning. Prefer to work collectively.	Attracted to law enforcement by civic contribution, availability of training opportunities, freedom and flexibility of not being tied to a desk, chances for teamwork and mentoring.
Generation X	Between the early 1960s and late 1970s	Baby Bust, Lost Generation	Latchkey kids, often from single-parent families who grew up with MTV and computers. Raised with technology. Believe hard work is the key to success. Value education. Defining events: fall of the Berlin Wall and AIDS.	Like question and answer sessions. Enjoy games and activities. Seek creative, challenging options. Trainer must earn their respect.	Seek competitive salaries, excellent benefits to assist their families, a steady shift assignment, more time off, and a structured career path.
Baby Boomers	Between the end of WWII and the early 1960s		Grew up in front of the TV. Optimistic and involved. Driven, soul-searching. Strong work ethic. Either love or hate authority figures. May exhibit a "know-it-all" attitude. Do have much experience. Defining events include Vietnam, Civil Rights Movement, Cold War, Space Race, Women's Liberation Movement and assassinations of Martin Luther King, Jr. and two Kennedy brothers.	Like problem solving in a nonauthoritarian environment.	
Veterans	Roughly between the ends of WWI and II	Traditionalists	Defined by the Great Depression, WWII, the Korean Conflict and labor unions. High degree of patriotism and reverence to the family. Raised in the age of radio and the Golden Age of Film. Dedicated, hard-working conformists. Conservative. Respect authority and adhere to rules. Often sought as mentors.	Enjoy stress-free, unhurried learning environment. Respond best to experienced instructors. Some are computer-phobic.	

Source: Data from Karen Less. "The Intergenerational Classroom in Law Enforcement Training." *The Law Enforcement Trainer,* May/June 2002, pp.20–24.

motivation, personality and personal objectives. The astute supervisor will be knowledgeable about each factor in each subordinate. Questions to ask regarding individual learners include: What is the officer's current skill level? What has the officer already learned? How far, realistically, can one expect this officer to progress in a given time? How motivated is this officer?

The typical law enforcement agency now has four distinct generations, each with its own individual defining characteristics, motivations, expectations and learning preferences. Table 7.1 summarizes the characteristics of these four generations.

A characteristic of Generation Y that significantly affects training is that it has been "left behind in the educational race," as Colaprete (2003, p.14) reports: "Almost half of all Americans between the ages of 21 and 25 lack basic literacy skills and are unable to balance a checkbook or read a map." He notes that most

Boomers and many Generation Xers are near retirement age and that Generation Yers now permeate the profession as officers, supervisors, soon-to-be administrators and trainers.

Supervisors have limited control over individual variables, but they must be sensitive to their importance. They must also be careful of stereotyping individuals. The information in this section is meant to provide only a guide.

Learning Styles People's preferred way of learning can differ.

 The three general categories of learners, or demonstration learning styles, are visual, auditory and kinesthetic.

Visual learners learn best through seeing. They like to read and take notes. They appreciate handouts. Auditory learners learn best through lecture. They feel the need to speak and welcome classroom discussion. Kinesthetic learners want to apply what they are learning, to take a hands-on approach to learning. They appreciate role playing, scenarios and simulations.

Adult Learners Research and common sense suggest that adults learn differently from children, differences delineated in the concepts of andragogy and pedagogy. Knowles (1970) set forth the idea that **andragogy,** the art and science of helping adults learn, is vastly different from **pedagogy,** the science of helping children learn. Adults are not grown children; they learn differently. Because of more advanced cognitive abilities, adults should not be given the "right" answer to a given problem but rather encouraged to think through a problem and to develop an appropriate response.

The principles of adult learning should be considered in training programs: "Adults differ distinctly in terms of such factors as motivation, interest, values, attitudes, physical and mental abilities, and learning histories" (Kennedy, 2003, p.1). Adult learners have a different self-image, more life experiences, fear of failure, greater expectation of immediately using the learning, diminished speed and retention of learning and some basic physical differences (Kennedy, p.1).

andragogy • the art and science of helping adults learn.

pedagogy • the science of helping children learn.

Task or Information Variables

Task or *information variables* relate to *what* is to be learned. This might involve knowledge, skills or attitudes.

The basic curriculum for recruits must be valid and job related. The first step in validation is to conduct a job analysis defining both the tasks that constitute the job and the knowledge, skills and abilities an individual must possess to perform the job effectively. To establish **content validity,** the direct relationship between tasks performed on the job, the curriculum and the test must be established.

content validity • the direct relationship between tasks performed on the job, the curriculum or training and the test.

 Job analysis is the key to determining the content to teach and test. When content relates directly to the tasks to be performed, it is considered valid. Tests that measure competence in these tasks are then also valid.

The next step is translating worker requirements into training/learning objectives. The result of these efforts is that police recruits are exposed to a curriculum that truly prepares them for a law enforcement career.

 Training can focus on knowledge, skills or attitudes.

Knowledge is often equated with book learning, theory and education and includes facts, ideas and information. This is referred to as the cognitive approach. The steps involved in loading and firing a gun or in obtaining information and then writing a report are usually first presented as facts—information. Officers are expected to apply most of the knowledge presented to them.

Skills generally involve applying knowledge. This is referred to as the behavioral approach. Skills may be technical or motor skills, such as firing a gun, or conceptual skills, such as actually writing a good report.

Attitudes are the most difficult to deal with through formal training. They are influenced primarily by the positive and negative examples set by managers, supervisors and others in the department. Officers may learn in training sessions that stress is a hazard of law enforcement work and that pessimism and cynicism are other occupational hazards. They may feel they are immune to stress, just as they may think they are immune to getting shot. This "it can never happen to me" syndrome so frequently attributed to law enforcement officers is not effectively dealt with through knowledge-centered training sessions.

Relevant questions about task or information variables include: How meaningful is the task or information? How difficult is it? How similar is it to tasks and information already mastered? How pleasant or unpleasant is the task? How is the instruction organized or presented?

Supervisors have great influence over this variable because they can try to ensure that the task or information being taught is seen as relevant, practical and indeed essential. Probably the most important variable, however, is the last one: how the instruction is organized or presented.

Environmental/Instructional Variables

Environmental/instructional variables refer to the *context* in which the training is provided. Common sense suggests that officers will learn better in a comfortable setting where they can see and hear what is happening and distractions are limited. The training environment should provide ample space and lighting, or low or no lighting if dealing with a nighttime issue; afford comfort and safety; be distraction free; and present an atmosphere where students can succeed (Cope, 2003, p.10).

Involving students in training is more difficult and time consuming and requires more teaching skill, creativity and a greater depth of instructor knowledge. However, it is widely accepted that application is an integral part of the training process. People learn by doing. Practical applications might include case studies and role playing, small-group activities, field trips and individual student performances (discussed shortly).

Common sense also suggests that the more practice officers get with a given task, the more proficient they will become. A critical factor is that they are practicing correctly. All too often practice does *not* make perfect; it makes an incorrectly practiced procedure *permanent* and therefore counterproductive.

Knowledge of results, or feedback, also greatly enhances learning. Feedback motivates and helps ensure that the correct learning has occurred. Incentives may be related to staying alive, becoming an exemplary officer, promotions, pay raises, threats or any number of factors. Chapter 9 deals with incentives and motivation.

Implications

Given the variables affecting learning, the bottom line is: *There is no one best way to instruct.* The most effective instruction is adapted to the individual officers; the specific knowledge, skill or attitude being taught; and the setting in which the training occurs.

Principles of Learning

As discussed, officers will exhibit a variety of learning styles. Several principles of learning have been stated or implied in the preceding discussion. They are summarized as follows:

 Principles of Learning:

- ■ Base training on an identified need.
- ■ Tell officers the learning objective.
- ■ Tell officers why they need to learn the material.
- ■ Make sure officers have the necessary background to master the skill (the **prerequisites**). Provide a way to acquire the prerequisites.
- ■ Present the material using the most appropriate materials and methods available. When possible, use variety.
- ■ Adapt the materials and methods to individual officers' needs.
- ■ Allow officers to be as active and involved as possible.
- ■ Engage as many senses as possible.
- ■ Break complex tasks into simple, easy-to-understand steps.
- ■ Use repetition and practice to enhance remembering.
- ■ Give officers periodic feedback on their performance.
- ■ Whenever possible, present the "big picture." Teach an understandable concept rather than relying on simple memorization or **rote learning.**

prerequisites • necessary background needed to master a given skill.

rote learning • memorization, not necessarily with understanding.

Familiarity with the basic principles of learning will help trainers express key concepts more effectively and enable trainees to absorb such concepts more fully.

Effective Trainers

"Great training leaders are clear about their expectations and are enthusiastic about communicating them" (Bell and Bell, 2003, p.56). Van Brocklin (2005, p.17) asserts: "Great trainers aren't necessarily the best spoken, the highest educated, the smartest or the smoothest, but they all have one thing in common—passion." She (p.18) recounts the oft-cited study by Albert Morabian at UCLA that concluded communication consists of 7 percent *what* we say, 38 percent *how* we say it (tone of voice, pitch, and the like) and 55 percent the *nonverbal stuff* (body language, gestures and demeanor).

Trainers must stay up to date on the ever-changing nature of law enforcement (Danaher, 2005, p.54). In addition, effective trainers follow the tenets of adult learning, delivering blended training covering the most prevalent learning styles, including cognitive, psychomotor and affective learning (Borrello, 2004, p.15). Dwyer and Laufersweiler-Dwyer (2004, p.24) recommend that trainers use recruits' experiences and involve them in setting their own educational objectives.

Learning is not a spectator sport, and effective trainers use active learning techniques with trainees. Effective trainers also give feedback promptly—knowing what you know and do not know sharpens learning. They also emphasize time on task and communicate high expectations. The more you expect, the more you will get. Finally, trainers must respect diverse talents and ways of learning.

Having looked at basic principles of effective training, next consider some common mistakes trainers make and some unsafe teaching styles and practices.

Training Pitfalls

The most common training mistakes include:

- Ignoring individual differences, expecting everyone to learn at the same pace.
- Going too fast.
- Giving too much at one time.
- Using tricks and gimmicks that serve no instructional purpose.
- Getting too fancy.
- Lecturing without showing.
- Being impatient.
- Not setting expectations or setting them too high.
- Creating stress, often through competition.
- Delegating training responsibilities without making sure the person assigned the task is qualified.
- Assuming that because something was assigned or presented, it was learned.
- Fearing subordinates' progress and success.
- Embarrassing trainees in front of others.
- Relying too heavily on "war stories."

Unsafe Teaching Styles and Practices

According to Murray (2005a, p.45): "The vast majority of training-related injuries and deaths can be attributed to a handful of unsafe teaching styles or practices in reality-based training:

- Uncontrolled experimentation
- Uneducated practice
- Play, disrespectful participation or frivolous activity
- Unsupervised and/or unorganized/disorganized role play
- Unqualified coaching
- Compressed training—cutting corners
- Honor system or lax safety protocols
- Student overload."

Rushing through training and taking shortcuts wastes the department's time and money and can place officers' lives in danger. The process of turning a fresh recruit into a competent officer must follow a logical course, often conceptualized as a learning curve.

The Learning Curve

Students and instructors should be familiar with the four stages of the learning curve (Cohen, 2004, p.2):

- Stage 1: Unconscious incompetence. This is the beginner who knows nothing, a new recruit.

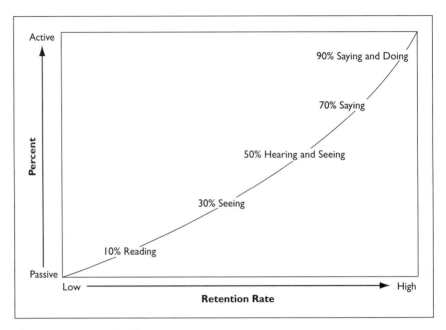

Figure 7.1 Retention Curve

- Stage 2: Conscious incompetence. With proper instruction and leadership, recruits realize the need to improve and to expand their skill or expertise.
- Stage 3: Conscious competence. Recruits now know what to do and how to do it, but have to think about it, which is fine for incidents with no stress.
- Stage 4: Unconscious competence. Recruits are in ready combat mode, the goal of defensive training. Recruits run on auto-pilot, with the unconscious mind taking over.

Many areas of training require this final level of competence, but of particular importance are situations involving officer safety: "It is naïve to believe that being able to demonstrate specific techniques in a training or evaluation setting (such as black belt grading) is the same as performing set techniques in a pressure situation" (Redenbach, 2005, p.67). This is where reality-based training (RBT) comes in. RBT for stressful situations has to be repeated so the response becomes automatic when a threat situation occurs (Mills-Senn, 2005a, p.45).

Retention

People retain 10 percent of what they read, 20 percent of what they hear, 30 percent of what they see, 40 percent of what they see and hear, 60 percent of what they discuss with others, 70 percent of what they experience personally, 80 percent of what they discover and solve individually or in groups and 95 percent of what they teach to someone else (Della, 2004, p.7). Figure 7.1 illustrates the correlation between various modes of learning and the percentage of information retained.

A key learning principle regarding retention is that of interval reinforcement. **Interval reinforcement** means presenting information several times, perhaps as follows:

interval reinforcement • presenting information several times, with breaks between the repetition.

First time: During the introduction of a lecture
Second time: In the middle of the lecture
Third time: At the end of the lecture in a summary or review
Fourth time: In a quiz a few days later, perhaps at roll call

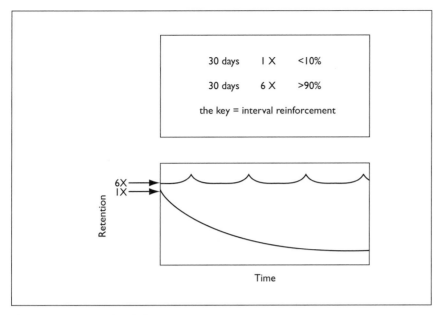

Figure 7.2   Interval Reinforcement

Source: Robert W. Pike. *Creative Training Techniques Handbook.* Minneapolis, MN: Lakewood Books, 1989, p.15. Used with permission of Robert W. Pike, President, Creative Training Techniques International, Inc., Eden Prairie, MN.

Fifth time:	During a review session a week later
Sixth time:	In an application of the information

Notice that the information is repeated with intervals between the repetitions. Studies have shown that if learners are presented information once, they remember only 10 percent after 30 days. If, on the other hand, they are exposed to the same information six times, they remember 90 percent after 30 days (Figure 7.2).

The *Law of Primacy* states that things learned first are usually *learned best*. The *Law of Recency* states that things learned last are *remembered best*. The implication is that key concepts should be presented early in the training and summarized at the conclusion of the training. These principles have a direct bearing on the instructional methods and materials used during training.

Instructional Methods

Many training methods are available. Which to select depends on the time available, the kind and amount of training needed, how many officers need to be trained and the cost.

 Instructional methods include lecture, question/answer sessions, discussion, videoconferencing, demonstration, hands-on learning, role playing, case studies and simulations.

Lecture

Lecture, direct oral presentation, is the traditional way to instruct. It is efficient, can be used with large numbers of people, is cost effective and is well suited to conveying large amounts of information. Because one instructor can reach a large number of students, lectures can reduce the cost of instruction—a relevant consideration for budget-conscious training departments.

Unfortunately, lecture is sometimes overused and sometimes abused. It can be boring and completely ineffective if skills are to be taught. Among the disadvantages of lectures are that they are passive and they cannot meet the needs of both fast and slow learners. A primary disadvantage of lecture is that it does not allow for learner participation. In addition, lecture does not provide the lecturer/trainer with feedback on how thoroughly learners are acquiring the desired information. Given these shortcomings, lectures should be short and supplemented with as many visual aids as possible.

Guided lectures enable students to assimilate more material while enhancing their note taking. Provide the lecture objectives before the lecture; then encourage students to put their pens down. Use the first half of the class time to deliver the lecture, and then ask students to briefly jot down as much material as they can recall. Next, place students into small groups and have them reconstruct the lecture based on their own notes. The cooperative interaction not only generates enjoyable discussion but provides students with notes that are superior to those produced individually.

Question/Answer Sessions

Q & A • question and answer method of teaching.

Question/answer sessions, or **Q & A** sessions, are of two basic types: Learners ask the instructor questions or the instructor asks the learners questions. Some lecturers will invite listeners to interrupt with questions that come to mind during the lecture. This is usually an effective way to break the monotony of a lecture, and it is usually the most appropriate place for the information. Other lecturers ask that listeners hold their questions until the end to make certain they cover all the information. The disadvantages of this approach are that people often forget their questions, the questions seem irrelevant later in the lecture or people are in a hurry to leave.

Another approach to using questions is for the instructor to ask the students questions, which helps keep the students awake and alert and provides feedback to both instructor and students. Trainers have three basic types of questions: factual, rhetorical or opinion based. *Factual questions* test students' grasp of the concepts presented, reinforcing learning through repetition. A factual question would be: "What are the elements of first-degree murder?" Instructors can move from factual questions that test *recall* to higher levels systematically: Test *knowledge* by asking "How are . . .?" Call for an *application*: "How could aspects of . . .?" Ask for *analysis*: "Why . . .?" Ask for *synthesis*: "If you had unlimited resources, what . . .?"

rhetorical questions • those to which answers are not expected. The purpose is to get the listener thinking about a topic.

Rhetorical questions are those to which an answer is not expected, asked to get the listener thinking about a topic. For example, "What are we doing here?" The questioner does not expect an answer because it would be only speculation until more information is provided.

Opinion-based questions get students to share their personal feelings about a topic. There are no right or wrong answers, but some are more plausible than others. For example, "What type of weapon is most effective for law enforcement officers to carry?" The resulting interchange of opinions, perhaps even arguments, could lead to another instructional method—discussion.

Discussion

Discussion is "an interactive training approach in which the participants generate much of the information and ideas" and the trainer serves as a facilitator and guide (Sullivan, 2003, p.22). The best discussions involve no more than 15 participants (Sullivan, p.23). Discussions allow learners to be active participants and are usually motivating. Effective discussions do not just happen. They require a skilled leader, usually the supervisor or trainer, to guide the discussion, keep it on track, control the amount of time devoted to each topic, ensure balanced participation by learners and summarize the key points at the end.

Law enforcement incident reviews of how specific cases were handled make excellent topics for discussion. The strengths and weaknesses of the cases can be identified and discussed, as can other approaches that might have been equally or more effective.

Videoconferencing

Videoconferencing is simultaneous, interactive audio and video communication. Although videoconferencing has advantages, the cost of purchasing the equipment is substantial, and lengthy booking dates may be required for a multipoint hookup. Other ways training can take place from a distance include computer-based training (CBT); satellite training and teleconferencing; simulators; electronic bulletin boards (EBBs); and online computer forums, discussed later in the chapter.

videoconferencing • simultaneous, interactive audio and video communication.

Demonstration

Many skills can be taught most effectively through *modeling* or *demonstrating* how to do something, such as how to give CPR, handcuff a suspect or frisk someone. An effective demonstration has the following characteristics:

- Everyone can see the demonstration.
- Each step is explained as it is slowly done.
- The purpose of the step is also explained.
- Questions are allowed along the way.
- Hazards or problems to anticipate are noted.

The demonstration is repeated at normal speed as many times as needed until everyone understands.

Hands-On Learning

Often, after a demonstration, learners are asked to do the procedure that was demonstrated. **Hands-on learning,** or actually doing what is required on the job, is an ideal form of training. It motivates learners and transfers to the real world. Whenever possible, theoretical information should be followed by some kind of actual performance.

hands-on learning • learning by doing.

Recalling the retention curve, people retain 10 percent of what they read compared with 90 percent of what they say and do. Sometimes, however, the real thing is not possible. In such instances role playing can be very useful.

Role Playing

As the name implies, role playing casts people into specific parts to act out. For example, one student might take the role of an arresting officer and another that of the person being arrested. Sometimes specific scripts are provided. Other times, just the general situation is described. Role playing is one of the most frequently used training tools, with recent surveys showing more than 80 percent of law enforcement agencies using some form of role playing in their training (Van Hasslet and Romano,

2004, p.12). It has become a "mainstay" in crisis negotiation skills training and evaluation. Role playing gives officers opportunities to improve communication skills, practice strategies and increase their chances of success (Maher, 2004, p.12).

In role playing the actors learn from doing and from class criticism. The watchers learn from what they see and from finding strengths and weaknesses in the performance. Role playing is especially useful in making officers more sensitive to how others feel and how their behavior affects others.

Case Studies and Scenario-Based Training

A *case study* is a detailed analysis of a specific incident used to instruct. It is a printed description of an atypical emergency or adversarial event that could occur within the trainees' normal workday, typically followed by a series of discussion points (Fuller, 2004b, p.44).

Scenario-based training is well-suited for senior and special courses, especially for criminal investigations. For example, scenario-based training can be used for interior and exterior crime scenes, for conducting interviews of suspects on videotape, for homicide and sexual assault investigations data entries and for drafting search warrants based on a crime scene scenario (Barath and Lenehan, 2005, p.26).

Simulations

simulation • imitation of a process.

A **simulation** or imitation of a process is yet another effective means of training. Simulation training has been used by law enforcement since the 1950s and includes such areas as driving, handcuffing and take downs, to name just a few of more than 50 types of simulation training now considered "indispensable" (Pivetta, p.25). Mills-Senn (2005b, p.50) contends: "Training in reality-based situations is critical to officer safety in the field." Simulations are devised to immerse participants in life-like events to elicit probable responses.

Training simulators have come a long way and continue to "push the envelope with new technological advances" (Hamilton, 2004, p.24). Current technology brings increasingly interactive simulation to driving, crisis resolution and force options (Bollig, 2004, p.7).

Judgment evaluation simulators can provide real-world critical incident experience (Oberlander, 2004, p.31). However, Messina (2005, p.29) calls attention to the fine line between realism and safety and notes that the adage that "under stress an officer will do what they are trained to do" is not quite right. He suggests a more accurate statement would be that "under stress, an officer will do what they are trained to do under stress."

Simulation is a valuable tool but never a replacement for good instruction (Bollig, p.9). "A skilled and dedicated trainer can make the difference between life and death for an officer who, within seconds, has to make a critical decision with permanent results" (Oberlander, p.33). Murray (2005b, p.70) cautions that simulations are a dual-edged sword that, used properly and appropriately, can be powerful training tools, but used improperly or inappropriately, can program officer behaviors that are unlikely to win a confrontation on the street.

Digital Game–Based Learning

Rogers (2004, p.116) describes digital game–based learning technology as a vehicle to immerse students into "simulated, real-time, slice-of-life, full-motion video learning scenarios." Says Rogers (p.116): "Through digital game-based learning

New multimedia technology is used in the continued training of law enforcement officers. Here one officer takes target practice using a simulator while another officer operates the computer to conduct the exercise.

students will actually step into a virtual reality situation." This allows experiential learning in the safety of cyberspace. It is most effective in areas that might be dangerous, costly or catastrophic if actually reenacted. In effect, it allows officers to "play it out before they live it out."

Combination

Usually a combination of instructional methods works best. The methods selected will depend on what is being taught. Colaprete (p.16) advocates taking an eclectic approach to training and defines **eclecticism** as the blending of the best teaching approaches to meet students' needs. Ninety percent of students would transfer new skills into use if theory, demonstration, practice, feedback and ongoing coaching were provided (Colaprete, p.16).

eclecticism • the blending of the best teaching approaches to meet students' needs.

Individual, Group or Entire Agency

Instructional methods also include whether the training should be individual, group or entire agency. Such decisions are based on similarities of officer behavior and schedules.

The individual, mentor, coach or field training officer (FTO) approach is a tradition within most local agencies and has been considered effective. Clearly, individual training is important and can be highly motivating. It is also very costly.

Group training has the advantage of giving everyone in the group the same basic knowledge and approach. Law enforcement officers must often rely on each other, sometimes without time or opportunity to discuss what action to take. Group training is more likely to produce the expected unspoken reaction. If each group member is trained to perform a specific way in a specific set of circumstances, officer safety is greatly enhanced. Group training is also more cost effective than individual training.

Some topics are important for everyone within the agency. In such instances training must be arranged to cover all shifts.

In addition to being familiar with instructional methods, trainers also need to know what instructional materials they might use.

Instructional Materials

 Instructional materials include printed information; visuals; bulletin boards; audiocassettes, videocassettes and DVDs; television programs; and computer programs.

Printed Information

Printed materials are by far the most common and most widely used. New recruits may receive a department policy and procedure manual to memorize. New policies and procedures are distributed in print, department-wide, for all employees to learn. When new equipment is purchased, instruction books frequently accompany it. When employees enroll in more formal training programs, they may have texts to read.

In addition, professional organizations have training materials on a wide variety of topics, as do other professional law enforcement institutions throughout the country. Self-study, correspondence courses or tutorial courses are also available to help officers learn information at their own rate and convenience.

Training bulletins are ideal for low-cost training on many subjects. One authoritative source of such bulletins is the International Association of Chiefs of Police (IACP), whose bulletins cover all aspects of law enforcement work at all levels. They are inexpensive and can be tailored to local department needs.

Printed materials are uniform, flexible and inexpensive. They also have disadvantages, however. They tend to be impersonal and can be boring.

Visuals

Appropriate visuals can enhance learning and help reduce barriers of time, space and language. Visuals are usually divided into two types: projected and nonprojected. Projected visuals include computer graphics, films, filmstrips, overheads, slides, videotapes and PowerPoint presentations. Nonprojected visuals include chalkboards, charts, diagrams, flipcharts, graphs, maps and models.

A picture is much more effective than words alone, and words and pictures together are even more effective. One reason visuals are so powerful is they fill a gap between the rate of speaking and listening, as Figure 7.3 illustrates.

Bulletin Boards

Bulletin boards can be effectively used for instruction. The key is to have someone responsible for maintaining the bulletin board and to have a long-range plan for what is to be presented each week or month. The bulletin board should be attractively arranged, be uncluttered and contain only up-to-date material. Each item posted on the board should have a removal date clearly marked in a uniform position.

Bulletin boards should be in a well-traveled area and continually update the training officers have received as well as inform them of available training courses. A separate bulletin board should be used for noneducational purposes,

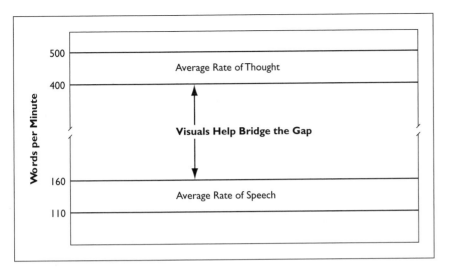

Figure 7.3 The Power of Visuals

Source: Robert W. Pike. *Creative Training Techniques Handbook*. Minneapolis, MN: Lakewood Books, 1989, p.34. Used with permission of Robert W. Pike, President, Creative Training Techniques International, Inc., Eden Prairie, MN.

for example, for department members wanting to sell used guns, cars or furniture, as well as for jokes, cartoons and announcements.

Audiocassettes, Videocassettes and DVDs

Audiocassettes, videocassettes and DVDs are becoming increasingly popular and affordable instructional media. Videos and DVDs offer a wealth of opportunity to learn new skills from instructors who may not be available locally (Kelly, 2004, p.40). They have the same advantages of printed material in that they allow for individual pacing and convenience of timing, but they have a further advantage in that many officers learn more easily from this method than from the more passive activity of reading. In addition, officers can listen to instructional tapes while on patrol or during quiet shifts.

Departments might want to build a library of audiocassettes, videocassettes and DVDs on relevant topics. The library might even include simulations and games that provide practice in problem solving and decision making as well as in manual dexterity.

Television Programs

Educational television has much to offer on general topics such as communication skills, dealing with people and cultural awareness. It is often also educational to watch popular cop shows to see the image of policing the public is watching.

 The Law Enforcement Television Network (LETN) is a private satellite television system that provides current programs on a variety of law enforcement subjects; it is available through subscription.

LETN programming is planned to reach each shift with identical information, providing uniformity of training. It is difficult if not impossible for local departments to provide training on each shift unless the shift managers or supervisors do the training. This usually means it is not presented the same way to each shift.

Computer Programs

Learners using computer programs are more active than when simply reading, listening to or viewing materials. The programs allow learners to proceed at their own pace, and most provide immediate feedback on the accuracy of responses. Many programs allow learners to skip material they can show they already know.

Other Training Options

 Other organizations available to assist with training include the American Society of Law Enforcement Trainers (ASLET), the National Association of Field Training Officers (NAFTO), the Federal Law Enforcement Training Center (FLETC), the National Center for State and Local Training, the FBI National Academy and the FBI.

The American Society of Law Enforcement Trainers (ASLET), founded in 1987, has approximately 2,500 members. The National Association of Field Training Officers (NAFTO) was chartered in 1991 to advance the interests of field training officers in all areas of criminal justice.

The Federal Law Enforcement Training Center (FLETC) seeks to provide high-quality, state-of-the-art law enforcement training for a broad spectrum of participating agencies in a cooperative, interagency manner. The Office of State and Local Training (OSL), a component of the Federal Law Enforcement Training Center, was established in 1982 to provide training in advanced topics and develop specialized law enforcement skills.

A major training program is the FBI National Police Academy. The FBI sustains all costs for sessions. The Academy started in 1935 and is located on the U.S. Marine Base at Quantico, Virginia. The Academy lasts 11 weeks and is offered four times a year. Each session includes 250 selected personnel. In addition, the FBI holds schools ranging from one hour to three weeks for local and state law enforcement officers. According to Stockton (2005, p.67): "Graduation from this prestigious institution is recognized throughout the world as indicative of a high-quality education for a law enforcement administrator."

Departments can also use local resources such as health professionals for training on stress, AIDS and the like; English teachers for assistance in report writing; and local attorneys for updates on new laws. The Federal Emergency Management Agency (FEMA) can provide courses on terrorism, disaster response and similar topics.

Training Standards

Standards for police training, how much is needed and what it should consist of, have been controversial since the early 1800s when Peel set forth his principles of reform. Compared with other professions, law enforcement does not require extensive formal training. Attorneys receive more than 9,000 hours of instruction and doctors receive more than 11,000 hours. Officers receive 400 to 800 hours.

In 1967 the President's Commission on Law Enforcement and the Administration of Justice recommended that Peace Officer Standards and Training (POST) commissions be established in every state. These boards were to set mandatory

Table 7.2   Recommended Basic Training Curriculum

Topic*	Number of Hours	Percent of Total Course
Introduction to the Criminal Justice System	32	8
Law	40	10
Human Values and Problems	88	22
Patrol and Investigation Procedures	132	33
Police Proficiency	72	18
Administration	36	9
TOTAL	**400**	**100**

*The specific subjects included in each topic were as follows:

Introduction to the Criminal Justice System: An examination of the foundation and functions of the criminal justice system with specific attention to the role of the police in the system and government;

Law: An introduction to the development, philosophy, and types of law; criminal law; criminal procedure and rules of evidence; discretionary justice; application of the U.S. Constitution; court systems and procedures; and related civil law;

Human Values and Problems: Public service and noncriminal policing; cultural awareness; changing role of the police; human behavior and conflict management; psychology as it relates to the police function; causes of crime and delinquency; and police-public relations;

Patrol and Investigation Procedures: The fundamentals of the patrol function including traffic, juvenile, and preliminary investigation; reporting and communication; arrest and detention procedures; interviewing; criminal investigation and case preparation; equipment and facility use; and other day-to-day responsibilities;

Patrol Proficiency: The philosophy of when to use force and the appropriate determination of the degree necessary; armed and unarmed defense; crowd, riot, and prisoner control; physical conditioning; emergency medical services; and driver training;

Administration: Evaluation, examination, and counseling processes; department policies, rules, regulations, organization, and personnel procedures.

Source: *Report on Police* (1973). Standard 16.3. p.394.

Source: Terry D. Edwards. "State Police Basic Training Programs: An Assessment of Course Content and Instructional Methodology." *American Journal of Police*, Vol. 12, No. 4, 1993, p.27.

minimum requirements and provide financial aid to governmental units to implement the standards.

 Peace Officer Standards and Training (POST) commissions exist in every state to set requirements for becoming licensed as a law enforcement officer.

Among the specific charges of the POST commissions were:

- Establishing mandatory minimum training standards (at both the recruit and in-service levels), with the authority to determine and approve curricula, identify required preparation for instructors and approve facilities acceptable for police training.
- Certifying police officers who have acquired various levels of education, training and experience necessary to adequately perform the duties of the police service.

Bradley (2005, p.37) explains: "The purpose of the POST agency is to set minimum requirements; individual agencies can expand these requirements to better address their local interests and needs." Table 7.2 provides a recommended basic training curriculum, as well as the specific subjects included in each topic.

Four Modes of Policing and Core Competencies

A survey of more than 400 law enforcement agencies identified four specific modes of policing activities by officers working in departments where problem-solving and community policing are practiced: (1) emergency response, (2) nonemergency response, (3) patrol activities and (4) criminal investigations (Hoover, 2004, pp.12-13). The survey also identified 15 activities officers perform, called *core competencies*. These core competencies are police vehicle operations, use of force, report writing, problem-solving skills, legal authority, officer safety, ethics, cultural diversity, conflict resolution, local procedures, leadership, civil rights, community-specific skills, communication skills and self-awareness. Many of these core competencies are included in the requirements for basic certification in many departments.

Basic Certification Instruction

Some agencies require a certificate or license before they will hire an individual. Others prefer to do the training themselves. In some instances state statutes specify a certain level of education and training before a person can become a law enforcement officer. One such state is Minnesota, whose Peace Officer Standards and Training (POST) Board accredits colleges to provide the academic subjects (education) and a skills program.

The *academic* learning objectives cover administration of justice, state statutes, criminal procedure, human behavior, juvenile justice, operations and procedures and cultural awareness. The *clinical skills* learning objectives cover techniques of criminal investigation and testifying, patrol functions, traffic law enforcement, firearms and defensive tactics.

Academy Training for New Recruits

Today, more than ever, law enforcement academies are challenged by increased workloads, complex antiterrorism and information sharing demands of the post-9-11 world, budget constraints and the threat of litigation requiring training standardization and quality controls (Myers, 2004, p.17). Roughly 626 state and local law enforcement academies exist in the United States, employing about 12,200 full-time and 25,700 part-time trainers (Hickman, 2005). Total expenditures in 2002 were an estimated $726 million, with per basic trainee costs averaging $13,100. The median amount of training was 720 hours, including 50 hours of firearms training, 50 hours on health and fitness, 45 hours on investigations, 44 hours on self-defense, 40 hours on criminal law, 40 hours on patrol procedures and techniques, 36 hours on emergency vehicle operations and 24 hours on first aid and CPR.

 Of the training models typically used for law enforcement recruits, experts recommend a blend of the paramilitary and the academic.

The type of people becoming officers has changed. Fewer have military backgrounds—more have college educations. The traditional boot-camp approach using stress in academy training flies in the face of what is known about how adults learn. Modern adult learning principles and self-image psychology suggest that applying pressure to create a stressful response before training is *counterproductive*. Applying extreme pressure before training is as ineffective as giving new recruits handguns and expecting them to qualify prior to firearms training.

The academic model, in contrast, trains recruits in the necessary knowledge and skill areas. They have little or no staff contact outside the formal training. A weakness of this model is that it fails to indoctrinate recruits into the law enforcement culture, an important part of their overall training.

On-the-Job Training

The most common and frequent training in law enforcement agencies is on-the-job training.

 On-the-job training (OJT) may occur during field training, in-house training sessions or roll call.

on-the-job training (OTJ) • occurs during field training, in-house training sessions and roll call.

Field Training

Field training may take several forms. It might consist of rotation, which provides opportunity for additional knowledge and increased competence in a specialized area. Rotating through various specialties provides opportunity for more of the total-person approach to learning.

 The most common type of on-the-job training for new recruits is done by the **field training officer (FTO)**.

field training • learning that occurs on the job, usually under the direction of a field training officer (FTO).

field training officer (FTO) • an experienced officer who serves as a mentor for a rookie, providing on-the-job training.

Rookie officers are assigned to an FTO who teaches them "the ropes." Recruits depend on their FTO and usually have a strong desire to please, fit in and be accepted. Most recruits see the FTO as a mentor, model and someone to emulate (Anderson, 2004, p.57).

Although FTO programs vary from state to state, most have four primary goals for supervised field training (Molden, 2004, p.4):
1. To transfer and apply classroom learning to the real problems and situations found on the street
2. To provide recruits an opportunity to become familiar with their working environment
3. To provide guidance, monitoring and evaluation
4. To provide a role model for recruits

Not all law enforcement officers make good FTOs; therefore, all FTOs should be carefully selected and then thoroughly trained before instructing others.

Coaching or counseling, both forms of one-on-one field training, can also take place on the job as the need arises, as can mentoring.

Subbing, another form of field training, takes place when individuals must be absent from their jobs for some reason. A law enforcement supervisor might be ill, and a senior patrol officer might take charge. Or the supervisor may be gone to a conference, and a subordinate may be left in charge. Supervisors should train their subordinates to the point that one could assume their job. This *does not* constitute a shirking of duties by the supervisor but is simply another step in developing better officers.

In-House Training Sessions

In-house training sessions, also called **in-service training,** are frequently used in local law enforcement departments. Specific portions of a shift may be set aside for training, which is repeated for each shift. Often trainers with the necessary knowledge, skills and ability to teach can be found within the department: "By using trained officers from within its agency a department can provide effective and cost efficient training in critical skills that will breathe new life into in-service training" (Lebreck, 2004, p.55).

in-service training • in-house training.

Consultants are used occasionally, although perhaps not as often as departments would like because of the expense. Consultants are used mainly for their expertise and

Training can take place in the field when experienced officers, who have been through the same situations as new officers, can share information, provide solid instructions and give constructive criticism to the new recruits.

ability to look at problems without local bias or obligations. In areas where several law enforcement departments exist in proximity, it is sometimes cost effective to share training. One department, for example, might be known for its outstanding work on community relations. Another might be known for its expertise in investigating gang-related criminal activity. Yet another might be known for its work with juveniles. These three departments might share their expertise during in-service training sessions.

Relationships might also be established with local, state and federal agencies to exchange instructors and perhaps materials on special problem areas such as drug investigations. They might also include prosecutors and courts, the coroner's office, private security consultants and social services personnel.

Roll Call

roll call • brief period before each shift when officers check in and receive their briefing prior to going on duty.

Roll call, the brief period before each shift when officers check in and receive their briefing before going on duty, can be a popular, economical time to provide training. The time must be used wisely because roll call generally lasts only 10 to 15 minutes. Nonetheless, training in short bursts is much more effective than long sessions for some subjects. Roll call is well suited to short topics of specific, immediate interest to the on-line officer, and that interest increases training success. Used wisely, those 15 minutes a day can add up to an extra 40 hours a year of training. Nowicki (2003a, p.30) stresses that roll call training be structured, well organized and documented carefully.

Training at the Management Level

Management on-the-job training can consist of using actual past department problems and requesting managers to offer solutions. These problems are related to the department in which the manager operates.

Of particular importance is effective training for newly promoted sergeants. This promotion is a critical and challenging adjustment for the officer who for the first time must supervise others. Supervisors should be trained in the same topics in which their line officers receive training (Nowicki, 2003b, p.40).

Fuller (2004a, p.41) recommends the "in-basket" exercise for supervisory training, a paper exercise where participants sequentially take notes, memos and orders from an in-basket and fill in a duty roster or work schedule based on the incoming information and instructions: "Done properly, the in-basket exercise can be a valuable training experience and is particularly suited for fine-tuning police supervisory decision-making."

Technical skill development at any management level can take place through reviewing the total law enforcement experience, then evaluating what was done and deciding how it could be done better. Managers can improve their human-relations skills by attending seminars, workshops, conferences or courses at colleges and universities.

A number of approaches to management training are available. Some departments rotate the manager through divisions. Job rotation, although sometimes painful, gives the police manager a total department experience. Other departments do not use rotation, and once managers are appointed, they remain in that position until their next promotion or retirement. Stagnation often reigns in such agencies. New managers may be assigned to experienced managers, who act as mentors.

Large city departments provide their own management training, tailored to their special problems and needs. Smaller agencies use a combination of methods: lecturers from federal, state and local law enforcement agencies or special management seminars. Smaller departments may band together in training groups to share resources.

Management and supervisory training is available externally at the federal, state and local levels. External law enforcement management courses are available through the International City Managers Association, the International Association of Chiefs of Police and the American Management Association. They are also available through local universities and colleges.

External Training

Attendance at training sessions and seminars outside the department is costly, but it introduces officers to new ideas and subjects not available locally. External training provides the opportunity to meet officers from other departments, to share and appreciate the universal nature of some law enforcement problems. Possibilities for external training include local college courses; the Federal Bureau of Investigation; the Northwestern Traffic Institute; the International Association of Chiefs of Police; the Bureau of Alcohol, Tobacco and Firearms; the Drug Enforcement Agency; and the U.S. military branches of service. Officers should document in writing their participation in such external training.

 External training may take the form of college classes, seminars, conferences, workshops, independent study and distance learning.

College Classes

Colleges and universities offer a wide variety of courses on subjects not taught by law enforcement departments. The department may pay for the tuition, fees, books and other costs, or officers may pay for them. In either case, such training usually takes place during officers' off-duty hours.

Ironically, some college-educated officers find varying degrees of acceptance by older officers in the department. Resentment is beginning to be minimized by the many candidates today with degrees in criminal justice and the number obtaining degrees while working. The debate surrounding the educational requirements for officers is discussed in Chapter 15.

Napier (2005, p.88) suggests that traditional university classes may be impractical and that taking a year or two off to finish an advanced degree is usually unpalatable if not impossible. The answer for many officers is distance learning.

Distance or E-Learning

Distance learning and training (DLT) has been around for many decades, beginning with the correspondence courses popular in the 1950s and 1960s. Distance learning has come a long way since then. The Internet has an ever-expanding number of online courses that use interactive processes like online discussions, audiovisual conferences and demonstrations and almost immediate feedback on work sent by e-mail and the Web (Nowicki, 2003c, p.36). Many colleges waive out-of-state tuition fees for students enrolling online, and some offer complete degree programs online: "Online programs offer the rigorous workload and testing requirements of the typical classroom setting without worrying about getting to class on time. That freedom is something anyone in law enforcement can appreciate" (Donofrio, 2003, p.56).

synchronous learning •
real-time, instructor-led online learning in which all participants are logged on at the same time and communicate directly with each other. Opposite of asynchronous learning.

asynchronous learning •
learning in which interaction between teachers and students occurs intermittently with a time delay. Opposite of synchronous learning.

One consideration in selecting distance learning courses is whether they provide synchronous learning or asynchronous learning. **Synchronous learning** is real-time, instructor-led online learning in which all participants are logged on at the same time and communicate directly with each other. **Asynchronous learning,** in contrast, is learning in which interaction between teachers and students occurs intermittently with a time delay.

E-learning, or training online, is fast becoming the standard for distance learning (Reiswerg, 2005, p.46). Such training offers several advantages, including login systems that track who is taking the training as well as the officer's progress. In addition, the course content is consistent and up-to-date. Finally, distance learning usually represents a cost savings.

Distance learning is not without its disadvantages, however, as it offers little or no face-to-face contact with instructors, demands more self-discipline in meeting deadlines and completing assignments and provides little or no hands-on experience for technical classes (Schanlaub, 2005, p.79).

Seminars, Conferences and Workshops

Pick up any law enforcement journal and the opportunities available for training through seminars, conferences and workshops become immediately apparent. Costs for seminars, workshops and conferences vary greatly, ranging from free (not very common) to hundreds of dollars per participant. Travel costs are also often involved. Nevertheless, this is sometimes the most effective alternative for obtaining needed expertise in a given topic. Many service clubs, such as Rotary, Kiwanis and Optimists, will financially assist law enforcement agencies with such educational opportunities.

Conferences for professional law enforcement organizations also offer sessions on a wide variety of topics and have the added advantage of allowing for the interchange of ideas among professionals from around the country. If budgets allow, attendance at state-level and even national conferences should be a part of the training program.

Who to send is often a key question. One way to decide is to consider who would make the best in-service instructor. Officers who attend conferences, workshops or seminars should be expected to share the information gained. Usually the officer who attends puts on a training session. This sharing improves the instructor officer's self-esteem and professional reputation, which is valuable in establishing credibility in court as an expert witness. Most of all it enhances the agency's reputation as one that employs quality people and trains them well.

Even if the budget will not allow officers to attend conferences and conventions, the information from them is often available through publications of professional organizations.

Ongoing Training—Lifelong Learning

Before getting the job, as a rookie, upon promotion to sergeant and beyond—throughout a law enforcement career—training should be ongoing. Regardless of the methods used, training must be continuous because people fail to remember a high percentage of what they learned: "Even the most experienced and highly qualified law enforcement officers need to periodically brush up their skills, particularly the ones they don't use very often" (Moore, 2005, p.102). New subjects continually arise that must be learned, including new laws and court decisions.

 Officers' training should be ongoing—lifelong learning.

Schofield (2003, p.34) contends: "It is conceivable that an officer could go through an entire career and never be reacquainted with the basics." Among the "basics" requiring periodic review are report writing, cultural diversity, Fourth Amendment and constitutional requirements and ethical dilemmas, in addition to the skills that are obvious, such as firearms qualification.

The Training Cycle

Because effective training is ongoing, it can be viewed as a cycle.

 The training cycle consists of need identification, goal setting, program development, program implementation, program evaluation and back, full circle, to assessment of need based on the evaluation.

Need Identification

Training programs must emphasize actual individual and department goals. Needs come to light from officers' conversations, supervisors' and managers' observations, complaints, officers' suggestions and other sources.

Training needs of officers at various levels of experience can be determined in a number of ways. Among the most common are:

- Reviewing new statutes that affect police operations and investigations.
- Taking department surveys.

- Reviewing reports and noting deficiencies.
- Reviewing internal and external complaints.
- Reviewing lawsuits against the agency.
- Analyzing specific law enforcement functions.
- Interviewing line officers and detectives.
- Interviewing managers and supervisors.
- Getting input from other agencies and the community.

These various methods of identifying training needs are likely to indicate which subjects are considered priorities, as well as various types and levels of training needed in any given department.

When identifying needs, planners should recognize that officers spend 10 percent of patrol activity on criminal-related matters and the remaining 90 percent on a variety of service-related calls (Paez, 2004, p.19).

Goal Setting

As with any type of goal setting, training goals should reflect specific training objectives that:

- Are specific and observable.
- Are measurable with a set criteria.
- Have a clear timeline for achievement.

Program Development

After the needs have been identified and goals and objectives specified, the actual training program must be developed or, for existing programs, revised based on the needs assessment. Rossett and Mohr (2004, p.38) recommend involving users: "Gain users' buy-in by including them in the design and development process." Usually the following steps are taken:

- Determine subject matter and objectives based on identified needs.
- Prepare the training.
- Select the most appropriate method(s).
- Select/write materials, audiovisual aids and tests.
- Select the instructor.
- Schedule the training.
- Reserve the facility.
- Present the training.
- Evaluate.
- Have learners apply new knowledge on the job.
- Evaluate.

Who Should Provide the Training? Managers, by their position, should be constantly providing individual, on-the-job training, helping subordinates grow and develop. Managers may also schedule more formal training sessions and present information themselves. They may seek assistance from an expert within the department. Or they may bring in someone from outside the department. Whether managers do the actual training or not, they are responsible for ensuring it is effective and meets their subordinates' needs. The ultimate responsibility is theirs.

Cost The amount of money budgeted for training varies greatly from department to department. In addition to the costs for instructors and materials, the cost of officers' salaries during training should also be factored in. Training costs can be cut by sharing resources with other departments, cohosting training, using FBI programs, seeking scholarships for officers to attend training and seeking sponsors for officers.

Facilities The type of training, method of instruction and audiovisuals will affect the physical facilities needed. The facility should be conducive to learning and to two-way communication. It should be well lit and well ventilated, contain adequate seating and writing surfaces and have good acoustics. Depending on the size of the group, a microphone may be necessary. If so, the most effective type is a small, wireless microphone.

Program Evaluation

Like training, evaluation should be continuous. The officers' grasp of the material should be tested in the classroom and on the job. Such evaluation will help determine whether further training is needed in a specific area.

One effective nontest way to evaluate training effectiveness is to compare officers' performance before and after training. Other before-and-after information that might reflect the effectiveness of training can be obtained from records of complaints, grievances, absenteeism, turnover and the like. Alternatively, evaluation instruments should include a pretest, posttest and follow-up field performance appraisal (Connor, 2004, p.41).

Trainers should consider having the trainees complete an evaluation of the session, including responding to such questions as these:

- How effective was the instructor?
- How interesting was the session?
- How relevant was the material?
- How was the pacing of the session?
- What did you like most about the training?
- What could be improved?

Benefits of Effective Training Programs

 Training programs can benefit individual officers, supervisors, managers, the entire department and the community.

Benefits for individual officers include improved chances for career success, increased motivation, improved morale, increased productivity, greater feelings of self-worth, reduced chances of injury on the job, greater confidence, pride, improved work attitudes and increased job satisfaction. In addition, Moore (2004, p.162) contends: "The well-trained officer is less likely to be brutal and less likely to cause departments to get sued for using too much force."

Among the many benefits supervisors of those trained might enjoy are getting to know officers better, furthering their own advancement and career, gaining more time, establishing better human relations, increased confidence in officers' abilities, increased flexibility, increased creativity, fewer discipline problems and mistakes and improved discipline.

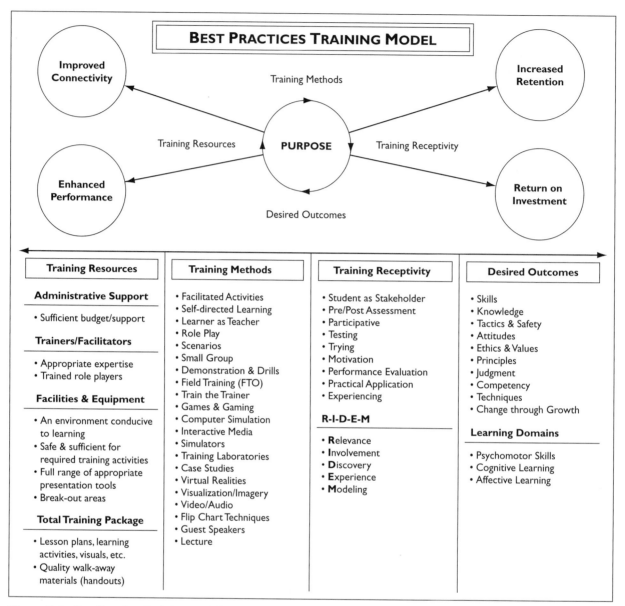

Figure 7.4 Best Practices Training Model

Source: Andrew Borrello and Jim Fraser. "The Best Practices Training Model." *The Law Enforcement Trainer,* September/October 2001, p.28. Reprinted by permission.

Many benefits enjoyed by individual managers also benefit the entire agency. In addition, the organization and ultimately the community benefit from training in more efficient, effective officers; increased quantity and quality of work; reduced turnover, absenteeism, waste, complaints and grievances; greater public support; and increased departmental pride.

Clearly, training is an important function of the effective manager/supervisor at all levels of the department. Figure 7.4 introduces a "Best Practices Training Model," which summarizes the main concepts presented in this chapter.

The Violent Crime Control and Law Enforcement Act of 1994

 The Violent Crime Control and Law Enforcement Act of 1994 authorizes major funding for law enforcement training.

The federal crime bill's Police Corps and in-service scholarship programs represent the largest federal investment in education for law enforcement personnel since the Law Enforcement Education Program in the late 1960s and 1970s. The act also puts hundreds more officers on the street in an effort to bolster community policing.

Training, Community Policing Services and Terrorism

The 1990s saw an urgency to respond to increases in crime, with no time to waste. The need to involve the community was recognized. Law enforcement agencies seeking to integrate the community policing philosophy into their departments faced a dilemma, however, for at the same time, the skills of policing were changing and a new way of policing was evolving—problem-solving policing (Scrivner, 2005, p.26).

A new federal agency, the Office of Community Oriented Policing (COPS), was created along with a network of Regional Community Policing Institutes (RCPIs) to develop a training capacity throughout the United States. As of 2005, 29 RCPIs were part of a network that has trained over 400,000 law enforcement officers and their community partners. Scrivner (p.30) contends that lessons can be learned from the success of the RCPIs to develop a similar training capacity for homeland security and intelligence-led policing, noting the parallels between the impetus for community policing—fear of crime—and that for homeland security—fear of suicide bombers or chemical attacks.

Just as the federal government recognized the need to assist law enforcement in its community policing efforts by establishing the COPS office, it recognized the need to assist law enforcement antiterrorism efforts by establishing the Department of Homeland Security. In addition, the Institute for Operational Readiness and Continuous Education in Security (iFORCES), a nationwide public and private sector consortium, has been established; its vision, as posted on its Web site (www.iFORCES.org), is:

> The tragic events of 9/11 have highlighted our Nation's need for unified and rapid responses to prepare and strengthen our Country against the greatest challenge of the new millennium: terrorism.
>
> The front lines in this new war are the men and women of our Law Enforcement, Military and First Responder communities as well as a vigilant and prepared citizenry.
>
> Our ability to swiftly advance and measure training, operational readiness, and human performance will be critical to our Nation's security in the coming years.

 SUMMARY

Training generally refers to vocational instruction that takes place on the job and deals with physical skills. Education generally refers to academic instruction that takes place in a college, university or seminar-type setting and deals with knowledge and understanding. Both training and education are needed for effective learning.

Developing human resources through ongoing training should be managers' single most important objective. Training not only improves productivity but also reduces liability. Keys to avoiding civil liability related to training are to provide first-rate training, to thoroughly document such training and to require thorough reports on any incident that could lead to a lawsuit.

Three variables that affect learning are individual variables, task/information variables and environmental/instructional variables. The three general categories of learners or learning styles are visual, auditory and kinesthetic. Training can focus on knowledge, skills or attitudes.

Job analysis is the key to determining the content to teach and test. When content relates directly to the tasks to be performed, it is considered valid. Tests that measure competence in these tasks are then also valid.

Important learning principles include the following: base training on an identified need; tell officers what the learning objective is; tell officers why they need to learn the material; make sure officers have the necessary background to master the skill (the prerequisites); present the material using the most appropriate materials and methods available; when possible use variety; adapt the materials and methods to individual officers' needs; allow officers to be as active and involved as possible during training; engage as many of the senses as possible during training; break complex tasks into simple, easy-to-understand steps; use repetition and practice to enhance remembering; and give officers periodic feedback on how they are performing. Whenever possible, present the "big picture"—teach an understandable concept rather than relying on simple memorization.

Effective learning depends on intelligent selection of methods and materials. Instructional methods include lecture, question/answer sessions, discussion, demonstration, hands-on learning, role playing, case studies and simulations. Instructional materials include printed information, visuals, bulletin boards, audiocassettes and videocassettes, television programs and computer programs. The Law Enforcement Television Network (LETN) is a private satellite television system that provides current programs on a variety of law enforcement subjects, available through subscription.

Other organizations available to assist with training include the American Society of Law Enforcement Trainers (ASLET), the National Association of Field Training Officers (NAFTO), the Federal Law Enforcement Training Center (FLETC), the National Center for State and Local Training, the FBI National Police Academy and the FBI itself. Peace Officer Standards and Training (POST) commissions exist in every state to set requirements for becoming licensed as a law enforcement officer.

Of the models of training typically used for law enforcement recruits, experts recommend a blending of the paramilitary and the academic. The most common training is on-the-job training. It may occur during field training, in-house training sessions or roll call. The most common type for new recruits is that done by the field training officer, or FTO. External training may take the form of college classes, seminars, conferences, workshops and independent study.

Officers' training should be ongoing, resulting in a training cycle consisting of needs identification, goal setting, program development, program implementation, program evaluation and back, full circle, to assessment of needs based on the evaluation. Training programs can benefit individual officers, supervisors, managers and the entire department and community.

The Violent Crime Control and Law Enforcement Act of 1994 authorizes major funding for law enforcement training.

 CHALLENGE SEVEN

Captain Hayley is responsible for the annual training plan for the Greenfield Police Department. During Chief Slaughter's crime-fighting tenure, Captain Hayley scheduled frequent training for all officers in the use of firearms, defensive tactics and enforcing criminal statutes. He scheduled training in pursuit driving and emergency medical response on a two-year rotation. Specialized training was provided to individual officers on an "as needed" basis. The training was usually conducted in an academy setting.

Chief Slaughter required his officers to train and qualify with their firearms every month—three times more often than required by POST. As a result, the department won the state shooting competition 10 years in a row. During those 10 years, Greenfield officers have fired their weapons on duty only to dispatch injured animals. Ammunition and officer overtime for training at the firearms range were the largest expenditures in the department's training budget.

The new chief has asked Captain Hayley to develop a training program with more emphasis on developing human resources and community policing. He suggested that some of the funds devoted to firearms training be used for other training.

1. Was the training provided by Chief Slaughter job related and appropriate for the tasks performed by his officers?

2. Captain Hayley should consider some fundamental changes in the training program if he wants to emphasize a community-policing strategy rather than a crime-fighting strategy. How might the blend of training verses educating change?

3. Suggest three specific topics for Captain Hayley's new training curriculum that relate to community policing.

4. The new chief is encouraging a participative management style within the department. In the past, the captains and Chief Slaughter determined the department's training needs. How can Captain Hayley reflect the department's new direction in how he selects training?

5. Training resources are often limited. POST-required and liability-driven training can consume a significant portion of the budget. What innovative training techniques might Captain Hayley explore to save money and ensure high-quality training? Describe three possible innovations.

6. If Captain Hayley reduces firearms training and adds communications training, he is likely to face resistance from the officers. Why? How can he circumvent a dispute over this change in the training curriculum?

DISCUSSION QUESTIONS

1. How would you compare and contrast training and education?

2. Which instructional methods do you think are most effective? Least effective?

3. Which instructional materials do you think are most effective? Least effective?

4. What is the role of the employee in self-development?

5. When would you use a group or conference method of training?

6. When would you use external training programs?

7. What are the major considerations in developing a law enforcement training program?

8. What would you include in a law enforcement training philosophy statement?

9. What five subjects do you consider most essential for a management development training program?

10. What training could be conducted during a cutback budgeting period and still provide reasonable training?

REFERENCES

Anderson, Jonathan L. "Managing Professional Relationships." *Law and Order*, June 2004, pp.56–58.

Barath, Irene and Lenehan, Mike. "Scenario-Based Training for Criminal Investigators." *The Law Enforcement Trainer*, April/May/June 2005, pp.26–27.

Bell, Chip R. and Bell, Bilijack R. "Great Training Leaders Are Clear about Their Expectations and Are Enthusiastic about Communicating Them." *Training and Development*, September 2003, p.56.

Bollig, Tim. "Trends in Training." *The Law Enforcement Trainer*, Fourth Quarter 2004, pp.6–9.

Borrello, Andrew. "Three-Ring Training: Next Generation Training Methods." *The Law Enforcement Trainer*, Fourth Quarter 2004, pp.12–15.

Bradley, Patrick L. "21st Century Issues Related to Police Training and Standards." *The Police Chief*, October 2005, pp.32–38.

Cohen, Arthur. "The Learning Curve." *ILEETA Digest*, April/May/June 2004, p.2.

Colaprete, Frank A. "Eclecticism: Blending the Best Adult Education Philosophies in Law Enforcement Training." *The Law Enforcement Trainer*, November/December 2003, pp.12–17.

Connor, Greg. "Training to Train or Training to Task?" *The Law Enforcement Trainer*, January/February 2004, pp.36–41.

Cope, Curtis J. "Building Training from Lessons Learned: A Checklist to Successful Training." November/December 2003, pp.8–10.

Danaher, Larry. "Who Are You?" *The Law Enforcement Trainer*, April/May/June 2005, pp.53–55.

Della, Brian C. "Nontraditional Training Systems: Realizing the Effectiveness of an Agency's Most Valuable Resource." *FBI Law Enforcement Bulletin*, June 2004, pp.1–9.

Donofrio, Andrew. "Online Learning." *Law Enforcement Technology*, February 2003, pp.56–61.

Dwyer, R. Gregg and Laufersweiler-Dwyer, Deborah L. "The Need for Change: A Call for Action in Community Oriented Police Training." *FBI Law Enforcement Bulletin*, November 2004, pp.18–24.

Fuller, John. "The In-Basket Exercise: An 'Oldie' Supervisor Training Method." *The Law Enforcement Trainer*, May/June 2004a, pp.41–43.

Fuller, John. "Scenario-Paper Exercises." *The Law Enforcement Trainer*, Third Quarter 2004b, pp.44–45.

Griffith, David. "On the Hook." *Police*, September 2005, pp.42–51.

Hamilton, Melanie. "Realistic Illusions." *Police*, June 2004, pp.24–29.

Harvey, William L. "From the Chief's Chair: The Chief's Role in Training for Small—Medium Departments." *The Law Enforcement Trainer*, May/June 2003, pp.42–46.

Hickman, Matthew J. *State and Local Law Enforcement Training Academies, 2002*. Washington, DC: Bureau of Justice Statistics, January 2005. (NCJ 204030)

Hoover, Jerry. "The Reno Model of Police Training Officer (PTO) Program." *The NAFTO News*, December 2004, pp.10–13.

Institute for Operational Readiness and Continuous Education in Security (iFORCES), retrieved February 1, 2006, from www.iFORCES.org.

Kelly, Perry William. "At the Flicks with the Flics: Videotape and DVD Training for Police Officers." *The Law Enforcement Trainer*, Third Quarter 2004, pp.37–40.

Kennedy, Ralph C. "Applying Principles of Adult Learning: The Key to More Effective Training Programs." *FBI Law Enforcement Bulletin*, April 2003, pp.1–5.

Knowles, M. S. *The Modern Practice of Adult Education: Andragogy vs. Pedagogy*. New York: Association Press, 1970.

Lebreck, Paul. "Doing More Training with Less Money." *Law and Order*, June 2004, pp.52–55.

Maher, James R. "Role-Play Training for Negotiators in Diverse Environments." *FBI Law Enforcement Bulletin*, June 2004, pp.10–12.

Martinelli, Ron. "How the 'Martinelli Decision' Will Affect Private Training Providers." *The Law Enforcement Trainer*, March/April 2004, pp.30–39.

Messina, Phil. "Confrontational Simulations." *The Law Enforcement Trainer*, July/August/September 2005, pp.28–29.

Mills-Senn, Pamela. "Making It Real Makes It a Reflex." *Law Enforcement Technology*, September 2005a, pp.38–48.

Mills-Senn, Pamela. "Real Training, Real Results." *Law Enforcement Technology*, January 2005b, pp.50–63.

Molden, Jack. "The Role of the Field Training Officer." *The NAFTO News*, December 2004, pp.4–5.

Moore, Carole. "Is Your Training Enough?" *Law Enforcement Technology*, August 2004, p.162.

Moore, Carole. "A New Year's Refresher." *Law Enforcement Technology*, January 2005, p.102.

Murray, Kenneth R. "Dangerous Teaching Styles: The Anatomy of Training Failures." *Police and Security News*, May/June 2005a, pp.45–52.

Murray, Ken. "Video Simulators: A Panacea or Pandora's Box?" *Law Officer Magazine*, September/October 2005b, pp.70–73.

Myers, Cory. "The 21st Century Law Enforcement Academy." *The Law Enforcement Trainer*, Third Quarter 2004, pp.17–20.

Napier, Mark. "The Need for Higher Education." *Law and Order*, September 2005, pp.86–94.

Nowicki, Ed. "Stretch Your Training Dollars." *Law and Order*, November 2003a, pp.30–32.

Nowicki, Ed. "Ten Things Every Chief Should Know about Training." *Law and Order*, October 2003b, pp.40–42.

Nowicki, Ed. "Training and Education via the Internet." *Law and Order*, September 2003c, pp.36–38.

Oberlander, Richard. "Judgment Evaluation and Force Option Training Simulators: Providing Real World Critical Incident Experiences." *The Law Enforcement Trainer*, May/June 2004, pp.31–35.

Paez, Anthony. "Lateral, Pre-Service and Entry-Level Recruits: Tips for the Field Training Officer." *The Law Enforcement Trainer*, Fourth Quarter 2004, pp.17–19.

Pivetta, Sue. "Bang-Bang You're Dead: A Case for Using Simulation in 911 Training." *The Law Enforcement Trainer*, March/April 2003, pp.25–29.

Redenbach, Robert. "Tactics vs. Athleticism." *The Law Enforcement Trainer*, April/May/June 2005, pp.66–79.

Reiswerg, Susan. "Distance Learning: Is It the Answer to Your Department's Training Needs?" *The Police Chief*, October 2005, pp.44–52.

Rogers, Donna. "WILL Interactive Helps Trainees 'Play It Out before They Live It Out.'" *Law Enforcement Technology*, March 2004, p.114–118.

Rossett, Allison and Mohr, Erica. "Performance Support Tools: Where Learning, Work, and Results Converge." *Training and Development*, February 2004, pp.35–39.

Rutledge, Devallis. "Chief Accountability." *Police*, October 2003, pp.94–96.

Schanlaub, Russ. "Degree or No Degree." *Law and Order*, September 2005, pp.76–85.

Schofield. "The Advanced Officer Skills Training Program (AOST)." *The Law Enforcement Trainer*, September/October 2003, pp.33–36.

Scott, Elsie. "Managing Municipal Police Training Programs with Limited Resources." *The Police Chief*, October 2005, pp.40–43.

Scrivner, Ellen. "Building Training Capacity for Homeland Security: Lessons Learned from Community Policing." *The Police Chief*, October 2005, pp.26–30.

Stockton, Dale. "The FBI National Academy: An Unbeatable Educational Experience." *Law and Order*, September 2005, pp. 66–74.

Stone, Michael P. and Berger, Marc J. "Police Trainers Cannot Be Held Civilly Liable for Trainees' Injuries during Training." *The Law Enforcement Trainer*, January/February 2004, pp.24–28.

Sullivan, Rick. "Talking Through: Discussion Basics." *Training and Development*, March 2003, pp.22–24.

Unkelbach, L. Cary. "Beware: Supervisor Individual Liability in Civil Rights Cases." *The Police Chief*, July 2005, pp.10–11.

Van Brocklin, Valerie. "Grab 'em by Their Hearts and They Will Follow: Training that Inspires." *The Law Enforcement Trainer*, January/February/March 2005, pp.16–19.

Van Hasslet, Vincent B. and Romano, Stephen J. "Role-Playing: A Vital Tool in Crisis Negotiation Skills Training." *FBI Law Enforcement Bulletin*, February 2004, pp.12–17.

CITED CASES

Board of County Commissioners v. Brown, 520 U.S. 397 (1997)

City of Canton, Ohio v. Harris, 489 U.S. 378, at 390, 109, S.Ct. 1197, at 1205 (1989)

Davis v. Mason County, 927 F.2d 1473 (9th Cir. 1991), cert denied, 502 U.S. 899, 112 S.Ct. 275, 116 L.Ed.2d 227 (1991)

Hamilton v. Martinelli & Associates, 2003 DJDAR 8199 (July 24, 2003)

BOOK-SPECIFIC WEB SITE

Go to the Management and Supervision in Law Enforcement Web site at www.thomsonedu.com/criminaljustice/bennett for student and instructor resources, including Internet Assignments and Case Studies.

CHAPTER 8

Promoting Growth and Development

None of us is as good as all of us.

Ray Kroc, founder of McDonalds

 DO YOU KNOW?

- What the workplace culture is?
- What norms are and why they are important?
- Where an officer's first loyalty must lie?
- How managers can shape the workplace culture?
- What the Johari Window describes?
- What a necessary first step for growth and development is?
- What personal goals specify and what areas they should include?
- What touchstone values and daily values are and how they are related?
- What a balanced performer manager is?
- What stages of growth people typically go through?
- How someone might develop a positive image?
- In what areas of cultural awareness law enforcement officers need development?
- What ethics entails and how to develop ethical behavior?
- What the key elements of corrupt behavior are?
- Why it is important to help officers grow and develop?

CAN YOU DEFINE?

balanced performer managers	hidden self	norms
balancing	holistic personal goals	open self
blind self	integrity	racial profiling
code of silence	interdependent	subconscious self
cultural awareness	job description	supernorms
daily values	Johari Window	synergy
ethical behavior	key result areas	touchstone values
ethics	majority worldview	unconditional backup
ghosting	mentor	undiscovered self
gratuity	minority worldview	workplace culture

Introduction

Law enforcement managers have two obligations as developers: developing themselves and developing their subordinates. Both are normally accomplished simultaneously. Because managing is getting work done through others, you will get the best from subordinates by developing their abilities. This is not always accomplished by being the "good guy." It is pleasant to have good interpersonal relationships with all workers, but it is not always possible. There are times for praise and times for discipline.

This chapter begins by discussing job descriptions and the workplace culture. Next it describes the importance of developing positive interpersonal relationships and of goal setting. This is followed by a look at balanced performer managers and how they might empower those who report to them. Next you will learn the stages of growth employees go through, the important managerial role of mentors, and approaches to developing positive attitudes, a positive image, cultural awareness and a sense of ethics and integrity. The chapter concludes with a discussion of the long-range importance of developing personnel; how managers can be motivators for change; and how they might evaluate the workplace climate for growth, development and change within their department.

Job Descriptions

A **job description** is a detailed, formally stated summary of duties and responsibilities for a position. It usually contains the position title, supervisor, education and experience required, salary, duties, responsibilities and job details. Job details make a specific position different from all others in an organization. Patrol officers' duties are different from those of detectives. Likewise, the duties of sergeants, lieutenants and chiefs differ.

job description • detailed, formally stated summary of duties and responsibilities for a position.

Job descriptions are not limiting or restrictive. They are simply minimum requirements, and the job description should make this clear. Employees who can expand these tasks or do them differently and better should be encouraged to do so. Job descriptions provide the basis not only for getting work done but also for setting expectations and standards for evaluation.

Tasks must be broadly stated and leave room for growth, change and expansion. They should also be reviewed at least annually, when some tasks may be eliminated and others added. For example, recently resources in many departments have shifted from the war on drugs to the war on terrorism. Law enforcement managers must respond to this national interest.

All law enforcement personnel have opportunities to expand their tasks and perform them better. Any law enforcement task can be done better, with greater total effect. Managers need to use every available resource to develop the best in each individual and the team. One key is a positive work culture.

The Workplace Culture

An organizational culture can be defined as "a shared basic assumption that the group has learned as it solved problems that has worked well enough to be considered valid and is, therefore, to be taught to new members as the correct way to perceive, think, and feel in relation to those problems" (Orrick, 2005, p.38).

The workplace culture is evident in any organization. Visit an engineering firm, and you are likely to encounter a well-dressed staff who greets you quite formally. Visit the local newspaper, and you are likely to encounter a casually dressed staff who greets you quite informally. Further, within many workplace cultures, subcultures exist. Within an advertising agency, for example, the sales force may dress up, whereas the creative staff may favor T-shirts and blue jeans. Each workplace develops its own culture.

workplace culture • the sum of the beliefs and values held in common by those within the organization that formally and informally communicate what is expected.

The **workplace culture** is the sum of the beliefs and values shared by those within the organization, serving to formally and informally communicate its expectations.

These beliefs and values are a type of "collective conscience" by which those within the group judge each other.

The Socialization Process

Young men and women entering law enforcement are usually idealistic and ready to make a difference in the world. They are eager to learn and emulate veteran officers. Inevitably, however: "Cops undergo a profound transformation while working as police officers that leaves them forever changed" (MacKenzie, 2005, p.72). This transformation of the police officer's identity and self-image may be more radical than in many other fields.

Research shows that police recruits come to the profession with high ideals and standards (Ford, 2003, p.85). However, with a short exposure to the occupation, attitudes and values undergo significant change and soon differ from attitudes of the general population. Socialization into police culture begins soon after a recruit's initial entry into the police academy, and the informal socialization continues and intensifies during the practical training and field training (Ford, p.85).

Many officers become furiously loyal to others in the department and begin to see a separation between themselves and society. They perceive, and often rightly so, that their very lives depend on supporting one another. This perspective is a defining element of the police culture.

The Police Culture

Whether it is called the Blue Wall, the Thin Blue Line, the Brotherhood or something else, it all means the same. If you carry a badge, you're family. All officers are bound by the oath they take when they become police officers. Anderson (2003b, p.104) explains that taking this oath bonds individuals to a fraternal order. This simple pledge, says Anderson (p.105): "transcends positions and rank, gender and race. It inspires the ethos of **unconditional backup**—psychological backup, emotional backup and ethical backup. It is this vow that binds one to the core ideals of the profession" (emphasis added).

unconditional backup • dictates that other officers must take action, get involved and back each other up ethically.

The police culture has been extensively written about and is often described as isolationist, elitist and authoritarian. Within some departments there is no clear mission statement, and conflict occurs between officers who see themselves as crime fighters and those who prefer the social-service role emphasized in community policing. Moskos (2003, p.9) points out the difference between old-school officers and new-school officers in many departments. The old-school officer believes in hitting back if someone disrespects them. The new school does not believe in hitting back, but rather believes in cuffing suspects and writing solid reports. According to Moskos: "Though we demand new-school behavior from our police most police officers are firmly old school" (p.9).

Although "street justice" is no longer standard procedure for most departments, research by Terrill et al. (2003, p.1003) indicates that officers who closely embody the values of the police culture are more coercive compared with those that differentially align with the culture, suggesting that police use of force is a function of officers' varying attitudinal commitment to the traditional values of police culture. These researchers (p.1007) conclude: "The traditional view of police culture posits that officers should almost uniformly, hold strongly unfavorable views of both citizens and supervisors, show disdain and resentment toward procedural guidelines, reject all roles except that which involves fighting crime, and value aggressive patrolling tactics and selectivity in performing their law enforcement duties." Hill (2005, p.142) cautions that department culture can become insular and linear—characteristics contrary to community policing—and suggests: "Community policing culture is built on the values of interaction and respect, both within the department and between the department and the community it serves."

Research suggests such a culture may be becoming more of a reality. Paoline (2003, p.199) reports that the traditional "blue" monolithic attitude and behavioral conceptualization of the police culture is a thing of the past. He (2004, p.205) also notes that analytically distinct groups of officers can be identified: tough cops, crime fighters, avoiders, problem solvers and professionals, as shown in Table 8.1.

Table 8.1   Attitudinal Expectations for Group Formation

	Group 1: Tough-Cops	Group 2: Clean-Beat Crime-Fighters	Group 3: Avoiders	Group 4: Problem-Solvers	Group 5: Professionals
Citizens	(−) citizens are hostile and uncooperative	(−) citizens are unappreciative	(−) citizens do not understand the police	(+) help citizens get to the root of problems	(+) maintain positive rapport with citizens
Supervisors	(−) supervisors are unsupportive	(−) supervisors are unsupportive	(−) or (+/−) pacify supervisors to keep out of trouble	(+) especially in more community policing departments	(+) value supervisory approval
Procedural guidelines	(−) they do more harm than anything	(+) value these due process safeguards	(−) viewed as obstacles	(−) too restrictive, impede efforts to solve problems	(+) accept the limitations placed on them
Law enforcement	(+) narrow role orientation that only includes law enforcement	(+) very rigid law enforcement orientation	(−) or (+/−) believe in only handling unavoidable (i.e., serious) crimes	(−) or (+/−) not the most important/defining function for an officer	(+) accept this role, though not rigid or inflexible
Order maintenance	(−) if handle, do so informally (not regarded as real police work)	(+) as long as they can handle them formally (i.e., ticket or arrest) part of role	(−) would only create more work	(+) expansive role orientation in handling citizen problems	(+) value roles beyond crime fighting
Community policing	(−) not real policing	(−) may impede their efforts to fight street crime	(−) would only create more work	(+) expansive role orientation	(+) expansive role orientation
Aggressiveness	(+) believe in aggressive style of patrol, part of image	(+) believe in aggressive style of patrol in controlling all illegality	(−) only increases chances to get into trouble	(−) usually only results in negative consequences for citizens	(−) or (+/−) exception rather than the norm
Selectivity	(+) believe in handling only real (i.e., serious) violations formally	(−) believe in pursuing and handling all forms (i.e., minor and serious) of illegal behavior	(+) believe in handling only unavoidable serious offenses that, if not handled, would bring undue negative attention to them	(+) discretionary informal judgment (over strict law enforcement) valued in handling problems	(−) handle full range of offenses, though do not feel the need to handle all formally (i.e., ticket or arrest)

Note: (+/−) indicates neutral attitudes.

Source: From Eugene A. Paoline, III. "Shedding Light on Police Culture: An Examination of Officers' Occupational Attitudes." *Police Quarterly,* June 2004, p.211. Reprinted by permission.

The first two groups describe what is often thought of as the traditional officer. Within a law enforcement agency, most or all of these groups can be found. Which group predominates will determine the dominant culture of that agency, which will also be reflected in its norms.

Norms What is important within any department is expressed as norms.

norms • attitudes and beliefs held by a group of individuals.

 Norms are the attitudes and beliefs held by the members of a group.

Norms are, in effect, what is "normal." Most people do not want to be considered "abnormal," so they do and say what others expect of them, for example:

- Do the job the way you're told.
- It's okay to be late.
- Never give so many citations; you make your colleagues look bad.

These norms are enforced by putting pressure on those who do not conform. Norms can hurt or help managers. Negative work norms can destroy morale and decrease performance; positive norms can heighten morale and improve performance. Two norms common in many police departments are a fierce loyalty to one another and the accompanying **code of silence,** the unwillingness to reveal any misconduct by fellow officers, discussed later in the chapter.

code of silence • encourages officers not to speak up when they see another officer doing something wrong.

The Us vs. Them mentality is usually present within the minds of those who participate in the code of silence. The code of silence and the Us vs. Them phenomenon often bond together. The result is intense loyalty, a positive feature of the police culture if it is loyalty to principles.

 An officer's first loyalty must be to defend the Constitution and laws of the United States, his or her state constitution and laws and local laws.

Changing the Workplace Culture

The most effective way to transform the organizational culture of a law enforcement agency into an atmosphere that embraces loyalty to principle above all else is a combination of leadership, role modeling and training.

 Managers can shape the workplace culture by doing the following:

1. Identify existing norms.
2. Evaluate the norms—do they work for or against the department's mission?
3. Encourage positive norms and try to eliminate negative ones through modeling and training.

Shaping the workplace culture requires the type of participatory management discussed earlier. Recognize, however, that when shaping the workplace culture, you can expect to encounter a kind of "Catch-22" in the form of **supernorms**—that is, overriding expectations of a given work group; for example, *never volunteer information* or *do not criticize.* Many of the communication skills discussed in Chapter 4 will help you deal with these supernorms and change those that are counterproductive.

supernorms • overriding expectations of a given work group, for example, *do not volunteer* or *do not criticize.*

You might also find the best subculture in your organization and hold it up as an example from which others can learn. Do not expect change overnight—it may take several years. Perhaps most important, live the culture you want. Walk the talk.

Within the workplace culture you and your people can grow and develop personally and professionally. The culture must expect, encourage and reward growth. Establishing a nurturing workplace culture depends on developing positive interpersonal relationships.

Developing Positive Interpersonal Relationships

Developing good manager–subordinate relations requires fairness, trust and confidence on everyone's part. It is not always the formal relationships, important as they are, that establish a rapport between manager and subordinate. It is a two-way feeling of respect, regard and trust.

Consider the employee who says: "I would do anything for the boss I have now. He demands a lot, but he is fair, and I trust that he will do what he says." More than likely this employee's manager has emotional maturity, displays confidence without being overbearing, knows his and the subordinate's job, would not ask the subordinate to do anything he would not do, expresses confidence in the subordinate and deals with the subordinate with compassion. Mutual respect develops when both manager and subordinate deal with each other in the same way.

Self-Disclosure and Feedback

An important part of developing relationships is for managers to get to know each member of the work unit better and, in the process, get to know themselves better. A model termed the **Johari Window** (named after the authors Joe and Harry) illustrates how people can learn more about others and themselves. The model is based on the premise that everyone has four parts to their identity, as Figure 8.1 illustrates.

Your **open self** is what you know about yourself and what you show to others. Your **hidden self** is the secret part that you do not share with others. Your **blind self** is the part of you that others can see but you do not know about yourself. Your **undiscovered** or **subconscious self** is the part of you that neither you nor others have yet discovered.

The Johari Window describes four parts of identity:

The open self

The hidden self

The blind self

The subconscious or undiscovered self

According to this model, through the process of self-disclosure and feedback—that is, honest interaction with others—you can widen the area of openness, reduce the hidden and blind parts and learn something about your undiscovered self.

Honest, open interaction with subordinates can help *everyone* within the workplace culture grow and develop. The direction this growth and development takes depends on the goals that are set.

Goal Setting

The importance of organizational goals has been discussed. Within organizational goals, managers should include growth and development, both individual and organizational. Remember that goals are targets: specific, measurable outcomes with a timeline.

Johari Window • a model to illustrate how people can learn more about others and themselves.

open self • what you know about yourself and what you show to others.

hidden self • that which is secret and which you do not share with others.

blind self • that part others can see but you do not know about.

undiscovered self • that part of you neither you nor others have yet discovered. Also called *subconscious self*.

subconscious self • that part of you neither you nor others have yet discovered. Also called *undiscovered self*.

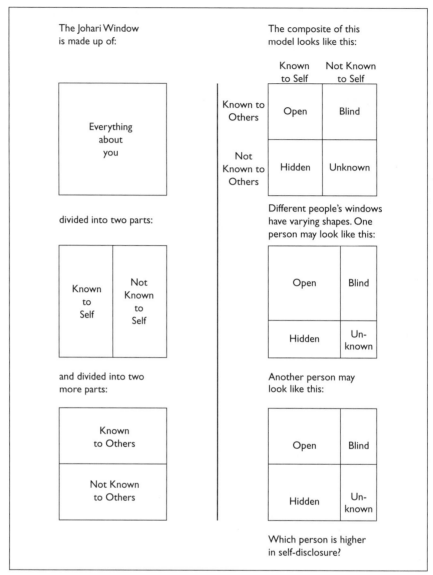

Figure 8.1 Johari Window

Source: Paul R. Timm. *Supervision,* 2nd ed. St. Paul, MN: West Publishing Company, 1992, p.52.

 Personal and organizational goals are a necessary first step for growth and development.

Goals should be (1) stated positively, (2) realistic and attainable and (3) personally important.

 A personal goal states what, when and how much.

The *what* is the specific result to achieve. The *when* is the target date by which the goal will be reached. The *how much* is, whenever possible, a quantifiable measure. Effective goals meet several of the following criteria: They are specific and realistic, action oriented, consistent with ability and authority and measurable. They should also include "stretch" and have a set deadline.

Law enforcement managers may set a goal of "talking to their subordinates about organizational and personal problems." They may help subordinates set their goals, which should be discussed and then written down. A specific time period should be established to accomplish the goals, and progress should be reviewed at the end of that period.

Goals should be specific. Vague, general goals are rarely accomplished. Saying you are going to "reduce crashes by 10 percent" is not necessarily a goal that you can achieve, desirable as it might be. You have no control over many variables associated with the goal, so select a realistic goal. Law enforcement officers in the field may set a goal of "increasing contacts with traffic violators by 10 contacts per day." This *would* be both realistic and achievable.

In the same vein, goals should not be excessively difficult. Excessively high goals destroy the chance for personal achievement. Goals must be attainable. If employees can help determine goals, they are more likely to achieve them. These goals may be higher than if managers establish them. An example of an unrealistic goal would be that all officers become expert sharpshooters. Varied levels of shooting ability exist. A more realistic goal would be that all officers take firearms range practice and qualify.

Goal setting, goal achievement and ultimate performance are directly related. It is exciting to realize that few people use more than 20 to 30 percent of their potential. People have few limits except those they impose on themselves. The 4-minute mile was considered impossible—until Roger Bannister ran it. The 7-foot high jump, the 17-foot pole vault—these are more examples of the impossible achieved.

Untapped potential exists in you and your people. The task is to create an exciting workplace in which people want to grow and develop and are helped to do so.

Holistic Goal Setting Although managers are not technically responsible for their subordinates' off-the-job activities and aspirations, people have much more to them than their jobs. Indeed, a common problem of law enforcement officers is that their jobs become all-encompassing, overshadowing other important aspects of life. Effective managers consider themselves and those they manage as "total" people. **Holistic personal goals** should include not only the job/career, but also any other areas of importance such as financial, social, avocational and the like. Strong (2004, p.65) asserts: "Balance is the key. Officers need to separate themselves from the profession's day-to-day grind. Otherwise we live the profession 24-7 which can result in becoming hardened and calloused toward society." Maintaining a balance between work and home will help officers focus on their mission of protecting and serving and will ensure healthy lives outside law enforcement (Strong, p.65).

holistic personal goals • include all aspects of a person's life: career/job, financial, personal, family/relationships and spiritual/service.

Managers will naturally be most concerned with the career/job-related goals such as learning new skills, but the other areas are also important. Managers should take care not to foster a lopsided workplace culture, focused entirely on career/job goals. Figure 8.2 illustrates the various aspects of each individual that might be part of any growth and development program.

Goals and Values

Closely related to goals are the values you hold—what is important to you. What are your **key result areas**—broad categories people often talk about as important? Figure 8.3 lists 20 key result areas commonly identified.

key result areas • the goals of an organization.

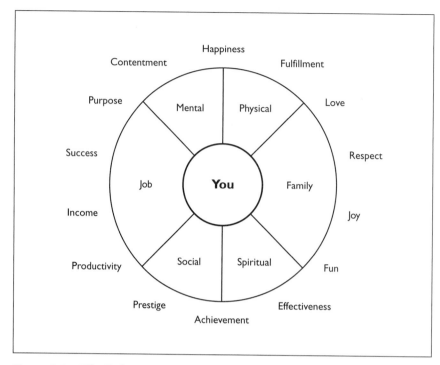

Figure 8.2   Life Circle

Source: Steven R. Covey. *The 7 Habits of Highly Effective People.* New York: Simon and Schuster, 1989, p.270. Copyright © 1989 by Steven R. Covey. Reprinted by permission of Franklin Covey Co.

touchstone values • what people say is important to them.

daily values • how people actually spend their time and energy.

Rank from 1 to 10 (1 being the most important) what you want. These are your **touchstone values.** Then rank how you actually spend the majority of your time, energy and money day to day. These are your **daily values.** How do the rankings compare?

 Touchstone values, what people say is important to them, and *daily values*, how people actually spend their time and energy, need to correlate.

Often what people value and what they spend the majority of their time on conflict. For example, a person may have family as his or her Number 1 touchstone value,

Achievement (sense of accomplishment)	Physical health (attractiveness and vitality)
Work (paying own way)	Emotional health (handle inner conflicts)
Adventure (exploration, risks, excitement)	Meaningful work (relevant/purposeful job)
Personal freedom (independence, choices)	Affection (warmth, giving/receiving love)
Authenticity (being frank and genuinely myself)	Pleasure (enjoyment, satisfaction, fun)
Expertness (being excellent at something)	Wisdom (mature understanding, insight)
Service (contribute to satisfaction of others)	Family (happy/contented living situation)
Leadership (having influence and authority)	Recognition (being well known; prestige)
Money (plenty of money for things I want)	Security (having a secure, stable future)
Spirituality (my religious beliefs/experiences)	Self-growth (continuing development)

Figure 8.3   Key Result Areas Achieved through Touchstone and Daily Values

Source: David G. Lee, Senior Consultant with Personal Decisions, Inc. of Minneapolis, MN. Reprinted with permission.

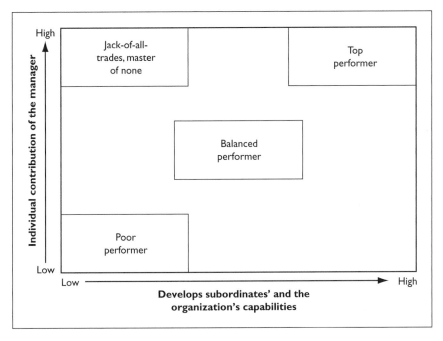

Figure 8.4   Balanced Performer

yet have work as the Number 1 daily value. Managers and those they manage need to examine their touchstone and daily values and seek a closer correlation between them.

Balanced Performer Managers and Empowerment

It cannot be repeated often enough: The most effective managers are those who accomplish priority tasks through their people. Managers who do everything themselves, no matter how well the tasks are done, are *not* effective managers, as Figure 8.4 illustrates.

Managers who concentrate on excelling themselves, on climbing up through the ranks rather than helping their subordinates to excel, are not balanced performers. Nor are the managers who do little or nothing themselves, relying on subordinates to carry the load but without providing an example for them to follow.

 Managers who contribute their efforts to accomplishing department goals while simultaneously developing their subordinates into top performers are superior **balanced performer managers** who empower others.

Managers who empower allow subordinates to grow to their fullest potential.

balanced performer managers • develop subordinates' and an organization's capabilities.

Stages of Growth

The stages of growth in a manager–employee relationship can be compared to that of a parent and child.

 The three stages of growth are dependent, independent and interdependent.

The first stage is the *dependent* stage. Rookies are initially learning the job and are very dependent on others. They watch, follow and need direction. The manager's role at this stage is usually to *tell* them what to do.

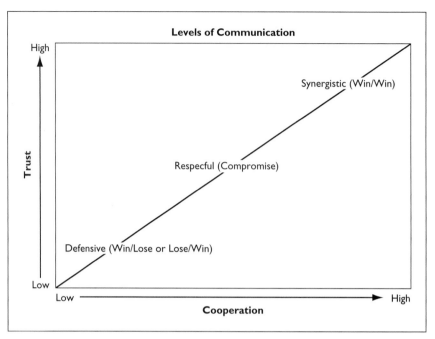

Figure 8.5 The Interaction of Cooperation, Trust and Open Communication to Produce Synergism
Source: Stephen R. Covey. *The 7 Habits of Highly Effective People.* New York: Simon and Schuster, 1989, p.270. Copyright © 1989 by Stephen R. Covey. Reprinted by permission of Franklin Covey Co.

As officers grow, develop and gain confidence, they become more *independent,* just as adolescents learn to be less dependent on their parents. The manager's role at this point is to allow more freedom and give more responsibility. Traditionally, managers who brought their people to this level felt they had done their job—moving their subordinates from dependence to independence.

More progressive managers, those who use participative leadership approaches, take their subordinates one step further, moving them to being **interdependent.** The role of the manager shifts to that of a collaborator—similar to the relationship of a parent to an adult son or daughter. In such a relationship levels of trust, cooperation and communication are high, producing **synergy,** where the whole is greater than the sum of its parts. It is the effect produced by a finely tuned orchestra. The relationship is illustrated in Figure 8.5.

One major problem for supervisors is adjusting techniques for handling personnel on the same shift who have diverse experiences. Supervising an officer with 10 years' experience demands different approaches than would be used with a new recruit. Veteran officers have knowledge, experience and self-confidence that rookies lack. Supervisors should seek input on decisions from these veteran officers, giving credit where merited, praising good work and mentoring rather than managing. Supervisors should not unknowingly punish veteran officers by overloading them because of their experience.

Education is one important way to move employees from dependence to independence and finally to interdependence. All members of the police department should be encouraged to continue their education through special seminars, undergraduate and graduate courses, in-service training, research, writing and teaching, as discussed in Chapter 7.

interdependent (stage of growth) • cooperate, care for, assist and support the team effort.

synergy • where the whole is greater than the sum of its parts.

Managers as Mentors

Every law enforcement organization has employees who need help to be better people and better employees. Managers can make that difference by assuming the role of **mentor**—being a role model, teacher, motivator, communicator, coach, resource person, counselor, supporter, advisor, talent developer, guide, demonstrator and protector (Colaprete, 2004, p.49). New employees in particular, at any level, can benefit from a mentor's knowledge of the history of the organization and its values, norms, policies, potential pitfalls and organizational culture (Deck, 2004, p.27).

Mentoring, introduced in Chapter 7, is commonly explained as a more experienced person helping a less experienced person to develop his or her capabilities and maximize potential (Crouch, 2005, p.69). It may be a formal or informal process. The best mentors are those with a passion for and thorough knowledge of a subject and the ability to pass on that passion and knowledge (Crouch, p.71). They are also able to hold in check the impulse to take over and do something quicker and perhaps easier.

Whomever is chosen to be a mentor, they should be familiar not only with the everyday tasks of the job but also with the administrative aspects of the job (Schembra, 2003, p.39). The mentor should identify and explain the types and kinds of supervisory or management problems and duties inherent in the new position. According to Colaprete (p.49): "Research indicates that mentored individuals perform better on the job, advance more rapidly within the organization, report more job and career satisfaction, and express lower turnover intentions than their non-mentored counterparts."

 A mentor is a wise, trusted teacher or counselor. Law enforcement managers are in an ideal position to be mentors.

Usually a mentor is of senior status and counsels a younger person, but sometimes mentors are of equal seniority. In fact, two people may be mentors to each other in different areas of work. Mentors help further the right type of education; express confidence in the other person; correct actions that, if continued, could be detrimental to advancement; and foster the right attitudes.

The purpose of mentoring is to help mentees reach their full potential. Most law enforcement officers who have worked their way to the top of the organization have had mentors along the way. They have also built up their career currency.

mentor • a more experienced person who helps a less experienced person develop his or her capabilities and maximize potential.

Developing Career Currency

Career currency is "the sum of all the professional qualities, characteristics, traits and skills an officer possesses" as well as what the officer does and how it is done (Borrello, 2004, p.94). Borrello (pp.96–100) compares career currency to a solid brick wall, built over time, brick by brick, and he offers several suggestions for building career currency beyond what is normally expected, including the following:

- Be a developer of others, perhaps an FTO, an instructor or a mentor.
- Become a subject matter expert.
- Become a published author.
- Maintain professional affiliations.
- Start networking with those who have notable recognition in law enforcement or are experts in their fields.
- Seek public speaking opportunities.
- Maintain personal and professional balance.

Career currency includes enhancing one's professional skills or helping others augment their skill sets. Here a CDU (civil disturbance unit) police officer (L) trains other members of the Washington DC police force at the Metropolitan Police Training Center in Lorton, Virginia.

Career currency can open doors to more assignments or positions and promotions: "The more career currency an officer has, the more he has to offer and the better position he will be in. Substantial career currency pays dividends by giving officers more options to choose from, which represents freedom within a career" (Borrello, p.100). An officer who invests time and energy in career currency is also likely to have a positive attitude toward his or her chosen profession and the future.

Developing Positive Attitudes

Effective managers are upbeat and positive. They see opportunities in setbacks. They encourage risk taking and are supportive when mistakes happen. And they encourage these attitudes in their subordinates.

Personality problems can be more devastating to employees than poor work performance. Managers must help certain employees to develop—those who are loners, who are sarcastic, who talk incessantly about themselves, who constantly complain or who have other personality problems. Directing them to outside counseling may be necessary. Managers have a responsibility to deal with problems in employee attitudes. Dealing with problem behaviors is the focus of Chapter 10.

Attitudes are not something managers can take away from someone. They are intangible. What people say and do and how they behave determine how others perceive them. Working with employees on specific negative attitudes can be an important part of their growth and development. British psychiatrist J. A. Hadfield illustrates the power of a person's mental attitude in his book *The Psychology of Power.* He describes having three people test the effect of mental suggestion on their strength, as measured by gripping a dynamometer. Hadfield first tested them for a baseline, giving no suggestions. The average grip was 101 pounds. He then hypnotized them and suggested they were very weak. Their average grip dropped to 29 pounds. He next suggested they were very strong, and the average grip jumped to 142 pounds.

Officers' attitudes are important personally, but they are also crucial to the public's perception of officers in general and the department they represent.

Developing a Positive Image

How people see themselves is their self-image. How others see them is their public image. The two often differ, as the Johari Window illustrated earlier.

A critical part of a subordinate's development is creating a positive public image. As Will Rogers noted: "You never get a second chance to make a good first impression." This is particularly true for law enforcement officers, who often have only one contact with individual citizens. Officers in a large city who make a traffic stop, for example, are unlikely to ever see that particular driver again. How they approach the driver, what they say and do, is the image the driver will retain of the officer. It may also become the image that person has of the entire law enforcement organization.

Managers must help subordinates learn to make favorable impressions whenever and wherever possible. Because law enforcement officers are so visible, they leave an impression even when they make no contact, merely by the way they patrol, their appearance, their manner and their attitude.

Their uniforms, their badges, their guns—all smack of authority. Add mirrored sunglasses, handcuff tie tacks and a swaggering walk, and a negative image is likely to be conveyed. Law enforcement officers should be encouraged to consider how they look, how they walk and how they talk to the public, especially when in uniform. The police uniform conveys power and authority. Officers can soften this image by considering the public as their "customers" or "clients" and treating them with respect.

Tinsley et al. (2003, p.42) suggest that strict *grooming standards* are needed to ensure safety, discipline and uniformity; to promote an *esprit de corps*; and to gain public respect. According to their survey of 200 citizens, fewer than 20 percent of those surveyed approved of male officers wearing plain stud earrings, having hair below the shirt collar, having a goatee and shaved head at the same time, having tattoos anywhere, wearing any jewelry, having pierced eyebrows, having a pierced nose or other facial piercing. For female officers, fewer than 20 percent of those surveyed approved of tattoos, earrings, dyed hair, jewelry, pierced nose, pierced eyebrows or other facial piercing. The majority of those surveyed felt that relaxing grooming standards would erode public confidence in the police and that respect, trust and pride would decrease.

 Law enforcement officers who have a professional appearance and act with competence and courtesy will leave a favorable impression with the majority of the public.

According to the *Sourcebook of Criminal Justice Statistics 2003* (p.115), 20 percent of those polled reported a "great deal" of confidence in police in 2003 to protect from violent crime, compared with 15 percent in 1981; 40 percent reported "quite a lot" of confidence in the police, compared with 34 percent in 1981. This is a large improvement. In 2004 (*Sourcebook*, p.113), 64 percent reported a great deal or quite a lot of confidence in the police.

Results of a study on the relationship between confidence in police and community policing suggest that minorities and younger people have a less favorable perception of police (Ren et al., 2005, p.55). Findings also suggest that citizen confidence is an area police management can use to measure the effectiveness of programs they implement. Frank et al. (2005, p.207) note that the relationship between the police and the public has taken on "added significance" under community policing. In addition, the police depend heavily on citizens to be successful in performing their duties (Rosenbaum et al., 2005, p.343). Research by Schafer et al. (2003, p.441) establishes a nexus between the public perception of police and their ability to achieve department goals and objectives. They (p.463) conclude that their findings "clearly demonstrate that the police can substantially improve their standing with the public by making efforts to ensure the public is satisfied with their specific interactions with the police."

Schanlaub (2004, p.141) further suggests that the public's perception of police can affect officers from entry level to command staff: "Politicians making funding decisions for pay, benefits, equipment and department manpower increases will listen to their constituents, the general public. Cooperation from the general public during investigations or events are obtained easier if there is a positive image of the local police."

Margolis and March (2004, p.25), likewise, stress that the police image "defines" the department's standing and affects the department's recruitment and retention, its budget and the support it receives from the city and community.

Research by Nofziger and Williams (2005, p.248) indicates that confidence in the police is influenced predominantly by impressions that crime has decreased or by having a positive encounter with police. Such confidence in police can significantly increase feelings of being safe.

The Police-Public Contact Survey 2002 reports that 45.3 million people had face-to-face contact with the police (primarily in traffic stops) and 90.1 percent of those surveyed believed police acted properly during their encounter. Management, through their training and supervision, can shape the relationship between residents and officers working the streets: "Whether police are polite or abrasive, concerned or aloof, or helpful or unresponsive to the people's obvious needs depends on actions taken by department leaders" (Skogan, 2005, p.298). Image is also important to officer safety, with many suspects openly admitting to "sizing up" an officer's ability to defend himself or herself by appearance alone (Blum, 2004, p.19).

A positive image will be greatly enhanced by treating all citizens fairly and equally. This often requires officers to recognize their personal biases and to deal with them. Much of officers' images are shaped by how they treat those who are different from themselves, be it a gender, racial or economic difference.

Developing Cultural Awareness and Sensitivity

Cultural awareness is another critical area of development for law enforcement personnel.

cultural awareness • understanding the diversity of the United States, the dynamics of minority–majority relationships, the dynamics of sexism and racism, and the issues of nationalism and separatism.

 Cultural awareness means understanding the diversity of the United States, the dynamics of minority–majority relationships, the dynamics of sexism and racism and the issues of nationalism and separatism.

Some difficulties arising from cultural differences were discussed in Chapter 4. Officers need to appreciate diversity both within their departments and in their communities. Most people understand and accept that our society is multicultural. Although the United States has been called a melting pot of people from all parts of the world, it is more like a salad bowl, where some enjoy majority status and others are viewed as minorities.

Members of the majority often view things quite differently from those in the minority. Elements of majority and minority worldviews have been outlined by the Minnesota Peace Officer Standards and Training (POST) Board. The **majority worldview** includes the following:

majority worldview • beliefs held by those in the majority.

- The majority views its philosophy and ideas as being the most legitimate and valid.
- Minority viewpoints, although their expression may be tolerated, lack the force and power of the majority and therefore are less valid than and secondary to the majority viewpoint.
- Minority members have the option of leaving society if they cannot abide by majority rule.
- Alternative viewpoints are often disruptive or disloyal.
- Power, status and wealth are the result of hard work and/or genetics.

The **minority worldview** includes the following:

minority worldview • beliefs held by those in the minority.

- Minorities must perform better to be accepted as average.
- Majority groups have power and control major institutions.
- Minority groups lack the power to control their own destiny.
- The minority views fairness as more valid than power, status and wealth.
- The minority views success as achievable only by working through the rules set by the majority.
- The minority world views the criminal justice system as biased against minorities.

Research by Weitzer and Tuch (2005, p.279) reports: "Race is one of the most consistent predictors of attitudes toward criminal justice institutions. . . . It is well established that African-Americans hold less favorable opinions than whites." Similar findings are reported by Tyler (2005, p.322), who found public trust and confidence in the police to be generally low with minority members. This may be the result of research findings such as those of Engel and Calnon (2004, p.49) showing that young black and Hispanic males are at increased risk for citations, searches, arrests and uses of force. Such findings often result in charges of racial profiling, discussed shortly.

In addition to members of minority groups who are U.S. citizens, the United States is faced with thousands of illegal immigrants of different races, ethnic groups, religions and cultures. Citizenship is an important issue for arresting officers because, under Vienna Convention rights, officers must notify noncitizens of their right to contact their consulate before making any postarrest statements.

Many immigrants may become victims, but because they come from cultures in which law enforcement officers are feared rather than seen as protectors, they are unlikely to cooperate with officers or to report when they are victimized.

In a sense, law enforcement officers are in a better position than many to understand minority status because they often view themselves as being in the minority, isolated from the mainstream of society. As law enforcement officers become aware of their own culture and as community policing gains ground, officers may seek to reduce this view of themselves as a minority, to interact more with the public and to see themselves as part of the mainstream.

© Michael Newman/PhotoEdit

Cultural awareness is a critical area of development for law enforcement personnel. Officers must appreciate the cultural diversity that exists within their communities. One way is for local patrol officers to interact with the people of their neighborhoods, like this officer who takes time to talk with a business owner who is an immigrant from the Philippines.

An important aspect of cultural awareness is understanding and respecting gender differences as well as differences in sexual preference. Cultural awareness also means identifying and respecting the rights of specific separatist/nationalist groups currently active in American society, including the Ku Klux Klan, the American Nazi Party, neo-Nazi skinheads, the Aryan Brotherhood/White Supremacists, Posse Commitatus, the National Socialist Party, the Black Muslim Movement, the American Indian Movement (AIM) and the Jewish Defense League (JDL). When such groups engage in terrorist activity, such as the 1995 bombing of Oklahoma City's Murrah Federal Building, it may be difficult to remain objective. When hate groups' words translate into criminal actions, they have gone well beyond exercising their civil rights.

Another challenge regarding immigrants is that they often settle in poor neighborhoods that have high crime rates and may therefore be associated with crime. Law enforcement personnel must guard against stereotyping such immigrants as criminals simply because they live in crime-infested neighborhoods. Such stereotyping may lead to racial profiling.

Racial Profiling

Racial profiling is defined by Batton and Kadleck (2004, p.31) as "the use of discretionary authority by law enforcement officers in encounters with minority motorists, typically within the context of a traffic stop, that result in the disparate treatment of minorities."

The *Sourcebook of Criminal Justice Statistics 2003* (p.126) reports that 53 percent of Americans believe racial profiling occurs when motorists are stopped on roads and highways, and only 31 percent believe such profiling is justified. A year-long study by Amnesty International found that nearly 32 million Americans, a number equivalent to Canada's population, have been victims of racial profiling, and 87 million Americans are at risk of being targeted because of their ethnicity or religious background (*Threat and Humiliation: Racial Profiling, Domestic Security and Human Rights in the United States*, 2004, p.vi). The literature is filled with studies confirming the "crime" of driving while black (DWB) or driving while Hispanic (DWH). President Bush has forbid racial profiling by the 70 federal law enforcement agencies, and several states have done likewise (Gardner and Anderson, 2004, p.269).

The Supreme Court decision in *Whren v. United States* (1966) affirmed that police officers can stop vehicles if they have reasonable suspicion of a traffic violation, even though they have no evidence of criminal activity. The officer's intent or pretext for stopping the vehicle is irrelevant. This decision places officers under pressure to have clear, bias-free policies regarding citizen stops. Cooke (2004, p.21) suggests the following model policy to avoid the appearance of racial profiling: "Officers shall not stop, detain, arrest, search or attempt to search anyone based solely upon the person's race, sex, sexual orientation, gender, national origin, ethnicity, age, or religion. Officers shall base all such actions on a reasonable suspicion that the person or an occupant of a vehicle has committed an offense."

Novak (2004, p.66) reports that police officers have suggested disproportionate contacts between officers and minorities may be an unanticipated byproduct of the war on drugs, the get-tough-on-crime movement, zero-tolerance policing or perhaps efficient operational policies. In addition, if police are deployed more heavily in minority communities, this will produce high rates of minority stops (Tomaskovic-Devey et al., 2004, p.3). Further, research by Lange et al. (2005, p.193) revealed that the racial makeup of speeding drivers on the New Jersey turnpike differed from that of nonspeeding drivers and closely approximated the racial composition of police stops: "Specifically, the proportion of speeding drivers who were identified as Black mirrored the proportion of Black drivers stopped by police."

It is interesting to consider that before 9-11 a majority of Americans condemned racial profiling, but since that fateful day, the majority of Americans approve of using profiling to identify terrorists (Rojek et al., 2004, p.126).

Profiling after 9-11 A 12-month study by Amnesty International USA found that the unlawful use of race in police, immigration and airport security procedures has expanded since the terrorist attacks of September 11, 2001: "Just as it is inaccurate to talk about racial profiling in the context of the 'War on Drugs' as simply 'Driving While Black or Brown,' it is wrong to characterize racial profiling committed in the name of the 'War on Terror' as simply 'Flying While Arab.'" Lewis (2004, p.ix) stresses: "[Racial Profiling] is a practice that strikes at the root of our national principles of fairness and violates the human dignity of those victimized. The attacks of September 11, 2001 neither justify nor excuse it." He suggests that

racial profiling • any police-initiated action that relies on the race, ethnicity or national origin rather than the behavior of an individual or information that leads the police to a particular individual who has been identified as being or having been engaged in criminal activity.

focusing on race, ethnicity, national origin or religion as a predictor of criminal behavior has always failed as a way to protect society. He cites the admission of Washington, DC, police Chief Charles Ramsey after the arrest of serial snipers John Allen Muhammad and John Lee Malvo: "We were looking for a white van with white people, and we ended up with a blue car with black people."

To avoid charges of racial profiling, officers must focus on a person's behavior in their "profiling." Boston's Logan Airport, from where two planes were hijacked and flown into the twin towers of the World Trade Center on 9-11, not only has spent more than $140 million on an in-line baggage screening system for explosives, it has also trained employees in Behavior Pattern Recognition (BPR), a security method based on two components: observing irregular behavior for the environment and targeting conversations with suspects (Heinecke, 2004, p.80). The method is similar to that used in Israeli airport security, where all passengers are interviewed. Heinecke (p.85) concludes: "Detection of irregular behaviors and persistent targeted conversations with suspects may prevent another 9/11."

Another way to avoid charges of racial profiling is to focus on intelligence regarding known or suspected terrorists. According to Carter (2004, p.iii): "The world of law enforcement intelligence has changed dramatically since September 11, 2001." Carter (p.198) acknowledges that intelligence operations are controversial, in part because of concern that, in their zeal to prevent terrorism, officers will abridge citizens' civil rights. Further controversies involve the fear that law enforcement agencies will gather and keep information about citizens who have not committed crimes but are exercising their civil rights on controversial issues. Carter (p.202) concludes: "America's law enforcement agencies are facing a new challenge. Throughout the history of policing challenges have been faced, they have been met with resolute determination, and America has been safer as a result. This new challenge is no different."

One concerted effort to gather accurate intelligence related to terrorism is that of the FBI's Terrorist Screening Center (TSC). The center was established on September 16, 2003, to facilitate and assist all law enforcement and intelligence agencies in protecting the United States from terrorist attack by:

1. Consolidating the U.S. government's approach to terrorism screening.
2. Maintaining a thorough, accurate, current and secure list of Terrorist Identities Information of known or appropriately suspected terrorists.
3. Providing appropriate and lawful use of that Terrorist Identities Information continuously to support all legitimate screening agencies.
4. Doing the above consistent with the provisions of the Constitution and applicable laws, including protecting the rights of all Americans ("Terrorist Screening Center Fact Sheet," 2005).

A new program, US-VISIT, for United States Visitor and Immigrant Status Indicator Technology, began in January 2005 and requires foreigners to have visas to enter the country and to be digitally fingerprinted and photographed at 115 airports and 14 shipping terminals (Moreno, 2004, p.A21).

After the terrorist attacks on London's subways and busses, many people called for racial, ethnic profiling. Epstein (2005, p.A11) reports the remarks of a New York Assemblyman: "They [terrorists] all look a certain way. It's all very nice to be politically correct, here, but we're talking about terrorism." Getlin (2005) quotes a city councilman with similar views: "There is a particular group who engages in these [terrorism] activities. They're not skinny balding Italian Americans from Staten Island." However, Getlin reports the remarks of the owner of a Middle Eastern herbal shop: "In this neighborhood we support all they do to fight terrorism. But if they single out Muslims just because of who we are, that would be unfair to all of us."

Something to think about: Actor James Woods shared a flight with some of the 9-11 terrorists in August 2001 and reported to the flight attendant that he thought the men were rehearsing a hijacking. Nothing came of Woods' report (Griffith, 2004, p.6). Griffith asks if Woods was paranoid when he reported on his fellow passengers: "Maybe. But on the morning of Sept. 11, 2001, his paranoia became a shining example of vigilance, the kind of nationwide neighborhood watch that we need to foil future terror attacks. And to paraphrase my former college professor, vigilance is a higher state of enlightenment." As long as suspicions are based on behavior, it is not racial profiling.

Profiling as a Legitimate Law Enforcement Tool The problem of racial profiling has, at its center, the fact that *profiling* has been a valuable tool in policing for decades. At airports, law enforcement and security personnel are taught to watch for certain traits—paying for a ticket in cash, no luggage, Middle Eastern descent, nervousness, etc.—to alert them to drug dealers or potential terrorists. Why is this suddenly approved conduct for law enforcement when using the same tactics to profile a drug dealer is not appropriate? It might be appropriate to rename "profiling" to "building a case" with race simply part of most suspect descriptions.

Gallo (2003, p.19) emphasizes the need to distinguish between profiling as a policing technique and as a politically charged term, noting that profiling is a useful tool: "The purpose of profiling is to provide a scientific method for focusing resources. . . . As a scientific method, profiling can be viewed as pattern recognition through systematically collecting, organizing and analyzing information collected by observation or measurement; drawing conclusions in assessing criminal suspicion and sharing data with others." The courts are generally supportive of race being included as one of several factors in identifying suspects. In *United States v. Weaver* (2000), a DEA officer stopped and questioned Arthur Weaver because he was a roughly dressed, young black male on a direct flight from Los Angeles who walked rapidly from the airport toward a cab, had two carry-on bags and no checked luggage, and appeared nervous. Weaver was carrying drugs and was arrested, but he challenged the legality of the officer's intervention. The Eighth Circuit Court of Appeals upheld the officer's conduct, explaining:

> Facts are not to be ignored simply because they may be unpleasant—and the unpleasant fact in this case is that he [DEA agent] had knowledge, based upon his own experience and upon the intelligence reports he had received from Los Angeles authorities, that young male members of the African-American Los Angeles gangs were flooding the Kansas City area with cocaine. To that extent then, race, when coupled with the other factors [the agent] relied upon, was a factor in the decision to approach and ultimately detain [the suspect]. We wish it were otherwise, but we take the facts as they are presented to us, not as we would wish them to be.

Despite such court support, officers must be educated on how to avoid unintentional racial profiling based on personal bias. It might be best to avoid the term *racial profiling,* because profiling has a legitimate place in law enforcement, and replace it with *racially biased policing,* which has no place in law enforcement.

One approach to identifying whether racially biased policing is occurring is to collect data on police-initiated stops of citizens. Most frequently this refers to traffic stops. In 1999 Connecticut was the first state to pass legislation requiring every municipal police agency and the state police to collect data on race for every police-initiated traffic stop. Such data collection presents supervisory challenges, including training officers to collect appropriate data, overcoming resistance to the practice, manipulating data and altering effective policing procedures.

balancing • unfairly stopping unoffending motorists to protect officers from the "statistical microscope" individually or collectively.

Resistance against legislation mandating data collection may result in **balancing,** unfairly stopping unoffending motorists to protect officers from the "statistical microscope" individually or collectively. The rationale is simple. If an officer stops a minority driver, he or she has to stop a certain number of white drivers to make the numbers come out right. This results in a great deal of unproductive work and may generate citizen complaints. **Ghosting,** falsifying patrol logs, might also occur to make the numbers come out right.

ghosting • falsifying patrol logs to make the numbers come out right to avoid charges of racial profiling.

Supervisors should watch for and correct any such practices before they result in formal complaints against the department. Supervisors face a significant challenge to maintain morale in implementing a practice viewed by many officers as an insult and to maintain productivity while ensuring appropriate data is collected.

The Police Executive Research Forum (Fridell, 2004) has published *By the Numbers: A Guide for Analyzing Race Data from Vehicle Stops.* This manual (p.1) defines racially biased policing as "the inappropriate consideration by law enforcement of race or ethnicity in deciding with whom and how to intervene in an enforcement capacity." The step-by-step report details what data sets to collect and how long to compile them before analysis. It explains various benchmarking methods for analyzing data.

In addition to helping subordinates develop a positive attitude, a positive image and cultural awareness and sensitivity, managers should foster a strong sense of integrity and ethical behavior.

Developing a Sense of Ethics and Integrity

ethics • standards of fair and honest conduct.

integrity • steadfast adherence to an ethical code.

Ruby Ridge, Waco, O. J. Simpson, Rodney King, Banner Louisa—these names and others have had the law enforcement community reeling from attacks on its integrity and ethical standards. **Ethics** refers to the rules or standards of fair, honest conduct. Ethics has become a primary focus in almost every profession and is the topic of countless articles, seminars and workshops. **Integrity** refers to steadfast adherence to an ethical code.

ethical behavior • that which is "moral" and "right."

Ethical behavior is that which is "moral" and "right." Law enforcement personnel must develop high ethical standards both on and off duty.

Strong (2005, p.69) suggests that when teaching the components of the "thin blue line," the qualities of loyalty, character, integrity and leadership need to be stressed.

According to Klockars (1983, p.427): "Some areas of human conduct develop their own distinct ethics while others do not." He suggests that special codes of ethics are developed if the area:

- Has some special features making it difficult to bring under the domain of general, conventional ethics. Police, for example, can use force, even deadly force, and may lie and deceive people in their work.
- Involves issues of concern not just to those who practice them, but also to others. They involve moral controversy.
- Involves certain types of misconduct that cannot or perhaps should not be controlled by other means.

Law enforcement fits all three conditions, partly because of its great discretionary power.

Kuidis (2005, p.20) contends: "If you have integrity, nothing else matters. If you don't have integrity, nothing else matters." Borrello (2005, p.65) explains integrity through the analogy of a balloon filled with all the primary elements of ethics—honesty, morals, standards, courage, principles, values. When the balloon is filled and the end is tied into a knot, airtight, uncompromised, the balloon would have *integrity*. Over time, unless care is taken, this integrity can be compromised or even lost.

A multitude of personal, departmental and external forces shape the dynamics of police integrity that ultimately affect each police officer's career. Personal forces that affect police personnel include economy/personal finances, diversity issues in the department, family values/moral literacy, experience with aggressive police tactics, the police subculture, community response to police activities and presence, frustration with the criminal justice system, peer influence and alcohol/drug abuse. Departmental forces that affect police personnel include the promotion system, leadership, reward structures, departmental values/policies, the accountability system, the quality of supervision, the disciplinary system, in-service training, entry-level training and the selection/hiring process. These departmental forces are influenced in part by external forces that affect the entire agency, such as civilian complaint boards, news media, political influences, community demands and other sectors of the criminal justice system (courts and corrections). See Figure 8.6.

To clarify the expectations regarding officer ethics and integrity, most law enforcement departments have a formal code of ethics, often framed and hanging on the wall. Such codes usually have at least three important themes:

- Justice or fairness is the dominant theme. Officers are not to take advantage of people or accept gratuities.
- Because of the importance of the law and the officer as tools of the Constitution, law enforcement behavior must be totally within the bounds set by the law.
- At all times, law enforcement officers must uphold a standard of behavior consistent with their public position.

The Law Enforcement Code of Ethics of the International Association of Chiefs of Police (IACP) (Figure 8.7) is an example of such a standard.

A code of ethics helps officers make decisions lawfully, humanely and fairly. However, ethics is not about what we say; it is about what we do. To determine whether an action is ethical, consider the following questions: Is it legal? Is it the best solution for the greatest number of people? How would you feel if it were made public? Does it follow the Golden Rule? Would you like such a decision directed at you? Is it the right thing to do? Blanchard and Peale (1988, p.27) set forth the following "ethics check" questions:

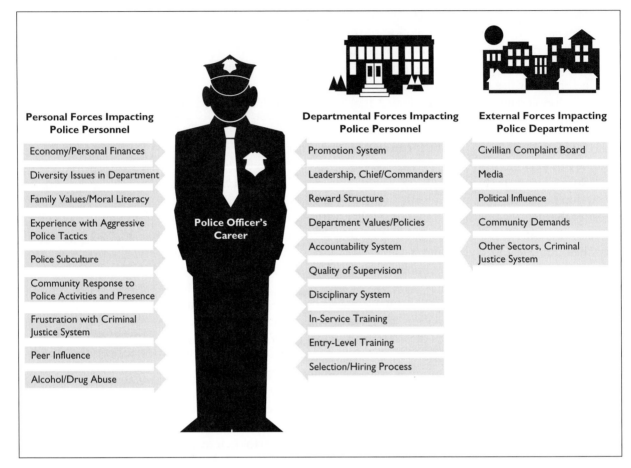

Figure 8.6   Dynamics of Police Integrity

Source: Stephen J. Gaffigan and Phyllis P. McDonald. *Police Integrity: Public Service with Honor.* U.S. Department of Justice. January 1997, p.92. (NCH 163811)

1. Is it legal? Will I be violating either civil law or company policy?
2. Is it balanced? Is it fair to all concerned in the short term as well as in the long term? Does it promote win–win relationships?
3. How will it make me feel about myself? Will it make me proud? Would I feel good if my decision was published in the newspaper? Would I feel good if my family knew about it?

Fair or not, the conduct of law enforcement personnel is expected to be above reproach. Many pressures in the real world push leaders toward compromise and expedience (Vernon, 2003, p.218). One area in which officer conduct may be called into question is in whether or not they accept gratuities.

Accepting Gratuities

gratuity • a favor or gift, usually in the form of money, given in return for service, for example, a tip given to a waiter in a restaurant.

Withrow and Dailey (2004, p.159) note: "Very few issues cause more heated debate among police scholars and practitioners than gratuities." A **gratuity** is defined as a favor or gift, usually in the form of money, given in return for service; for example, a tip given to a waiter in a restaurant. Common arguments for and against gratuities have been set forth.

Law Enforcement Code of Ethics*

All law enforcement officers must be fully aware of the ethical responsibilities of their position and must strive constantly to live up to the highest possible standards of professional policing.

The International Association of Chiefs of Police believes it is important that police officers have clear advice and counsel available to assist them in performing their duties consistent with these standards and has adopted the following ethical mandates as guidelines to meet these ends.**

Primary Responsibilities of a Police Officer: A police officer acts as an official representative of government who is required and trusted to work within the law. The officer's powers and duties are conferred by statute. The fundamental duties of a police officer include serving the community; safeguarding lives and property; protecting the innocent; keeping the peace; and ensuring the rights of all to liberty, equality and justice.

Performance of the Duties of a Police Officer: A police officer shall perform all duties impartially, without favor or affection or ill will and without regard to status, sex, race, religion, political belief or aspiration. All citizens will be treated equally with courtesy, consideration and dignity.

Officers will never allow personal feelings, animosities or friendships to influence official conduct. Laws will be enforced appropriately and courteously and, in carrying out their responsibilities, officers will strive to obtain maximum cooperation from the public. They will conduct themselves in appearance and deportment in such a manner as to inspire confidence and respect for the position of public trust they hold.

Discretion: A police officer will use responsibly the discretion vested in the position and exercise it within the law. The principle of reasonableness will guide the officer's determinations and the officer will consider all surrounding circumstances in determining whether any legal action shall be taken.

Consistent and wise use of discretion, based on professional policing competence, will do much to preserve good relationships and retain the confidence of the public. There can be difficulty in choosing between conflicting courses of action. It is important to remember that a timely word of advice rather than arrest—which may be correct in appropriate circumstances—can be a more effective means of achieving a desired end.

Use of Force: A police officer will never employ unnecessary force or violence and will use only such force in the discharge of duty as is reasonable in all circumstances.

Force should be used only with the greatest restraint and only after discussion, negotiation and persuasion have been found to be inappropriate or ineffective. While the use of force is occasionally unavoidable, every police officer will refrain from applying the unnecessary infliction of pain or suffering and will never engage in cruel, degrading or inhuman treatment of any person.

Confidentiality: Whatever a police officer sees, hears or learns of, which is of a confidential nature, will be kept secret unless the performance of duty or legal provision requires otherwise.

Members of the public have a right to security and privacy, and information obtained about them must not be improperly divulged.

Integrity: A police officer will not engage in acts of corruption or bribery, nor will an officer condone such acts by other police officers.

The public demands that the integrity of police officers be above reproach. Police officers must, therefore, avoid any conduct that might compromise integrity and thus undercut the public confidence in a law enforcement agency. Officers will refuse to accept any gifts, presents, subscriptions, favors, gratuities or promises that could be interpreted as seeking to cause the officer to refrain from performing official responsibilities honestly and within the law. Police officers must not receive private or special advantage from their official status. Respect from the public cannot be bought; it can only be earned and cultivated.

Cooperation with Other Officers and Agencies: Police officers will cooperate with all legally authorized agencies and their representatives in the pursuit of justice.

An officer or agency may be one among many organizations that may provide law enforcement services to a jurisdiction. It is imperative that a police officer assist colleagues fully and completely with respect and consideration at all times.

**Adopted by the Executive Committee of the International Association of Chiefs of Police on October 17, 1989, during its 96th Annual Conference in Louisville, Kentucky, to replace the 1957 code of ethics adopted at the 64th Annual IACP Conference.*
***The IACP gratefully acknowledges the assistance of Sir John C. Hermon, former chief constable of the Royal Ulster Constabulary, who gave full license to the association to freely use the language and concepts presented in the RUC's "Professional Policing Ethics," Appendix I of the Chief Constable's Annual Report, 1988, presented to the Police Authority for Northern Ireland, for the preparation of this code.*

Continued

Figure 8.7 Law Enforcement Code of Ethics

Source: Reprinted from *The Police Chief*, Vol. LVII, No. 6, page 10, June 1990. Copyright held by the International Association of Chiefs of Police, Inc., 515 N. Washington St., Alexandria, Virginia 22314. U.S.A. Further reproduction without express written permission from IACP is strictly prohibited.

Personal/Professional Capabilities: Police officers will be responsible for their own standard of professional performance and will take every reasonable opportunity to enhance and improve their level of knowledge and competence.

Through study and experience, a police officer can acquire the high level of knowledge and competence that is essential for the efficient and effective performance of duty. The acquisition of knowledge is a never-ending process of personal and professional development that should be pursued constantly.

Private Life: Police officers will behave in a manner that does not bring discredit to their agencies or themselves.

A police officer's character and conduct while off duty must always be exemplary, thus maintaining a position of respect in the community in which he or she lives and serves. The officer's personal behavior must be beyond reproach.

Allowing Gratuities Gratuities help create a bond between officers and the public, thus fostering community policing goals. They represent a nonwritten form of appreciation and usually are given with no expectation of anything in return. Most gratuities are too small to be a significant motivator of actions. The practice is so deeply entrenched that efforts to root it out will be ineffective and cause unnecessary violations of the rules. A complete ban makes officers appear as though they cannot distinguish between a friendly gesture and a bribe. Finally, some businesses and restaurants insist on giving gratuities. However, many contend that accepting gratuities is often the first step in officers' engaging in unethical behavior and from there into actual corruption.

Banning Gratuities Accepting gratuities violates most departments' policies and the law enforcement code of ethics. Even the smallest gifts create a sense of obligation. Even if nothing is expected in return, the gratuity may create an appearance of impropriety. Although most officers can discern between friendly gestures and bribes, some may not. Gratuities create an unfair distribution of services to those who can afford them, voluntary taxing or private funding of a private service. Finally, it is unprofessional. Moore (2005, p.122) cautions: "Your integrity and that of your agency is worth much more than the cost of a cup of coffee." Table 8.2 summarizes the main arguments for and against accepting gratuities. In some departments, accepting gratuities is considered a form of misconduct.

Table 8.2   Arguments for and against Gratuities

Allowing Gratuities	
■ They help create a friendly bond between officers and the public, thus fostering community-policing goals.	■ The practice is so deeply entrenched that efforts to root it out will be ineffective and cause unnecessary violations of the rules.
■ They represent a nonwritten form of appreciation and usually are given with no expectation of anything in return.	■ A complete ban makes officers appear as though they cannot distinguish between a friendly gesture and a bribe.
■ Most gratuities are too small to be a significant motivator of actions.	■ Some businesses and restaurants insist on the practice.

Banning Gratuities	
■ The acceptance violates most departments' policies and the law enforcement code of ethics.	■ Although most officers can discern between friendly gestures and bribes, some may not.
■ Even the smallest gifts create a sense of obligation.	■ They create an unfair distibution of services to those who can afford gratuities, voluntary taxing or private funding of a public service.
■ Even if nothing is expected in return, the gratuity may create an appearance of impropriety.	■ It is unprofessional.

Source: Mike White. "The Problem with Gratuities." *FBI Law Enforcement Bulletin,* July 2002, p.21.

Misconduct

Son and Rome (2004, p.179) contend: "Police misconduct has been a social issue in the United States for much of the 20th century." This interest continues today. Police misconduct involves a broad spectrum of behavior including mistreatment of offenders, discrimination, illegal search and seizure, violation of suspects' constitutional rights, perjury, evidence planting and other forms of corruption.

Research has found that nearly 70 percent of the police officers surveyed observed someone accepting free coffee or food or speeding unnecessarily (Son and Rome, p.199). Much less common were more serious and unacceptable forms of misconduct, the most frequent of which was racial harassment, with 17 percent of officers having personally witnessed such harassment.

Unethical Behavior and Corruption

The Knapp Commission, the Mollen Commission Report, the Christopher Commission, the Rampart Board of Inquiry—all found extensive unethical behavior and corruptions in the police departments investigated. Unethical behavior may include taking overlong breaks, abusing sick time, arriving late for work, falsifying time sheets, lying, tampering with evidence, compromising an investigation, being disrespectful to the public, drinking on the job and the like. Corruption goes beyond unethical behavior in that it is done for personal gain.

 The key elements of corrupt behavior are that it (1) is prohibited by law or rule, (2) involves misuse of position and (3) involves a reward or personal gain for the officer.

The Slippery Slope Sherman's Slippery Slope of Corruption posits that police corruption begins with a lowering of ethical expectations and values to attain a gratuity of minor value, for example, accepting a free cup of coffee. Although this action in itself is most likely harmless and inconsequential as a corrupting force, it may over time produce a snowball effect, leading an officer to accept gratuities of larger magnitude. Furthermore, such practices often lead those providing the "freebies" to expect preferential treatment by recipient officers.

Noble Cause and Ends versus Means Another facet of unethical behavior concerns the noble cause corruption dilemma, in which officers believe unlawful means are justified when the result is the protection of human life or some other noble cause. Unquestionably, law enforcement officers face difficult decisions daily.

Because officers are granted awesome coercive authority, it is imperative that police officers exercise their power responsibly and ethically. When confronted with the really "bad guys," it may be tempting to take advantage of this power and the discretion granted to not administer "street justice." It takes moral courage and strong ethical principles to resist the "ends justifying means" pitfall.

Above the Law The public understands that the police are granted special privileges and exceptions from obeying the law. Officers can exceed speed limits, violate traffic controls and carry concealed weapons in the line of duty. During the socialization process, some officers receive the message they are special and above the law. However, "equality under the law" is the foundation of the American criminal justice system. Officers who believe they are above the law subvert the essence of our criminal justice system.

Bad Apples or a Bad Barrel? Often the argument is heard that just as a few "bad apples" can ruin the entire barrel, so a few bad cops can ruin the entire department. Managers must examine their department and find ways to promote integrity and ethical behavior that adheres to this higher standard. According to Trautman, director of the National Institute of Ethics: "The most destructive form of police misconduct is administrators ignoring obvious ethical problems" (Griffith, 2003, p.72). Trautman's research has found that when the "brass" ignores bad cops, a culture of corruption begins to flourish in the department.

The Code of Silence According to Nowicki and Punch (2003, p.330): "To some officers, the most serious aspersion that can be cast upon another officer is to say that he or she breached the code of silence and provided information to internal affairs investigators." Griffith (p.74) suggests: "Police loyalty known as the 'blue wall' or the 'code of silence' has forced many officers to jeopardize their careers and their liberty to cover up another officer's misconduct. The results are often tragic." Quinn (2004) also cautions:

> As terrible as it is, there is no escaping the Code. It is as inevitable as your childhood diseases and just as necessary. Each stinging battle with the Code will be either an inoculation of the spirit and an opportunity to grow stronger or a crippling injury to your integrity. Regardless of the outcome there will be vivid images you can't erase from your memory. There will always be the mental and physical scars to remind you of your battles.
>
> But, each encounter can leave you better prepared both physically and mentally for the tough challenges ahead, if you are willing to admit you're not superman, and you recognize your "dark side" for what it is. Because only when we know the Code of Silence for what it is can we gain some control over it. Either way, you won't escape unscathed because at some point in time you are going to "Walk with the Devil" in order to get the job done [p.27].
>
> Every day is a new challenge and ethical police conduct is often an uphill battle. Even the best of cops have days when they want to give up and do whatever it takes to put a child molester, baby murderer, or other lowlife in prison. When you sit inches away from these scum and they brag about the truly horrific things they have done to an innocent it's easy to abide by the Code—if that's what it takes. When the evidence isn't perfect, you just use a little creative report writing and this guy will never harm another person again. Illegal searches, physical abuse, or even perjury, you know you will be in the company of many good cops who have done the same. But are they really good cops?
>
> The choice of being a "Peace Officer" means there will be many battles in solitary combat with other cops and with yourself. You will not win them all— you cannot—the cards are stacked against you. There will be no medals, awards ceremonies or cheering crowds for the battles you do win. But there will be honor and integrity—in your life and in your work. [pp.13–14.]

Griffith (p.74) quotes Trautman as saying: "Misconduct and the code of silence are the most destructive forces in law enforcement. It is far more likely that an officer's career will be cut short by these things than by a bad guy with a knife in the alley."

Promoting Ethical Behavior and Integrity

A good starting point for promoting ethical behavior and integrity is to eliminate the code of silence. Anderson (2003a, p.120) points out: "When a fellow officer falls into harms way ethically, the ethos of unconditional backup dictates that other officers must take action, get involved, and back each other up ethically." Robinson (2004, p.76) contends that whenever unethical conduct, corruption or brutality occurs, both the employees of the agency and the profession are tainted: "An essential element of a profession is the requirement of self-policing, and each officer and employee of a law enforcement agency has the shared responsibility of policing the actions of other employees."

As a symbolic statement of commitment to ethical behavior, the IACP has recommended a Law Enforcement Oath of Honor:

> *On my honor, I will never betray my badge, my integrity, my character, or the public trust.*
>
> *I will always have the courage to hold myself and others accountable for our actions.*
>
> *I will always uphold the constitution and community I serve.*

In addition to the oath, numerous departmental policies and procedures have been shown to help foster an environment of ethical behavior and officer integrity.

Training and encouraging officers to make ethical decisions is a vital element in promoting community policing and problem solving. Trautman (2003, p.54) further stresses that administrators must openly hold themselves accountable for addressing any obvious ethical problems of the department.

The Long-Range Importance of Developing Personnel

 Developing individuals and team players is important because most future law enforcement managers will come from the lower levels of the organization.

If officers are not self-developed or developed by managers at all levels, where will future executives come from?

Managers as Motivators for Change

Law enforcement organizations are similar to all other organizations. They constantly change. If they are to flourish, they must embrace change and make it work for them. Sometimes change occurs in a revolutionary manner, but most often it is evolutionary. Law enforcement managers at all levels play a significant role in this process, which may involve change in the organizational structure, its goals and its objectives; its members; or in the community it serves. Change involves alteration of attitudes and work behavior as individuals, as team members and as members of the department.

Evaluating the Climate for Growth, Development and Change

Law enforcement managers who want to evaluate their workplace culture and its conduciveness to growth, development and change can use the brief survey in Figure 8.8.

Evaluate Your Organization

1. Inflexible: discourages the new and unusual	1	2	3	4	5	6	7	Open to new ideas; receptive	_____
2. Focused on present or past	1	2	3	4	5	6	7	Future oriented; anticipates future	_____
3. No way to train further or develop new skills	1	2	3	4	5	6	7	Many opportunities to learn new skills	_____
4. Individual effort more important than group effort	1	2	3	4	5	6	7	Cooperative efforts, participation in group is important	_____
5. Little planning and communication	1	2	3	4	5	6	7	Active planning, with involvement of others	_____
TOTAL									_____

If your organization scored between 5 and 19, it is *not* conductive to growth and development. If your organization scored between 20 and 29, the growth and development environment is positive but needs improvement. A score of 30 and above indicates that your organization values growth and development.

Figure 8.8 Evaluate Your Organization Survey

McPherson (2004, p.137) recommends: "Fostering ethical competence among police professionals does not mean sending agency personnel to an ethics seminar. It involves daily lessons in ethics, utilizing learning moments that occur in the course of everyday work."

SUMMARY

The workplace culture is the sum of the beliefs and values shared by those within the organization, serving to formally and informally communicate its expectations. These group attitudes and beliefs are called norms. An officer's first loyalty must be to defend the Constitution of the United States, his or her state constitution and laws, and local laws.

To shape the workplace culture, managers should identify existing norms, evaluate them and then encourage positive norms and try to eliminate negative ones through modeling and training. A positive workplace culture promotes good interpersonal relationships. Such relationships must be built on self-understanding. A model, the Johari Window, shows how people can learn more about themselves and others. The Johari Window describes four parts of a person's identity: the open self, the hidden self, the blind self and the subconscious or undiscovered self.

Personal and organizational goals are a necessary first step for growth and development. A personal goal states what, when and how much. Holistic goal setting should include career/job, financial, personal, family/relationships and spiritual/service. Goals should also consider values. Touchstone values, what people say is important to them, and daily values, how people actually spend their time and energy, need to correlate.

Managers who contribute to accomplishing department goals while simultaneously developing their subordinates into top performers are superior balanced performer managers who empower others. As managers help their people grow and develop, they should be aware of the three stages of growth. Employees initially are dependent. As they grow and develop they become independent and finally interdependent. Managers can often help their people through these stages by mentoring. Law enforcement managers are in an ideal position to be mentors. As mentors, managers should help their subordinates develop positive attitudes, a positive image, cultural awareness and a strong sense of ethics.

In addition to possessing the knowledge and skills required to do the job, law enforcement officers who have a professional appearance and act with competence and courtesy will leave a favorable impression with the majority of the public. To create such positive impressions, law enforcement personnel must develop cultural awareness and sensitivity. They must understand the diversity of the United States, the dynamics of minority–majority relationships, the dynamics of sexism and racism and the issues of nationalism and separatism.

Another important area for growth and development is in ethics. Ethical behavior is that which is "moral" and "right." Law enforcement personnel must develop high ethical standards both on and off duty. The key elements of corrupt behavior are that the conduct (1) is prohibited by law or rule, (2) involves misuse of position and (3) involves a reward or personal gain for the officer. Developing individuals and team players is important because most future law enforcement managers will come from the lower levels of the organization.

CHALLENGE EIGHT

As the new police chief of the Greenfield Police Department, you expected some resistance from officers during the transition from a crime fighting philosophy to a community policing philosophy. Several veteran officers oppose the change. Most younger officers are willing to try community policing and enjoy interacting with the community. Unfortunately, they worry about being rejected by the veteran officers. Most younger officers do not want to buck the prevailing police culture and informal hierarchy.

Officer Blake, a senior officer and vocal opponent of community policing, is an informal department leader. You decide to ride along with him on a patrol shift. He's an honest guy who tells you exactly what is on his mind. Officer Blake was the department shooting champion and unhappy with the cutbacks in firearms training. He thinks the old way of doing things was working just fine. They kept people in line, and the crime rates reflected it. He tells you that community policing is social work, not police work, and that his job is making arrests and keeping the streets safe.

As you listen to Officer Blake, he patrols a park where a group of young Asian men are gathered. He drives by slowly and stares at them. They look down, not making eye contact. Officer Blake looks at you and says, "I don't trust those guys. They're up to something." Officer Blake drives through the parking lot and back past the young men. "I always make sure they know I'm watching them." The young men begin playing soccer.

Officer Blake's next stop is Ruby's Bar and Grill. Several other squads are parked in front of the building. You learn this is their regular break location and that coffee is free, food is half price and a booth is reserved for cops.

1. How would you encourage the new officers' enthusiasm for community policing and help them buck the prevailing culture?

2. Is Officer Blake a good candidate to be a mentor for a new officer?

3. Officer Blake is clearly entrenched in the crime fighting mode of law enforcement. How would his encounter with the young men in the park affect your department's public image?

4. Isolating police officers in squad cars creates a barrier to good communications and can thwart cultural awareness. How could an emphasis on community policing have changed this encounter?

5. As a new chief attempting to implement a community policing strategy, how would you address the issue of gratuities?

DISCUSSION QUESTIONS

1. How would you describe an ethical person? Who might be role models in our society?

2. What would you include in a job description for a law enforcement officer? A sergeant? A chief or sheriff?

3. What norms would you like to see in the law enforcement agency you work for?

4. What do you consider the five most important touchstone values listed in Figure 8.3?

5. What are your three most important touchstone values? Your three most important daily values? Do they correlate? If not, what should you do?

6. What ethical problems have you faced in your life?

7. Have you had any mentors in your life? Been a mentor to someone else? If so, what seemed to enhance the experience?

8. How prevalent do you believe racial profiling is in your community? Your state? The country?

9. Should officers accept gratuities? If so, what is acceptable?

10. What skills would you like to further develop? How important would this be to your law enforcement career?

REFERENCES

Anderson, Jonathan. "Ethical Backup." *Law and Order*, October 2003a, pp.118–120.

Anderson, Jonathan. "The Oath." *Law and Order*, November 2003b, pp.104–105.

Batton, Candice and Kadleck, Colleen. "Theoretical and Methodological Issues in Racial Profiling Research." *Police Quarterly*, March 2004, pp.30–64.

Blanchard, Kenneth and Peale, Norman Vincent. *The Power of Ethical Management.* New York: William Morrow and Company, Inc., 1988.

Blum, Jon. "Image Is not Everything—But It Helps." *The Law Enforcement Trainer*, January/February 2004, pp.19–22.

Borrello, Andrew. "Defining the Building Blocks of Ethics." *Law and Order*, January 2005, pp.65–68.

Borrello, Andrew. "Ten Ways to Develop a Police Career." *Law and Order*, October 2004, pp.94–100.

Carter, David L. *Law Enforcement Intelligence: A Guide for State, Local, and Tribal Law Enforcement Agencies.* Washington, DC: Community Oriented Policing Services Office, November 2004.

Colaprete, Frank A. "The Case for Investigator Mentoring: The Rochester Experience." *The Police Chief*, October 2004, pp.49–52.

Cooke, Leonard G. "Reducing Bias in Policing: A Model Approach in Virginia." *The Police Chief*, June 2004, pp.18–22.

Crouch, Robert. "Mentoring in the Auburn Police Department." *Law and Order*, June 2005, pp.68–74.

Deck, Elaine. "Mentoring for Success." *The Police Chief*, March 2004, pp.27–31.

Engel, Robin Shepard and Calnon, Jennifer M. "Examining the Influence of Drivers' Characteristics during Traffic Stops with Police: Results from a National Survey." *Justice Quarterly*, March 2004, pp.49–90.

Epstein, Edward. "Calls for Racial, Ethnic Profiling Renewed after Transit Attacks; Critics Say it Unfairly Singles Out Minorities." *San Francisco Chronicle*, August 10, 2005, p.A11.

Ford, Robert E. "Saying One Thing, Meaning Another: The Role of Parables in Police Training." *Police Quarterly*, March 2003, pp.84–110.

Frank, James; Smith, Brad W.; and Novak, Kenneth J. "Exploring the Basis of Citizens' Attitudes toward the Police." *Police Quarterly*, June 2005, pp.206–228.

Fridell, Lorie A. *By the Numbers: A Guide for Analyzing Race Data from Vehicle Stops.* Washington, DC: Police Executive Research Forum, 2004.

Gallo, Frank J. "Profiling vs. Racial Profiling: Making Sense of It All." *The Law Enforcement Trainer*, July/August 2003, pp.19–21.

Gardner, Thomas J. and Anderson, Terry M. *Criminal Evidence: Principles and Cases*, 5th ed. Belmont, CA: Wadsworth Publishing Company, 2004.

Getlin, Josh. "Profiling Fears Surface in Subway." *Los Angeles Times*, August 8, 2005.

Griffith, David. "Cracking Down on Bad Cops." *Police*, October 2003, pp.68–74.

Griffith, David. "Watching the Neighborhood." *Police*, April, 2004, p.6.

Heinecke, Jeannine. "Adding Another Layer to the Security Blanket." *Law Enforcement Technology*, March 2004, pp.78–85.

Hill, C. Ellen. "How to Build a Culture." *Law and Order*, September 2005, pp.142–146.

Klockars, Carl B. *Thinking about Police: Contemporary Readings*. New York: McGraw-Hill, 1983.

Kuidis, Debbie. "The Start of a New Lifestyle: A Police Officer's Mission." *FBI Law Enforcement Bulletin*, March 2005, pp.18–21.

Lange, James E.; Johnson, Mark B.; and Voos, Robert B. "Testing the Racial Profiling Hypothesis for Seemingly Disparate Traffic Stops on the New Jersey Turnpike." *Justice Quarterly*, June 2005, pp.193–223.

Lewis, Timothy K. "Foreword." In *Threat and Humiliation: Racial Profiling, Domestic Security, and Human Rights in the United States*. New York: Amnesty International USA, September 2004.

MacKenzie, John. "The Siren's Call." *Police*, January 2005, p.72.

Margolis, Gary J. and March, Noel C. "Creating the Police Department's Image." *The Police Chief*, April 2004, pp.25–34.

McPherson, Nancy. "Reflections from the Field on Needed Changes in Community Policing." In *Community Policing: The Past, Present, and Future*, edited by Lorie Fridell and Mary Ann Wycoff. Washington, DC: The Annie E. Casey Foundation and the Police Executive Research Forum, 2004, pp.127–140.

Moore, Carole. "Free Cup of Coffee." *Law Enforcement Technology*, April 2005, p.122.

Moreno, Sylvia. "Border Security Measures to Tighten Next Month." *Washington Post*, October 15, 2004, p.A21.

Moskos, Peter. "Old-School Cops in a New School World." *Law Enforcement News*, October 15/31, 2003, p.9.

Nofziger, Stacey and Williams, L. Susan. "Perceptions of Police and Safety in a Small Town." *Police Quarterly*, June 2005, pp.248–270.

Novak, Kenneth J. "Disparity and Racial Profiling in Traffic Enforcement." *Police Quarterly*, March 2004, pp.65–96.

Nowicki, Dennis E. and Punch, Maurice E. "Fostering Integrity and Professional Standards." *Local Government Police Management*, 4th ed. Edited by William A. Geller and Darrel W. Stephens. Washington, DC: International City/County Management Association, 2003, pp.315–352.

Orrick, Dwayne. "Police Turnover." *The Police Chief*, September 2005, pp.36–40.

Paoline, Eugene A., III. "Taking Stock: Toward Richer Understanding of Police Culture." *Journal of Criminal Justice*, Vol. 31, No.3, 2003, p.199.

Paoline, Eugene A., III. "Shedding Light on Police Culture: An Examination of Officers' Occupational Attitudes." *Police Quarterly*, June 2004, pp.205–236.

The Police-Public Contact Survey (PPCS) 2002. Washington, DC: Bureau of Justice Statistics, 2002.

Quinn, Michael W. *Walking with the Devil: The Police Code of Silence* (*What Bad Cops Don't Want You to Know and Good Cops Won't Tell You*). Minneapolis, MN: Quinn and Associates, 2004.

Ren, Ling; Cao, Liqun; Lovrich, Nicholas; and Gaffney, Michael. "Linking Confidence in the Police with the Performance of the Police: Community Policing Can Make a Difference." *Journal of Criminal Justice*, Vol. 33, No. 1, 2005, p.55.

Robinson, Patricia. "Shared Responsibility: The Next Step in Professional Ethics." *The Police Chief*, August 2004, pp.76–81.

Rojek, Jeff; Rosenfeld, Richard; and Decker, Scott. "The Influence of Driver's Race on Traffic Stops in Missouri." *Police Quarterly*, March 2004, pp.126–147.

Rosenbaum, Dennis P.; Schuck, Amie M.; Costello, Sandra K.; Hawkins, Darnell F.; and Ring, Marianne I. "Attitudes toward the Police: The Effects of Direct and Vicarious Experience." *Police Quarterly*, September 2005, pp.343–365.

Schafer, Joseph A.; Huebner, Beth M.; and Bynum, Timothy S. "Citizen Perception of Police Services: Race, Neighborhood Context, and Community Policing." *Police Quarterly*, December 2003, pp.440–468.

Schanlaub, Russell. "Public Perception of Police." *Law and Order*, July 2004, pp.140–141.

Schembra, John. "Transitional Training." *Law and Order*, June 2003, pp.38–42.

Skogan, Wesley G. "Citizen Satisfaction with Police Encounters." *Police Quarterly*, September 2005, pp.298–321.

Son, In Soo and Rome, Dennis M. "The Prevalence and Visibility of Police Misconduct: A Survey of Citizens and Police Officers." *Police Quarterly*, June 2004, pp.179–204.

Sourcebook of Criminal Justice Statistics—2003. Washington, DC: Bureau of Justice Statistics, 2003.

Strong, Paul. "Ethics." *Law and Order*, January 2004, pp.65–66.

Strong, Paul. "Teaching the Thin Blue Line." *Law and Order*, January 2005, pp.69–71.

Terrill, William; Paoline, Eugene A., III.; and Manning, Peter K. "Police Culture and Coercion." *Criminology*, November 2003, pp.1003–1034.

"Terrorist Screening Center (TSC) Fact Sheet." http://www.fbi.gov. Accessed August 2, 2005.

Threat and Humiliation: Racial Profiling, Domestic Security, and Human Rights in the United States. New York: Amnesty International USA, September 2004.

Tinsley, Paul N.; Plecas, Darryl; and Anderson, Gregory S. "Studying Public Perceptions of Police Grooming Standards." *The Police Chief*, November 2003, pp.42–45.

Tomaskovic-Devey, Donald; Mason, Marcinda; and Zingraff, Matthew. "Looking for the Driving While Black Phenomena: Conceptualizing Racial Bias Processes and Their Associated Distributions." *Police Quarterly*, March 2004, pp.3–29.

Trautman, Neal. "Self-Accountability: The Ultimate Integrity Tool." *Law and Order*, January 2003, pp.52–58.

Tyler, Tom R. "Policing in Black and White: Ethnic Group Differences in Trust and Confidence in the Police." *Police Quarterly*, September 2005, pp.322–342.

Vernon, Robert. "Inspirational Leadership and Ethics." *Law and Order*, October 2003, p.218.

Weitzer, Ronald and Tuch, Steven A. "Determinants of Public Satisfaction with the Police." *Police Quarterly*, September 2005, pp.279–297.

Withrow, Brian L. and Dailey, Jeffrey D. "A Model of Circumstantial Corruptibility." *Police Quarterly*, June 2004, pp.159–178.

CITED CASES

United States v. Weaver, 234 F.3d 42, 46 (D.C. Cir. 2000)

Whren v. United States, 517 U.S. 806 (1966)

BOOK-SPECIFIC WEB SITE

Go to the Management and Supervision in Law Enforcement Web site at www.thomsonedu.com/criminaljustice/bennett for student and instructor resources, including Internet Assignments and Case Studies.

CHAPTER 9

Motivation and Morale

The convict's stroke of the pick is not the same as the prospector's.

Antoine de Saint-Exupéry

You can buy a man's time; you can buy his physical presence at a given place; you can even buy a measured number of his skilled muscular motions per hour. But you cannot buy enthusiasm . . . you cannot buy loyalty . . . you cannot buy the devotion of hearts, minds, or souls. You must earn these.

Clarence Francis

 DO YOU KNOW?

■ What motivation is?

■ What theories of motivation have been proposed by Maslow? Herzberg? Skinner? Vroom? Morse and Lorsch? McDonald?

■ Which kind of reinforcement is more effective?

■ When reinforcement should occur?

■ What the most common external motivators are?

■ What internal motivators include?

■ How the law enforcement job can be made more interesting?

■ What morale is?

■ What factors might indicate a morale problem?

■ What factors might be responsible for morale problems?

■ Who is most able to improve or damage individual and department morale?

■ How morale might be improved?

■ What promotions should be based on?

■ What three phases an assessment center typically uses for law enforcement personnel?

■ Whether promotions should be from without or within?

CAN YOU DEFINE?

assessment center	incentive programs	motivation
contingency theory	intangible rewards	motivator factors
expectancy theory	internal motivators	negative
external motivators	job enlargement	reinforcement
Hawthorne Effect	job enrichment	perception
hierarchy of needs	job rotation	perks
hygiene factors	morale	

continued

Introduction

Why do some law enforcement officers arrive at work ahead of time, eager to perform? Why do others arrive just in the nick of time? Why do some perform at a high level without direction and others need constant direction? Why are some upbeat and others chronic complainers? What motivates such behavior?

Consider the following conversation between two officers, one who had just completed an especially frustrating shift. This officer asked the other, "Why do we come here day after day and put up with this crap?" The other officer thought for a moment and then answered, "I don't know. I think it has something to do with house payments." Most people do need to work to survive. What will make them also enjoy their work and do their best? What will motivate them?

This chapter begins with an examination of the turnover problem in law enforcement. The remainder of the chapter looks at motivation and morale, two keys to officer retention. First motivation and self-motivation are defined. Next the motivational theories of Maslow, Herzberg, Skinner, Vroom, Morse and Lorsch and McDonald are discussed. This theoretical discussion leads into a more practical examination of the causes and symptoms of an unmotivated work force followed by a discussion of external, tangible motivators and internal, intangible motivators. This is followed by a look at the law enforcement career as a motivator and the benefits of motivated personnel.

The discussion then turns to morale and its definitions, both individual and organizational. Next indicators of morale problems are presented, along with a discussion of some reasons for such problems. Specific suggestions for building morale are then outlined, followed by a discussion of the relationship between promotions and morale. The chapter concludes with an example of one innovative program geared to improve morale inexpensively.

Officer Retention, Motivation and Morale

Researcher Haarr (2005, p.431) points out: "Resignation of police officers is a significant concern among police executives because of the direct financial costs of recruiting, selecting and training police personnel as well as the indirect costs related to disruption of services and organizational efficiency, time spent waiting for police recruits to achieve a 'streetwise' competence and providing fewer services to citizens." Law enforcement agencies throughout the country are experiencing increased rates of staff turnover, a problem that is approaching critical levels for many agencies. Factors that contribute to high turnover include poor pay and tough competition in the labor market (Orrick, 2005, p.36).

Koper (2004, p.4) reports that although overall attrition rates were not unusually high (less than 8 percent), unanticipated vacancies caused difficulty for about half the responding agencies: "Retaining new hires seems to have been a significant part of this problem, particularly in small agencies, where two-thirds of departing officers had served for 5 or fewer years."

Recall that the average cost of training a new recruit was $13,100 (Hickman, 2005), and the problem intensifies with the loss of more experienced officers. It is not only costly to lose officers, but in time agencies with higher turnover and therefore less experienced officers often suffer reduced productivity, lower quality service delivery, more frequent complaints and more lawsuits.

Agencies are not the only ones who suffer when officers leave. Haarr (p.449) found that police recruits who voluntarily resigned within the first 16 months experienced conflict and cognitive dissonance when their academy training, field training and police work were "inconsistent with or contradictory to" their sense of self and their belief about what police work should be. In addition, for female recruits, gender discrimination was part of their decision to resign.

On a more positive note, Koper (p.6) reports that the Community Oriented Policing Services (COPS) goal of adding 100,000 peace officers through grants appears to be successful. As of the summer of 2000, about three quarters of agencies with expired hiring grants had kept their funded positions for at least one to two years.

Furthermore, staff turnover need not always have negative consequences, for it allows the department to spread its leadership influence, initiate changes within the organization's culture and replace ineffective or unethical staff (Orrick, p.36). Nonetheless, retaining good officers is a key concern and challenge of police managers. Effective motivation and a climate of high morale are vital to retention efforts and are a primary responsibility of supervisors (Johnson, 2004, p.134).

Motivation Defined

motivation • an inner or outer drive or impetus to do something or to act in a specified manner. An inner or outer drive to meet a need or goal.

 Motivation is an inner or outer drive to meet a need or goal.

Self-motivation is derived from within an individual. Outer motivation is provided from external sources to influence an individual or to furnish a reason for another person to do a desired act in a desired way. A *motive* is an impetus, an impulse or an intention that causes a person to act, individually or collectively with others, in a directed manner.

Motivation and *morale* are terms often used in management but not easily defined or understood. Lack of motivation is often the reason for low morale. Research psychologists have outlined factors that affect motivation and morale. Incentives must be worthwhile to employees, they must be reasonably attainable and employees must feel a sense of responsibility to achieve them. In modern police terms, employees must be empowered. Motivation requires a sense of well-being, self-confidence and accomplishment. To keep levels of motivation and morale high, managers must give recognition.

Can managers motivate their subordinates? According to some, motivation can come only from within. A story from business helps illustrate the point. A young salesperson was disappointed because he had lost an important sale. Discussing it with the sales manager, the man lamented, "I guess it just proves you can lead a horse to water, but you can't make him drink." To which the sales manager replied, "Your job isn't to make him drink. It's to make him thirsty."

Managers can create an environment that will motivate people by creating opportunities for success and recognizing accomplishments.

Self-Motivation

When employees know an agency's goals and choose to help meet them, this is self-motivation. Fortunately for management, most employees want to do a good job. It is management's job to help and to provide additional motivation when needed. For example, an officer who works long after the shift is over to make certain a victim is adequately taken care of may be rewarded by being given time off during the next shift. Many incentives other than monetary ones encourage employees and cost nothing. They take little time, yet are seldom used. Most employees have pride in their work. They want to satisfy themselves and their employers.

Self-motivated law enforcement officers work for personal job satisfaction. Law enforcement work gives them a sense of accomplishment and personal value. Self-motivated officers are dedicated to their work and make every hour on the job count.

Job satisfaction remains a basic reward of working, even though not many employees would mention it as a benefit. Recreation and time for home life, children and rest are equally important. Self-motivated employees are more apt to work toward organizational as well as personal goals because the melding of both provides even more job satisfaction. Leadership researchers Konzes and Posner (2002, pp.59–60) report that the most motivated employees have values aligned closely with the organization's values. The second most motivated group of employees had a highly defined set of personal values even though their agencies did not have such clearly defined values.

Not all jobs provide an enjoyable environment. Many people work only to make a living, to provide security for their families and to supply the funds to enjoy the other things in life. Many work at jobs they do not like. Not all law enforcement officers like their work. In these situations managers need to be motivators.

Many theories of motivation have been developed based on extensive research of employees in the work environment. These studies reveal that although monetary rewards are a necessary part of jobs, money is not the major consideration as long as it is basically adequate for living.

Motivational Theories

Each individual has needs, even though a person may not have a list of needs or even have consciously thought about them. These needs make each of us what we are and cause us to do what we do. Each individual takes action to meet these needs.

The 1960s saw the development of many theories about motivation. Knowledge of these theories helps us understand what people can do for themselves and what managers can do for employees. The results of studies by human-behavior researchers apply as much to law enforcement as to any other profession.

The Hierarchy of Needs—Abraham Maslow

One of the best-known studies of human needs was conducted by Abraham Maslow in 1962. He concluded that every human has five basic needs, which he assembled into a hierarchy, as Figure 9.1 illustrates. At the base of the hierarchy are *physiological needs*: air, food, water, sleep, shelter and sex. It is mandatory that

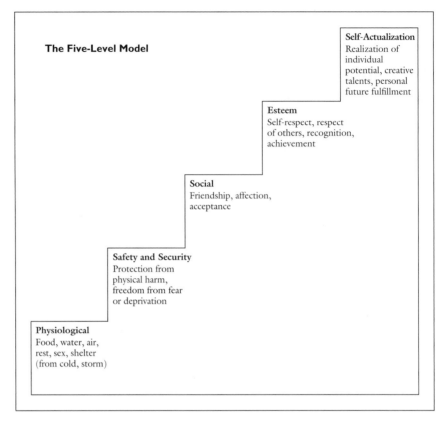

Figure 9.1   Maslow's Hierarchy of Needs

at least air, food, water and sleep be satisfied, or a person could not function or proceed to the next level. Some segments of the world's population live their entire lives just trying to satisfy this level of need. Shelter could be added to the list because it is more than merely a place to sleep; it is protection from the elements.

 Maslow's **hierarchy of needs** is, in the order they need to be met, physiological, safety and security, social, esteem and self-actualization.

hierarchy of needs • Maslow's motivational theory that people have certain needs that must be met in a specific order going from basic physiological needs to safety and security, social, esteem and self-actualization needs.

The second level, *safety and security*, includes protection from serious injury and death, freedom from fear and a clear authority structure. Humans function better in an environment free from fear. It has long been known that children need a set of standards even though they tend to rebel against them. Adults also need a set of standards, an authority structure, even though they, too, sometimes rebel. People want a level of certainty, to know where they stand. This translates at work to safety from accidents, a reasonable promise of job security and an opportunity for increases in pay and promotions.

The third level, *social*, includes friendship, love, affection and group and team belonging. These are important needs for everyone. Workers want peer acceptance, approval, sharing and friendship.

The fourth level, *esteem*, includes self-respect, respect and recognition from others, status, a title, added responsibility, independence and recognition for job performance.

self-actualization • refers to achievement, to meeting individual goals and fulfilling one's potential.

The fifth level, *self-actualization*, refers to achievement, meeting individual goals and fulfilling one's potential. **Self-actualization** is what you do when all the

An important need is that of social acceptance by one's peers and a sense of belonging among coworkers. Here, officers from various law enforcement agencies throughout Florida satisfy not only their need to build social bonds with each other but also to participate in a charitable cause; running to raise funds for the Special Olympics in Putnam County, Florida.

other needs are satisfied. It is fostered by the chance to be creative and innovative and by having the opportunity to maximize skills and knowledge.

According to Maslow's theory, people's wants are always increasing and changing. Once an individual's basic (primary) needs have been satisfied, other needs take their place. The satisfied need no longer acts as a motivating force. If a number of needs are unsatisfied at any given time, an individual will try to satisfy the most pressing one first. Maslow believed that all levels of needs probably exist to some degree for individuals most of the time. Rarely is any one need completely satisfied, at least for long. Hunger, for example, may be satisfied after eating, but it emerges again later.

Maslow's theory of needs is popular because it makes sense. People can identify these needs in their own lives. In addition, the needs can be seen operating on the job. In many jobs, including law enforcement jobs, the first two levels of needs are automatically provided. Safety, for example, is extremely important in law enforcement. The law enforcement organization must do everything possible to ensure its officers' safety—and the officers should know what steps have been taken.

Satisfied needs do not necessarily become inactive needs. If law enforcement officers receive salary increases, they may raise their standard of living, and then another salary increase is as welcome as the first.

Law enforcement organizations may meet the needs of the group but not of individuals. For example, with a minimal number of promotions, other means of satisfying the need for recognition must be found. Managers can play an important role in providing on-the-job authority structure. They can provide respect through praise and recognition for tasks well done.

Managers can help subordinates meet even the highest goals, fulfilling individual potential through training and on-the-job educational opportunities.

Complex	Self-actualization	Challenging job
		Creativity
		Achievement in work
		Advancement
		Involvement in planning
		Chances for growth and development
	Esteem	Merit pay raises
		Titles
		Status symbols/awards
		Recognition (peer/boss)
		Job itself
		Responsibility
		Sharing in decisions
	Social	Quality supervision
		Compatible co-workers
		Professional friendships
		Department pride/spirit
	Safety/Security	Safe working conditions
		Sound department policies
		Protective equipment
		General salary increases
		Job security
		Feeling of competence
Basic	Physiological	Heat/air conditioning
		Base salary
		Cafeteria/vending machine
		Working conditions
		Rest periods
		Efficient work methods
		Labor-saving devices
		Comfortable uniform

Figure 9.2   Maslow's Levels of Needs and Job Factors

Officers seek challenging opportunities to provide service to the community. If their performance is good, they expect fair compensation and rewards. The agency should provide clear goals that have been mutually agreed upon, and officers should expect to meet those goals, both individually and as a group. Maslow's five levels of needs and their translation into specific job-related factors are illustrated in Figure 9.2.

Orrick (p.39) contends that Maslow's hierarchy does not allow officers to move into or be motivated by higher-ordered needs such as belongingness, self-esteem or self-actualization until lower ordered needs of physical needs and security are satisfied. He suggests that departments will never be able to retain and motivate staff until the survival mentality socialized into new officers is addressed. New officers are socialized and indoctrinated on the dangers inherent in law enforcement and focus their attention on "making it home at the end of the day without being complained about, disciplined, sued, injured or killed." Service and problem solving, not combat, should be the focus of academy instruction and socialization for new officers (Orrick, p.39). Such a shift in focus would be in keeping with the motivational theory set forth by Herzberg.

Two-Factor Hygiene/Motivator Theory—Herzberg

Another behavioral psychologist, Frederick Herzberg, developed the **two-factor theory**, or the hygiene/motivator theory. Herzberg's theory divides needs that require satisfaction through work into two classes: hygiene factors and motivator factors.

 Herzberg's **hygiene factors** are **tangible rewards** that can cause *dissatisfaction* if lacking. **Motivator factors** are **intangible rewards** that can create *satisfaction*.

Dissatisfaction and satisfaction are not two ends of a continuum, because people can experience lack of dissatisfaction without necessarily being satisfied.

Tangible rewards pertaining basically to the hygiene factors do *not* provide satisfaction. They simply prevent dissatisfaction. Having officers who perform only because they are not dissatisfied is seldom conducive to high performance. Providing more tangible rewards is highly unlikely to accomplish better results.

The hygiene factors are similar to Maslow's lower-level needs. People assume these factors will be met. If they are not, people will be dissatisfied. Company policies, job security, supervision, a basic salary and safe working conditions are extrinsic factors that do not necessarily motivate people to do better work. They are expected.

Herzberg's hygiene factors help to explain why many people stick with jobs they do not like. They stay because they are not dissatisfied with the tangible rewards such as the pay and the retirement plan even though they are definitely not satisfied with the work itself.

Industry found that when many of the wage increases, fringe benefits, seniority and security programs were initiated, they did not substantially reduce the basic problems of low productivity, high turnover, absenteeism and grievances. Herzberg claimed that approach was wrong. Instead, jobs should provide greater control over outcomes of work, have clearly established goals and have more to do rather than less. Figure 9.3 shows the relationship between Maslow's hierarchy of needs theory and Herzberg's two-factor theory.

As Herzberg (1978, p.49) pointed out: "A man whose work possesses no contentment in terms of self-fulfillment, but exists exclusively to fulfill the purposes of the enterprise or a social organization, is a man doomed to a life of human frustration, despite a return of animal contentment. You do not inspire employees by giving them higher wages, more benefits, or new status symbols. It is the successful achievement of a challenging task which fulfills the urge to create. . . . The employer's task is not to motivate his people to get them to achieve; he should provide opportunities for people to achieve so they will become motivated."

Herzberg's theory, like Maslow's, does not consider differences in people, for the same motivators will not motivate everyone. Law enforcement managers, for example, will find that not all patrol officers are motivated by the same needs. Managers have to adjust motivational approaches to the individual.

Most employees still believe that satisfying work is more important than increased salary and advancement, *if* the basic salary is adequate. The job itself—law enforcement work—is a good example: The work is satisfying because what officers do is meaningful to them and to the community they serve. Most law enforcement officers are *not* in it for the money.

two-factor theory • Herzberg's motivational theory that employees' needs can be classified as hygiene factors and motivator factors.

hygiene factors • tangible rewards that can cause dissatisfaction if lacking.

tangible rewards • external motivators such as salary, bonuses, insurance, retirement plans, favorable working conditions, paid vacation and holidays, titles and adequacy of equipment.

motivator factors • intangible rewards that can cause satisfaction.

intangible rewards • internal motivators such as goals, achievement, recognition, self-respect, opportunity for advancement or to make a contribution and belief in individual and department goals.

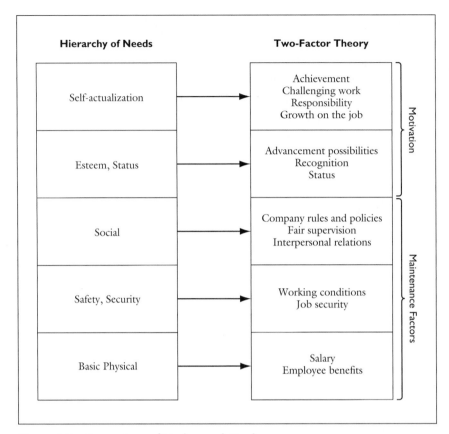

Figure 9.3   Comparison of Maslow and Herzberg

Source: Stan Kossen. *Supervision,* 2nd ed. St. Paul, MN: West Publishing Company, 1991.

Reinforcement Theory—Skinner

Extremely influential writings by B. F. Skinner suggest that behavior can be shaped and modified using positive and negative reinforcement. Skinner's pioneering work in behavior modification was first described in his book *The Behavior of Organisms*, published in 1938, and expanded in *Walden Two*, published in 1948. A key conclusion of Skinner's research is that behavior is a function of its consequences. The ethics behind modifying behavior became highly controversial in the 1960s. Nonetheless, Skinner's theories *are* still relevant to managers, are implicit in the motivational theories just discussed and seem to be simple common sense.

positive reinforcement • rewards following a desired behavior that tend to increase that behavior.

negative reinforcement • punishment following an undesired behavior that tends to decrease the behavior.

reinforcement theory • B. F. Skinner's motivational theory that behavior can be modified by using positive and negative reinforcement.

In reinforcement theory employees are rewarded for good behavior—**positive reinforcement**. They repeat the behavior to achieve the reward, and it becomes a learned behavior. **Negative reinforcement** is designed as an activity that will stop a given stimulus from happening. If there is a loud noise and a person presses a lever to stop the noise, and the noise stops, the pushing behavior will be reinforced. For police officers, if they seem angry, it may prevent sarcastic remarks. So, the more anger displayed, the greater (in theory) the reduction in sarcastic remarks from people they are working with. Removing an undesirable stimulus may reinforce behavior (Conroy, 2006).

 Skinner's **reinforcement theory** suggests that positive reinforcement rewards and increases a given behavior; negative reinforcement decreases a given behavior by reinforcing another, desired behavior.

Use of both positive and negative reinforcement is readily seen on the job. Often both are used, and both make sense. Negative reinforcement is not to be confused with punishment. They are *not* the same.

 Reinforcement is usually more effective than punishment. Also, the closer in time to the behavior, the more effective the reinforcement will be.

What is the problem with punishment? With a history as old as the human race, it is the belief that the harsher the punishment, the greater its effectiveness in changing behavior. Many managers, including those in penology, still adhere to this belief.

The means to inflict punishment have changed, with the whip, the rack and the stock falling into disfavor. Today's punishments are more subtle but have the same effect. Punishment-oriented managers might use techniques such as criticizing or ridiculing someone in public, ignoring a job well done, withholding needed information or avoiding discussion on an expected promotion or raise.

Although the punishments have changed, the problems associated with using a punishment-oriented management style have not. First, and perhaps most important, punishment can cause a get-even attitude. This can take the form of "fight"—where the employees cause problems by what they say or do. Or it can take the form of "flight," where the workers "quit but stay." They simply put in the required time and do as little as possible.

A second problem is that managers have to be constantly watching over employees. If vigilance is relaxed, the negative behavior is likely to recur.

A third problem is that subordinates may come to associate punishment with the manager's presence and may dread seeing the manager coming around. They may become defensive every time the manager appears.

Yet another problem with punishment is that sometimes any kind of attention, even punishment, is considered more positive than being ignored. Teachers are well aware of this phenomenon with "problem" students who act up merely for the attention they get when they do. Law enforcement officers who crave acknowledgment of their existence by their superiors may feel that criticism is preferable to being totally ignored.

Another principle of reinforcement theory that managers need to consider is the time factor. Many incentives once thought to be powerful motivators are delayed—and scheduled. A good example is the paycheck. A law enforcement officer may conduct an excellent investigation on the first of the month but not be paid until the fifteenth of that month. In such cases, the paycheck is not seen as related to the investigation.

That is why incentives such as praise and recognition, given *immediately,* can be powerful motivators. Positive reinforcement can be highly motivating, but the theory also has some disadvantages. It does not consider human needs and tends to simplify behavior and rewards. It does not consider that employees may be motivated by the job itself, may be self-motivated or may consider rewards as manipulation, which they will eventually reject. Failing to reward can lead to decreased production, and failing to punish poor performance can reinforce that behavior.

The Expectancy Theory—Vroom

Victor H. Vroom's expectancy theory looks at options employees have on the job. It combines some features of the preceding theories and advances the ideas that employees believe good work on the job will lead to high job performance and that high job performance will lead to job rewards.

Regardless of the chief individual motivating factors, if employees believe that performance will lead to satisfying motivational needs, they will work hard. Naturally, employees must be able to perform. According to Vroom's theory of motivation, employees become motivated to take action when the following three-step process takes place:

1. A motivating factor—a need to satisfy or goal to achieve—exists that is important to the employee.
2. The employee believes that by putting in the required or requested effort, the job can be performed.
3. The employee believes that by successfully performing the job as requested, the need will be satisfied or the goal will be achieved.

Employees have an effort expectancy and a performance expectancy. If managers clearly define the tasks and help employees with direction and skill training to perform the job, effort expectancy will rise. Managers can help achieve performance expectancy by providing means of satisfying individual needs.

Managers must know what opportunities specific jobs offer before they can use them as motivational opportunities for employees. These may be money, opportunity for educational or job growth, praise or peer recognition. Expectancies vary even with individuals doing the same job. Expectancy theory integrates ideas about employee motivation.

expectancy theory • Vroom's motivational theory that employees will choose the level of effort that matches the performance opportunity for reward.

 Vroom's **expectancy theory** suggests that employees will choose the level of effort that matches the performance opportunity for reward.

For example, if a law enforcement officer investigating a crash that happened one-half hour before shift change realizes that completing the investigation will take an hour, he or she can complete it, ask another officer to take over the investigation or do a poor job by leaving the investigation before obtaining the needed information.

The officer knows doing the complete job will receive recognition by the sergeant. He or she knows asking someone else to complete the investigation will lead to complications in obtaining facts and completing reports. He or she knows that leaving the scene without information for proper reporting will be reason for reprimand. The officer will probably choose to put in the extra time and complete the report because the rewards are a better expectancy than a reprimand. It will also look better on his or her record. The officer should also understand that making repeated comments to those involved in the crash that "this is on my own time" are negative and may result in a complaint. On the other hand, the satisfaction of a job well done and the good inner feeling that results may be motivating in themselves.

Contingency Theory—Morse and Lorsch

Closely related to the expectancy theory is the contingency theory developed by John J. Morse and Jay W. Lorsch. They built on McGregor's Theory X/Theory Y (Chapter 2) and Herzberg's motivation and maintenance factors in their research on how an organizational task fit affects and is affected by task performance and employees' feelings of *competence*. The four key components of the contingency theory are the following:

- People have a basic need to feel competent.
- How people fill this need varies and will depend on how the need interacts with other needs and the strengths of those needs.
- Competence motivation is most likely to exist when task and organization "fit."
- Feeling competent continues to be motivating even after competence is achieved.

 Morse and Lorsch's **contingency theory** suggests fitting tasks, officers and the agency's goals so that officers can feel competent.

contingency theory • Morse and Lorsch's motivational theory that suggests fitting tasks, officers and agency goals so that officers can feel competent.

Contingency theory further suggests that highly structured tasks might be performed better in highly structured organizations that have a management structure that resembles McGregor's Theory X approach. Conversely, highly unstructured tasks might be performed better in more flexible organizations whose management structure resembles the Theory Y approach. In law enforcement work, both kinds of tasks occur. Consequently, flexibility in management style becomes very important.

The Rule of Four—McDonald

McDonald's Rule of Four also revolves around contingencies and focuses on how managers react to subordinates' behavior. Some studies have identified as many as 127 skills managers need to be effective (McDonald, 2005, p.26). Once the "clutter" is cut through, what becomes important is what a manager does *after* someone does something. McDonald suggests there are only four possibilities.

 McDonald's Rule of Four says managers have these options to influence people's behavior at work: (1) reward good behavior (positive reinforcement), (2) punish bad behavior (negative reinforcement), (3) threaten people exhibiting bad behavior and (4) ignore the bad behavior. The most effective option is to reward good behavior.

McDonald reports on research showing that managers do the following, from most often to least often:
- They ignore the behavior.
- They punish bad behavior.
- They threaten their people.
- They reward good behavior.

He notes that punishing people may result in less bad behavior, but no one will feel good about it. Threatening people usually creates a toxic environment, and ignoring negative behavior leaves employees adrift and may inadvertently reward bad behavior. "The most effective management tool we have—the one that gets you more of the behavior you want and creates a positive environment—is rewarding people for their good behavior. But this is what managers do least of all!" (McDonald, p.26). Making a conscious effort to reverse the preceding order will get better results.

Motivational theory has important implications for law enforcement managers and supervisors. No matter which theories they believe have the most credence, managers must understand that certain external, tangible motivators and certain internal, intangible motivators are important in accomplishing goals through others.

Causes and Symptoms of an Unmotivated Work Force

Causes of an unmotivated work force might include overwork, downsizing, endless restructuring, boredom, frustration, promotions—who gets them and why—work conditions and the court system.

Symptoms of an unmotivated officer include absenteeism, constant complaining, lack of care for equipment, lack of respect for other officers, lack of respect for rules and regulations, low morale, sleeping or loafing on duty, slovenly appearance and tardiness. Dealing with these symptoms is the focus of the next section. In addition to recognizing the causes and symptoms of lack of motivation, managers must also understand and know how to use the knowledge that certain external, tangible motivators and certain internal, intangible motivators are important in accomplishing goals through others.

External, Tangible Motivators

Although external motivators no longer have the power they once had, they are expected. As Herzberg's theory states, basic needs must be met or dissatisfaction will result. This is not to say that lack of dissatisfaction will be motivating. It is likely, however, to keep people on the job and to keep them from counterproductive behavior.

external motivators • tangible rewards such as salary, bonuses, insurance, retirement plans, favorable working conditions, paid vacation and holidays, titles and adequacy of equipment.

Among the most common **external motivators,** or tangible rewards, are salary, bonuses, insurance, retirement plans, favorable working conditions, paid vacation and holidays, titles and adequate equipment.

The Compensation Package

The law enforcement profession is not known for its great salaries. Nonetheless, money is important to most employees. They want and need enough salary to be comfortable and to meet their basic financial responsibilities. Some officers work two jobs until they have the amount of money they consider necessary. It is true that money talks. What managers must remember, however, is that it says different things to different people.

Although pay in the law enforcement profession is not at the top of the scale, the entire compensation package is usually competitive. One important factor is an equitable procedure for raises. In a well-managed department, employees would not have to ask for raises. They would know what to expect— and when—in return for their performance and dedication. Given the hazardous nature of law enforcement work, the compensation package should include health, disability and life insurance.

Perks

perks • tangible rewards.

Perks, or tangible rewards, can be as large as a luxury cruise for the "training suggestion of the year" or as small as a reserved parking spot. Little extras can contribute much to making jobs more attractive. Some perks cost nothing, and others are relatively inexpensive. Consider the following:

- Cards or small gifts for special occasions such as birthdays or service anniversaries
- Tickets to sporting events and shows for outstanding performance

- Free coffee and snacks
- Facilities and equipment for heating meals, such as microwave ovens
- Daily newspapers and magazines, including professional journals
- Personal notes for achievements—on the job and off
- Support for league teams such as softball and bowling
- Smiles

Incentive Programs

Incentive programs can also be used to motivate. For example, fast-track career paths, flexible work hours, ongoing training, spot bonuses and travel incentives, as well as anything that makes balancing work and personal life easier, such as dry cleaning, child-care allowances or a fitness membership.

incentive programs • programs designed to motivate.

Working Conditions and Schedules

Employees expect adequate heat, light, ventilation and working hours. They also expect a well-maintained squad car and up-to-date equipment. Having a desk or a private office can also be rewarding. Inadequacies in working conditions can cause great dissatisfaction.

The work environment can have a great impact on morale. People appreciate working in a clean, attractive and healthy environment. A local florist might be approached to donate some plants to brighten up the offices. Seasonal decorations can help add to appropriate holiday spirit. Attractive artwork can liven up otherwise drab hallways. Interested employees might want to form a committee, organize a garage sale to raise money and decorate certain areas of the department according to a planned schedule. The options are limitless.

In addition, flexible hours and job sharing opportunities, when possible, are attractive motivators to many officers, especially those trying to balance the job with family life.

Security

Although this may seem like an internal reward—or motivator—many aspects of security are indeed external, tangible and expected. Among them are fair work rules, adequate grievance procedures, reasonable department policies and discipline, and seniority privileges. Some aspects of the compensation package such as insurance and retirement plans also meet basic security needs.

Social

Like the need for security, employees' social needs can fall within the external, tangible category when such things as parties, picnics, breaks and social gatherings are considered. Opportunities to mix with one's peers and superiors, sometimes including spouses, may be very rewarding.

Status

The need for status can also be partially met by external, tangible rewards such as privileges, titles, private offices, awards and other symbols of rank and position. These external, tangible factors are sometimes called *maintenance* factors. Provided in adequate quantity and quality, they merely prevent dissatisfaction. The best managers can hope for is a "fair day's work for a fair day's pay." To get subordinates to truly perform, managers usually need to provide internal, intangible motivators as well.

Internal, Intangible Motivators

Internal, intangible motivators can spark employees to give their best effort to accomplish individual and department goals. "The majority of officers entering the force are motivated by intangible factors all directly related to leadership. Motivation, positive attitude and enthusiastic work environment are much more important than brand new equipment or a shiny new station" (Stainbrook, 2004, p.34).

internal motivators • include goals, achievement, recognition, self-respect and the opportunity for advancement or to make a contribution.

Internal motivators, or intangible rewards, include goals, achievement, recognition, self-respect, opportunity for advancement, opportunity to make a contribution and belief in individual and departmental goals.

Goals and Expectations

Goals need to be set and met. Specific goal setting results in greater accomplishment. Goals should make officers reach to their levels of competence. Different goals are often needed for individual officers. The reason some students fail in school is because goals are too easy and they become bored. On the other hand, the same goals may be too high for other students to achieve and they become frustrated. Students who achieve to their level of competence will be motivated.

The highly touted management by objectives (MBO) relies on clear, meaningful goals, both for individual officers and for the organization. Goals establish future direction of effort. Accomplishing goals provides room for creativity, innovation, diversity and a sense of accomplishment.

Operational goals should be set by first-line and middle managers, with the participation of patrol officers. Goals should be consistent and communicated. Realistic goals, proper resources to do the job, employee communication and a personal and organizational sense of accomplishment all play a major role in law enforcement motivation. Closely related to goals are expectations. To illustrate the importance of expectations, recognize the **Pygmalion Effect:** What managers and supervisors expect of their officers and how they treat them largely determine their performance and career progress.

Pygmalion Effect • what managers and supervisors expect of their officers and how they treat them largely determine their performance and career progress.

Encouragement

Encouragement can be extremely motivating. Consider the story of a group of frogs traveling through the woods. Two fell into a deep pit. All the other frogs gathered around the pit and, upon seeing how deep the pit was, told the two they would never get out and would die there. The two frogs ignored their comrades and tried to jump out while the other frogs kept telling them to stop wasting their energy. Finally one frog paid attention and simply gave up, fell down and died. The other frog continued to jump as hard as he could despite his comrades yelling at him to stop the pain and suffering. This just made him jump even harder, and he finally jumped out. Amazed, his comrades asked him why he kept jumping. To which the frog replied he was deaf and thought they were encouraging him.

The lessons to be learned: (1) Destructive words to someone who is down can be what it takes to kill them. (2) Encouraging words to someone who is down can lift them up and help them make it through the day.

Achievement, Recognition, Growth and Advancement

Achievement is a motivator. It can be a series of small accomplishments or one accomplishment that ultimately grows to a larger one. It can be a task done well for the first time, something done better than before, a higher score or committing fewer errors.

Recognition is also a motivator, whether it comes from peers or managers. Recognition is most effective if it can be related to a person's personal qualities rather than to the performance itself. For example, rather than saying "Good job on solving the XYZ case," emphasize the personal qualities involved, such as, "I admire your determination to keep working on the XYZ case until you got it solved."

Recognize accomplishment. Too often managers fail to use this reward that costs nothing. Recognition of something well done, offered at the time of accomplishment, is a powerful motivator: "Thank you for working overtime to get that report to me." "I have just reviewed your case report. It is excellent and reflects a lot of thought." Some employees report that their managers have never complimented or praised them in an entire year. Some managers cannot bring themselves to praise subordinates either because it is not in their nature or they are too busy.

The importance of recognition was established by the well-known experiment conducted from 1927 to 1932 by Elton Mayo at the Western Electric Company's Hawthorne Plant in Cicero, Illinois. This study's major finding was that almost regardless of the experimental manipulation used, the workers' production improved. One reasonable conclusion is that the workers were pleased to receive the researchers' attention, a phenomenon that became known as the **Hawthorne Effect.** Production increased not as a consequence of actual changes in working conditions introduced by the plant's management but because management showed interest in such improvements. (The Hawthorne Effect also needs to be taken into account when research is being conducted.)

> **Hawthorne Effect** • workers are positively affected by receiving attention. This affects research efforts.

In addition to recognition, employees want growth and advancement in their jobs. These do not have to be promotions or pay raises. They can even be little things: giving personal responsibility for a task, giving a title, showing concern for employees' health and welfare or giving deserved praise for a not-so-important task done well. All can contribute to a critical motivator: self-esteem.

Self-Esteem

Self-esteem involves self-confidence, a feeling of self-worth. As individual tasks are successfully accomplished, self-esteem builds. A sincere compliment by another person on your ability to perform a task also builds self-esteem. It is law enforcement managers' responsibility to build self-esteem in their team. The more self-esteem individuals in the agency have, the higher the organizational esteem will be. Recall Maslow's hierarchy of needs and, specifically, the fourth level labeled "esteem."

Officers with low self-esteem will perform low-level work. If they have been told they are incompetent, they probably will not perform well. This has been referred to as a **self-fulfilling prophecy.** People tend to behave and eventually become what they think others expect of them. Law enforcement managers need to apply the implications of the self-fulfilling prophecy to everyday employee/law enforcement task performance. As one poster reads: "Every job is a self-portrait of the person who did it. Autograph your work with excellence."

> **self-fulfilling prophecy** • the theory that people live up to expectations. If people believe they can do a job, they usually can. If people believe they cannot do a job, they usually cannot.

Officers' perceptions of themselves and other people directly influence how the officers conduct themselves in public. This is important because law enforcement is a "people" profession. Officers' attitudes directly influence how they handle other people. Officers with low self-esteem are overly concerned with themselves because they fear failure and know they are not functioning as well as they should.

Managers can build individual self-esteem in the following ways:

- Do not embarrass subordinates, especially in front of others.
- Recognize and build on individual accomplishments.
- Give praise for things done well at the same time as you give criticism for things not well done.
- Give personal attention.
- Ask employees' opinions on problems.
- If an employee gives an opinion or suggestion, act on it in some way. Do not ignore it.
- Help individuals develop to their potential.
- Give employees breathing room for ideas, creativity and innovation.
- Give special task assignments.
- Get to know employees as individuals.
- Give certificates of appreciation when deserved.
- Truly listen.
- If employees express ideas, write them down in their presence.
- If someone has complimented an officer, pass it on.
- Assign part of the next departmental meeting to different officers.
- Share important information. Let everyone be "in the know."
- Acquire a piece of equipment that will help officers do a better job.

A Feeling of Importance

Managers must let their subordinates know they count. One manager used the following memo to let his employees know how valuable they were:

"You Arx A Kxy Pxrson" Xvxn though my typxwritxr is an old modxl, it works vxry wxll—xxcxpt for onx kxy. You would think that with all thx othxr kxys functioning propxrly, onx kxy not working would hardly bx noticxd; but just onx kxy out of whack sxxms to ruin thx wholx xffort.

You may say to yoursxlf—"Wxll I'm only onx pxrson. No onx will noticx if I don't do my bxst." But it doxs makx a diffxrxncx bxcausx to bx xffxctivx an organization nxxds activx participation by xvxryonx to thx bxst of his or hxr ability.

So thx nxxt timx you think you arx not important, rxmxmbxr my old typxwritxr. You arx a kxy pxrson.

(*Pasadena Weekly Journal of Business*, 155 S. El Molino Ave., Suite 101, Pasadena, CA, 91101. Reprinted by permission.)

One of the best ways managers and supervisors can let their people know they are important is to *listen* to them. Chapter 4 emphasized the role listening plays in communication. Law enforcement managers who truly listen to their subordinates will learn a great deal about their needs and feelings. The more managers know about their officers and their needs, the more they can help them meet those needs.

The more managers concentrate on the person talking to them, the more they show how much they value that person. Psychiatrists usually spend most of a patient's time listening. They understand this primary need of the patient to unburden, to let it all out. At the same time they learn a tremendous amount of information about the patient.

Effective listening is an *active* form of communication. You must work at it. Physically show your attentiveness. Ask questions. Clarify. Take notes. Maintain eye contact. If you do not believe that listening is active, the next time someone tries to tell you something, do not pay attention; excuse yourself and start to make a phone call; or simply look away from the person, in no way encouraging them to continue the conversation. The person will immediately be able to tell that you are not interested.

Being Involved, Included and "In" on Things

The importance of participative management has been discussed. The more employees feel a part of a department, the harder—and better—they will work. To establish and maintain involvement, use a team approach and encourage suggestions.

The Law Enforcement Career as a Motivator

Law enforcement work itself can be a motivator. Many officers find that law enforcement tasks, in and of themselves, are a basis for **self-motivation.** When a law enforcement applicant appears before an interviewing board and is asked, "Why do you want to be a law enforcement officer?" the answer is invariably a variation of "Because I like to work with people," or "I want to provide a service, and I think law enforcement work is an opportunity to do that."

self-motivation • acting in an expected way from personal choice.

Herzberg identified several factors that could lead to dissatisfaction on the job, including inadequate pay, difficult work schedules, inadequate benefits, poor working conditions and the like.

Herzberg also noted that job satisfaction is primarily a reflection of personal growth factors in one's workplace assignment. He identified three primary sources of job satisfaction: (1) the importance of the work itself, (2) the sense of responsibility while doing the work and (3) the feeling of recognition for that work.

Law enforcement entails a great variety of skills: handling an automobile, using weapons, conversing with all types of people, interviewing and interrogating, using computers and computerized information, setting up case investigations and so on. Everything law enforcement officers do provides task significance. They have a high degree of autonomy in their decisions and actions. Decisions are often instantaneous and permanent. In addition, their actions are highly visible because of their uniforms. This visibility should provide motivation to do the best possible job at all times.

Personal growth can be achieved by providing opportunities for departmental training, seminars, college classes or public talks to civic organizations and youth groups. These types of job enrichment opportunities can also provide a higher degree of self-motivation and self-control in performing law enforcement tasks in emergencies, without close manager control.

The law enforcement job is generally not perceived as boring and routine. If it becomes that way, it is generally the officer's fault because ample opportunities exist to make it more exciting. Even routine foot and vehicle patrol should not be boring. Many exciting things happen on a shift or at least have the potential for happening.

Orrick (p.40) suggests that one way to guide an employee through a promising career is with a mentoring program. Such programs have been shown to "increase new officer success rates, build confidence, anchor officers to the department and reduce turnover."

The importance of interesting work is illustrated by the story of a man visiting Mexico who found in a little shop a very comfortable, attractive, reasonably priced handcrafted chair. Extremely pleased, the tourist asked the shop manager if he could make him a dozen chairs just like it. The Mexican nodded and, obviously displeased, said, "But the señor knows that I must charge much more for each such chair."

The tourist, astonished, exclaimed, "More? In the United States if you buy in quantity, you pay less. Why do you want to charge me more?"

The reply, "Because it is so dull to make twelve chairs all the same."

Managers should make the law enforcement job itself more interesting and challenging for officers, provide goals and make challenges out of routine work. Law enforcement tasks can be studied and made more interesting. Assignments can be made more efficiently and with greater variety to make the total job more satisfying. Community policing offers an opportunity to make a difference.

Giving more responsibility, providing opportunity for employees to perform the job without being directly told what to do, treating each employee according to his or her own needs—these actions are motivating.

 Law enforcement work can be made more interesting and motivating in three important ways:

- Job rotation
- Job enlargement
- Job enrichment

Job Rotation

job rotation • changing the job assignment or shift.

Job rotation can make the job more challenging. Job rotation also serves as a training opportunity and provides variety—an opportunity to understand the total law enforcement job. Different things happen on the day shift than on the night shift or middle shift. Job tasks are different in the patrol, detective, juvenile, narcotics and administrative divisions.

Job rotation is often done on a temporary basis. Such cross-training not only provides a better understanding of the total law enforcement effort but also gives supervisors more flexibility to deal with absences and requests for vacations. Job rotation also prepares officers for promotions and can serve as a motivator as such officers begin to feel competent doing new and different tasks.

Job Enlargement

job enlargement • assigning additional responsibilities to an existing job.

Job enlargement, giving additional responsibilities, such as making a survey of vehicle licenses to determine the number of outsiders in the community, can provide helpful information for the department, other departments or the community. Increasing the number of tasks may be perceived as a threat. Given the right training and tools, officers should perceive job enlargement as motivating, giving them renewed interest in and enthusiasm for law enforcement work.

Building on Herzberg's work, Hackman and Oldham (1976) set forth their theory of job enrichment, specifying five core job characteristics underlying job satisfaction: task identity, task significance, skill variety, job feedback and autonomy. Certainly all of these can be provided through police work.

Job Enrichment

Job enrichment is similar to job enlargement, except that in job enrichment the focus is the *quality* of the new jobs assigned rather than the quantity. Job enrichment emphasizes adding variety, deeper personal interest and involvement, increased responsibility and greater autonomy. Job enrichment is appropriate for any highly routine job.

For some officers, however, job enrichment might also be perceived as threatening. Some officers do not want enrichment. They do not need more challenges because they may already be working to capacity. They may be comfortable in their routine, or they may be burned out.

Not all officers will want to do all law enforcement tasks. Maybe they are satisfied with routine tasks. The lower level of tasks may satisfy their needs of security, money and group belonging. Even if given the opportunity for change, they may prefer one division over another. Not all officers want promotions. They would rather be responsible for only what they do, not for getting results from other people.

job enrichment • similar to job enlargement, except that in job enrichment the focus is on the quality of the new jobs assigned rather than on the quantity. Emphasizes adding variety, deeper personal interest and involvement, increased responsibility and greater autonomy. Appropriate for any highly routine job.

Job Satisfaction and Community Policing and Problem Solving

One benefit often attributed to community policing and problem solving is that officers are more motivated and morale is heightened. This is a result of officers feeling they are making a significant difference in the community: "Officers who fix problems and do not merely treat the symptoms can make a bigger difference in their communities and have more rewarding careers" (Orrick, p.40). Officers in departments embracing community policing report greater job satisfaction, as discussed in Chapter 3.

Benefits of Motivated Personnel

The benefits of having highly motivated personnel are numerous—less sick leave, better coverage, more arrests and better investigations. In fact, most of the numerous benefits listed in Chapter 7 as resulting from an effective training program would also result from effective motivation. With both effective training and motivational programs, these benefits are highly probable. The price of not paying attention to motivation is often low morale and a generally negative environment.

Morale: An Overview

An office poster designed to inspire employees to greater efforts reads: "You can— if you will!" Beneath it, someone had scrawled, "And you're canned if you won't!" Both sayings relate directly to morale and employees' attitudes toward their jobs. This brings to mind the military aphorism: "The beatings will continue until morale improves."

morale • a person's or group's state of mind, level of enthusiasm and involvement with work and with life. How employees feel, in contrast to discipline, how employees act.

 Morale is a person's or group's state of mind, level of enthusiasm and amount of involvement with work and with life.

Morale can make or break an individual or an organization. As Napoleon observed, referring to his army: "An army's effectiveness depends on its size, training, experience and morale . . . and morale is worth more than all the other factors combined."

Morale is *always* present. It might be high, low or on an even keel, but it exists perpetually. Management's responsibility is to keep morale as high as possible and to be alert to signs that it may be dropping. The morale of individuals, work units and an entire agency concerns managers and supervisors.

McAndrew (2003, p.9) contends that low morale is "one readily identifiable culprit" for police department's inability to retain qualified personnel—"to say nothing of its link to other organizational problems such as corruption and inefficiency."

Achieving high morale is a complex challenge, with different problems depending on the department's size and leadership style. Even within the same agency, morale, as it relates to job satisfaction, can differ from one position to another.

Morale is somewhat elusive and difficult to define. Individuals and organizations differ greatly, and what would induce high or low morale in one might be the opposite in another. Good or poor morale is generally attributed to individuals, whereas high or low morale characterizes the entire organization.

Good or high morale is a *can-do* attitude. As Admiral Ben Morrell says: "Morale is when your hands and feet keep on working when your head says it can't be done." The right kind of persistence *does* pay. Coaches stress the importance of that "second effort" in winning games. The willingness to make another try when the first one fails distinguishes the average player and employee from the star. A Chinese proverb proclaims: "The person who says it cannot be done should not interrupt the person doing it."

Douglas MacArthur, the general so instrumental in helping win World War II, might never have gained his status without persistence. When he applied for admission to West Point, he was turned down, not once but twice. He persisted, however, applied a third time, was accepted and marched into history.

Morale can be measured by observing the actions and statements of employees. Are they positive and upbeat? Do people take pride in their work? Are they supportive? Or are they negative? The quality of officers' work will be affected as much by their morale as by their skills. Effective managers know that people's job performance is directly related to how they feel about the job, themselves, their peers, their managers and their agency.

Maintaining good morale should be a priority because "low morale can do more damage to an agency than a city council armed with budget cuts. And it leads to high turnover, mistakes and bad press" (Moore, 2004, p.162). Although improved morale will not always increase employees' effectiveness and productivity, it puts employees in the frame of mind to be productive. Given good supervision and good working conditions, employees with high morale will be extremely effective. As legendary race car driver, engineer, entrepreneur and former CEO and president of STP Corporation Andy Granatelli noted: "When you are making a success of something, it's not work. It's a way of life. You enjoy yourself because you are making your contribution to the world."

Indicators of Morale Problems

Knowing where an agency stands is the first step in improving morale (Stainbrook, p.32). Good managers are always alert for changes in work attitudes that may indicate trouble. They might notice sullenness, irritability, indifference, tardiness or increased absenteeism. Among the most common indicators of morale problems are a noticeably less positive attitude, loss of interest and enthusiasm, negativism and lack of respect. Other indicators are excessive absenteeism, sick leave and turnover; longer lunch hours and/or breaks; and coming in late and leaving early. Still other indicators include low productivity, less attention to personal appearance, many grievances and complaints, and many accidents.

 Indicators of low morale include lack of productivity, enthusiasm and cooperation; absenteeism; tardiness; grievances; complaints; and excessive turnover.

Managers may recognize these red flags in individual officers, or they may be pervasive throughout the department. In the latter case, the manager faces a much greater challenge. A first step is to identify *why* morale might be low. Seldom is the answer simple or singular.

To identify causes of morale problems, some managers distribute a survey that includes questions such as the following (to which respondents answer strongly disagree, disagree, uncertain, agree or strongly agree):

1. This is a good department to work for.
2. My supervisor understands me.
3. My supervisor listens to my concerns.
4. I have the training I need to do a good job.
5. I have the equipment I need to do a good job.
6. I am proud to be a member of this department.

Such a survey not only helps identify areas that might be causing morale problems but also lets employees communicate their feelings and know that these feelings are important to the department. However, the survey results must be *used*. Employees who think the department is insensitive might use a lack of follow-through to support their contention.

Surveys are not the only way to identify factors contributing to a morale problem. Managers who communicate well with their subordinates can often discover problems simply by having an open-door policy and listening to what people say. The closer managers are to their employees, the easier it will be for them to recognize a negative change in morale before it becomes disruptive.

Reasons for Morale Problems

The underlying causes of morale problems are not always easy to determine. Individual morale can be low and the organizational morale high, or the reverse can be true. Some people point out that morale is related to happiness and well-being. Others say it is more related to work benefits. Still others believe it is a philosophical problem of self-fulfillment. In general, employees who work toward organizational goals are deemed to have high morale, and those who do not are deemed to have low morale.

If a law enforcement agency has inadequate, nonequitable salaries and fringe benefits; lacks modern equipment; and does not provide adequate resources, morale is likely to be low. Measures must be taken to correct these inadequacies. If all these factors are met and morale is still low, the problem is probably centered in individual needs.

Most of the blame for low morale can be placed on controllable factors such as poor management, internal politics and favoritism by supervisors: "The most important component in an agency's morale is the attitude and management style of the department's chief executive" (Moore, p.162).

 Causes for low morale include poor management, job dissatisfaction and failure to meet important individual needs.

In many departments, the source of what is driving officer morale down is clear: "An uncaring police administration and rude or disrespectful supervisors" (McAndrew, p.9). In a survey of several hundred uniformed members of the New York Police Department, only 5.6 percent of officers considered police administrators to be responsive to and supportive of their needs. More than half indicated they did not receive appropriate recognition from their supervisor for unusually good jobs, and more than a quarter saw their supervisors' performance expectations as unrealistic: "Unsupportive administrators and ill treatment by supervisors were common themes in written comments. . . . There is considerable consensus in the literature of policing that management is one of the principal causes of low morale among officers, and the findings from this research support that consensus" (McAndrew, p.10).

Another important cause of low morale is job dissatisfaction. Among the job-related factors contributing to low morale are lack of administrative support; ineffective supervision; lack of necessary equipment or training to perform effectively; lack of promotion opportunities; political interference; corruption within the department; the criminal justice system itself, which may appear to be a revolving door for criminals; and the image of the police frequently portrayed by the media.

In addition, police wages and salaries have never been high, although the total benefit package and sense of job security have always made the job desirable. Given that police endure a high level of stress, most certainly face an abnormal risk of injury or death on the job and have a higher rate of burnout than most workers, police positions are underpaid.

When individual morale is low, employees should first examine themselves. Mental attitudes toward superiors, fellow workers and the public have a great deal to do with job satisfaction.

perception • how one views or interprets things.

Perception, the angle from which people view things, makes a tremendous difference in what they see. For example, the difference between a cute little mischief maker and a juvenile delinquent is whether the child is yours or someone else's.

A story about a young couple who opened a salmon cannery in Alaska also illustrates this point. They were having a hard time selling their salmon, despite an extensive advertising campaign. The problem was that their salmon was grey, not the pink salmon customers were used to. They pondered the problem for several days and then had a brainstorm. They changed the can's label, putting in bold letters right under the brand name "The only salmon guaranteed not to turn pink in the can." It worked.

A similar situation exists in how subordinates rate certain job factors and how managers rate the same factors. Consider the survey results summarized in Table 9.1.

Table 9.1 Worker and Supervisor Ratings Compared

Job Conditions	Worker Rating	Supervisor Rating
Full appreciation of work done	1	8
Feeling "in" on things	2	10
Sympathetic help on personal problems	3	9
Job security	4	2
Good wages	5	1
Work that keeps you interested	6	5
Promotion and growth in company	7	3
Personal loyalty to workers	8	6
Good working conditions	9	4
Tactful disciplining	10	7

Source: William B. Melincoe and John P. Peper. Supervisory Personnel Development. California State Police
Officers Training Series, #76, Sacramento, CA, p.87.

Full appreciation of work done and feeling "in" on things led the workers' list.
These same factors were at the bottom of the supervisors' ratings. Similarly, good
wages were at the top of the supervisors' list and in the middle of the workers' list.
Such information is critical for managers to know.

For those who firmly believe in Abraham Maslow's hierarchy of needs, it may be
time to check the employees' needs for affiliation, achievement and self-actualization.

Building Morale

McAndrew (p.10) asserts: "Overall, improving morale comes down to administrative factors and not negative issues." Key areas include salary, the quality of
supervision, organizational/public support, physical conditions at work and
nepotism/favoritism. He notes: "Addressing these problems in the current environment of declining budgets and dramatically increasing responsibilities presents a momentous challenge to leaders in both law enforcement and politics."

Despite these challenges, managers can build morale with strong leadership
and open communication: "Morale within a department falls squarely on the
shoulders of its leaders" (Stainbrook, p.32).

 The individual most able to raise or lower individual and department morale is the
manager/supervisor through leadership and open communication.

Improving morale requires certain attitudes on the manager's part. First, managers must believe that subordinates *can* grow and change—they can improve
their attitudes/morale given the right circumstances. Managers must be like the
tailor, who, according to George Bernard Shaw, is the "only person who behaves
sensibly because he takes new measurements every time he sees me."

Second, managers must be open and honest with their subordinates, treat
them with respect and seek to understand them. Finally, managers must understand themselves. They must recognize their own prejudices, their own strengths
and weaknesses, their own obstacles to high morale and their critical role as a
model for others.

The story is told of the Reverend Billy Graham visiting a small town and asking
a young boy how to get to the post office. After receiving directions, Dr. Graham

invited the lad to come to the church and hear him explain to the townsfolk how to get to heaven. The boy declined, saying, "I don't think so. You don't even know how to get to the post office."

Credibility is crucial. Managers who seek to build morale must exhibit high morale themselves. Only then can they hope to raise the work unit's morale. Several options for morale building are available to managers and supervisors.

 Options for building morale include:

- Being positive and upbeat.
- Setting clear, meaningful goals and objectives.
- Setting appropriate standards.
- Being fair.
- Making no promises that cannot be kept.
- Providing the necessary resources.
- Developing organizational and personal pride.
- Providing a sense of participation—teamwork.
- Treating each person as an individual.
- Giving deserved recognition.
- Criticizing tactfully.
- Avoiding the "boss" attitude.
- Communicating effectively.

People enjoy working with a cheerful, optimistic boss. Like magnets, people are drawn to the positive and repelled by the negative. An upbeat attitude is contagious—as is a negative attitude. A shoe manufacturer recently ran an ad for slippers that read: "Keeps your feet from getting cold." The ad was a total flop. When the copy was changed to read "Keeps your feet warm and comfortable," sales doubled.

You have heard it before, but goals and objectives are at the heart of most management areas, and this certainly includes morale. Companies with the least employee turnover and the highest morale are those that have successfully communicated the company's mission and goals. Law enforcement executive managers should set department goals and objectives with the input of their subordinates—and this includes the line officers. The moment officers get the feeling they are not sharing in the department's goals, in what is going on, morale will drop, productivity will decrease and serious problems will arise.

Reasonable, clear, fair employee standards for conduct and behavior also should be established, published and made known. Employees expect this, and the law enforcement organization cannot function without these standards. As obvious as it may sound, it is critical that managers be fair in all aspects of the job. Most employees do not mind reasonably strict rules and procedures if they make sense and apply equally to everyone. Fairness is a common denominator for increased employee morale.

Likewise, managers should never promise things they cannot deliver. They should not be overly optimistic, trying to please their subordinates or telling them what they want to hear simply to keep them happy. It is very tempting to do so and to hope that things will work out for the best, but this can lead to problems.

Law enforcement employees need resources to do a good job and to feel good about themselves and what they do. Training is essential. All employees need to feel competent in the tasks for which they are responsible. Training also needs to be ongoing so officers are up to date. Their equipment should also be current and in good working condition.

The appearance of the station, the squad cars and insignia on the door, identification or name signs on each room in the station, desk name signs, uniforms that leave a favorable impression—all reflect morale. Many of these are not expensive, but they can make a significant difference in how officers feel about themselves and their organization.

Organizational and personal pride are closely related. Employees like to work for an organization they can be proud of. All law enforcement organizations have individual identities based largely on management goals and objectives. Bring up the subject of department and personal pride at staff and department meetings. Do not just think you are the best; really work at being the best. Often, competing in intradepartmental competitions such as sharp-shooting, physical fitness or intradepartmental sports can contribute to a feeling of pride. These can also foster a sense of participation, another factor contributing to high morale.

Despite an emphasis on teamwork, every employee is an individual and must be recognized as such. Call employees by the names they prefer, including nicknames in appropriate situations. Take an interest in their problems. Employees who have problems at home cannot function at full efficiency on the job. Although managers cannot usually *do* anything about such problems, they can lend a sympathetic ear.

Too many law enforcement managers criticize when things go wrong but fail to praise when things go right. This is illustrated in the story about the first month of World War I, when generals were handling huge armies under unprecedented circumstances. On the Western Front, the Battle of the Marne ended the German advance, stabilized the front and saved France. Leading the French armies was Marshal Joffre, a soldier viewed by most as unimaginative.

Years later when the battle was analyzed, military commentators tried to decide who should receive credit for this decisive victory. The commentators could come to no agreement other than that surely some general had made a crucial move at the correct moment. They decided to ask Marshal Joffre who was responsible. Joffre's reply was: "I really don't know who ought to get credit for the victory at the Marne. I know only one thing. If we had been defeated, everyone would have agreed at once that the fault was mine."

Show judgment in giving credit and praise. It can be carried to extremes so that subordinates come to rely on it for every task they complete. Such people are like the little boy who said to his dad, "Let's play darts. I'll throw and you say 'Wonderful.'"

A wise manager once said, "That criticism is best which sounds like an explanation." It is easy to be critical. The real management challenge is to come up with constructive alternatives. Several other considerations are important when criticism is necessary.

- Be certain of the facts. Do not make mountains out of molehills.
- Correct in private; praise in public.
- Be objective and impersonal. Do not compare one officer unfavorably with another.

- Ask questions; do not accuse. Allow those you are correcting to explain themselves.
- Focus on the action that needs correcting, not on the individual officer. Emphasize what is to be done, not what is wrong.

The legitimate purpose of criticism is *not* to humiliate but to help subordinates do better next time. Remember that criticism is seldom as effective as praise in changing behavior. Before managers give a person a "kick in the pants," no matter how much it is deserved, they should raise their sights and *try* to give a pat on the back instead.

Managers should also avoid the "boss" attitude, striving to be friendly yet businesslike, and to think of "We" instead of "I." When appropriate, they should smile and be enthusiastic.

Finally, and most importantly, managers must communicate effectively: "Communication may be the single most important aspect of building good morale in any organization" (Stainbrook, p.36). Employees want to know what is going on and how they are doing. Employees cannot act or react in a vacuum. Department newsletters, letters of commendation, constructive criticism, news releases, department bulletin boards, personal conversations, department or staff meetings—all are forms of communication.

It is demoralizing for officers to hear inside information from news media rather than from their superiors. It is essential that police administrators keep their officers informed. Among the ways to do this are newsletters, attending roll call, going on ride-alongs and simply walking around the department, sometimes referred to as Management by Walking Around (MBWA). Administrators who take this approach should be prepared to hear negative comments, especially at first.

Promotions and Morale

Management positions within the law enforcement profession are more limited than in almost any other profession. This can cause severe morale problems. The promotion process must be fair, and those who want promotions must be helped in their quest.

Not everyone is management material. Those who are not should be guided into seeking satisfaction on the job in other ways, perhaps in developing a specialty the agency needs. The future of law enforcement agencies rests in making the best use of personnel. Those who are best suited for management—who have leadership qualities and communication skills—are those who should be promoted.

 Promotions must be fair and based on management qualities, not on technical skills or seniority.

Written examinations have been the most frequently used technique to make promotional selections of mid- to lower-level police positions. Any examination should be validated for the type and size of the agency using it. Written examinations, oral examinations and on-the-job performance ratings can be used for promotional decisions.

Most law enforcement agencies use a civil service examination, both written and oral. It is common to require minimum or maximum ages, terms of service, specific types of experience and other criteria for eligibility to take the examination. Most merit systems provide similar examinations. Final selection of the top three candidates (or any pre-established number) is made from the written and oral examinations. The Civil Service Commission, the city manager, the mayor with the city council's approval or the law enforcement chief executive officer then makes the choice.

Promotion panels often consider formal education level, amount and type of specialized training, specific skills, length of employment, previous evaluations, productivity or performance levels, personal appearance, department awards and recognition and discipline/reprimand history (Cormican, 2005, p.152).

Assessment Centers

A trend is to use an **assessment center** to select those eligible for promotion, especially at the upper levels. Properly designed and administered assessments are not only more reliable than traditional testing methods for evaluating supervisory, managerial and administrative potential but can also be adapted to all types of positions and assignments and, for the most part, are widely accepted and favored by candidates (Hale, 2005, p.18).

The multi-faceted, structured process used in an assessment center can take the guesswork out of finding the right person for a job opening (McLaurin, 2005, p.18). Furthermore, a properly planned and implemented assessment center will be seen as a fair, objective process for promoting the most qualified officer. However, used incorrectly, an assessment center can become "stigmatized" as unreliable and unfair and could result in civil litigation. Examples of the methods used in assessment centers are contained in Table 9.2.

assessment center • places participants in the position of actually performing tasks related to the anticipated position. Incorporates situational techniques in a simulated environment under standardized conditions.

Table 9.2 Typical Management Assessment Center Methods

Method	Description	Example Traits Analyzed
Management game or simulation	Participants perform in a simulated setting, sometimes with a computer simulation, make necessary decisions and analyze the results.	Organizing ability, financial aptitude, decision making, efficiency under stress, adaptability and leadership capacity
Leaderless group discussions	Participants in a group with no formally appointed leader are asked to solve a business problem.	Aggressiveness, persuasiveness, verbal skills, flexibility and self-confidence
In-basket exercise	A mail in-basket for an ill executive is given to the participants to analyze, to set priorities and to take action on.	Organizing ability, decision making under stress, conceptual skills, ability to delegate and concern for others
Role playing	Participants are asked to take the roles of hypothetical employees, as in a performance evaluation interview.	Insight, empathy to others, human and technical skills and sensitivity to others
Psychological testing	A series of pencil-and-paper instruments is completed by the participants.	Reasoning, interests, aptitudes, communication tendencies, leadership and group styles, motivation profile and the like
Case analysis	Participants are given a case to analyze individually and present to a group of evaluators.	Verbal ability, diagnostic skills, conceptual skills, technical skills and so on
In-depth interviews	Participants are interviewed by raters—usually after some of the above exercises have been completed—regarding a variety of personal interests, skills and aptitudes.	Verbal ability, self-confidence, managerial skills, commitment to career and so on

Source: International City Managers Association, 1120 G Street, NW, Washington, DC, p.253. Reprinted by permission.

The total assessment typically is organized into three phases.

 Assessment centers use three phases:

1. Testing: written examination, verbal screening and psychological testing
2. Oral board interview, situational testing, leaderless group discussion and individual psychological interview
3. Polygraph examination, background check, physical examination and officer/staff interviews

During the second phase, candidates confront hypothetical problems that managers typically encounter. At the end of the second phase, candidates are ranked using the information from the first two phases. A predetermined number are selected in rank order to complete the third phase.

Whether an assessment center is used or the promotions are done in-house, whenever possible it is usually best to promote from within the agency. This is not always easy. Sometimes this decision is not up to the immediate supervisor or manager. But studies and common sense show that passing over qualified personnel to bring in an outsider almost invariably erodes morale.

 When possible, promotions should be from within.

Seeing colleagues receive a promotion can be highly motivating for those who also want to be promoted and can improve department morale. Another morale booster is to provide police/family programs for officers.

Police/Family Programs

The police career is difficult to keep separate from officers' personal lives. Tasks and experiences are often intermixed with family well-being. Job stress is often family stress. Traumatic experiences do not end with the termination of the shift or on arriving home. Incidents that result in shooting a suspect or end with an officer being injured or killed on duty are endured by the family as well as by the officer. Police family members often have no more understanding of the police job than the average layperson. To compound the problem, police spouses often have careers in addition to family responsibilities. The officers' daily interactions with the seamy side of life and with problem people may cause a distorted, unbalanced view of society. In severe cases this can lead to alcoholism, drug abuse, separation, divorce or even suicide.

To cope with these problems, a number of police departments have experimented with police-spouse seminars to explain work shifts; police jargon; salaries; fringe benefits; types of police incidents; types of people police come in contact with; police equipment; police training; and panel discussions on selected subjects, with the panel consisting of officers, spouses and experts on the subject. Expectations and fears of officers and their spouses are discussed freely. Spouses often form support groups that meet regularly or when a crisis arises.

Table 9.3 MPO Requirements of the Pierce County Sheriff's Department (Tacoma, Washington)

Phase I	Entry Level Requirements

1. Three years as a Deputy Sheriff with the Pierce County Sheriff's Department.
2. Last two evaluations must have a total score of 70 or better. A current evaluation from within the last 12 months must be provided.
3. Candidates must apply with a typewritten letter, which must be endorsed by his/her immediate supervisor.

Phase II	Advanced Patrol Officer Requirements

1. A total of six years with the department, 50 percent of which must have been spent in the field force.
2. Upon completion of the sixth year, a candidate's last two evaluations must be 80 or above with no individual factor below 70.
3. An average shooting score of expert or better while in this phase.
4. At least four points accumulated as an accident-free driver (entry-level time included).
5. Three years to complete this phase.

Education: Sixteen points total required with a minimum of eight points from any approved law enforcement training classes. Points may be accumulated for higher learning achieved prior to coming into the department.

Experience: Fifteen points total with a minimum of six from specialized support assignments from within the department.

Major involvement: No points necessary for this segment. However, points may be earned for use in Phase III.

Phase III	Master Patrol Officer Requirements

1. A total of ten years minimum with the department, 70 percent of which must have been spent in field force patrol (3 years advanced and 4 years master phase).
2. Accumulate a total of seven years of accident-free driving points.
3. Shooting scores shall average expert or better during this 4-year phase.
4. Typewritten letter requesting consideration as an MPO and showing that all requirements have been met.
5. Evaluations must be 80 percent or above with no individual factor below 70 percent.

Education: Eight additional points accumulated from law enforcement training classes.

Experience: Twelve points total with three points required from specialized support assignments within the department.

Major involvement: Six points total.

Source: Paul D. Thrash. "An Incentive Program: Boosting Morale of Veteran Officers." *Law Enforcement Technology,* October 1992, p. 53. © PTN Publishing Co. *Law Enforcement Technology,* October 1992. Reprinted by permission.

An Innovative Program for Maintaining Veteran Officers' Morale

Promotions are extremely hard to come by in law enforcement, and many officers do not want them, preferring to drive a squad car rather than sit behind a desk. Administrators are often faced with the difficult task of keeping morale high for patrol officers who have been on the job for several years. One innovative approach to this challenge was developed by the Pierce County Sheriff's Department in Tacoma, Washington—the Master Patrol Officer (MPO) program. This program has three distinct phases: the Entry level, the Advanced Patrol Officer level and the MPO level. Table 9.3 describes the requirements for each. The MPO point system gives credit for education, experience and involvement in law enforcement service or in the community. Table 9.4 gives the highlights of the MPO point system. Physical recognition of MPO status is provided by double chevrons or corporal stripes worn by MPOs.

Table 9.4 The MPO Point System

Education		Major Involvement	
AA degree or 90 quarter hours	4 pts	In House participation or service on:	
BA degree	6 pts	Board of Professional Standards	*2 pts per year*
MA degree	8 pts	FTO Advisory Board	*2 pts per year*
PhD degree	10 pts	FTO Advisory Board	*2 pts per year*
Approved law enforcement classes	1 pt per 8-hr class	Accident Review Board	*2 pts per year*
		Radio Users Committee	*2 pts per year*
Mandatory or refresher classes do not receive points. A maximum of four points for a one-week school and eight points for a two-week school.		Special Project Boards or Committee	*1 pt per project*
		Publish an article in a law enforcement-related magazine or journal	*1 pt per article*

Experience	
Accident-free driving record	*1 pt per year*
Master shooter (96 percent and above)	*2 pts*
No sick leave usage	*0.5 pt per year*
Medal/awards	*3 pts per year*
Specialized support assignments (K-9, Juvenile, Civil, Traffic, DARE, Warrants, etc.)	*3 pts per year (maximum 6 pts)*
Field Training Officer (FTO)	*5 pts per year (maximum of 10)*
Assigned responsibilities (SWAT, Bomb Squad, Dive Team, Search/Rescue)	*2 pts per year (maximum of 6)*

Community Involvement	
Involvement in any community service project or social service project as a leader or board member	*2 pts per project*
a) sports	
b) other civilian non-profit organization	
c) Military Reserve Service	
Involvement as an officer (1-year minimum)	*2 pts per project*
a) union/guild	
b) law enforcement	
c) any statewide or national law enforcement support group approved by the MPO board	
Serves as president of any of the above organizations for a minimum of one year	*3 pts per office*

Source: Paul D. Thrash. "An Incentive Program: Boosting Morale of Veteran Officers." *Law Enforcement Technology,* October 1992, p.56. © PTN Publishing Co. Law Enforcement Technology, October 1992. Reprinted by permission.

SUMMARY

Motivation is an inner or outer drive to meet a need or goal. Researchers who have studied motivation and proposed theories about it include Maslow, Herzberg, Skinner, Vroom and Morse and Lorsch.

Maslow's hierarchy of needs is, in the ascending order they need to be met, physiological, safety and security, social, esteem and self-actualization. Herzberg's hygiene factors are tangible rewards that can cause dissatisfaction if lacking. Motivator factors are intangible rewards that can create satisfaction.

Skinner's reinforcement theory suggests that positive reinforcement rewards and increases a given behavior; negative reinforcement decreases a given behavior by reinforcing another, desired behavior. Reinforcement is usually more effective than punishment. In addition, the closer in time to the behavior, the more effective the reinforcement will be.

Vroom's expectancy theory suggests that employees will choose the level of effort that matches the performance opportunity for reward. Morse and Lorsch's contingency theory suggests fitting tasks, officers and the agency's goals so that officers can feel competent. McDonald's Rule of Four says managers have these options to influence people's behavior at work: (1) reward good behavior (positive reinforcement), (2) punish bad behavior (negative reinforcement), (3) threaten people exhibiting bad behavior and (4) ignore the bad behavior. The most effective option is to reward good behavior.

No matter what theory or combination of theories law enforcement managers subscribe to, external and internal rewards are important. Among the most common external motivators or tangible rewards are salary, bonuses, insurance, retirement plans, favorable working conditions, paid vacation and holidays, titles and adequacy of equipment. Internal motivators or intangible rewards include goals, achievement, recognition, self-respect, opportunity for advancement, opportunity to make a contribution and belief in individual and departmental goals. Law enforcement work can be made more interesting and motivating in three important ways: job rotation, job enlargement and job enrichment.

Morale is a person's or group's state of mind, level of enthusiasm and amount of involvement with work and life. Indicators of low morale include lack of productivity, enthusiasm and cooperation; absenteeism; tardiness; grievances; complaints; and excessive turnover. Causes of low morale include job dissatisfaction and failure to meet important individual needs.

The individual most able to raise or lower individual and department morale is the manager/supervisor. Options for building morale include being positive and upbeat; setting clear, meaningful goals and objectives; setting appropriate standards; being fair; making no promises that cannot be kept; providing necessary resources; developing organizational and personal pride; providing a sense of participation—teamwork; treating each person as an individual; giving deserved recognition; criticizing tactfully; avoiding the "boss" attitude; communicating effectively; and accepting what cannot be changed.

One important factor affecting morale is promotions. Promotions must be fair and based on management qualities, not on technical skills or seniority. Some law enforcement agencies use assessment centers to determine promotions. Such centers typically involve three phases: (1) testing: written examination, verbal screening and psychological testing; (2) oral board interview, situational testing, leaderless group discussion and individual psychological interview; and (3) polygraph examination, background check, physical examination and officer/staff interviews. When possible, law enforcement administrators should promote from within to improve overall morale.

 CHALLENGE NINE

After several months on the job as the Greenfield police chief, you observe a lack of motivation and low morale among a core group of officers. They are resistant to the concept of community policing and just want to be left alone to do "real" police work—arresting crooks. During the previous administration, officers received monthly awards for making the most arrests and writing the most traffic citations.

One of your captains tells you the disgruntled officers are influential in the department's informal hierarchy. Some are veterans who have taken promotional exams but were never selected. Others never even took the exams. The captain says they are skilled officers who could have been promoted if they had worked harder and better prepared themselves. He thinks their lack of success has left them bitter.

The captain suggests you issue a directive ordering the entire department to implement one community policing project each month. Those who do not comply will be progressively disciplined. He thinks the threat of discipline will motivate the disgruntled officer to accept community policing.

1. As the Greenfield Police Department chief, what changes would you implement to improve morale and increase motivation among officers not pursuing supervisory positions?

2. Is resistance to change a sign of low morale and lack of motivation?

3. What affect will your captain's suggested directive have on the department?

4. How can community policing improve morale?

5. How does your role (police chief) as a motivator differ from the role of a sergeant as a motivator?

DISCUSSION QUESTIONS

1. What motivates you?

2. What do you consider your basic needs? Write down the top five.

3. What are five motivators that make you do better work?

4. What would not motivate you?

5. Do you agree or disagree with the following statement: "It is not possible to motivate anyone." Why?

6. What makes your on-the-job morale go down? Go up?

7. What are some ways to give personal recognition for a job well done?

8. What job conditions make you feel best?

9. How do morale and motivation interact?

10. If you could make one change in your life that would improve your morale, what would that change be?

REFERENCES

Cormican, Russell. "Interview Tips for Promotions and Transfers." *Law and Order*, September 2005, pp.151–155.

Haarr, Robin N. "Factors Affecting the Decision of Police Recruits to 'Drop Out' of Police Work." *Police Quarterly*, December 2005, pp.431–453.

Hackman, J.R. and Oldham, G.R. "Motivation through the Design of Work: Test of a Theory." *Organisational Behaviour and Human Performance*, Vol.16, No.2, 1976, pp.250-279.

Hale, Charles. "Pros and Cons of Assessment Centers." *Law and Order*, April 2005, pp.18–21.

Herzberg, Frederick. *One More Time: How Do You Motivate Employees?* Boston: Harvard Business Review (no date).

Herzberg, Frederick. *Motivation, the Organizational Environment and Productivity*, 1978.

Hickman, Matthew J. *State and Local Law Enforcement Training Academies, 2002.* Washington, DC: Bureau of Justice Statistics, January 2005. (NCJ 204030)

Johnson, Robert Roy. "Motivating Senior Officers." *Law and Order*, July 2004, pp.134–138.

Konzes, James E. and Posner, Barry Z. *The Leadership Challenge*, 3rd ed. San Francisco: Jossey-Bass, 2002.

Koper, Christopher S. *Hiring and Keeping Police Officers.* Washington, DC: National Institute of Justice Research in Practice, July 2004. (NCJ 202289)

McAndrew, John. "Morale Stinks. Here's Why. Now What?" *Law Enforcement News*, February 28, 2003, pp.9–10.

McDonald, Tom. "The Rule of Four." *Successful Meetings*, September 2005, p.26.

McLaurin, Michael. "How to Run an Assessment Center." *Police*, March 2005, pp.18–26.

Moore, Carole. "Maintaining Positive Morale." *Law Enforcement Technology*, July 2004, p.162.

Orrick, Dwayne. "Police Turnover." *The Police Chief*, September 2005, pp.36–40.

Stainbrook, Mark G. "Rallying the Troops." *Police*, August 2004, pp.32–38.

BOOK-SPECIFIC WEB SITE

Go to the Management and Supervision in Law Enforcement Web site at www.thomsonedu.com/criminaljustice/bennett for student and instructor resources, including Internet Assignments and Case Studies.

CHAPTER 10

Discipline and Problem Behaviors

I would rather try to persuade a man to go along, because once I have persuaded him, he will stick. If I scare him, he will stay just as long as he is scared, and then he is gone.

Dwight D. Eisenhower

 DO YOU KNOW?

- How morale and discipline differ?
- What the purpose of discipline is?
- What the foundation for most disciplinary actions is?
- What a fundamental management right is?
- What the 10/80/10 principle is?
- How a problem employee is characterized?
- What types of personalities might be likely to result in problems?
- How managers can deal with problem people?
- What serious problems managers must deal with?
- What a primary rule for the timing of discipline is?
- What should be considered when assessing penalties?
- What steps are usually involved in progressive discipline?
- What balance of consequences analysis is?
- What consequences are most powerful?
- How managers can use the balance of consequences?
- What the PRICE Method consists of?
- How much time effective praise and reprimands require?
- What ratio of praise to blame is usually needed?
- What strokes managers can use?

CAN YOU DEFINE?

appeal	dismissal	one-minute	self-discipline
balance of conse-	general orders	managing	sexual harassment
quences analysis	gunnysack approach	passive resistance	stroke approach
comprehensive	insubordination	positive discipline	summary discipline
discipline	marginal performer	PRICE Method	summary
decoupling	negative discipline	progressive	punishment
demotion	negligent retention	discipline	suspension
discipline	nonactor liability	reprimand	termination

Introduction

Managers are challenged in the area of discipline as in no other. Values have changed, and court decisions have supported more liberal views of discipline over the past decades. The days of autocratic, despotic discipline are gone.

Imposing some form of discipline is invariably part of a law enforcement manager's responsibilities, one the manager must be prepared to exercise when necessary. Most people assume that when discipline is discussed, it refers to punishment, but discipline is far broader than punishment.

This chapter begins with a definition of discipline, followed by a description of positive, constructive self-discipline and a look at the typical rules and regulations for law enforcement departments. Of importance when considering discipline is the tension between clarity of role and creativity, as well as common problem behaviors you can anticipate. Then the challenge of managing difficult people as well as those who commit serious offenses are discussed.

Next, the need for managers to accept that positive discipline is not always effective and to recognize the need for negative discipline/punishment is examined, including guidelines for administering negative discipline, for using progressive discipline, for using summary punishment and for providing a process to appeal and important legal considerations. This is followed by a discussion of comprehensive discipline, including such systems as the balance of consequences analysis, the PRICE Method, one-minute managing and the stroke approach. The chapter concludes with a brief description of a fair disciplinary system.

Discipline Defined

discipline • training expected to produce a desired behavior—controlled behavior or administering punishment. Also a state of affairs or how employees act, in contrast to morale, which is how employees feel.

self-discipline • self-imposed rules for self-control.

Discipline is training expected to produce a desired behavior—controlled behavior. Discipline should never be an end in itself. It should be used to develop highly trained, efficient law enforcement officers. Those officers with the highest performance have a high level of determination, pride, confidence and self-discipline. **Self-discipline** is a set of self-imposed rules governing a person's self-control. Leaders throughout the world set degrees of discipline, as do religions. Discipline can be a form of voluntary obedience to instructions, commands or expected demeanor.

Discipline is closely related to morale. As discussed in Chapter 9, morale is a state of mind, an employee's attitude. Discipline, in contrast, is a state of affairs, or how employees act.

 Morale is how a person feels; discipline is how a person acts.

Morale and discipline are closely related because the level of morale affects employees' conduct. The higher the morale, the fewer the discipline problems. Conversely, the lower the morale, the more likely discipline problems will erupt.

 The purpose of discipline is to promote desired behavior, which may be done by encouraging acceptable behavior or punishing unacceptable behavior.

Positive, Constructive Self-Discipline

Positive, constructive self-discipline, like self-motivation, is usually most effective. **Positive discipline** uses training to foster compliance with rules and regulations and performance at peak efficiency.

positive descipline • uses training to foster compliance with rules and regulations and performance at peak efficiency.

Maintaining Positive Discipline

It is to law enforcement managers' advantage to maintain a high degree of self-discipline within subordinates. They might begin by exercising self-discipline as an example.

When employees willingly follow the department's rules and regulations and put forth full effort to accomplish their individual and departmental goals, positive discipline prevails. The Navy would call this a "taut ship." But officers need to know the rules and what is expected of them.

Knowledge of Rules, Regulations and Expected Behaviors

Everybody should understand what they can and cannot do. The more employees know, the more able they are to conduct themselves as expected. To inform employees, managers might post rules on bulletin boards, distribute Standard Operating Procedure (SOP) manuals and discuss the rules at meetings.

Officers should have input on rules. If they have a voice in establishing the rules, they are more likely to support them. Having a few rules that everyone supports is better than having many rules that are violated.

Typical Rules and Regulations for Law Enforcement Departments

Rules and regulations are often established by civil service boards and will vary with each department. Officers should be aware of all rules and regulations, and all members of the agency are subject to disciplinary action if they violate these.

General Conduct Officers are expected to report for duty at the designated time and place. They must not engage in disorderly conduct or accept gifts from suspects, prisoners or defendants. Officers must refrain from using unnecessary force on any person. Officers must object and refuse to obey an immoral or illegal order.

Performance of Duty Officers must preserve the law; protect life and property; and enforce federal statutes, state laws and county and city ordinances. Officers are required to discharge their duties calmly and firmly, to act together and to assist and protect each other to maintain law and order. Any officer who fails to comply, by act or omission, with any order, procedure, rule or regulation of the department or who acts in the performance of official duties in a way that could discredit himself or herself, the department or any other member of the department may be considered in neglect of duty. Officers must be courteous and respectful in dealing with the public and respond promptly to all calls for assistance from citizens or other officers.

Restrictions on Behavior Officers must not knowingly make a false report, either oral or written. For unionized law enforcement organizations, relevant provisions of

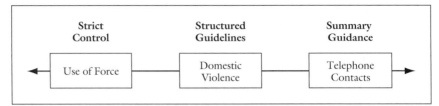

Figure 10.1 The Continuum of Policy: Levels and Examples

Source: Geoffrey P. Alpert and William C. Smith. "Developing Police Policy: An Evaluation of the Control Principle." *American Journal of Police,* 1994, p.9. Reprinted by permission.

the labor agreement must be considered. Some supervisors fear that with a union contract they cannot make discipline stick. This is *not* true. No union contract protects workers from discipline when a valid work rule is violated: "Discipline is a fundamental, indispensable tool of management" (Johnson, 2004, p.97).

 Maintaining discipline is a fundamental management right.

Policy versus Discretion

Although clear policies and procedures are necessary, they can be overdone. Too often the policy and procedure manual collects dust on the shelf because it is just too big. Effective managers recognize when control is necessary and when discretion should be allowed. Policies should be made to cover high-risk, low-frequency police functions, for example, use of deadly force and high-speed pursuits. Other police functions, such as most domestic dispute calls, require discretion within guidelines. Yet other functions, such as telephone contacts with citizens, may actually be hindered by controlling policies. Figure 10.1 shows a continuum on which control and discretion may be viewed.

Policies and Procedures Revisited

 An agency's policy and procedure manual is the foundation on which most discipline must be based.

Policies and procedures were introduced in Chapter 1. At the heart of an effective discipline system and high morale are clear written policies and procedures that guide officers yet allow for discretion in unique circumstances. The writing style should be concise and understandable by all personnel. Furthermore, procedures should be written so they apply during the day or night and on week days or weekends and holidays (McLaurin, 2005, p.26). Finally, policies and procedures must reflect not only federal, state and local laws; they must also comply with the Americans with Disabilities Act (ADA).

Updating of policies and procedures should be regularly scheduled rather than as a reaction to some crisis. A survey by Sharp (2004, p.72) found that 96 percent of the respondents had changed policies and procedures in direct response to an event that occurred in their jurisdiction. In addition (p.73) 93 percent said that outdated and poorly worded policies and procedures are potential magnets for opposing counsel to file lawsuits against agencies and officers.

General Orders

Grattet (2004, p.63) explains that **general orders** formalize a department policy on a particular issue and are a central mechanism to law enforcement leadership confronting recurring and potentially problematic enforcement issues. Grattet notes that all departments face discrepancies between their formal policies and informal practices, referred to as **decoupling:** "Decoupling occurs when an organization adopts a splashy new policy but then never really implements it to change how the work gets done."

Grattet (p.63) recommends that general orders be based on accurate, simple descriptions of the situations to which they apply and be clear and inclusive. They should also be credible and durable.

Clarity of Role versus Creativity

Specific rules and regulations leave little doubt as to what is expected of officers. This emphasis on formal rules is the result of three developments: the need for due process in discipline, protection against civil litigation and the accreditation movement. Despite this emphasis on rules and regulations, the question arises: Do such written directives help officers learn the correct way to do law enforcement work and motivate them to do so, or do they send a message to officers that they are not trusted?

An excessive number of rules may discourage innovation, risk taking, imagination and commitment to the department's mission. The trend in business is just the opposite. Control is achieved not through formal, written rules and regulations but by developing team spirit and a commitment to shared values.

The administrator's challenge is to lead by instilling the desired values and culture within the organization. This might include gearing recruiting, selecting and socializing toward basic departmental values and basing assignments, promotions and other rewards on these basic values. Administrators also sometimes deal with problem behaviors.

Dealing with Problem Employees

When dealing with problem employees, it is helpful to keep the 10/80/10 principle in mind.

 The 10/80/10 principle divides the work force into three categories: 10 percent self-motivated high achievers, 80 percent average achievers and 10 percent unmotivated troublemakers who cause 90 percent of management's problems.

Employees have many reasons for exhibiting objectionable behavior. A formerly excellent employee may change behavior due to physical illness or emotional or mental breakdown. This may not be exhibited violently or suddenly but subtly and over a long period. A change in behavior may also occur in response to disruptive and objectionable changes in department rules or regulations.

A key question is: Are problem employees too costly to retain, or is it wiser to change their behavior? Changing behavior is usually more cost-effective than replacing employees, so managers must learn more about employee assistance programs (EAP) and their underlying philosophy. Many law enforcement agencies

general orders • formalize a department policy on a particular issue and are a central mechanism to law enforcement leadership confronting recurring and potentially problematic enforcement issues.

decoupling • discrepancies between an agency's formal policies and informal practices; occurs when an organization adopts a splashy new policy but then never really implements it to change how the work gets done.

operate their own EAPs. Others contract with outside agencies to provide services such as counseling and peer support, as discussed in Chapter 12.

 A problem employee exhibits abnormal behavior to the extent that the behavior is detrimental to organizational needs and goals as well as the needs and goals of other law enforcement personnel.

Such behavior reduces the department's effectiveness and the desired professional level of law enforcement service to the community and results in numerous conflicts. Miller (2003, p.53) notes that when personal quirks irritate others or derail the success of those who display them, career consequences can be ruinous in a highly demanding profession such as policing.

marginal performer • employee who has demonstrated ability to perform but who does just enough to get by.

A **marginal performer** is an employee who has demonstrated ability to perform but does just enough to get by. Sometimes an elder officer is thought to be a marginal performer when, in actuality, the officer has been to countless fights, horrific car crashes, grizzly homicides and has "seen it all." As Oldham (2005, p.33) explains: "A calm surrounds this officer that does not exist in less experienced hands."

Often employees themselves are responsible for their problems because of their mental attitude, physical condition and emotional well-being. The manifestations of such problems are laziness, moodiness, resistance to change, complacency, absence or tardiness and disorganization. These problems could probably be altered with changes in attitude, physical condition or emotional well-being.

Many factors affect employees and determine their behavior. New law enforcement employees enter the field with expectations of becoming professionals and often already have some college education or a college degree. In addition, new officers expect law enforcement education courses that are more directly related to their career while on the job. Many of today's officers plan to attend college-level criminal justice courses after employment. With education comes higher expectations of special tasks, promotions, specialized assignments and higher salaries.

Dealing with Difficult People

Personality problems such as hostility, excessive sensitivity or bad attitudes can disrupt a law enforcement organization. In severe cases it may be necessary to refer an employee to outside counseling or assistance. With hostile employees it is best to listen and make arrangements to discuss the matter later when emotions have subsided. During later discussion managers should make it clear that the behavior is unacceptable because of its effect on other employees and operations.

Conflict often results from personality clashes. Personality types can be placed on a continuum ranging from those who are always in total agreement to those who are always in total disagreement. In the middle are those who are noncommittal, never taking one side or the other (see Figure 10.2).

 Difficult people include yes people, passives, avoiders, pessimists, complainers, know-it-alls, exploders, bullies and snipers.

Yes people are vocally supportive in your presence but rarely follow through. They smile, nod and do nothing. They always have excuses when a deadline rolls around. Yes people have a high need for acceptance and usually avoid open conflict. They

Figure 10.2   Personality Types

tell you what they think you want to hear. Tactfully confront the no-action behavior. When you make an initial request, give them time to say no. If they do not,
have them put the commitment in writing or say exactly when they will complete
the project. Do not allow them to make unrealistic promises. Build incremental
steps, deadlines and checkpoints. Follow up and monitor the expected results.
Show your approval when the promised action is taken.

Passives are silent, unresponsive people who seldom offer their own ideas or
opinions, keeping their thoughts to themselves. Their responses are usually short
and noncommittal. Some will put in writing what they will not say. Working with
passives can be frustrating. The major coping strategy is to get them to open up and
talk to you. Comment on their quietness. Help reduce their tension. Ask open-
ended questions and wait for them to answer, and then thank them for their ideas.

Avoiders put things off; they procrastinate or physically absent themselves to
avoid getting involved. To deal with indecisive avoiders, find out why they are
stalling. Probe. Question. Listen. Move away from vagueness toward specificity.
Express the value of decisiveness. Explore alternatives. Help them make decisions,
and then give support after they have made a decision.

Pessimists always say "no," are inflexible and resist change. Structure their work
relationships so they have little contact with other workers. Closely related to pessimists are *complainers*—those who find fault with everything and everyone. These
people continually gripe but take no personal responsibility for anything. Some
people are basically negative about everything. Griping has become a habit—a
chronically dismal way of looking at one's department, supervisor and fellow officers. Some people just are not happy unless they are complaining. Managers
who have such subordinates should recognize the problem and make a concerted
effort to at least not let the negative attitude affect others. Among the tactics managers might use are the following:

- Do not overreact to the negativism. When possible, ignore it.
- Relax tension. Negative people often make those around them feel stressed.
  Do not let that happen. Break the tension with a little humor.
- Promptly undo any damage. Negative workers often stir up their peers and dis-
  rupt the department or work group. If this happens, send the negative person
  out of the common work area and get everyone else back on track.

- Make your expectations clear. Have a heart-to-heart talk with the negative person. Try to find out why he or she is so negative. Let the person know you expect the negativism to be kept out of the department.
- Set an example. Be as optimistic and upbeat as possible. Encourage your subordinates to act positively, too.

Confront them, interrupt the complaining and have them detail the problem. Acknowledge and understand the complaint, but do not agree with it, argue about it or accept blame for it. Discuss the realities of the situation and focus on solving it.

Know-it-alls are highly opinionated, egotistical, speak with great authority, are sure of themselves, have all the right answers (or think they do) and are impatient with others. Know-it-alls have a strong need for order and structure, to be right (or at least to never be wrong), to be seen as competent and to be admired and respected. Use the know-it-alls' expertise and at the same time be sure your ideas are fully considered and used. Acknowledge their expertise, but help them see their effect on others. Show them how their ideas are helpful and yet not necessarily the only way to view an issue. Avoid being a counter-expert, but do your homework and know your facts. Raise questions without confrontation. Let them save face.

Exploders yell and scream. They are overemotional and sometimes even hysterical. Because you cannot talk to people who are yelling and screaming, first disarm the anger. Stand up and face them squarely. Do not let them go on for more than 30 seconds, but do not tell them to calm down. Put your hand out to stop them. Call them by name and keep repeating the name until they stop yelling. Validate their feelings: "I understand you are angry. I want to work with you but not this way." Help them regain self-control. Let them cool off. Ask, "What do you need right now?" As a last resort, simply walk away from them.

Bullies attack verbally or physically, using threats and demands to get their way. They are like steamrollers, using unrelenting, hammering arguments to push people to back down. They have a strong need to be correct and are impatient with others. Stand your ground without being aggressive, and avoid a head-on fight. Do not argue or worry about being polite. Use low-key persistence. Do not let them interrupt. Establish eye contact, call them by name and be clear about what you do and do not want.

Snipers are hostile, aggressive people who do not attack openly like the exploder and bully but rather engage in guerrilla warfare, using subtle digs, cheap shots and innuendos. Like exploders and bullies, snipers have a strong judgmental view of how others should think and act, but they choose to stay hidden and attack covertly. Neutralize sniping without escalation into open warfare. Meet in private and avoid countersniping. Bring them out into the open while avoiding a direct confrontation by saying things such as, "Are you trying to make a point?" "What are you trying to say?"

 To deal with problem people, get their attention, identify the problem behavior, point out the consequences, ask questions, listen and explain expectations. Avoid defensiveness.

Serious Problem Behaviors

In local law enforcement agencies, the most frequent charges are intoxication on the job, insubordination, frequent tardiness, negligence, prohibited moonlighting, incompetence or unsatisfactory performance, improper handling of evidence, violation of a municipal ordinance, conduct unbecoming an officer, use of abusive/racial/ethnic language, failure to report for duty or leaving duty without permission, abusive actions against prisoners or people under arrest and careless operation of a vehicle.

 Among the most challenging and serious problem behaviors are abuse of sick leave, substance abuse, corruption, insubordination, sexual harassment and use of excessive force.

Abuse of Sick Leave

Although the abuse of sick leave may seem relatively insignificant compared with such problem behaviors as corruption and use of excessive force, the abuse of sick leave can cost a department at least an additional 150 percent over the budgeted amount to cover the vacancies with overtime pay (Orrick, 2004, p.39). In additional to the financial impact, abuse of sick leave has an organizational impact, reducing the effectiveness and efficiency of the department. According to Orrick, it can also have an ethical impact because when employees misrepresent themselves as being sick, it reflects on their integrity and diminishes their peers' and supervisor's confidence in them.

To effectively manage sick leave, managers need a good records system that tracks when employees take leave and the reasons for the absence. Orrick (p.41) describes an Attendance Enhancement Program (AEP) that reversed a continuous increase in use of sick leave in the Ottawa, Ontario, Police Service. In 2000 the cost to the department of use of sick leave equaled the cost of 57 full-time employees. The AEP program involved offering officers monetary rewards or recognition or both for showing perfect or strong attendance. The program also gave supervisory staff the information, procedures and tools needed to monitor attendance. The program was successful, with use of sick leave dropping by 1.6 days per employee, a gain of approximately 2,500 days of productive work and $540,000 in increased productivity.

Substance Abuse

Aronsohn (2003, p.34) contends: "The dangers of substance abuse are well known. Nationwide, employers lose thousands of work hours every year due to drug- and alcohol-related ailments. In addition to the health hazards, substance abuse in the workplace hinders morale, judgment and safety and frequently contributes to discrimination and harassment claims."

Ferraro and Judge (2003, p.94) note that preventing substance abuse in the workplace, including drugs and alcohol testing, can protect employees and the public and can lower an organization's operational costs. They point out that federal or state law, collective bargaining agreements and contractual obligations may enter into the decision as to which drugs to test for. Federal regulations allow testing for alcohol and five controlled substances: marijuana, cocaine, amphetamines, opiates and PCI, collectively referred to as the Department of Health and Human Services-5 (DHHS-5).

Telltale signs of substance abuse in the workplace include an increase in absenteeism, employee grievances, employee theft, accidental injuries and workers' compensation claims. Other signs include a decrease in job interest, productivity and quality of work.

Managers should recognize the symptoms of alcohol or drug abuse. If they suspect an employee is abusing alcohol or drugs, they should never accuse the employee of doing so, because this could open the manager and department to a slander or defamation of character lawsuit. Rather, focus on job deficiencies and corrective action. Show a genuine concern for the employee's problem and attempt to refer him or her to a qualified specialist. Give officers ample opportunity to seek assistance. Follow up if an employee enters a treatment program.

Corruption

The problem of corruption was discussed in detail in Chapter 8 and is only briefly reviewed here. Corruption is of concern because officers in the field are exposed to numerous opportunities to benefit personally from actions they take against criminals. They may be offered bribes or come across huge amounts of drugs or cash. They may feel overworked, underpaid and therefore entitled to take what they consider just compensation for the risks they face on the job. Yet, whenever one member of a police department is found to be corrupt, the hundreds of thousands of honest, hardworking officers suffer. The problem of police corruption affects agencies of all sizes, in all areas of the country.

Insubordination

insubordination • failure to obey a lawful and direct order from a supervisor.

Policing has traditionally followed a quasi-military structure, with higher-ranking officers authorized to give lawful orders to lower-ranking officers that must be obeyed, whether they personally agree with them or not. Failure to carry out such direct, lawful orders can expose an officer to discipline for **insubordination**.

Sexual Harassment

sexual harassment • unwelcome, unsolicited and deliberate action of a sexual nature that occurs in the workplace or extension of the workplace.

Sexual harassment has increased in visibility and has also resulted in numerous lawsuits. **Sexual harassment** is a type of sex discrimination prohibited by Title VII of the Civil Rights Act of 1964, as well as by most state laws. The federal government defines sexual harassment as "unwelcome sexual advances, requests for sexual favors, and other verbal or physical conduct of a sexual nature" ("Preventing Sexual Harassment," p.1).

The Equal Employment Opportunity Commission Web site states: "Unwelcome sexual advances, requests for sexual favors, and other verbal or physical conduct of a sexual nature constitutes sexual harassment when submission to or rejection of this conduct explicitly or implicitly affects an individual's employment, unreasonably interferes with an individual's work performance or creates an intimidating, hostile or offensive work environment." The Commission notes that sexual harassment can occur in a variety of circumstances, including but not limited to the following:

- The victim as well as the harasser may be a woman or a man. The victim does not have to be of the opposite sex.
- The harasser can be the victim's supervisor, an agent of the employer, a supervisor in another area, a co-worker, or a nonemployee.
- The victim does not have to be the person harassed but could be anyone affected by the offensive conduct.
- Unlawful sexual harassment may occur without economic injury to or discharge of the victim. The harasser's conduct must be unwelcome.

There are two legally recognized types of sexual harassment. One type, *quid pro quo harassment*, usually involves a supervisor's demand for sexual favors from an employee in return for a job benefit. For example, you will pass probation, get a promotion, get a good performance evaluation, not be written up for doing something wrong, etc., if you will engage in some type of sexual behavior.

The second type, *hostile-environment harassment*, as the name implies, involves a hostile environment (whether created by co-employees or by supervisors). According to the National Center for Women and Policing (www.womenandpolicing.org): "A hostile environment consists of unwelcome sexual behavior, such as jokes, cartoons, posters, banter, repeated requests for dates, requests for sexual favors, references to body parts, or physical touching that has the purpose or effect of unreasonably interfering with an individual's work performance or creating an intimidating, hostile, or offensive working environment. Isolated acts that are not severe will not rise to the level of a hostile environment." Two conditions determine liability for employers in cases of hostile environment sexual harassment: (1) The employer knew or should have known about the harassment, and (2) the employer failed to take appropriate corrective action.

Sexual harassment may occur as "indirect" or "third party" when one employee witnesses the repeated sexual harassment of another or when an employee is not directly harassed but the harassment of others adversely affects the workplace (Holtz, 2003b, p.118). Third-party sexual harassment may be either quid pro quo or hostile environment. Quid pro quo third-party sexual harassment occurs when employees who are not the target of harassment lose potential job benefits to other less qualified employees who submit to harassment. Hostile environment third-party sexual harassment occurs when employees who are not themselves harassed must work in an atmosphere where such harassment is pervasive. If employees who grant sexual favors are given preferential treatment, other employees' motivation and performance may suffer.

The police environment may be more conducive than others to sexual harassment because of the nature of the work, for example, investigating sex crimes and pornography rings. Some evidence also suggests that sexual harassment is significantly higher in male-dominated occupations. Women who report sexual harassment run the risk of the situation getting worse or of other officers refusing to talk to her or to cover her when she calls for backup. Retaliation against an employee who opposed sexual harassment or made a charge or participated in an investigation is prohibited under Title VII. However, as the National Center for Women and Policing cautions, such retaliation does occur in such forms as the following:

- Shunning/ostracizing—no one will talk to her, or she is prevented from receiving information important to the performance of her job or important to her personal safety.
- Stalking/harassing incidents—obscene telephone calls, telephone calls where the caller says nothing, hang-up calls at all hours of the day and night, threatening or harassing letters or notes, damage to her automobile, articles left on her desk or in her work area that are intended to intimidate or harass.
- Becoming the subject of rumors of sexual activity or other demeaning information.
- Being held to a higher standard of performance—her evaluation reports become more critical and she is held to a different standard than others.
- Harassing internal affairs complaints are filed against her by members of the organization or by citizens who have been enlisted to help the harasser.

- Denial of training opportunities.
- Denial of transfer to specialty jobs.
- Denial of promotion.
- Failure to provide back-up in emergency situations. This is the ultimate form of retaliation. When it becomes apparent that she will not receive backup in a timely manner, the woman often leaves the organization because she is in fear for her life.

To prevent charges of sexual harassment, departments need a clear policy that identifies conduct that may constitute sexual harassment. The policy should also include a statement that such conduct will not be tolerated and that those found guilty of prohibited conduct will be subject to appropriate disciplinary action.

First-line supervisors are key facilitators in the battle against sexual harassment (Holtz, 2003a, p.126). How a manager investigates a sexual harassment complaint may determine the outcome of a harassment lawsuit. Managers should take every sexual harassment complaint seriously and collect all the facts from both sides, keeping the investigation confidential. As they investigate, they should document everything: memos, conversations, reports and the like. If the charge of harassment is substantiated, appropriate discipline should be undertaken, according to department policy.

Research by Collins (2004) found that sexual harassment is likely to flourish in organizations that fail to take complaints seriously, engage in retaliation against the complainant or refuse to take meaningful action. An agency's failure to impose corrective action perpetuates the perception that sexual harassment is acceptable.

Use of Excessive Force

Use of excessive force has always been a cause of problems, resulting in numerous lawsuits. Use of force is sometimes a necessary part of the job, but determining what is reasonable is highly subjective.

Luna (2005, p.4) provides the following definitions:

- *Force.* Any nonnegotiable use of police authority to influence citizen behavior. Includes low-level force options (verbal commands, use of restraints) through high-level force options (deadly force). The mere presence of an officer, because of the implied authority of the uniform, is included.
- *Justifiable force.* Force used in accordance with law; force that was reasonable in light of the circumstances faced and known by the officer at the time it was used.
- *Excessive force.* The illegal or unreasonable use of force, with reasonableness determined by whether a reasonably prudent officer would have used the same amount of force in the same situation, in light of the information available to the officer at the time.
- *Deadly force.* Force likely to cause serious bodily injury or death.

Survey results reported by Durose et al. (2005) stated that 21 percent of those surveyed (45.3 million people) had a contact with police and that only 1.5 percent of such contacts involved police use of force. Of these, about three fourths (75.4 percent) felt the force used or threatened by police was excessive.

The landmark case in use of force is *Graham v. Connor* (1989), in which the Court said the right to make an arrest or investigatory stop carries with it the right to use some degree of physical coercion or threat thereof to effect it. The Court

Bob Boyle, secretary of the Boston Police Patrolmen's Association, and Jamarhl Crawford, Boston chairman of the New Black Panther Party, discuss police shootings of citizens, September 12, 2002. Discussions such as these help create and maintain clear policies regarding the use of force.

also held: "The calculus of reasonableness must embody allowance for the fact that police officers are often forced to make split-second judgments—in circumstances that are tense, uncertain, and rapidly evolving—about the amount of force that is necessary in a particular situation." The standard established by this decision is the "reasonably objective officer." The more "heinous" a person's activities or threat level, the more force an officer may justifiably use (Gundy, 2003, p.63). Beasey (2004, p.106) points out: "There are times when shooting someone or striking them with a baton is absolutely necessary and absolutely reasonable." However, the public viewing such actions may disagree and view a brutal appearance with brutality. Beasey stresses: "Police work is, at times, bone breaking, bloody, flesh-tearing, bruising, sweaty, lethal, and ugly." These realities must be considered in any department's use-of-force policies. Moore (2004, p.110) recommends that managers review their use-of-force policies and training procedures often—annually at minimum.

Research by Alpert et al. (2004) found that decisions by officers to use some type of force appear to depend on the type of call, offense and level of perceived authority over the suspect. They report that reviews of the literature show that use of force is most likely to occur when the suspect shows signs of alcohol or drug intoxication or engages in hostile behavior.

The majority of excessive force claims are filed against police officers and agencies under Section 1983. Claims arise in three major areas: arrests and seizures of criminal suspects, post-arrest or pretrial detention and postconviction confinement.

Perhaps the best known use-of-force case is that of *Rodney King v. Los Angeles* (1992). Both the city and the officers involved were sued under Section 1983. In addition, other officers who stood by and did nothing to prevent the alleged wrongful acts were involved under the **nonactor liability** provisions. That is, officers who

nonactor liability • when an officer present at a scene where use of force is in question and is obviously excessive and the nonactor officer did nothing to prevent it, that officer is also held liable by the courts.

were present at a scene at which use of force was in question or where force was obviously excessive yet did nothing to prevent it have also been held liable by the courts.

The key to avoiding a charge of excessive force is being able to justify the type and amount of force used. Rutledge (2004, p.59) stresses the importance of the accuracy and completeness of any force reports, not only for internal investigations, but also for criminal and civil liability and public relations. Research by Terrill (2005) suggests that to judge the appropriateness of police force, the extent to which force is applied proportionately and incrementally should be measured and considered.

One way to reduce the force needed might be using K-9s. However, police canine tracking or searching for a wanted subject is a serious use of force and must be properly managed (Nowicki, 2005, p.61). Department policy should state when a canine can be used and against whom.

Use-of-Force Continuums

Use-of-force continuums have been evolving for over three decades and are used as a "graphical interface" to explain the complex, inflammatory realm in which police are faced with using force. Aveni (2003, p.75) points out that such continuums have their shortcomings, attempting to create a black-and-white menu of options from a "world of grey facts and circumstances."

Many departments use a linear force continuum, suggesting that officers work through a series of alternatives, ascending the continuum until they use the most appropriate response. Figure 10.3 shows a linear use-of-force continuum. Fridell (2005, pp.47–48) contends that currently law enforcement professionals are re-evaluating the traditional linear (incremental) use-of-force continuum as a tool for training and as a way to articulate force policy. She lists the following complaints about linear continuums:

- They do not consider every factor that might affect an officer's choice of response.
- They imply that an officer must exhaust all efforts at one level on the continuum before proceeding to the next. Even if informed they are allowed to "jump steps," the continuum is sometimes explained in court as one requiring step-by-step ascension.
- They are complex and difficult to remember, potentially leading to dangerous moments of delay by an officer during a critical incident.

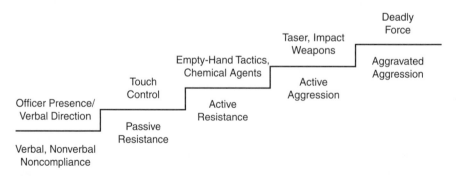

Figure 10.3 A Linear Use-of-Force Continuum

Source: Lorie A. Fridell. "Improving Use-of-Force Policy, Policy Enforcement and Training." In *Chief Concerns: Exploring the Challenges of Police Use of Force*, edited by Josua A. Ederheimer and Lorie A. Fridell. Washington, DC: Police Executive Research Forum, April 2005, p.48.

Figure 10.4   A Circular Use-of-Force Continuum

Source: Lorie A. Fridell. "Improving Use-of-Force Policy, Policy Enforcement and Training." In *Chief Concerns: Exploring the Challenges of Police Use of Force*, edited by Josua A. Ederheimer and Lorie A. Fridell. Washington, DC: Police Executive Research Forum, April 2005, p.50.

Some departments have instituted circular use-of-force models to replace the linear continuum. Figure 10.4 illustrates a circular use-of-force model. Many of the circular use-of-force models place the force options in random order to prevent any implication that officers escalate to greater force in a given sequence. Whether a department uses any type of force continuum, it should not replace a carefully crafted use-of-force policy. Law enforcement managers need three essential elements in dealing with use of force in their agencies: (1) a sound policy, (2) effective mechanisms for enforcing the policy and producing accountability and (3) integrated training that teaches officers when and how to use force appropriately (Fridell, p.55). The question of use of force often arises in situations involving demonstrations and sit-ins.

Passive Resistance

Passive resistance is a form of civil disobedience reflecting a philosophy of nonviolence. Protestors and demonstrators using passive resistance can pose a "substantial challenge" for police officers, and law enforcement officers often face civil lawsuits alleging excessive force following such events (Zigmund, 2005, p.10).

Departments should establish clear policies on how passive resistance is to be approached. Because nonviolent protestors generally pose no immediate threat to the safety of officers or others, law enforcement officers must carefully select use-of-force tactics and properly control their application as specified in department policy (Zigmund, p.12).

Having looked at some of the most serious problem behaviors managers might confront, consider next what options managers have for dealing with the behaviors. Often some form of negative discipline or punishment is called for.

passive resistance • a form of civil disobedience reflecting a philosophy of nonviolence. Often used by protestors and demonstrators.

Negative Discipline/Punishment

negative discipline • punishment or reprimand in an effort to compel expected behavior.

Law enforcement managers at all levels will sometimes find it necessary to use negative discipline. **Negative discipline** uses reprimands and punishments for wrong behavior in an effort to compel expected behavior. In nonemergency situations, managers should make reasonable efforts to gain voluntary compliance. If that fails, managers must exercise the disciplinary responsibilities of their position.

The purpose of negative discipline is to help offenders correct behavior and to send a message to others that such behavior is not acceptable. The ultimate decision to bring a disciplinary action may arise because an employee commits a number of minor violations or an obviously serious one. Those being disciplined must fully understand what they are being disciplined for and why. Managers must have the authority to exercise discipline and be willing to proceed through hearings and appeals if necessary. The discipline recommended should fit the offense and be neither excessively harsh nor lenient.

 A primary rule of effective discipline is that it should be carried out as close to the time of the violation as possible.

Delays cause further problems. Witnesses may have left employment, different versions may be manufactured, or facts may be forgotten.

Disciplinary actions should be carried out in private to avoid embarrassment and defensiveness. One exception to the privacy rule is if an employee openly confronts a manager in front of others. In such cases the manager must take immediate, decisive action to maintain respect and control of the department.

Most cases of misconduct involve errors in judgment and do not rise to the level of ethical or criminal transgression requiring severe discipline (Serpas et al., 2003, p.22). In such instances, most employees welcome the chance, at the earliest possible time, to come forward, admit their mistake, accept a reasonable sanction for the mistake and move forward in their careers. When engaging in corrective discourse, a manager should address the problem behavior, not the officer's character (Johnson, 2004, p.98). In addition, during corrective discourse a genuine leader will help the individual find within themselves the most appropriate answers and sanctions (Field, 2005, p.66). Open-ended questions rather than offering quick solutions or imposing sanctions help managers accomplish this. Field (p.70) contends that because managers have different experiences and personalities, they should not give advice, because what works for one person may not for another: "Asking the right questions, at the right time, can lead people to find self-inspired answers—unique answers that are suited to individual needs and circumstances."

Any initial disciplinary action should be *corrective*. Only when corrective discipline, training and counseling have little or no effect should disciplinary action be punitive. Punishment has the disadvantage of showing what should not be done, rather than reinforcing what should be done.

Supervisors first need to identify which officers, through their actions or lack thereof, deserve punishment or other disciplinary action. They must then determine which action is most appropriate and how to administer it.

Identifying the Problem Performer—Early Intervention Systems

Although most officers in a department readily cooperate with supervisors and their performance requests, some resist supervisory requests by repeatedly challenging and questioning orders, and still others outright fail to perform. Weitzel (2004, p.27) contends: "Without a doubt, every organization has at least one problem employee." Slahor (2004, p.90) states: "Studies repeatedly indicate that it is a disproportionately small number of officers in a department who are responsible for the majority of complaints."

What is needed is a way to identify these problem officers early. Early intervention systems (EISs), commonly referred to in the past as early warning systems (EWSs), focus on problems and discipline and are data-driven management tools to identify police officers with performance problems and intervene to correct those problems (Walker et al., 2005, p.5). However, first and second line supervisors may see such a system as an abrogation of their authority to supervise and discipline: "EWSs centralize the function of discipline over which line supervisors need to control and supervise. The need to teach and hold supervisors accountable—not take away their authority—then becomes primary to the issue of EWS as a support system" (Colaprete, 2004, p.66).

Peed and Wexler (2005, p.vii) contend that although EISs have been around for over a quarter century, their recent evolution is having increasing success in solving personnel problems. They suggest that the two key components of an effective EIS are (1) well-trained supervisors (especially first-line supervisors) and (2) availability of a broad range of interventions to help address the numerous difficulties facing officers on the street.

EIS is a powerful, multifaceted tool that typically exists in the form of an electronic data base (Walker et al., p.1). Among the common data elements recorded are officer's use of sick leave, the number and type of community complaints and the number and type of use-of-force incidents. Walker et al. (pp.5–6) cite five guiding principles of EISs:

1. An EIS should be part of an agency's larger effort to support and improve officer performance.
2. First-line supervisors are the lynchpin of EISs.
3. For EISs to be effective, intervention options should vary to meet the wide range of officers' needs.
4. The chief executive ultimately is responsible for the success or failure of EISs.
5. EISs are a valuable administrative tool that can enhance accountability and integrity in a law enforcement agency.

Walker et al. (p.10) stress: "The buy-in and support of supervisors is critical to the success of EIS because they can have significant influence over the officers whom they supervise." They (p.14) also point out that the power of an EIS is its ability to identify patterns of officer performance that allow supervisors to intervene early to prevent more serious problems from developing.

The availability of a range of interventions is also critical to an EIS. Counseling by an officer's immediate supervisor is the most common intervention. Other effective interventions include training, professional counseling, peer support groups, crisis intervention teams, reassignment and relief from duty (Walker et al., p.21). The many benefits of EISs include improved supervision, help to officers in overcoming personal or professional problems that affect job performance, earlier identification of potential problems with personnel, a strengthened culture of integrity and accountability within agencies, improved community relations, reduced litigation costs and adoption of proven best practices that help bring agencies to the forefront of the field (Walker et al., p.47).

The Community Oriented Policing Services (COPS) Office and the Police Executive Research Forum (PERF) have published *Strategies for Intervening with Officers through Early Intervention Systems: A Guide for Front-Line Supervisors* (Walker et al., 2006). This guide provides practical strategies for front-line supervisors to work with employees identified as needing assistance to correct deficiencies in behavior. If interventions are unsuccessful, penalties may be imposed.

Determining Penalties

Many variables enter into penalty determination; for example, is it a first offense or a repeated offense? Are there extenuating circumstances? Each case must be decided on its own facts, and penalties must be assessed in the same way. No single penalty will do justice to every set of circumstances. The penalty should have a legal and moral basis and should include an appeal process. Penalties should also be reasonable. If they are viewed as too lenient, they probably will not be enforced because it is not worth the effort. If they are too harsh, they may not be enforced because they are too severe.

 The offense and offender, how the offense was committed and the offender's attitude and past performance are important considerations in assessing penalties.

Most law enforcement departments have either departmental or civil service rules and regulations that define which behaviors are violations and the penalty for each. Punishments vary from warnings to termination of employment. Some departments use a table of offenses, penalties and application of appropriate disciplinary actions. Appendix A contains a sample of such a table. Such tables are not to be used automatically. Supervisors must consider the specific circumstances carefully when evaluating offenses and penalties, including the employee's work history, contribution to the agency and probability of rehabilitation. *Each case must be considered individually.*

The most frequent disciplinary actions in municipal law enforcement employment are oral or written reprimands, efficiency rating demerits, summary punishment for minor offenses, withholding part or all of an officer's salary for a specified time, decrease of seniority rights, a fine, suspension, demotion in rank or dismissal.

Progressive Discipline Many departments operate under the concept of progressive discipline. Employees are usually given a light penalty for the first infraction of a rule, a more severe penalty for the next infraction and so on. The primary objective of progressive discipline is to give employees a chance to voluntarily improve performance and to clearly inform employees that stronger disciplinary actions will be taken if they do not correct the behavior.

progressive discipline • uses disciplinary steps based on the severity of the offense and how often it is repeated. Steps usually are oral reprimand, written reprimand, suspension/demotion, dismissal.

 Progressive discipline uses disciplinary steps based on the severity of the offense. The steps usually are:

- Oral reprimand.
- Written reprimand.
- Suspension/demotion.
- Discharge/termination.

reprimand • formal criticism of behavior. May be oral or written.

The most frequent type of penalty is an oral or a written *warning* or **reprimand**. An *oral reprimand* is a conversation between a supervisor and an employee about a specific aspect of the employee's performance. It informs employees that continued behavior or level of performance will result in more serious action. The supervisor must provide specifics. Employees should know what to correct and how, and they must have sufficient time to make the correction before other action is taken. Normally employees cooperate and problem behavior is eliminated.

If the warning is important, the supervisor should make a written record and place it in the personnel file. A *written reprimand* is a formal written notice to the employee regarding significant misconduct, specific inadequate performance or repeated offenses for which the employee has received an oral reprimand. The same conditions apply as for a warning. The violation should be stated in detail, along with what actions will correct the behavior, a time limit, whether there have been previous oral warnings for the same conduct and what will occur if the employee does not correct the violation. A written reprimand is usually recommended for a violation that must be corrected immediately. It should be given by at least a first-line supervisor and perhaps a middle-line manager, with the supervisor as a witness. The employee should receive a copy of the written reprimand.

A warning or a reprimand sends a signal to employees that management has disapproved. It is best to handle all employee penalty matters in person. The procedure may permit the employee to state his or her position before management takes final action.

A **suspension,** being barred from a position, is the next most serious punishment. Suspensions may be with or without pay. Normally, suspensions are given after consultation with the middle manager and the executive manager. Suspensions with pay normally are given to provide time for management to investigate a situation. It is not in any way a finding of wrongdoing. For example, an officer who shoots and kills a suspect may be suspended with pay while the matter is investigated. A coroner's jury will probably convene, and management will consider its findings in making a final decision. If the officer's action was justified, the officer is returned to duty as though no action had been taken.

Suspensions may usually be appealed to the executive manager, city manager, civil service board or a special board. They may also be a matter for union support or denial.

The most serious forms of punishment are *demotion* and *dismissal* or *termination*. These actions are taken by the head of the law enforcement department or the government jurisdiction and are also subject to appeal. These actions are end-of-the-road punishments, administered in very serious first offenses or in situations in which the employees have disregarded other warnings, reprimands and suspensions.

A **demotion** places an employee in a position of lower rank and pay and can seriously impede the remainder of the employee's career. **Dismissal** or **termination** is the most serious penalty. It is used when management decides strong action must be taken in the best interests of the organization and its other employees. Termination is necessary when employees do not respond to attempts to correct behavior that violates written rules and regulations and of which the employee was provided proper notice. Incompetence and inability to get along with other employees are two major reasons for termination. Other major reasons are dishonesty or lying and insubordination.

Technically, dismissal and termination are slightly different. *Dismissal* is an action taken by a hiring and firing authority. It is not voluntary on the part of the employee. It is, in effect, a discharge or firing. *Termination* is also an end to employment, but it

suspension • being barred from a position for a period of time. May be with or without pay. Often part of progressive discipline.

demotion • places an employee in a position of lower responsibility and pay. Often a part of progressive discipline.

dismissal • termination of employment. Usually the final step in progressive discipline.

termination • being fired from employment. Usually the final step in progressive discipline.

may be voluntary or involuntary. Employees may terminate employment due to such reasons as illness or accepting a different job. The differences are basically a matter of semantics.

Terminations are costly to the organization. Replacement selection costs are high, and training is a long-term commitment. Unfortunately, in some situations termination is the only recourse. Most managers will say that firing an officer is one of their most distasteful responsibilities.

Although firing someone is seldom easy, it is almost always easier than keeping them. Normally termination occurs only after a serious offense; after repeated offenses by the same employee; or after a series of the same type of offense where warnings, oral and written reprimands, suspension or similar previous disciplinary actions went unheeded.

Wrongful termination lawsuits have been rising in the past decade. These actions arise from the due process clause of the Fourteenth Amendment, which prohibits persons acting as agents or employees of the state or its political subdivisions from depriving a person of property or liberty without due process. A person has the right not to be terminated from employment except for good or just cause. Title 42, U.S.C., Section 1983, provides a procedure by which a person employed by a state, county or municipal government can bring suit against a department or supervisor for violating the person's constitutional rights in the termination process. Due process requires a valid reason for termination, procedural action, notification of the person to be terminated and an opportunity for a hearing.

Difficult as termination is for police managers, it remains their responsibility. Failure to exercise it when justified results in the ultimate failure of manager effectiveness. Should a manager fail to terminate an officer when justified, and the officer does anything "wrong" in the public's eyes, the manager and the entire department could be sued for **negligent retention.**

negligent retention • failing to terminate an employee when justified.

Discharge should be presented so that employees can retain self-esteem, if possible. They should be told whether they can expect references for what they did well while on the job, when the termination takes effect, how the announcement will be made and whether they can resign voluntarily for the record. Any actions taken should center on the behavior or offense rather than on the individual.

Summary Punishment

Not all disciplinary actions fall within the realm of progressive discipline. Managers must have the authority to exercise *summary* discipline when certain infractions occur. **Summary discipline,** or **summary punishment,** is discretionary authority used when a supervisor thinks an officer is not fit for duty or when, for any reason, the supervisor thinks immediate action is needed.

summary discipline • discretionary authority used when a supervisor feels an officer is not fit for duty or for any reason the supervisor feels a need for immediate action. Also called *summary punishment.*

Summary punishment may require officers to work a day or two without pay or may excuse them from duty for a day without pay. Officers who receive summary punishment have a right to a hearing.

Guidelines for Administering Negative Discipline

When you use negative discipline, what you do *not* do is often more important than what you do. Officers may become defensive and less concerned with listening than defending themselves. Communication skills and tact are essential in these situations. The following guidelines apply when using negative discipline:

- Get the facts first. Consider the circumstances. Was the misbehavior accidental? Did the person know the rules? Was this the first offense? Keep adequate records.
- Be calm. Allow tempers to settle. Avoid sarcasm. Do not threaten, argue or show anger.
- Know your powers as outlined in your job description.
- Check on precedents for similar offenses.
- Suit the disciplinary action to the individual and the situation. Know each subordinate and his or her record. The severity of the discipline should match the seriousness of the offense.
- Focus on the behavior, not on the person. Be sure the behavior is something the person has control over or can change.
- Do not ascribe intent to the behavior or imply it was done on purpose. Focus only on the behavior.
- Be sure the person is attentive and emotionally ready to listen.
- Be clear, specific and objective. Use actual examples of problem behavior.
- Check for understanding by asking questions. How is the person taking the criticism?
- Respect the employee's dignity.
- End with expectations for changed behavior.
- Follow up.

Effective discipline is more easily maintained with a written set of guidelines such as the preceding. Managers should coordinate their disciplinary efforts. Every manager should enforce every rule, regulation and policy equally. Unenforced or unenforceable rules should be changed or cancelled. Further, managers should set the example, letting their subordinates know they mean what they say.

Supervisors should avoid the **gunnysack approach** to discipline, accumulating negative behaviors of a subordinate and then dumping them all on the officer at the same time rather than correcting them as they occur. Accumulated, they may be serious enough to warrant dismissal. However, handled one at a time, the officer might have had a chance to change.

gunnysack approach • occurs when managers or supervisors accumulate negative behaviors of a subordinate and then dump them all on the employee at the same time rather than correcting them as they occurred.

Steps in Administering Negative Discipline

To apply discipline, write down your main goal in taking disciplinary action— change the employee's behavior and reduce the chances of the behavior happening again. Write down the violation and what conduct was involved, much the same procedure used in making a charge against a citizen. State the reason for the action, specifically, what has been violated and how. Show how the behavior creates a problem. State how you feel about it.

Listen to the employee's explanation. Remember that to err is human. To blame somebody else is even more human. Anticipate this and help employees sort out their responsibilities. Also recognize that if an excuse is good enough, it becomes a reason. Managers and supervisors cannot know everything. They, too, can make mistakes. If this happens, managers must openly admit their mistake and offer a sincere apology for the *misunderstanding*.

Suggest corrective action and, if possible, involve the person in the suggestion. Be firm but fair. Fairness does not mean treating everyone equally. A rookie will make mistakes that might not be tolerated if made by a veteran officer. State exactly what action you are going to take and explain that further violations will bring more severe results. Offer assistance in resolving the present problem. Describe how you value the person as an individual and as an important part of the work group and the entire department. Secure a commitment to future positive behavior.

McGregor (Theory X/Theory Y) says the lessons learned from a hot stove should be present in effective discipline. When a person touches a hot stove (violates a rule or regulation), the burn (punishment) is immediate, consistent (it happens every time) and impartial (it is the same for everyone). Further, the severity of the burn depends on the length of time the stove and victim remain in contact and the heat of the stove. The burned individual may initially feel anger at the stove, but in reality, the anger is an indictment of oneself and the carelessness causing the burn. The anger will lessen, and the victim will have a healthy respect for the stove in the future.

The final step is to tell the individual how to appeal the decision. The right to appeal should be inherent in any disciplinary action.

Appeal

appeal • request for a decision to be reviewed by someone higher in the command structure.

An **appeal** is a request for a decision to be reviewed by someone higher in command. The most frequent appeals are to a review board or department disciplinary board. Appeals can also be made to a civil service board review, a district or high court and, in some cases, a management–labor board. Many departments use an internal review procedure, including the following steps.

Step One The employee requests a face-to-face meeting with the immediate supervisor within five working days. The supervisor and employee meet, and the supervisor decides to withdraw or stand by the disciplinary action.

Step Two An employee who is not satisfied with the results of Step One presents the written reasons for dissatisfaction to the department head within five days. The department head sustains or rescinds the disciplinary action within three working days.

Step Three An employee who is not satisfied with the results of Step Two presents the written reasons for dissatisfaction with the department head's response to the top-level manager of the jurisdiction. Within five days the manager or representative either sustains or rescinds the disciplinary action. This is the final step.

Departments may also have a process for employees to appeal disciplinary actions to a civil service commission. This process usually involves the employee appearing for a hearing before a board that rules in the matter. Such hearings may be closed to the public. The decision and findings of the commission are in writing and are considered final.

Legal Considerations

Disciplinary actions are subject to specific procedures as established by civil service or department rules and regulations. If an officer is charged with a criminal offense, the legal procedure is the same as for any citizen. In these cases, violation of civil service rules and regulations of the law enforcement department would, in all probability, await the outcome of the criminal action even though they are completely separate actions.

In general, violations of department rules and regulations are investigated using the same basic procedures as those accorded criminal violations. All facts must be carefully documented. Search warrants should be obtained when legally required to secure evidence. Gathering evidence, taking statements, seeking witnesses and adhering to legal procedures of handling evidence are all important.

Civil service hearings are similar to criminal hearings. Legal procedures vary, but the charges are read in an open hearing, witnesses are called and the employee is present. Employees may or may not testify because they are not required to give incriminating evidence against themselves.

Past personnel records may be introduced into evidence if relevant. Proper, detailed documentation of the facts supporting any violation of department rules and regulations is the key to justice. Most disciplinary action cases overturned by the courts have involved situations in which proper documentation was lacking, prejudice was involved, the violation was based on an action deemed a discretionary matter on the officer's part or violations of due process procedures were involved. Formal investigations of officer behavior and the legal issues involved are discussed in Chapter 11.

Comprehensive Discipline

Comprehensive discipline uses both positive and negative discipline to achieve individual and organizational goals. Several specific approaches to comprehensive discipline have been developed, including the balance of consequences analysis, the PRICE method, the one-minute management approach and the stroke approach.

comprehensive discipline • uses both positive and negative discipline to achieve individual and organizational goals.

The Balance of Consequences Analysis— Wilson Learning Corporation

Building on Skinner's reinforcement theory and Vroom's expectancy theory, Wilson Learning Corporation developed the **balance of consequences analysis.**

For example, Officer Jones is a popular foot patrol officer. He spends lots of time chatting with citizens on his beat, having made friends with shopkeepers and owners of business establishments as well as area residents. The problem is that he is always late with his incident reports. Investigators complain that they do not have the reports when they need them. Further, Jones often has to put in unpaid overtime to get his paperwork done.

balance of consequences analysis • a grid used to analyze problem behavior and the consequences that follow the behavior in an attempt to understand how the consequences might be to altered to change the problem behavior.

His sergeant does not want to lose him because he is a skilled officer, and his friendliness and popularity are an asset to the department. But the lateness of his reports is causing problems. The sergeant analyzes the consequences operating in this situation.

First, what are the rewards Jones receives from socializing?
- Pleasant visits with citizens
- Satisfaction from knowing people like him
- Praise from peers and superiors for being people oriented

Against this list, the negative consequences of the behavior must be looked at. These include:
- Complaints from the investigators.
- Overtime (unpaid).
- Reduced chances for promotion.

BEHAVIOR	
Undesired (current) Late reports	**Desired** Reports on time
Positive Consequences Pleasant visits Satisfaction Praise	**Positive Consequences** Less criticism Less overtime Promotion more likely
Negative Consequences Criticism Overtime Promotion less likely	**Negative Consequences** No pleasant visits Less praise More work

Figure 10.5   Officer Jones' Balance of Consequences Analysis

Source: Steve Bucholz. *The Positive Manager.* p.125. Copyright ©1985 by John Wiley & Sons, Inc., New York. Reprinted by permission.

Next consider what positive results would occur if Jones stopped socializing and got his reports done on time:

- Investigators would stop complaining.
- Unpaid overtime would stop.
- Chances for promotion would increase.

On the other hand, what negative consequences might result?

- Miss the good times socializing
- Miss the praise for being people oriented
- More actual work to do

The balance of consequences grid would look like Figure 10.5.

 The balance of consequences analysis considers behavior in terms of what positive and negative results the behavior produces and then focuses on those results.

A final piece of information is needed to complete the analysis—the strength of the consequences. Consequences fall into one of three either/or categories. Every consequence is either:

- Personal or organizational (P or O).
- Immediate or delayed (I or D).
- Certain or uncertain (C or U).

 Personal, immediate and certain (PIC) consequences are stronger than organizational, delayed or uncertain (ODU) consequences.

Look at Jones' positive consequences for the undesirable behavior:

- Pleasant visits with citizens—personal, immediate, certain (PIC)

- Satisfaction from knowing people like him—personal, immediate, certain (PIC)
- Praise from peers and superiors for being people oriented—personal, delayed, certain (PDC)

Compare this with the positive consequences if he should do less socializing and get his paperwork done on time:
- Investigators would stop complaining—personal, delayed, certain (PDC).
- Overtime (unpaid) would stop—personal, delayed, certain (PDC).
- Chances for promotion would increase—personal, delayed, uncertain (PDU).

Clearly, the positive consequences for the *undesirable behavior* are stronger than those for the desirable behavior. The same is true for the negative consequences. The negative consequences associated with the undesirable behavior are delayed and uncertain. The negative consequences for less socializing are immediate and certain. The message for management:

 Change the balance of consequences so that employees are rewarded for desired behavior and punished for undesired behavior—not vice versa.

Managers can change the balance of consequences by:
- Adding positive consequences for desired behaviors.
- Adding negative consequences for undesired behaviors.
- Removing negative consequences for desired behaviors.
- Removing positive consequences for undesired behaviors.
- Changing the strength of the consequences—that is, changing an organizational consequence to a personal one, a delayed consequence to an immediate one or an uncertain consequence to a certain one.

Consider the following situation: A law enforcement department is doing an analysis of its efficiency and has asked all officers to complete time sheets at the end of their shifts. One shift sergeant is having difficulty getting her officers to turn in their sheets. The officers see the sheets as busywork, interfering with efficiency rather than helping to improve it, so they often leave work without completing them. The sergeant then has to track them down the next day to get them to fill them in. As a solution to the problem, the sergeant gets on the P.A. system at the beginning of the shift, reads the names of those who did not complete their time study and asks them to report to the front desk to fill them in. Examine the following list of consequences of the described behavior.
- Filling out the sheets takes a few minutes past quitting time.
- This results in getting caught in a traffic jam.
- Officers may get chewed out by the sergeant if they do not fill in the sheet.
- Officers are given time at the beginning of their next shift to fill in the sheets.
- Officers get their names read over the P.A. system.
- Colleagues clap and cheer when the names are read.
- The efficiency study will not be reliable if all officers do not complete the time sheets.
- The sergeant has to spend time getting officers to comply with the request.

This problem can be looked at using the balance of consequences analysis. A key to using this tool is to look at the behavior through the eyes of the beholder—in this instance, the problem officers. The analysis will look like the chart in Figure 10.6. In this case it is obvious that reading the names over the P.A. system is positively reinforcing the undesired behavior, not punishing it. Peer pressure

BEHAVIOR	
Undesired (current) Not filling in time sheets	**Desired** Filling in time sheets
Positive Consequences Get time next shift (PIC) Get name announced (PIC) Collegues cheer (PIC)	**Positive Consequences** NONE
Negative Consequences Make supervisor unhappy (ODC) Unreliable survey results (ODU)	**Negative Consequences** Caught in traffic (PIC) Name will not be read (PIC)

Figure 10.6   Balance of Consequences Analysis—Time Sheet Problem

might be brought to bear on those who do not participate. Or those who turn their sheets in as desired could be rewarded in some way.

The PRICE Method

The PRICE Method, developed by Blanchard (1989, p.18), is a five-step approach to employee performance problems such as attendance.

 The **PRICE method** consists of five steps:

- **P**inpoint
- **R**ecord
- **I**nvolve
- **C**oach
- **E**valuate

PRICE method • Blanchard's five-step approach to employee performance problems: Pinpoint, Record, Involve, Coach, Evaluate.

The five steps are applicable to most problem behaviors. The first step is to *pinpoint* the problem behavior and make certain the employee knows about it. Say, for example, an officer frequently uses profanity in public. This unacceptable behavior needs to be changed. Exactly what constitutes profanity must be specified.

The second step is to *record* how often and when the problem behavior occurs. Under what circumstances does the officer use the profanity? Who else is usually present? What triggers it? How often does it happen? At any certain time of day? This record establishes the behavior as problematic and also provides a baseline from which to work.

Third, *involve* the officer in setting a goal to eliminate the problem behavior and deciding on specific strategies to meet this goal. The strategies should include a specific timeline as well as incentives for specific accomplishments toward goal achievement.

Fourth, *coach* the officer regularly and consistently. According to Blanchard (p.18): "This is the most critical part of the plan. It is also the step where managers most frequently stumble." Provide positive reinforcement whenever the officer substitutes an acceptable word for what would normally elicit a profanity. Enlist the aid of other officers to help provide positive reinforcement. Make certain others do not use profanity without being criticized. Double standards will undermine the PRICE Method.

Finally, *evaluate* the performance according to a predetermined schedule to monitor progress.

One-Minute Managing

The *One Minute Manager*, for which Blanchard is perhaps best known, suggests that managers can use **one-minute managing,** including both praise and reprimands, to get their subordinates to perform at peak efficiency with high morale.

Both praise and reprimands can be effectively accomplished in one minute.

one-minute managing • Blanchard's approach to giving one-minute praises and reprimands.

Blanchard and Johnson (1981, p.44) suggest that *one-minute praising* works well when managers:
1. Tell people *up front* that you are going to let them know how they are doing.
2. Praise people immediately.
3. Tell people what they did right—be specific.
4. Tell people how good you feel about what they did right and how it helps the organization and the other people who work there.
5. Stop for a moment of silence to let them "feel" how good you feel.
6. Encourage them to do more of the same.
7. Shake hands or touch people in a way that makes it clear that you support their success in the organization. (Any such physical contact should be done in a way that could never be construed as sexual harassment.)

Blanchard and Johnson (p.59) suggest that *one-minute reprimands* work well when managers:
1. Tell people *beforehand* that you are going to let them know how they are doing in specific terms.
   The first half of the reprimand:
2. Reprimand people immediately.
3. Tell people what they did wrong—be specific.
4. Tell people how you feel about what they did wrong—in specific terms.
5. Stop for a few seconds of uncomfortable silence to let them *feel* how you feel.
   The second half of the reprimand:
6. Shake hands or touch them in a way that lets them know you are honestly on their side. (Again, with any physical contact, avoid any appearance of sexual harassment.)
7. Remind them how much you value them.
8. Reaffirm that you think well of them but not of their performance in this situation.
9. Realize that when the reprimand is over, it's over.

Figure 10.7 illustrates how one-minute praisings and reprimands constitute a comprehensive disciplinary approach.

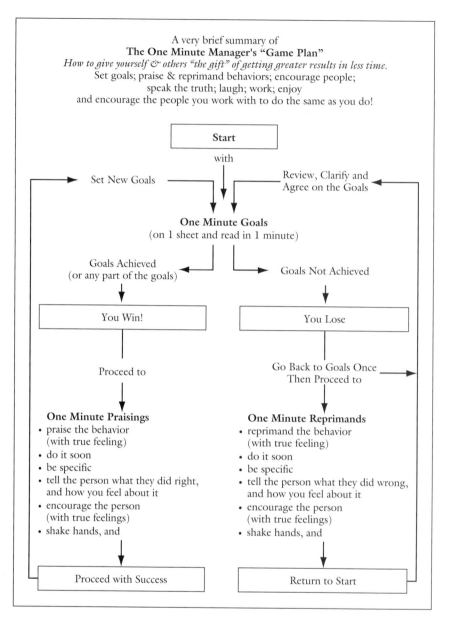

Figure 10.7 The One-Minute Manager's "Game Plan"

Source: Kenneth Blanchard and Spencer Johnson. *The One Minute Manager.* p.101. Copyright © 1981 by William Morrow and Co. Used by permission of William Morrow and Company, Inc., Publishers, New York.

Blanchard cautions that simply knowing the secrets of one-minute praising and reprimanding is not enough:

> To use these tools well, you must understand some specific management techniques. . . .
>
> Giving an equal amount of praise and criticism may not be enough to save you from being thought of as a bad boss. In most groups, there's a need for four times as many positive interactions—that is, praising—as negative interactions.
>
> A reprimand has such a powerful effect that it takes four positive words to balance one negative word.

An effective manager usually gives four times more praise than blame.

Blanchard describes a corporation he worked with where criticism and praise were approximately equal. The employees thought their relationship with their boss was "totally negative." Even when the ratio was changed to two praisings for every one reprimand, people still thought their boss was "all over them." Only when the ratio became four praisings to one criticism did the employees feel they had a "good relationship" with their boss.

The Stroke Approach

The Better Than Money Corporation is founded on the principle that management has available to it several options that are "better than money" to motivate employees. This principle carries over into the corporation's main business, consulting on excellence in customer service. Its **stroke approach** includes five kinds of strokes:

- Positive—any sincere, positive comment or expression. Clearly a warm fuzzy.
- Negative—any negative action or word that is clearly a cold prickly.
- Absent—lack of any word or recognition.
- Crooked—a positive stroke followed by a negative one, for example, "That's a beautiful dress you have on. I wonder when it will be in style."
- Plastic—a comment given as a ritual, for example, "How are things going?"

stroke approach • using positive strokes rather than negative, crooked or plastic strokes.

 Managers can give strokes that are positive, negative, absent, crooked or plastic. They should focus on positive strokes.

To use strokes effectively, managers should concentrate on the positive strokes as much as possible. Figure 10.8 shows how a manager might set "stroking objectives" each day.

STROKING OBJECTIVE FOR:

Date:_____

1. Give out two Positive Strokes per day.
       Genuine
       Sincere
       Specific
       Timely

2. Identify one top performer in your work group.
   Name _____

   Give two Positive Strokes per week. (Do not combine with #1).

3. Identify one marginal performer in your work group.
   Name _____

   Give two Positive Strokes per week. (Do not combine with #1).

   _____

Figure 10.8   Using Strokes to Discipline Positively

Source: Copyright © 1980 by John Tschohl, Better than Money Corporation. Courtesy of Service Quality Institute, Minneapolis, MN. Reprinted by permission.

A Fair Disciplinary System

A fair, equitable disciplinary system has the following characteristics:

- Reasonable and necessary policies, procedures and rules to govern employees' conduct at work and promote both individual and organizational goals. Regular review of these standards.
- Effective communication of these policies, procedures and rules as well as the consequences for noncompliance.
- Immediate, impartial and consistent enforcement of the policies, procedures and rules.
- An appeals procedure.

 SUMMARY

Discipline and morale are closely related. Morale is how a person feels; discipline is how a person acts. The purpose of discipline is to promote desired behavior. This may be done by encouraging acceptable behavior or punishing unacceptable behavior. An agency's policy and procedure manual is the foundation on which most discipline must be based. Discipline is a fundamental management right.

The 10/80/10 principle divides the workforce into three categories: 10 percent who are high achievers, 80 percent who are average achievers and 10 percent who are unmotivated troublemakers and cause 90 percent of management's problems. A problem employee exhibits abnormal behavior to the extent that the behavior is detrimental to organizational needs and goals as well as the needs and goals of other department personnel. In addition to problem employees, law enforcement managers must also be able to deal with people who, although not technically "problem" employees, are extremely difficult to work with. These include yes people, passives, avoiders, pessimists, complainers, know-it-alls, exploders, bullies and snipers. To deal with problem people, get their attention, identify the problem behavior, point out the consequences, ask questions, listen and explain expectations. Avoid defensiveness.

A primary rule of effective discipline is that it should be carried out as close to the time of the violation as possible. Progressive discipline uses disciplinary steps based on the severity of the offense. The steps are usually (1) oral reprimand, (2) written reprimand, (3) suspension/demotion and (4) discharge. The offense and offender, how the offense was committed and the offender's attitude and past performance are important considerations in assigning penalties.

Discipline, either positive or negative, depends on the use of consequences. The balance of consequences analysis considers behavior in terms of what positive and negative results the behavior produces and then focuses on those results. Personal, immediate and certain (PIC) consequences are stronger than organizational, delayed or uncertain (ODU) consequences. Managers should change the balance of consequences so that employees are rewarded for desired behavior and punished for undesired behavior—not vice versa.

The PRICE Method consists of five steps: (1) pinpoint, (2) record, (3) involve, (4) coach and (5) evaluate. Both praise and reprimands can be effectively accomplished in one minute. An effective manager usually gives four times more praise than blame. Managers can also give strokes. These strokes might be positive, negative, absent, crooked or plastic. The focus should be on positive strokes.

CHALLENGE TEN

The new Greenfield police chief has asked Captain Blair to review and update the policy and procedure manual. The chief wants her to develop a manual that reflects the departments' community policing philosophy. The current manual is several inches thick, steeped in fine details and includes rules and procedures for nearly every circumstance. It was initially modeled after a manual written in the 1960s for a large police department in another part of the country.

Captain Blair knocks the dust off her copy of the manual and starts reading. She realizes that she hasn't read the entire manual since she was hired as an officer twenty years ago. Some language and policies in the manual are unrelated to the activities of the Greenfield Police Department. Captain Blair knows that most members of the department aren't familiar with all the policies and procedures in the manual and certainly aren't complying with them.

Captain Blair notes that the policy on breaks at restaurants requires officers to sit facing the entrance door for officer safety. The policy regarding traffic stops requires officers to approach vehicles with their hand on their gun as they listen for noise from the trunk and visually check back seats. An entire section of the manual is devoted to riot control, something the Greenfield Police Department has never experienced.

1. Do lengthy and detailed policy and procedure manuals enhance tight discipline?
2. Do lengthy and detailed policy and procedure manuals protect departments from litigation?
3. What basic changes should Captain Blair consider if she rewrites the manual?
4. How should she change the tone or philosophy of the manual?
5. What is a good strategy for gaining officers' acceptance of a new manual?
6. Should all policies and procedures be written with the same detail?

DISCUSSION QUESTIONS

1. Why is discipline a broader term than punishment?
2. What level of law enforcement manager should investigate the majority of discipline problems?
3. What is constructive discipline?
4. Do you think written departmental rules and regulations are necessary? For what areas?
5. What behaviors would be severe enough violations to warrant termination?
6. What would be a constructive law enforcement department philosophy for discipline?
7. Are there too many departmental rules and regulations? Not enough? What are the most important ones?
8. Why is discipline necessary for individual functioning? For organizational functioning?
9. Choose a problem behavior you would like to change and do a balance of consequences analysis. Are there changes you can make to reduce or eliminate the problem behavior?
10. As a manager, what types of positive and negative discipline would you be inclined to use?

REFERENCES

Alpert, Geoffrey P.; Dunham, Roger G.; and MacDonald, John M. "Interactive Police-Citizen Encounters that Result in Force." *Police Quarterly*, December 2004, pp.475–488.

Aronsohn, Audrey J. "Substance Abuse: Is Your Company's Policy Up-To-Date?" *Loss Prevention & Security Journal*, June 2003, pp.34–35.

Aveni, Thomas J. "The Force Continuum Conundrum." *Law and Order*, December 2003, pp.74–77.

Beasey, Dale. "Brutal v. Brutality." *Law and Order*, October 2004, pp.104–108.

Blanchard, Kenneth. "A PRICE That Makes Sense." *Today's Office*, September 1989, p.18.

Blanchard, Kenneth and Johnson, Spencer. *The One Minute Manager*. New York: William Morrow and Company, 1981.

Colaprete, Frank. "Early Warning Systems." *Law and Order*, October 2004, pp.64–68.

Collins, Sue Carter. "Sexual Harassment and Police Discipline: Who's Policing the Police?" *Policing: An International Journal of Police Strategies and Management*, Vol. 27, No. 4, 2004.

Durose, Matthew R.; Schmitt, Erica L.; and Langan, Patrick A. *Contacts between the Police and the Public: Findings from the 2002 National Survey*. Washington, DC: Bureau of Justice Statistics, April 2005. (NCJ 207845)

Ferraro, Eugene and Judge, W. J. "Put Your Drug Policy to the Test," *Security Management*, May 2003, pp.94–101.

Field, Mark. "The Art of Asking Questions." *Law and Order*, March 2005, pp.66–70.

Fridell, Lorie A. "Improving Use-of-Force Policy, Policy Enforcement and Training." In *Chief Concerns: Exploring the Challenges of Police Use of Force*, edited by Joshua A. Ederheimer and Lorie A. Fridell. Washington, DC: Police Executive Research Forum, April 2005, pp.21–56.

Grattet, Rykett. "Making the Most of General Orders." *The Police Chief*, February 2004, pp.63–66.

Gundy, Jess. "The Complexities of Use of Force." *Law and Order*, December 2003, pp.60–65.

Holtz, Larry. "Harassment Policies." *Law Enforcement Technology*, April 2003a, p.126.

Holtz, Larry. "What Is Sexual Harassment?" *Law Enforcement Technology*, March 2003b, p.118.

Johnson, Robert Roy. "Corrective Interaction." *Law and Order*, August 2004, pp.97–100.

Luna, Andrea Morrozoff. "Introduction." In *Chief Concerns: Exploring the Challenges of Police Use of Force*, edited by Joshua A. Ederheimer and Lorie A. Fridell. Washington, DC: Police Executive Research Forum, April 2005, pp.1–20.

McLaurin, Michael. "Write a Policy Manual." *Police*, September 2005, pp.22–26.

Miller, Laurence. "Police Personalities: Understanding and Managing the Problem Officer." *The Police Chief*, May 2003, pp.53–60.

Moore, Carole. "Excessive Force." *Law Enforcement Technology*, November 2004, p.110

Nowicki, Dennis. "K-9 Deployment as a Serious Use of Force: Handler-Controlled Alert Methodology." In *Chief Concerns: Exploring the Challenges of Police Use of Force*, edited by Joshua A. Ederheimer and Lorie A. Fridell. Washington, DC: Police Executive Research Forum, April 2005, pp.60–61.

Oldham, Scott. "Experience Counts." *Law and Order*, March 2005, pp.33–34.

Orrick, Dwayne. "Controlling Abuse of Sick Leave." *The Police Chief*, March 2004, pp.39–42.

Peed, Carl R. and Wexler, Chuck. "Foreword." *Supervision and Intervention within Early Intervention Systems: A Guide for Law Enforcement Chief Executives*. By Samuel Walker, Stacy Osnick Milligan and Anna Berke. Washington, DC: Officer of Community Oriented Policing Services and the Police Executive Research Foundation, December 2005, pp.vii–viii.

"Preventing Sexual Harassment." St. Paul, MN: Equal Opportunity Division, Department of Employee Relations, no date.

Rutledge, Devallis. "Use of Force on Prisoners." *Police*, January 2004, pp.58–59.

Serpas, Ronal; Olson, Joseph W.; and Jones, Brian D. "An Employee Disciplinary System That Makes Sense." *The Police Chief*, September 2003, pp.22–28.

Sharp, Arthur. "Keep Policies and Procedures Updated." *Law and Order*, June 2004, pp.72–75.

Slahor, Stephanie. "Earlier is Better When Solving Problems." *Law and Order*, June 2004, pp.88–90.

Terrill, William. "Police Use of Force: A Transactional Approach." *Justice Quarterly*, March 2005, pp.107–138.

Walker, Samuel; Milligan, Stacy Osnick; and Berke, Anna. *Supervision and Intervention within Early Intervention Systems: A Guide for Law Enforcement Chief Executives*. Washington, DC: Officer of Community Oriented Policing Services and the Police Executive Research Foundation, December 2005.

Walker, Samuel; Milligan, Stacy Osnick; and Berke, Anna. *Strategies for Intervening with Officers through Early Intervention Systems: A Guide for Front-Line Supervisors*. Washington, DC: Police Executive Research Forum, 2006.

Weitzel, Thomas Q. "Managing the Problem Employee: A Road Map for Success." *FBI Law Enforcement Bulletin*, November 2004, pp.25–32.

Zigmund, Edmund. "Police Use of Force: The Problem of Passive Resistance." *The Police Chief*, April 2005, pp.10–12.

CITED CASES

Graham v. Connor, 490 U.S. 386 (1989)

Rodney King v. Los Angeles, 1992

BOOK-SPECIFIC WEB SITE

Go to the Management and Supervision in Law Enforcement Web site at www.thomsonedu.com/criminaljustice/bennett for student and instructor resources, including Internet Assignments and Case Studies.

CHAPTER 11

Complaints, Grievances and Conflict

*A complaint is an opportunity to prove the kind of stuff you and your department
are made of, a chance to cement a relationship so solidly it will last for years.
That's much more important than who's right and who's wrong.*

Anonymous

DO YOU KNOW?

- Who may register a complaint?
- What categories of law enforcement misconduct are often included in external complaints?
- How complaints might be avoided?
- What the most common causes of internal complaints are?
- How job satisfaction, communication and performance are related?
- What the Pinch Model illustrates?
- When complaints do not need to be taken seriously?
- What two functions are served by a careful complaint investigation?
- How officers may protect themselves legally when under investigation?
- What the majority of grievances concern?
- What the outcome of a complaint or grievance might be?
- Whether conflict must be negative?
- What possible benefits conflict might generate?
- What major sources of conflict exist in the law enforcement organization?
- What management's responsibility in conflict situations is?
- How conflicts that arise during crises should be dealt with?
- What the confrontation technique is and what to expect from it?
- What healthy conflict does?
- What the keys to maintaining healthy conflict are?
- What the intersubjectivity approach to resolving conflict involves?

CAN YOU DEFINE?

arbitration	exonerated	intersubjectivity approach	positive conflict
complainant	external complaints	mediation	principled negotiation
complaint	Garrity protection	negative conflict	reframing
conflict	grievance	pinch	sustained
confrontation technique	grievant	Pinch Model	unfounded
crunch	healthy conflict internal complaints		

Introduction

Chapter 10 discussed problem behaviors perceived by managers. This chapter reverses the perspective and looks at problems perceived by subordinates and by those outside the law enforcement organization. These perceived problems may result in complaints or grievances.

It is an organizational fact of life that most law enforcement supervisors must deal with complaints as part of their responsibilities. How supervisors react to complaints will directly affect the organization's ability to function effectively. If complaints are not dealt with promptly, thoroughly and fairly, the result will be serious negative consequences for the entire organization.

Managers must also deal with conflict, both internal and external. One reason is that our society has become increasingly complex. Choices used to be simpler. What kind of weapons? Squad cars? Investigative equipment? Another reason conflict is inevitable is that managers deal with people, and within the law enforcement agency people have strong egos and are used to speaking their minds and getting their way. But they are also people who depend on each other to get results—sometimes to stay alive.

A third reason conflict is inevitable is that resources are limited, and the law enforcement organization is no exception. Choices must be made as to allocation of human resources (who is assigned to what shift) and monetary resources (salaries, perks).

Indeed, all organizations, including law enforcement, will have conflict. Individual and organizational goals; differences in employee lifestyles and individual needs; varied interpretations of rules and regulations; physical, social and psychological differences; and variations in viewpoints all exist and contribute to disagreement and conflict.

This chapter begins with definitions that differentiate between complaints and grievances. It then examines the difference between external and internal complaints, as well as complaint policies and how complaints are handled and investigated, including the role of internal affairs investigations and the civilian review board. Next, grievances are discussed, including their causes and resolutions, mediation and arbitration, followed by an examination of the disposition of complaints and grievances. The chapter then discusses the legal rights and procedures for officers named in disciplinary actions.

This is followed by a closer look at the conflicts law enforcement managers must deal with, including some contrasting views of conflict, sources of conflict and the responsibility of managers to reduce negative conflict and make positive conflict work for the organization's benefit. Next is a discussion of recognizing and acknowledging conflict and managing crisis conflict. Then the probability of role conflict within the organization is examined, followed by a look at external conflicts and politics, both internal and external. The chapter concludes with a discussion of maintaining healthy conflict and the importance of conflict resolution skills.

complaint • a statement of a problem.

grievance • a formally registered complaint. A claim by an employee that a rule or policy has been misapplied or misinterpreted to the employee's detriment.

Complaints and Grievances Defined

A **complaint** is a statement of a problem. A **grievance** is a formally registered complaint. By definition, a complaint and a grievance are basically synonymous. Either can be described as a criticism, charge, accusation or finding of fault. Complaints and grievances may also be described as circumstances or conditions thought to be unjust, whether real or imagined.

A complaint or grievance is an action taken by someone against a person or an organization for a perceived wrong. Whether real or imagined, the wrong is sufficient in the mind of the person complaining that the matter must be brought to the attention of the proper authority. The action taken may be an oral criticism, a written statement, a listing of wrongs, a civil service procedure, a meeting demand, a hearing demand or formal legal action.

Complaints

Complaints are an unavoidable part of being a manager. Even the most efficient managers get their share of complaints.

 A complaint may be made by the general public, by people arrested or by employees of the law enforcement department, including peers or managers. The person or group filing the complaint is called the **complainant.**

complainant • a person or group filing a complaint.

Complaints may be external or internal.

External Complaints

Law enforcement departments exist to serve their communities. With this basic premise, citizens can be thought of as consumers of law enforcement services, and, like any business, departments should "aim to please." Research suggests that customers who have bad experiences tell approximately 11 people about it; those with good experiences tell just 6. Managers should recognize that it is impossible to please everyone all the time. Some citizens, rightly or wrongly, will perceive a problem and register a complaint.

External complaints are those made by citizens against a law enforcement officer or officers, a supervisor, support staff and/or the entire department. The complaint may be made by an individual or a group. It may be as "trivial" as a citizen receiving what he or she perceives to be an unjustified parking ticket or as serious as a charge of brutality or racism.

external complaints • statements of a problem made by a person or group outside the law enforcement organization.

Studies have found that complaints are not filed evenly by people across demographic parameters. A complainant profile generated by such studies shows that nonwhite, unmarried, low-income males under age 30 are most likely to complain about the police. In fact, nearly 75 percent of all complaints against officers come from this group.

Studies also revealed that the officers most likely to receive complaints against them were those under age 30 assigned to uniformed patrol duties with fewer than 5 years of police experience and only a high school education.

People who call in complaints without leaving a name are generally not as credible as those who identify themselves. This does not mean, however, that anonymous complaints should be ignored. With the drug problem as serious as it has become, with intimidation, injuries and in some cases death threatening those who provide information, it is understandable that people may not want to give their names.

An employee who receives a complaint should obtain all possible information about the incident. Sometimes the complainant may be under the influence

Table 11.1 Disposition of Allegations against the Police

	Exonerated	Unfounded	Not Sustained	Sustained	Totals
Excessive force	55	1	14	3	73
Attitude/Language	8	6	31	11	56
Conduct unbecoming a police officer	13	5	22	38	78
Attention to duty (Substandard performance)	1	0	0	0	1
Lack of police service					
Violations regarding reports	1	1	0	0	2
Other	17	1	36	65	119
Totals*	95	14	103	117	329
Summary of Disciplinary Actions Taken in Response to Sustained Allegations					
Dismissed from the department					1
Suspended					25
Written reprimand					32
Oral reprimand					2
Referred to training					10
Counseling					23
Psychological evaluation					5
Off-duty employment ban					1
Officers resigned					3
Total					102

*There are 25 cases pending disposition.

of alcohol or other drugs and, if interviewed later, may give a considerably different story. Many departments have dispatcher complaint forms. Others automatically record all calls into and out of the department.

The Police Executive Research Forum has published a model policy statement for handling citizen complaints. The intent of the policy statement is to provide precise guidelines to ensure fairness to officers and civilians alike. It seeks to improve service quality in three ways: (1) by increasing citizen confidence in the integrity of law enforcement actions, (2) by permitting law enforcement officials to monitor officers' compliance with department procedures and (3) by clarifying rights and ensuring due process protection to both citizens and officers.

Causes of External Complaints Specific categories of misconduct subject to disciplinary action need to be clearly defined.

 Categories of officer misconduct often included in external complaints are crime, excessive force, false arrest, improper entry, unlawful search, harassment, offensive demeanor and rule infractions.

The annual report of a large, urban police department included information about complaints, including the types of complaints processed and their disposition, as summarized in Table 11.1. The most common complaint in this department, and also the most frequently sustained complaint, was conduct unbecoming an officer. The most common disciplinary action taken was written reprimand. Interestingly, the second most frequent allegation, and the most frequently exonerated, was excessive force. Suspension and counseling were other frequently used disciplinary actions. Such reports tell the public that police agencies do not take officer wrongdoings lightly and support the fact that police departments have in-house procedures to investigate public and individual complaints about officer conduct and actions.

Reducing External Complaints Preventing misconduct is a primary way to reduce complaints. Agencies should make every effort to eliminate organizational conditions that may foster, permit or encourage improper behavior by officers.

 Complaints can be reduced through effective recruitment and selection, training, policy and procedures manuals, effective supervision, community outreach and data collection and analysis.

Data collection and analysis might reveal problem behavior before complaints are registered. If complaints do occur, mediation is often successful in resolving the problem.

Mediation Walker et al. (2002, p.1) describe **mediation** as a form of alternative dispute resolution (ADR): "Mediation involves the informal resolution of a complaint or dispute between two parties through a face-to-face meeting in which a professional mediator serves as a neutral facilitator and where both parties ultimately agree that an acceptable resolution has been reached." Table 11.2 summarizes the *potential* benefits of mediation.

mediation • bringing in a neutral third party to assist in negotiations.

Table 11.2 Potential Benefits of Mediation

Benefits for Police Officers
1. Better understanding of interactions with citizens.
2. Opportunity to explain actions to citizens.
3. Greater satisfaction with complaint process.
4. Empowerment.
5. Chance to learn from mistakes.

Benefits for Citizen Complaints
1. Greater opportunity to meet goals.
2. Greater satisfaction with complaint process.
3. Better understanding of policing.
4. Empowerment.

Benefits for Police Accountability
1. Greater responsibility for one's action.
2. Positive changes in police subculture.

Benefits for Community Policing
1. Goals consistent with those of community policing.
2. Problem-solving process.
3. An opportunity for dialogue.

Benefits for Complaint Process
1. More efficient complaint process.
2. Cost savings.
3. Higher success rate.

Benefits for Criminal Justice System
1. More trust in justice system.
2. Lower crime rate.

Source: Samuel Walker, Carol Archbold and Leigh Herbst. *Mediating Citizen Complaints against Police Officers: A Guide for Police and Community Leaders.* Washington, DC: Community Oriented Policing Services Office, 2002, p.5.

Table 11.3 Mediation

Approach	When to Use
Ask employees to pinpoint the root of the problem	To build cooperation
	To pave the way for yielding to an employee's suggestion
	To maintain harmony and good will
Take charge of the situation	In an emergency where quick action is vital
	To implement unpopular ideas
	To enforce rules or discipline (Use sparingly.)
Work toward a reasonable compromise	When other methods aren't working
	To establish a middle ground
	To get quick group agreement
Integrate all parties into a creative solution	To benefit from merging insights of people with different perspectives
	To get long-term commitment from everyone involved
Step back from the whole situation	An issue is trivial
	Someone else can be more effective
	The issue is part of a bigger problem that must be solved separately

Source: Adapted from Dorothy Simoneli. "War of the Workers." *IB (Independent Business)*, May–June 1994, pp.72–73. Copyright 1994 by Group IV Communications, Inc., 125 Auburn Court, Suite 100, Thousand Oaks, CA 91362.

Community mediation centers have provided low-cost or free conflict resolution services since the early 1970s (Coletta, 2003, p.72). Over 550 mediation centers have trained thousands of volunteer mediators to help resolve disputes. Coletta estimates that about 85 percent of cases that go to mediation reach some sort of resolution.

The National Association for Community Mediation (NAFCM) is a Washington, DC–based organization that promotes community mediation and maintains an extensive library of resources on conflict resolution and training. Its Web site reports 19,500 volunteer community mediators and 76,000 citizens trained by community mediation programs. More than 97,500 cases are referred annually.

How to approach mediation often depends on the specific circumstances. Table 11.3 provides basic approaches to mediation and when each might be appropriate.

Internal Complaints

internal complaints • statements of problems made by officers or employees within a law enforcement agency.

Complaints by officers or employees, **internal complaints,** are generally brought to the attention of the next highest manager. If the complaint is against a manager, it is brought before the next highest manager. If the complaint is against the department head, it is brought before the city manager or other head of local government, following the chain of command.

When investigating internal complaints against specific employees, the primary purpose should be to correct the behavior and make the employee a contributing member of the department. Employees are a tremendous investment. Everything reasonable should be done to reach a conclusion satisfactory to management and the employee.

The following guidelines might assist in handling internal complaints: always be available, listen carefully and gather all the facts. Address the problem, and if an apology is called for, do so immediately. Explain your decision and why it was made as well as how it can be appealed.

A manager's attitude toward complaints can mean the difference between a temporarily rocky road and a permanent dead end. Recall that many complaints may be symptomatic of low morale or of problems with employees' feelings of self-worth.

Causes of Internal Complaints Law enforcement officers are not known to be "cry babies." They usually pride themselves on being tough, disciplined and able to take whatever they need to. They may, however, be harboring feelings of dissatisfaction that manifest themselves in observable behaviors. A number of conditions can cause officers to complain.

 Most internal complaints are related to working conditions or management style.

Officers may be dissatisfied with safety conditions, condition of vehicles, lack of equipment needed to do the job or other work conditions. They may also think their managers are too strict or too lenient, have too high or too low standards, oversupervise or undersupervise, give too little credit and too much criticism, will not accept suggestions, show favoritism or make unfair job assignments. The discussions of motivation and morale in Chapters 9 and 10 include signs that officers are unmotivated and/or experiencing low morale—instances in which complaints and grievances are likely to appear.

One challenging area of internal complaint managers sometimes must deal with is a charge of disability discrimination under the Americans with Disabilities Act (ADA). Lyman (2005, p.75) points out that in 2004, 15,346 charges were filed with the Equal Employment Opportunity Commission on the basis of an employer's failure to make reasonable accommodation for a disabled employee. Lyman (p.80) lists the following possible reasonable accommodations:

- Job restructuring
- Part-time or modified work schedules
- Reassignment to a vacant position
- Acquisition or modification of equipment or devices
- Appropriate adjustment or modification of examinations or training
- Appropriate adjustment or modification of policies

Employers should be flexible and reasonable, but they do not need to meet the accommodation request of a disabled employee if it would present an "undue hardship." The ADA is discussed in depth in Chapter 15.

Reducing Internal Complaints When signs of employee dissatisfaction appear, preventive action is needed. When managers sense that "things are not going right," it may be time to set up a personal talk or a shift or department meeting. Determine the type of discontentment and the cause. Pay special attention to what employees are saying in small groups. Talk with individual officers. Make it known that you are available to discuss matters formally or informally. For years researchers have looked for a correlation between satisfaction and performance (Buchholz and Roth, 1987, pp.70–71). Studies have examined satisfaction levels with self, job, peers, management and organizations and have found a person could be satisfied with all of these and still not perform well (hygiene factors). A breakthrough came when satisfaction was correlated to communication as follows:

Satisfaction	Communication	Performance
High	high	highest
Low	high	high
High	low	low
Low	low	lowest

Satisfied employees who talked about it performed the best; dissatisfied employees who did not talk about it performed the worst—findings you might expect.

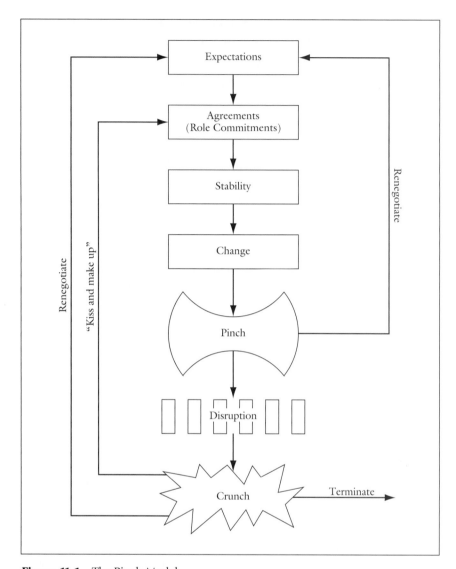

Figure 11.1   The Pinch Model

Source: Steve Buchholz and Thomas Roth. *Creating the High Performance Team,* p.73.
Copyright 1987 by John Wiley and Sons, Inc. Reprinted by permission.

Surprisingly, however, those who were satisfied but did not talk about it were ranked lower in overall performance than those who were dissatisfied but talked about it. This means that even people who may not be fully satisfied but have an environment where they can *communicate* about their dissatisfaction perform better than those who may be satisfied but are in a climate that lacks open communication.

 Communication is directly related to job performance. Those who are dissatisfied on the job and communicate perform better than those who are satisfied and do not communicate.

Pinch Model • illustrates the importance of communication in dealing with complaints and the consequences of not communicating effectively. A pinch, a minor problem, can turn into a crunch, a major problem.

Open communication will not only help employees be more satisfied but also help identify problems before they become major. This is illustrated in the **Pinch Model,** Figure 11.1, which illustrates the importance of open communication and the likely consequences of its absence.

The lines of communication within a department must be kept open. Encouraging communication can help keep a pinch from becoming a crunch.

A **pinch** is a small problem between individuals, a situation in which an individual or individuals feel something is wrong. It's not a full-blown problem—yet. Pinches result from such things as the supervisor changing the rules, changing the schedule, failing to provide expected support or feedback or failing to keep a promise. They can also result from misunderstandings and failure to clarify expectations on the job. If small problems are handled effectively, major problems can be avoided. If they are not dealt with, they may accumulate and disrupt performance and relationships, usually leading to a major confrontation, or **crunch.**

A crunch occurs when the problem becomes serious. It is marked by strong emotional reactions from both sides. This may be a heated argument or total avoidance. At this point two alternatives often exist. First, those involved in the crunch may "kiss and make up" but without dealing with the root problem. This results in a vicious cycle, with pinches leading to crunches and more confrontation. Or it may result in transfer or termination. The Pinch Model suggests that when pinches or crunches occur, managers and subordinates need to renegotiate, starting with an open discussion of expectations.

pinch • a minor problem.

crunch • a major problem.

 The Pinch Model illustrates the importance of communication in dealing with complaints and the consequences of not communicating effectively.

In addition to keeping communication lines open and encouraging subordinates to express their concerns, managers can help reduce complaints in other ways. They can help employees improve their education and their work conditions; inspect and improve equipment and determine what additional equipment can be requested in the next budget; and give praise when it is deserved. When criticism is deserved, they can make it constructive criticism delivered in private.

Often people with complaints have tunnel vision and have not considered points on the other side. A complaint is usually nothing personal. Regard it as a chance for successful change. Be positive rather than negative. Surprisingly, most complaints can be worked out if they are not allowed to proceed too far. Complaints handled inappropriately often become grievances.

Complaint Policies

Any manager who wants to operate efficiently and maintain high morale must take every complaint seriously. No matter how trivial or unreasonable a complaint may seem to a manager, it does not appear that way to the person making it: "It remains critical to the integrity of an agency that it accept and fully investigate all complaints" (Kelly, 2003, p.6).

 A basic rule: *Never* take a complaint lightly.

"The way complaints are handled by an organization and its managers is critical" (Slatkin, 2003, p.125). Every police department should have a written complaint review policy explaining procedures used to investigate complaints, the roles and responsibilities of the supervisors and the officer complained against, the function of internal affairs, possible dispositions and the appeal process. It is essential that citizens support and have confidence in the police department.

A complaint policy not only establishes a plan but also states the department's philosophy regarding public complaints. Police administrators know that police–civilian encounters will inevitably cause problems. Police have unique authority in the community, as well as considerable discretionary power. The agency, community, employee and complainant all benefit from a fair, open investigation policy of complaints against the police.

Regardless of its origination, whether external or internal, the complaint must be investigated and resolved.

Handling and Investigating Complaints

Complaints can be received from any source, in person, by mail or by phone. Even complaints from juveniles, anonymous sources and arrestees should be accepted if the facts warrant.

Making a complaint should be easily accomplished. A clearly marked, easily accessible office should be open from early morning until evening. Often this is the internal affairs (IA) office. Phone complaints should be accepted any time.

Whenever possible, complaints should be in writing. If this is not possible, the department should complete a complaint description form and send it to the complainant to be reviewed, signed and returned to the agency.

A complaint against an officer, support staff or the entire department must be investigated thoroughly, following the same principles as in a criminal investigation. This is true whether the complaint is from someone outside or within the department. The investigation and adjudication of complaints will depend on the specific charge and on the past record of the officer involved. The investigation process should have a definite time limit, such as 120 days, with a one-time, 30-day extension possible.

 A careful investigation of a complaint instills confidence in management's fairness and protects those accused of wrongdoing.

Complaints require action. In some cases the basis for the complaint is readily discernible and easily verified. In other cases, however, the facts are not as clear or even in dispute. These matters are considerably more difficult to resolve. In yet other situations the complaint is completely irrational, but it must be dealt with rationally.

Most complaints about minor infractions such as discourtesy or sarcasm can be investigated by the accused officer's first-line supervisor. More serious allegations should be assigned to the department's internal affairs department, discussed shortly.

In dealing with complaints, determine the exact nature of the complaint. What specifically occurred that caused the complainant to take action? An investigation must support the specifics and must involve the person complained against.

If a police officer is charged with a violation of rules and regulations and thinks the charge is unjust, the officer can request a hearing. If the charge is upheld at the hearing, the appeal procedure will vary from department to department. The hearing may be with the city manager, city council, police complaint board or civil service commission. If upheld by one of these hearing authorities, it may be possible to appeal to the District Court. Officers' rights regarding complaints and grievances are discussed later in the chapter.

The person assigned to the investigation must be able to draw a conclusion from the specifics of the complaint. All complaints against law enforcement employees must be investigated within the constraints of the legal process. Inquiries must be objective. Conclusions and final decisions should be avoided until all facts are available. Despite their seemingly minor nature, complaints may have a major impact on department morale if not investigated properly. It is necessary to investigate complaints to clear the person complained against as well as to serve the interests of justice. Considerations in the investigation include investigating immediately and collecting both positive and negative facts; interviewing those complained against as well as the complainant; and taking written statements, if necessary, checking personnel records of those accused as well as previous complaints of the person accusing and then conducting a fair hearing.

Good complaint investigations not only protect the reputation of the department and any accused employee but also provide an opportunity for the complainant to be heard and the public to be notified of the results. Immediate disposition of such incidents builds public confidence, law enforcement morale and a general sense of justice.

Actions to be taken, offenses deemed to be wrongs, the status of the employee until the case is decided and other matters are often defined in the department rules and regulations or grievance procedures established by union contracts.

Internal Affairs Investigations

Policing the police is a difficult job. Most police officers see internal affairs as a "necessary evil" and refer to them as "the rat squad" (Griffith, 2003, p.76). However, while internal affairs investigators protect the public from abusive police, they also tread the fine line of protecting individual officers from unfounded allegations.

Internal affairs sections traditionally are reactive, responding to citizen complaints and reports of misconduct and policy violations from other department members (Dees, 2003, p.88). Kelly (p.5) lists five functions of the internal affairs process: (1) protecting the public, (2) protecting the department, (3) protecting the employee, (4) removing unfit personnel and (5) correcting procedural problems. Colaprete (2003, p.100) asserts: "The internal affairs investigation is the most complex and sensitive investigation conducted by a police organization." He (2005, p.112) emphasizes: "Police administrators are constantly faced with political pressure, media attention, the requirements of legal and collective bargaining agreements, and the protection of the community in the conduct of all internal investigations." He points out three major legal considerations: criminal, internal and civil.

If there is even a hint of criminal behavior on the part of the employee, the matter should be separated into both a criminal and an administrative investigation. The criminal investigation should be conducted first, including the *Miranda* warning if applicable. This is followed by the administrative investigation, including a *Garrity* warning if applicable.

The first step is to review all evidence. Next, obtain copies of all associated elements of the case. These can include a copy of the crime or arrest report, a computer printout of the call-for-service, a copy of radio transmissions and any other retrievable items. A fundamental component of most investigations is interviewing all involved parties.

Officers' Rights and Legal Procedures

The nature of police work makes officers vulnerable to a variety of legal actions. The National Association of Police Organizations (NAPO) provides legal resources to police defendants and their attorneys. Established in 1978 to protect officers' legal and constitutional rights, it attempts to put police officers on a level playing field with everybody else. According to its Web site, NAPO represents more than 2,000 police unions and associations, 236,000 sworn law enforcement officers, 11,000 retired officers and more than 100,000 citizens.

A variety of legislation has also protected due process rights of officers involved in disciplinary hearings and other court actions. In addition, several states have enacted Law Enforcement Officers' Bills of Rights (LEOBR). The Violent Crime Control and Law Enforcement Act of 1991 contains proposed federal legislation concerning mandated due process rights afforded peace officers who are subject to internal investigations that could lead to disciplinary action. In other jurisdictions, contracts resulting from collective bargaining provisions may affect the investigative process when police officers are involved.

In general, a Police Officers' Bill of Rights gives law enforcement officers, sheriffs and correctional officers the right to be notified of any pending disciplinary action within a reasonable time before the action takes effect, to be treated with a specific minimum standard of fairness while under investigation, to request a hearing if an investigation results in a recommendation of disciplinary action and to advance review and comment on any adverse material being placed in the officer's personnel file.

The self-incrimination clause of the Fifth Amendment to the U.S. Constitution prohibits forcing individuals to provide evidence against themselves in a criminal matter. The due process clause of the Fourteenth Amendment makes this requirement applicable to the states. The Supreme Court ruled in *Garrity v. New Jersey* (1967) that a violation of the Fourteenth Amendment occurs when the government uses a police officer's statement in a criminal trial against that officer. Officers accused of misconduct can be threatened with loss of their jobs if they do not cooperate with an internal investigation. In other words, anything used in a criminal trial may be used in an administrative trial, but the reverse is not true.

Under the Garrity Rule: "An employer has the right to require employees to answer questions regarding their conduct as long as those questions are narrowly drawn and directly related to the duties they were hired to perform. The employer may use these statements in disciplinary actions involving the employee which could result in termination of employment." However, if the employer uses Garrity to compel an officer to answer questions, they are prohibited from giving this information to police or having it used during a criminal trial. The officer must request Garrity protection. They can protect themselves by getting in writing a **Garrity protection,** a written notification that they are making their statement or report involuntarily:

> On (date) at (time) at (place), I was ordered to submit this report (give this statement) by (name and rank). Consequently, I submit this report (statement) involuntarily and only because of that order as a condition of continued employment.
>
> I believe the department requires this report (statement) exclusively for internal purposes and will not release it to any other agency or authority.
>
> I hereby specifically reserve my constitutional rights to remain silent under the Fifth and Fourteenth Amendments. Further, I rely specifically upon the protection afforded to me under the doctrines set forth in *Garrity vs. New Jersey* (1967).

Garrity protection • a written notification that an officer is making his or her statement or report in an internal affairs investigation involuntarily.

This protects the officer should the matter become a criminal issue. The statement or report could not be used against the officer. It might also help break the code of silence.

 While under investigation, officers may find legal protection from a Law Enforcement Officer Bill of Rights (LEOBR), if one has been enacted in that state, and under the Garrity protection.

Civilian Review Boards

In some communities, civilian review boards have been designated to investigate and dispose of complaints against law enforcement officers. Civilian review boards were introduced in Chapter 3.

Law enforcement agencies usually have opposed such civilian review boards on the grounds that they erode the authority of the responsible law enforcement manager. At the heart of the debate regarding the civilian review boards is the question of whether police possess the ability, the structure and the will to police themselves. Those in favor of review boards think they take pressure off the police to investigate their own and help reduce public belief that the police will whitewash wrongdoing within the agency. Further, because the review board is an external agency, it can be more independent in its investigation. In addition, review board membership can represent more elements of a diverse community.

Police, on the other hand, believe that the department can police its own, that it has its own complaint-handling procedures through existing department policies

AP/Wide World Photos

U.S. Attorney General Alberto Gonzales, right, listens to New Orleans Police Chief Warren Riley, left, as St. Bernard Parish Sheriff Jack Stephens looks on, center, while they meet in Chalmette, Louisiana, Thursday, Oct. 20, 2005, at the Disaster Recovery Center set up in the parking lot of a WalMart Store that was closed by flooding. Rapid, well-coordinated responses to emergencies and natural disasters, as well as listening to the concerns and immediate needs of residents in the wake of such crises, is critical to avoiding citizen complaints and keeping public support for the department high.

and that the police have governed themselves in the past and will continue to do so. Many police executives think that civilian review boards substantially reduce the effectiveness of the police agency administration. Accountability is the essence of the issue. Police believe they have accountability through the existing structure of first-line supervisor; middle manager; upper-level manager; and, finally, chief of police.

Despite the controversy, many larger cities have civilian review boards. According to one account, approximately 100 municipalities throughout the country use civilian panels to investigate complaints.

Civilian review boards typically have the power only to make recommendations to the police chief executive, not to impose discipline. Some, however, advocate modifying such boards, from a strictly reactive body to one more involved in preventing incidents leading to complaints.

It is conceivable that citizens might expect more sympathy from a panel of other civilians, yet such findings support the notion that civilian review boards are capable of making fair, objective, unbiased decisions regarding complaints, not automatically and disproportionately siding with the citizen complainant to the detriment of the officer or the department. In addition to resolving complaints, managers must also answer to grievances filed against the department.

Grievances

Grievances are as much a part of law enforcement managers' responsibilities as complaints. Grievances can come only from law enforcement employees, not from the public. A grievance is a claim by an employee that a rule or policy has been misapplied or misinterpreted to the employee's detriment. The person filing the grievance is known as the **grievant.**

grievant • the person or group filing a grievance.

Grievances are a right of employees. Formal grievance procedures are not provided to cause problems but rather to promote a more harmonious, cooperative relationship between employees and management.

Managers' decisions are not always correct. Different interpretations can be made of rules, regulations, policies and procedures. The grievance procedure provides a means of arriving at decisions concerning these varied interpretations. In most instances the final decision may be more satisfactory to all parties involved because it involves input from a number of sources and is not just one person's opinion. Law enforcement managers should not treat employees who file grievances any differently from any other employee.

Causes

 Dissatisfaction with physical working conditions and equipment causes the majority of grievances. Almost a third are caused by dissatisfaction with management's actions.

Vehicle condition, quality and timeliness of repair, equipment used in emergencies, lighting conditions, office space, excessive reports, type of acceptable firearm, protective equipment such as armored vests and tear gas and other physical items are the subject of much debate and dissatisfaction. Law enforcement supervisors need to discuss these matters at staff meetings because they are generally budget items that depend on decisions made by higher-level managers.

Roughly 30 percent of grievances result from some management behavior or action. This includes plural standards of conduct, failure to recognize good work, obstinate dealing with subordinates, failure to use procedures uniformly and fairly, use of obscene language, discrimination and other types of objectionable manager behavior.

Grievances concerning rules, regulations, policies and procedures center primarily on violations of civil rights. In the early years of policing, requirements were harsh concerning hairstyle, facial hair and off-duty employment. Employees realize some rules and regulations are necessary for the common good of management, employees and the community. They object, however, to what they consider over-regulation. Many also object to off-duty conduct regulations. They believe that stricter regulations should not apply to officers simply because of their profession.

Civil and criminal actions against law enforcement officers have tended to force standardized procedures in these areas. In general, objections are low if the rules and regulations are communicated to the entire department and a two-way discussion is held concerning limitations and reasons.

The management's failure to do what employees expect also causes employee dissatisfaction. Employees, in general, want to do a good job and resent too many impediments. Among perceived impediments are:

- Failure to communicate and to train employees to do the job effectively.
- Failure to explain procedures and then blaming employees for not doing it right.
- Failure to praise when it is deserved.
- Managers' failure to set a good example for subordinates.

Managers should not penalize employees for actions not directly related to performance of duty or to the best interest or safety of other department employees and not specifically in the rules, regulations, policies or procedures.

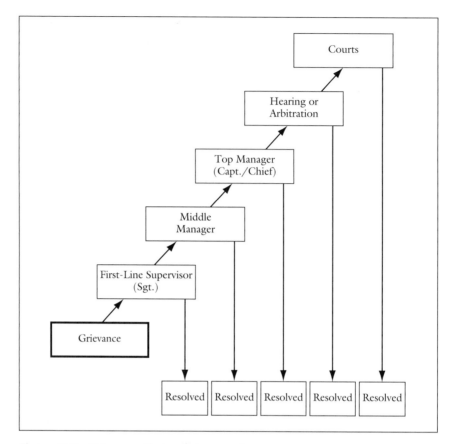

Figure 11.2 Grievance Chain of Command

Source: "Conflict Management and the Law Enforcement Professional in the 1990s." *Law and Order*, May 1994. Reprinted by permission of the publisher.

Resolving Grievances

Most noncontractual grievances are resolved at the first-line supervisor level. These are matters not associated with salaries, fringe benefits or conditions negotiated by the labor union or an employee group representative. The first-line manager talks to the grievant or the group filing the grievance. Through two-way communication, an objective approach by both sides, common sense, fair play and discussion of all issues and alternatives, the matter may be resolved at this level.

If the matter is not resolved at the first level, a formal grievance is filed and forwarded to the next level manager. If not resolved at this level, it proceeds to the head of the department. If it fails to be resolved at this level, the matter proceeds to voluntary arbitration, civil service board proceedings or other assigned hearing boards. Figure 11.2 illustrates the chain of command a grievance may go through.

Many law enforcement departments have ordinances, statutes or formal procedures for handling grievances. Following is an example of a grievance ordinance.

Informal Grievance Procedure. Any employee or group of employees having a grievance should first discuss the grievance with their immediate supervisor within five working days of the occurrence that caused the grievance. Within five working days, the supervisor should reply. If the supervisor's answer does not satisfactorily adjust the grievance, the employee should follow, within five working days, the formal grievance procedure outlined in the next section.

Formal Grievance Procedure. The following steps are used in the formal grievance procedure.

Step 1. The grievance is submitted in writing to the employee's immediate supervisor. The supervisor meets and discusses the grievance with the employee and/or their representative, if any, and replies in writing to the employee within five working days.

Step 2. If a settlement is not reached, the written grievance will be presented within five working days to the next level of supervision. The second level supervisor or their representative has five working days to investigate and render a written decision.

The procedure continues in this fashion, going up the hierarchy to the department head, the city manager and finally the civil service commission.

The ordinance provides employees an opportunity and right to bring dissatisfactions to management. It does not necessarily mean the grievance is justified, but it provides a procedure for having the matter heard and decided. It is an orderly procedure that applies to all employees equally and is free from interference, restraint, coercion or reprisal. The intent is to make grievances an aboveboard matter for discussion rather than a behind-the-back approach to problems.

The ordinance's wording makes it clear that employees have a chance to be heard. Grievance procedures are provided to avoid having problems fester, grow and become unmanageable. The results of such a procedure are most often positive for employees, management and the organization.

Mediation and Arbitration

Sometimes mediation or arbitration is used to settle grievances. Mediation, as previously discussed, brings in a neutral outside third party who tries to reconcile the two sides after hearing both and recommending a solution, which is not binding on either party.

Arbitration also brings in a neutral outside third party who, like the mediator, listens to both sides. The arbitration hearings may be informal or formal. After hearing both sides, the arbitrator recommends a solution. Unlike the mediator's recommendation, however, the recommendation of the arbitration is often binding.

arbitration • turning a decision over to an individual or panel to make the final recommendation.

Disposition of Complaints and Grievances

 A complaint or grievance investigation usually results in one of four findings: sustained, not sustained, exonerated or unfounded.

A **sustained** complaint or grievance is one in which the investigative facts support the charge. If the investigative facts are insufficient, that is, the evidence does not support the accusations, the complaint or grievance is *not sustained*. An **exonerated** complaint or grievance is one in which the investigation determines that the matter did occur but was proper and legal. An **unfounded** complaint or grievance is one in which either the act did not occur or the complaint was false.

Most cases are disposed of in a relatively short time, either as sustained or not sustained. A surprisingly small number have little basis for further action. If a complaint or grievance is sustained against an individual, progressive discipline

sustained • complaint or grievance in which the investigative facts support the charge.

exonerated • a complaint or grievance in which the investigation determines that the matter did occur, but was proper and legal.

unfounded • complaint or grievance in which the act did not occur or the complaint/grievance was false.

such as that discussed in Chapter 10 is recommended. If corrective measures are necessary, they must be executed as soon as possible. At a set future time, the matter must be rechecked to determine whether further action is needed.

In addition to the challenges of complaints and grievances, managers often face less clearly defined problems in the form of conflict.

Conflict

conflict • a mental or physical fight.

Conflict is normal in all organizations and becomes negative only when left unresolved (Pruitt, 2003, p.129). **Conflict** is a struggle, a mental or physical fight, a controversy, a disagreement or a clash. Conflict can range from an internal struggle within a person over whether to smoke a cigarette or take a drink to armed combat between nations over boundaries or religious beliefs.

Controversy and conflict can be fleeting or prolonged, conscious or subconscious, destructive or constructive. Conflict may be:

- *Approach–approach conflict*—selecting one of two positive alternatives.
- *Approach–avoidance conflict*—selecting one positive alternative that will also produce a negative consequence.
- *Avoidance–avoidance conflict*—selecting one of two negatives, commonly referred to as "the lesser of two evils."

Because conflict is inevitable for managers and supervisors, they must have the skills to manage it effectively.

Contrasting Views of Conflict

Conflict has always existed between people and organizations. Most people believe conflict is always negative because they see the destructive results of conflict in wars, in marriages, in organizations and among individuals. Law enforcement departments also have traditionally regarded conflict as inherently bad. Administrators note its damaging effects. Morale decline, lower productivity, lack of creativity, poor performance and many other ills have been blamed on **negative conflict.** The prevailing attitudes are to avoid or eliminate conflict by adding more and more rules and regulations. Law enforcement agencies in which conflict reigns are regarded as poorly administered. In departments in which conflict is poorly handled, it is a destructive force. Excessive conflict without resolution *is* negative and can lead to disunity in individual and organizational purpose, decreased morale and lower productivity.

negative conflict • disagreements that are destructive.

This need *not* be the case, however. Conflict does not have to be destructive. If it is recognized for what it is, conflict can be a positive influence because it can bring attention to problems that need to be resolved. **Positive conflict** can result in personal or organizational growth.

positive conflict • challenges the status quo and offers constructive alternatives.

How managers approach conflict determines whether it is a negative or a positive force within the organization.

Although organizations with badly managed conflict are hamstrung with dissension, those with *no* conflict are in an equally unproductive situation. Organizations with no conflict are dormant, static, unimaginative, unable to change and in danger of becoming obsolete.

A healthy amount of conflict, properly handled, motivates individuals and organizations. It exposes problems, defines causes, obtains input from those involved toward constructive solutions and may develop new outlooks.

Conflict is constructive if it:
- Encourages better decision making and/or change.
- Makes life more interesting.
- Reduces irritation.
- Enriches a relationship.
- Increases motivation to deal with problems.
- Is stimulating.

Conflict can be agitating and exciting, indicating organizational vigor. It can keep a groove from turning into a rut.

 Conflict that opposes without antagonizing can be extremely beneficial to a law enforcement organization, keeping it innovative and responsive to change.

It is usually not disagreement that creates anger and hostility; rather, it is the manner in which the disagreement is handled. As George Bernard Shaw noted: "The test of breeding is how people behave in a quarrel." The challenge to managers is not to suppress conflict but to minimize its destructiveness and to transform the anger often associated with it into positive, creative forces.

Sources of Conflict

Conflict originates from several sources. In law enforcement organizations the most common forms of conflict are internal, between two or more individuals, between organization and officer, between groups within the organization or between officers and other agencies and the public.

 Conflict may come from individual, interpersonal or job-related sources as well as from sources outside the organization. Change is a major source of conflict.

Individual Sources

Individual, internal conflict exists because of uncertainty, lack of knowledge, criticism, pressures of superiors or the organization, differing opinions on organizational goals or the fear of doing something wrong.

Personal problems at home can be brought to the workplace, for example, problems with children, financial matters, one's spouse and the like.

Interpersonal Sources

Interpersonal sources of conflict result because personnel come from different cultures, have different backgrounds and have different dominant needs. Many conflicts arise because of personality differences and may be the result of prejudices or biases or of different perceptions and values. Much conflict results from the various ways people view the world—ways that reflect the individual's upbringing, culture, race, socioeconomic class, experience and education. Such conflict is often expressed this way: "He has never done anything to me, but I just can't stand him."

Table 11.4 Intergenerational Diversity in the Workplace

Trait	Traditional Employees Born 1900–1942	Baby Boomers Born 1943–1960	Generation X Born 1961–1983	Millennials Born 1984–1999
Perception	Lifetime career in a single field, usually with same employer; seeks to make a lasting contribution; heads down, onward and upward attitude, built today's workplaces	Eighty million strong; extended the work week from a standard 38 hours to 60 hours; at a crossroads in trying to balance overwhelming need to succeed in career track with the current desire to slow down and enjoy the fruits of their labors	Believe they have to prove themselves constantly; projects image of being overly ambitious, disrespctful, and irreverent; learned from their parents' experience that going by the company rules doesn't guarantee you a job	Unique mix of technology savvy and social conscience, just entering the workforce but are expected to change the landscape of the workplace
Career goal	Leave a legacy	Build a stellar career	Balance work life with personal life; build a repertoire of transferable skills and experience; have a portable career; flexible schedules; independence; professional growth; interesting work and time off	Build parallel careers, multi-tasking, seek to pursue more than one line of work at the same time
Expected feedback from employer	None, expects very little in employer performance evaluation	Regularly scheduled employer performance evaluation; one a year enough	Instantaneous, immediate feedback; tell me how I am doing all the time	Feedback at a push of button; send an e-mail–or better yet, an instant message–to me about how I am doing
Workplace values	Formality; top-down chain of command; more likely to write a memo; prefer to make decisions based on what worked in the past	Competitive; willing to sacrifice for success; tend to favor top-down approach; personable communication that builds rapport; reshaped corporate culture with casual dress codes and flexible schedules	Work/life balance top of list; values efficiency and directness; expectations are immediate and instantaneous; cut to the chase and avoid unnecessary meetings; low tolerance for bureaucracy and rules	Highly collaborative and optimistic; emphasis on work/life balance; comfortable with technology; can-do positive standpoint; need voice in decisions

Source: Reprinted from *The Police Chief*, Vol. LXXI, No. 10, p.104, ©2004. Copyright held by the International Association of Chiefs of Police, 515 North Washington Street, Alexandria, VA 22314 USA. Further reproduction without express written permission from IACP is strictly prohibited.

Sullivan (2004, p.99) points out that for the first time in history four different generations of employees are found in law enforcement departments. The work ethic of each generation can lead to a number of "clashpoints." Some differences in these generations were explained in Chapter 7. Table 11.4 summarizes the intergenerational diversity in the workplace.

In more general terms, Pruitt (pp.129–130) explains that police departments have a contingent of the "old guard" and a much larger contingent of the "new guard," which is predominately younger and better educated: "The old guard feels unappreciated and pushed aside by the new guard." The two groups mistrust and compete with each other, a major challenge to management.

Sometimes a large group is dissatisfied, usually as a result of factors such as low pay, inadequate benefits, poor working conditions or exceptionally strict discipline. Frequently, whole group dissatisfaction arises during contract negotiations, and management must communicate openly during such times.

Job-Related Sources

Job-related conflicts usually involve organizational and administrative objectives, goals, rules and regulations; the hierarchy structure; differences on how to use resources; and conflicts between personnel and groups.

Groups within the organization may be promoting self-interests ahead of organizational interests. Internally, departments such as administration, dispatch, juvenile, investigation and patrol compete for allocated budget funds.

Competition also adds to conflict. Most officers seek recognition and promotion, which may result in extremely destructive interpersonal conflicts. Conflict may arise when an officer of less seniority is promoted over an officer of more seniority, when a patrol officer turns over a case to an investigator and never hears anything more about the case, or when one officer does the work and the shift manager takes the credit. Conflict may also arise when a senior patrol officer gets a smaller salary than a starting detective, when a senior officer is assigned to patrol in a new squad car or when officers are given preferential shift assignments.

Sources of Conflict External to the Law Enforcement Organization

Municipalities have limited resources to operate the total city government. The law enforcement organization is one agency competing for a share of these resources. If law enforcement personnel perceive they are not obtaining sufficient resources for reasonable operation, conflict will arise. If, for example, the fire department receives more money than the law enforcement department or vice versa, heated disagreement is likely.

Responsibility for Conflict Management

Law enforcement agencies have a number of levels at which conflict may be resolved. Supervisors are the front line to resolve conflict at its source and are directly responsible for most personnel. Yet personnel are the most frequent source of conflict, and personnel conflicts should be resolved at this level when possible.

Supervisors are also essential to conflict management because they are usually the first to know that conflict exists in the ranks. It is their responsibility to mediate these conflicts unless they believe the conflicts are deeper and more involved than the shift level of management can handle.

Group conflicts may have to proceed to middle or upper management. Using higher-level authority sometimes resolves a situation temporarily but may not always identify the problem.

If there is conflict in the relationships of manager and subordinates, such as a past problem or personal prejudices, the matter should be sent to the next management level. If conflicts exist between supervisors, responsibility shifts to middle-management level. All conflicts could potentially shift to the executive manager, city manager, civil service proceedings or the courts. Resolution at the lowest level is preferable.

Recognizing and Acknowledging Conflict

Regardless of the level of intervention, the best method to resolve conflict is usually to deal directly with those involved, determine the cause of the conflict and seek a solution. Delaying the inevitable only increases the probability of a worse problem.

 A manager's responsibility is to recognize conflict when it occurs, have a system for reporting conflict and take action as soon as possible.

Evading an issue does not resolve the conflict. Transferring or isolating individuals does not identify a conflict either and may interfere with the entire organization's operation. Some managers avoid conflict by seeking out employees who are not apt to "rock the boat"; using the authority of their position autocratically; increasing feelings of agreement but never actually agreeing; or stalling for time, hoping the problem will go away.

Managing Crisis Conflict

Conflict is a constant concern of management. Usually it is best handled through discussion, exploration of causes and alternatives and participatory leadership. In crises, however, such conflict management is not possible.

 Conflicts that arise during crises must be managed by following established procedures and the chain of command.

Crisis management is usually reactive rather than proactive. Procedures must be established to minimize conflicts and to resolve those that occur during a crisis. The following guidelines might assist:

- Anticipate the kinds of conflict and who might be involved. Establish precedents.
- Make certain one person is clearly in charge.
- Make certain all officers know what they are responsible for doing.
- Let no one shirk assigned responsibilities.
- Keep lines of communication open. Keep everyone involved informed, including your superior, but also control the flow of information.
- Make decisions that allow the most options.
- If the crisis is prolonged, be sure personnel get rest and can attend to personal needs.
- If the crisis is prolonged, put someone in charge of routine duties that still must be performed while the crisis continues.
- As the crisis winds down, expect delayed stress reactions (depression, irritability, irrational outbursts). Hold debriefings.
- Return to normal operations as soon as possible.
- Evaluate performance and identify conflicts that should have been avoided or handled differently.

Handling Personal Attacks

If you find that you are becoming angry, acknowledge it out loud: "This is starting to really irritate me." This gives the other person fair warning that you may blow up and is another way to buy time while you maintain control. *Respond* to the person rather than *react*. Listen to what the person is asserting. Could it be right? Ask clarifying questions. State your own position clearly.

Defuse the other person's anger. Get on the same level physically: sit if the person is sitting; stand if the person is standing. Be quiet and allow the person to vent. Empathize by saying something such as: "I can see how you might feel that way." But do not patronize.

Focus on the present and the future, on resolving the conflict rather than on placing blame. It takes two people to make a conflict. Open the lines of communication and keep them open, but do not exceed your level of authority. Make only promises that you can keep.

If the person continues to be angry and confrontational, ask, "What do you expect me to do?" or "What do you want?" Such statements may disarm a vindictive troublemaker. They may also help you discover a person's genuine concerns. If the person asks for something you cannot deliver, say so.

If all the preceding fail, accept that this person must want the conflict to continue for some reason. At this point seek intervention from a higher level of authority or suggest that the attacker get help from another source. Distance yourself from people who seem intent on making your job more difficult, and limit their access to you.

It is probably a truism that no one truly "wins" an argument. This is illustrated by the law enforcement lieutenant who was hardworking, conscientious and highly skilled but had not received a promotion in 10 years. Asked to explain his failure to advance, he replied, "Several years ago I had an argument with the chief. I won."

Handling Disagreements between Others in the Department

The first step in handling disagreements between two subordinates is to decide whether intervention is wise. Some conflicts are truly personality clashes rather than problem centered. In such cases it is fruitless to intervene and will only weaken your leadership when conflicts involve true problems rather than simply personalities. Some managers rely on the confrontation technique to handle such disputes.

 The **confrontation technique,** insisting that two disputing people or groups meet face-to-face to resolve their differences, may effectively resolve conflicts, or it may make them worse.

confrontation technique • insisting that two disputing people or groups meet face-to-face to resolve their differences.

Sometimes those in conflict will resolve their differences themselves. Often, however, the differences intensify, positions harden, people become angry and defensive and logic gives way to personal attacks. Those in conflict refuse to back down on any points. The adversaries bluff, not wanting to show their true feelings.

Managers might intervene in conflicts if employees cannot reach a solution or the solution does not end the conflict. They should intervene if the conflict is disrupting the department. Once you decide it would be beneficial to intervene, meet with each person privately to discuss issues and to confirm the willingness of both parties to resolve the conflict. Then select a neutral meeting location.

If the conflict is truly disruptive, consider using the power of your position and issue an ultimatum to stop the bickering: "Come to an agreement by the end of the shift, or I'll come up with one for you that neither of you will probably like." At other times one subordinate may be clearly in the right on a given issue. In such instances an effective manager will serve as a mediator between the conflicting employees to resolve the conflict as rapidly as possible.

Most often, however, both subordinates are partially right and partially wrong. In such instances, the following guidelines may be helpful:

- Listen to both sides to understand the issues.
- Do not take sides.
- Separate the issue from personalities.
- Do not speak for one to the other.
- Get the parties to talk with each other and to listen.
- Point out areas of misunderstanding, but place no blame.

AP Photo/Diane Bondareff

Law enforcement personnel often come into conflict with angry citizens and must try to diffuse the situation. New York City police officers block a wall of angry anti-war protesters near the United Nations Headquarters on February 5, 2003.

- Get the parties to reverse roles to see the other's point of view.
- Search for areas of agreement.
- Allow both to save face in any solution reached.
- Stress the importance of resolving the conflict.
- Monitor any solution agreed upon.
- If no solution can be reached, suggest a third-party mediator or negotiator.

Although conflict can be healthy, it can also be destructive. You cannot row a boat in two directions at the same time. Law enforcement employees have to pull together to accomplish their goals and objectives. It is management's job to see that they do so most of the time.

Dealing with External Conflicts

External conflicts can be with other agencies or with the public.

Conflicts with Other Agencies

External conflict may exist between law enforcement organizations at municipal, county, state and federal levels, as well as with private police and security agencies. Disagreements over jurisdictional authority, powers of arrest, who is in charge at the scene of an incident involving several jurisdictions, specialized and technological duties at the scene of a crime and many other issues cause conflict. Often it is the same basic conflict that exists internally within a law enforcement organization, that is, a lack of understanding and communication that deteriorates into a personality conflict. The goal of providing the best possible public service is lost.

Conflicts with the Public

Law enforcement personnel often come into conflict with angry citizens with complaints, people being arrested or given a citation or citizens angry about a general law enforcement situation they have heard about.

The potential for conflict between officers and the public exists because officers' perception of their duties may differ from the public's. Officers on traffic patrol may enforce speeding laws. Offenders given citations may ask, "Why are you picking on me for going 5 miles over the speed limit on this open stretch of road? I'm not hurting anyone. Why aren't you over by the school where you could do some good?" Or "Why aren't you picking up criminals?" Officers rarely see vehicle crashes happen, but they are expected to determine who is in the wrong—a potential for conflict of opinion.

Dispatchers or desk personnel are often on the receiving end of such complaints. How they handle them may be important to present and future public relations. Over the years a number of approaches for handling angry complainants have been developed.

People involved in these conflicts have learned that the first stages are important to defusing the situation. Except when the complainant is intoxicated or emotionally or mentally disturbed, the defusing phase takes from one to five minutes. Things have either calmed down by that time or the complainant is not going to be satisfied with anything you try to do.

Dealing with Internal and External Politics

Dealing with conflicts, internal or external, can be hazardous to managers, even if they are not directly involved. Intraagency and interagency conflicts inevitably involve politics. People take sides; battle lines are drawn. Managers who attempt to stay out of conflict may be perceived as wishy-washy or fence sitters. In the midst of the conflict, managers have to keep their employees functioning efficiently.

To do so, managers should first separate their responsibility from the political games going on, focusing on the tasks to be accomplished. They should refrain from discussing any politically sensitive situation with subordinates. This is quite a different matter from keeping your people "in the know." Managers should also respect the chain of command even if they tend to side with the position taken by someone lower in the hierarchy. In addition, managers should say the same thing to everyone involved. They must remain honest and objective and not simply tell people what they want to hear. Finally, when the conflict ends, as it inevitably will, managers must help smooth the return to normalcy. When it's over, it's over.

Police chiefs should become politically active in supporting political issues affecting delivery of law enforcement services.

Maintaining Healthy Conflict

Law enforcement managers seek to control destructive conflict, but at the same time they should maintain healthy conflict to improve performance and productivity.

 Healthy conflict challenges the status quo and offers constructive alternatives.

healthy conflict • challenges the status quo and offers constructive alternatives.

Healthy conflict breeds change and improvement. In fact, bringing conflict into the open is often one of the healthiest things you can do because it clarifies issues, reduces stress, clears the air, stimulates decision making and brings things to a forum where they can be dealt with, enabling relationships to continue to grow. Such opposition is a help. Kites rise against the wind, not with it.

 Keys to maintaining healthy conflict include open, two-way communication; receptivity to new ways of doing things; and encouragement of risk taking.

Healthy conflict in law enforcement organizations may include:

- Brainstorming sessions to develop new techniques for patrol and investigations.
- Contests for creative and innovative ideas on law enforcement projects and programs.
- Idea-developing sessions for improving task performance.

The secret in organizational conflict is establishing a balance between none and too much. Law enforcement departments with a balance of conflict are active, progressive organizations.

Avoiding the Suppression of Conflict

Some managers avoid conflict, preferring instead to always act as peacemakers. This is certainly appropriate in many instances, but sometimes it may result in delaying the resolution of arguments or finding the best solution to problems. Recall the discussion of the Abilene Paradox in Chapter 5 and groupthink.

Understanding

A key to positive conflict is to pursue agreement with understanding. Those involved should agree to agree or agree to disagree, but understanding is a must. The classic failure in interpersonal communications is the failure to recognize the other person's right to believe in the good sense of his or her point of view. A problem-solving approach to conflict would include the following:

- Understand each party's views.
- Identify underlying needs and concerns.
- Search for potential solutions.
- Enumerate probable consequences.
- Select manageable alternatives that satisfy all parties.
- Develop mechanisms to monitor and adjust.

Learning more about each other and about the task required of those involved in a conflict is helpful. Lack of understanding of each other's jobs increases conflict. Some departments rotate officers between shifts and patrol zones to provide a broader understanding of the total problems of the community. This also applies to divisions. For example, transferring some patrol personnel to investigations may help patrol understand problems of the investigating division.

Another solution is to have each person or group state what they would do if they were the other person or group in the conflict. In other words, force them to perceive the issue from the other side. It is much the same approach as having others state how they perceive you and comparing this with how you perceive yourself. Such an approach can be very revealing.

Another approach to solving group conflict is intersubjectivity. This refers to people mutually understanding and respecting each others' viewpoints, a kind of reciprocal empathy. In this approach, each person's most important ideas about the problem and its solution are recorded on separate 3-by-5-inch cards. From the total set of cards, about 40 are chosen to represent all contributions.

The group involved in the conflict meets, and each person is given a set of cards and asked to organize them in a meaningful way. Most people arrange their cards on the table in plain view, and discussion arises as to how each is sorting and arranging. The power of the exercise is not in what each person does with the cards but in the discussion it produces. This provides a basis for deepening mutual understanding and for the eventual merging of different perspectives.

 The **intersubjectivity approach** uses 3-by-5-inch cards as a means to get people in conflict to share their most important ideas about a problem and to come to a mutual understanding of and respect for each other's viewpoints.

intersubjectivity approach • uses 3-by-5-inch cards as a means to get people in conflict to share their most important ideas about a problem and to come to a mutual understanding of and respect for each other's viewpoints.

Conflict Resolution Skills

Conflict is inevitable, so managers must learn to deal with it effectively and manage it positively. Conflict resolution skills should be part of every officer's training because they are invaluable on the streets as well as in interactions within the organization.

Pruitt (p.131) recommends that conflict management skills training be part of annual in-service training, including problem solving, conflict de-escalation skills, mediation skills, negotiation skills and cultural awareness issues. He stresses that the edge needed for organizations to not only survive but thrive in our fast-changing, stressful times is found in the strength of human relationships and the positive connections that bring people closer together for achievement and increased teamwork: "Negative conflict that remains unresolved is a thief that steals away productivity, achievement, teamwork and cooperation."

Conflict can result in one of three situations: win-lose, lose-lose and win-win. In *win-lose situations*, the supervisor uses command/control authority, giving orders and expecting them to be carried out. The subordinate must either obey or face disciplinary action. This is how conflicts have traditionally been managed within law enforcement organizations. Win-lose can produce frustration.

In *lose-lose situations*, a conflict is settled through an ineffective compromise, with neither side feeling they have accomplished their purpose. The underlying philosophy is that "something is better than nothing" and that direct confrontation should be avoided. Such short-term solutions may result in even greater conflict in the future.

In *win-win situations* the focus is on the basic merits of each side rather than on interpersonal haggling. Research from the Harvard Negotiating Project has resulted in a method known as **principled negotiation,** a higher-level approach to effective mediation that focuses on mutually satisfying options. One key is separating the people from the problem. The participants should see themselves as working together to solve a particular problem.

Principled negotiation proceeds in four basic steps, each involving both theory and practice, as Figure 11.3 illustrates. First, clearly identify the problem. Is the problem actually the heart of the conflict or merely a symptom of a deeper problem? Once you have identified the problem, analyze it to determine its underlying causes. The third step is to discuss alternative approaches to resolving the conflict. Fourth, reduce these alternative approaches to action ideas—steps that you can implement to resolve the conflict.

principled negotiation • pays attention to basic interests and mutually satisfying options. Avoids positional bargaining that tends to produce rushed agreements that can lead to damaged relationships.

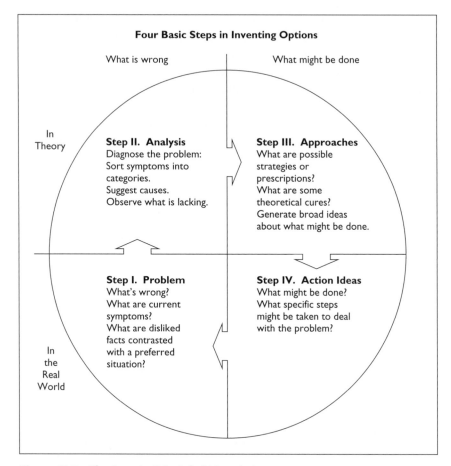

Figure 11.3 The Steps in Principled Negotiations

Source: Joseph Billy, Jr., and Ronald J. Stupak. "Conflict Management and the Law Enforcement Professional in the 1990s." *Law and Order,* May 1994, p.39. Reprinted by permission of *Law and Order.*

reframing • a conflict resolution skill; a psycholinguistic technique that shifts a person's perspective to recast conflict as a positive, rather than a negative, force.

Another conflict resolution skill is **reframing**, a psycholinguistic technique that shifts a person's perspective. Many factors influence the direction of personal and organizational perspective, including an individual's unique life experiences and the workplace culture. Slatkin (p.126) explains: "Reframing means to relabel something, to cast it in a different light and give it new meaning to the parties. The same moon looks very different from the opposite end of a telescope." Complainers do not operate in a vacuum. They may be a lone voice in a department that covertly supports their views but are too timid or cynical to complain aloud. Says Slatkin: "The complainer is often an organizational barometer." By viewing the complainer as a resource, conflict can be dissipated. Complaints can be listened to, investigated, evaluated and acted on. With reframing, conflict can become a positive rather than a negative force.

 SUMMARY

A *complaint* is a statement of a problem, whereas a *grievance* is a formally registered complaint. A complaint may be made by the general public; by people arrested; or by employees of the law enforcement department, including peers or managers. The person or group filing the complaint is called the complainant.

Complaints may originate externally or internally. External complaints are those made by citizens against a law enforcement officer or officers, a supervisor, support staff and/or the entire department. Categories of officer misconduct included in external complaints are crime, excessive force, false arrest, improper entry, unlawful search, harassment, offensive demeanor and rule infractions. External complaints can be reduced through effective recruitment and selection, training, written directives, manuals, supervisory responsibility, community outreach and data collection and analysis.

Most internal complaints are related to working conditions or management style. Many could be avoided if communication were improved. Communication is directly related to job performance. Those who are dissatisfied on the job and communicate their discontent perform better than those who are satisfied and do not communicate. The Pinch Model illustrates the importance of communication in dealing with complaints and the consequences of not communicating effectively.

A basic rule is to *never* take a complaint lightly. A careful investigation of a complaint instills confidence in management's fairness and protects those accused of wrongdoing. While under investigation, officers may find legal protection from a Law Enforcement Officer Bill of Rights (LEOBR), if one has been enacted in that state, and under the Garrity protection.

A grievance is a claim by an employee that a rule or policy has been misapplied or misinterpreted to the employee's detriment. The person filing the grievance is known as the grievant. Dissatisfaction with physical working conditions and equipment causes the majority of grievances. Almost a third are caused by dissatisfaction with management's actions.

Mediation and arbitration bring in a neutral outside third party to intervene in grievance proceedings. A complaint or grievance investigation usually results in one of four findings: sustained, not sustained, exonerated or unfounded.

In addition to complaints and grievances, managers often are faced with conflict. How managers approach conflict determines whether it is a negative or a positive force within the organization. A healthy amount of conflict, properly handled, motivates individuals and organizations. It exposes problems and may create a forum in which people can define the problem's causes. Those involved can provide input that leads to constructive solutions and developing new outlooks. Conflict that opposes without antagonizing can be extremely beneficial to law enforcement organizations, keeping them innovative and responsive to change.

Conflict may come from individual, interpersonal or job-related sources as well as from sources outside the organization. The manager's responsibility is to recognize conflict when it occurs, have a system for reporting conflict and take action as soon as possible. Conflicts that arise during crises must be managed by following established procedures and the chain of command.

Conflict need not be negative. To bring conflict into the open, some managers use the confrontation technique, which brings two disputing people or groups face-to-face to resolve their differences. It may either effectively resolve conflicts or make them worse. Healthy conflict challenges the status quo and offers constructive alternatives. Keys to maintaining healthy conflict include open, two-way communication, receptivity to new ways of doing things and encouragement of risk taking. One way to foster healthy conflict is the intersubjectivity approach, which uses 3-by-5-inch cards as a means to get disputing parties to share their most important ideas about a problem and to come to a mutual understanding of and respect for each others' viewpoints. Managing conflict is a great responsibility.

CHALLENGE ELEVEN

Lieutenant Smith is in charge of the investigations unit of the Greenfield Police Department. He received a phone call from a citizen complaining about Detective Smug. The citizen did not want to give his name or file a formal complaint, but wanted to report that Detective Smug was rude and obstinate. The caller said he was the victim of a crime, and Detective Smug was assigned the case. The citizen hung up without giving further details.

Lieutenant Smith had fielded many complaint calls from angry citizens. He understood that detectives didn't always have the luxury of treating everyone courteously. He also felt that officers deserved the benefit of the doubt when complainants refused to identify themselves. Lieutenant Smith jotted a note to himself about the call and went on with his business.

Later that day, Lieutenant Smith had a meeting with Sergeant Davis. Sergeant Davis was recently promoted and is Detective Smug's direct supervisor. Lieutenant Smith mentioned the anonymous complaint in passing, and Sergeant Davis nodded. Lieutenant Smith detected concern in Sergeant Davis' response and asked if something was troubling her. Sergeant Davis said that during the previous month she had received several similar complaints from citizens about Detective Smug. She said he had also made rude comments to a couple of the other detectives. Sergeant Davis said she tried to talk to Detective Smug about his behavior, but he was dismissive and gave her the brush-off. Since no one had filed an actual complaint, she dropped the issue. She thinks Detective Smug's rude behavior may be the result of being passed over for the detective sergeant position even though he had more seniority and experience than Davis.

1. Was it appropriate for Lieutenant Smith to discuss an anonymous complaint regarding a minor infraction with Detective Smug's supervisor?

2. Why should the Greenfield Police Department be concerned about something as minor as a complaint of rude behavior?

3. Should Lieutenant Smith direct Sergeant Davis to personally address Detective Smug's behavior?

4. Is it a good idea to keep complaints and their resolutions a secret?

5. How should Lieutenant Smith deal with Detective Smug?

6. What should Lieutenant Smith do if he continues to receive complaints about Detective Smug's rude behavior?

DISCUSSION QUESTIONS

1. How are complaints and grievances similar? Different?

2. Why is it important to investigate complaints immediately?

3. Can you think of an example of some pinches in your work? Crunches?

4. What are some steps to reduce conflict?

5. What are examples of destructive conflict? Constructive conflict?

6. What are sources of conflict among law enforcement agencies at different levels of government?

7. What are possible sources of conflict between the police and the public?

8. Can you identify "difficult people" you know who fit the categories described in this chapter?

9. Do you know of instances in which conflict has produced positive results? Would these results have been accomplished without conflict?

10. How do the behaviors discussed in this chapter relate to those discussed in Chapter 10?

REFERENCES

Buchholz, Steve and Roth, Thomas. *Creating the High-Performance Team.* New York: John Wiley and Sons, 1987.

Colaprete, Frank. "The Necessary Evil of IA." *Law and Order,* May 2003, pp.96–100.

Colaprete, Frank. "Internal Affairs Interviews." *Law and Order*, June 2005, pp.112–115.

Coletta, Craig. "How Police Departments Can Benefit from Referral to Community Mediation Programs." *The Police Chief*, August 2003, pp.72–77.

Dees, Tim. "Internal Affairs: Management Software." *Law and Order*, May 2003, pp.88–95.

Griffith, David. "Policing the Police." *Police*, October 2003, pp.76–79.

Kelly, Sean F. "Internal Affairs Issues for Small Police Departments." *FBI Law Enforcement Bulletin*, July 2003, pp.1–6.

Lyman, Stephen W. "How to Handle Disability Issues." *Security Management*, October 2005, pp.75–82.

National Association for Community Mediation (NAFCM) Web site: http://www.nafcm.org. Accessed December 5, 2005.

National Association of Police Organizations (NAPO) Web site: http://www.napo.org. Accessed December 5, 2005.

Pruitt, David K. "Conflict Management." *Law and Order*, October 2003, pp.129–131.

Slatkin, Arthur. "Complainer: Troublemaker or Constructive?" *Law and Order*, October 2003, pp.125–127.

Sullivan, Bill. "Can Traditional Work Standards and the Contemporary Employee Coexist?" *The Police Chief*, October 2004, pp.99–104.

Walker, Samuel; Archbold, Carol; and Herbst, Leigh. *Mediating Citizen Complaints against Police Officers: A Guide for Police and Community Leaders*. Washington, DC: Community Oriented Policing Services Office, 2002.

CITED CASE

Garrity v. New Jersey, 385 U.S. 493 (1967)

BOOK-SPECIFIC WEB SITE

Go to the Management and Supervision in Law Enforcement Web site at www.thomsonedu.com/criminaljustice/bennett for student and instructor resources, including Internet Assignments and Case Studies.

CHAPTER 12

Stress and Related Hazards of the Job

Your day-by-day—sometimes minute-by-minute—contact with criminals, complainants and citizens alike who are crying, cursing, bleeding, puking, yelling, spitting . . . and just plain crazy subjects your system to repeated onslaughts of disturbance.

Charles Remsberg, *The Tactical Edge*

DO YOU KNOW?

- Whether stress must always be negative?
- What common sources of stress are?
- What the four categories of stress are?
- What a major source of stress may be?
- Which law enforcement officers face stress from additional sources?
- What posttraumatic stress disorder (PTSD) is? Who is most at risk for PTSD?
- What physical problems stress is related to?
- What possible major negative effects of stress might be?
- What the symptoms of burnout are?
- How managers can help prevent burnout?
- How stress can be reduced?
- How alcohol, drugs and smoking relate to stress?
- What programs can reduce stress?
- What departments can provide to help officers?

CAN YOU DEFINE?

acute stress	cumulative stress	split-second
afterburn	distress	syndrome
blue flame	diurnal	stress
burnout	employee assistance	traumatic stress
burst stress	program (EAP)	type A personality
chronic stress	eustress	type B personality
circadian system	homeostasis	
critical incident	posttraumatic stress	
critical incident	disorder (PTSD)	
stress debriefing	psychological	
(CISD)	hardiness	

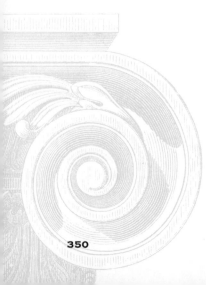

Introduction

Law enforcement is a stressful profession. Police officer stress can manifest itself in many ways that can hurt officers, their loved ones, their department, and the public: burnout, lower tolerance levels, poor judgment, substance abuse, health problems, deteriorating relationships with family and friends, low productivity, high turnover, use of excessive force, citizen complaints and increased rates of workers' compensation claims, to name just a few (Torres et al., 2003, p.110). In fact: "Stress is killing and incapacitating more police officers than bullets. Along with body armor, every man and women entering this profession deserves a 'stress vest' that provides them with the knowledge, skills and on-going services to combat the deadly consequences of stress" (Fox, 2003, p.9).

This chapter begins by defining stress and identifying some major sources of stress as well as sources of stress specific to the law enforcement profession. Next is an in-depth discussion of reactions to stress or the symptoms likely to be present, including physical, psychological, behavioral and on-the-job. The results of excessive levels of stress are then described, including divorce, alcohol problems, depression and suicide. Next, the chapter examines ways to cope with stress and how stress levels can be reduced. The chapter concludes with descriptions of how organizations can reduce stress, effective programs to manage stress and an examination of the manager's/supervisor's role in minimizing the negative effects of stress.

Stress Defined

Stress means different things to different people. To a mechanical engineer, it means the point at which objects break or deteriorate from excessive pressures or physical tension. Stress is not that different in humans. A single high-stress incident or recurring minor stress can cause the mind or physical body to deteriorate or break down completely. **Stress** is generally thought of as tension, anxiety, strain or pressure. It is the body's internal response to a situation a person perceives as threatening.

> **stress** • tension, anxiety or worry. Can be positive, eustress, or negative, distress.

Hans Selye, MD (1907–1982), the father of the stress field, originally defined *stress* as the body's nonspecific response to any demand placed on it. He later said stress was simply the wear and tear caused by living. Stress, like conflict, has both a positive and a negative aspect. In ancient China the symbol for stress included two written characters—one for opportunity and one for danger.

 Stress can be helpful (eustress) or harmful (distress), depending on its intensity and frequency as well as how it is mediated.

Eustress is positive stress that enables people to function and accomplish goals. It allows law enforcement officers to react instantaneously in life-threatening situations, to feel the excitement, the energy and the heightening of the senses. **Distress,** in contrast, is negative stress that can lead to numerous diseases, including depression.

> **eustress** • helpful stress, stress necessary to function and accomplish goals.
>
> **distress** • negative stress.

Although stress can be positive, most people equate stress with distress. The remainder of this chapter will use the term in this sense because it is the negative stress that managers must try to manage effectively. Lost hours, illness and reduced performance are costly to an organization. Law enforcement workers' compensation claims have increased substantially due to stress-related disorders. Too many high-stress incidents are occurring at home and at work with no chance to "come back to normal" between incidents. Stress can become overpowering.

Table 12.1   The Anatomy of Stress

Natural Response	Original Benefit	Today's Drawback
■ Release of cortisone from adrenal glands.	■ Protection from an instant allergic reaction or from a dustup with an attacking foe.	■ If chronically elevated, cortisone destroys the body's resistance to the stresses of cancer, infection, surgery, and illness. Bones are made more brittle by cortisone. Blood pressure can be elevated.
■ Increase of thyroid hormone in the bloodstream.	■ Speeds up the body's metabolism, thereby providing extra energy.	■ Intolerance to heat, shaking nerves to the point of jumpiness, insomnia, weight loss and ultimately exhaustion or burnout.
■ Release of endorphin from the hypothalamus.	■ Identical to morphine, a potent pain killer.	■ Chronic, relentless stresses can deplete levels of endorphin, aggravating migraines, backaches, and the pain of arthritis.
■ Reduction in sex hormones— testosterone in the male and progesterone in the female.	■ Decreased fertility. In wartime, decreased libido made both partners lives more bearable.	■ Obvious anxieties and failures when intercourse is attempted. Premature ejaculation in male, failure to reach orgasm in female.
■ Shutdown of the entire digestive tract. Mouth goes dry to avoid adding fluids to the stomach. Rectum and bladder tend to empty or jettison any excess load prior to battle.	■ Acts as a vital "self-transfusion," allowing person to perform superordinary feats of muscular power.	■ Dry mouth makes it difficult to speak with authority. The drawback of the "jettison response" is obvious.
■ Release of sugar into the blood, along with an increase in insulin levels to metabolize it.	■ Quick, short-distance energy supply.	■ Diabetes can be aggravated or even started.

Source: Adapted from Peter G. Hanson. *The Joy of Stress*. Kansas City, MO: Universal Stress Syndicate Company, 1995, pp.19–27.

---

homeostasis • the process that keeps all the bodily functions in physiological balance.

The biological concept of homeostasis helps explain how stress occurs. **Homeostasis** is the process that keeps all bodily functions, such as breathing and blood circulation, in balance. To see homeostasis at work, run in place for a few minutes and then sit down. The running mildly stresses your body, temporarily putting it out of balance. After you rest, however, your body returns to normal. The same thing happens in acute stress.

acute stress • severe, intense distress that lasts a limited time, and then the person returns to normal.

traumatic stress • severe, extremely intense distress that lasts a limited time, and then the person returns to normal. Sometimes called *acute stress.*

Acute stress is severe, extremely intense distress that lasts a limited time, and then the person returns to normal. It is sometimes called **traumatic stress.** Acute stress is temporary and may result in peak performance. Adrenaline rushes through the body; heart rate increases; blood pressure, brain activity, breathing rates and metabolic rates increase—preparing the body for fight or flight. Thousands of years before we became "civilized," our bodies were faced with the challenge of simple survival, for which either a "fight or flight" response was appropriate. Table 12.1 presents an explanation of the anatomy of stress: the physical and psychological changes that occur, how they were previously advantageous and how they now have become detrimental.

Cortisone, which is released into the body during times of stress, has the negative effects of breaking down muscle tissue and encouraging fat storage and weight gain, properties that were beneficial when survival under extreme conditions was at stake but which have become unnecessary in today's modern society (Danielsson, 2005, p.19).

chronic stress • less severe than acute stress, but continuous.

cumulative stress • less severe but continues and eventually becomes debilitating. Sometimes called *chronic stress.*

In contrast to acute stress, **chronic stress** is less intense but continues and eventually becomes debilitating. It is sometimes called **cumulative stress.** Garrett (2006, p.42) explains: "In policing there is a constant drip, drip, drip of stress,

Table 12.2   Rank Order of 14 Stressor Variables (N = 415) (5 = highest; 1 = lowest)

Stressor	Mean
Child Beaten/Abused	4.39
Harming/Killing Innocent Person	3.93
Conflict with Regulations	3.90
Harming/Killing Another Police Officer	3.89
Domestic Violence Calls	3.89
Another Officer Killed	3.71
Hate Groups/Terrorists	3.67
Poor Supervisor Support	3.64
Riot Control	3.43
Public Disrespect	3.41
Barricaded Subjects	3.28
Shift Work	3.08
Another Officer Hurt	3.08
Hostage-Takers	2.96

Source: Dennis J. Stevens. "Police Officer Stress." *Law and Order*, September 1999, p.79. Reprinted by permission.

and it starts to wear on you." Many of the sources of stress are continuous and may not even be noticed.

Sources of Stress

Stress comes from several sources, many of which are work related.

 Stress commonly arises from change and uncertainty, lack of control and pressure.

Change and uncertainty are an unavoidable part of life and of law enforcement. Officers responding to a call often have no idea what awaits. They may be unsure of who they can trust or believe. *Lack of control* may be seen when law enforcement officers apprehend suspects they believe to be guilty and see these suspects not prosecuted or found not guilty. Officers must work with assigned partners they did not select. They must be polite to surly citizens.

Pressure is also abundant in law enforcement, with work overloads, paperwork, sometimes unrealistic expectations from the public and the responsibility to protect life and property and to preserve "the peace."

In addition to these general categories of stressors, sources of stress can also be found by looking at a person's lifestyle, personality and job. The rank order of 14 stressor variables is shown in Table 12.2.

Many lists of stressors have been generated, including stressors specific to the police profession. Most of the stressors fall into four main categories, although some overlap exists.

 Sources of stress for police officers include:

- Internal, individual stressors.
- Stressors inherent to the police job.

■ Administrative and organizational stressors.

■ External stressors from the criminal justice system, the citizens it serves, the media and the family.

Internal, Individual Stressors

Internal stressors vary greatly and can include officers' worries about their competency to handle assignments as well as feelings of helplessness and vulnerability. An especially pertinent source of stress today is that generated by an officer's racial or gender status among peers, discussed shortly. Some common stress producers of daily living are changing relationships, a lifestyle inconsistent with values (too committed), money problems (credit-card debt, poor investments), loss of self-esteem (accepting others' expectations) and fatigue or illness (poor diet, lack of sleep or lack of exercise).

Personality may also affect stress levels. Psychologists often divide individuals into two types: **type A personality,** an aggressive, hyperactive "driver" who tends to be a workaholic; and **type B personality,** who has the opposite characteristics. The type A person is more likely to experience high stress levels.

type A personality • describes people who are aggressive, hyperactive "drivers" who tend to be workaholics.

type B personality • describes people who are more laid back, relaxed and passive.

Stress Related to Police Work

Stressors inherent in police work include constant threat to safety, entering dark buildings in which armed suspects are believed to be hiding, high-speed pursuits, continual exposure to victims in pain as well as unsavory criminals, the immense responsibilities of the job, the authorization to take a life, the ability to save a life and the need to remain detached yet be empathetic.

The police role itself is often vague and contradictory, with few, if any, accurate methods to assess performance. Many people become police officers to fight crime, not to do social work. They are surprised to see how much "service" is actually involved in police work. They are also surprised to learn that their efforts are often not appreciated and that, in fact, their uniform is an object of scorn and derision. The police badge may weigh only a few ounces, but it carries a heavy weight to those who wear it. One of the greatest stressors is being responsible for one another's lives; a line-of-duty death has been ranked as the number one stressor in some police departments (Garcia et al., 2004, p.38).

Line-of-Duty Deaths During the last century 14,153 officers were killed in the line of duty. The deadliest year was 1974, when 273 officers were killed. The deadliest day in law enforcement was September 11, 2001, when 72 officers were killed while responding to the terrorist attacks on America ("Police Facts," 2005). Table 12.3 shows the number of law enforcement officers killed in the past 10 years.

The top 10 leading causes of law enforcement fatalities during the past century were firearms (49 percent), automobile crashes (15 percent), motorcycle accidents (7 percent), being struck by a vehicle (7 percent), job-related illness (4 percent), aircraft accidents (2 percent), stabbings (1 percent), falls (1 percent), drowning (1 percent) and being beaten (1 percent). Figure 12.1 shows the causes of officer fatalities from 2000 to 2004.

In the last three decades there has been a 36 percent decrease in firearm deaths and a 40 percent increase in vehicle collision deaths (Floyd, 2005, p.21). These trends hold important implications for law enforcement training.

Line-of-duty deaths place a tremendous strain on a department. Although any line-of-duty death will affect an agency, the death of a partner can be especially

Table 12.3 Law Enforcement Officers Killed in the Line of Duty/Past Ten Years (1995–2004)

Year	Felonious Deaths*	Accidental Deaths	Total Deaths
1995	86	93	179
1996	66	73	139
1997	80	89	169
1998	67	101	168
1999	51	92	143
2000	62	95	161
2001	148	87	235
2002	68	83	156
2003	63	83	146
2004*	69	84	153
Total	760	880	1649
Average	(76 per year)	(88 per year)	(164 per year)

*Based on preliminary information

Source: The Law Enforcement Trainer, July/August/September 2005, p.74.

devastating. Every department should be properly prepared to handle such tragedies. Written policies should detail how to notify the family, assist with funeral arrangements, help the family complete paperwork required to receive benefits and provide continuing support to the survivors. Officers should understand the Public Safety Officers' Benefits (PSOB) program, which was designed to offer peace of mind to men and women seeking careers in public safety and to make a strong statement about the value American society places on the contributions of those who serve their communities in potentially dangerous circumstances. The program awards death, disability and education assistance benefits to the survivors

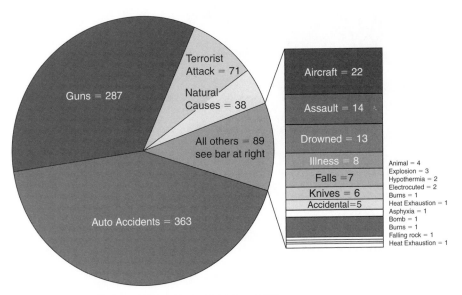

Figure 12.1 Officer Fatalities 2000–2004 (n = 853)
Source: Officer Down Memorial Page

of law enforcement officers killed or permanently and totally disabled in the line of duty.

Frequently line-of-duty deaths are part of a critical incident, another source of extreme stress for many officers.

critical incident • an extremely traumatic event such as a mass disaster or a brutally murdered child.

burst stress • to go from complete calm to high activity and pressure in one "burst."

split-second syndrome • a condition that affects police decision making in crisis. Asserts that if a person has intentionally or unintentionally provoked or threatened a police officer, at that instant the provoker rather than the police should be viewed as the cause of any resulting injuries or damages.

Critical Incidents A **critical incident** is any event that elicits an overwhelming emotional response from those witnessing it and whose emotional impact goes beyond the person's coping abilities. Officers need to be in constant emotional control. They also experience what is referred to as **burst stress**, that is, having to go from relative calm to high intensity, sometimes life-threatening activity.

This is closely related to what Fyfe (1986) refers to in his classic **split-second syndrome** that affects police decision making in crisis. The split-second syndrome asserts that if a person has intentionally or unintentionally provoked or threatened a police officer, at that instant the provoker rather than the police should be viewed as the cause of any resulting injuries or damages. In such situations, all that can reasonably be asked is that officers respond quickly and that a high percentage of inappropriate decisions should be expected and accepted.

A critical incident need not be a life-and-death situation, nor must it necessarily involve a *crisis*. A broader definition that seems to apply well to those in law enforcement is "any situation in which an individual believes that justice has not been

© AP/Wide World Photos

Police are under sudden and excessive stress, and frequently investigate incidents involving confrontation and violence. Little Rock, Arkansas, police officers comfort Tory Kennedy, 10, center, after he was held hostage in a Little Rock neighborhood in 2002. The child, one of four, escaped through a window before three others were released by the man holding them.

served for that individual or another" (Conroy, 2006). This expanded definition of *critical incident* includes such things as a criminal going free on a technicality.

Officers routinely deal with incidents involving confrontation and violence, which create stress equal to or higher than that in most occupations. Many participants in these incidents have been involved in violence before the officers arrive, and often the violence continues after they arrive. Domestic disputes, disorderly conduct, rape and gang activities are examples of such confrontations.

During emergencies, officers receive orders and act on them, or they give orders, but they seldom have a chance to discuss events during the crisis. The quasi-military nature of law enforcement structure prevents them from questioning orders. Although officers have legal authority and responsibility to carry out their duties, they often have to repress how they feel when dealing with the public. For example, intoxicated persons often verbally abuse officers, and although the officers may make an arrest, they normally accept such verbal abuse as part of the job. Because most of these situational feelings can be discussed only with other officers, police officers tend to feel isolated from the rest of society, which can produce stress.

Officer-involved shootings have been identified in numerous studies as critical incidents that cause considerable stress in officers. Officers involved in shooting incidents may experience a wide range of effects, including perceptual disturbances such as tunnel vision, sense of time slowing down or speeding up, sense of sounds diminishing or increasing in volume and memory loss. Muscular control may also be affected. Leg muscles can tremble or lock, hands can shake and muscles in the upper back and shoulders can go into spasm. Perhaps the most traumatic aspect of an officer-involved shooting involves the treatment of the officer after the incident, as they often face uncertainty about criminal charges, job security and civil litigation (Conroy). Adding to the stress is the fact that many departments lack a policy on how to treat officers following a shooting.

Especially traumatic for officers are confrontations with individuals who want to die. Campbell (2005, p.60) suggests that these extremely dangerous people fall into three primary classes: (1) terrorists on a suicide mission, (2) criminals who won't be taken alive, and (3) emotionally disturbed people who want to take their own lives and choose a police officer to help them out, known as "suicide by cop" (SBC) incidents, sometimes referred to as death by indifference. Suicide-by-cop is a growing phenomenon that has become so pervasive it is called a number of different things, including victim-precipitated homicide and police-assisted suicide (Gallo, 2004a, p.13). No matter how the death is classified, the officer who pulls the trigger is likely to experience tremendous stress, guilt and self-defeating second-guessing in the form of thoughts such as "I should have been able to see this coming and stop it" (Conroy). This self-doubt can haunt an officer for a long time.

Critical incidents may involve a death that requires the officer to notify the next of kin, an aspect of the police job that can be extremely stressful.

Death Notifications Delivering the news of a tragic death is never easy: "The shock, denial and other intense emotions family members and friends experience when receiving a death notification can test even veteran officers" (Dewey-Kollen, 2005, p.12). Survivors should never be notified of a death by telephone. Instead, it is recommended that two officers perform the notification, one of them in uniform. One officer should convey the information while the other officer observes reactions and offers support (Holtz, 2003, p.218).

Every year thousands of officers face the grim task of breaking the "world's worst news": "It's a duty most don't immediately associate with the profession. As an issue, it's fertile ground for liability" (Moore, 2003, p.106).

Fear of a Lawsuit Another source of stress for officers is fear of legal action against them and their agency. Every arrest is a possible basis for a lawsuit. Once publicized, a lawsuit suggests that the officer was wrong even though the suit may have no legal basis. Some officers choose to be less aggressive in confrontational situations, and others have been reluctant to use the necessary physical force to subdue violent criminals for fear of a lawsuit. Yet another stressor, one that seldom makes headlines but has been clearly identified as harmful to officers, is fatigue.

Fatigue and Shift Work Rodriguez (2004, pp.9–10) comments: "As a police officer myself, I have worked the midnight shift, the overtime, the court time and the extra duty days while trying to juggle a 'normal' life with my family at home. It is not easy. As a general rule, no single factor is solely responsible for police officer fatigue; it is typically the result of a combination of factors, along with the stresses of police work itself."

Ninety percent of law enforcement officers surveyed reported driving on duty while drowsy, and 25 percent reported actually falling asleep at the wheel (Rosenberg, 2005, p.115). Research indicates that being awake for 17 to 19 hours produces impairment equivalent to a .05 blood alcohol level and a reduced reaction time that is almost 50 percent worse than alcohol consumption (Rosenberg, p.116).

diurnal • day-oriented. Humans are by nature diurnal in their activities.

circadian system • the body's complex biological timekeeping system.

Humans are naturally day-oriented (**diurnal**) in their activity patterns. They are equipped with a complex biological timekeeping system (the **circadian system**). This system's major function is to prepare the body for restful sleep at night and active wakefulness during the day. The circadian system has a resetting mechanism that realigns it, but that mechanism is designed to cope with a "fine tuning" of *only* one hour or so per day. It is *not* designed to cope with the gross changes characteristic of moves to and from night work.

The brain relies on outside influences, such as daylight, social contact, regular meal times and sleep, to keep its circadian rhythm functioning effectively. When these timekeeping clues are altered through shift work, the body's circadian rhythm is negatively affected and fatigue can result. Fatigue may wear down the body's defenses, thus magnifying the effects of other stressful events.

Morgan (2005, p.106) notes that coffee is often used to counteract effects of sleep deprivation, but excessive caffeine intake can make an individual jittery and anxious and actually decrease mental performance. A study by the National Academy of Science's Institute of Medicine concludes: "Taking large doses of caffeine to offset lack of sleep, especially in situations where public safety and health could potentially be compromised, cannot be justified" (Morgan, p.106).

In addition to fatigue, shift work is associated with other complicating factors. Shift work may contribute to isolation from family and friends and contribute to the "blue wall" and "code of silence" perceptions some have. Studies indicate that officers who work overtime have a greater number of complaints filed against them. Monthly shift rotations necessitate not only physical adaptations such as getting used to sleeping different hours, but also adaptations in officers' social and personal lives. Shift work also obviously involves change, which in itself can be stressful.

Change In law enforcement work, change is constant—a change of shift, assignment to a new manager, change of patrol partner, placing computers in the squad cars—many types of changes affect officers. Technological advances have introduced a variety of equipment. Laws and court decisions are constantly in dispute and changing. When change occurs in administration or operations, managers tend to be more involved with the organizational aspects of the change than with human relations. The organization changes, but the organization is people. It is how people react to change that is important.

The first reaction to change is usually reluctance to accept it or fear it will not work. Management must explain changes and provide training so personnel can make a successful transition. Failure to explain change will bring resistance. Managers should explain not only that a change will be made but also that input from employees is desired and that there will be a follow-up and assessment. Many other aspects of the organization have also been identified as causing stress for officers.

Administrative and Organizational Stressors

Fox (p.9) contends: "The most common and debilitating source of stress in law enforcement comes from within the agency itself." Research has suggested the most significant stressor on law enforcement officers is administrative stress, for although line-of-duty deaths and other critical incidents do happen, they are relatively rare, whereas administrative and organizational forces are omnipresent and pervade every aspect of the job (Conroy).

 A major source of employee stress may be upper-level management.

Many management practices and organizational factors can cause stress specific to law enforcement. Stress frequently arises from having to operate from a set of policies and procedures drawn up by individuals who do not have to carry them out. Seldom is the on-line officer's opinion on operational policies and procedures sought, even though it is the individual officer who must carry out these policies and procedures. Research by Morash et al. (2006, pp.35-36) found that a lack of control over work activities stood out as an important predictor of stress: "The second strongest predictor of stress was feeling a lack of influence on how police work is accomplished. Officers who felt stressed said they could not influence the way policing was done and could not influence department policies and procedures."

Other common criticisms of the work environment are internal politics, favoritism and interpersonal treatment, and internal surveys reveal that working in a paramilitary structure depersonalizes and marginalizes people from top to bottom: "Decision-making structures that deprive them of input embitter officers and breed cynicism. They resent supervisors who treat them as numbers, who have no consideration for their personal or family lives, who play favorites in terms of choice assignments, shifts and recognition. They doubt whether or not they will be backed up by their superiors in times of trouble" (Fox, p.9).

Lack of support from administration when a questionable action is taken, the unavailability of needed resources and the poor condition of equipment also cause stress for officers. Other stressors include excessive paperwork, adverse work schedules, unfair discipline, lack of promotional opportunities and the autocratic quasi-paramilitaristic model. Scott (2004, p.237) studied stress among rural and small town patrol officers and found that the strongest predictor of stress stemmed from a change in the department's top management positions.

A phenomenological study of law enforcement officers and the stresses they encounter has identified 12 major sources of administrative stress:

1. Feeling of inadequate support—hampered by the court system, public misunderstanding and lack of administrative support.
2. Unfair or unequal treatment—in shift assignments, time off, promotions.
3. Decisions overruled—higher authorities, especially sergeants, overrule a decision made by a patrol officer on the street, often in regard to an arrest.
4. Civil suits—often the policy is a "negotiated settlement," deciding it is more cost effective to settle, leaving the impression the officer was in the wrong.
5. Mixed messages—officers are expected to fight crime (be reactive) and at the same time engage in community policing efforts (be proactive).
6. Department policy versus discretion—a two-inch thick rule book lays out all the policies and procedures, but officers are expected to use discretion. A violation of any policy is grounds for disciplinary action. However, if following policy results in a negative circumstance that could or should have been avoided had the officer used discretion, the officer is again in trouble.
7. The administration as an adversary—this is worse than an administration being viewed as nonsupportive. Patrol officers are most often likely to feel this way, with middle management caught in the middle. It is also a common complaint of officers who represent the department for the union.
8. Hiring standards lowered—as the pool of candidates decreases, some departments have, indeed, lowered their standards. Affirmative action hiring also causes problems when less-qualified individuals are hired because they are a member of a minority group.
9. Differing goals—officers may see themselves trying to alleviate victims' pain, but see administrators as trying to sway politicians. Officers see themselves as trying to save lives and administrators as trying to save dollars.
10. Miscommunication—administration may communicate one thing to officers and another thing to the public. The court notification process also causes friction, with officers being told to show up on a certain day, but not at a certain time, often during their time off.
11. Punitive transfers—often officers who are very satisfied in their present positions are transferred because of some minor infraction or because they do not get along with their supervisor.
12. Lack of input—the administration often makes decisions without consulting those who are expected to carry them out—in most instances the patrol officer (Conroy and Hess, 1992, pp.176–185).

Although the research was conducted over a decade ago, these administrative sources of stress still exist in many departments throughout the country (Conroy). External stressors are also persistent and pervasive in law enforcement.

External Stressors

The criminal justice system and society at large also can induce stress in police officers. Officers are often faced with the court's scheduling of police officers for appearances, prosecutors decisions not to prosecute a case, defendants "getting off" because of a loophole in the law, the court's perceived leniency, the early release of offenders on bail or parole, corrections' failures to rehabilitate criminals re-sulting in "revolving door" justice, the exclusion of police officers when plea bar-gaining is used and the perceived lack of appreciation for the role of law enforce-ment. One police officer put it this way: "I think the crowning blow was to see that it's almost futile to go out there and do anything about it. You keep putting 'em away, and they keep letting 'em out. And then new people come along, and it just doesn't stop, and it will never stop."

Not only do the failures of the criminal justice system cause stress for police, these failures are often perceived as partially the fault of law enforcement officers. In addition, law enforcement officers are seen as authority figures. People deal with them differently and treat them differently. They often are isolated. Wearing a badge, uniform and gun makes a law officer separate from society. An additional stressor is that many citizens have unrealistic expectations of what law enforcement officers can do, based on a distorted view of police work presented by the media.

The *media* display this distorted view repeatedly. Approximately one third of regular television programming deals with some aspect of the criminal justice sys-tem. If a TV cop can solve three major crimes in an hour, why can't the local po-lice at least keep prostitutes off the street, or find the person who vandalized the school? Unrealistic expectations can carry over into family life and other personal pursuits.Moore (2004, p.146) observes: "Between mandatory training, court, call duty and shifts that ricochet an officer from his or her usual eight or 10 hours into overtime, police often find themselves trapped in a profession that doesn't allow room for family and recreational pursuits. Duty-related tasks occupy so much of their time, their home lives suffer. They miss anniversaries, their kids' concerts and school open houses. This dearth of time for personal development can translate into divorce, suicide, alcoholism or burn-out."

Even when officers' schedules allow them to attend important family events, they may not be able to transition as easily into "after-hours" activities as people who work in other professions. Lindsey and Kelly (2004, p.3) note: "Each day of-ficers gird themselves for the dangers and rigors of the job. When they go off duty, the process of 'coming down' begins to take effect on the body and mind. Having been hypervigilant for the duration of the shift, the body demands downtime to preserve itself. However, family life and the day-to-day activities of living require the body to continue pushing. Officers constantly face the inability to come down from a hypervigilant state, causing their bodies to deteriorate further and faster."

In addition, the aftermath of a stressful incident can greatly affect an officer's family and leave damaging emotional scars, a phenomenon identified as **after-burn.** Risk factors that make a police family vulnerable to stress include limited knowledge of police work among family members, a conflict between job and family priorities and isolation felt by the officer and spouse. Protective factors that may help police families better handle the stress of police work include an aware-ness of job-related stress factors, a negotiated family structure with clear roles and responsibilities, conflict resolution skills and a social support system.

afterburn • a stressful incident that greatly affects an officer's family and leaves damaging emotional scars.

The Interplay of Stressors

Garcia et al. (p.43) studied stressors during a period of decreasing crime and found similar stressors to those already discussed: "The top ranked stressor—concern for a fellow officer being injured or killed—is consistent with similar findings in the literature and reinforces the frequent perceived potential for crisis situations, even

Table 12.4 Police Officer Stressors Ranked by Mean Scores

	Organizational	Job-related	External	SD
Fellow officers being injured or killed		54.42		31.04
Public criticism of police			53.62	29.85
Family demands			51.36	31.09
Making important on-the-spot decisions		49.39		26.99
Fellow officers not doing their job		48.57		30.52
Responding to a felony in progress		43.33		29.30
Incompatible partner		41.13		35.10
Job conflict with rules (i.e., by the book vs. the situation		40.70		29.41
Exposure to death		37.88		27.29
Sustaining a serious physical injury on the job	37.73		29.55	
Threat of lawsuit			37.00	34.42
Situations requiring use of force		36.53		30.69
Assignment of increased responsibility	35.98			26.91
Transfer to another assignment area	35.01			30.85
Department/unit recognition	33.62			26.87
Promotion competition	33.30			33.48
Racial conflicts			33.20	30.21
Subject of internal affairs investigation	28.79			33.54
Shift work		27.38		32.99
Undercover work		22.45		26.26
Personal thoughts of suicide*			9.56	21.35
Scales total/means			36.81	18.04
		37.93		18.25
	33.10			20.35
Total index 35.43				16.80

*Although not significant among the stressors, 20% of respondents (i.e., 210 officers) indicated having some thoughts of suicide during the previous 12 months, and 7% (i.e., 73 officers) specified that it had caused them moderate or high levels of stress.

Source: National Law Enforcement Officers Memorial Fund, Washington, DC.

during a period of low crime. This aspect continues to differentiate police work from most other occupations." They (pp.45–46) also found:

- Public criticism is indicative of the contemporary stressors experienced by police officers.
- Family demands for personal time and involvement continue to be a significant stressor for police officers.
- Organizational stressors are less of a factor for officers in the early (less than 5 years) and later (more than 20 years) stages of their career. Officers with more than 20 years of experience are also significantly less susceptible to job-related and overall stressors than those with fewer years on the job.
- Working the late shift results in more job-related stress than other shifts.

Garcia et al. surveyed over 1,000 police officers about the amount of stress caused by organization, job-related and external sources on a scale of 1 to 100 (high level). Table 12.4 summarizes the mean (average) amount of stress from most to least. Interestingly, no organizational factors ranked among the top 10 stressors. It is also of interest that only three sources of stress had a mean of more than 50. The researchers conclude that their results indicate generally moderate levels of stress.

Law Enforcement Personnel with Additional Stressors

Some officers are placed in high-stress assignments such as narcotics, undercover work and SWAT units. Stress levels vary tremendously depending on the assignment, the area and the shift.

Additional stress is often experienced by women officers, minority officers, investigators, officers in small towns and rural areas, and managers.

Women Officers

In addition to the stress experienced because of the job they have selected, female officers have some stressors not faced by their male counterparts, for example, male chauvinism, lack of respect and support, higher rate of turnover, citizen negativism and sexual harassment. Additional stress for females is caused by lack of acceptance by predominantly white, male forces with subsequent denial of information, alliances and protection as well as a lack of role models and mentors.

In 2000 women represented 13 percent of all sworn officers, an increase of 4.9 percent from 1990. In addition, women currently hold only 7.3 percent of top command assignments (Garcia, 2003, p.336). Garcia reports what so many researchers have found: "No matter what behaviors women display or what tasks women police have accomplished, they are damned if they do and damned if they don't [act feminine]."

Recruiting and Retaining Women: A Self-Assessment Guide for Law Enforcement notes: "The military model, which places value on strict, unquestioning adherence to rules, is not only contrary to the skills desired in community policing officers, it is a culture foreign to most female recruits." And when hazing, shunning and humiliation are considered acceptable techniques to tear recruits down before building them up, "it is very easy for sexual harassment to join that acceptable list."

Another stressor on female officers, seemingly more so than for males, includes personal issues related to home life and the issue of who is expected to care for family members.

Minority Officers

Minority police officers may experience more stress than majority police officers because they are expected to be more tolerant of community problems within their minority population, yet are also expected to enforce the law impartially. They may also be expected to join a minority organization within the department, separating them from the majority of the force. And, like their female counterparts, minority officers face the additional stress of lack of acceptance by a predominately white force with subsequent denial of information, alliances and protection as well as a lack of role models and mentors. In addition, plainclothes minority officers are at greater risk of being mistaken for criminals by other officers in large departments, where officers in one precinct do not necessarily know officers in another precinct.

Research by Dowler (2005) found, for example, that African police officers are more likely to feel criticized and more likely to believe they are perceived as militant. However, they are also less likely to feel negative or depressed about the police job.

Rural and Small-Town Patrol Officers

Research by Scott found that, as in larger departments, stress stemming from the organization was among the most problematic for rural and small-town patrol officers, with internal departmental politics and the department's leadership leading the list of stressors. Stressors not commonly reported among larger departments but rating high in rural and small-town departments were lack of department resources, coming into conflict with a well-known community member, pulling over/arresting or citing a personal acquaintance (relatives and friends), public contacting them while off duty and time/distance for backup to arrive.

Oliver and Meier (2004, p.46) identify four stress factors unique to rural patrol: security, social factors, working conditions and inactivity. They note that because of geographical isolation and limited number of officers on duty, rural officers face more stress related to their personal safety and security. The second stressor, social factors, is the result of everyone they encounter on or off duty knowing they are police officers, a phenomenon called the "fishbowl effect." Stressful working conditions include low pay and inadequate equipment and training. The final stress factor is long hours of inactivity, more so than in a larger department.

An additional stress factor is that officers in small departments are essentially on-call 24/7. The stress that comes from never being able to get away from the job can be overwhelming (Conroy).

Investigators

Several stressors accompany the responsibilities of being a criminal investigator. They may have to investigate several cases at once, often within short timeframes, because suspects can be incarcerated for only a short time without sufficient evidence. Many investigators work long hours, often on their own time, which can lead to fatigue and eventually burnout. They commonly take their cases home with them, which can cause severe tension in their family life. Furthermore, for investigators working undercover, long hours away from family compound their stress, and deep immersion into the criminal world can lead to intense internal conflict (Conroy).

Investigators may also become frustrated with the court system and the perception of a revolving door criminal justice system. In addition, they may be under constant scrutiny of citizens who expect cases to be solved rapidly. Investigators may not get needed backup or may have less sophisticated equipment than the criminals they are investigating. Finally, they may question society's values as they deal with horrible, inhumane crimes.

Managers/Supervisors

When officers are promoted, they assume the added stress of being managers. Promotion often involves managing officers who formerly were peers. Sometimes these relationships are difficult because of close, even social friendships, or prior antagonistic relationships. Most officers, however, understand what is required of the law enforcement manager position. They know that managers have to discipline and correct.

The amount of stress managers face varies with the position, level and assigned duties. First-line supervisors often work in the field with the officers they supervise, performing the same duties, especially in smaller departments. Gove (2004, p.104) suggests that first-line supervisors need to learn to manage people rather than trying to handle situations. It is easiest to return to what is familiar and for the supervisor to handle situations, incidents and calls for service, but they need to have faith in their officers and help them develop their skills.

Because managers are responsible for not only themselves but for every officer they supervise or manage, this is stress producing. The higher the level of law enforcement manager, the more stress there is in developing programs, preparing budgets, making speeches, settling personnel grievances and complaints, resolving citizen complaints and many other duties. Top managers have more control over their work and less stress from lack of control. Middle and first-line managers generally have more stress because of lack of control over their work.

Effects of Stress—An Overview

It is difficult to assess the total effect of going from boredom to high stress, dealing with conflict and confrontation, coping with the criminal element, facing the adversity of courtroom tactics, dealing with the spin-off effects on family members, writing tedious reports, handling criticism by managers and many other everyday pressures of the job.

Stress demands a response, which may range from minimal to serious. Stress affects people in numerous ways: physical, emotional and psychological.

Physical

The average life expectancy in the United States is 74.4 years for men and 80.1 years for women (Lindsey and Kelly, 2004, p.3). However, a 40-year study found that police officers with 10 to 19 years of service had an average age of death of 66 years. Officers with 30 years on the job increased their mortality rate more than three times (Violanti, 2002). This research found a "significantly increased risk of digestive and hematopoietic cancers among police officers who have 10 to 19 years" on the job, agreeing with other studies theorizing the link between cancer and stress (p.3). This same employment period linked stress with such maladaptive behaviors as alcohol and tobacco use and with significantly higher risk of death from esophageal cancer as well as significantly elevated risk of cirrhosis of the liver, as discussed shortly.

Law enforcement managers need to recognize signs of stress in their subordinates and in themselves. Symptoms of stress appear differently in different people.

 Stress is related to heart problems, hypertension, cancer, ulcers, diabetes, chronic headaches, anxiety-related disorders, asthma, excessive eating, decreased sex drive, fatigue, dizziness, muscle aches and tics, backaches and frequent urinating.

Stress can cause these medical conditions, or the conditions can be prolonged, increased in severity or aggravated by stress. Living in our complex, fast-paced society results in many stress-related diseases. An estimated 85 percent of all illnesses are stress related.

Psychological

Psychological symptoms of stress include boredom, defensiveness, delusions, depression, apathy, emotional illness, hostility, loneliness, nervousness, paranoia, sudden mood changes and tension. One of the most debilitating psychological effects is posttraumatic stress disorder.

Posttraumatic Stress Disorder (PTSD) As they wage war on crime and violence, law enforcement personnel may have a problem similar to that experienced by military combat personnel. During World War I, soldiers were *shell-shocked*. In

World War II, they suffered from *combat fatigue* and *battle stress*. Psychologists gradually came to realize that civilians involved in major catastrophes such as earthquakes, fires and rapes experienced similar stress disorders. Traumatic events such as these (1) are likely to be sudden and unexpected, (2) threaten officers' lives, (3) often include loss (partner, physical ability or position) and (4) may abruptly change officers' values and self-confidence. An estimated one third of law enforcement officers in the United States suffer from PTSD (Goss, 2005, p.54). Symptoms included diminished responsiveness to their environment, apathy, disinterest, pessimism and diminished sex drive.

posttraumatic stress disorder (PTSD) • a psychological ailment following a major catastrophe such as a shooting or dealing with victims of a natural disaster. Symptoms include diminished responsiveness to the environment; disinterest; pessimism; and sleep disturbances, including recurrent nightmares.

 Law enforcement officers may experience **posttraumatic stress disorder (PTSD)**, a clinical name associated with a debilitating condition suffered by Vietnam War veterans.

The first phase after a traumatic incident, the initial impact phase, may last a few minutes or a few days. Attention is on the present, with the officer stunned or bewildered and having difficulty coping with normal situations.

This phase may be followed by the recoil phase of wanting to retell the experience and attempt to overcome it through this retelling. The need is for support from fellow officers. Personal reactions may be withdrawal, anxiety, hopelessness, insomnia and nightmares. Other reported symptoms commonly experienced are flashbacks, depression, sexual dysfunction, obsessive behavior (particularly with alcohol and drugs) and fear.

Those who can be of greatest assistance are fellow officers; immediate supervisors; unit commanders; peer counselors; chaplains; mental health professionals; the officer's family; and, in some cases, the media and citizens. Those who assist should be good listeners, show empathy and concern, offer reassurances and support and provide group grief sharing.

 Officers in larger law enforcement departments and those assigned to more difficult and violent tasks, such as murders, SWAT teams or narcotics teams, are the most likely candidates for PTSD.

Cross and Ashley (2004, p.24) contend: "Law enforcement officers face traumatic incidents daily. These events, typically unexpected and sudden, fall well beyond the bounds of normal experiences; hence, they can have profound physical, emotional and psychological impacts—even for the best trained, experienced and seasoned officers." Posttraumatic stress disorder is a concern when dealing with emergencies, but it can also result from other aspects of police work.

Clagett (2004, p.42), a police sniper, describes how, after being forced to kill a suicidal subject, he found himself "snared in a web of legal proceedings and personal guilt." For example, when he went to shave: "I try to look in the mirror. I realize I can't look myself in the eye. Nothing like this has ever happened to me before, and I don't like it" (p.46). He (p.49) says: "Let me sum up by saying that surviving as a police sniper involves two problems. Problem number one is properly making the shot so an innocent life is saved. Problem number two is surviving everything that comes after that shot. Please trust me when I tell you that problem number two is much tougher than problem number one."

Trying to hurry through or ignore altogether the emotional turmoil that follows a traumatic incident can have serious consequences, with some officers turning to alcohol and drugs to help dull the pain: "Certainly, not every officer deals with stress and trauma by abusing chemicals, and not every officer who chooses to abuse chemicals does so to numb the effects of trauma. However, overwhelming evidence suggests that the two factors often *are* linked, particularly in the high-stress environment of police work" (Cross and Ashley, pp.24–25).

In addition to the maladaptive response of substance abuse, some officers choose to forego what could be life-saving, or at least career-saving, counseling because they fear being diagnosed with mental illness (PTSD) and the impact such a diagnosis would have on subsequent job assignments, promotional opportunities or civil litigation (Conroy).

Behavioral

Behavioral symptoms of stress include accident-proneness, anger, argumentativeness, blaming others, drug and/or alcohol abuse, excessive violence, irritability, inability to concentrate, lack of control, neurotic behavior, nail biting, obsession with work, rage, rapid behavior changes, uncontrollable urges to cry and withdrawal. Most people, after reading about the common symptoms of stress just discussed, would probably comment, "I've had all these symptoms." It is only when the symptoms appear in excess or several appear simultaneously that problems arise.

On the Job

Stress reactions found among police officers include repression of emotion, displacement of anger, isolation and unspoken fears. In addition, police officers may behave inappropriately under stress, for example, becoming verbally or physically abusive, looking for any excuse to call in sick, arguing with other officers, placing themselves in danger or engaging in "choir practice" (heavy drinking with peers). They may argue with supervisors, criticize the actions of fellow officers and supervisors, lose interest in the job or sleep on duty. At its most extreme, stress may result in burnout.

Burnout When stress continues unremittingly for prolonged periods, it can result in the debilitating condition referred to as *burnout*. **Burnout** has occurred in a person who is "used up or consumed by a job," made listless through overwork and stress. A once-motivated, committed employee experiences physical and emotional exhaustion on the job brought about by unrelieved demands. The person experiences a persistent lack of energy or interest in his or her work. Officers who are burned out are at extremely high risk of being injured or killed on duty because they are usually not safety conscious. They are also at risk for depression or suicide.

burnout • occurs when someone is exhausted or made listless through overwork. It results from long-term, unmediated stress. Symptoms include lack of enthusiasm and interest; a drop in job performance; temper flare-ups; a loss of will, motivation or commitment.

 Symptoms of burnout include lack of enthusiasm and interest; decreased job performance; temper flare-ups; and a loss of will, motivation or commitment.

Those most likely to experience burnout are those who are initially most committed. You cannot burn out if you have never been on fire. To those in police work, the **blue flame** is the symbol of a law enforcement officer who wants to make a difference in the world. The enthusiasm shown by rookie officers as they recover their first occupied stolen vehicle or make their first collar is like a torch being lit. The key is knowing how to keep the flame burning throughout the many stresses of an entire law enforcement career.

blue flame • the symbol of a law enforcement officer who wants to make a difference in the world.

Burned out employees can often be helped by a change—something to motivate them. Sometimes changes in the job itself help—adding new dimensions to old tasks. Expert assistance is usually needed at this level, and counseling may be necessary.

 To avoid burnout, keep the work interesting, give recognition, provide R and R (rest and relaxation), avoid "other duties" and limit the assignment.

Other Possible Major Effects of Stress

 Police officers' stress may cause alcohol and substance abuse problems, higher rates of domestic abuse and divorce, depression and even suicide.

Alcoholism and Substance Abuse

As many as one in four officers have alcohol abuse problems (Fox, p.9). "We all know," says Miller (2005, p.21), "that alcohol is often part of the cop culture and that a good deal of brotherhood-of-the-badge-type bonding takes place at the local tavern." Moore (2005, p.210) suggests: "Traditionally, choir practice—or having a few drinks after shift's end—has been a rite of passage for rookie officers. Alcohol has always been a factor in this business."

A study by Violanti cited earlier found that for those who drank heavily, cirrhosis of the liver was elevated in officers with only nine years on the job. According to Cross and Ashley (pp.27–28), abuse of alcohol and other drugs has both overt and covert social and economic costs: "lost productivity and wages; increased family problems, including risks of domestic violence." They note that when public safety members are substance abusers, the problems multiply: "Employees can become unable to perform their sworn duties, administrators can find themselves increasingly overburdened trying to deal with a problem that can result in negative perceptions of their agencies, and the public can lose faith and trust in the system." They contend that officers who use alcohol and other drugs to deal with stress often cannot perform their duties adequately. They may become agitated, hypervigilant or aggressive. Or they may feel tired, overwhelmed and unable to concentrate. Family problems increase, and officers may become isolated. Accelerated substance use often results in progressive lateness and absenteeism: "Ultimately, the end result is a tremendous increase in the risk of suicidal ideation, which studies have linked strongly to alcohol and other drug use among law enforcement officers," as discussed shortly (Cross and Ashley, pp.27–28).

Management must ensure that the department does not downplay, rationalize or deny the seriousness of drug abuse or its existence. Supervisors should be alert to signs of substance abuse. Moore suggests the following red flags to watch for signifying alcohol abuse: officers whose physical appearances deteriorate, who are frequently out sick or injured, who are shunned by their peers, who have more than their share of automobile accidents or who are frequent targets of civilian complaints. Debt overload can also lead to alcohol abuse.

Officers who abuse drugs face another potential problem. Page (2005, p.180) explains that officers who begin as recreational users are at risk of becoming trapped in a "user driven cycle" of corrupt behavior. A major federal report on drug-related police corruption has found that on-duty officers engaged in "serious criminal activities, including unconstitutional searches and seizures, stealing drug money and/or drugs from drug dealers, selling stolen drugs, protecting drug operations, providing false testimony, and submitting false crime reports" (Page, p.180). As noted, abuse of alcohol and other drugs can also play a role in domestic violence and divorce.

Domestic Violence and Divorce

Griggs (2004, p.60), founding director of the National Police Family Violence Prevention Project, in an interview with *Law Enforcement News* (Gallo, 2004b, p.60), contends: "Domestic violence in police families has always been one of the original 'don't ask, don't tell' issues, alternately ignored, hidden or denied firmly protected by the blue wall of silence." Griggs reports that many retired law enforcement personnel have described police domestic violence as "just another off-shoot of a stressful job, as prevalent and as unfortunate as alcoholism or drug use." She (p.64) believes domestic violence is "endemic" to law enforcement, explaining: "When the responsibility of power, authority and upholding the law is combined with stress, fatigue, inappropriate coping mechanisms and possibly dysfunctional social responses, the results can be deadly" (Gallo, 2004b, pp.60–64).

Graves (2005, p.108) stresses: "No agency can afford the negative ramifications that come with a domestic abuse incident by one of their own. An insufficient or complete lack of a police increases risk of civil litigation stemming from unaddressed domestic violence issues involving agency personnel." He recommends that a well-written policy of zero tolerance for domestic violence will protect the department.

Another common effect the high-stress lifestyle of policing has on officers is divorce. The national divorce rate is 50 percent, but research shows police officers suffer a substantially higher divorce rate, with estimates ranging between 60 and 75 percent (Goldfarb, 2004). Some estimate that police officers divorce twice as often as the national average. Goldfarb also reports that police officers going through a divorce are five times more likely to commit suicide than an officer in a stable marriage. Officer suicide is discussed shortly.

Depression

Depression is a serious, life-threatening medical illness that can affect anyone. Unfortunately our society places a stigma on having depression or seeking help for it. As with PTSD, a diagnosis of depression may impact an officer's future. And since many officers are skeptical about the confidentiality of medical records, they resist seeking professional help (Conroy). Because depression is a medical illness, an imbalance of chemicals in the brain, medication can often be prescribed to treat it. But often people do not recognize the symptoms.

Symptoms of depression include significant changes in appetite and sleep patterns; irritability, anger, worry, agitation and anxiety; loss of energy and persistent lethargy; unexplained aches and pains; feelings of guilt, worthlessness and/or hopelessness; inability to concentrate; indecisiveness; inability to take pleasure in former interests; social withdrawal; pessimism or indifference; prolonged sadness or unexplained crying spells; excessive consumption of alcohol or use of chemical substances; recurring thoughts of death; or suicide.

The difficulty lies in getting people to recognize the symptoms and to seek treatment. "Bringing Depression into the Light" (2002, pp.2–3) explains:

> If you've ever had major depression, you will recognize its hallmarks. You feel
> constantly sad or burdened, you lose interest in all activities, even those you

used to enjoy. Work, school, relationships and other aspects of your life get derailed or put on hold indefinitely because you just don't have the energy for them. . . .

Trying to "snap out" of a severe depression is like trying to talk yourself out of a heart attack. . . .

Depression and alcohol abuse often go hand-in-hand. Occasionally, drinking excessively is a symptom of severe clinical depression. More often, depression results from excessive drinking. Prolonged alcohol abuse and alcoholism can lead to prolonged periods of depression. It becomes a vicious circle of suffering. . . .

Because depression involves a biochemical imbalance in the brain, medications that restore the balance can be an important tool in your recovery. More than 70 percent of people with depression improve with medication therapy. . . .

For some people with depression, talk therapy—alone or with medication—can help.

Depression must be treated, because it is one of the leading causes of suicide. In at least 90 percent of all suicides, untreated depression is believed to be the major factor.

Suicide

Researchers report the following about suicide by law enforcement officers:

- "Police kill themselves at twice the rate that they are killed in the line of duty" (Nislow, 2004a, p.1).
- "Suicide in law enforcement is three times greater than the national average" (Lindsey and Kelly, p.1).
- "More law enforcement officers are slain by their own hands than any other cause" (Hamilton, 2003a, p.18).
- "Why do police officers kill themselves with their sidearms? Because they can" (Hamilton, 2003b, p.24).

Researchers at the University of Buffalo found that police officers are eight times more likely to commit suicide than to be killed in a homicide (Fox, p.9). Alcohol, family problems, the breakup of relationships and stress all contribute to the high rate of police suicide, about 30 percent higher than what is found in the general population. Some authorities feel that police suicides are underreported because fellow officers are usually the first on the scene and may cover up the suicide to save the family further pain or embarrassment or for insurance purposes.

The following factors contribute to officer suicide: alcohol abuse, posttraumatic stress disorder, failing relationships, suspension from the force, internal investigations into corruption or other malfeasance, career stagnation and clinical depression (Griffith, 2003, p.6; Nislow, 2004a, p.1). According to Hamilton (2003c, p.25): "One of the main reasons cops murder themselves is because they are under investigation. While many see the suicide as an admission of guilt, experts say it's more likely caused by an officer's fear of losing his or her badge, his or her identity as a cop." Officer suicide may also be rooted in control issues: "Sometimes it is the only thing the officer has control over, and we know how important control is to cops" (Conroy).

Among the warning signs of suicide are a high number of off-duty accidents, an increase in citizen complaints, a change in personality, the dispersing of gifts and writing a will. Pinzzotto et al. (2005, p.14) list the following potential indicators of suicide:

- Verbalized intentions of self-destruction
- Longings or interest in death
- Prior attempted suicides
- Prior medical or psychiatric care
- Death of a spouse, significant other or friend
- Substantial loss of funds or outstanding and pressing debts
- Divorce
- Pending or actual loss of a job, including retirement
- Imminent arrest of the individual or a close friend/associate
- Health problems

The victims of suicide are not the people who take their lives but the people left behind: "They're the ones who are left with the anger, and the guilt, and the sense of abandonment. Suicide survivors are so damaged by the deaths of their loved one that they often take their own lives" (Griffith, p.6).

Having looked at the major sources of stress and possible reactions to it, consider what managers can do for themselves and what they can do for their subordinates and department.

Coping with Stress

No one escapes stress. How people *deal with* it determines whether they cope and develop or deteriorate. Stress in its more severe stages can be totally devastating. The severity of stress must be taken into account when considering how best to reduce its effects to a tolerable, manageable level.

Covey (2003, p.133), author of *The 7 Habits of Highly Effective People*, states: "Police officers must learn to become the gatekeepers of their own well-being. The job can lead to early deaths, high rates of divorce and alcohol abuse, a predisposition to disease and depression, and in extreme cases, even suicide. *Sharpening the saw* is the habit that increases our capacity to survive the career and retire to live a healthy, balanced life. It is the habit that allows us to live all the other habits of effective people."

Take definite steps to reduce stress. Most people need to work to earn a living but may need to change their attitudes about their work or about the people they work with. The symptoms of stress are often obvious, but its cause is more difficult to determine and even more difficult to change. Unfortunately, we tend to treat the symptoms rather than reduce the causes of stress.

Reducing Stress Levels

Grossi (2005, p.38) recommends: "A healthy diet, giving up the cigarettes and booze, making regular exercise a part of your life style, even just power-walking every couple of days is going to help."

 Stress levels can be reduced through physical exercise, relaxation techniques, good nutrition, taking time for oneself, making friends, learning to say no, staying within the law, changing one's mental attitude, keeping things in perspective and seeking help when it is needed.

Physical exercise improves the body's stamina to deal with stress and provides time away from work temporarily, which is also healthy.

Relaxation techniques are often helpful. Most consist of removing all distractions, closing your eyes, imagining yourself in a peaceful setting and breathing slowly and deeply for 10 to 20 minutes. Courses on relaxation are often offered through community health programs. Some people meditate as a relaxation technique.

Good nutrition also helps reduce stress. A diet that improves general health will help reduce stress. Information on diets is available from physicians, community health programs or libraries. Reducing cholesterol levels requires one type of diet, whereas losing weight or dealing with a specific physical condition may require another type of diet.

Take time for yourself. Take vacations. Try to keep your mind off job-related matters when not on duty. Develop hobbies and outside interests; volunteer. Some officers write poetry to relieve stress. Take walks, listen to music or go window-shopping. You will accomplish more at work if you are mentally and physically recharged by some time off.

Make friends both within and outside the department. Get active in a club or civic group. Problems and worries become smaller if you have others to share them with.

Learn to say no. Do not be taken advantage of. A sweatshirt bears the message: "Stress—what happens when your gut says 'no' and your mouth says 'Of course, I'd be glad to.'" Do not volunteer for more than you can reasonably carry.

Stay within the law, no matter what temptations arise. Yes, law enforcement officers can and do perform illegal acts, and this adds to job tension. Consider what you do not only from a legal but also from an ethical standpoint. Doing "right" things reduces stress; doing "wrong" things increases stress. There is no "right" way to do a "wrong" thing.

A *change in mental attitude* can provide release from stress. As the adage says, "Accept what you cannot change." The power of the mind is strong. Positive attitudes provide a new outlook on life and your cause of stress. Negative attitudes can be self-defeating.

Keep things in perspective. If you think something is threatening, it is almost as dangerous as if it were. Do not blow things out of proportion. Be realistic. Your mistakes almost never last in others' minds as long as they do in your own.

Seek help if you need it. Law enforcement officers deal with life-threatening situations as part of their job. If you need help coping with the job's dangers, seek counseling. Talk about the problem with other officers and see how they deal with it. It is as real to them as to you. Mental stress is often more difficult to deal with than physical stress. Officers should be encouraged to seek confidential counseling even without a diagnosis of a mental illness (Conroy).

Other ways to reduce stress include getting plenty of sleep, setting personal goals, making a "to-do" list and taking things one at a time, smiling and laughing to lighten your day, saying positive things to yourself, taking time to recharge by taking mini timeouts, volunteering or helping others. Finally, *do NOT smoke,* and if you drink, *drink in moderation. AVOID drugs* to control stress unless recommended by a qualified physician.

 Alcohol, drugs and smoking increase stress over time and can also seriously affect physical health.

Especially important is assuming responsibility for your own well-being. Stressful situations are not necessarily permanent. Situations change, as do levels of stress. You have a role to play in determining what happens. Develop a personal strategy for dealing with your stress. Reexamine your personal goals. Maybe you have set them too low or too high or need to change them completely. If necessary, change your lifestyle. Get plenty of rest and eat right. And don't take yourself too seriously. Confront situations, deal with them and put the unknown behind you. You will be better able to get on with the important things.

How the Organization Can Reduce Stress

The law enforcement administration can do much to reduce employee stress. Managers must pay attention not only to the victims of stress but also to the conditions that created it. In law enforcement the source may be an incident, a citizen, a manager, a fellow officer or other sources. Having identified the source of the stress, study all methods of relieving stress and determine what might work best.

Implementing a stress management and prevention program may require increased use of personnel and resources, but such a program can lead to long-term cost savings, high productivity and morale and enhanced community–police relations: "The inescapable conclusion of many studies is that stress affects the bottom line" (Torres et al., p.114). Therefore, concern for an officers' ability to manage stress should be a consideration in the selection process.

Testing and Selection

Administrators can continue the strong testing already in use to select candidates most likely to cope well with stress by being physically fit, mentally stable and emotionally well balanced. Law enforcement employees who start healthy have a good foundation for remaining healthy during their careers. Administrators need to demand tests designed specifically for the needs of law enforcement personnel selection.

Law enforcement budgets provide training, weapons and vehicles, and they should provide funds for keeping fit. As in the medical profession, those in law enforcement must sometimes cope with emergency situations that demand immediate yet highly analytical responses. In both professions life may depend on the actions taken. Psychological testing and interviews can help screen out mentally and emotionally weak or unstable applicants. Doing so is not only good for the department but is also best for the candidates, even though they may not believe so at the time. The department benefits by less sick leave and absenteeism, greater productivity, better employee relationships, fewer resignations, fewer new hirings (with the associated costs) and more work hours available due to less new officer training time. Potential employees are saved from attempting a career likely to fail, loss of time spent in the wrong vocation or possible public humiliation in a critical situation.

Managers can also learn to recognize the warning signs of individuals under stress both during the selection process and after employees are hired. The Dallas Police Department has developed a list of 15 common warning signs for stress (see Table 12.5).

Training

Blum and Polisar (2004, p.49) urge that programs to train field training officers and supervisors in tactical decision making under stress can help eliminate many

Table 12.5 The 15 Most Prevalent Stress Warning Signs

Warning Signs	Examples
1. Sudden changes in behavior usually directly opposite to usual behavior	From cheerful and optimistic to gloomy and pessimistic
2. More gradual change in behavior but in a way that points to deterioration of the individual	Gradually becoming slow and lethargic, possibly with increasing depression and sullen behavior
3. Erratic work habits	Coming to work late, leaving early, abusing compensatory time
4. Increased sick time due to minor problems	Headaches, colds, stomach aches, etc.
5. Inability to maintain a train of thought	Rambling conversation, difficulty in sticking to a specific subject
6. Excessive worrying	Worrying about one thing to the exclusion of any others
7. Grandiose behavior	Preoccupation with religion, politics, etc.
8. Excessive use of alcohol and/or drugs	Obvious hangover, disinterest in appearance, talk about drinking prowess
9. Fatigue	Lethargy, sleeping on job
10. Peer complaints	Others refuse to work with the officer
11. Excessive complaints (negative citizen contact)	Caustic and abusive in relating to citizens
12. Consistency in complaint pattern	Picks on specific groups of people (youth, blacks, etc.)
13. Sexual promiscuity	Going after everything all of the time—on or off duty
14. Excessive accidents and/or injuries	Not being attentive to driving, handling prisoners, etc.
15. Manipulation of fellow officers and citizens	Using others to achieve ends without caring for their welfare

Source: Reprinted with permission of the Psychological Services Unit, Dallas Police Department.

of the errors made in the field by teaching all personnel to control their judgment and decision making under crisis conditions. They recommend:

- An ongoing and permanent system to train all agency personnel in stress-exposure management to help prevent stress reactions and posttraumatic stress disorder in police officers and executives.
- That to ensure that every employee has the necessary skills to manage crisis incidents and extraordinary events, supervisors and trainers should emphasize adaptive expertise, which allows for the immediate recognition that a change in tactics is required by changes in the conditions encountered and the alteration of tactics in real time.
- That ongoing training should teach officers and others to adapt to the unexpected. Officers will then be experts in adapting to both routine and crisis encounters.

Blum and Polisar recommend a system of training and practice that makes police personnel experts and well-conditioned in management stress-exposure incidents to substantially decrease the frequency and severity of errors in tactical responses and substantially lower physical or emotional injuries often suffered from these conditions. The agency's liability costs will also be substantially lowered when law enforcement personnel are experts in managing stress exposure, without any degradation in their performance or health.

Stress-Exposure Management Training (SEMT) Blum and Polisar (p.52) explain the three overriding principles on which SEMT is founded:

1. Police officers must develop a working knowledge of, and familiarity with, the reactions of their brains and bodies under stress-exposure conditions. They need to be shown—through the video-recorded reactions they demonstrate

in response to, for instance, ambush conditions—how their performance is affected by precisely the same conditions that they would encounter in the field.

2. Officers must be shown how to countermand the negative effects of stress. They must be taught to control and mediate their reactions to stressful events in real time.

3. All officers must build a great deal of self-confidence in their performance in order to succeed in police work. . . . The increase in self-confidence and skill officers feel as they see themselves control conditions in which they initially were helpless will be of great benefit.

They conclude: "The individual who is expert, practiced and conditioned to peak performance in stress-exposure management and work performance under adverse conditions, will respond properly to many more difficult or problematic tasks than one who lacks such expertise." They stress such training must be ongoing, because, like physical fitness, stress-exposure management techniques are highly perishable skills.

Ongoing Psychological Support

Periodic psychological fitness-for-duty evaluations are also important. Psychological reviews should be available for employees who have developed mental or emotional problems after employment. They should also have psychological assistance available after a killing or other severely traumatic event while on duty.

Some agencies have full-time police psychologists. Others have regular access to confidential psychological services. Many agencies are now using self-help groups for police plagued with problems such as alcoholism and PTSD. In addition some areas have treatment centers for law enforcement personnel with job-related stress disorders and other types of psychological problems. Some agencies use a psychologist jointly with the county or state. Smaller departments may obtain the assistance of a retired psychologist in the community as a volunteer or on a small retainer.

Officers may resist psychiatric help because they view it as a sign of weakness. They may be reluctant to admit they have stress-related problems for fear of losing their co-workers' respect or lessening their chances for promotion. For these reasons, ensuring privileged communication is essential in working with officers after a trauma.

Programs to Prevent/Reduce Stress

The business world has implemented stress-reduction programs such as athletic club memberships, physical activities, flex time, free time and company gripe sessions. Some of these programs might be options for law enforcement organizations. Other programs include peer support groups, critical incident stress debriefing, organizational consultant programs and chaplain programs.

Peer Support Groups

 Peer support groups are a particularly effective type of stress-reduction program.

Police departments of all sizes are implementing peer support programs to help officers deal with stress and emotional difficulties. A peer support group was started in New York by Detective Richard Pastorella. In 1982 Pastorella was left blind, half deaf and missing a hand from a failed attempt to disarm a terrorist bomb. As he lay recuperating in his hospital bed, alone, depressed, feeling utterly worthless, he decided other officers in similar circumstances should not have to suffer alone as he was. Three months after his discharge from the hospital he started the Police Self-Support Group. The group's membership included officers wounded by criminal violence, injured in traffic or other accidents, or traumatized by seeing a fellow officer go down. Almost all suffered from PTSD.

No amount of police machismo can deflect the cold, hard reality of PTSD. Like a relentlessly corrosive force if left unattended, PTSD can gnaw away at one's psychological bridges until they collapse. A similar type of program aimed at alleviating stress, particularly PTSD, is critical incident stress debriefing.

In 1998 Congress created the Public Safety Officers' Educational Assistance (PSOEA) Program, which also makes benefits available to spouses and children of public safety officers killed or permanently and totally disabled in the line of duty. Another resource is Concerns of Police Survivors (COPS), Inc., a national support group founded in 1984 for spouses and children of officers killed in the line of duty. In addition to providing support groups, COPS sends approximately eight mailings a year to its members. Regular mailings are also sent to the 4,000 agencies in its database.

Peer support and support groups are helpful in many ways. Veteran members may advise new members on available financial benefits and can shepherd them through the complex paperwork and procedures. They can make referrals for local services for everything from a funeral home to a counselor. Support groups may hold regular meetings during which problems and issues can be discussed.

© Michael Newman/PhotoEdit

Police departments nationwide have implemented peer support groups to help officers deal with problems. Officers are more willing to confide in their colleagues because they share the same set of stresses.

Critical Incident Stress Debriefing

Critical incident stress debriefing (CISD) is another effective way to prevent or reduce stress. In CISD, officers who experience a critical incident such as a mass disaster, a crash with multiple deaths or a particularly grizzly murder are brought together as a group for a psychological debriefing soon after the event. A trained mental health professional leads the group members as they discuss their emotions and reactions. This allows officers to vent and to realize they are not going crazy but are responding normally to a very abnormal situation.

A CISD should take place within 24 to 72 hours after a critical incident. Earlier is usually too soon for full emotional impact to have occurred. If only one officer is involved in the critical incident, he should be joined in the CISD by volunteers from the department who have experienced a similar incident or have been trained in PTSD.

To overcome officers' reluctance to participate in a mental health program, attendance at a CISD should be mandatory. A CISD should not become an operational critique. The groups should be small and everything said kept confidential.

 Law enforcement departments should include an **employee assistance program (EAP)** or provide referrals to outside agencies for psychological and counseling services and to assist officers with stress, marital or chemical dependency problems.

Help for those at risk of suicide within the department includes counseling units, peer counseling groups and police chaplains. Outside the department help might be sought from physicians; priests, ministers, rabbis, etc.; attorneys; and family.

Chaplain Corps

When troubled or stressed, many people turn to their faith for guidance and solace. Some departments make chaplains available to officers who need a place to turn in times of stress. However, these chaplains must be trained in police work and must know the difference between spiritual guidance and religion (Conroy).

Other Stress Management Programs

 Health programs and stress management seminars are another means to help law enforcement officers prevent destructive stress or at least reduce it.

Health programs include medical and psychological services and fitness programs. Law enforcement administration can also provide in-service health and fitness training and weight control classes.

Law enforcement management should provide an opportunity for employees to attend stress management seminars. All personnel, including dispatchers, should attend. A distinct benefit from attending such seminars is a better understanding of the nature of stress and ways to prevent, cope with or reduce its effects. The FBI has all new agents complete a Stress Management in Law Enforcement (SMILE) course to help them better understand the stress they may encounter on the job. Through such exposure they become more aware of the emotional and psychological dangers of the job, beyond the physical ones most expect to find in law enforcement.

Individuals who can successfully cope with stress have what psychology has termed **psychological hardiness.** Such individuals believe they can influence and control their lives and accept change as normal and positive.

critical incident stress debriefing (CISD) • officers who experience a critical incident such as a mass disaster or crash with multiple deaths are brought together as a group for a psychological debriefing soon after the event.

employee assistance program (EAP) • may be internally staffed or use outside referrals to offer help with stress, marital or chemical-dependency problems.

psychological hardiness • the ability to successfully cope with stress.

Programs for the Family

An ingredient missing from many employee assistance programs is the orientation and preparation of family and friends for new officers' transition into the police culture (Torres et al., p.110). By providing such knowledge and insight, departments can hope to help families and friends of new officers come to (1) understand the potential pitfalls of policing, (2) acquire insight into the potential attitudinal and behavioral changes in the new officer, (3) be alert to personality and behavioral changes that may require action, and (4) be familiar with resources available for intervention before the situation deteriorates too far and family relationships are irreparably damaged.

The orientation might include the swearing in ceremony and reception for new officers, an orientation packet with material on stress and how it can be most successfully dealt with, a tour of the department and a ride-along. Such an orientation program can demonstrate that the department cares about the new police families while introducing them not only to police work and the potential pitfalls of the job but also to the rewards of a law enforcement career (Torres et al., p.112).

The Role of the Manager/Supervisor

In addition to promoting the programs just described, law enforcement managers have another important role in minimizing the effects of stress in themselves and their subordinates. First-line supervisors are in daily contact with shift officers; they need to work with them to reduce stress and have concern for their problems.

Establishing rapport with all officers is essential to reducing stress. Law enforcement managers can provide both positive reinforcement and constructive criticism if there is a foundation of respect and communication. They should keep in close touch with their subordinates and recognize the symptoms of stress. If an officer shows such symptoms, the manager should be ready to assist and reduce to whatever level possible the degree of stress. Sometimes just having someone to talk to is the most helpful. If counseling or psychological assistance is needed, it should be provided or information furnished regarding local sources of assistance.

Managers must also "walk the talk," keeping themselves physically and mentally fit as role models. Controlling stress may seem overwhelming, but the good news is that you can do a lot to minimize the stress in your life and in the lives of your officers. You are in charge.

 SUMMARY

Stress can be helpful (eustress) or harmful (distress), depending on its intensity and frequency as well as how it is mediated. Stress often arises from change and uncertainty, lack of control and pressure. Four categories of law enforcement stress are internal, individual stressors; stressors inherent to the police job; administrative and organizational stressors; and external stressors from the criminal justice system, the citizens it serves, the media and the family. A major source of employee stress may be upper-level management. Additional stress is also often experienced by women officers, minority officers, investigators, rural and small-town patrol officers and managers.

Stress affects people in numerous ways: mental, physical, emotional and psychological. Stress is related to heart problems, hypertension, cancer, ulcers, diabetes, chronic headaches, depression, anxiety-related disorders, asthma, excessive eating from nervous tension, decreased sex drive, fatigue, dizziness, muscle aches and tics, backaches and frequent urinating. An estimated 85 percent of all illnesses are stress related.

Symptoms of burnout include lack of enthusiasm and interest; decreased job performance; temper flare-ups; and a loss of will, motivation or commitment. To avoid burnout, keep the work interesting, give recognition, provide R and R (rest and relaxation), avoid "other duties" and limit the assignment.

Law enforcement officers may experience posttraumatic stress disorder (PTSD), a clinical term associated with a debilitating condition suffered by Vietnam War veterans. Officers in larger departments and those assigned to the more difficult and violent tasks, such as murders, SWAT teams or narcotics teams, appear to be the most likely candidates for PTSD.

Stress levels can be reduced through physical exercise, relaxation techniques, good nutrition, taking time for oneself, making friends, learning to say no, staying within the law, changing one's mental attitude, keeping things in perspective and seeking help when needed. Alcohol, drugs and smoking increase stress over time and also can seriously affect physical health.

Support groups are one particularly effective type of stress-reduction program. Critical incident stress debriefing (CISD) is another effective way to prevent or reduce stress. Law enforcement departments should include employee assistance programs (EAP) or provide referrals to outside agencies for psychological and counseling services and assistance for officers with stress, marital or chemical dependency problems. Health programs and stress management seminars are other means to help officers prevent or reduce destructive stress.

 CHALLENGE TWELVE

Lieutenant Smith is meeting with Detective Smug to discuss several complaints concerning Smug's rude behavior toward citizens and other detectives. Smug has been with the department for 15 years and a detective for 10 years. He has a good service record and is generally liked by his peers. He has no history of behavior problems. During the past several months, he has offended citizens with his obstinate attitude and curt remarks. A fellow detective has privately told Lieutenant Smith that Smug is quick to anger and often condescending. Smug's behavior seems out of character for him.

Prior to the meeting, Lieutenant Smith learned that Detective Smug's wife left him six months ago for an officer on a neighboring department. Smug has not shared this with other officers, but the rumors spread quickly. Smug was also recently passed over for detective sergeant. A younger female detective with less experience was promoted.

Lieutenant Smith begins the meeting by telling Detective Smug about the series of complaints. He asks Smug if he is aware of the behavior and what may be causing it. Detective Smug is defensive and denies being rude to anyone. He says if there is a problem, it's the new chief and all the changes he's throwing at people. Smug says he's heard rumors that the detectives are going to rotate shifts every month.

Lieutenant Smith observes that Detective Smug seems withdrawn and tired. He's usually a snappy dresser, but now he's a bit disheveled. His attendance record shows an increased use of sick time.

1. As a skilled manager, Lieutenant Smith should be cognizant of potential signs of stress. What indicators are apparent in Detective Smug?

2. Identify three obvious sources of stress in Detective Smug's life.

3. If Lieutenant Smith suspects that stress is the root cause of Detective Smug's problem behavior, should he excuse it?

4. How can Lieutenant Smith and the department help Detective Smug deal with his stress?

5. Police officers face a variety of job-related stressors. Discuss one that is unique to Detective Smug's job.

DISCUSSION QUESTIONS

1. What do you consider the five most stressful aspects of work in law enforcement?

2. What are major stressors in your life right now?

3. How would you reduce your level of on-the-job stress?

4. Has your level of stress changed with job changes? Age changes? Changes due to a singular incident? Changes due to a series of similar incidents?

5. Have you taken any psychological tests? Which ones?

6. Are you a type A or a type B personality? What significance does that have to your work in law enforcement?

7. Have you ever participated in a support group? How effective was the experience?

8. Do you know anyone who has burned out? Can you explain why?

9. How does stress at the management level differ from that at the line level?

10. Does your local law enforcement agency have an EAP or other forms of employee support to reduce stress?

REFERENCES

Blum, Lawrence N. and Polisar, Joseph M. "Why Things Go Wrong in Police Work." *The Police Chief*, July 2004, pp.49–52.

"Bringing Depression into the Light." *Discover*, Spring 2002.

Campbell, R. K. "Don't Go with Them." *Police*, May 2005, pp.60–63.

Clagett, Russ. "After the Echo." *Police*, March 2004, pp.42–49.

Conroy, Dennis L. Personal correspondence with the author, review of the chapter, February 2006.

Conroy, Dennis L. and Hess, Kären M. *Officers at Risk: How to Identify and Cope with Stress.* Placerville, CA: Custom Publishing, 1992.

Covey, Stephen R. "Enhancing Public Trust." *The Police Chief*, April 2003, pp.128–133.

Cross, Chad L. and Ashley, Larry. "Police Trauma and Addiction: Coping with the Dangers of the Job." *FBI Law Enforcement Bulletin*, October 2004, pp.24–32.

Danielsson, Matt. "Lighten the Load." *Tactical Response*, May–June 2005, pp.18–19.

Dewey-Kollen, Janet. "Death Notification Training." *Law and Order*, May 2005, pp.12–14.

Dowler, Kenneth. "Job Satisfaction, Burnout, and Perception of Unfair Treatment: The Relationship between Race and Police Work." *Police Quarterly*, December 2005, pp.476–489.

Floyd, Craig W. "Police Week 2005." *The Police Chief*, May 2005, p.21.

Fox, Robert A. "The Blue Plague of American Policing." *Law Enforcement News*, May 15/31, 2003, p.9.

Fyfe, James J. "The Split-Second Syndrome and Other Determinants of Police Violence." In *Violent Transactions*, edited by Anne Campbell and John Gibbs. New York: Basic Blackwell, 1986.

Gallo, Gina. "Decedent as Perpetrator, Killer as Victim." *Law Enforcement News*, January 2004a, pp.13–14.

Gallo, Gina. "The National Police Family Violence Prevention Project Helps Departments Address Domestic Abuse in Police Families." *Law Enforcement Technology*, 2004b, pp.60–64.

Garcia, Luis; Nesbary, Dale K.; and Gu, Joann. "Perceptual Variations of Stressors among Police Officers during an Era of Decreasing Crime." *Journal of Contemporary Criminal Justice*, February 2004, pp.33–50.

Garcia, Venessa. "'Difference' in the Police Department: Women, Policing, and 'Doing Gender.'" *Journal of Contemporary Criminal Justice*, August 2003, pp.330–344.

Garrett, Ronnie. "Don't Cowboy Up." *Law Enforcement Technology*, February 2006, pp.40–51.

Goldfarb, Daniel. "The Effects of Stress on Police Officers." Speech to union delegates. http://www.heavybadge.com. Accessed May 10, 2004.

Goss, Cynthia. "Mental Health Aftermath of Simulated Attacks." *Law and Order*, May 2005, pp.48–55.

Gove, Tracey. "Unique Challenges to the New Supervisor." *Law and Order*, November 2004, pp.100–105.

Graves, Alex. "Law Enforcement Involved Domestic Abuse." *Law and Order*, November 2005, pp.108–111.

Griffith, David. "Suicide Is Not Painless." *Police*, May 2003, p.6.

Grossi, David. "Fitness and Wellness." *The Law Enforcement Trainer*, April/May/June 2005, pp.38–40, 77.

Hamilton, Melanie. "Cop Killer." *Police*, May 2003a, pp.18–32.

Hamilton, Melanie. "Eating a Gun." *Police*, May 2003b, p.24.

Hamilton, Melanie. "Losing Yourself." *Police*, May 2003c, p.25.

Holtz, Larry. "Policy Goes a Long Way in Death Notification." *Law Enforcement Technology*, December 2003, p.218.

Lindsey, Dennis and Kelly, Sean. "Issues in Small Town Policing: Understanding Stress." *FBI Law Enforcement Bulletin*, July 2004, pp.1–7.

Miller, Laurence. "Driven to Drink." *Law and Order*, November 2005, p.21.

Moore, Carole. "Breaking Bad News." *Law and Order*, May 2003, pp.106–109.

Moore, Carole. "Never Enough Time." *Law Enforcement Technology*, September 2004, p.146.

Moore, Carole. "Cutting Down on Choir Practice." *Law Enforcement Technology*, September 2005, p.210.

Morash, Merry; Haarr, Robin; and Kwak, Dae-Hoon. "Multilevel Influences on Police Stress." *Journal of Contemporary Criminal Justice*, February 2006, pp.26–43.

Morgan, Eugenia M. Kolasinski. "The Science of Sleep." *Law and Order*, July 2005, pp.106–113.

Nislow, Jennifer. "An Alarming Body Count? Questions Surround Data on Police Suicides." *Law Enforcement News*, October 2004a, pp.1, 15.

Nislow, Jennifer. "Before the Going Gets Too Tough. . ." *Law Enforcement News*, November 2004b, pp.1, 15.

Oliver, Willard M. and Meier, Cecil A. "The Four Stress Factors Unique to Rural Patrol Revisited." *The Police Chief*, November 2004, pp.46–54.

Page, Douglas. "Drug Screening of Police: On the High Road." *Law Enforcement Technology*, September 2005, pp.180–187.

Pinizzotto, Anthony J.; Davis, Edward F.; and Miller, Charles E., III. "Suicide by Cop: Defining a Devastating Dilemma." *FBI Law Enforcement Bulletin*, February 2005, pp.8–20.

"Police Facts." National Law Enforcement Officers Memorial Fund Web site. Updated November 25, 2005. http://www.nleomf.com. Accessed December 12, 2005.

Recruiting and Retaining Women: A Self-Assessment Guide for Law Enforcement. Los Angeles, CA: National Center for Women & Policing, no date.

Rodriguez, Dennis. "When Police Ethics Is Spelled with a Zzzz…." *Law Enforcement News*, October 2004, pp.9–10.

Rosenberg, Russell. "Working the Beat When You Are Beat." *Law and Order*, July 2005, pp.115–117.

Scott, Yolanda M. "Stress among Rural and Small-Town Patrol Officers: A Survey of Pennsylvania Municipal Agencies." *Police Quarterly*, June 2004, pp.237–261.

Selye, Hans. *The Stress of Life.* New York: McGraw-Hill, 1956.

"Ten Reasons Cops Are Different." http//:www.heavybadge.com. Accessed December 12, 2005.

Torres, Sam; Maggard, David L., Jr.; and Torres, Christine. "Preparing Families for the Hazards of Police Work." *The Police Chief*, October 2003, pp.108–114.

Violanti, John M. "Study Concludes Police Work is a Health Hazard." *American Police Beat*, November 2002.

BOOK-SPECIFIC WEB SITE

Go to the Management and Supervision in Law Enforcement Web site at www.thomsonedu.com/criminaljustice/bennett for student and instructor resources, including Internet Assignments and Case Studies.

CHAPTER 13

Deploying Law Enforcement Resources and Improving Productivity

The deployment of police strength both by time and area is essential.

Basic Tenet of the Peelian Reform Act of 1829

DO YOU KNOW?

- What organizational contradiction exists in most law enforcement agencies?
- How area assignments are determined?
- How patrol size is determined?
- Why rapid response may be important?
- What basic premise underlies random patrol?
- What the Kansas City study of preventive patrol found?
- What methods of patrol might be used?
- What the crime triangle is?
- How to most effectively channel resources to fight crime?
- What predisaster plans should include?
- What the strategic goals of the Department of Homeland Security are?
- What the first line of defense against terrorism is?
- How law enforcement productivity can be measured?
- How law enforcement productivity has traditionally been measured?
- How law enforcement productivity may be improved?
- What the single most important factor in high productivity and morale is?

CAN YOU DEFINE?

aggressive patrol	incivilities	proportionate
civilianization	lag time	assignment
CompStat	management	quotas
cone of resolution	information	random patrol
crime triangle	system (MIS)	shift
dog shift	productivity	watch
hot spots		

Introduction

Law enforcement agencies exist for a purpose—to fulfill a specific mission. Management, in conjunction with line personnel, sets forth this mission and the requirements for accomplishing it. Missions mean little without action, and in most businesses, including law enforcement, that means schedules. The link between mission and schedules is illustrated in Figure 13.1.

As Johnson (2005, p.71) points out: "Middle managers are the conduit between upper management and the rank and file." It is the sergeants, lieutenants and captains who convey the department's mission to those who will accomplish it. A key middle management function is determining allocation of personnel. The characteristic that distinguishes law enforcement personnel allocation from most business and industrial situations is the manner in which tasks are generated. In most non–law enforcement situations, the tasks to be performed are known in advance, and the number of people required to complete them is easily determined. For example, if a shoe manufacturing plant needs to produce 10,000 pairs of shoes next week to meet orders, the number of people needed to produce them can be determined.

Some law enforcement tasks are also predictable. For example, escorting distinguished visitors or maintaining order along a parade route are services known ahead of time. Most law enforcement tasks, however, can be predicted only in terms of the likelihood of their occurring at a specific time and place. Such tasks make up the bulk of law enforcement work and are the basis of the personnel allocation problem.

This chapter begins by examining the key management function of deploying personnel, including how they have traditionally been deployed, factors affecting deployment, assignment rotation and research findings about deployment and response time. Next is a look at differentiated response and random patrol, including the results of the Kansas City Preventive Patrol Experiment, followed by

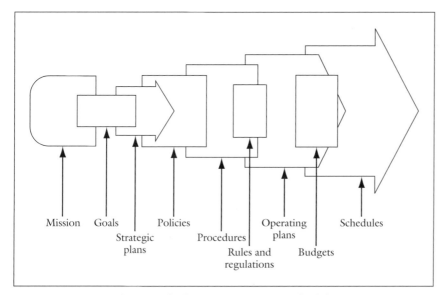

Figure 13.1 How Plans Interlock: From Missions to Schedules

Source: Lester R. Bittel. *The McGraw-Hill 36-Hour Management Course.* New York: McGraw-Hill Publishing Company, 1989, p.77. Reprinted by permission.

a presentation of the methods of patrol currently in use. Then ways the law enforcement personnel pool might be expanded are discussed, including involving citizens through citizen police academies, citizen patrols and reserve units; using departmental volunteers; and civilianizing departmental positions. Next is a discussion of deploying resources to fight crime, for emergencies and to enhance homeland security.

The discussion then turns to an examination of law enforcement productivity. A definition of productivity is presented as well as some symptoms of productivity problems and how such problems might be addressed. The chapter concludes with a return to previous discussions of leadership, discipline, motivation and morale as they relate to productivity.

Deploying Personnel

The largest division in any law enforcement agency is the uniformed patrol unit, which provides services 24/7. Other specialized divisions have fewer officers and often provide services for only portions of the day. Specialized personnel are assigned by demand based on frequency of incidents and cases requiring a specific service. A typical division of personnel is illustrated in Figure 13.2.

Patrol officers have the most important job in the department and are expected to handle competently a "mind-boggling array of calls" (Sweeney, 2003, pp.89–90). In addition: "Challenging, important and hazardous though patrol work may be, the laborious routine and onerous schedule prevent it from getting the prestige it deserves" (Sweeney, p.90). In fact, in most departments the most crucial officers in the agency are lowest on the totem pole.

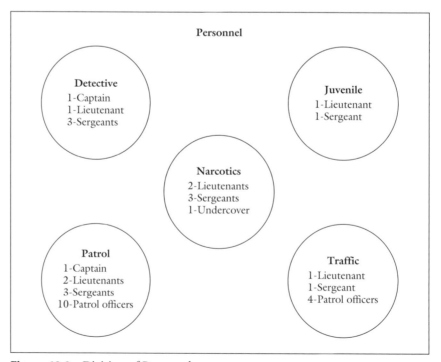

Figure 13.2   Division of Personnel

Source: Henry M. Wrobleski and Kären M. Hess. *Introduction to Law Enforcement and Criminal Justice,* 8th ed. Belmont, CA: Wadsworth Publishing Company, 2006, p.198.

The fact that patrol officers, those primarily responsible for accomplishing the department's goals, are lowest in status and in pay results in a serious organizational contradiction.

Why the contradiction? Some administrators disregard the importance of the patrol function. Others think patrol is not sufficiently stimulating, rewarding or challenging to keep the most able officers satisfied. In addition, many officers want to be transferred because of the unsavory schedule. Patrol officers work nights, weekends and holidays. Such schedules can be especially troublesome to married officers whose spouses work normal hours. Many patrol officers seek transfers to other divisions or into management not only for a better schedule but also to escape the hazards of patrol and to receive higher pay and increased status both inside and outside of the department. Keeping patrol officers motivated and productive is a considerable management challenge. And, as noted, how officers are scheduled can greatly influence their level of satisfaction.

Patrol is typically scheduled based on analysis of service call data.

Police Logs

When managers analyze service call data, they can easily observe variations in how patrol officers are being deployed. Personnel assignment should match those variations as much as possible. The logs need not be complicated. They can simply list requests for services, time, nature of the request and time the incident was completed. Time logs provide information for studying the types of incidents that occur and how to assign personnel where they are needed most.

Sharp (2003, p.124) contends: "Finding the ideal shift schedule for law enforcement agencies is about as easy as teaching a K9 to fly a police helicopter." The ideal work schedule does not exist. Among the variables affecting scheduling are staffing shortages caused by illness, injury, vacations, training and court time. Nonetheless, managers must schedule personnel to accomplish the department's mission.

Because of the 24/7 scheduling needs of law enforcement, manual scheduling of personnel is both time consuming and error prone (Dees, 2005, p.122). Davis (2005, p.92) calls scheduling a "thankless job," that is "a labor-intensive juggling act and the results rarely please few if any employees." Fortunately, software scheduling programs are now available that allow officers to check a database to see when they can schedule vacations. Approval or denial of requests for leave are more easily justified without accusations of favoritism. If emergency callouts of personnel are required, computerized scheduling programs can show who is available.

Shifts

Patrol traditionally has three 8-hour shifts, with officers working a shift five days a week, with two days off. A **shift** is simply the time span to which personnel are assigned. Some departments call it a **watch**. One common division is 7 a.m. to 3 p.m.; 3 p.m. to 11 p.m.; and 11 p.m. to 7 a.m. (the **dog shift**).

In recent years 10- and 12-hour shifts have become common and have frequently resulted in higher officer satisfaction and easier scheduling. The *10-hour shift* is an attractive scheduling option as it provides more days off (52 additional days a year) than eight-hour schedules, and the workdays are more tolerable than 12-hour shifts (Oliver, 2005, p.102). In addition, 10-hour shifts increase the number of officers on duty while the shifts overlap. These overlapping shifts can be

shift or **watch** • time span to which personnel are assigned.

dog shift • late night, early morning shift.

matched to the periods of greatest activity on the streets, better matching coverage to workload. For example, if a department's peak period of activity is from 3 pm to 9 pm, two shifts can overlap to double the coverage:

Day shift: 11 a.m. to 9 p.m.

Evening shift: 3 p.m. to 1 a.m.

Night shift: 1 a.m. to 11 a.m.

Ten-hour shifts can be effective in maintaining proper coverage around the clock while reducing overtime, eliminating overstaffing and ensuring acceptable service levels (Oliver, p.103).

Another alternative is the *12-hour shift*. In a typical 3/12 shift plan, an officer works a 12-hour shift three days a week for three weeks. The fourth week generally involves four 12-hour shifts, and then it is back to three days a week for three weeks, and so on. Such shift formats appear popular with officers and citizens alike. In addition to being economical, the format improves officer morale and productivity.

Many departments rotate shifts and area assignments or both. The three general shift rotation options are nonrotating, forward (with the clock) and backward (against the clock). Not rotating remains best because almost any change in daily sleep routines tends to increase fatigue. Backward shift rotation is the hardest to adapt to because the body's circadian rhythm is slightly predisposed to rotating forward. Other departments, especially those using community policing, assign permanent shifts, areas or both, believing this allows officers to become more familiar with their assignment and therefore more effective.

Some departments simply divide personnel into three equal shifts, but this is seldom effective. Rarely should personnel be equal on all shifts. Assignment of personnel by day of week and determining days off should be based on data. Assignments must maintain a balance between actual needs and the effects of some assignments on morale. Because computers allow rapid statistical data to be developed, personnel changes can be made at any time from one area to the other, resulting in proportionate assignment.

Proportionate Assignment

proportionate assignment • area assignments are determined by requests for services, based on available data.

Area assignments are determined by requests for services based on available data. This is called **proportionate assignment.** No area should be larger than the time it takes a car to respond to emergency calls in a reasonable time.

Area boundaries should be primary arteries, if possible, to provide faster access. Car assignments generally follow the size of the areas to be patrolled and the frequency of requests for services in those areas.

A number of factors determine proportionate assignment. A first step is to list those items requiring time and to weigh the importance of each. For example, felonies are generally weighted heavier than misdemeanors. In recent years drug offenses and related problems have required specialized personnel and increased training of regular officers. Even more recently homeland security efforts have become a priority.

To determine patrol area size, consider square miles, street miles, amount of crime and disorder, and response time.

The Response

Two important factors managers consider when making decisions about appropriate responses to calls for service are how rapid the response should be and who should respond.

Response Time

Most statistical breakdowns provide information on patrol areas and response times. A federal study released in the 1960s stated that a response time of one minute or less was needed to increase arrests at crime scenes. Few law enforcement departments can guarantee a response time of less than three minutes on all calls for service. Reasons other than on-scene arrests, however, also require rapid response.

 A response as rapidly yet as safely as possible builds public confidence in law enforcement capabilities and competence. It also places officers at the scene to protect evidence before people or the elements destroy it. It increases the chances of locating witnesses and making arrests. Further, it increases the chances of providing lifesaving emergency first aid to crime victims.

Other considerations in response time are barriers to patrol such as ditches, hills, water, number of officers available, total patrol area size, types of offenses and types and quantity of service requests. Safety is of utmost importance. The response should not pose a more significant threat to society than the incident to be investigated.

An even more important factor than police response time is the time between the occurrence of the incident and the report to the police, commonly referred to as **lag time,** over which police have no control. Another time factor important to total response is the time between when the dispatcher receives the call and dispatches it to a patrol car. Perhaps the most important factor, however, is citizen expectation.

lag time • time elapsed between the occurrence of an incident and it being reported to the police.

The Kansas City Response Time Analysis study found that a large proportion of crimes were not discovered until some time after they occurred and were therefore unaffected by rapid police response. The Police Executive Research Forum (PERF) replicated the Kansas City study over three years and confirmed the findings. This information is the basis for many agencies using differentiated response.

Differentiated Response

It is only logical that the type of call influences the response. After a literature review and a survey of over 200 police departments serving jurisdictions of more than 100,000, a group of police practitioners and researchers were charged with developing a model for police response to citizen calls for service. The result was the Differential Police Response Strategies Model, which consists of three key components:

- A set of characteristics to define an incident type
- A time factor to identify the relationship between the time the incident occurred and the time the police received the call
- A full range of response strategies, going from an immediate response by a sworn officer to no response, with numerous alternatives in between, as shown in Figure 13.3.

Type of Incident/Time of Occurrence

Response Alternatives			Major Personal Injury			Major Property Damage/Loss			Potential Personal Injury			Potential Property Damage/Loss			Minor Personal Injury			Minor Property Damage/Loss			Other Minor Crime			Other Minor Noncrime		
			In-Progress	Proximate	Cold	In-Progress	Proximate	Cold	In-Progress	Proximate	Cold	In-Progress	Proximate	Cold	In-Progress	Proximate	Cold	In-Progress	Proximate	Cold	In-Progress	Proximate	Cold	In-Progress	Proximate	Cold
	Sworn	Immediate																									
		Expedite																									
		Routine																									
	Nonsworn	Appointment																									
		Immediate																									
		Expedite																									
		Routine																									
	Nonmobile	Appointment																									
		Telephone																									
		Walk-In																									
		Mail-In																									
		Referral																									
		No Response																									

Figure 13.3   General Differential Response Model

Source: Raymond O. Summrall et al. *Differential Police Response Strategies.* Washington, DC: Police Executive Research Forum, 1981, p.9. Reprinted by permission.

Kinds of Patrol

Patrol officers are often engaged in either random preventive patrol or directed aggressive patrol.

Random Preventive Patrol

During preventive patrol, officers frequently establish a pattern, which can become known to criminals and used to their advantage. To overcome this potential problem, many departments use **random patrol,** that is, patrol by random number selection.

random patrol • officers on patrol are unsystematically assigned areas to cover.

One type of random patrol uses a computer to select random numbers. Officers going on duty are provided an envelope with these numbers, which they select at random. Officers then patrol the area designated by that number for no longer than 10 minutes and then select another number. The numbers may be repeated to eliminate the possibility of a criminal thinking once an area has been patrolled, it will not be patrolled again. Criminals cannot know where officers will patrol because the officers themselves do not know until they select the next area number.

 The basic premise of random patrol is to place officers closer to any potential incident or request for service before it happens, based on data provided by experience. Goals are to reduce response time and erase set patrol pattern habits.

The Kansas City Preventive Patrol Experiment Although the Kansas City Preventive Patrol Experiment was conducted more than 30 years ago (1972), it remains the most comprehensive study of preventive patrol. The experiment divided 15 beats in Kansas City into three groups, each having five beats:

Group 1—Reactive beats: no preventive patrol, responding only to calls for service

Group 2—Control beats: maintained their normal level of preventive patrol

Group 3—Proactive beats: doubled or tripled the level of preventive patrol

 The Kansas City Preventive Patrol Experiment found that increasing or decreasing routine preventive patrol had no effect on crime, citizen fear of crime, community attitudes toward the police on delivery of police services, police response time or traffic accidents (Klockars, 1983, p.160).

Klockars (p.130) commented on the results of the Kansas City experiment: "It makes about as much sense to have police patrol routinely in cars to fight crime as it does to have firemen patrol routinely in fire trucks to fight fire." However, E. Sweeney (2004, p.23) notes that when preventive patrols are cut, preventable crimes and traffic crashes, including fatalities, increase. He (p.24) recommends that officers patrol smarter, not less.

Research by Famega et al. (2005) found that, on average, more than three quarters of a patrol officer's shift is unassigned. During this time most officers patrol routinely or back up other officers on calls to which they were not dispatched. Only 6 percent of unassigned time was directed by supervisors, dispatchers, other officers or citizens. When supervisors did provide directives, they were often vague and general, not proactive, problem oriented or community policing oriented. They (p.540) reach two conclusions: (1) a very significant proportion of patrol officer time is spent uncommitted and could be better utilized doing proactive, problem-oriented policing activities and (2) supervisors need to provide much more detailed directives, based on sound crime analysis, to capitalize on the underutilization of patrol officer time.

Directed Aggressive Patrol

"Driving around aimlessly is not necessarily the best way to patrol," says Sweeney. He suggests that officers concentrate on locations where high numbers of crashes are occurring, areas of the beat with the highest incidences of crime or calls for service, and critical infrastructures that are potential targets for terrorists. This is the emphasis in directed or aggressive patrol. **Aggressive patrol** focuses on preventing and detecting crime by focusing attention on problem areas and by investigating suspicious activity.

aggressive patrol • proactive patrol, focuses on preventing and detecting crime by investigating suspicious activity. Also called *proactive patrol*.

The premise behind aggressive patrol is that through purposeful contact with individuals, officers will build an intelligence base of information regarding who lives and works on their beat, where problems are occurring and possible reasons for the problems. An application of such patrol is aggressive traffic enforcement of suspicious vehicles (those driving at night without headlights, speeding or weaving through traffic), which often leads to arrests: "All officers know America's highways are often haunted by criminals. They use them as escape routes, as a place to find victims, and as a way to traffic their own nefarious brand of commerce—drugs, guns, stolen property and cash" (Hustmyre, 2003, p.113).

Aggressive patrol fits well with the proactive approach to community problems inherent in the community policing philosophy. It also may dictate what method of patrol is used.

Table 13.1 Summary of Patrol Methods

Method	Uses	Advantages	Disadvantages
Foot	Highly congested areas Burglary, robbery, theft, purse snatching, mugging	Close citizen contact High visibility Develop informants	Relatively expensive Limited mobility
Automobile	Respond to service calls Provide traffic control Transport individuals, documents and equipment	Most economical Greatest mobility and flexibility Offers means of communication Provides means of transporting people, documents and equipment	Limited access to certain areas Limited citizen contact
Motorcycle	Same as automobile, except that it can't be used for transporting individuals and has limited equipment	Maneuverability in congested areas and areas restricted to automobiles	Inability to transport much equipment Not used during bad weather Hazardous to operator
Bicycle	Stakeouts Parks and beaches Congested areas	Quiet and unobtrusive	Limited speed
Mounted	Parks and bridle paths Crowd control Traffic control	Size and maneuverability of horse	Expensive
Air	Surveillance Traffic control Searches and rescues	Covers large areas easily	Expensive
Water	Deter smuggling Water traffic control Rescues	Access to activities occurring on water	Expensive
Special-terrain	Patrol unique areas inaccessible to other forms Rescue operations	Access to normally inaccessible areas	Limited use in some areas
Segway scooter	Same as foot, but faster and less tiring	Close citizen contact, high visibility, quiet and maneuverable	Limited access to certain areas, not used during bad weather

Source: Henry M. Wrobleski and Kären M. Hess. *Introduction to Law Enforcement and Criminal Justice,* 7th edition. Belmont, CA: Wadsworth Publishing Company, 2003, p.183.

Methods of Patrol

Given the wide range of circumstances encountered during patrol, a variety of patrol methods have been devised. The most common remains automobile patrol. Table 13.1 provides a summary of patrol methods.

 Common methods of patrol include automobile, bicycle, motorcycle and foot patrol. Other methods include air, mounted, water, special-terrain and Segway patrol.

Managers may need to consider several issues involving automobile patrol, namely whether to use one-officer or two-officer patrol units and whether the department should implement a take-home policy for squad cars.

One-Officer versus Two-Officer Patrol Units

Officer safety is at the core of the argument favoring two-officer patrol units, which also make a shift less boring and provide a chance for officers to develop working relationships. However, officer productivity and operational efficiency are increased using one-officer patrol units. If two officers are needed, two squads can be sent on a call.

Using one-officer units with appropriate delay procedures for another car to arrive at a scene is an effective administrative and budgeting procedure. The use of

Bicycle patrols are reported to be more effective than automobile patrols in certain instances. Officers on bicycles can cover larger sections of the community, and bikes can go places vehicles cannot go and are very maneuverable.

electronic patrol car locators can enhance officer safety in a one-officer unit. Such locators are also of great value in deploying patrol personnel. According to Wrobleski and Hess (2006, p.193):

> The one-officer unit offers several advantages, including cost-effectiveness in that the same number of officers can patrol twice the area, with twice the mobility, and with twice the power of observation. In addition, officers working alone are generally more cautious in dangerous situations, recognizing that they have no backup. Officers working alone also are generally more attentive to patrol duties because they do not have a conversational partner. The expense of two cars compared to one, however, is a factor.

Experiments by the Police Foundation using both types of unit staffing in a large city police department revealed that officers in two-officer units were more likely to be assaulted by a citizen, be injured in the line of duty and have a suspect resist arrest. Studies that have looked at the frequency of assaults and injuries to patrol officers have upheld these findings that single-officer units tend to be safer.

Some districts may require two-officer units and, under specific instances and for short periods, more than two. Sometimes union contracts dictate that two-officer units be used, which can seriously hinder management as it plans for the most effective deployment of personnel.

Another controversial area is whether officers should be allowed to take their patrol car home.

Take-Home Patrol Cars

Allowing officers to take their patrol cars home offers many advantages to officers and their agencies (Scoville, 2005, p.38). These officers tend to take better care of their cars and be more responsible with them, resulting in lower maintenance and repair costs. The practice also increases the visibility of police officers in their neighborhoods. In addition, the department can use the take-home program as a perk for already employed officers as well as a recruiting tool for those interested in joining the department. One of the biggest advantages is that officers with take-home cars are readily deployed to critical incidents while off duty.

Take-home car programs are not without disadvantages, however. While the officer is off duty, the car is not in service, necessitating a much larger vehicle fleet. Also of concern is the security of the car and its contents. Deciding whether to allow patrol officers to take their vehicles home and use them as rolling police offices and personal transportation is one of the most important decisions an agency has to make about its patrol cars (Scoville, p.38).

Expanding the Law Enforcement Personnel Pool

Agencies have expanded their personnel pool through the use of citizen police academies, citizen patrols, reserves and volunteers within the department—frequently retired individuals, including retired police officers. Another trend is the civilianization of certain law enforcement functions.

Citizen Police Academies

Several police departments seeking to implement community policing have started citizen police academies (CPAs), described in Chapter 3. Since the organization of the first recorded U.S. citizen police academy in Orlando, Florida, in 1985, many communities have developed their own academies, each with its own unique focus. Many academies also include ride-along programs for participants.

A logical extension of the Citizen Police Academy is the Citizen Police Academy Alumni Association (CPAAA), an organization that can further deepen community relationships and leverage local volunteer resources (Aryani et al., 2003, p.52).

Citizens on Patrol

In many jurisdictions community policing strategies include citizen patrols. One such citizen patrol, operating in Fort Worth, Texas, encouraged community residents to patrol their own neighborhoods and be directly responsible for reducing crime. The program currently has over 2,000 patrollers, representing more than 87 neighborhoods in the city.

In Delray Beach, Florida, a city with a population of 50,000, the police department's largest volunteer project is the Citizens Observer Patrol (COP), whose three primary goals are to:

- Effectively reduce crime and disorder in selected communities.
- Establish a working relationship between the Delray Beach police and its citizenry.
- Empower people to take ownership of their communities to reduce crime.

The Delray Beach Citizens Observer Patrol has 850 members in 21 sectors. Crime has markedly diminished in every area.

Reserves

Reserve officers, sometimes called part-timers, auxiliaries, specials or supernumeraries, are valuable assets to police departments in the effort to expand law enforcement resources. The number of reserve officers is increasing throughout the country as agencies use this cost-effective means to add personnel (Fielden, 2004, p.28). In 2004 there were approximately 400,000 sworn law enforcement reserve officers (volunteer and paid) in the United States.

Reserve officer programs vary considerably from department to department. In some jurisdictions reserve officers have powers of arrest and wear the same uniform as law enforcement officers except for the badge, which says "reserve." They may even purchase their own firearm and ballistics vest and drive their personally owned vehicles during operations. Some jurisdictions recruit reserves from those retiring from their full-time ranks. Many reserve units function in specialized roles, for example, search-and-rescue operations. Fielden (p.32) asserts: "Reserve officers are a force multiplier that is very effective. By assigning reserves to duties such as crowd control, departments can free up full-time personnel for more pressing operations." A trend that has become increasingly popular is using reserve officers for bike patrol: "Due to their inherent qualities of speed, stealth and easy penetration of congested areas, bikes offer an effective weapon in the fight against urban terror" (Williams, 2005, p.85).

Issues exist regarding the use of reserves, particularly in labor and liability concerns. To allay labor concerns, some departments have a contract with full-time officers stating that reserves are used only if a regular officer turns down the overtime or wants to take "comp" time off. To address liability issues, most agencies require reserves to complete rigorous training courses. Some, in fact, require reserves to go through the full basic academy, not accepting the reserve academy training as adequate.

Volunteers

The three groups of law enforcement personnel just discussed—citizen police academy participants, citizen patrols and reservists—consist primarily, if not solely, of volunteers. And their numbers are increasing.

Volunteers supplement and enhance existing or envisioned functions, allowing law enforcement professionals to do their jobs more effectively (Kolb, 2005, p.23). They can provide numerous benefits to a department, including maximizing existing resources, enhancing public safety and services, and improving community relations. Other services volunteers may provide include fingerprinting children, patrolling shopping centers, checking on homebound residents, and checking the security of vacationing residents' homes. Additional functions volunteers might perform include clerical and data support, special event planning, search and rescue assistance, grant writing, and transporting mail between substations (Chouinard, 2003, p.26).

In 2002, the Volunteers in Police Service (VIPS) initiative was created as a joint effort of the U.S. Department of Justice and the International Association of Chiefs of Police. The VIPS Program works to enhance the capacity of state and local law enforcement to use volunteers and serves as a gateway to resources and information for and about law enforcement volunteer programs. The VIPS Program is a partner of Citizen Corps, an initiative helping to make communities across America safer, stronger and better prepared for emergencies of all kinds. The mission of Citizen Corps is to harness the power of every individual through education and outreach, training and volunteer services. It is a vital part of USA Freedom Corp ("Citizen Corp," 2005).

Another program of the USA Freedom Corps initiative is the Community Emergency Response Team (CERT) program, created to provide opportunities for individuals to assist their communities in emergency preparation through volunteering. It is managed by the Department of Homeland Security. In 2005 there were more than 1,100 CERT teams across the country (*Law Enforcement and Community Emergency Response Teams*, 2005).

Kolb (p.23) cautions that establishing and maintaining a volunteer program is not cost free, but that the return on the investment is substantial. She gives as an example the San Diego Police Department, which reported that in 2004 it spent about $585,000 on the staffing, equipment and management of its four volunteer programs, but estimates the value of the hours contributed by volunteers at more than $2.65 million. In another example, the Billings (Montana) Police Department was helped by volunteers doing computer work at what is estimated at a billable value of $30,000 (Kingman, 2005, pp.4–5).

Aryani (2005, p.75) recommends that effective agency-provided volunteer training and periodic refresher sessions are paramount in decreasing costs and liabilities and increasing the effectiveness of volunteer resources. He (p.76) stresses: "It is paramount that [volunteers] conduct themselves in a safe, professional, ethical, and competent manner reflecting positively on the agency and furthering the mission of the program."

As with the concern over using reserves, some paid, full-time officers are hesitant to embrace volunteers. To overcome staff resistance to volunteer programs, managers should emphasize that volunteers are used to make officers' jobs easier, not to take work away from them. Keeping officers on the streets is what a volunteer program is about.

Explorers

Yet another way to expand and or support sworn officers' efforts is through an Explorer program. Most departments provide extensive training in personal conduct, first aid, police procedures, weapons familiarization, crime scene investigation, traffic control, interpersonal communication, criminal law and specialized police duties.

Civilianization

civilianization • hiring citizens to perform certain tasks for law enforcement agencies.

Civilianization, which has been occurring over the past 40 years, is the hiring of nonsworn personnel to replace or augment the work of sworn police officers (Schander, 2003, p.57). Civilians have typically been employed in such functions as dispatch, forensic services, planning and research, budget and finance, information systems, legal counsel, jail/corrections, human resources and public information (Schander, p.57).

Civilianization is a cost-effective way to make use of the numerous and varied capabilities of citizens, while at the same time freeing up law enforcement personnel to concentrate their efforts on tasks they have been specifically trained for. Many routine functions performed by officers do not require their expertise nor their special authority and arrest powers. Animal-control officers, dispatchers, jailers and others might be civilians, rather than sworn peace officers. One function glamorized by television programs is that of the crime scene investigator, who may or may not be a sworn law enforcement officer.

Deploying Resources to Fight Crime

Many individuals in law enforcement and probably the majority of the citizens they serve consider crime fighting as a primary responsibility of their agency. It is. Advances in technology have enhanced these efforts, especially advances in mapping crime.

Mapping Crime

Law enforcement's ability to understand the extent of crime and patterns to its occurrence is continuously evolving, and with it has come an enhanced capacity for police to tailor their response to suit a community's specific crime problems. Diamond (2004, p.42) notes: "Crime-mapping technology gives agencies nationwide the intel to efficiently deploy officers and prevent crime." Crime tends to cluster, forming **hot spots** in certain geographic areas. Hot spots are found at the neighborhood level, which helps local law enforcement allocate patrols to areas most in need of a police presence.

According to Diamond (p.42): "Computers have revolutionized the art of crime mapping. Once just an exercise of sticking pins into a map glued to a bulletin board, crime mapping is now built on a foundation of 'geographic information systems,' or GIS, a fancy term for creating, updating and analyzing computerized maps. The relevance of GIS to law enforcement is that these maps can be easily overlaid with strategic and tactical information such as recent burglaries." Furthermore, GIS is used to better protect departments' officers and deploy them more efficiently (Diamond, p.46).

Networks and their associated databases have also allowed law enforcement to expand their use of GIS beyond crime mapping, enabling them to use generic Web browsers, or Intranets, to share information and resources more rapidly and cost-effectively: "Intranet mapping is not just about policing; it is also about community redevelopment and effectively coordinating governmental services and resources for both homeland security and economic development" (Lutz, 2003, p.122).

Another innovation in manipulating data is **CompStat,** short for "computer statistics" or "comparison statistics," a multi-faceted police operations management system first used in 1994 by the New York City Police Department (Schick, 2004, p.17). According to Walsh and Vito (2004, p.57): "CompStat is a goal-oriented, strategic-management process that uses information technology, operational strategy and managerial accountability to guide police operations. As designed by the New York City Police Department, the original model asserts that the primary police mission is the reduction of crime and the enhancement of a community's quality of life."

CompStat has been successfully implemented in several major metropolitan jurisdictions throughout the country and "represents a sea change in managing police operations . . . perhaps the most radical change in recent history" (McDonald, 2004, p.33). Results of a study by Weisburd et al. (2004, p.15) confirm what many police observers have noted: that "CompStat has literally burst onto the American police scene." Thirty-three percent of large departments (100 or more sworn officers) have implemented a CompStat-like program, and another 26 percent are planning such a program (Weisburd et al., p.15). The results of this study are presented in Table 13.2.

The success of the CompStat Process lies in its foundation, being based on the four crime-reduction principles of (1) accurate and timely intelligence, (2) effective tactics, (3) rapid deployment of personnel and resources and (4) relentless follow-up and assessment (Shane, 2004a, p.13). These four underlying principles are coupled with accountability and discretion at all levels of the law enforcement agency (Shane, 2004b, p.12). Data from participating agencies confirms the effectiveness of the CompStat process: "Crime rates among the cities practicing CompStat reveal

hot spots • specific locations with high crime rates.

CompStat • a strategic crime-control technique centered around four principles: (1) accurate and timely intelligence, (2) effective tactics, (3) rapid deployment of personnel and resources and (4) relentless follow-up and assessment.

Table 13.2   Has Your Department Implemented a CompStat-Like Program?

Department Size	Percent Yes	Percent No, but Planning	Percent No
Small (50–99 Sworn)	11.0	29.3	59.8
Large (100+ Sworn)	32.6	25.6	41.8

Due to rounding, rows may not add to 100.

Source: David Weisburd, Stephen D. Mastrofski, Rosann Greenspan and James R. Willis. "The Growth of CompStat in American Policing." *Police Foundation Reports*, April 2004, p.6. Reprinted by permission.

the program's true success. In New York City over the last 10 years, crime came down 64 percent; in Philadelphia, crime fell 23 percent between 1995 and 2002; in Baltimore, crime decreased 31 percent between 1995 and 1999; and in Newark, crime declined 51 percent between 1995 and 2001" (Shane, 2004c, p.20).

The Crime Triangle

One tool to help law enforcement tackle crime through problem solving is the crime triangle, shown in Figure 13.4. The basis for the crime triangle is Cohen and Felson's Routine Activities Theory, which proposes that crime occurs during the intersection, in time and space, of motivated offenders and suitable victims (or targets), under circumstances of absent or inadequate guardianship. Crime is presumed amenable to suppression if any of the three legs of the triangle is removed or neutralized.

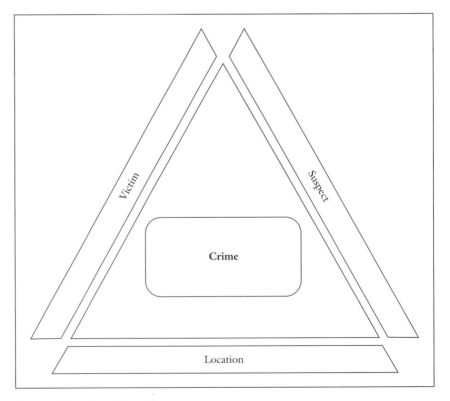

Figure 13.4   The Crime Triangle

Source: Ralph B. Taylor. "Crime and Small-Scale Places: What We Know, What We Can Prevent, and What Else We Need to Know." In Taylor et al. *Crime and Place: Plenary Papers of the 1997 Conference on Criminal Justice Research and Evaluation*, July 1998, p.2.

The **crime triangle** is a model that illustrates how all three elements—motivated suspect, suitable victim and adequate location—are required for a crime to occur.

crime triangle • a model illustrating how all three elements—motivated suspect, suitable victim and adequate location—are required for crime to occur.

One side of the crime triangle, the suspect, is most often the focus of crime-fighting efforts.

Focus on Criminals Just as managers are beginning to tap into the resources of their community, they are also beginning to do more partnering with other agencies to apprehend criminals. A prime example of such a partnership is that between the Metro-Dade Police Department in Miami and the Bureau of Alcohol, Tobacco and Firearms (ATF), Miami District Office. The program is called Project Achilles because they target career criminals who are known to possess firearms. This possession of firearms makes them vulnerable, putting them within both the state and the federal criminal justice system. The program grew out of studies that indicate that 6 percent of the criminals arrested commit up to 70 percent of all serious crime.

 Focusing on career criminals is a logical approach to fighting crime. Equally promising in crime-fighting efforts is a focus on high-crime locations.

Focus on Location In the crime triangle, location is a critical element. Some criminal justice researchers and practitioners have begun to focus on *places* where offenses occur, identifying hot spots, a term borrowed from geology to designate a region of potentially volatile geologic, or volcanic, activity. A hot spot can be a single address, a cluster of addresses, part of a block, an entire block or two or an intersection. To organize data about crime over time at various levels of analysis, criminologists have applied the concept of the **cone of resolution** (Figure 13.5), this time borrowing from geography.

cone of resolution • narrowing in on the geographic locations of crime.

Borrowing another concept, this time from ecology, Braiden (1998, p.8) suggests another way to view the significance of location—"the hunt and the habitat":

I can't think of two special-interest groups more philosophically opposed to each other than hunters and animal rights activists, yet there are two things

Figure 13.5 The Cone of Resolution

Source: Ralph B. Taylor. "Crime and Small-Scale Places: What We Know, What We Can Prevent, and What Else We Need to Know." In Taylor et al. *Crime and Place: Plenary Papers of the 1997 Conference on Criminal Justice Research and Evaluation*, July 1998, p.2.

they totally agree upon: The species will survive the hunt; it will not survive loss of its habitat.

What can policing learn from this basic principle of nature? Well, if the ultimate goal is to eliminate the criminal species forever, surely the best way to do that is to eliminate the habitat that spawns and sustains that species. Structured as it is, the criminal justice system puts 95 percent of its resources into the hunt while the habitat is left almost untouched. We can never win working that way, because the habitat never stops supplying new customers for the hunt.

incivilities • signs of disorder.

Another way of viewing the role of habitat or location as an element of crime causation is to consider **incivilities,** or signs of disorder. Wilson and Kelling's classic "broken windows" theory suggested that such incivilities lead to higher crime rates, victimization rates and residents' perception of the fear of crime. A focus on the third side of the crime triangle—the victims and reducing their suitability as targets—brings community policing into the scene, as discussed later in the chapter.

A more recent way of analyzing crime is the *criminal event perspective* (CEP), formulated in the late 1990s. Criminal events differ from criminal acts in that criminal events include circumstances before, during and after the event as well as the social context of the act. Criminal event analysis also considers time (weekends, night), geography, economic and political pressures, and community characteristics that increase the likelihood of crime. CEP challenges offender-based theories and argues in favor of an integrated perspective, including offender, victim and context (Marshall, 2004, p.344). In addition, CEP is a tool theorists and researches can use to construct models containing the variables related to crime and used to explain crime (Anderson and Meier, 2004, p.416). Law enforcement managers can structure their efforts to prevent or reduce crime on these variables.

In addition to their crime-fighting responsibilities, law enforcement agencies frequently have to deploy resources in emergencies.

Deploying Resources in Emergencies

During normal deployment, law enforcement managers have time to use statistics and studied judgment to determine allocation requirements, but during emergencies, present circumstances and experience largely dictate which personnel are deployed. Results depend on what managers in the field decide during those first minutes at the scene.

Law enforcement managers must be trained in emergency procedures, including medical emergencies, earthquakes, tornados, hurricanes, flooding, radioactive waste accidents, hostage taking, bomb threats, terrorist attacks, aircraft crashes, large fires, gas leaks, riots or other large crowd disturbances and snipers. They must be familiar with Civil Emergency Preparedness plans and the availability of assistance locally and from other agencies. They must be aware of the availability of emergency equipment and the location of area hospitals and rescue squads. This information should be condensed into written predisaster plans.

Predisaster Plans

Moore (2005, p.98) points out: "While no natural event can be programmed, an agency's response can be, within reason."

Predisaster plans should include the following:

- Which emergencies to prepare for
- What must be done in advance (supplies on hand, agreements with other agencies, etc.)
- What specific functions must be performed during the emergency and who is responsible for performing them, including outside organizations and agencies that might help
- What steps need to be taken to restore order after an emergency has ended
- How to evaluate a response

The plan should be made by top management in conjunction with those who would be involved in implementing it, including government officials, fire department personnel, health care personnel and so on.

Many jurisdictions use a three-level approach, with *Level 1* for minor events that can usually be handled by on-duty personnel. *Level 2* is for moderate to severe situations requiring aid from other agencies and perhaps other jurisdictions. *Level 3* is for catastrophes in which a state of emergency is proclaimed and county, state and perhaps federal assistance is requested. In such instances the National Guard may be called. The emergency plan should identify the levels of emergencies that might occur and the level of response required. Increasingly, law enforcement agencies across the country are devising and implementing Incident Command Systems (ICSs) to coordinate their emergency response.

Unfortunately, many managers place emergency planning as a low priority, thinking that such emergencies are unlikely to happen in their jurisdiction. But they could, and when they do, most citizens expect their law enforcement agencies to alert them, deal with it and keep them informed.

Managers should not only have predisaster plans and *practice* them but should also be familiar with establishing command posts, furnishing information to the press and obtaining intelligence information on which they can make decisions. Accurate information is needed to know whether to evacuate, provide extra security, treat injured people, prevent looting, put up barricades or redirect traffic. Most law enforcement departments have experienced managers who have been involved in similar incidents. No fixed rules will serve in every situation, but there are guidelines. A great deal of independent decision making occurs in these moments. Law enforcement decision makers must be prepared for short, intense incidents or long-term sieges involving many hours. A unified command structure should include all departments within the jurisdiction responsible for critical services, including law enforcement, fire, emergency medical services, power and gas, streets or highways departments, water services, sewer, the city manager and the media. Managers should also be familiar with federal assistance available for emergency planning and response.

Available Assistance

The National Incident Management System (NIMS) introduced in Chapter 1 can also be of assistance in planning for and responding to emergencies. Herron (2004, p.20) explains that the NIMS recognizes the ongoing need for federal government responders to effectively work with state and local authorities for both incidents of terrorism and other emergencies. Accordingly, the NIMS represents a "core set of doctrine, principles, terminology and organizational processes to enable effective, efficient, and collaborative incident management at all levels" (Jamieson, 2005, p.68).

Jamieson (p.69) describes the four phases of an NIMS adoption. Although intended for federal agencies, states as well as local and tribal agencies will find it helpful in designing their NIMS implementation process. Phase 1 is initial staff training, which might include completing the Federal Emergency Management Agency's (FEMA) independent NIMS and ICS (Incident Command System) courses. Phase 2 consists of evaluating plans, policies and procedures to identify what needs to be changed to comply with NIMS. Phase 3 involves modifying emergency response plans; emergency operation plans; and other relevant plans, procedures and policies to reflect NIMS concepts. Phase 4 involves credentialing and certifying personnel and equipment based on NIMS Integration Center standards.

Mutual aid agreements are a key component of the NIMS and must be updated regularly so that officers know exactly what they have the authority to do (Weiss and Davis, 2005, p.121). *Mutual Aid: Multijurisdictional Partnerships for Meeting Regional Threats* (2005) describes mutual aid agreements as being comprehensive, formalized and far reaching, intended for sharing resources and services during periods of natural or manmade disasters. Sharing resources during such unusual circumstances is far more efficient and cost effective than having overlapping and duplicative services in each jurisdiction that may be infrequently or sparsely used.

Closely related to mutual aid agreements are Emergency Management Assistance Compacts (EMACs). Chudwin (2005) describes how Illinois's EMAC helped them respond to the request for assistance "as soon as possible" from Louisiana officials. Illinois was ready when the call came in. One hundred fifty officers from throughout the state formed a task force to respond to the request. When they arrived they were sworn in as special Louisiana state police officers, granting them authority to enforce the law everywhere in the state. They received a copy of the Louisiana criminal code to be sure they understood local law, concentrating on use of force issues regarding arrest, looting and deadly force. Chudwin (p.46) observed: "Life as Americans know it ceased to exist. The fabric of society was torn, and only the law and order provided by these men and women who did not budge held the thin blue line."

Another source of assistance in emergencies is FEMA, whose mission is to reduce loss of life and property and protect our nation's critical infrastructure from all types of hazards through a comprehensive, risk-based, emergency management program of mitigation, preparedness, response and recovery. On March 1, 2003, FEMA became part of the Department of Homeland Security, with the three strategic goals of:

1. Protecting lives and preventing the loss of property from natural and technological hazards.
2. Reducing human suffering and enhancing the recovery of communities after disaster strikes.
3. Ensuring that the public is served in a timely and efficient manner (FEMA Web site).

FEMA recommends communities address the following functions in disaster plans: (1) communication, (2) transportation, (3) public works, (4) firefighting,

(5) intelligence efforts to assess damage, (6) mass care for those people displaced from their homes, (7) resource support (contracting for the labor needed to assist in a disaster), (8) health and medical, (9) search and rescue, (10) hazardous materials, (11) food or feeding and (12) energy. Communication should be the number one priority.

Some emergencies can be anticipated, as was the case with hurricane Katrina. In such instances the prep work may start slowly, with line officers making mental notes of the personnel gear they will need while middle management starts thinking about scenarios and contingencies, recognizing that the primary mission during the first 72 hours will be search and rescue but that officers will be expected to provide law enforcement and humanitarian services as needed (Daugherty, 2005, p.42). Furthermore, every level of the organization has a different function that depends on the levels above and below.

Responding to an Emergency

The first law enforcement manager at the scene must take control, regardless of rank. Stalling for a manager of higher rank to take over could be fatal to people who need evacuation or rescue or to people being threatened. Normally, time is on the side of law enforcement in criminal or hostage situations. Subterfuge to gain time is important. Direct confrontation should be avoided unless it is the last resort. Each incident of this type has individual elements to consider, and no matter how many incidents an officer has been called on to resolve, a surprise element usually requires a considered, different decision.

Daugherty (p.45) suggests the following for middle managers: (1) Personnel are assets, not equipment. Take care of the personnel and they will take care of the equipment. (2) Trust that people below you and above you are doing their best. Your performance depends on theirs. (3) If you are not a line officer, your role is support. They provide the service. Everything managers do should be in support of them. (4) It is all right to go to extremes to help one person or one family. Individual actions make a difference. (5) No matter how fast you get to an impact area, it is not fast enough. Someone is already in need. (6) Start organized. Work organized. Finish organized. (7) Have compassion for the community and none for those that prey upon them.

Technological Aids A variety of technological devices are helping law enforcement better cope with resource deployment during and following emergencies. For example, in the hurricane-vulnerable region of the Florida Keys, rugged PC mobile laptop computers were used by sheriff's deputies during an evacuation to help with radio time, security-sensitive data and prioritizing who needed to be evacuated from the barrier island chain first. Personal digital assistants (PDAs) can put everything officers need in the palms of their hands, including computer-aided dispatch information, while away from their cruisers.

The consequence of failed communication was vividly evidenced during Hurricane Katrina as "unadulterated chaos" (Careless, 2005, p.115). The loss of the city of New Orleans' radio system isolated officers in the field, disrupting the command and control structure for police, fire and EMS, seriously compromising officers' ability to do their jobs in the very worst of conditions (Careless, p.117). The few usable frequencies were overwhelmed with two or three channels

Computers and other technological advances have made the jobs of patrol officers more efficient and safe. They can enter license numbers and addresses to find out almost instantly whether they are dealing with a wanted person. A Maryland State Police officer demonstrates the capabilities of voice activation technology in December 2002.

and 4,000 people trying to use them. While other agencies responded to the nationwide "911" and brought with them their own communication systems, none were so compatible as to allow intercommunication: "Ideally a national communication system will exist in the near future so major catastrophes can be managed more efficiently" (Arey and Wilder, 2005, p.90).

Another technological aid that helps law enforcement handle medical emergencies is the automated external defibrillator (AED). Because medical research has shown that up to half of all sudden cardiac arrest (SCA) deaths could be prevented with early defibrillation, and officers commonly arrive on the scene of an SCA before paramedics or other personnel, many departments believe it makes sense to have AEDs and officers trained in their use. The American Heart Association (AHA) says that first responders must administer care to a person within eight minutes of a sudden cardiac arrest for them to have more than a 4 percent chance of survival.

After the Emergency

After the emergency, the focus should be on returning to normalcy as soon as possible and on attending to the mental health needs of those who responded. Hamilton (2005, p.38) comments on the enormity of what Gulf state law enforcement officers were asked to do during and after hurricanes Katrina and Rita: "No amount of training could protect officers from the physical and emotional toll of working after losing homes and contact with family amid flood waters" (p.42). Critical incident stress debriefings as discussed in Chapter 12 are essential.

Many of the management responsibilities related to deploying personnel in emergencies are similar to what would be needed during and after a terrorist attack. In addition, managers must be knowledgeable of their responsibilities in homeland security.

Deploying Resources for Homeland Security

Time has passed since 9-11. Yet, as Buhrmaster (2005, p.45) stresses: "Time can be both a friend and an enemy. If you use it to prepare for action, it can prove priceless. If you allow it to corrode your tactical edge, however, it can prove extremely dangerous." As a starting point, it is important to understand the Department of Homeland Security and how it affects law enforcement management.

The Department of Homeland Security

As a direct result of 9-11, on October 8, 2001, the Department of Homeland Security (DHS) was established, reorganizing the departments of the federal government. Some 180,000 people from 22 different agencies joined to form the DHS (Davies and Plotkin, 2005, p.1), the three-part mission of which is "to prevent terrorism attacks within the United States, reduce America's vulnerability to terrorism, and minimize the damage from potential attacks and natural disasters." The DHS serves in a broad capacity, facilitating collaboration between local and federal law enforcement to develop a national strategy to detect, prepare for, prevent, protect against, respond to and recover from terrorist attacks within the United States. Figure 13.6 provides the organizational chart for the DHS.

 The strategic goals of the Department of Homeland Security are awareness, prevention, protection, response, recovery, service and organizational excellence.

- *Awareness*—identify and understand threats, assess vulnerabilities, determine potential impacts and disseminate timely information to our homeland security partners and the American public.
- *Prevention*—detect, deter and mitigate threats to our homeland.
- *Protection*—safeguard our people and their freedoms, critical infrastructure, property and the economy of our nation from acts of terrorism, natural disasters or other emergencies.
- *Response*—lead, manage and coordinate the national response to acts of terrorism, natural disasters or other emergencies.
- *Recovery*—lead national, state, local and private sector efforts to restore services and rebuild communities after acts of terrorism, natural disasters or other emergencies.
- *Service*—serve the public effectively by facilitating lawful trade, travel and immigration.
- *Organizational Excellence*—value our most important resource, our people. Create a culture that promotes a common identity, innovation, mutual respect, accountability and teamwork to achieve efficiencies, effectiveness and operational synergies.

The DHS' mission statement and goals provide the framework for the department's six-point agenda.

DHS Six-Point Agenda The six-point agenda that guides the department seeks to (1) increase overall preparedness, particularly for catastrophic events; (2)create better transportation security systems to move people and cargo more securely and efficiently; (3) strengthen border security and interior enforcement and reform immigration processes; (4) enhance information sharing with our partners; (5) improve DHS financial management, human resource development, procurement

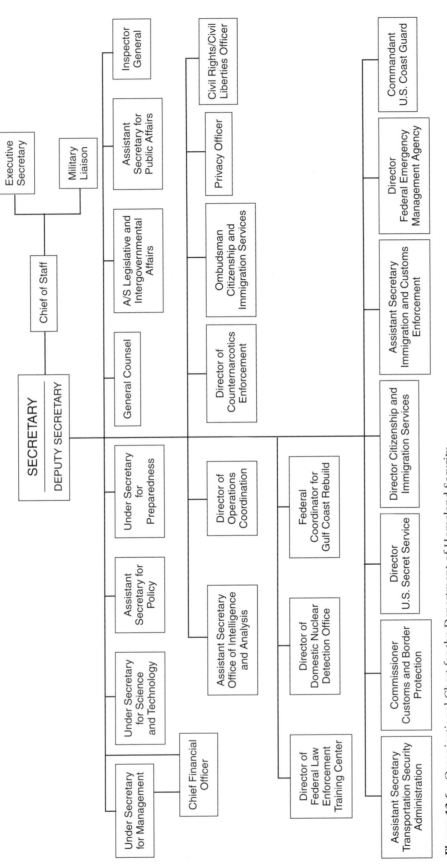

Figure 13.6 Organizational Chart for the Department of Homeland Security

Source: Department of Homeland Security, www.dhs.gov.

and information technology; and (6) realign the DHS organization to maximize mission performance.

The USA PATRIOT Act

On October 26, 2001, President Bush signed into law the Uniting and Strengthening America by Providing Appropriate Tools Required to Intercept and Obstruct Terrorism (USA PATRIOT) Act, giving police unprecedented ability to search, seize, detain or eavesdrop in their pursuit of possible terrorists. The law expands the FBI's wiretapping and electronic surveillance authority and allows nationwide jurisdiction for search warrants and electronic surveillance devices, including legal expansion of those devices to e-mail and the Internet.

The USA PATRIOT Act significantly improves the nation's counterterrorism efforts by:

- Allowing investigators to use the tools already available to investigate organized crime and drug trafficking.
- Facilitating information sharing and cooperation among government agencies so they can better "connect the dots."
- Updating the law to reflect new technologies and new threats.
- Increasing the penalties for those who commit or support terrorist crimes.

According to Boyter (2003, p.17): "The law [the PATRIOT Act] has come under increasing attack from groups across the political spectrum. Some members of Congress and civil liberties groups say the act has given federal agents too much power to pursue suspected terrorists, threatening the civil rights and privacy of Americans."

Report from the Field: The USA PATRIOT Act at Work (2004, p.1) states: "Since the USA PATRIOT Act was enacted, the Department of Justice—ever cognizant of civil liberties—has moved swiftly and vigorously to put its new tools into practice. As of May 5, 2004, the Department has charged 310 defendants with criminal offenses as a result of terrorism investigations since the attacks of September 11, 2001, and 179 of those defendants have already been convicted." After an extension from its expiration at the end of 2005, the Senate voted 29-10 to renew the act on March 2, 2006. The House followed suit on March 7, voting 280-13, days before the law was set to expire on March 10 (Greene, 2006, p.6). On March 9, President Bush signed into law the USA PATRIOT Improvement and Reauthorization Act.

As Devanney and Devanney (2003, p.10) explain: "The intent of the Patriot Act, when it was passed in 2001 as an immediate response to the 9/11 attacks, was to provide *federal* law enforcement with better means to defend against terrorism" (emphasis added). They note: "Even in the first days after 9/11, federal officials recognized the importance of local officers in defense against terror. In October 2001, President Bush signed executive Order 12321, which called for federal agencies to reach out to state and local agencies." The concern about local involvement was later incorporated into the Homeland Security Act (HSA) in November 2002. But again, this act focused on reorganizing 22 agencies to defend against terrorism. Unquestionably, the efforts of local law enforcement agencies are critical in the fight against terrorism.

The Critical Role of Local Law Enforcement in Homeland Security

The International Association of Chiefs of Police (IACP) contends that current homeland security strategies have a "fundamental flaw": they do not incorporate the input of state, tribal and local agencies. Their publication *From Hometown Security to Homeland Security* (2005, pp.3–6) rests on five principles:

1. All terrorism is local.
2. Prevention is paramount.
3. Hometown security is homeland security.
4. Homeland security strategies must be coordinated nationally, not federally.
5. The importance of bottom-up engineering; the diversity of the state, tribal, and local public safety community; and noncompetitive collaboration.

The importance of collaboration among the 17,000 law enforcement agencies staffed by 700,000 sworn police officers, deputy sheriffs and criminal investigators is vital:

- "It is vital that patrol officers correctly see themselves as the country's first line of defense against terrorist attacks" (Gardner, 2003, p.6).
- "When it comes to homeland security, every law enforcement officer can play a vital role. . . . A single law enforcement officer can indeed foil a devastating terrorist attack" (Wexler, 2003, p.30).
- "The 700,000 American law enforcement officers could become the eyes and ears of intelligence agencies, the first line in homeland defense" (White, 2004, p.5).

 The first line of defense against terrorism is the patrol officer in the field.

Berkow (2004, p.25) suggests:

American policing is well into the new post-September 11 era of new duties. Before the attacks, the world of counterterrorism, site security and intelligence gathering were generally restricted to either the largest of police agencies or those departments that were responsible for specific identified threats. Most police agencies in the United States were neither trained to carry out these tasks nor focused on them. Since the attacks, every agency in the United States regardless of size or location has accepted these new homeland security missions to some degree. Every agency has now added a counterterrorism mindset to their regular mission and is focused on building and enhancing that capability.

Our country's critical infrastructure—those deemed most critical to national public health and safety, governance, economic and national security, and retaining public confidence—now include agriculture, banking and finance, chemical and hazardous waste, defense industrial base, energy, emergency services, food, government, information and telecommunications, transportation, postal and shipping services, public health, and water (*Assessing and Managing the Terrorism Threat*, 2005, p.5). Key assets now include national monuments and icons, nuclear power plants, dams, government facilities and commercial assets. Each locality should identify its own critical infrastructures and assets and assess their risk potential.

In addition, because the private sector owns and protects 85 percent of the nation's infrastructure, law enforcement–private security partnerships can put vital information into the hands of those who need it: "To effectively protect the nation's infrastructure, law enforcement and private security must work collaboratively because neither possesses the necessary resources to do so alone" (*Engaging the Private Sector to Promote Homeland Security*, 2005).

Table 13.3   Best Practices and Trends in Homeland Security by Phases of Emergency Management

Mitigation	Preparedness
Federal assistance programs	Assignment of emergency management responsibilities
U.S. Homeland Security Advisory System	Emergency plans and possible hazards
Threat assessment	Mutual aid agreements
Building design and physical structures	Simulated-disaster exercises
Municipal and county building codes	Training for local government employees
Nonstructural safety measures	Use of the Incident Command System
Pedestrian and vehicular evacuation routes	
Response	**Recovery**
Contributions and donations management	Crime scene security
Damage assessment practices	Crisis counseling
Early-warning notification systems	Disaster assistance to property owners and citizens
Emergency shelters and assistance	Management of fatalities
Evacuation practices	Rebuilding private structures and spaces
Geographic information systems	Restoration of public infrastructure and open spaces
Medical services and equipment	
On-site command and control	
Public information and the news media	

Source: Roger L. Kemp. "The Future of Homeland Security." In *Homeland Security: Best Practices for Local Government,* edited by Roger L. Kemp. Washington, DC: International City/County Management Association, 2003, p.136. Reprinted by permission.

Best Practices in Homeland Security: An Overview

In the years since 9-11, agencies throughout the country have focused efforts on homeland security, efforts that usually fall into one of four phases: mitigation (lessening the threat), preparedness, response and recovery. Table 13.3 summarizes approaches that have been identified as effective in each of the four areas.

Mutual Aid Agreements Mutual aid agreements, commonly used to prepare for emergencies (as discussed earlier in the chapter) can play a greater role in preventing and responding to the threat of terrorism according to the Post–9-11 Policing Project ("Police Mutual Aid Agreements Seen as Key to Fighting Terrorism," 2006, p.3). This project is a collaboration of the IACP, the National Sheriffs' Association, the National Organization of Black Law Enforcement Executives, the Major Cities Chiefs Association and the Police Foundation. Established in 2004, its aim is to help local law enforcement agencies "proactively manage a changed and continually changing police environment" to take on the vast new responsibilities following the September 11, 2001, terrorist attacks.

The Project stresses that command and control issues must be addressed as both an operational necessity and a legal consideration in view of the possibility that civil liability may arise from decisions made regarding who is in charge.

Mutual Aid stresses that jurisdictions who provide services and resources without a written mutual aid agreement do so "at their own risk." Among the liability-related problems that might occur are liability for wear and tear on, damage to, or loss of equipment; injured personnel; civil liability stemming from the actions, inactions or omissions of responding officers; and the costs of services and resources. Failure to address such issues ahead of time could have negative consequences for both responding and requesting agencies.

Training in Homeland Security Efforts In October 2005, the Department of Homeland Security's Office for Domestic Preparedness launched its Cooperative Training Outreach Program (CO-OP) The intent of the program is to expand first-responder preparedness training across the country by permitting the states to identify and approve institutions within their states, territories or tribal entities that can adopt and deliver DHS standardized training courses (*Cooperative Training Outreach Program*, 2005). The training should include recognizing routine crimes that could signal terrorist activity planning.

Terrorism and Crime Savelli (2004, pp.65–66) points out: "Keep in mind, any law enforcement officer can potentially come in contact with a terrorist at any time, whether investigating an unrelated crime, conducting normal duties or responding as a back-up for another law enforcement officer. Also, keep in mind how many of the 9-11-01 hijackers had contact with law enforcement officers in various parts of the country and how many unsuspecting law enforcement officers, in any capacity, may have such contact with terrorists today or in the future." Savelli (pp.65–66) provides the following examples:

- Sept. 9, 2001 Ziad Jarrah, hijacker of the plane that crashed in Shanksville, Pennsylvania, was stopped by police in Maryland for speeding. He was driving 90 mph in a 65 mph zone. He was issued a ticket and released.
- August 2001 Hani Hanjour, who hijacked and piloted the plane that crashed into the Pentagon, killing 289 persons, was stopped by police in Arlington, Virginia. He was issued a ticket for speeding and released. He paid the ticket so he would not have to show up in court.
- Mohammed Atta, who hijacked and piloted the plane that crashed into the north tower of the World Trade Center, was stopped in Tamarac, Florida, for driving without a valid license and issued a ticket. He didn't pay the ticket so an arrest warrant was issued. A few weeks later he was stopped for speeding but let go because police did not know about the warrant.

Despite the ever-present threat of a terrorist attack, a poll conducted by the IACP revealed a concerning lack of preparedness on the part of our nation's law enforcement agencies. Of the 4,500 agencies that responded to the survey, 71 percent reported being "not at all prepared" or "somewhat unprepared" to prevent terrorism. A mere 1 percent claimed that they were "adequately prepared" (Garrett, 2004, p.6).

Although the events of 9-11 unquestionably expanded the scope of law enforcement's responsibility, it did not automatically include a corresponding increase in personnel or resources to affect the police mission. Consequently, law enforcement productivity—already a considerable management concern—has endured new scrutiny and encountered unprecedented challenges.

Law Enforcement Productivity

productivity • converting resources to results in the most efficient and effective way possible.

Productivity from the law enforcement department, one of the most costly municipal services, is expected. Managers' effectiveness is judged by the results they obtain using the available resources. **Productivity** is converting resources to achieve results efficiently and effectively. Productivity measures results gained from a specific amount of effort. An efficient use of resources alone may not be effective or meet a desired need. An effective use of resources may not be efficient or sufficient in overall impact. Productivity planning helps to balance efficiency and effectiveness guided by an overall desire for value.

Measuring Law Enforcement Productivity

Law enforcement services are not as measurable as production-line efforts. Production lines measure productivity in units manufactured; businesses measure it in profits.

 Law enforcement productivity is measured by the quality and quantity of services provided.

Increased productivity is a high priority. A balance between management and worker expectations has to be achieved without abandoning the concept that work must be productive. Reasonable standards must be determined. Desired management productivity and employee performance capability must be balanced. Once this balance is determined, employees have a standard against which management can measure them. If accurate records are kept, employees will know where they stand in relation to what is expected and to all other employees who perform the same functions.

 Law enforcement productivity has traditionally been measured by arrests, stops, traffic citations, the value of recovered property and reduction of crashes and crime.

The main concern with these productivity measurements is that law enforcement officers may not have much control over them. Reduction in crashes or crime may be short term, or there may be no reduction at all, but this does not necessarily mean that officers are not productive.

Quotas versus Performance Standards Productivity normally involves setting minimum standards, which, in law enforcement, brings up the question of quotas. A **quota** is a specific number or proportional share that each is expected to contribute. It is difficult not to use arrests, tickets issued, number of service calls answered and number of reports and activities initiated by officers as a basis for productivity because these are what officers do. But also important are how these tasks are executed, the quality of reports and the public's perception of the officers.

quota • a specific number or proportional share that each officer is expected to contribute or receive.

Productivity Problems

Symptoms of productivity problems are similar to those of motivation/morale problems: high absenteeism and turnover, high levels of waste, high accident rates and unreasonable complaints and grievances. The Internet is often a time waster. Server logs record all Internet activity on a network, including who visited what Web site, how long they stayed, what they looked at, what they searched for and where they went next. Examining server logs can reveal whether employees are less productive because of time spent on nonwork-related Internet activities.

Improving Productivity

Often the difference between promising ideas and productive results is a good manager. Productivity is directed from the top and accomplished at the bottom of the organizational hierarchy. Such productivity can be improved by:

- Clearly explaining organizational goals.
- Permitting more decisions to be made at the "doing" level.
- Supporting creativity and innovation.
- Increasing individual control over the tasks for which officers are responsible.

Furthermore, managers and supervisors at all levels must set performance expectations and then insist that those they oversee meet these expectations. Each department level must hold the next level accountable.

 Law enforcement productivity can be improved by:

- Training and experience.
- Rewards and incentives.
- Improved equipment.
- Technology.
- Intelligence-led policing.

Training and experience can improve productivity by helping people do tasks more efficiently. Productivity can also be increased through a reward system. Deserved praise, commendations and personal recognition are rewards. Monetary rewards, although effective, may not be as effective as personal rewards that build self-esteem and self-worth. All the concepts in Chapter 9 related to motivating employees are relevant.

In addition, improved law enforcement productivity can be accomplished by introducing improved equipment. An up-to-date communications and computer center can assist officers; however, the equipment should be procured based on a realistic cost assessment in relation to expected benefit. Many smaller, less costly pieces of equipment can increase patrol productivity. For example, cell phones for each unit, radar installed in most beat cars and a car desk or lighted clipboard for report writing are small items that can increase productivity.

Implementing mobile computing systems has several benefits, including higher crime-solution rates, greatly reduced clerical costs and, most important, increased officer safety. Such systems are excellent examples of ways in which technology can increase productivity.

Technology

Productivity can be increased without adding employees by using technology presently or soon to become available. Taping reports to be recorded later by clerk typists, using computers, installing improved 911 and computer-assisted dispatch (CAD) systems, superhighway police information systems and a host of other future technologies will vastly enhance police productivity.

management information system (MIS) • software programs that organize data to assist in decision making.

Computers can be used in a variety of ways to enhance productivity, for example, record keeping, data analysis, word processing, investigating, inventorying property rooms and maintaining stolen-property files. One way computers are improving departments' productivity is by facilitating the organization of data through a management information system (MIS). A **management information system (MIS)** provides data for planning and decision making. MIS procedures include collecting, analyzing and reporting past, present and projected information from within and outside the organization. Figure 13.7 illustrates the components of a management information system.

Integrated justice systems are improving not only the productivity of law enforcement but also that of the entire criminal justice system. The goal is to have the original information, collected by the officer on the street, flow into every other application used by every other step in the justice system.

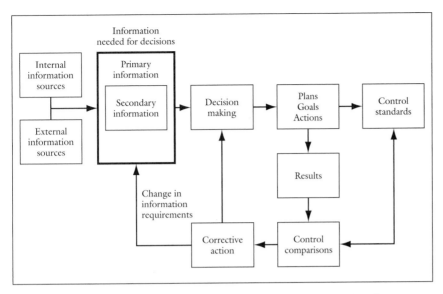

Figure 13.7 Components of a Management Information System (MIS)

Source: Lester R. Bittel. *The McGraw-Hill 36-Hour Management Course.* New York: McGraw-Hill Publishing Company, 1989, p.234. Reprinted by permission.

To keep up with technology, managers might use the National Aeronautics and Space Administration's (NASA) Technology Utilization Program, established in the early 1960s by congressional mandate to promote the transfer of aerospace technology to other areas. For example, a Pennsylvania police department called upon NASA's ability to enhance ATM films so the images were sufficiently sharpened to identify a car and driver, resulting in the arrest of a kidnapper/murder. Another promising approach to improving productivity is intelligence-led policing.

Intelligence-Led Policing

Intelligence-Led Policing: The New Intelligence Architecture (2005) states: "Traditional, hierarchical intelligence functions need to be reexamined and replaced with cooperative, fluid structures that can collect information and move intelligence to end users more quickly. Intelligence in today's policing environment must adapt to the new realities presented by terrorism and conventional crimes." The document stresses that new realities require increased collaboration in information gathering and intelligence sharing.

Critical community infrastructures such as food, agriculture, public health, telecommunications, energy, transportation and banking are now partners in terrorism prevention and crime control. Likewise, community and problem-oriented policing must be integrated into intelligence operations to address conventional crime issues. The intelligence process itself consists of six steps: Planning and direction, collection, processing/collation, analysis, dissemination, and reevaluation, as shown in Figure 13.8. An important aspect of intelligence-led policing is the concept of fusion centers, an emerging trend in law enforcement that is discussed in detail in Chapter 17.

Before leaving the discussion of productivity, consider previous discussions related to productivity.

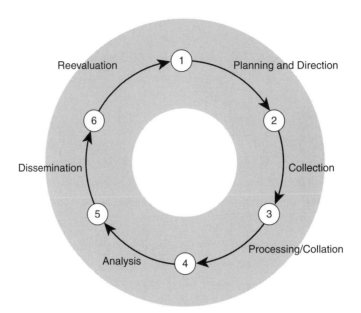

Figure 13.8   The Intelligence Process

Source: *Intelligence-Led Policing: The New Intelligence Architecture.*
Washington, DC: Bureau of Justice Statistics, September 2005, p.6.

Leadership, Discipline, Motivation and Morale Revisited

An anonymous quote reads: "Interest and attention are just as important to people as grease and oil are to a machine. Without it they don't run smoothly, never reach top speed and break down more frequently."

Developing a spirit to perform is one of management's jobs. Law enforcement managers use four motivating techniques: redesigning the law enforcement job; providing productive work and an opportunity for achievement and recognition; stating clear, concise and achievable goals; and providing some form of reward and enticement system for excellent performance. Intrinsic as well as extrinsic rewards can be used.

 The quality of management in the organization is the single most important factor for high productivity and morale. They are integrally related.

Cresie (2003, p.88) stresses: "The leadership philosophy that advocates the creation of high performance organizations through employee empowerment and team building is right on target." Sarver (2003, pp.46–52) presents 12 steps managers can take to improve subordinates' productivity:

1. Try to see things from the line officer's point of view.
2. Include them in decision-making activities and listen to them.
3. Give them responsibility and hold them accountable.
4. Reward them for contributions, and give credit where it is due.
5. Publicly commend their accomplishments.
6. Mentor and support them.
7. Challenge them to explore new ideas.
8. Treat them as they want to be treated.
9. Be firm when necessary.

10. Be honest with them.
11. Be part of their activities.
12. Care about them.

The department's mission is accomplished through the line officers. It is up to management to provide this bridge between mission and accomplishments.

 SUMMARY

The fact that patrol officers, those primarily responsible for accomplishing the department's goals, are lowest in status and in pay results in a serious organizational contradiction. A key management function is deploying personnel to patrol the jurisdiction. Area assignments are determined by requests for services based on available data. This is called proportionate assignment. No area should be larger than the time it takes a car to respond to emergency calls in a reasonable time. To determine patrol area size, consider square miles, street miles, the amount of crime and disorder and response time. Although rapid response may not deter crime or increase the apprehension of criminals, it is important because fast response builds public confidence in law enforcement capabilities and competence. It also places officers at a scene to protect evidence before people or the elements destroy it. It increases the chances of locating witnesses and making arrests. Further, it increases the chances of providing lifesaving emergency first aid to victims of crimes.

Most law enforcement departments use some form of random patrol, the basic premise of which is to place officers closer to a potential incident or request for service before it happens, based on data from experience. Goals are to reduce response time and erase set patrol pattern habits. However, the Kansas City Preventive Patrol Experiment found that increasing or decreasing preventive patrol had no effect on crime, citizen fear of crime, community attitudes toward the police on delivery of police services, police response time or traffic accidents. Common methods of patrol include automobile, bicycle, motorcycle, foot and air patrol. Other methods use mounted, water and special-terrain patrol.

Many managers, in an attempt to expand their employee base, have begun using alternative personnel resources, including citizen patrols, reserves and volunteers, in addition to civilianizing some law enforcement functions. Civilianization refers to hiring citizens to perform certain tasks for the law enforcement department.

Managers are expected to fulfill their responsibility to deploy resources to fight crime. The crime triangle is a model illustrating how all three elements—motivated suspect, suitable victim and adequate location—are required for crime to occur. Focusing on career criminals (suspects) is one logical approach to fighting crime. Focusing on specific locations with high crime rates, areas known as hot spots, is another approach. Focusing on victims brings community policing into the crime-fighting scene.

Managers also must be prepared to deploy resources during times of emergency and, therefore, should have carefully formulated predisaster plans. These plans should include, at minimum:

- Which emergencies to prepare for.
- What needs to be done in advance (supplies on hand, agreements with other agencies, etc.).
- What specific functions must be performed during the emergency and who is responsible for performing them, including outside organizations and agencies who might help.
- What steps need to be taken to restore order after the emergency has ended.

■ How the response is to be evaluated.

A relatively new area of responsibility is participating in homeland security efforts. The strategic goals of the Department of Homeland Security are awareness, prevention, protection, response, recovery, service and organizational excellence. The first line of defense against terrorism is the local law enforcement officer on patrol.

Law enforcement productivity is measured by the quality and quantity of services provided. It has traditionally been measured by arrests, traffic citations, value of recovered property and reduction of crashes and crime. Law enforcement productivity can be improved by training and experience, rewards and incentives, improved equipment and technology. One means to improve productivity is through a management information system (MIS), which provides data for planning and decision making.

The quality of management in the organization is the single most important factor for high productivity and morale. They are integrally related.

CHALLENGE THIRTEEN

The Greenfield Police Department has changed its mission statement to reflect the city's current service needs. The new mission emphasizes community-based, problem-solving policing. As the new police chief, you have reviewed the performance of the different units within the department. The detective unit is primarily reactionary and investigates crime reports taken by the patrol unit. They also conduct frequent prostitution stings at a local hotel, for which they have received several commendations. Records for the previous five years indicate no citizen complaints regarding prostitution. The only reports of prostitution were generated during the sting operations. The arrested prostitutes all worked for outcall services in other cities and traveled more than 20 miles to reach the hotel where they were arrested.

The patrol division devotes most of its time to preventive patrolling. They have an excellent response time to emergency calls. Patrol officers have been evaluated by the number of arrests they make and the number of tags they issue. Officer Swanson, a patrol officer for 20 years, has never received a service award. He has received several poor evaluations for spending too much time on calls and not writing enough tags. Officer Swanson knows everyone in town and often stops to chat at local businesses. He sometimes takes long coffee breaks at the senior citizens' home and has been seen dropping kids off at school. Citizens often specifically ask dispatch to send Officer Swanson to assist them. Although he receives consistently low evaluations from his supervisors, his file is packed with positive letters from citizens.

1. Is it possible for officers to do an excellent job at the tasks they are assigned and be unproductive?

2. Do you recognize a potential problem with the detectives' emphasis on prostitution stings?

3. Considering the Kansas City Preventive Patrol Experiment, why not reduce the strength of patrol shifts?

4. How can Greenfield's patrol strategy be changed to reduce preventive patrol and enhance community policing?

5. Is it possible that Officer Swanson may be more productive than his supervisors realize?

DISCUSSION QUESTIONS

1. What factors should be considered in determining personnel assignment to shifts?
2. What is your opinion of the random patrol method of deploying law enforcement personnel?
3. Do you favor one- or two-officer patrol units? Why?
4. Does your law enforcement agency use civilianization? If so, for what positions? Could this be expanded?
5. What emergencies should be planned for in your jurisdiction?
6. Have you ever been involved in a disaster or emergency that required law enforcement officers? If so, how effectively did they perform?
7. What proportion of resources do you feel should be allocated to "fighting crime"?
8. What innovative ideas can you think of to increase effectiveness and productivity?
9. How does your law enforcement agency use computers?
10. When are you highly productive? What factors are present during those times?

REFERENCES

Anderson, Amy L. and Meier, Robert F. "Interactions and the Criminal Event Perspective." *Journal of Contemporary Criminal Justice*, November 2004, pp.416–440.

Arey, James and Wilder, Ann. "Strategies Following a Catastrophe." *Law and Order*, November 2005, pp.90–94.

Aryani, Giant Abutalebi. "Guidelines for Police Volunteers." *Law and Order*, April 2005, pp.74–77.

Aryani, Giant Abutalebi; Alsabrook, Carl; and Garrett, Terry. "Homeland Security and Police Volunteers." *Law and Order*, April 2003, pp.52–56.

Assessing and Managing the Terrorism Threat. Washington, DC: Bureau of Justice Statistics, September 2005. (NCJ 210680)

Berkow, Michael. "The Internal Terrorists." *The Police Chief*, June 2004, pp.25–30.

Boyter, Jennifer. "Attorney General Ashcroft Defends Patriot Act." *The Police Chief*, September 2003, p.17.

Braiden, Chris. "Policing—The Hunt and the Habitat." *Law Enforcement News*, October 31, 1998, pp.8, 10.

Buhrmaster, Scott. "It's Not Over." *Law Officer Magazine*, July/August 2005, pp.42–45.

Careless, James. "Katrina: Four Years after 9/11 and Little Progress." *Law and Order*, October 2005, pp.114–120.

Chouinard, Carrie. "One Department's Volunteer Experience." *The Police Chief*, August 2003, pp.26–30.

Chudwin, Jeff. "Patroling the Pieces: Officers Share Observations and Lessons from Hurricane Katrina Deployment." *Law Officer Magazine*, November/December 2005, pp.44–51.

"Citizen Corp." Washington, DC: Bureau of Justice Assistance Program Brief, 2005. (NCJ 203669)

Cooperative Training Outreach Program. Washington, DC: Department of Homeland Security, 2005.

Cresie, John. "Creating High Performance Organizations." *Law and Order*, October 2003, pp.88–90.

Daugherty, Jack. "Hurricane Katrina Disaster Response: A Mid-Management View." *The Law Enforcement Trainer*, October/November/December 2005, pp.42–45.

Davies, Heather J. and Plotkin, Martha R. *Protecting Your Community from Terrorism, Vol. 5: Partnerships to Promote Homeland Security*, Washington, DC: Community Oriented Policing Services and the Police Executive Research Forum, November 2005.

Davis, Bob. "Principal Decision Systems International." *Police*, August 2005, pp.92–93.

Dees, Tim. "In Time Enterprise Solutions." *Law and Order*, July 2005, pp.122–123.

Devanney, Joe and Devanney, Diane. "Homeland Security and Patriot Acts." *Law and Order*, August 2003, pp.10–12.

Diamond, Joe. "Connecting the Dots." *Police*, April 2004, pp.42–47.

Engaging the Private Sector to Promote Homeland Security: Law Enforcement-Private Security Partnerships. Washington, DC: Bureau of Justice Statistics, September 2005. (NCJ 210678)

Famega, Christine N.; Frank, James; and Mazerolle, Lorraine. "Managing Police Patrol Time: The Role of Supervisor Directives." *Justice Quarterly*, December 2005, pp.540–559.

FEMA Website: http://www.fema.gov. Accessed February 13, 2006.

Fielden, Scott. "How to Run a Reserve Program." *Police*, December 2004, pp.28–32.

From Hometown Security to Homeland Security: IACP's Principles for a Locally Designed and Nationally Coordinated Homeland Security Strategy. Alexandria, VA: International Association of Chiefs of Police, May 17, 2005.

Gardner, Gerald W. "Getting Ready for the Big One: Terrorism Can Happen Anywhere, at Any Time." *Police*, October 2003, p.6.

Garrett, Ronnie. "The Wolf Is at the Door: What Are We Waiting For?" *Law Enforcement Technology*, March 2004, p.6.

Greene, Kevin E. "Congress Reauthorizes Anti-Terrorism Law." *Subject to Debate*, April 2006, p.6.

Hamilton, Melanie. "Taking a Toll." *Police*, November 2005, pp.38–42.

Herron, Shawn M. "The National Incident Management System." *The Police Chief*, November 2004, pp.20–28.

Hustmyre, Chuck. "Catching Criminals on the Highway." *Law and Order*, September 2003, pp.113–117.

Intelligence-Led Policing: The New Intelligence Architecture. Washington, DC: Bureau of Justice Statistics, September 2005. (NCJ 210681)

Jamieson, Gil. "NIMS and the Incident Command System." *The Police Chief*, February 2005, pp.68–78.

Johnson, Robert Roy. "Middle Management's Obligation and Opportunity." *Law and Order*, December 2005, pp.70–73.

Kingman, Ken. "Volunteers: Three Ingredients for Success." *Community Links*, Winter 2005, pp.4–5.

Klockars, Carl B. *Thinking about Police: Contemporary Readings*. New York: McGraw-Hill, 1983.

Kolb, Nancy. "Law Enforcement Volunteerism: Leveraging Resources to Enhance Public Safety." *The Police Chief*, June 2005, pp.22–30.

Law Enforcement and Community Emergency Response Teams (CERT): How Agencies Are Utilizing Volunteers to Address Community Preparedness Goals. Volunteers in Police Service, 2005. www.policevolunteers.org. Accessed February 13, 2006.

Lutz, William. "The Powerful Combination of Intranets and Mapping." *Law Enforcement Technology*, June 2003, pp.118–122.

Marshall, Ineke Haen. "Introduction." *Journal of Contemporary Criminal Justice*, November 2004, pp.344–347.

McDonald, Phyllis P. "Implementing Compstat: Critical Points to Consider." *The Police Chief*, January 2004, pp.33–37.

Moore, Carole. "Responding to the Perfect Storm." *Law Enforcement Technology*, November 2005, p.98.

Mutual Aid: Multijurisdictional Partnerships for Meeting Regional Threats. Washington, DC: Bureau of Justice Statistics, September 2005. (NCJ 210679)

Oliver, Bruce. "Ten-Hour Shifts: A Good Fit." *Law and Order*, July 2005, pp.102–105.

"Police Mutual Aid Agreements Seen as Key to Fighting Terrorism." *Criminal Justice Newsletter*, January 17, 2006, pp.3–4.

Report from the Field: The USA PATRIOT Act at Work. Washington, DC: Department of Justice, July 2004.

Sarver, Steven J. "Twelve Steps to Getting the Most Out of Your Employees." *The Police Chief*, October 2003, pp.46–52.

Savelli, Lou. *A Proactive Law Enforcement Guide for the War on Terrorism*. Flushing, NY: LooseLeaf Law Publications, Inc., 2004.

Schander, Mary L. "Civilian Career Advancement." *The Police Chief*, January 2003, pp.57–59.

Schick, Walt. "CompStat in the Los Angeles Police Department." *The Police Chief*, January 2004, pp.17–23.

Scoville, Dean. "Personal Transportation." *Police*, April 2005, pp.38–44.

Shane, Jon M. "CompStat Process." *FBI Law Enforcement Bulletin*, April 2004a, pp.12–21.

Shane, Jon M. "CompStat Design." *FBI Law Enforcement Bulletin*, May 2004b, pp.12–19.

Shane, Jon M. "CompStat Implementation." *FBI Law Enforcement Bulletin*, June 2004c, pp.13–21.

Sharp, Arthur. "The Ideal Work Schedule." *Law and Order*, September 2003, pp.124–127.

Sweeney, Earl M. "Maintaining Traffic Patrols in the Face of Rising Energy Costs." *The Police Chief*, August 2004, pp.23–24.

Sweeney, Thomas J. "Patrol." In *Local Government Police Management*, 4th ed., edited by William A. Geller and Darrel W. Stephens. Washington, DC: International City/County Management Association, 2003, pp.89–133.

Walsh, William F. and Vito, Gennaro F. "The Meaning of CompStat." *Journal of Contemporary Criminal Justice*, February 2004, pp.51–69.

Weisburd, David; Mastrofski, Stephen D.; Greenspan, Rosann; and Willis, James J. "The Growth of CompStat in American Policing." *Police Foundation Reports*, April 2004.

Weiss, Jim and Davis, Mickey. "Mutual Aid When Disaster Strikes." *Law and Order*, August 2005, pp.114–121.

Wexler, Sanford. "Homeland Security: Think Locally." *Law Enforcement Technology*, January 2003, pp.30–35.

White, Jonathan R. *Defending the Homeland: Domestic Intelligence, Law Enforcement and Security*. Belmont, CA: Wadsworth Publishing Company, 2004.

Williams, Gene. "Reserve Officers on Bikes." *Law and Order*, April 2005, pp.82–86.

Wrobleski, Henry M. and Hess, Kären M. *Introduction to Law Enforcement and Criminal Justice*, 8th ed. Belmont, CA: Wadsworth Publishing Company, 2006.

BOOK-SPECIFIC WEB SITE

Go to the Management and Supervision in Law Enforcement Web site at www.thomsonedu.com/criminaljustice/bennett for student and instructor resources, including Internet Assignments and Case Studies.

CHAPTER 14

Budgeting and Managing Costs Creatively

Budget—a mathematical confirmation of your suspicions.

A. Latimer

 DO YOU KNOW?

- What purposes a budget serves?
- Who is responsible for preparing the budget?
- How most budgets are developed?
- Whose input is vital to any budget?
- What categories are typically included in a budget?
- What the greatest cost in a law enforcement budget usually is?
- What cutback budgeting involves?
- What common cost choices most organizations face?
- What the first step in managing costs is?
- Who is responsible for reducing costs?
- How subordinates might be involved in managing costs creatively?
- How a department might reduce costs? Increase revenues?
- How asset forfeiture and the Eighth Amendment are related?
- Who the lead federal funding agency is for law enforcement?

CAN YOU DEFINE?

accounting
accounting period
activity-based
  costing (ABC)
all-levels budgeting
assets
audit trail
balance sheet
block grant
bottom-line
  philosophy
budget

capital budget
certified public
  accountant (CPA)
common costs
contingency funds
cutback budgeting
depreciation
direct expenses
discretionary budget
discretionary grant
financial budget
financial statements

fiscal year
fixed costs
flexible budget
formula grant
generally accepted
  accounting
  principles
  (GAAPs)
indirect expenses
line-item budgeting
line items
operating budget

operating expenses
overhead
performance
  budgeting
petty cash fund
program budgeting
semi-variable costs
sunk costs
variable costs
variance analysis
zero-based
  budgeting

Introduction

The principal mechanisms for controlling an organization's financial resources are the *budget* and the *cost accounting system.* The budget sets out a planned use of expenditures for the organization and is usually approved annually by a higher political authority. The cost accounting system measures the flow of expenditures through the organization and assigns them to specific activities (Stephens, 2003, p.59).

Budgeting has become more of a challenge as agencies are asked to "do more with less." After 9-11 the government spent billions of dollars creating the Department of Homeland Security. One in four cities had to shift money from its public safety budget to cover homeland security costs (Whitehead, 2004, pp.103–104). In addition, as Scoville (2004, pp.76–77) points out, law enforcement agencies are feeling the strain of finding money and personnel for both homeland security and street patrol. He notes that the first phase of the Iraq War alone cost $79 billion and that more than $100 billion may be spent on the reconstruction of Iraq: "The reallocations of the federal dollar have had—and will continue to have—serious implications for states and their law enforcement agencies" (p.78).

The budget must reflect an agency's mission. When it comes to prioritizing law enforcement's dollar, public safety has to be number one, which means: "Each agency and municipality must evaluate for itself the tradeoff between terrorism and emergency preparedness and law enforcement's ability to respond to calls for assistance, remove felons from the streets, maintain bomb squads and crime labs, and field adequate patrols" (Scoville, p.82).

This chapter begins with a definition of budgets and a description of the purposes of budgets. Next is a listing of basic budgeting and accounting terminology. This is followed by a discussion of who is responsible for preparing the budget and the budgeting process. The chapter then focuses on budgeting systems and budget categories, followed by an explanation of the importance of communication in seeking support for the budget as well as how to present the budget for approval. Next is a look at monitoring the budget and the possibility of cutback budgeting. The discussion then turns to managing costs creatively, including ways to reduce costs and to increase revenues. The chapter concludes with a discussion of grants: the various types available, where to learn about them and how to apply for them.

Budget Defined

budget • a list of probable expenses and income during a given period, most often one year.

financial budget • a plan or schedule adjusting expenses during a certain period to the estimated income for that period.

A **budget** is a list of probable expenses and income during a given period, most often one year. A **financial budget** is a plan or schedule adjusting expenses during a certain period to the estimated income for that period. Brock et al. (1990, p.G-1) define budgeting as: "The process of planning and controlling the future operations of a business by developing a set of financial goals and evaluating performance in terms of these goals." A budget is a working document, a tool to be used, not to be cast in stone or held in reverence. A budget, in effect, is a planning and control document, including stated financial expenditure amounts in accordance with a predetermined revenue or income. It is subject to approval by a higher authority than the person or department presenting the budget proposal.

The budget is a critical instrument in law enforcement planning, administration and operations. Preparing the budget is made difficult because most law enforcement services are intangible. Budgets are synonymous with monetary resources, which in turn are synonymous with personnel, equipment, supplies and, ultimately, the ability to provide comprehensive, continuous law enforcement services. Each agency has developed guidelines, budget forms and formats. In addition, many computer software budgeting programs are in use by law enforcement agencies at all governmental levels.

Budget can also be a verb, as in, "Let's budget money for this particular project." Usually, however, it is a noun that refers to an estimate of money to be spent during a year.

Types of Budgets

Most departments have two types of budgets. The **operating budget** deals with all expenses needed to run the department: salaries, insurance, electricity and the like. The **capital budget** deals with "big ticket" items such as land, buildings and improvements to systems; vehicles; and office equipment. To be included in the capital budget, items must have the following three characteristics: (1) be a tangible asset (can be felt/touched), (2) have a life expectancy or useful life of more than one year and (3) exceed a minimum cost threshold established by the department (Orrick, 2005, p.233).

operating budget • a budget that contains projections for income statement items as well as expenses.

capital budget • deals with "big ticket" items such as major equipment purchases and vehicles.

Some departments also have a **discretionary budget,** which sets aside funds to be used as needed. Discretionary funding in law enforcement agencies is a favorite target in annual budget battles (Estey, 2004, p.6).

discretionary budget • funds available to be used as the need arises.

Budgets are familiar tools to most people. They are used not only by law enforcement agencies, businesses and other organizations but also in personal lives. They are often viewed as negative, restrictive, something to be tolerated. But they also serve some extremely important purposes.

Purposes of Budgets

Budgets control and guide how resources are used and make those in charge of them responsible for their wise use.

Budgets serve as a plan for and a means to control resources.

Budgets establish financial parameters for department needs. The vast majority of plans and projects of the department depend on finances. Budgets permit decision making at lower levels to work upward through the law enforcement hierarchy. First-line supervisors can present budget ideas that may ultimately be transformed into street operations. For example, the supervisor who develops an accident-prevention program and receives funding to put the program into action must be mindful of budget controls during the entire program.

Budgets also help reduce the tendency for divisions of a department to build their own little empires by establishing a maximum line item for each division. The detective division, the patrol division and the juvenile division may each have an allotted amount of funds. Any one division can spend only the funds approved for that division. Without budgeting, serious competition for total funds could be detrimental to the department's overall objectives.

Budgets provide an opportunity to compare expenditures with services provided. For example, the investigative division can compare personnel and other operational costs with the number of cases investigated, cases successfully closed, arrests made and property recovered.

Budgeting is a continuous process and a written commitment. Budgets are a law enforcement agency's work plan transformed into dollars, which translate into salaries, fringe benefits, equipment and special projects.

Budgets are formally approved statements of future expenses throughout the fiscal year. Expenses are constantly balanced against the approved budget allocations. Budgets control available resources and assist in their efficient use. In essence, budgets are a monetary Bible whose First Commandment is: "Thou shalt not spend more than is herein allocated."

Not less than monthly, executive managers receive itemized expenses and a statement of the balance remaining in each budget category. Some communities operate on a **bottom-line philosophy,** which permits departments to shift funds from one category to another as long as the total budget bottom line is not exceeded. Other communities consider each category as separate line items. Any shifting of funds from one category to another must be approved.

Budgets also reflect the political realities of law enforcement agencies and their jurisdictions. More effective managers are more likely to obtain approval for their programs and projects than less effective managers or those with less political clout. Before looking at who is responsible for preparing the budget and the process involved, take time to familiarize yourself with some basic terminology.

> **bottom-line philosophy •** allows shifting funds from one expense category to another as long as expenses do not exceed the total amount budgeted.

Budgeting and Accounting Terminology

Law enforcement managers must have a working knowledge of the vocabulary of financial management. The following definitions are adapted from Brock et al. (pp.G-1–G-8), with the term *agency* substituted for *business* in many instances. (Reprinted by permission of Glencoe, a division of McGraw-Hill.)

Accounting—the process by which financial information about an agency is recorded, classified, summarized, interpreted and then communicated to managers and other interested parties.

Accounting period—the time covered by the income statement and other financial statements that report operating results.

Assets—items of value owned by an agency.

Audit trail—the chain of references that makes it possible to trace information about transactions through an accounting system.

Balance sheet—shows an agency's financial position at a specific date by summarizing the agency's assets and liabilities.

Certified public accountant (CPA)—an accountant licensed by a state to do public accounting work.

Common costs—expenses not directly traceable to a segment of an agency such as a department or division; they might include a municipality's insurance costs.

Depreciation—the process of allocating the cost of a long-term asset to operations during its expected useful life. For example, squad cars will decrease in value as they are used.

Direct expenses—operating costs that can be identified specifically within individual departments. Includes such items as salaries and benefits.

Financial statements—periodic reports that summarize an agency's financial affairs.

Fiscal year—the 12-month accounting period used by an agency. A calendar year, from January 1 through December 31, may or may not be the same as an agency's fiscal year.

Fixed costs—expenses that do not vary in total during a period even though the amount of service provided may be more or less than anticipated, for example, rent and insurance.

Flexible budget—a projection that contains budgeted amounts at various levels of service.

Generally accepted accounting principles (GAAPs)—the rules of accounting used by agencies in reporting their financial activities.

Indirect expenses—operating costs not easily assigned to a particular department when transactions occur. Some indirect expenses, such as depreciation, have a meaningful relationship to individual departments and can be allocated based on this relationship. Other indirect expenses must be allocated on the most logical basis possible.

Operating expenses—costs that arise from an agency's normal activities.

Petty cash fund—a cash fund of a limited amount used to make small expenditures for when it is not practical to write checks.

Semi-variable costs—expenses that have characteristics of both fixed costs and variable costs. For example, utility expenses are semi-variable costs because they occur monthly but the amount varies.

Sunk costs—historical costs already incurred and thus irrelevant for decision-making purposes, for example, the purchase of a K-9. Other costs associated with the dog, however, will continue.

Variable costs—expenses that change in total directly with the amount of service provided, for example, personnel costs including overtime.

Responsibility for Preparing the Budget

Budget preparation may be the responsibility of the records department; a financial officer assigned to planning; or, in large departments, a separate division. In smaller law enforcement agencies, executive managers may prepare the budget. In larger departments, a person of next lower rank, a staff person or a special fiscal division is assigned to prepare the budget details and present it to the executive manager, who then holds staff meetings or budget workshops to complete the budget.

Executive law enforcement managers should encourage managers in all divisions and at all levels to monitor budget expenditures and justify expenses within their assigned responsibilities. Such a policy encourages budget preparation participation because managers can visualize the total process.

Executive managers or assigned staff need input from all employees. Requested budget information at various levels should be in a form and language understandable to people not directly connected to preparing the final budget. In a problem-oriented department, the budgeting process will be more participatory and bottom-up than it is in a traditional department (Stephens, p.59).

The all-levels process of budgeting preparation is becoming common in many agencies. First-line supervisors know the needs of street-level law enforcement services and will include potentially overlooked items.

 Managers at each level should be responsible for the budget they need, based on input from their subordinates. This results in **all-levels budgeting.**

all-levels budgeting • everyone affected by the budget helps prepare it.

If all levels of employees and managers have input into the budget, they will understand it and be more aware of revenue and expenditure balancing. They also become part of not only the process of budget preparation but also the goal development on which the budget is based and the subsequent budget review and possible revisions.

What people help to create, they are likely to support. The budget is one area in which support is critical. Normally the employees' most active interests will be in the areas of salaries and fringe benefits. In reality, some other budget items more severely affect their day-to-day work activities. Effective managers demonstrate this to employees and ensure that subordinates do not focus solely on budget areas that directly affect them but rather on the whole picture.

Budgets will be more accurate and complete if they are prepared using a logical process beginning with the department's lowest levels and working upward. If the total budget exceeds the amount approved for the agency, the budget must be reviewed line item by line item, and items must be eliminated that will have the least effect on total services provided. Support of all involved is needed to make such cuts without negative effects.

Typical Levels in Developing a Budget

Budget development usually starts at the level of area commands where budget requests originate. Such requests are either (1) funded within the department's base budget, (2) disapproved or (3) carried forward for management review. At the division level, managers review the area requests, make needed adjustments and submit a consolidated request to the budget section.

Within two to three months, the budget section identifies proposals for new funding that have department-wide impact and passes them on to the executive level. The commissioner and aides review the figures along with those from other city departments and agree on a budget to submit to the city manager.

The Budgeting Process

Developing a budget is an art, not a science: "Mastering the budgeting process is critical for the success of the police organization. Budgeting is not a complicated process. However, it is a learned skill that requires ingenuity, creativity, attention to detail and good communication skills" (Orrick, p.239). In addition to serving as the funding process for department operations, a budget can also be viewed as a:

- Planning document—It is the funding document for what the organization plans to accomplish during the next year.
- Political document—It is a financial expression of our values.
- Living document—The conditions and events impacting the department change. The organization must be flexible and respond to these conditions (Orrick, p.239).

Budgeting is a year-round process. It begins with the department's mission, goals, objectives, and work plans and the resources needed to carry them out.

Determining Personnel Costs

Since personnel costs make up the largest item in an agency's budget, determining staffing levels is a critical step. Once staffing levels are determined, the cost of personnel services can be calculated by obtaining information on base salary, merit or longevity increases, cost of living increases, Federal Insurance Contributions Act (FICA—7.5 percent of salary withheld and matched by employer), worker's compensation, retirement, health/dental/life insurance, overtime and any other compensation-related benefits.

Review of Last Year's Budget

Budget preparation often includes a review of the previous year's budget. These expenditures were approved and probably apply to the new budget. Accurate figures of total costs related to successful accomplishment of past goals provide a foundation for future predictions. These figures are then adjusted to allow for increased costs due to inflation and reduced costs due to wider use, greater availability of the product or competition. The figures should be placed on a computer spreadsheet so revisions can be easily made.

The next task is to compare cost increases, line item by line item, and adjust, eliminate or add items. These changes should be based on carefully thought-out assumptions. Each year new items and programs appear, and the total amount of available funds varies, but the main budget format remains.

 Most law enforcement budgets are developed by revising the previous year's budget based on logical assumptions.

Most budget items are short term, that is, applicable to current-year activities. Because estimated costs are more stable over short periods, short-term expenditures are easier to plan for than long-term expenses. Carryover, or continued items or programs from previous budgets, must include inflationary costs, including cost-of-living salary increases, additional fringe-benefit costs and spin-off costs from increased vacation or sick-leave programs.

Law enforcement budget preparation is a series of events involving hearings, city council workshops, input meetings, cost estimating and a host of other technical details. The process generally involves presentation by the finance department at a governmental entity department staff meeting or by written instructions sent to the department head. Sample forms for preparing budgets are included. Dates are set for various levels of preparation, discussions and workshops.

Law enforcement agencies repeat the process with their own personnel. Any changes in procedure from previous budgets are discussed. Dates and times for different levels of completion must be established, or procrastinators will submit at the last minute, resulting in lower-quality preparation and consideration. This may lead to omitting items important to continued effective operations.

Law enforcement agencies operate for extended periods with tasks and functions varying from day to day, month to month and year to year. It is difficult to foresee all situations that eventually must be converted into cost factors. For example, who can predict whether a squad car will be involved in a crash and "totaled"; or whether 20 inches of sleet and snow will fall, creating numerous crashes;

Records help police officers identify areas where expenditures are needed. Using facts, officers can present their budget requests to their superiors. Input from all levels results in the best budget, and it helps make the budget acceptable to officers at all levels.

contingency funds • money allocated for unforeseen emergencies.

or whether a natural disaster or a terrorist attack will occur, requiring hundreds of hours of overtime? **Contingency funds** are set aside for such unforeseen emergencies, but the precise total of allowable expenditures is difficult to ascertain.

Priorities must be weighed. Rarely are revenues sufficient to support all requests, and rarely are all requests justifiable. Justification includes the reasons the item is needed and the effect it would have on the department's operations if eliminated. Items that can be accurately cost-determined should include the source of the cost estimate. The more specific the cost and justification, the less likely the expense is to be criticized.

Some items are mandated by state and federal regulations, collective bargaining agreements and the Fair Labor Standards Act. Some items are directly linked to safety issues, increasing chances a proposed expenditure will not be cut. Sometimes prices have risen, for example, rising fuel costs. Training is a common target for cuts because: "Agencies need firearms, computers and patrol cars, but training is an abstract that can't be seen or touched" (Nowicki, 2003, p.30). Indeed, training is often the first area to experience sharp cuts, but "in our world of school shootings and threats of terrorism the demand for training of officers has never been greater" (Lebreck, 2004, p.52). Nowicki cautions that cutting the training budget can be "a disaster waiting to happen." A suggested rule of thumb to increase funding chances is that the department gets a return of ten dollars for every dollar spent on training (Orrick, p.236).

Some communities are using outcome-based budgeting, requiring the department to justify budget requests based on the output of the department's services (Smith, 2005, p.82). Officer workload must be differentiated from call load: "Workload is a weighted measure of the types of calls as well as the amount of time and number of officers involved. Call load is merely the number of dispatch calls" (Smith, p.82). The importance of measuring more than call load or workload was discussed in Chapter 13. Staffing analysis is a key component of budget preparation.

Even if all requests are justifiable, final decisions must be based on available revenues. Tough decisions are often mandatory. Moreover, not all factors can be measured in dollars. Budgets involve intangibles, such as cost in morale and performance. In some budget preparations, the manager closest to the origin of the financial request is given the total list of requests, the estimated costs and the maximum funding available. Managers are asked to decide what to eliminate.

This prioritization often involves consulting with all employees for whom the manager is responsible. If priorities are set with employees' input, they are more acceptable. Further, employees understand the total budgeting process, which ultimately translates into their everyday operational capabilities for the budget year. Input may be given at one or several stages of the budget process.

Budget preparation should be an ongoing process of planning, setting goals and objectives, itemizing, obtaining input on needs and comparing the data with past budgets. Information to be used in developing the budget should be collected continuously.

 All law enforcement employees should contribute ideas related to budget items as specific needs arise.

Subordinates should submit their ideas to their most immediate manager. At the proper time, managers submit summaries of these suggestions to the next level manager, and so on up to the executive manager. If such ideas are submitted during times of actual need, they will more accurately represent reality when the final budget is developed. Waiting until the last few months before budget presentation time and then rushing to obtain all the necessary information is not good budgeting procedure.

Even with this base, managers may approach budgets with reluctance and apprehension. This is partly because various internal divisions compete, and the agency's total budget competes with all other government departments for available tax revenue dollars. One way to ease the mental anguish of budgeting is to not expect perfection. Having a specific step-by-step procedure for looking at specific areas within the budget can also help lessen anxiety.

Budgeting Systems

Law enforcement budgets may take several forms. One of the most common is **line-item budgeting,** initiated in the 1900s and still popular. In this system, specific categories (**line items**) of expenses are identified and dollars allocated for each. Line-item budgets are usually based on the preceding year's budget and a comparison between it and actual expenses.

line-item budgeting • identifies specific categories (line items) and dollars allocated for each.

line items • specific expense categories, for example, personnel, maintenance, training.

performance budgeting • allocates dollars based on productivity.

program budgeting • identifies programs and allocates funds for each.

overhead • expenses that do not vary in total during a period even though the amount of service provided may be more or less than anticipated, for example, rent and insurance.

activity-based costing (ABC) • a modern version of the program budgeting system, except that rather than breaking costs down by program, the approach breaks down costs by activity.

zero-based budgeting (ZBB) • begins with a clean slate, justifying each expenditure anew.

Performance budgeting allocates dollars based on productivity. Those divisions that perform most effectively are allotted a greater share of the budget. **Program budgeting** identifies the various programs an agency provides and allocates funds for each. A percentage of administrative costs, support costs and **overhead** (operating expenses exclusive of personnel) are assigned to each program. This budgeting approach requires much paperwork, and many managers feel it is unproductive. However, it can help preserve programs in the face of budget cut pressure. **Activity-based costing (ABC)** is a modern version of the program budgeting system, except that rather than breaking down costs by program, the approach breaks down costs by activity. ABM refers to activity-based management, a logical outgrowth of this approach to analyzing costs. ABC breaks up overhead into neat little cost drivers, the factors that determine the final cost of an operation.

Zero-based budgeting (ZBB) requires justifying all expenditures, not only those that exceed the prior year's allocations. All budget lines begin at zero and are funded according to merit rather than according to the level approved for the preceding year. Zero-based budgeting requires management to articulate objectives and then identify alternative methods of accomplishing those objectives, systematically analyzing the effects of various funding levels. Such an approach to budgeting makes comparison of competing programs easier.

Budget Categories

Regardless of the budgeting system, the budget is usually divided into two classes of expenses: variable, which will change depending on the level of service provided, and fixed, or overhead, which is relatively constant. Within these two categories, subcategories of expenses can be identified.

 Common budget categories include salaries and wages, services and supplies, training and travel, contractual services and other or miscellaneous.

The miscellaneous category should not be treated as a catchall but should be used for small items such as journal subscriptions or books. Budgets also often contain special one-time requests for capital equipment, such as new police vehicles or investigative equipment.

Typical Allocations to Various Categories

In most budgets, salaries and wages account for the largest expenditures, typically 80 to 85 percent. Of this amount, fringe benefits usually amount to 25 percent of the allocation.

 Personnel costs usually account for at least three fourths of the operating budget.

Salaries and wages predominate primarily because of the personnel needed to provide extended-time law enforcement services. Equipment is also used for the same extended time and consequently must be replaced more frequently. For example, a simple item such as a dispatcher's chair used 24/7 is going to need replacement much faster than one used during a 5-day, one-shift week. Figure 14.1 shows a typical public safety department's expenditures.

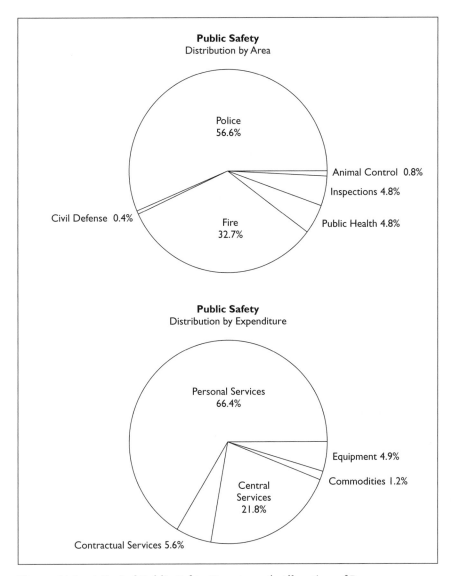

Figure 14.1 A Typical Public Safety Department's Allocation of Resources

Communication and Budget Support

Open, meaningful communication with neighborhood groups, citizens, elected officials, other departments and agencies, and line officers is critical to securing an adequate budget. Of particular importance is effective communication with elected officials, the public and line staff when dealing with financial matters. Police administrators should encourage those elected officials with budgetary authority to ride with patrol officers: "Reading annual reports or listening to answers being given at a council meeting is no substitute for seeing first hand what officers face and hearing what citizens fear" (Boertien, 2004, pp.130–131).

To increase the likelihood of budget approval, those preparing the budget should consider forming an advisory committee representative of the community and the local governing body to ensure a diversity of viewpoints and information.

They might also consider surveying the community to provide back up and provide information to counter any claims by hostile officials.

Presenting the Budget for Approval

The law enforcement budget process generally culminates in presentation to the city council or city manager. Here it competes for revenues with all other departments. Many factors come into play at this point—some factual, some political.

Budget presentations should be made realistically and honestly because the law enforcement budget must be sold to a higher body for final approval. Political decision makers need accurate information. Padding the budget is often discussed, but in reality city managers, city councils and finance departments are well aware of this tactic. Managers must request funds based on needs, provide a spirit of cooperation and candor and try to avoid serious conflicts. Without factual, accurate information, decisions will likely be made based on personal contacts, innuendo and community pressure.

Haberfeld (2006, p.165) emphasizes the importance of both facts and emotions in a budget presentation and suggests that most successes in law enforcement agencies come from winning not only minds, but also hearts. The competencies needed in both areas are summarized in Table 14.1.

Presenting the budget is similar to making a sales pitch, but managers are cautioned that "shooting from the hip doesn't work" (Goldsmith, 2005, p.24). The presentation should be practiced and rehearsed with a colleague, a spouse or in front of a mirror. Orrick (2003, p.24) suggests: "Never underestimate the power of an effective budget presentation, in writing or in person." He suggests police managers can be very persuasive by following two simple rules. First, be prepared. Know what the hot issues are, have a response ready when they surface, and use high-quality visual aids in every presentation. Second, keep your cool. Budget hearings can become emotional: "Never demonstrate anger or indignation toward an elected official" (Orrick, p.24). In addition, those representing the department should never argue with the elected body. This shows a lack of restraint and professionalism.

Table 14.1   Art of Winning Minds and Hearts: Leadership Competencies Needed

Art of Winning Minds	Art of Winning Hearts
Objective: Convincing people—make them understand the purpose	*Objective:* Moving people—increase their commitment/motivation
Medium: Information	Medium: Emotion
■ Relevance	■ Authenticity
■ Cogency	■ Empathy
■ Showmanship	■ Listening
■ Questioning	■ Rapport
■ Dialogue	■ Optimism
■ Promotion of discovery	■ Trust in intuition
■ Atmosphere of intellectual safety	■ Atmosphere of emotional safety

Source: M. R. Haberfield. *Police Leadership.* Upper Saddle River, NJ: Pearson, Prentice Hall, 2006, p.165. Reprinted by permission.

After the budget is approved, it must be implemented by converting dollars and cents into law enforcement services rendered. It is the manager's responsibility to make sure these dollars are wisely used as budgeted.

Monitoring

The budget is a *tool*, not a document to be approved and then filed. After the budget is passed, the most important task is to monitor spending. **Variance analysis** consists of comparing actual costs against what was budgeted and analyzing differences.

varience analysis • comparing actual costs against what was budgeted and examining the differences.

Budget execution can be compared with firing a weapon (Orrick, 2005, p.238). The sight alignment and trigger squeeze may be correct, but rounds may be grouped to one side at the 7-yard mark. If no corrective action is taken, the officer will miss the target from 15 or 25 yards. The same is true with a department's budget. If a line item is 2 percent over budget after the first month and no corrective action is taken, it may be 24 percent over at the end of the year. Expenditures must be monitored monthly.

Variances in the budget are caused by one of three things: (1) price change (either higher or lower), (2) volume (using more or less of a line item) or (3) efficiency of operation (equipment is operating more or less efficiently than anticipated) (Orrick, p.239). Differences should be contained in a variance report and made known to everyone who directly or indirectly influences the costs. A variance is not necessarily a sign the budget is wrong. Rather, it signals a need for control over income or expenses. Reporting budget variances is an opportunity to provide guidance to management. Variance reports should be made monthly. Problems or deviations should be identified and recommendations made for corrective action. Forms such as those in Figure 14.2 might be used to report variances and requests for budget revisions. Budgeting is a guideline, not an infallible indicator of the future. No one can do better than an estimate, and variances *will* arise.

Cutback Budgeting

Estey (p.6) contends: "Law enforcement agencies of all sizes and makeup are facing an imminent financial crisis of monumental proportions." Most departments are being asked to provide more services with fewer funds. Whether called budget reduction, cutback budgeting or reduced expenditure spending, it means added frustration and anxiety for police managers.

 Cutback budgeting means providing the same or more services with less funding.

cutback budgeting • providing the same or more services with less funding. Also called *budget reduction* or *reduced expenditure spending*.

"Doing more with less" is the mandate of the future for most law enforcement agencies. Even successful programs have been discontinued because of lack of funding. To a large extent, budgets control an organization's potential and capabilities.

Causes of Cutback Budgeting

Cutbacks are caused by several factors, the most familiar being that the problem is considered solved. A second cause is erosion of the economic base, seen especially in the United States' older cities and the Northeast, in the growth of dependent populations and shifts from the Frostbelt to the Sunbelt. Other causes

Variance Report

Account: _____

Date: _____

Year-To-Date

Actual	Budget	Variance	±%

Variance Analysis

Date: _____

	Actual Results	Budget Assumptions	Variance	%
I: Prior year-to-date				
_____				
_____				
_____				
Total				
II: Current month				
_____				
_____				
_____				
Total				

Figure 14.2   Forms for Reporting and Analyzing Variances

include inflation, taxpayer revolts and actual limits to growth. Whatever the cause, cutback management poses special challenges.

Doing More with Less

Orrick (pp.235–236) describes several approaches to budget cuts:

- Cut all requests for personnel increases.
- Cut equipment viewed as luxuries.
- Use precedent—cut items that have been cut before.
- Recommend repair and renovation, not replacement.
- Recommend a study to defer the costs.
- Cut all costs by a fixed amount (for example, 5 percent).
- Cut departments with a bad reputation.
- Don't cut when the safety of staff or the public is involved.

Request for Budget Revision

Account _____   Date _____

Year-to-date Actual $ _____

Year-to-date Budget $ _____

Variance $ _____ % _____

This variance is caused by: _____

_____

_____

_____

_____

_____

_____

This budget should be changed to: _____

_____

_____ Effective date _____

_____

Approved _____

Title _____ Date _____

Figure 14.2 (continued)   Forms for Reporting and Analyzing Variances

 Common cost choices that management must make include whether to:

- Resist or smooth cuts.
- Make a deep gouge or small decrements.
- Share the pain or target the cuts.
- Budget for efficiency or equity.

In each case, the best choice from a management viewpoint may not make sense politically or from a team-building viewpoint. Levine (p.10) presents possible solutions, such as reassigning functions to county or state governments and the following:

> Some services can be "privatized" by installing fees, user charges and contracting arrangements for special skills, and some services can be consolidated to achieve economies of scale. Services can be "civilianized" through the use of volunteers and nonsworn personnel. Some services can be reduced or eliminated by careful monitoring of the differences between citizen "needs" and citizen "wants." And expenses can be trimmed through overtime control, "downtime management," self-insurance and new pension arrangements.

"The enemies of responsible management in these difficult times," says Levine (p.10), "are complacency, convenience and wishful thinking." Compounding the problem are the political dynamics with "entrenched interests and neighborhood groups fight[ing] to maintain services at prevailing levels against emerging groups with new demands." Three steps suggested by Levine might be considered by managers facing cutback budgeting (pp.11–12):

1. Assume a positive attitude toward innovation; be willing to experiment.
2. Become convinced that fiscal stress can be managed; prioritize services and projects.
3. Develop a marketing strategy to sell taxpayers on the importance and quality of public services.

Each government agency has its sources of revenues and its requirements for services. When revenue sources do not meet the cost of requirements for services, a cutback budgeting situation develops. New revenues must be designated or services cut. Cost reductions might include cutting overtime; reducing capital outlay purchases; reducing travel; initiating hiring freezes; or, in extreme instances, laying off personnel or promoting early retirement.

Seeking new revenues is another solution. A combination of cutback budgeting procedures and new revenues may be necessary. Managers might look at how budgeting is done in the private sector, with requests for proposals and bidding an integral part of major purchases. Many businesses also use cooperative purchasing, joining together for better pricing.

The same can be done in law enforcement. For example, several agencies could go together in purchasing police vehicles, thereby getting a better price.

Managing Costs Creatively

Perhaps without even realizing it, you have already learned about one of the most creative ways to manage costs—managing time. People and their time are a manager's greatest resource. The following discussion assumes that the manager is already paying careful attention to this aspect of budgeting.

Identifying Common Cost Problems

 The first step in solving cost problems is to identify waste areas.

Absenteeism and turnover are major cost problems in most organizations. Managers concerned with controlling costs should have a very clear idea of just how much each subordinate is worth in dollars per day. This figure, coupled with absenteeism, is very important to managers as they look at their budgets.

Other costs managers should target are equipment maintenance, mail, duplicating, computer and telephone. Are employees using these facilities for personal business? If so, might it make sense to establish a mechanism so they could pay for the convenience? This works well in many organizations. Meetings are another area, already mentioned, where much waste occurs. Many resource management experts suggest that at least one fourth of all time (and dollars) spent on meetings is wasted. Paperwork is another obvious, yet frequently overlooked, area of waste.

 Reducing costs is all employees' responsibility.

Employees should understand where waste is occurring and how they might help reduce it. In addition to this reactive approach to cost containment, a more proactive approach might also be used.

Employee Cost Improvement Suggestion Programs

The idea of a suggestion system is certainly not new, for such systems have been successfully operating for decades in business and industry. A typical system includes guidelines for acceptable suggestions, a mechanism for making the suggestions and rewards for those suggestions selected as feasible.

 Employees can suggest ways to cut costs through an employee cost improvement suggestion program.

Successful employee suggestion programs share several common features, including clearly informing all employees of the program's details and procedures; providing fair, meaningful rewards; and continuously publicizing the program and its objectives.

Such programs are in keeping with the team concept introduced in the first section of this text and emphasized throughout. Costs must be managed if law enforcement agencies are to provide the services citizens expect and require.

A financial crisis can also present opportunity as managers look for innovative ways to stretch existing budgets: "People learn to improvise, adjust and jury rig" (Griffith, 2004, p.6). As one police chief commented: "I'm a firm believer that tight financial times often are the genesis for creative ideas. If you're flushed with money, the tendency is just to sort of continue to do business as usual" (Griffith, quoting Chief James Montgomery, Bellevue (Washington) Police Department, p.6).

Many law enforcement agencies are using the budget crunch as an impetus to conserve resources and develop new, efficient programs that may not ever have been developed: "They focus on mitigating the outflow of money and maximizing opportunities for revenue" (Hamilton, 2004a, p.60).

Creative Ways to Reduce Costs

Creativity can be an asset in a department's ongoing quest to reduce costs. For example, the chief of a three-officer department stretches the agency's dollars by going online ("e-Bay-Savvy Chief Makes Budget-Dollars Go Further," 2005, p.14): He bought Vascar timing devices, used for catching speeders, for $100 each when they usually cost $3,500; laptop computers were purchased for $150 instead of $3,200; and a 2000 Ford Crown Victoria was acquired for $4,500, while the same model with the same mileage would have cost $7,000 from the U.S. General Services Administration. Going online might work well for a small department, but larger departments usually need other ways to reduce costs.

A forum sponsored by the National Criminal Justice Association revealed the following ways agencies are able to sustain services in a time of shrinking resources ("Doing the Best with Less," 2003, p.9):

- Increase flexibility to respond to needs quickly.
- Increase use of e-mail publications to share information and cut printing costs.
- Partner with state higher education institutions to meet research, evaluation, training and curriculum development needs.

- Combine resources with other community, faith-based, and state agencies to help meet treatment, education and housing needs of ex-offenders.
- Increase use of specialized courts, such as reentry, mental health, community and drug courts.
- Increase use of long-distance, Web training.
- Use funding to sustain, not expand.
- Use seed money to fill gaps in funding and minimize use of state funds.
- Use community volunteers through programs such as Volunteers for Police Service and Neighborhood Watch.
- Increase use of regional and multi-state training.
- Use special conditions on grants to encourage efficiency.
- Tie funding to project performance.

 Reduce costs by sharing resources, using a regional approach or consolidating services, establishing community resource centers, contracting, using a Quartermaster system, using volunteers and privatizing.

Sharing Resources

Hanson (2004, p.151) believes the current fiscal state for public entities has reached a crisis and is so profound as to now touch every operation factor of policing. Furthermore, the competition for funds among the various publicly funded agencies, such as public schools, mental health services, social service agencies and the criminal justice system, is dangerous and detrimental to all involved, and it is recommended that leaders in these areas be challenged to explore the best ways to achieve interdisciplinary cooperation (Hanson, p.151).

An example of interagency cooperation is provided by joint task forces and SWAT teams that save money and personnel by pooling resources. All agencies involved benefit by spending less on training and equipment than if each funded its own unit (Hamilton, 2004c, p.70). Another way agencies can share resources is to pass on or trade out extra equipment. For example, since 1995 the Defense Logistics Agency's Law Enforcement Support Office (LESO) has been responsible for transferring excess Department of Defense equipment suitable to counter-drug and counterterrorism activities to federal, state and local law enforcement. The LESO program has provided departments with such items as cars, surveillance equipment, uniforms and boots (Kress, 2005, p.24).

The Regional Approach or Consolidating Services

Regional approaches to common problems allow multiple jurisdictions to pool their resources to form and share teams not needed full time, for example, SWAT, scuba, accident reconstruction and crime scene units. In addition, departments might make use of equipment from the Regional Intelligence Sharing System (RISS), a program funded by the Department of Justice that provides equipment and analytical support for law enforcement throughout the country. Many agencies are developing regional consortia: groups of departments with mutual interest in such things as funding a large-scale interoperability project (Miller, 2003, p.97).

Similar to the regional approach, consolidation allows jurisdictions to share staff and services. Cities and towns with small to medium police departments might consolidate emergency services. They might also share training rooms and actual training. Many communities have a single public safety complex where police, fire and emergency medical service (EMS) personnel are located. In other communities, firefighting and EMS functions are performed by one team.

Community Resource Centers

Another approach to reducing costs is to establish a community resource center, or more than one for large jurisdictions. Combining police services with social services can provide on-site counseling, educational tutoring, legal services, health care and after-school programs.

Contracting

Contracting, providing law enforcement services by one government entity to another, has come into its own. Departments should consider whether having one agency be responsible for all law enforcement activities is more efficient than having several separate special-purpose agencies. Organizational pride may play a role in this decision, as may community attitudes toward having an entity other than their local police provide law enforcement services.

The Quartermaster System

When examining the best way to equip a department and outfit their officers, many law enforcement administrators face a choice: provide officers with a uniform allotment or use the Quartermaster system, where the agency keeps a storehouse of uniforms. Although stocking such inventory may have some drawbacks, such as limited flexibility for special needs, the Quartermaster system has important advantages. Placement of a single large-quantity order provides a supply of identical stock from the same dye lot and usually affords higher level of quality for a lower price. Another consideration is that officers frequently are reluctant to spend their allotment on uniforms, spending it in other ways.

Research shows that 53.5 percent of police officers receive some kind of allotment to purchase essential gear, apparel or equipment. However, nearly 60 percent of officers from agencies with four or fewer officers do not receive allotments, perhaps because they tend to be union negotiated. Most agencies purchase ammunition and body armor, but most officers buy their own boots and footwear, either from their allotments or out of pocket (Griffith, 2005, p.33).

Volunteers

Use of volunteers is increasing in law enforcement departments across the country, as discussed in Chapter 13. The Bellevue (Washington) Police department usually has about 60 volunteers who contribute approximately 11,000 hours annually, saving the department roughly $187,000 a year (Hamilton, 2004c, p.68). Using volunteers does more than just save money—it adds value to department services and enhances community policing efforts.

Privatization

Another way to do more with less is through privatization. Agencies might use private correctional facilities to cut costs. They might contract with private agencies to respond to burglar alarms or to provide extra security at special events. In addition to reducing costs, managers should look for ways to increase revenues.

Increasing Revenue

Managers should examine variations between in-house and outsourcing costs for every task their department does. Avenues to explore include free training opportunities, becoming a warranty repair center for the department's vehicles, contracting police services for other municipalities and holding prisoners for other agencies. Talk to other departments to find out why they have money (Sanow, 2005, p.6).

 Departments might increase revenue by fundraising, donations, charging for some services, using asset forfeiture statutes to their advantage and seeking grants.

Fundraising

The primary source of revenue for law enforcement agencies is provided by the jurisdiction served by the agency. Local police departments, for example, are supported primarily by tax dollars of that locality. Many police departments find they are able to increase the dollars available to them by raising funds themselves. Among the methods agencies have used to raise funds are dues to a crime prevention organization and seeking support from civic groups for specific projects, such as K-9 units.

One example of a successful fundraiser is the Crown Point (Indiana) Police Department's Adopt-A-Car Program, started in 1995 when this small department needed to purchase 10 new cars but found itself $125,000 short. A lieutenant came up with the idea of asking local businesses to donate $1,500 each (tax deductible) to equip the vehicles. In return, the department painted "This vehicle equipped by (business name)" in 1 1/2-inch high letters on the back of the car. In less than two days, the department had enough sponsors to outfit its new cars and refurbish the old ones.

A similar program in Springfield, Florida, allows corporations to sponsor patrol cars in return for having their advertisements featured on the vehicle's hood, trunk and quarter panels for three years (Mollenkamp, 2003, p.83). The program allows any appropriate sponsor to advertise on the vehicles and excludes alcohol, tobacco, firearms, gaming and other inappropriate sponsors. Not everyone supports the program, however. As one police chief said, "Some things are too important to be for sale. Police are one of them."

In one midwestern community, a citizen crime prevention association has an annual used book sale. Collection boxes are placed in businesses, schools and churches throughout the community, and citizens donate their used books. Each spring, space is donated by a local business, and volunteers conduct a week-long book sale. Profits are in the thousands of dollars. One purchase made with the funds was a K-9 for the police department. The officers named the dog "Books."

Some police departments secure funds to purchase Automated External Defibrillators (AEDs) for their patrol cars from local chambers of commerce, insurance companies, civic organizations such as the Rotary Club and the Lions Club, banks and hospitals. The American Heart Association and the American Red Cross provided training on their use. Putting AEDs in patrol cars can save countless lives from sudden cardiac arrest (Hamilton, 2003, p.16).

Donations

Accepting money or donations from local businesses or community members might appear to be a simple, obvious solution to budget shortfalls. However, accepting donations can be a "political and ethical minefield" (Hamilton, 2004b, p.72). Nonetheless, many departments gladly accept donated bicycles, helmets, AEDs and the like.

Weissenstein (2003) reports: "Police departments with shrinking budgets and a growing list of missions are using nonprofit foundations to solicit funding for new, and sometimes controversial, initiatives." He cites as an example the New York Police Department, which is using funds from such entities as Pfizer, Motorola and other donors to the New York City Police Foundation, a charity whose marriage of private philanthropy and public security is being replicated nationwide. Police and foundations officers acknowledge that the mix of private money and policing has inherent risks, particularly the possibility that wealthy donors can gain undue influence (Weissenstein).

Charging for Services

Some agencies have begun charging for traditional services, such as DUI arrests. Other departments are billing the hosts of loud parties if the police are called back to the party within 12 hours. In addition to raising revenues, some departments have noticed a 75 percent reduction in second calls about loud parties. Other departments are recouping their costs for extraordinary police services, that is, police services rendered during parades and athletic events or in natural disasters or criminally caused catastrophic events such as bombings or hostage incidents.

An increasingly popular avenue in some jurisdictions is charging sentenced prisoners an incarceration fee. The Juneau County (Wisconsin) Sheriff's Department charges other counties $45 a day to house inmates, which brings in an estimated one-half-million dollars annually. It also provides extra after-hours security to local organizations and businesses, for a fee (Hamilton, 2004a, p.62).

Other options for creative managers to increase revenues include selling department products, assets or services, for example, auctioning surplus equipment or unclaimed items from the property room, or providing security at sporting and entertainment events. Departments might also charge fees for services such as reports, photographs, fingerprinting, license checks and responding to alarms. Besides collecting such fees, departments may also economize by taking advantage of the rapidly expanding electronic commerce technologies available over the Internet or via networked kiosks similar to ATMs. Such transactions might include ordering reports, issuing licenses and so on.

Some agencies have found that accepting credit cards rather than insisting on cash bail has increased revenues collected. Other departments have formed special police assessment districts.

Asset Forfeiture

One source of additional revenue is asset forfeiture. The practice of attaching guilt to objects used in committing a crime may have originated with Greek and Roman law. If, for example, a sword was used to kill a man, it was believed to possess an evil quality independent of the killer. The sword would be confiscated and sold, with the proceeds used for good deeds.

Asset forfeiture as a way to combat crime gained momentum during the 1980s and 1990s and is now a commonly accepted practice among law enforcement agencies (Clingermayer et al., 2005, p.319). The main factors in forfeiture decisions are the connection between the asset and the crime and the asset's value.

One defense of asset seizure is the Innocent Owner Defense—the assets of an owner who had no knowledge of the prohibited activity, either by act or omission, are not subject to forfeiture. The Supreme Court has ruled that asset forfeiture is governed by the Eighth Amendment and, as such, must not be so severe as to constitute cruel and unusual punishment.

 The Supreme Court considers asset forfeiture to be governed by the Eighth Amendment, which forbids cruel and unusual punishment. It is up to the states to make this determination.

In addition to the preceding means of increasing revenues, many departments seek grants to finance specific needs.

Grants

Shane (2003, p.12) notes: "Using grant funds to supplement departmental budgets provides a perfect route toward achieving their goals." Numerous grant opportunities exist for law enforcement agencies at both the federal and state levels. To improve the chances of receiving a grant, it is important to understand the types of grants available and which federal, state and local agencies fund such grants. There are two basic types of grants: a **formula** or **block grant,** which is awarded to states or localities based on population and crime rates and a **discretionary grant,** which is awarded based on the judgment of the awarding agency.

formula grant • awarded to states or localities based on population and crime rates. Also called a *block grant.*

block grant • awarded to states or localities based on population and crime rate. Also called a *formula grant.*

discretionary grant • awarded based on the judgment of the awarding state or federal agency.

Federal Grant Money Formula and block grant programs are awarded to states or local government units according to an established formula based on population or crime statistics (Pate, 2003, p.517). The most significant of the programs are the Edward Byrne Memorial State and Local Law Enforcement Assistance Formula Grant Program (Byrne Formula Grant Program) and the Local Law Enforcement Black Grants (LLEBG), both federal grant programs.

A key to grant hunting is getting on government mailing lists for up-to-date information on federal grants. The federal government's fiscal year ends September 31, so October is a good time to start researching new grant opportunities.

 The Department of Justice's (DOJ) Office of Justice Programs (OJP) is the lead federal funding agency for law enforcement.

Eight offices within OJP make grants available to law enforcement agencies: the Bureau of Justice Assistance (BJA), the Office of Juvenile Justice and Delinquency Prevention (OJJDP), the Bureau of Justice Statistics (BJS), the Office for Victims of Crime (OVC), the National Institute of Justice (NIJ), Violence against Women, the Corrections Program Office and the Community Oriented Policing Services (COPS) office.

The BJS has three primary sources of funding. LLEBG, created by Congress in 1994, provide funds to local government units to support projects to reduce crime and improve public safety. Funds go directly to local jurisdictions, distributing approximately $500 million per year. It is a 10 percent matching program; that is, for every $9 the government provides, the recipient must match it with $1.

The Byrne Formula grants were first funded under the Omnibus Crime Control and Safe Streets Act of 1968. Grants are awarded in 28 purpose areas and support a comprehensive range of projects to improve the criminal justice system, with an emphasis on drug-related crime, violent crime and serious offenders. The Edward Byrne Formula Grant Program is based on a state's population.

States receive .25 percent of approximately $500 million as a base proportion. After that, the grant size is based on population and crime rate. Byrne formula grants represent the single largest source of law enforcement–related funding Congress makes available to states. This is a 25 percent match program.

The third program, the Edward Byrne Discretionary Grant Program, grants about $50 million to innovative programs that are within the government's high priority areas. The Byrne Discretionary Grants Program focuses on training and technical assistance for crime and violence prevention and control, with grants able to be awarded to states, local government units, tribes and tribal organization, individuals, educational institutions and private nonprofit organizations (Pate, p.519). The BJA also has a Bulletproof Vest Partnership (BVP) grant that pays up to 50 percent of the cost of NIJ-approved vests (Labbe, 2005, p.183).

The BJA Web site (www.ojp.usdoj.gov/BJA/) offers information on everything from counterterrorism training to partnerships and programs to help departments with limited financial resources.

The COPS program, established in 1994, has been controversial but has already distributed $8.8 billion dollars in grants to help fight crime in high-risk areas. COPS grants have consistently contributed between 10 and 13 percent to the yearly reductions in violent crime at the height of their funding (*Interim Report on the Effects of COPS Funds*, 2005, p.11). A broad, exhaustive survey of 13,133 local law enforcement agencies found "clear, significant statistical links between COPS grants increasing the number of sworn officers, preventing crimes by having more officers on the beat, and encouraging the adoption of new police practices" (*Interim Report*, p.11). The survey also found that COPS grant funds were associated with significant increases in average reported levels of community policing–style practices, including problem-solving, place-oriented practices, crime analysis and community collaboration.

From 2001 to 2004 the LLEBG, the Edward Byrne Memorial Grant Program and the COPS program have been cut by $1.2 billion, a 50 percent cut to these "crucial programs" (Estey, p.6). Boyter (2004, p.8) notes that in 2005, the Byrne grants and the LLEBG were combined into a single program known as the Edward Byrne Memorial Justice Assistance Grant (JAG). Figure 14.3 shows the decrease in federal funding for law enforcement agencies under COPS/LLEBG/Byrne and JAG.

Slahor (2005c, p.101) notes: "The new grants landscape is moving away from the traditional processes to an emphasis on homeland security." Furthermore: "Federal grants are undergoing significant changes as the DHS becomes more rigorous in enforcing the collaboration of law enforcement agencies to strengthen national security" (Rotondo, 2004, p.73). The Department of Homeland Security has three main programs from which law enforcement agencies can obtain funds: the State Homeland Security Grant (SHSG) program, the Law Enforcement Terrorism Prevention Program (LETPP) and the Urban Area Security Initiative (UASI) (Voegtlin and Boyter, 2004, p.8). SHSG funds are distributed to the states, with 80 percent required to be passed on to local governments. The funds are not solely for law enforcement but can fund a wide range of other public safety agencies. LETPP funds are designated solely for use by state and local law enforcement agencies and can be used to cover the cost of homeland security–related planning, organization, training, exercises and equipment. UASI funds are provided to only 50 urban areas.

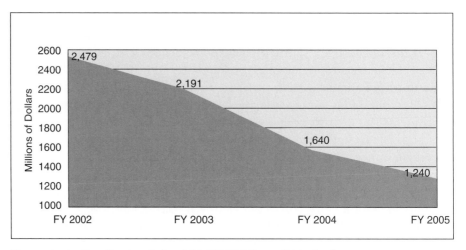

Figure 14.3 Funding Levels for COPS/LLEBG/Byrne/JAG Fiscal Years 2002–2005

Source: Reprinted from *The Police Chief*, Vol. LXXI, No. 12, p.8, ©2004. Copyright held by the International Association of Chiefs of Police, 515 North Bureaugard Street, Alexandria, VA 22314 USA. Further reproduction without express written permission from IACP is strictly prohibited.

In January 2006 the DHS announced a change in how it will award funds through UASI, its largest grant program, with awards now being based on a city's measurable risk factors. This is in response to critics who complained that sparsely populated states such as Wyoming were receiving a proportionally greater share of Homeland Security money than populous jurisdictions, including Washington, that are much more likely to be attacked (Eggen, 2006, p.A1).

Sharp (2003, p.182) notes that homeland security funding must be spent on specialized equipment that might be needed for specific events such as chemical or biological attacks. Sixty-four percent of the respondents in his survey reported they acquired antiterrorism-related equipment, with gas masks and face mask respirators being the most popular items, followed by chemical escape suits, hazardous material devices and communications devices.

The DHS Federal Emergency Management Agency (FEMA) disaster grants provide funding for terrorism prevention for high-density urban areas for transportation security. It also provides funds for first responder training (Slahor, 2005a, p.36).

Another federal funding source is the Weed and Seed program, which weeds out crime from designated neighborhoods, moves in with a wide range of crime and drug prevention programs and then seeds these neighborhoods with a comprehensive range of human service programs that stimulate revitalization.

The availability of discretionary grants is advertised in the Federal Register. The Federal Register is the official daily publication for rules, proposed rules and notices of federal agencies and organizations offering grants (Labbe, p.183). This source, published Monday through Friday, also provides the application criteria and details about the grants. Most major libraries subscribe to this publication.

The National Criminal Justice Reference Service (NCJRS) is a valuable source of information for funding available at the federal level. An agency can request to be put on the NCJRS mailing list for proposal solicitations and other information, and the agency will then receive all solicitations disseminated by OJP and the COPS office. Administrators can access the NCJRS Web site at http://www.ncjrs.org

or contact NCJRS by e-mail at askncjrs@ncjrs.org. Another source is www.grants.gov, a single, secure, reliable Internet source managed by the U.S. Department of Health and Human Services for finding and applying for federal grants.

State Grant Money Funding may also be sought at the state level. The governor's office generally houses contact points for law enforcement–related grants. Managers must be aware that the appropriate "administrative agency" for grants varies from state to state (Shane, p.19). In New Jersey, for example, it is the State Division of Criminal Justice; in California it is the Office of Criminal Justice Planning. Shane notes that the state's administrative agency is responsible to pass through federal funds to local jurisdictions.

In addition, almost every state has a grant specialist in the Attorney General's Office or in the State Emergency Preparedness Office. At a minimum, each state has a contact point for the BJA's Edward Byrne Formula Grants Program.

The 670-page No Child Left Behind (NCLB) Act has poured billions of new federal dollars into education and, in recognizing that youths commit most street crime and are victims of many of them, has made funds available to law enforcement, giving a proportional share to each state (Pekow, 2003, p.83). The list of programs authorized in the education bill provides many opportunities and hundreds of millions of dollars to solve both problems.

The NCLB Act provides block grants in which each state gets a share. States, in turn, must give 95 percent of their share in grants to local communities for programs to provide homework help, counseling, recreation and mentoring (Pekow, p.83). Police-sponsored Boys and Girls Clubs, Police Athletic Leagues, YMCA and other community organizations qualify for such funding. States can provide grants for three to five years, with a $50,000 minimum. This is another area law enforcement departments might want to explore at the state level, especially if they have police liaison officers in the schools.

To improve the chances of receiving any of the multitude of grants available, it is important that managers acquire skills in writing grant proposals.

Writing a Grant Proposal Newell (2005, p.189) explains: "A grant proposal is a formal, written request for funds to support a specific program or project." Newell cautions that most proposals are submitted in a highly competitive forum and suggests that grant writers view their proposal as a document with at least two goals: (1) to inform the reader of their plans and (2) to persuade the reader that their project is worthy of funding. Grant writers should sell their reader on the following points:

- The need or problem they will attempt to "fix" with the grant money is significant and worthy of funding.
- The project or program the funds will be used for is well planned and has a good chance of success.
- The agency requesting the funds is capable of successfully managing the funds and completing the proposed project on schedule.

Volz (2005, p.10) suggests: "Granting agencies decide how to award funds in similar ways to an investment banker looking for sound investments." He (p.12) suggests that grant writers include compelling statistics to support the problem, cause and long-term effects. Shane (p.16) recommends that grant writers should use statistics to quantify ideas and give them numerical precision.

Proposals should not be written in a vacuum but, rather, should be collaborative efforts, including people from different agencies (Slahor, 2005b, p.19). The more people and agencies who have input and stand to benefit, the greater the chances of receiving funding: "Federal grant applicants would be well served by coordinating projects with their respective regions to improve their chances of winning federal monies" (Rotondo, p.75). Becoming a pilot project to benefit many other agencies and stakeholders in the public and private sectors can enhance funding success and should be highlighted in the narrative of the grant application (Slahor, 2005d, p.25).

The first step in writing a grant proposal is to read the solicitation carefully and follow the instructions exactly: "Know the rules. Follow the rules" (Slahor, 2005e, p.25). Where applicable, graphs and charts should be included to help communicate ideas and present data. Showing local support is also important. It is often advisable to partner with a local university. Professors skilled in grant writing can lend credibility to the project.

The six components of most proposals, unless otherwise specified, are (1) a statement of need, (2) how this need can be met—the objectives of the project, (3) who will accomplish the tasks, (4) what timeline will be followed, (5) what the cost will be and (6) how the results will be evaluated. The key element in grant writing is attitude: "You have to believe that you can take it as far as you want to as long as you're willing to work hard" (Henson, 2005).

Do not be discouraged if your proposal is turned down. The key to successful grant writing is to learn from your mistakes. Many very worthwhile and successful programs were rejected repeatedly before eventually being funded. Grant seeking takes knowledge, preparation, patience and endurance. It is not easy, and the competition is keen, but the effort can be rewarding.

Other Sources of Funding

Other sources of funding for law enforcement include direct corporate giving programs, usually foundations, and community-service groups such as the Rotary, Kiwanis and Elks that focus on crime prevention programs, child abuse, drug abuse, senior citizen safety and the like. The Hillsborough County (Florida) Sheriff's Office obtained a $1 million community development block grant from the U.S. Department of Housing and Urban Development (HUD).

Additional income may be obtained from company-sponsored foundations, private foundation funds, individual gifts of equipment or money and individual operating foundations. Thousands of private foundations fund hundreds of program areas each year. These can be found on the Internet or the library, or through a research company such as Research Grant Guides (Shane, p.19). A quick and easy way to find grant information is via the Internet. Check any of the OJP offices by indicating the office at the end of their Web address. For example, the Bureau of Justice Assistance would be found at www.ojp.usdoj.gov/BJA/. Information may also be obtained by calling the OJP Grants Management System hotline at 888-549-9901.

SUMMARY

Budgets serve as a plan for and a means to control resources. Managers at each level should be responsible for the budget they need, based on input from their subordinates.

This results in all-levels budgeting. Most law enforcement budgets are developed by revising the previous year's budget based on logical assumptions. All law enforcement employees should contribute ideas related to budget items as specific needs arise.

Three kinds of resources must be identified: human, direct and indirect. Common budget categories include salaries and wages, services and supplies, training and travel, contractual services and other or miscellaneous. Personnel costs usually account for at least three fourths of the operating budget. Once the budget is developed, it should be used to monitor costs.

Cutback budgeting means providing the same or more services with less funding. Managers need new strategies that involve making choices as to whether to resist or smooth cuts, to cut deeply or in small decrements, to share the pain or target the cuts and to budget for efficiency or equity. The first step in solving cost problems is to identify waste areas. All employees are responsible for reducing costs. Employees can suggest ways to cut costs through an employee cost improvement suggestion program. Costs can also be reduced by using a regional approach or consolidating services, establishing community resource centers, contracting, using a Quartermaster system, using volunteers and privatizing.

Many departments are increasing revenues, including conducting fundraisers, charging for some services, using asset forfeiture statutes to their advantage and seeking grants. The Supreme Court considers asset forfeiture to be governed by the Eighth Amendment, which forbids cruel and unusual punishment. It is up to the states to make this determination. The Office of Justice Programs (OJP) is the lead federal funding agency for law enforcement.

 CHALLENGE FOURTEEN

Captain Jones is responsible for preparing the budget for the Greenfield Police Department. The new chief has asked her to review the entire budget and find long-term and short-term cost reductions. He wants to shift some resources to community policing projects and would also like to create an undercover drug unit. He encourages her to be creative and bold because he does not anticipate any increases in the budget during the next few years.

The Greenfield Police Department is a medium-sized suburban department. Three neighboring cities have comparable departments performing similar functions. Each of the four departments has their own booking and short-term holding facility and their own dispatch center. The county sheriff's department operates a detention center for felons and long-term prisoners. Arresting officers transport their prisoners to the county facility and are often out of service for several hours during this process.

Each city has its own SWAT team. The teams' equipment was purchased through a federal grant, but the personnel costs are each department's responsibility. The teams train frequently, but the cities do not often have incidents that require a SWAT response. The county sheriff's department also has a SWAT team that responds when requested by local police departments. None of the departments has an undercover drug unit. They refer drug cases to state and federal agencies, but those agencies are often too busy for a timely response.

A review of the Greenfield Police Department activity logs reveals that officers spend considerable time standing by for vehicle tows, directing traffic at civic functions and delivering documents to city council members.

1. How should Captain Jones begin the process of preparing a new budget?

2. Assuming that the Greenfield officers are still relying on preventive patrol, how could a change in strategy benefit the budget?

3. Suggest some major long-term cost savings Captain Jones could consider regarding dispatch and booking services.

4. Is the continued support of a seldom-used SWAT team a good use of Greenfield Police Department resources?

5. What other sources of creative funding may be available to support a drug unit?

6. How could Captain Jones use volunteers and reserve officers to increase man-power?

DISCUSSION QUESTIONS

1. Do you have a personal budget? If so, what are your main categories?

2. Do you belong to any organizations that have a budget? If so, what are their main categories?

3. How do budgets restrict? Provide freedom?

4. What things in addition to money might a law enforcement agency budget (e.g., space)?

5. Is your law enforcement department functioning under cutback budgeting?

6. What percentage of a city's total budget goes to the law enforcement department?

7. Which department gets the largest share of the city's budget?

8. What methods might be used to raise funds for your local law enforcement agency?

9. What suggestions do you have for cutting the cost of providing law enforcement services?

10. Why must the budget be updated annually?

REFERENCES

Boertien, Robert. "Rapid Growth: Desirable but Challenging." *Law and Order*, July 2004, pp.130–132.

Boyter, Jennifer. "Congress Omnibus Appropriations Bill; State and Local Law Enforcement Assistance Funds Cut by 24 Percent." *The Police Chief*, December 2004, p.8.

Brock, Horace R.; Palmer, Charles E.; and Price, John Ellis. *Accounting Principles and Applications*, 6th ed. New York: Gregg Division, McGraw-Hill Publishing Company, 1990.

Clingermayer, James C.; Hecker, Jason; and Madsen, Sue. "Asset Forfeiture and Police Priorities: The Impact of Program Design on Law Enforcement Activities." *Criminal Justice Policy Review*, Vol. 16, No. 3, 2005, p.319.

"Doing the Best with Less." *NCJA Justice Bulletin*, August 2003, p.9.

"e-Bay-Savvy Chief Makes Budget Dollars Go Further." *Law Enforcement News*, April 15, 2005, p.14.

Eggen, Dan. "D.C. May Benefit as DHS Bases Grants on Risk." *Washington Post*, January 4, 2006, p.A1.

Estey, Joseph G. "Act Now to Help Forestall Coming Financial Crisis in Policing." *The Police Chief*, December 2004, p.6.

Goldsmith, Barton. "10 Tips for Making a Pitch." *Successful Meetings*, March 2005, pp.24–25.

Griffith, David. "Two Sides of the Coin." *Police*, November 2004, p.6.

Griffith, David. "Who Really Pays for Your Gear?" *Police*, July 2005, pp.32–36.

Haberfeld, M. R. *Police Leadership*. Upper Saddle River, NJ: Pearson, Prentice Hall, 2006.

Hamilton, Melanie. "How to Acquire ADEs." *Police*, January 2003, pp.16–22.

Hamilton, Melanie. "Brother, Can You Spare a Few Mil?" *Police*, November 2004a, pp.60–64.

Hamilton, Melanie. "Getting the Goods." *Police*, November 2004b, pp.72–74.

Hamilton, Melanie. "Staffing Shortage." *Police*, November 2004c, pp.66–70.

Hanson, Ellen T. "Community Policing during a Budget Crisis: The Need for Interdisciplinary Cooperation, Not Competition." In *Community Policing: Past, Present, and Future*, edited by Lorie Fridell and Mary Ann Wycoff. Washington, DC: The Annie E. Casey Foundation and the Police Executive Research Forum, November 2004, pp.151–158.

Henson, Kenneth. "Grant Writing in Higher Education." Presentation at the Text and Academic Authors Association in Las Vegas, June 22, 2005.

Interim Report on the Effects of COPS Funds on the Decline in Crime during the 1990s. Washington, DC: Office of Community Oriented Policing Services, 2005. http://www.gao.gov/new.items/d05699r.pdf. Accessed December 24, 2005.

Kress, Joy. "Obtaining Excess Department of Defense Equipment." *The Police Chief*, December 2005, pp.24–28.

Labbe, Corenne. "An Introduction." *Funding and Grant Resources. A Police Chief's Desk Reference.* Washington, DC: The International Association of Chiefs of Police and the Bureau of Justice Assistance, 2005, pp.181–185.

Lebreck, Paul. "Doing More Training with Less Money." *Law and Order*, June 2004, pp.52–55.

Levine, Charles H. "Cutback Management in an Era of Scarcity: Hard Questions for Hard Times." *Executive*

Police Development. Washington, DC: Department of Justice, National Institute of Justice and the FBI, no date.

Miller, Christa. "Stretching Your Resources." *Law Enforcement Technology*, April 2003, pp.97–101.

Mollenkamp, Becky. "Corporate Sponsorship for Law Enforcement." *Law and Order*, January 2003, pp.80–83.

Newell, Bridget. "Grantwriting." In *A Police Chief's Desk Reference*. Washington, DC: The International Association of Chiefs of Police and the Bureau of Justice Assistance, 2005, pp.188–195.

Nowicki, Ed. "Stretch Your Training Dollars." *Law and Order*, November 2003, pp.29–32.

Orrick, W. Dwayne. "Justifying Police Budgets in a Sluggish Economy." *The Police Chief*, August 2003, pp.21–24.

Orrick, W. Dwayne. "Budgeting in Small Police Agencies." In *A Police Chief's Desk Reference*. Washington, DC: The International Association of Chiefs of Police and the Bureau of Justice Assistance, 2005, pp.228–239.

Pate, Anthony. "External Resources." In *Local Government Police Management*, 4th edition, edited by William A. Geller and Darrel W. Stephens. Washington, DC: International City/County Management Association, 2003, pp.515–558.

Pekow, Charles. "Obtaining Grants." *Law and Order*, January 2003, pp.83–85.

Rotondo, Rick. "Winning Grants to Fund Mobile Data Networks." *Law Enforcement Technology*, March 2004, pp.72–76.

Sanow, Ed. "Show Me the Money." *Law and Order*, August 2005, p.6.

Scoville, Dean. "Slicing the Pie." *Police*, November 2004, pp.76–82.

Shane, Jon M. "Writing a Winning Grant Proposal." *FBI Law Enforcement Bulletin*, May 2003, pp.12–21.

Sharp, Arthur. "Training Funding and Equipment." *Law and Order*, October 2003, pp.178–183.

Slahor, Stephenie. "FEMA Disaster Grants." *Law and Order*, August 2005a, p.36.

Slahor, Stephenie. "Grants for Small Communities." *Law and Order*, June 2005b, pp.17–20

Slahor, Stephenie. "Grants 101." *Law and Order*, May 2005c, pp.96–101.

Slahor, Stephenie. "Information Technology Grants." *Law and Order*, November 2005d, pp.25–27.

Slahor, Stephenie. "Performance Measuring the Grant." *Law and Order*, September 2005e, pp.25–26.

Smith, Eric. "Patrol Staffing Analysis." *Law and Order*, December 2005, pp.80–85.

Stephens, Darrel W. "Organization and Management." In *Local Government Police Management*, 4th ed., edited by William A. Geller and Darrel W. Stephens. Washington, DC: International City/County Management Association, 2003, pp.27–65.

Voegtlin, Gene and Boyter, Jennifer. "2005 Federal Budget Proposal Released; State and Local Law Enforcement Assistance Programs Face Cuts." *The Police Chief*, March 2004, p.8.

Volz, David. "No Stone Unturned." *Law Enforcement Technology*, March 2005, pp.8–14.

Weissenstein, Michael. "Police Departments Turn to Private Funding." *Staten Island Advance*, July 19, 2003.

Whitehead, Christy. "Budget Cuts: More than Layoffs." *Law and Order*, August 2004, pp.102–104.

BOOK-SPECIFIC WEB SITE

Go to the Management and Supervision in Law Enforcement Web site at www.thomsonedu.com/criminaljustice/bennett for student and instructor resources, including Internet Assignments and Case Studies.

CHAPTER 15

Hiring Personnel and Dealing with Unions

Nobody's perfect except when filling out a job application.

Anonymous

 DO YOU KNOW?

- What steps are involved in the selection process?
- What the most common screening methods used in the hiring process are?
- What major employment legislation affects hiring for law enforcement agencies?
- What the EEOC is and how it affects hiring practices?
- What goal the Americans with Disabilities Act (ADA) seeks to guarantee?
- What kinds of inquiries or evaluations are prohibited by the ADA?
- What an affirmative action program is?
- In what areas of management EEO and affirmative action policies are important?
- What the National Labor Relations Act requires of management?
- What the National Labor Relations Board is?
- What the primary purpose of unions is?
- Why people join unions?
- What levels of negotiation are usually involved in collective bargaining?

CAN YOU DEFINE?

adverse impact
affirmative action
   program (AAP)
background check
bona fide
   occupational
   qualification
   (BFOQ)
Civil Rights Act
   of 1964
closed shop
collective bargaining
delaying tactics

Equal Employment
   Opportunity
   Commission
   (EEOC)
Fair Labor Standards
   Act of 1938
halo effect
just cause
Landrum-Griffin
   Act of 1959
National Labor
   Relations Act of
   1935 (Wagner Act)

National Labor
   Relations Board
   (NLRB)
negligent hiring
Norris-LaGuardia Act
reverse
   discrimination
right-to-work laws
special employment
   groups
Taft-Hartley Act
   of 1947
union

continued

Introduction

"One of the greatest challenges facing law enforcement organizations today is the successful recruitment and retention of highly qualified employees" (McKeever and Kranda, 2005, p.289). Considering that it takes more time, effort and expense to train the wrong person than it does to hire the right person, managers should regard the recruiting task as one of their most critical functions (p.293).

Today's law enforcement agencies seek a new breed of officer—a balance of brawn and brains—one who possesses not only the physical qualities tradition-ally associated with policing, such as strength and endurance, but also the emo-tional and intellectual characteristics needed to effect public order in an ever-changing and increasingly diverse society. "People skills" have become a critical tool for law enforcement officers.

The qualities the public expects in its law enforcement officers include higher ed-ucation and training, the ability to cope with myriad problems and apply discre-tion, serving and protecting, impartiality, and honesty (Guthrie, 2004, p.24). A sur-vey conducted in St. Paul, Minnesota, to determine what character traits the citizens of that city wanted in their police professionals revealed the desire for officers who were enthusiastic, creative, self-motivated, understanding, self-confident, indepen-dent, courageous, tenacious, respectful, compassionate, honest, loyal, interactive, re-sponsible and able to exercise good judgment (Conroy and Placide, 2003, p.10).

This chapter begins with a discussion of the critical importance of hiring well to avoid litigation from vicarious liability or negligent hiring and many other problems. The chapter then suggests steps departments can take to hire well, be-ginning with recruiting and continuing through the selection process: the appli-cation, testing, background checks and interviews. Next, the use of assessment centers and employment criteria departments might consider are discussed. After looking at the selection process, you will learn about laws that affect the process, including the Americans with Disabilities Act (ADA) and affirmative action. The chapter concludes with a look at how labor laws and unions affect both the se-lection process and the functioning of the department.

The Importance of Hiring Well

The hiring process is so critical in law enforcement in part because of **vicarious li-ability,** which refers to the legal responsibility one person has for the acts of an-other. Managers, the entire agency and even the jurisdiction served may be legally responsible for the actions of a single officer. Vicarious means "taking the place of another thing or person, substituting for." Law enforcement officers have always been responsible for their individual wrongdoings, criminally or civilly. Civil lia-bility most frequently involves violation of the Civil Rights Act, specifically Statute 42 of the U.S. Code, Section 1983, which states:

> Every person who, under color of any statute, ordinance, regulation, custom, or
> usage, of any State or Territory, subjects, or causes to be subjected, any citizen of

vicarious liability • the legal responsibility one person has for the acts of another.

the United States or other person within the jurisdiction thereof to the deprivation of any rights, privileges, or immunities secured by the Constitution and
laws, shall be liable to the party injured in an action at law, suit in equity, or
other proper proceeding for redress.

In other words, anyone acting under the authority of law who violates another
person's constitutional rights can be sued. In 1978 in *Monell v. New York City Department of Social Services,* the court ruled that local municipalities were also liable
under Section 1983 (Title 42, U.S.C.).

It is now accepted that local government may be responsible for the wrongdoing of a subordinate enforcing a local ordinance, regulation or policy. In cases
in which law enforcement managers directed, ordered or participated in the acts,
they are equally liable. In addition, if upper-level managers are negligent in hiring, assigning, training, retaining, directing or entrusting, they may be liable even
if they were not present.

Negligent hiring litigation is becoming more common. Law enforcement
managers and supervisors have been held liable for negligence in hiring personnel unqualified or unsuited for law enforcement work. The majority of these cases
involve failure to use an adequate selection process or to check for prior offenses
or misconduct.

negligent hiring • failure to
use an adequate selection
process resulting in hiring personnel unqualified or unsuited
for law enforcement work.

Negligent hiring and retention have become major problems because of numerous court cases that have resulted in significant judgments. Conducting background investigations, hiring qualified personnel and then developing them into
permanent employees can help reduce such lawsuits. Negligent supervision, negligent training and negligent retention have been discussed.

Recruiting

Recruiting is more difficult currently because of a shrinking pool of qualified candidates. To successfully recruit in today's highly competitive job market, agencies
must first look at what they have to offer and then select from a variety of recruiting strategies.

The Shrinking Applicant Pool

Egan (2005) notes: "In a generation's time, the job of an American police officer, previously among the most sought-after by people with little college background, has
become one that in many communities now goes begging." He points out that the
career has little appeal among many young people and that those who are interested
are frequently lured away by aggressive counteroffers from the military or by better
pay at entry-level jobs in the private sector. The supply of good police recruits is down
throughout the country, with more than half of small agencies and two thirds of large
agencies reporting a lack of qualified applicants (Koper, 2004, p.2).

Additional recruiting challenges include appealing to a new generation of applicants, dispelling misconceptions caused by the mass entertainment media regarding the real job, and understanding that law enforcement has changed from
the once traditionally blue-collar job to a challenging profession requiring technical skills (Ellis et al., 2005, p.20).

The generational transition currently underway and at the center of the workforce
crisis has resulted from the convergence of two trends: the growing number of aging
baby boomers and the much smaller cohort of younger people, the generation Xers,

who follow behind them (Henchey, 2005, p.108). Members of the 102 million-strong millennial generation (born between 1982 and 2002) have yet to fully impact the law enforcement workplace, but they will be the majority of new police officers and deputies hired in the coming decade: "By the year 2020, most police officers will be members of the millennial generation" (Henchey, p.108).

When force numbers need to be increased, organizations tend to lower their standards and hire the needed numbers, sacrificing quality for quantity. However, this "solution" does not necessarily equate to better police work: "When in doubt, do not hire—keep looking" (Haberfeld, 2006, p.234).

Self-Appraisal

The first essential step in the recruitment process is an honest self-appraisal (McKeever and Kranda, p.290). What does the agency have to offer recruits? Symposium participants at the 205th session of the FBI National Academy on recruitment, when asked to rank the top five items that new employees want, responded with: (1) salary; (2) benefits—leave time, medical coverage and retirement; (3) job security; (4) career development—specialization and promotion; and (5) job satisfaction—pride, excitement and community (Vest, 2003, p.13). In addition: "Participants from larger agencies indicated that job security; personal growth opportunities; and pay, benefits, and retirement coverage represented the most important factors" (Vest, p.13).

Recruiting Strategies

Departments take a variety of approaches in recruiting. Traditional activities include handouts, military recruiting, advertisements (TV, radio, newspapers), job fairs and visits to colleges. National recruiting newsletters may also assist, including the National Employment Listing Service and Knights. Recruiting graduates of college criminal justice programs is one major source of candidates, and implementing college internships can be a valuable aid to recruitment. Web sites also offer employment listings. The International Association of Chiefs of Police (IACP) has a job Web site, www.iacppolicejobs.com, where departments can list job openings for a monthly fee. Job searches by potential applicants are free.

A study of police officer recruitment in North Carolina found that the most frequently used recruitment technique was word-of-mouth, used by 95 percent of the agencies surveyed (Yearwood and Freeman, 2004, p.43). The least frequently used technique was radio/TV ads, used by 25.4 percent. The other recruitment techniques included newspaper ads (83.1 percent), community college visits (71.8 percent), Internet postings (62.9 percent), personnel listings (61.3 percent), auxiliary/reserve force (57.3 percent), job fairs (49.2 percent) and Police Corps (35.5 percent). Respondents also rated the effectiveness of recruiting techniques on a scale of 0 to 9. Word-of-mouth received the highest rating: 6.83, followed by community colleges, 5.62; newspaper ads, 5.38; and auxiliary/reserve force, 5.32. Rated lowest were radio/TV ads, .85.

Another avenue in recruiting police candidates is to seek out second-career officers. For example, the Appleton (Wisconsin) Police Department actively recruits new officers from other professions, not necessarily because of their knowledge of police work but because of their maturity and stability. The impending retirement of veteran officers presents yet another recruiting opportunity for departments: recruiting reserve officers from their full-time ranks.

Recruitment efforts should not overlook a department's civilian employees as well as participants in its programs such as the reserves, explorers or citizen police academies.

Recruiting for Diversity

As departments recognize the value of diversity within their ranks, recruitment efforts often focus on attracting ethnic minorities and women.

Recruiting Racial/Ethnic Minorities Strandberg (2004, p.40) points out: "The widespread distrust of law enforcement in many minority communities, whether a result of cultural predispositions or bad experiences, compounds the problem of recruiting minorities. Although many minorities view police as the 'enemy' and would never consider joining their ranks, others view law enforcement as a way to a better life." An African-American police lieutenant from Atlanta explains why he became a police officer: "You got out of my neighborhood without ending up dead or in prison by either becoming a minister or a cop. I always fell asleep in church so I decided to become a cop."

The Delaware State Police uses troopers from throughout the state in their recruiting efforts, sending officers into minority community centers and developing their own job fair. Other likely places to recruit are Latino festivals, Urban leagues, NAACP meetings and minority churches. The Sacramento (California) Police Department taps and trains interested minority citizens to recruit potential officers in their neighborhood (Johnson, 2005, pp.16–20). In addition to finding qualified candidates, the citizen recruiters sponsor their recruits if selected, meeting with them during the academy, meeting with their family to offer support, and participating in the academy graduation ceremony: "This program stands as a fresh approach to the old problem of attracting qualified minorities into policing" (Johnson, p.20).

Recruiting Women Recruiting, hiring and retaining female officers is vital to a balanced, effective department. However: "Recruitment of women into the gendered organization of policing has been slow" (Garcia, 2003, p.330). Tests of physical strength often wash out qualified candidates, especially women. Viverette (2005, p.6), the first woman president of the IACP, reports that only 12 to 13 percent of the nation's police officers in 2005 were women: "Things have gotten better, but we still have a long way to go." Jones (2004, p.165) suggests: "To successfully increase the number of women in policing, law enforcement agencies should develop a specific plan of action that targets women in the recruiting process and emphasizes the agency's desire to significantly increase the number of women in their ranks."

Strategies specific to recruiting women include revising recruiting brochures to include photos of female officers; organizing career fairs specifically for women; and displaying recruiting posters in gyms, grocery stores and other places women are likely to see them. Departments should reach out to physically active women by posting flyers in places such as gyms; locker rooms of women's sport teams; and facilities for rock climbing, karate and similar activities. Women might also be recruited at community colleges, especially those with criminal justice and social service degree programs.

Recruiting advertisements geared to the crime fighting, law-enforcing aspects of the profession and the warrior image may be ineffective: "In order to recruit more women into policing, law enforcement agencies must overcome the common perception that policing is a 'male-oriented profession' limited to duties that require only physical strength" (*Recruiting & Retaining Women*, p.43). In contrast, an emphasis on the helping aspects of the job might be very appealing. Departments must take care, however, not to turn off highly qualified male applicants.

If recruiting efforts are successful, the law enforcement agency will receive numerous applications from which to select those best suited for their particular agency.

The Selection Process

Spawn (2003, p.20) notes: "The officer candidate selection process—from the written test to the agility test, to background investigations, psychological evaluations and polygraph examinations—is intensive and expensive." A person wanting to become a police officer must usually go through several steps in the selection process. Although procedures differ greatly from agency to agency, several elements are common to most selection processes.

 The selection process is based on carefully specified criteria and usually includes completing an application form, undergoing a series of tests and examinations, passing a background check and successfully completing an interview.

A typical sequence of events in the employment process is illustrated in Figure 15.1. Unfortunately, this process is sometimes lengthy, and the best-qualified candidates are not willing to wait months for a decision.

The Application

The initial application is an important document to determine a candidate's competence for the job. The consent statement provides the right to verify any information on the application. The application should also have an employment-at-will provision indicating that no contract guarantees permanent employment.

Many law enforcement departments use a civil service–type application and selection process. A sample application is contained in Appendix B.

Restricted Subjects The following subjects are *not* allowed for either an application form or an employment interview: race, religion, national origin, gender, age (you may ask whether the applicant is between the ages of 18 and 70), marital status and physical capabilities. Administrators must be able to show that all questions are relevant to the position they are seeking applicants for.

Testing/Screening

Applicant testing usually progresses from the least expensive method, the written examination, to the most expensive, the background investigation, with the number of qualified recruits being narrowed at each step. Because several trips are needed to complete the process, the selection process is difficult for anyone living any distance from the hiring agency. Some agencies have revised their selection process so that it can be completed in one trip.

 The most common screening methods for selection are basic skills/written tests, medical examinations, background investigations, psychological examinations and physical fitness tests.

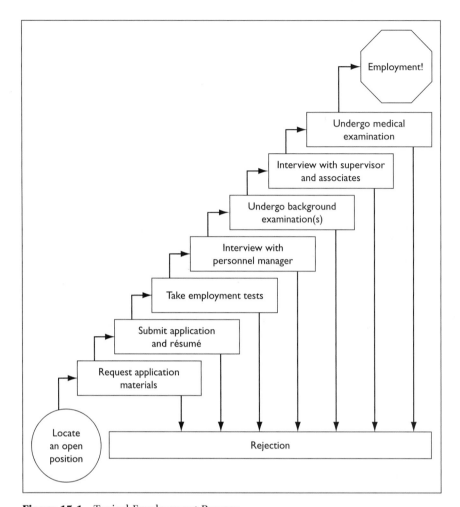

Figure 15.1   Typical Employment Process

Source: J. Scott Harr and Kären M. Hess. *Seeking Employment in Criminal Justice and Related Fields*, 4th ed. Belmont, CA: Wadsworth, 2003, p.176.

Other methods used with less frequency included oral boards/oral interviews, polygraphs, chief's and/or command interviews and writing tests: "Selecting the right entry-level examination process is inseparably linked to the identification of the best candidates to hire" (Legel, 2005, p.66).

Written Tests Basic skills in math and reading can be assessed using standardized tests. Writing skills are also important to assess: "Poor writing skills can damage a department's reputation. Worse, sloppy report writing can result in problems in the courtroom" (Moore, 2004, p.82). Although report writing skills can be taught, they do take time to develop and master. A recruit who already possesses strong written communication skills can help a hiring manager decide between two or more otherwise equally qualified candidates. Writing skills can be tested by having candidates write an autobiography or an essay explaining why they want to become a law enforcement officer. Although many conventional written test formats are available, some departments are using innovative written exam alternatives to assess not only applicants' basic skills but also their compatibility with the profession.

A screening test called the "Police Officer Screening Test for the 21st Century," or "POST-21," is an "add-on exam" consisting of four parts: (1) an evaluation of the applicant's policing orientation, (2) a series of questions to test flexibility in responses, (3) an evaluation of the applicant's realistic expectations of police officer duties and (4) an essay section on problem-solving techniques. This screening test, in effect, assesses applicants for aptitude in community policing (Dwyer and Laufersweiler-Dwyer, 2004).

The Medical Examination The medical examination assesses overall applicant health and includes more specific tests for vision, hearing and cardiovascular fitness. Departments do allow applicants to have corrected vision with glasses or contact lenses; however, an emerging issue that many agencies are wrestling with has been whether to permit vision correction by laser surgery. The debate centers on the as yet unknown long-term effects of laser correction surgery. Drug testing may be part of the medical examination.

Background Investigations Candidates should undergo a thorough **background check,** usually conducted by a member of the agency. Background checks can prevent many potential problems and save the cost of training an unsuitable employee: "A thorough background investigation not only ensures that the most qualified candidates are hired, but also can help a department avoid damaging legal actions and give an indication of an individual's competence, motivation and personal ethics. . . . A thorough background investigation can make the difference between putting a qualified individual on the streets to protect and serve society or an unqualified, tainted individual who can cause harm to himself, society and the hiring department" (Fuss and Snowden, 2004, p.60).

> **background check** • investigating references listed on an application as well as credit, driving record, criminal conviction, academic background and any professional license required.

The background check includes past employers and references. The person who conducts the background check should contact every reference, employer and instructor. No final candidates should be selected until reference checks are made. Reference checks should be done from not only those who provided letters of recommendation but others as well. The same inquiries should be made for each candidate, and the questions must be job related.

The background check might also include queries regarding credit, driving record, criminal conviction, academic background and any professional license required. Most states have passed laws making it difficult, if not impossible, for ex-offenders to acquire employment as police officers (Harris and Keller, 2005, p.6). Candidates might be asked to sign a release and authorization statement such as that illustrated in Figure 15.2. A request should also be made for documents such as diplomas, birth certificates and driver's licenses. Applicants should be photographed and fingerprinted. Military duty should be confirmed, along with a copy of discharge papers.

One controversial area explored during the background check is past experience with controlled substances. Sharp (2003, p.80) notes: "Many potential officers' dreams of careers in law enforcement may have gone up in smoke because they tried marijuana, either recently or long ago." Traditionally law enforcement agencies have opposed hiring candidates who have used marijuana, regardless of when or how many times. However, many managers recognize that times are changing, and departments currently vary greatly in what they will allow before disqualifying a candidate. The chief of the Akron (Ohio) Police Department notes that they recruit a lot of college graduates and that it is difficult to find a college

---

Sample Release and Authorization Statement

In connection with this request, I authorize all corporations, companies, former employers, credit agencies, educational institutions, law enforcement agencies, city, state, county and federal courts, military services, and persons to release information they may have about me to the person or company with which this form has been filed and release all parties involved from any liability and reponsibility for doing so.

I also authorize the procurement of an investigative consumer report and understand that it may contain information about my background, mode of living, character, and personal reputation. This authorization, in original or copy form, shall be valid for this and any future reports or updates that may be requested. Further information may be available on written request within a reasonable period of time.

_____   _____
Applicant's signature   Date

Figure 15.2   Sample Release and Authorization Statement

Source: © 1991 American Society for Industrial Security, 1655 North Fort Myer Dr., Suite 1200, Arlington, VA 22209. Reprinted by permission from the April 1991 issue of *Security Management.*

graduate who has not at least experimented with marijuana. Bradley (2005, p.37) notes: "As the Ritalin generation matures, the acceptability of persons who have had drug use in their background will be more common."

A related concern is whether applicants who smoke cigarettes should be disqualified. Some departments notify potential recruits of their tobacco-free policy. Other departments have no such policy, fearing it would greatly reduce the number of applicants. Currently, banning smokers in the recruiting process is not widespread, but it appears to be picking up steam (Sharp, 2004, p.55).

Psychological Examinations The IACP Psychological Service Section recommends that pre-employment psychological assessments should be used as one component of the overall selection process ("Pre-Employment Psychological Evaluation Services Guidelines," 2005, p.68). Nearly all departments recognize a need for psychological screening of final candidates for a police position, but because of cost or lack of suitable psychologists, it may not be done. Only the leading candidates are evaluated psychologically to keep costs down. The IACP guidelines state: "Except as allowed or permitted by law, only licensed or certified psychologists trained and experienced in psychological test interpretation and law enforcement psychological assessment techniques should conduct psychological screening for public safety agencies."

Holzman and Kirschner (2003, p.85) assert: "In the area of law enforcement psychological evaluations have proven invaluable as one of the necessary pre-employment activities for prospective officers. Due to the nature of law enforcement work, psychological evaluations serve a unique role by being able to identify potential officers who may not adjust successfully."

The psychological tests often include cognitive ability; quantitative and language reasoning; and the Minnesota Multiphasic Personality Inventory (MMPI), the most widely used psychological assessment test in the country. Most psychological tests measure social maturity and self-control, social tolerance, emotional stability/stress tolerance, confidence/assertiveness, personal insight, empathy, effectiveness in work relationships, conventionality and tendency to abide by rules, nondefensiveness, health and achievement/motivation.

Psychologists who work with police departments must be familiar with validity and reliability measures of tests and the legal requirements imposed by affirmative action and the ADA, as well as pertinent case law and guidelines. When a candidate's psychological tests indicate abnormalities, a department must consider these seriously before hiring. When testing indicates unsuitability or lack of stability, it is best not to hire.

Physical Fitness Tests Collingwood et al. (2003, p.49) note: "The public's expectation of a responding officer in a situation requiring physical effort, especially in a use of force situation, is the ability to provide the requisite service. They expect and deserve a fit officer because in a situation with injury and life and death consequences having those physical capabilities can minimize those threats."

Using data collected in the last 15 years from 34 physical performance standards and validation studies performed on more than 5,500 officers, Collingwood et al. (2004, p.33) identified frequent and critical physical tasks required of law enforcement officers: walking, running short and long distances, running up and down stairs, running over uneven terrain, heavy lifting and carrying, jumping or vaulting over obstacles, climbing fences and stairs, dodging around or crawling under or through obstacles, dragging objects, extracting and dragging victims, pushing heavy objects such as cars, bending and reaching, using restraining devises, using hands and feet in self-defense and short- and long-term use of force.

Fitness can become a legal issue too. The people and property the police are paid to protect depend on officers being able to do their job. If they cannot, they could be sued. In *Parker v. The District of Columbia* (1988), the jury awarded $425,046 to a man shot by a police officer who was arresting him. As part of its ruling, the court noted: "Officer Hayes simply was not in adequate physical shape. This condition posed a foreseeable risk of harm to others."

Research has found a striking lack of agreement regarding the physical capabilities that should be tested (Lonsway, 2003, p.237). A survey of 62 agencies indicated that the vast majority (89 percent) used some form of physical agility testing for entry-level selection, and agencies with a test had 31 percent fewer sworn women than agencies without such a test.

Physical-agility tests are most often of the military type and frequently include an obstacle course. The Broward Community College Criminal Justice Institute's testing center, for example, uses the physical-agility course shown in Figure 15.3.

In addition, Broward uses the following strength and endurance tests:

- Trigger pull—strong hand 18, weak hand 12
- Ten push-ups
- A standing jump based on the person's height
- Three pull-ups (from dead hang, palms facing away)
- Vehicle push—20 feet (push from rear of vehicle)
- Mile run (5 minutes maximum time)

Whether the criteria for passing should be the same for males and females is open to debate. If different standards are set, then the Civil Rights Act of 1991 might be used to claim disparate treatment. This act states: "It shall be an unlawful employment practice . . . in connection with the selection or referral of applicants or candidates for employment or promotion, to adjust the scores of, [or] use different cutoff scores . . . on the basis of race, color, religion, sex or national origin."

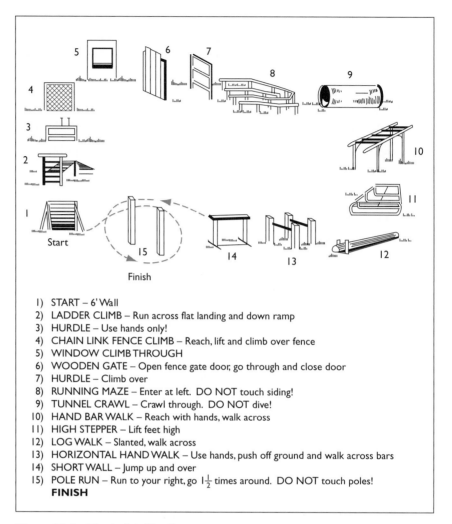

1) START – 6' Wall
2) LADDER CLIMB – Run across flat landing and down ramp
3) HURDLE – Use hands only!
4) CHAIN LINK FENCE CLIMB – Reach, lift and climb over fence
5) WINDOW CLIMB THROUGH
6) WOODEN GATE – Open fence gate door, go through and close door
7) HURDLE – Climb over
8) RUNNING MAZE – Enter at left. DO NOT touch siding!
9) TUNNEL CRAWL – Crawl through. DO NOT dive!
10) HAND BAR WALK – Reach with hands, walk across
11) HIGH STEPPER – Lift feet high
12) LOG WALK – Slanted, walk across
13) HORIZONTAL HAND WALK – Use hands, push off ground and walk across bars
14) SHORT WALL – Jump up and over
15) POLE RUN – Run to your right, go $1\frac{1}{2}$ times around. DO NOT touch poles!
FINISH

Figure 15.3   Physical-Agility Course

Source: Criminal Justice Institute, Broward Community College, Ft. Lauderdale, FL. Reprinted by permission.

The Interview

Finnimore (2003, p.23) notes: "In the business world, poor communication skills can cost companies revenue. In law enforcement, a lack of quality communication skills could prove deadly." The interview can assess a candidate's communication skills.

In-person interviews should be held with each applicant, during which the department can explain the nature and benefits of the position to be filled. In return, the applicant can explain his or her interest in law enforcement and, specifically, the hiring department. Managers should provide an opportunity for the applicant to ask questions, as most have questions about salary, benefits, overtime, promotions, uniform allowances and the like.

Civil Service Commission representatives or other selection board personnel usually conduct the final interview. Whether an individual or a panel conducts the interview, those responsible should be familiar with what they can and cannot ask. The same questions prohibited on the application are also prohibited during the interview. Interviewers should also take certain steps before, during and after the interview to make it most effective.

Before the Interview Interviewers should review the application forms, letters of recommendation, references, notes and all other application materials. They might be asked to do a preliminary ranking of specific factors. Such materials and information should not be discussed with others in the organization and should be kept secured.

Decide the questions to ask or general areas to cover as well as who will ask each question or cover each area. The questions should be designed to determine the "fit" between the candidate and the position. Consider asking the following questions:

- Why do you want to become a law enforcement officer?
- What do you think you will contribute to the department?
- What do you think are the most significant trends in law enforcement?
- How have your education and experiences prepared you for this position?
- What plans do you have for self-development in the next 12 months?
- Why did you select this department/agency?

In framing the questions, consider the following general guidelines:

- Avoid asking questions that call for yes or no answers (closed questions).
- Ask open-ended questions. Interviewers want to hear how candidates think and to see their ability to do so under stress.
- Avoid asking leading questions. Instead ask questions that use "why," "how," "what" and "describe" or "tell me about."
- Avoid asking about any of the prohibited information protected by the Equal Employment Opportunity Act (to be discussed shortly).
- Keep questions job related.

During the Interview The first step is to establish rapport, a feeling of mutual understanding and trust. A warm greeting, friendly handshake, sincere smile and some small talk are appropriate to establish a relaxed atmosphere.

The next step is usually to explain how the interview will proceed or to set the agenda, including a general time frame. Next the job and the organization are described, followed by the asking of predetermined questions.

During the question/answer portion of the interview, an interviewer's listening skills are critical. Some suggest that interviewers should talk no more than 25 percent of the time. Candidates should do most of the talking. Silences should not be sources of anxiety because candidates often need time to formulate their responses. Wait patiently.

Consider tape recording the interview if several are to be conducted. This can help refresh your memory later. Candidates whose interviews you are recording should be notified of this before the interview begins. Recording all applicants and then listening to them in one sitting allows for better comparisons.

To ensure that interviews are nondiscriminatory:

- Ask the same general questions and require the same standards for all applicants.
- Treat all applicants fairly, equally and consistently.
- Be professional and consistent in addressing men and women. If using first names, do so for all candidates.
- Never indicate a particular interest in hiring a woman or minority person to improve the agency's Affirmative Action/Equal Employment Opportunity profile. It is unlawful and insulting to apply different standards based on a candidate's gender or minority status.

Maintaining eye contact, listening carefully and taking notes are ways to show candidates you are paying attention to their responses. It is often best to take notes on a clipboard held in your lap so candidates do not see what you are writing.

Do not form an opinion early in the interview. Stay neutral throughout. Avoid the **halo effect**—the tendency to assume that candidates who are strong (or weak) in one area will also be strong (or weak) in other areas. Allow time at the end of the interview for candidates to ask questions. Conclude the interview with a thank you and an indication of when you might make a decision.

Some agencies use interview rating forms such as that in Appendix C.

After the Interview After the successful candidates are selected, notified and have accepted the position, all other candidates should be notified of the decision. All selection process materials such as ratings, reference check notes and the actual application files should be returned immediately to the personnel office or other appropriate location. Successful candidates are usually required to pass a stringent medical examination before the job offer is final.

Selection is an expensive, time-consuming process for any agency. It is also a time-consuming and frustrating process for candidates. Often eligibility lists are obtained even though no actual position may be open. Elapsed time between taking an examination and obtaining a position may vary from weeks to years.

Some states have considered giving statewide examinations, permitting any participating law enforcement agency within the state to draw candidates from this list. This would eliminate much individual recruiting and selecting and also reduce costs. However, a strong desire for local testing based on local needs remains. A future consideration could be metropolitan, regional or statewide examinations, with each community making its final selections from this list.

Assessment Centers

Assessment centers are nothing new. Both the Allies and the Axis used them during World War II to train their spies. Hale (2005, p.86) asserts: "There is usually a strong correlation between a candidate's score in an assessment center and how well that candidate will perform." Assessment centers were discussed in Chapter 9.

Employment Criteria

To comply with Equal Employment Opportunity requirements and avoid legal problems, law enforcement agencies must hire personnel to meet very specific standards directly related to the job. A **bona fide occupational qualification (BFOQ)** is one that is reasonably necessary to perform a job. An example of a bona fide occupational qualification in law enforcement might be that the applicant has normal or correctable-to-normal hearing and vision or that the person be able to drive a vehicle.

Educational Requirements

One requirement that may pose difficulties is requiring a certain level of education. As far back as 1916 August Vollmer, father of modern policing, emphasized education for officers. Again in 1937 the Wickersham Commission and in 1967 the President's Commission on Law Enforcement and the Administration of Justice recommended education beyond high school. Yet the majority of local police

halo effect • tendency to rate one who performs above average in one area above average in all areas or vice versa.

bona fide occupational qualification (BFOQ) • a requirement reasonably necessary to perform the job.

departments, almost 90 percent, require only a high-school diploma or its equivalent (Bruns, 2005, p.97).

Bradley (p.35) asserts: "In this century it is highly likely that all police officers will be encouraged to have a college-level education." In some states, such as Minnesota, a two-year college degree is required. A U.S. Department of Justice study reported that in 2000, approximately 37 percent of large police agencies required applicants to have some college when applying, compared with 19 percent requiring some collage just 10 years prior in 1990 (Schanlaub, 2005, p.79). Another study found: "Higher education reduces time required for movement in rank and assignment to specialized positions and was positively correlated to promotion into supervisory and administrative posts. Implications are that higher education will enhance an officer's probability of rising to the top regardless of whether the agency requires a college degree as a precondition of employment" (Polk and Armstrong, 2001, p.77). Napier (2005, p.94) goes further in stating: "When we rationally look at what is required of law enforcement today, it is clear that higher education is not a luxury, not simply desirable, not a bonus—it is a necessity."

The most common reason for not requiring higher education is the fear the requirement would be challenged in court or through labor arbitration. A landmark case was *Griggs v. Duke Power Company* (1971), in which Griggs, an African-American employee, claimed that the requirement of having a high school diploma and passing two aptitude tests discriminated against him. The court ruled that any requirements or tests used in selecting or promoting must be job related.

A similar case occurred in *Davis v. City of Dallas* (1978). The Dallas Police Department at the time required applicants to have completed 45 semester hours of college credit with a "C" average. In this case the court ruled in favor of the police department, because the city introduced evidence supporting the educational requirement. Numerous nationwide studies have examined setting education requirements for police departments with favorable conclusions.

Clearly, not everyone agrees that college education enhances patrol officer performance. The biggest objections are that there are not enough promotions to satisfy a college-educated employee, the college-educated employee would be less likely to accept authority and that such a requirement would lower the pool of applicants for police positions and would be detrimental to potential minority applicants. Still, the advantages of advanced education appear to outweigh the disadvantages.

Various recruitment and scholarship programs have been developed throughout the country to attract and educate those who are interested in criminal justice professions. One national scholarship program, the Police Corps, recruits and trains college graduates to serve as community police officers.

One concern of those seeking higher education while employed as officers is how to pursue a course of study without taking time off from work. A solution is available through the Internet and distance learning, as discussed in Chapter 7. A question facing applicants and administrators alike is, if a degree is sought, what type of degree is most beneficial? Should it be a degree in liberal arts or in criminal justice? Opinions are mixed on this issue.

Research looked at the question "Are street smarts better than books smarts?" and found that officers with bachelor of science degrees were below the average in frequency of commendations and above the average in all the negative work habits of traffic collisions, sick time use and discipline. Officers with bachelor of arts degrees, in contrast, were above the average in the frequency that they received commendations and below the average in traffic collisions, sick time use and frequency of discipline (Bostrom, 2005, pp.18, 23).

A partial explanation offered for this disparity is the fact that a bachelor of arts degree emphasizes problem solving, develops understanding of how perceptions influence behavior, increases a person's comfort with ambiguity and assumes the things going on the world are fluid and interrelated (Bostrom, p.24). Officers with a bachelor of science degree, in contrast, tend to be rewarded for collecting verifiable facts and drawing conclusions based on those facts. Bostrom (p.25) then posits that perhaps the type of degree does not matter. The difference may be the type of person who chooses to pursue a bachelor of arts degree rather than a bachelor of science degree.

Another item of contention is how much advanced education is recommended for officers of varying ranks. Some experts think that experience in other law enforcement agencies should substitute for education. What this ratio of experience to education should be is not clear. An officer who has both education and experience is obviously the most desirable.

Whatever the decision, a clear policy documenting that a specific level of education is a bona fide occupational qualification (BFOQ) should be established. In addition, it is becoming more common for promotion to be contingent upon a higher level of education.

Because managers hire and promote, they must be thoroughly familiar with laws related to employment.

Laws Affecting Employment

Several laws affect employment, including the following:

- The *Equal Pay Act of 1963 (EPA)* prohibits discrimination in wages on the basis of gender for all employers.
- The *Civil Rights Acts of 1964 and 1970* prohibit race discrimination in hiring, placement and continuation of employment for all private employers, unions and employment agencies.

Civil Rights Act of 1964 • prohibits discrimination based on race, color, religion, sex or national origin by private employers with 15 or more employees, governments, unions and employment agencies.

> Title VII of the Civil Rights Act of 1964, as amended by the Equal Employment Opportunity Act (EEOA) of 1972, prohibits discrimination based on race, color, religion, gender or national origin for private employers with 15 or more employees, governments, unions and employment agencies.

- The *Age Discrimination in Employment Act (ADEA) of 1967*, amended in 1978, prohibits discrimination based on age for people between the ages of 40 and 70.
- *Title IX of 1972 Education Amendments* prohibits discrimination in education benefits based on race, color, religion, gender and national origin.
- The *Rehabilitation Act of 1973*, amended in 1980, prohibits discrimination against handicapped individuals for federal contractors and the federal government.
- The *Pregnancy Discrimination Act of 1978*, an amendment to Title VII, prohibits discrimination in employment on the basis of pregnancy, childbirth and related conditions for all private employers with 15 or more employees, governments, unions and employment agencies.
- The *Civil Service Reform Act of 1978* requires a federal government "workforce reflective of the nation's diversity."

- The *Immigration Reform and Control Act of 1986* prohibits discrimination against qualified aliens or on the basis of national origin.
- The *Americans with Disabilities Act (ADA) of 1990* prohibits discrimination based on physical or intellectual handicap for employers with 15 or more employees.

The legislation guaranteeing rights for people with disabilities provides only for fair and equal treatment in the workplace based on ability. Private employers or government agencies are not required to hire candidates for employment who are not qualified to perform essential job functions. The ADA is discussed in detail following this overview.

 The **Equal Employment Opportunity Commission (EEOC)** enforces laws prohibiting job discrimination based on race, color, religion, gender, national origin, handicapping condition or age between 40 and 70.

Equal Employment Opportunity Commission (EEOC) • enforces laws prohibiting job discrimination based on race, color, religion, sex, national origin, handicapping condition or age between 40 and 70.

If a department has a selection standard or requirement that results in rejection of a greater percentage of a certain class of applicants such as minorities or women, an adverse impact has occurred (Nowicki, 2003, p.362). An **adverse impact** is when the *rate* of selection is different for special classes than for the most selected class of applicants. The rule of thumb is that an adverse impact occurs when the selection rate, or percentage passing, of any special class of persons is less than 80 percent of the selection rate of the top scoring group (Nowicki, p.362).

adverse impact • when the *rate* of selection is different for special classes than for the most selected class of applicants.

The Family and Medical Leave Act of 1993

This law requires companies of 50 or more employees to allow employees 12 weeks of unpaid leave of absence for parenting or medical reasons.

The Uniformed Services Employment and Reemployment Rights Act of 1994

The Uniformed Services Employment and Reemployment Rights Act (USERRA) of 1994 provides that returning service members are to be reemployed in the job they would have attained had they not been absent for military service, with the same seniority, status and pay as well as other rights and benefits (Brown, 2004, p.33). USERRA also requires that employers provide COBRA-like continuation of group health coverage for up to 18 months for employees on military leave and their covered dependents who would otherwise lose their coverage.

The Americans with Disabilities Act of 1990

The Americans with Disabilities Act (ADA) of 1990, Title I, became effective in 1992. Title II, which involves discrimination in employment practices, went into effect in 1994 and applies to all agencies with 15 or more employees.

 Law enforcement is directly affected by the ADA's goal of guaranteeing individuals with disabilities access to employment and to governmental programs, services and activities.

The ADA prohibits employers from discriminating against a *qualified individual with a disability (QID)* in all areas of employment, including hiring, training, promoting, terminating and compensation. It also prohibits discrimination in nonemployment areas and requires accessibility to all services and facilities of public entities. Table 15.1 contains a brief explanation of key terms commonly used in the ADA. Notice especially the definitions for *disability* and *otherwise qualified*.

Table 15.1   Terms Associated with the ADA

The ADA uses numerous terms to describe its requirements and the obligations of those covered by the law. Here is a brief index and short explanation of some of the key words and phrases commonly used in the ADA.

Disability	(1) A mental or physical impairment that substantially limits a major life activity; (2) a record of having such an impairment; (3) being regarded as having such an impairment.
Impairment	A physiological or mental disorder.
Substantial limitation	When compared to the average person: (1) an inability to perform a major life activity; (2) a significant restriction on how or how long the activity can be performed; or (3) a significant restriction on the ability to perform a class or broad range of jobs.
Major life activity	Basic functions that the average person in the general population can do with little or no difficulty such as walking, seeing, hearing, breathing, speaking, procreating, learning, sitting, standing, performing manual tasks, working or having intimate sexual relations.
Otherwise qualified	A person with a disability who satisfies all of the requirements of the job such as education, experience, or skill and who can perform the essential functions of the job with or without reasonable accommodation.
Essential functions	The fundamental, not marginal, duties of a job.
Reasonable accommodation	A change in the application process, work environment, or job descriptions involving marginal functions of the job, or the use of modified or auxiliary devices that enable a person with a disability to perform the essential functions of the job without causing an undue hardship or direct threat to the health and safety of herself or himself or of others.
Undue hardship	Significant difficulty or expense relative to the size and overall financial resources of the employer.
Direct threat	A significant risk of substantial harm based on valid, objective evidence and not mere speculation.

Source: Paula N. Rubin. *The Americans with Disabilities Act and Criminal Justice: An Overview.* Washington, DC: National Institute of Justice, Research in Action, September 1993, p.4.

The ADA also establishes the following excluded disorders that are not caused by a physical impairment and thus are not considered disabilities: bisexuality, compulsive gambling, exhibitionism, gender-identity disorders, homosexuality, kleptomania, pedophilia, pyromania, sexual behavior disorder, transsexualism, transvestism and voyeurism.

Employment Issues This act has had a significant impact on the recruiting process. Most agencies have had to reorganize some of their recruiting procedures. To be in compliance, administrators should identify "essential functions" in job descriptions. Based on these, they should next develop selection criteria—ways to measure an applicant's ability to perform each essential job function.

 The ADA prohibits medical inquiries or evaluations, including some psychiatric evaluations, until after a job offer has been made.

The medical examination remains an important part of the application process, however. Serious consequences could arise as a result of a police officer not having the ability to perform essential job functions. If an applicant's disability would cause a direct threat to the applicant or public safety, the risk must be identified and documented by objective medical evidence as well.

Not all psychological examinations are disallowed under the ADA. Only those tests or scales specifically designed to disclose an impairment are disallowed. The ADA does not address polygraph tests and does not consider physical agility tests to be medical examinations; therefore, such tests are not governed by the ADA. Applicants may be subjected to drug testing. Further, employers may hold illegal drug users and alcoholics to the same performance standards as other employees.

Reasonable Accommodations Employers must make "reasonable accommodations" for any physical or mental limitations of a QID unless the employer can show that such accommodation would create an undue hardship or could threaten the health and safety of the QID or other employees. Reasonable accommodations might include modifying existing facilities to make them accessible, job restructuring, part-time or modified work schedules, or acquiring or modifying equipment. However, reasonable accommodations are not required when providing them causes an undue hardship for the agency.

It is unlikely that police agencies will be required to make substantial accommodations in the hiring process because the nature of police work requires some degree of fitness that can be substantiated through a job analysis. However, a reasonable accommodation goes beyond modifying job descriptions. It also means making buildings accessible to the physically disabled. Accessibility applies not only to employees but to nonemployees as well and involves parking lots, the building itself, the front desk, the elevator and staff. Appendix D contains an accessibility checklist.

Nonemployment Issues The ADA regulates all services and programs provided by public entities, which includes law enforcement agencies. Police agencies report that the greatest difficulties they face when responding to people with disabilities are citizens' misunderstanding of the police role in dealing with persons with disabilities; difficulty reaching help on weekends and evenings; and mistaking disabilities for antisocial behavior.

The ADA does not prohibit officers from enforcing the law, including use of force necessary to protect officer or public safety. However, the ADA does require officers who question suspects at the police station to provide communication and to delay questioning hearing-impaired suspects or witnesses until such assistance is available.

Enforcement of the ADA The regulating agencies for the ADA are the Department of Justice (DOJ), the Architectural Transportation Compliance Board (ATCB), the Equal Employment Opportunity Commission (EEOC) and the Federal Communications Commission (FCC). Agencies out of compliance may face civil penalties up to $50,000 for the first violation and $100,000 for subsequent violations, in addition to being ordered to modify their facilities to be in compliance.

Affirmative Action

Not only must employers avoid discrimination in the hiring process, but in some instances they must actively seek out certain people and make certain they have equal opportunities to obtain jobs.

 An **affirmative action program (AAP)** is a written plan to assist members of traditionally discriminated-against minority groups in employment, government contracts and education.

affirmative action program (AAP) • a written plan to ensure fair recruitment, hiring and promotion practices.

According to Walker et al. (2004, p.129): "The most controversial aspect of employment discrimination is the policy of affirmative action. The Office of Federal Contract Compliance defines affirmative action as 'results-oriented actions [taken] to ensure equal employment opportunity [which may include] goals to correct under-utilization . . . [and] back pay, retroactive seniority, makeup goals and timetables.'"

Ho (2005, p.471) contends: "Undoubtedly, the implementation of affirmative action has contributed to the progress of recruiting racial minorities as police officers across the nation." He (p.472) argues that police departments will successfully recruit racial minorities, regardless of the proportion of racial minorities in the communities, if the departments continue to implement their affirmative action polices. He also points out that implementing affirmative action in the selection process has been criticized for lowering recruitment standards.

Scuro (2004, p.24) notes: "In numerous prior decisions, the United States Supreme Court has held that mandatory quotas established to meet an affirmative action plan's racially motivated goals are unlawful and thereby unconstitutional under federal law." In *Griggs v. Duke Power Company* (1971) the Court clearly ruled that racially based quotas violated federal law.

In 1978 the Supreme Court, in *Regents of University of California v. Bakke*, allowed use of race as a factor among many in admissions to achieve diversity. Alan Bakke, a 37-year-old white male engineer, was denied admission to the medical school at the University of California at Davis, although his Medical College Admission Test score and grade-point average were higher than those of several of the 16 minority students admitted under a set-aside. In a 5–4 decision, the Court voted to invalidate the Cal-Davis quota system and admit Bakke to medical school. However, it endorsed affirmation action in principle.

During the 2002–2003 term the Supreme Court handed down two landmark decisions regarding affirmative action. In *Grutter v. Bollinger* (2003) the Court upheld the University of Michigan's law school admissions' racially based affirmative action plan which permitted race to be one factor used in the admissions process. However, in *Gratz v. Bollinger* (2003) it declared unconstitutional the University of Michigan's undergraduate admissions program because it made race a "final and critically decisive factor and used a point system in which the race of an undergraduate applicant was factored into the final score upon which final admission was predicated" (Scuro, p.26).

Affirmative action programs are mandated by several employment laws. Their intent is to undo the damage caused by past discrimination. The affirmative action policy of one agency states:

> The Anytown Police Department realizes that discrimination and the prejudice from which it results are deeply ingrained within our culture. Concentration on the mere prevention of discrimination can result in the implementation of practices that provide only superficial equality. Such practices, while possibly within the letter of the law, do not enact the full intent of the federal and state legislation, presidential and gubernatorial executive orders or the courts' interpretation of these mandates. It is, therefore, the intent of the Anytown Police Department to organize and implement policies, procedures, practices and programs that aid in overcoming the effects of past discrimination in regard to all of the protected groups.

special employment groups • groups included in affirmative action programs such as African Americans, Asians, Eskimos, Hispanics, homosexuals, immigrants, individuals with AIDS, individuals with disabilities, Middle Easterners, Native Americans, religious group members, substance abusers, Vietnam veterans, whites (reverse discrimination), women and young and aging individuals.

Among the **special employment groups** included in affirmative action programs are African Americans, Asians, the elderly, Eskimos, Hispanics, homosexuals, immigrants, individuals with AIDS, individuals with disabilities, Middle-Easterners, Native Americans, religious group members, substance abusers, war veterans, women and youths.

From this listing, one conclusion is obvious: anyone can fit into a "special employment group." Those responsible for hiring must take precautions to be fair and unbiased. They should recognize existing biases and ensure that biases do not enter into the process—a difficult task. If, for example, an affirmative action plan requires that all members of certain groups, such as minority group members, be given a personal interview, this may cause members not within this group to claim reverse discrimination. **Reverse discrimination** refers to giving women and minorities preferential treatment in hiring and promoting to the detriment of white males.

reverse discrimination • giving preferential treatment to women and minorities, to the detriment of white males, in hiring and promoting.

Several court decisions have struck down affirmative action initiatives as discriminatory. In 1996 both Texas and California (Proposition 209) struck down race-based admissions policies in their universities. The Berger Court sought a middle ground regarding affirmative action, supporting the basic concept but rejecting rigid application. The Rehnquist Court took a more negative view of affirmative action but has not rejected the concept totally.

Some departments use a form such as that contained in Appendix E to gather needed affirmative action data.

Equal employment opportunity and affirmative action policies begin with recruiting and selecting but are also important in assigning, training, promoting, disciplining and firing personnel.

Because these EEO and AA policies are important in so many areas of management, it is critical that managers understand their own policies as well as the policies and ordinances or statutes of their municipality, state and the country. Such knowledge is critical during the selection process. Possible resources are the director of personnel, the city attorney, law enforcement advisory boards, other law enforcement agencies and the International Association of Chiefs of Police.

In addition to laws related to hiring, many managers also must take into consideration restrictions imposed by unions.

Labor Laws and Unions

A **union,** in the broadest context, is any group authorized to represent the members of the law enforcement agency in negotiating matters such as wages, fringe benefits and other conditions of employment. Most states require by statute that certain conditions be met to be recognized as a union or bargaining unit. A **union shop** refers to a situation in which people must belong to or join the union to be hired.

union • any group authorized to represent the members of an agency in negotiating such matters as wages, fringe benefits and other conditions of employment.

union shop • must belong to or join the union to be hired.

Several laws ensure fair compensation standards as well as employees' rights to bargain collectively with management. Unions have existed in the United States for more than 200 years, beginning in 1792 when shoemakers formed a local union in Philadelphia. In 1932, the **Norris-LaGuardia Act** was passed to regulate employers' use of court injunctions against unions in preventing work stoppages. The Act also made yellow-dog contracts illegal. A **yellow-dog contract** forbids new employees to join a union. To do so would be grounds for discharge.

Norris-LaGuardia Act • regulated court injunctions against unions and made yellow-dog contracts illegal.

yellow-dog contract • makes union membership illegal under the penalty of discharge.

Another major law, sometimes called the "Magna Carta of organized labor," was enacted in 1935.

National Labor Relations Act of 1935 (Wagner Act) • legalized collective bargaining and required employers to bargain with the elected representatives of their employees.

The **National Labor Relations Act of 1935 (Wagner Act)** legalized collective bargaining and required employers to bargain with the elected representatives of their employees.

This act sets forth rules and procedures for both employers and employees. Its intent was to define and protect the rights of employees and employers and to encourage collective bargaining.

Fair Labor Standards Act (FLSA) of 1938 • established the 40-hour week as the basis of compensation and set a minimum wage.

The **Fair Labor Standards Act (FLSA) of 1938** established the 40-hour week as the basis of compensation and set a minimum wage. Police officers generally are covered by the FLSA. Brooks (2004, p.24) explains other provisions of the act. The FLSA requires covered employees to be compensated for overtime at the rate of one and one-half times their regular hourly wage. Time spent engaged in training, which primarily benefits the employer or is done at the employer's direction, is compensable. Brooks (p.30) notes that employees may be given one and one-half hour compensatory time off for every hour of overtime worked, but public safety employees may be allowed to accumulate only 480 hours of compensatory time. In *Christensen v. Harris County* (2000) the Supreme Court ruled that the FLSA allows a public employer to order an employee to take compensatory time off whenever the employer chooses to do so. Devanney and Devanney (2004, p.28) note that the FLSA does not require a public employer to allow its employees the use of comp time on days specifically requested by the employee. It requires only that comp time be permitted within a reasonable time after the employee requests its use.

Generally, time spent on-call is not compensable under the FLSA unless the employees are required to remain at the employer's premises or are so restricted they cannot engage in personal activities. Time spent commuting from home to work is not compensable, nor is time spent caring for equipment. In addition, volunteers are not covered by the FLSA.

Taft-Harley Act of 1947 • balanced the power of unions and management by prohibiting several unfair labor practices, including closed shops, which prohibited management from hiring nonunion workers.

closed shop • prohibits management from hiring nonunion workers.

right-to-work laws • make it illegal to require employees to join a union. Established by the Taft-Hartley Act of 1938.

Landrum-Griffin Act of 1959 • required regularly scheduled elections of union officers by secret ballot and regulated the handling of union funds.

National Labor Relations Board (NLRB) • the principal enforcement agency for laws regulating relations between management and unions.

The **Taft-Hartley Act of 1947** was passed to balance the power of unions and management by banning several unfair labor practices, including closed shops. A **closed shop** prohibits management from hiring nonunion workers. In effect, this act allowed states to pass their own **right-to-work laws,** making it illegal to require employees to join a union. In addition, the **Landrum-Griffin Act of 1959** required regularly scheduled elections of union officers by secret ballot and regulated the handling of union funds.

 The **National Labor Relations Board (NLRB)** is the principal enforcement agency for laws regulating relations between management and unions.

McPherson (2004, pp.137–138) advises: "There is no single formula for ensuring successful relationships between management and labor unions." When these relations are successful, it is the result of hard work by two committed, value-based leaders: the police chief and the union president. McPherson stresses that union leaders be treated as police professionals. A respectful relationship, despite differences that will inevitably arise, is in the best interest of the department and the union.

Strong feelings for and against unions are common in the general public and among those in law enforcement. For many law enforcement agencies, unions are a positive force; for others, they create problems and dissension; and in yet others, they are nonexistent. Even in agencies without unions, however, the possibility of employees becoming unionized is always there. Managers need to understand the current nature of unions and how they can benefit the mission of a law enforcement agency.

Nowicki (p.382) suggests that unions are often the result of poor management, that management practices may antagonize employees and cause them to seek more control over the workplace through collective bargaining.

A Sheriff's Association Union meeting in Grant County, Iowa. Creating and maintaining a respectful relationship, despite inevitable differences, serves the best interests of both the department and the union.

Collective Bargaining

The primary purpose of unions is to improve employment conditions through collective bargaining.

Collective bargaining is the process whereby representatives of employees meet with representatives of management to establish a written contract that sets forth working conditions for a specific time, usually one to three years. The contract deals not only with wages and benefits but also with hours of work and overtime, grievance procedures, disciplinary procedures, health and safety, employees' rights, seniority and contract duration. Most states have laws restricting officers from going on strike.

Law enforcement managers must recognize that officers have a right to join a union and to negotiate with management. Unions have caused administrators to re-examine their roles in negotiations, roles that have varied from remoteness to direct involvement at the bargaining table. In more recent years, both sides have engaged outside experts to represent their positions in negotiations, both at the bargaining table and during arbitration proceedings.

Most state collective bargaining statutes divide the scope of bargaining into three categories: (1) voluntary subjects that may be negotiated if both parties agree, (2) mandatory subjects that must be negotiated and (3) forbidden subjects that cannot be negotiated (Nowicki, p.384). *Voluntary topics* include issues such as safety, union security and productivity. *Mandatory subjects* usually include all

collective bargaining • the process whereby representatives of employees meet with representatives of management to establish a written contract setting forth working conditions for a specific time, usually one to three years.

matters directly affecting wages, hours, and terms and conditions of employment. *Excluded subjects* generally include the mission and functions of the agency, how the work is to be done and the equipment that will be used.

The union is obligated to protect the union employees' interests. Management is obligated to manage and control the agency. The ultimate goal of both should be excellent law enforcement services. At times the relationship develops into a struggle for power, with each assuming an adversarial position. By working together, management and unions can achieve the agency's mission to provide effective service to the community.

Key Contract Clauses Although all clauses of the contract are important, five clauses deserve special attention: (1) a management rights clause, (2) the definition of a grievance and the procedure for filing one and a procedure for handling disciplinary matters, (3) a no-strike provision, (4) a "zipper clause" and (5) a maintenance-of-benefits clause (Nowicki, p.385).

Managements' rights clauses usually include the right to plan, direct and control all police operations and set department policy, goals and objectives. This includes the right to hire, discipline, promote, train, fire, determine standards of conduct and the like.

Grievance clauses generally define what constitutes a grievance, the steps in the process and time limits. In collective bargaining, part of the disciplinary process is the basic principle of **just cause.** Under the just cause principle, a disciplinary case must be presented in two distinct parts. First, management must prove that the act in question was actually committed and that it violated some rule or policy. Second, management must show that the discipline imposed was not arbitrary, capricious, unreasonable or discriminatory (Nowicki, p.386).

No-strike clauses put the union on record as being against strikes and, properly written, could allow the department to seek monetary damages from the union in case of a strike. A *zipper clause* clearly states that the contract is a complete, full agreement between the two parties and neither party is obligated to negotiate on other items during the term of the contract. A *maintenance-of-benefits clause* identifies and describes in detail the specific benefits that will be maintained under the new contract.

Midterm Bargaining In states with collective bargaining, if management wants to make material changes to existing rules or implement new rules, it should involve the union bargaining unit before the effective date of the new rules or regulations: "Under most collective bargaining laws, a public employer is required to give to employee bargaining representatives (unions) both notice and an opportunity to bargain before unilaterally establishing or changing rules or policies that involve or affect mandatory subjects of bargaining" (Collins, 2004, p.12).

Types of Law Enforcement Unions

Law enforcement labor representation groups include local department benevolent associations that act on behalf of personnel, independent unions with a regional or state affiliation and nationally supported and organized labor unions such as the American Federation of Labor–Congress of Industrial Organizations (AFL-CIO).

Many law enforcement labor organizations simply evolved. A social group would be formed to discuss the interrelationships of a department and plan social

just cause • a reasonable, fair, honest reason.

zipper clause • clearly states that the contract is a complete, full agreement between the two parties and neither party is obligated to negotiate on other items during the term of the contract.

events for the year, often including family members. Over the years these groups started discussions concerning perceived department problems and eventually grew into benevolent associations.

One highly debated issue concerning union membership has been who should belong. What ranks should be included? Should managers and supervisors belong to the same union as line officers because their interests in wages and benefits are largely the same? Is there a conflict of interest?

Some studies indicate that 85 percent of law enforcement unions include both patrol officers and sergeant levels or above, which means that only 15 percent consist solely of patrol–level officers. As long as issues are mainly concerned with wages and benefits, this is not a problem. But when issues involve taking more control of what management considers its rights, such as one-officer versus two-officer patrol cars, transfers and promotions, working-hour assignments and the like, conflict can occur. Some agencies have formed separate management-level units within the same umbrella as the rank-and-file union to overcome the objections to a single unit.

Some managers would rather not have unions. If unions are to exist, most managers would rather they be local and independent. Local union membership provides opportunity for personal, face-to-face discussions about local department problems; lower dues; more control over who is to represent the department; and control over all expenditures.

On the other hand, national union representation allows national research on wages, benefits and other issues; outside representation at discussions; and greater political influence. Legal assistance is often available. Outside representation prevents union conflict issues spilling over into everyday performance and personal relationships. The main national union groups are:

- *International Union of Police Associations*—affiliated with the AFL-CIO.
- *Fraternal Order of Police*—the oldest police organization in the United States; emphasizes collective bargaining in some areas and socializing in other areas.
- *National Association of Police Officers*—consists of police unions opposed to affiliation with the AFL-CIO.
- *International Brotherhood of Police Officers*—founded in Rhode Island in 1969; emphasizes collective bargaining.
- *International Brotherhood of Teamsters*—a private union.
- *American Federation of State, County and Municipal Employees*—a union for public employees founded in 1936, affiliated with the American Federation of Labor.

Each organization decides what kind of union to have and often bases its selection on past local management–rank-and-file relationships. Attitudes toward management have often been as much a reason for union membership as other conditions of employment.

Reasons for Joining Law Enforcement Unions

A common reason for joining a union is a perceived lack of communication, inaction or deliberate disregard for the feelings and reasonable desires of the majority of employees. Other frequently mentioned reasons are lack of concern for the employees' general needs, lower wages and fewer benefits than comparable departments, peer pressure, general frustration, conditions of equipment or employment, imagined wrongs, lack of concern for legitimate grievances, badly handled personnel problems, inadequate communications, favoritism, lack of formal grievance procedures, distrust between management and the rank and file, disregard of job stress factors, past bad-faith bargaining and negotiating, lack of recognition for a job well done and a lack of leadership by management.

> People join unions to ensure fair treatment, to improve their economic situation and to satisfy social needs.

Management versus Employee Rights

Controversy between management and unions revolves largely around what is perceived as reasonable management and employee rights or demands. Managers must have specific functions reserved. On the other hand, management depends on employees to do the job. The better law enforcement tasks are performed, the better the managers and employees are perceived by the community they both serve. The better the community perception and rating of the agency, the greater the acceptance of law enforcement needs in terms of wages, benefits and general support.

The most frequently reserved management rights are determining staffing and staffing levels; determining work schedules, patrol areas and work assignments; controlling police operations; establishing standards of conduct on and off duty; establishing hiring, promoting, transferring, firing and disciplinary procedures; setting work-performance standards; establishing department goals, objectives, policies and procedures; and establishing training programs and who should attend. Management should not have these rights unreasonably infringed upon at the bargaining table. Contracts are long-term instruments that affect not only the present regime but future managers as well. Management must possess sufficient rights to fulfill the agency's mission to the community.

The most desirable way to avoid management–employee conflict is to resolve issues at the lowest level possible. Primarily, this means between first-line supervisors and patrol officers (or equal rank). The vast majority of issues should be resolved at this level, and the first-line supervisor must have the responsibility and authority to do so.

Others perceive a more basic conflict—a distinct difference between the professional law enforcement stance and that advocated by unions. The professional model would be: we look to lateral entry and professional skills rather than time on the job in our selections. We want to expand the entire profession. The union model would be: We protect our people no matter what happens. If we have to pick between the young, educated professional and the old, established worker, we go with the old one every time.

Management, Unions and Politics

Management would like to believe that they can administer a law enforcement agency without being involved in politics. Many administrators say, "I try to stay out of politics." If "politics" is perceived as actively supporting candidates during political campaigns, it is possible. But to remove oneself from all politics is virtually impossible. Locally elected government officials approve law enforcement budgets. Passage of desirable ordinances and statutes depends on elected officials.

Gaining the respect and support of these officials after they are elected is a necessity to law enforcement administration. In some cities, unions are also very active in elections and in supporting specific candidates.

Law enforcement management involvement in politics is less likely in communities with a council/manager form of government because the chief executive officer reports directly to the city manager. The city manager is a buffer between law enforcement managers and the city's elected officials.

City management has many departments and varied personnel concerns. Even though city government may sympathize with law enforcement demands, it must balance the demands of all departments. City administration may resist binding arbitration for this reason. Final decisions are made by people not associated with the local government and who have no personal stake in how the decision may be implemented financially or managerially.

Levels of Bargaining

Bargaining may take place at various levels ranging from discussion to court settlements. At the most cooperative level, *open discussion* resolves issues and results in a win-win situation, with a contract that both sides consider fair. If discussion does not resolve all the issues, the next level may be *mediation*, bringing in a neutral third party to assist in the discussion. A mediator helps the two sides reach an agreement.

If the negotiation process stalls, the matter may be referred to *arbitration*, with the consent of all parties. Usually three arbitrators are appointed, and a majority makes the decision. Either a statute or agreement of all parties determines the method of selection. Arbitration should be a last resort. Beyond arbitration, the matter can sometimes be appealed to the courts.

 Negotiations usually proceed through these levels: discussion, mediation, arbitration and the courts.

Management and Unions Working Together

Law enforcement management/union decision making may involve mayors, councils, city managers and often outside negotiators, arbitrators, grievance committees and even the courts. Although law enforcement officers usually do not have the right to strike, they may accomplish similar results through actions such as "blue flu" or slowdowns. Bargaining units of some type are a fact of administrators' lives. It is better to form good relationships that lead to positive results for both sides than to begin with adversarial attitudes. Working within the confines of the written contract is important at all levels of supervision and management, from sergeant to chief.

Open communication, reasonable expectations, honest cooperation, upfront presentations, a sincere desire to negotiate and common objectives are all evidence of good-faith bargaining. Both sides should avoid **delaying tactics** such as failing to disclose important demands until the end; deliberately withholding information; deliberately providing misinformation, untruths or distortions; providing only information that weakens the others' position; or deliberately exhibiting unwillingness to resolve the issues so as to throw the process into binding arbitration.

delaying tactics • stalling during negotiations.

Successful management/union negotiations begin with a positive atmosphere within the agency during everyday activities and normal routine, for it is here that the tone for mutual respect is established. Everyday problems have a way of developing into grievances, which may then become issues in management/union negotiations. When first-line supervisors have open dialogue and communication about problems and this continues up the hierarchy, an avenue is established for later openness in labor relations as well.

Negotiations should be entered into far ahead of budget deadlines. Timing should also avoid city and union elections. Both sides should agree on rules for negotiation procedures; maintain open channels of communication; present logical, reasonable justification for their positions; and prepare areas of agreement as well as disagreement. Areas of agreement should be disposed of as soon as possible to focus energies on differences. Both sides should recognize the emotions involved and resist overreactions. Officials on both sides should be aware that off-the-cuff, unsupportable statements can stop negotiations. Items for negotiation should not be discussed outside negotiation proceedings. No individual department head should have the authority or responsibility for final settlement. Lay the past contract and the proposed contract side by side and compare wording, additions and deletions, word for word, page by page.

The most equitable negotiations take place in an atmosphere of openness, cooperation, faith and trust. Seek fairness and focus on the main goals of both sides.

Collective Bargaining, Arbitration and the CEO

CEOs (chiefs of police, sheriffs, superintendents, directors of public safety or any other title denoting head of an agency) might take several positions in collective bargaining negotiations. At the very least, CEOs should be available to describe how a prior contract has affected the agency or how changes in the community or the agency require changes in the new contract. During negotiation stages, the CEO or the management representatives should be informed about how matters under discussion might affect their operations.

In some instances CEOs may be facilitators or advisors. In this role they can tell negotiators how specific actions would affect management's ability to administer the agency. In other instances CEOs may actively participate in the prenegotiation stages but become interested bystanders during actual negotiations, or they may actively participate in the negotiations.

In all discussions, mediations and arbitrations, retain careful records. What occurs at one level of negotiations is likely to be reviewed at the next level. In addition, what is stated at any time in the process is usually subject to appeal. After the negotiation process is complete, a contract is written containing the specific terms of the agreement. Everyone affected by the contract should receive a copy and understand its terms.

 SUMMARY

Selection of law enforcement personnel is a critical management function. The selection process is based on carefully specified criteria and usually includes completing an application form, undergoing a series of tests and examinations, passing a background check and successfully completing an interview. The most common screening methods for selection are basic skills/written tests, medical examinations, background investigations, psychological examinations and physical fitness tests.

Selection is often affected by laws related to equal employment, affirmative action and labor (unions). Title VII of the Civil Rights Act of 1964, as amended by the Equal Employment Opportunity Act (EEOA) of 1972, prohibits discrimination based on race, color, religion, gender or national origin for private employers with 15 or more employees, governments, unions and employment agencies. The Equal Employment Opportunity Commission enforces laws prohibiting job discrimination based on race, color, religion, gender, national origin, handicapping condition or age between 40 and 70. Law enforcement is directly affected by the ADA's goal of guaranteeing individuals with disabilities access to employment and to government programs, services and activities. The ADA prohibits medical inquiries or evaluations, including some psychiatric evaluations, until after a job offer has been made.

An affirmative action program (AAP) is a written plan to assist members of traditionally discriminated against minority groups in employment, government contracts and higher education. Equal employment opportunity and affirmative action policies begin with recruiting and selecting but are also important in assigning, training, promoting, disciplining and firing personnel.

The National Labor Relations Act of 1935 (Wagner Act) legalized collective bargaining and required employers to bargain with the elected representatives of their employees. The National Labor Relations Board (NLRB) is the principal enforcement agency for laws regulating relations between management and unions.

The primary purpose of unions is to improve employment conditions through collective bargaining. People join unions to ensure fair treatment, to improve their economic situations and to satisfy social needs. Negotiations usually proceed through discussion, mediation, arbitration and the courts.

CHALLENGE FIFTEEN

The Greenfield Police Department's hiring process has not changed in many years. Officer applicants, without exception, must have a two-year law enforcement degree to be eligible to apply. Applicants are initially screened with a standardized written exam testing general knowledge. The test uses language not specific to the Greenfield Police Department and appears to be a test developed decades ago by another department. The test includes outdated references to technology and police procedures. The test emphasizes officer qualities suited for a traditional "crime fighting" strategy.

The interview portion of the hiring process consists of a panel of police managers reading general questions to the applicants. Each applicant is given a certain amount of time to respond. Follow-up questions are discouraged, and the managers are provided with the preferred answers to use in assessing the applicant.

Successful applicants are required to pass a rigorous physical fitness test. The applicants are tested for strength, endurance and agility. It is common knowledge within the department that many of the current officers could no longer pass the test.

You have recently been promoted to captain. The new chief has asked you to study the hiring procedure and to offer suggestions for updating it. The chief wants a process that reflects the department's emphasis on community policing.

1. The Greenfield Police Department has a requirement that applicants must have a two-year degree in law enforcement. Can you think of any potential negative consequences resulting from this requirement?

2. What changes should you suggest for the written exam?

3. What are the benefits of adding an essay to the written test?

4. How could you improve the interview portion of the hiring process?

5. Do you see any pitfalls with the physical fitness test?

DISCUSSION QUESTIONS

1. During which stages of the selection process is discrimination most likely to occur?

2. Compare and contrast the Equal Employment Opportunity Act and an affirmative action plan.

3. Have there been any civil suits related to law enforcement employment in your area in the past few years? In your state?

4. What is the most difficult part of the selection process?

5. What questions would you ask during an employment interview?

6. How much education should an entry-level position in law enforcement require? A management position?

7. What are other bona fide occupational requirements for an entry-level position in law enforcement? For a management position?

8. Have you ever belonged to a union? If so, what were your reactions to it?

9. Do you favor unions for law enforcement employees? What are the advantages and disadvantages for management?

10. Is the law enforcement agency in your jurisdiction unionized? How does management feel about it?

REFERENCES

Bostrom, Matthew D. "The Influence of Higher Education on Police Officer Work Habits." *The Police Chief*, October 2005, pp.18–25.

Bradley, Patrick L. "21st Century Issues Related to Police Training." *The Police Chief*, October 2005, pp.32–38.

Brooks, Michael E. "The Fair Labor Standards Act and Police Compensation." *FBI Law Enforcement Bulletin*, June 2004, pp.24–32.

Brown, Judith. "Military Leave: Supporting Employees." *The Police Chief*, November 2004, pp.30–33.

Bruns, Diana. "Patrol Officers' Opinions on the Importance of a College Degree." *Law and Order*, September 2005, pp.96–99.

Collingwood, Thomas; Hoffman, Robert J.; and Smith, Jay. "The Need for Physical Fitness." *Law and Order*, June 2003, pp.44–50.

Collingwood, Thomas; Hoffman, Robert J.; and Smith, Jay. "Underlying Physical Fitness Factors for Performing Police Officer Physical Tasks." *The Police Chief*, March 2004, pp.32–37.

Collins, John M. "Labor Relations: Promulgating a New Rule." *The Police Chief*, June 2004, p.12.

Conroy, Dennis and Placide, MaCherie. *Prevention of Racially Biased Policing Accountability and Supervision: Technical Assistance Guide*. City of Saint Paul (Minnesota) Police Department, 2003.

Devanney, Joe and Devanney, Diane. "Recent Cases in Employment Law." *Law and Order*, July 2004, p.28.

Dwyer, R. Gregg and Laufersweiler-Dwyer, Deborah L.

"The Need for Change: A Call for Action in Community Oriented Police Training." *FBI Law Enforcement Bulletin*, November 2004, pp.18–24.

Egan, Timothy. "Police Forces, Their Ranks Thin, Offer Bonuses, Bounties and More." *The New York Times*, December 28, 2005.

Ellis, Gene; Skinner, Chris; and Smith, Gary. "Using Visual Technology for Recruitment." *The Police Chief*, January 2005, pp.20–24.

Finnimore, Ian J. "Learning and Applying Good Communication Skills." *The NAFTO News*, Spring 2003, pp.23–24.

Fuss, Timothy and Snowden, Lynne. "Importance of Background Investigations." *Law and Order*, March 2004, pp.58–63.

Garcia, Venessa. "'Difference' in the Police Department: Women, Policing, and 'Doing Gender.'" *Journal of Contemporary Criminal Justice*, August 2003, pp.330–344.

Guthrie, Edward L. "Qualities and Traits of the Professional Law Enforcement Officer." *FBI Law Enforcement Bulletin*, December 2004, pp.23–24.

Haberfeld, M. R. *Police Leadership*, Upper Saddle River, NJ: Pearson, Prentice Hall, 2006.

Hale, Charles. "Candidate Evaluation and Scoring." *Law and Order*, December 2005, pp.86–87.

Harris, Patricia M. and Keller, Kimberly S. "Ex-Offenders Need Not Apply: The Criminal Background Check in Hiring Decisions." *Journal of Contemporary Criminal Justice*, February 2005, pp.6–30.

Henchey, James P. "Ready or Not, Here They Come: The Millennial Generation Enters the Workforce." *The Police Chief*, September 2005, pp.108–118.

Ho, Taiping. "Do Racial Minority Applicants Have a Better Chance to Be Recruited in Predominately White Neighborhoods? An Empirical Study." *Police Quarterly*, December 2005, pp.454–475.

Holzman, Arnold and Kirschner, Mark. "Pre-Employment Psychological Evaluations." *Law and Order*, September 2003, pp.85–87.

Johnson, Kevin. "The Community Recruiter." *The Police Chief*, June 2005, pp.16–20.

Jones, Robin. "Recruiting Women." *The Police Chief*, April 2004, pp.165–166.

Koper, Christopher S. *Hiring and Keeping Police Officers*. Washington, DC: National Institute of Justice, July 2004. (NCJ 202289)

Legel, Chad. "Evaluating an Entry-Level Exam." *Law and Order*, December 2005, pp.66–69.

Lonsway, Kimberly A. "Tearing Down the Wall: Problems with Consistency, Validity and Adverse Impact of Physical Agility Testing in Police Selection." *Police Quarterly*, September 2003, pp.237–277.

McKeever, Jack and Kranda, April. "Best Practices Guide for Recruitment and Retention of Qualified Police Personnel." In *A Police Chief's Desk Reference*. Washington, DC: The International Association of Chiefs of Police and the Bureau of Justice Assistance, 2005, pp.288–299.

McPherson, Nancy. "Reflections from the Field on Needed Changes in Community Policing." In *Community Policing: The Past, Present, and Future*, edited by Lorie Fridell and Mary Ann Wycoff. Washington, DC: The Annie E. Casey Foundation and the Police Executive Research Forum, November 2004, pp.127–139.

Moore, Carole. "Strong Report Writing Presents Positive Image." *Law Enforcement Technology*, January 2004, p.82.

Napier, Mark. "The Need for Higher Education." *Law and Order*, September 2005, pp.86–94.

Nowicki, Dennis E. "Human Resource Management and Development," In *Local Government Police Management*, 4th ed., edited by William A. Geller and Darrel W. Stephens. Washington, DC: International City/County Management Association, 2003, pp.353–390.

Polk, O. Elmer and Armstrong, David A. "Higher Education and Law Enforcement Career Paths: Is the Road to Success Paved by Degree?" *Journal of Criminal Justice Education*, Spring 2001, pp.77–99.

"Pre-Employment Psychological Evaluation Services Guidelines." *The Police Chief*, September 2005, pp.68–86.

Recruiting & Retaining Women: A Self-Assessment Guide for Law Enforcement. Washington, DC: National Center for Women & Policing, no date.

Schanlaub, Russ. "Degree or No Degree." *Law and Order*, September 2005, pp.76–82.

Scuro, Joseph E., Jr. "Supreme Court Redefines Affirmative Action." *Law and Order*, February 2004, pp.24–26.

Sharp, Arthur. "Departmental Divergences on Marijuana Use and New Recruits." *Law and Order*, September 2003, pp.80–84.

Sharp, Arthur. "Recruits and Smoking." *Law and Order*, December 2004, pp.52–55.

Spawn, Mark A. "Recruitment Strategies: A Case Study in Police Recruitment." *FBI Law Enforcement Bulletin*, March 2003, pp.18–20.

Strandberg, Keith. "Conquering Recruiting Challenges: Finding the Best Candidates for the Job." *Law Enforcement Technology*, January 2004, pp.40–45.

Vest, Gary. "Closing the Recruitment Gap: A Symposium's Findings." *FBI Law Enforcement Bulletin*, November 2003, pp.13–17.

Viverette, Mary Ann. "Diversity on the Force." *The Police Chief*, December 2005, p.6.

Walker, Samuel; Spohn, Cassia; and DeLone, Miriam. *The Color of Justice: Race, Ethnicity, and Crime in America*, 3rd ed. Belmont, CA: Wadsworth Publishing Company, 2004.

Yearwood, Douglas L. and Freeman, Stephanie. "Recruitment and Retention of Police Officers in North Carolina." *The Police Chief*, March 2004, pp.43–49.

CASES CITED

Christensen v. Harris County, 529 U.S. 576 (2000)

Davis v. City of Dallas (1978)

Gratz v. Bollinger, No. 02-516, decided June 23, 2003

Griggs v. Duke Power Company, 401 U.S. 424 (1971)

Grutter v. Bollinger, No. 02-241, decided June 23, 2003

Monell v. New York City Department of Social Services, 436 U.S. 658 (1978)

Parker v. The District of Columbia (1988)

Regents of University of California v. Bakke, 438 U.S. 265 (1978)

BOOK-SPECIFIC WEB SITE

Go to the Management and Supervision in Law Enforcement Web site at www.thomsonedu.com/criminaljustice/bennett for student and instructor resources, including Internet Assignments and Case Studies.

CHAPTER 16

Measuring Performance: Assessment and Evaluation

Excellence is not a standard; it is a frame of reference, a state of mind.

Anonymous

DO YOU KNOW?

- What the basic purpose of evaluation is?
- What purposes are served by performance appraisals?
- What the three usual forms of inspection are?
- What purposes performance appraisals serve? What their main purpose should be?
- Who should conduct a performance appraisal?
- What function job standards serve? In what areas they may be established?
- What lawsuits may be brought against agencies that do not have fitness tests, standards or programs?
- What a by-the-numbers evaluation is?
- What consequences evaluations should have?
- What common types of performance evaluations are?
- What the main purpose of a performance interview is?
- How frequently to evaluate performance?
- What problems may occur in evaluations?
- How to evaluate the entire organization?
- What accreditation is and who does it?

CAN YOU DEFINE?

accreditation
behaviorally
    anchored rating
    scales (BARS)
by-the-numbers
    evaluation
cybernetics

descriptive statistics
evaluate
halo effect
horn effect
inferential statistics
performance
    appraisal

performance
    interviews
pre-evaluation
promotability/
    assignment factors
standards
valid

Introduction

We are constantly evaluating others and being evaluated ourselves. People evaluate, in varying degrees, every time they meet someone. The opinion they form of others, even in a social situation, is an informal evaluation. In the business world, people are evaluated as potential customers. People who wager on racing evaluate the horses and the jockeys before they bet. At election time, people evaluate the candidates for office. Law enforcement officers evaluate people's behavior to determine if they might be up to something.

This chapter begins with an overview of evaluation and the evaluation cycle. It then discusses specific purposes of evaluation and the criticality of clearly stated and job-related performance criteria or standards. This is followed by a discussion of inspections and performance appraisals. Next the chapter examines a variety of surveys and rating forms and the type of information sought during evaluations as well as common types of performance evaluations. The discussion then turns to performance interviews, guidelines for evaluating and problems to anticipate during evaluations. This discussion is followed by a look at the benefits of evaluation. The chapter then examines evaluating the teams within a department, evaluation training, evaluating the entire department and the potential role of accreditation in evaluation. The chapter concludes with a discussion of recognizing value in policing, measuring citizen satisfaction with police services and a look at evaluation and research.

Evaluation: An Overview

Evaluation and *appraisal* are synonyms. Both refer to measuring performance or outcomes. To **evaluate** means to determine the worth of something, be it an individual's performance, a training program or an agency.

evaluate • to determine the worth of, to find the amount or value of or to appraise.

 The basic purpose of evaluation is to determine how well an agency is accomplishing its mission and to make improvements.

The importance of having a stated mission has been stressed throughout this text. Evaluation assesses how well individuals, teams, units and the entire department are contributing to this mission. Integral to this assessment are the training efforts and the innovations a department undertakes as well as perceptions of the citizens an agency seeks to serve and protect.

Evaluation can be as informal as a manager pointing out to a subordinate a job well done or as formal as an annual performance review. Evaluation can be as simple as an inspection of the patrol officers at roll call before they hit the streets or as complex as the process involved in seeking accreditation.

Evaluations must be objective, seeking to identify not only strengths but also weaknesses. It is only through such objectivity that improvements can be made. As improvements are made, their effectiveness should also be assessed, resulting in a cycle of evaluation.

The Evaluation Cycle

For evaluation to be effective, the results must be used. Evaluation must be perceived as a means to determine strengths and weaknesses of individuals as well as programs within an agency and how well each is contributing to total agency efforts. The evaluation cycle is diagrammed in Figure 16.1.

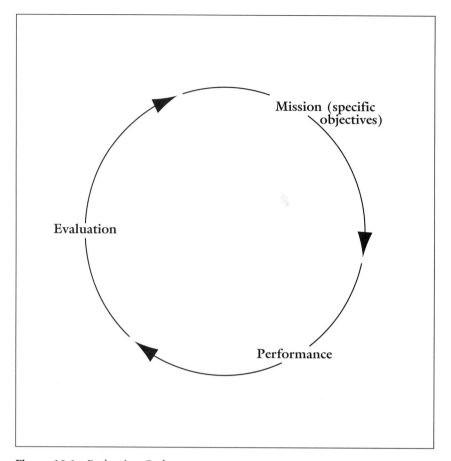

Figure 16.1 Evaluation Cycle

Purposes of Evaluation

Evaluation provides an objective assessment of how individual officers and managers are performing. It also can provide an objective assessment of teams or units within the department as well as innovations and training efforts being implemented. It can provide an assessment of the entire agency and determine whether it is accomplishing its stated mission. It can also provide an assessment of citizen satisfaction.

 Evaluation can provide an objective assessment of individual officers, managers, innovations, programs and the entire agency. It can provide information related to the budget. It can also help defend against lawsuits and assess citizen satisfaction with the service provided.

One of the most common types of evaluation used in law enforcement agencies is the inspection.

Inspections

 The three typical forms of inspections are line inspections, spot inspections and staff inspections.

Line Inspections

A line inspection is the day-to-day review of a subordinate's appearance. Such an inspection serves two purposes: (1) it lets the supervisor know that the subordinate's uniform and equipment or business attire meet established standards, and (2) it provides supervisors a chance to demonstrate to subordinates that they are interested in how subordinates look and that the supervisors are going to adhere to established standards (Marcum, 2005, p.120).

A type of line inspection often missed by supervisors is direct observation of officers performing day-to-day tasks by riding along with an officer from time to time (Marcum, p.120).

Spot Inspections

Spot inspections are like line inspections but are done by someone other than the inspected person's chain of command (Marcum, p.121). They are unannounced and give the inspectors a true picture of how things are actually being done. They also assess if a supervisor is handling reports and other paperwork properly. Spot inspections may lead to discipline, but they usually document an officer's or supervisor's good work (Marcum, p.121).

Staff Inspections

Staff inspections are more formal than line or spot inspections. Staff inspections are proactive and complement and augment the line inspection (Fuller, 2004, p.66). Most staff inspections have six objectives:

1. To determine whether the department's procedures and policies are being properly implemented
2. To determine whether the department's procedures and policies are adequate to attain the department's goals
3. To determine whether the department's resources (such as personnel) are being used fully and sensibly
4. To determine whether the department's resources are adequate to attain the department's goals
5. To discover any deficiencies in integrity, training, morale or supervision
6. To help operating line units plan their line inspections

A correctly conducted staff inspection can uncover potential problems before they reach proportions that negatively affect the department (Fuller, p.66). The focus should be on how things are being done, not necessarily on the people who are doing them. Such a distinction can negate the common perception that staff inspections are spy operations intended to detect personnel shortcomings.

Every unit and activity should be inspected, but certain areas need regularly scheduled attention: human resources; crime reporting and statistics; evidence handling and storage; firearms, drugs, money and other valuables; agency vehicles, interior and exterior; emergency equipment in patrol vehicles; personal defense and restraint systems; unit work stations; case presentation and officers' testimony; overtime payments; and accuracy of roll-book entries (Fuller, pp.70–72).

In addition to inspections, one of the most important types of evaluation is the performance appraisal.

Performance Appraisals

A field training officer provides continuous informal evaluation while helping rookies learn to perform tasks efficiently. The time comes, however, when the rookies will have to pass a test—a formal evaluation of their skills. Both types of evaluation are necessary.

Informal evaluation is thought by some experts to be better than formal evaluation. They do not believe that evaluating on a precise date is truly how to evaluate. It is better to make judgments whenever necessary. Thus, evaluation should be continuous. They also point out that evaluating at the time behavior occurs is more apt to consider the behavior rather than personality. Informal evaluations, such as a sergeant praising a patrol officer, can be motivating, as discussed in Chapter 9. Informal evaluations can also help identify behaviors that might become serious problems if not dealt with early, as discussed in Chapter 10.

Formal evaluations may be in the form of checklists and rating forms. A performance appraisal is intended to represent an accurate, objective accountant of an employee's performance during a stated time period (Hilgenfeldt, 2004, p.90). There are various ways of measuring performance: quality of task performance, productivity measurements, attendance records or individual testing. Basically, managers need to know what subordinates are doing, how well they are doing it and how strong performance can be continued and weak areas improved.

Regardless of the rating form selected, managers must observe subordinates performing their assigned tasks and conduct a **performance appraisal**. They must find some form of comparison and measurement and assess employees' development.

performance appraisal •
formal evaluation of on-the-job functioning; usually conducted annually.

Law enforcement managers' attitudes toward performance appraisals and their ability to assess are critical factors for a successful evaluation system. Will employees be rated as individuals, in comparison with other employees doing similar tasks or by state or national standards?

 Managers who provide the most immediate direction of subordinates should do the evaluation.

Immediate supervisors can most directly observe employee behavior at the level at which the majority of required tasks are performed. In most cases, the police sergeant evaluates patrol officers. The administrative sergeant or lieutenant evaluates dispatch personnel. The investigative sergeant or lieutenant evaluates investigative personnel.

If employees are transferred during a rating period, each responsible manager should put in writing the evaluation for the period of responsibility. A system to establish time periods for evaluation and reminders should be devised, often based on the hiring anniversary date. Some type of immediate follow-up and feedback should be provided between formal ratings as needed. Law enforcement managers are motivators, and motivation is one reason for evaluation.

Purposes of performance appraisals include promoting common understanding of individual performance levels, needs, work objectives and standards; providing feedback and suggesting specific courses of action to improve, including training; setting objectives for future performance; and helping in making decisions about promotions, reassignments, disciplinary actions and terminations.

Performance appraisals are not intended to cause undue burdens to managers but rather to provide consistent criteria for improving employee performance.

When employees understand how they are doing, know that what they are doing contributes to the organization and know what they are doing correctly, performance levels will justify the evaluation effort.

Most managers who do performance evaluations do not know how to do them correctly because they were never taught adequately (Mulder, 2004, p.100). A trained evaluator has the skill and ability to successfully observe, accurately record and objectively articulate observed behaviors (Hilgenfeldt, p.90).

Some managers claim that evaluations take too much time, that employees resent it or that to do an evaluation is a "pain." The truth is, managers must evaluate employees—either by means of formal rating systems or informally. If managers correct employees on the job, they are in fact evaluating task performance. If they fail to correct a situation that needs correcting, they are not accepting responsibility.

 The main purpose of performance evaluation is to improve employee performance.

Performance Criteria/Standards

Performance appraisals must be based on clearly stated job descriptions and clearly stated performance standards. If job descriptions change, evaluations must reflect these changes. Evaluation forms and standards *must* fit the job. What tasks are rated? What level of performance is required? As many criteria as possible should be written.

The manager's job is to help everyone achieve their level of competence. Although some evaluation systems rank order employees, usually they should not be rated on a curve but individually. It is possible to have all excellent employees (or the reverse). Employees who meet established standards at the required level should be provided an acceptable rating regardless of how other employees perform.

Standards may involve quality of performance, quantity and meeting established goals. In law enforcement work, quality rather than quantity is usually most important. Competence and courtesy in handling requests for service are important factors. Without performance standards supervisors may be inconsistent and unfair in promotions, awards and discipline. Performance standards allow supervisors to be consistent and fair.

standards • targets to be met, including level of performance.

Performance standards should be mission related, measurable, attainable and practical to monitor. Such standards let officers know what to expect, remove personality from ratings and provide a basis for objective appraisal with a minimum of inconsistencies.

 Job standards make it easier for employees to meet requirements and for managers to determine whether they have been met.

Obviously, numerical or quantity standards are easier to meet and evaluate, but many law enforcement tasks do not lend themselves to quantitative standards. Traditional measurements such as crime rates, clearance rates, tickets issued and the like measure only events, not whether the activities were completed efficiently and effectively. When standards are established, they must be made known to employees so that employees know what is expected. As noted, managers must accompany subordinates in the field periodically to know what they are doing and how well. They cannot do this from behind a desk.

Reports can also be used to measure performance. Activity reports indicate types and numbers of tasks performed. The number of citizen complaints or commendations also indicate performance quality.

 Standards may include areas such as physical energy to perform and emotional stability while performing law enforcement tasks; individual judgment; reliability; loyalty and ability to get along with the public, fellow employees and managers; creativeness and innovation; attitude; knowledge of tasks; competence; and amount of required management.

Standards vary considerably among federal, state, county and municipal organizations.

Quotas One controversial area related to performance standards is whether an agency uses a quota system to evaluate an officer's performance. A survey of 30 law enforcement agencies found that none had a quota system, nor had they ever had such a system for arrests and traffic stops (Sharp, 2005, p.14). Nonetheless, programs such as "Click It or Ticket" (a program promoting use of seatbelts) lead to a persistent belief among citizens that law enforcement agencies *do* use quota systems (Sharp, p.14). In the "Click It or Ticket" program, officers have to make contact with at least three violators per hour to receive federal funds. The manager of the Washington State program says it is not a quota but is rather a performance standard: "Officers must make three contacts an hour, but that doesn't mean writing three tickets."

The consensus of the survey respondents was that quotas in any form (e.g., points) should not be used as a motivational tool or to judge an officer's performance (Sharp, p.18). As one respondent observed, the use of quotas elicits an atmosphere of quantity rather than quality: "When a measure is placed, solely by a number, the pressure to meet that quota may supersede the quality of what the initial task is intended to accomplish."

Fitness-for-Duty Evaluations Fitness-for-duty evaluations (FFDE) usually include physical and psychological fitness. Whether a law enforcement agency should have mandatory physical fitness standards (MPFS) is controversial. A poll of 32 agencies of various sizes revealed that MPFS are a concern but they are not a high priority, even though 93 percent of the respondents said there should be mandatory standards for at least some department members. However, only 37 percent had in-service standards in place, and only 30 percent of those standards were mandatory. The principal reason for this lack of standards was lack of funds (Sharp, 2003, p.59).

Collingwood et al. (2004, p.32) contend: "Few if any law enforcement personnel disagree with the notion that physical fitness is necessary for the safe and effective performance of certain critical and essential job functions." The question is: how fit must officers be, and how can this be measured?

Physical fitness is important, not only for officer safety, but also to ensure that officers can perform their jobs effectively. The Cooper Institute for Aerobics Research (CIAR) has worked with law enforcement fitness programs since 1976 and suggests that agencies be concerned with fitness because it relates to:

- The ability of officers to perform essential functions of the job.
- Minimizing the risk of excessive force situations.
- Minimizing the known health risks associated with the public safety job.

- Meeting many legal requirements to avoid litigation and have a defensible position if challenged in court.

Current legislation requires that fitness standards and programs be job related and scientifically valid (Cooper Institute). To demonstrate job relatedness, a fitness standard must be an underlying factor for performing essential and/or critical physical functions of the job and it must *predict* who can and cannot perform these functions.

The Institute notes that fitness tests/standards/programs must be accepted in the field of exercise science as meeting the "standard of ordinary care" of the American College of Sports Medicine (ACSM). The Institute reports that several public safety studies consistently show 29 to 30 strenuous/critical physical tasks that are job related and recommends the following fitness test battery: 1.5 mile run, 300 meter run, vertical jump, 1 RM (range of motion) bench press and/or maximum pushups, 1 minute sit up. Testing for body fat and flexibility does not predict a person's ability to perform essential tasks in public safety (Cooper Institute).

As has been discussed, tests, standards and programs cannot discriminate against protected classes as established by the Civil Rights Acts of 1964 and 1991, the Americans with Disabilities Act (ADA) or the Age Discrimination in Employment Act (ADEA). However, the Cooper Institute stresses: "If job relatedness is established and documented, then the fitness tests, standards and programs *can* discriminate against anybody. It is important to implement tests/standards/programs that do discriminate between those *who can and cannot do the job* regardless of age, gender, race, or handicap condition."

The Institute also suggests two levels of legal concern. The first concern involves *safety.* An agency must document that their policies and procedures meet the "standard of ordinary care" by following ACSM guidelines. The second area involves liability for an agency that does not have fitness tests, standards and programs. Agencies who do not address fitness requirements and needs of officers are susceptible to litigation for the following:

- Negligent hiring—failure to hire applicants who are fit to do the job
- Negligent training—failure to train recruits and incumbents so they are physically capable of doing the job
- Negligent supervision—failure to supervise incumbents to ensure they can meet the physical demands of the job
- Negligent retention—failure to reassign officers who cannot meet the physical demands of the job

 Law enforcement agencies that do not have fitness tests, standards or programs may face charges of negligence in hiring, training, supervision or retention.

In addition to physical fitness standards, most states have statutes that define *psychological fitness* for peace officers. The issue of mental stability comes under the purview of the Americans with Disabilities Act (ADA), whose primary benchmark is whether an individual's condition prevents him or her from performing "essential job functions." The pre-employment psychological assessment was discussed in Chapter 15. A psychological FFDE is a formal, specialized examination of an employee that results from (1) objective evidence that an employee may be unable to safely or effectively perform a defined job and (2) a reasonable basis for believing that the cause may be psychological ("Guidelines for Police Psychological Services,"

2005, p.70). A psychological FFDE requires the informed consent of the person to be examined. Circumstances that may trigger a psychological FFDE include officer-involved shootings and any other critical incidents that might have profound psychological impacts.

In addition to assessing whether individuals are "fit for duty," performance assessments must measure how individuals actually have performed and are performing using various instruments.

Instruments for Performance Appraisals

Whether a department creates its own assessment instrument or adopts one from another department, the instrument should be objective, comprehensive, reliable and current. (See Appendix F for sample evaluation forms.) An objective evaluation form, for example, might rate an officer's proficiency on a numerical scale of 1 to 7, with 1 indicating least proficient and 7 most proficient. The values of 1, 4 and 7 are designated as "anchors," with 1 representing *unacceptable*, 4 *acceptable* and 7 *outstanding*. Raters need not comment on any factor unless it is rated 7 or less than 3.

by-the-numbers evaluation • makes evaluations more objective by using a numerical scale for each characteristic or dimension rated.

 By-the-numbers evaluation makes evaluation more objective by using a numerical scale for each dimension.

Promotability/assignment factors attempt to make the evaluation "count for something."

promotability/assignment factors • an attempt to make evaluation "count for something."

 Evaluations should have consequences. Those who rate highly might be considered for promotions, special assignments or pay raises. Those who rate below the acceptable range might be given counseling; training; a demotion; salary reduction; probation; or, in extreme cases, termination.

For instance, in the Redondo Beach (California) Police Department, a simple mathematical formula is used based on the individual ratings assigned to each factor. The rating counts toward 25 percent of the promotional process and 50 percent of the selection process for special assignments. In addition, the evaluation has other consequences, with those having acceptable or higher overall ratings being considered for special training.

pre-evaluation • a procedure to allow those being evaluated to have input by completing a form outlining their accomplishments.

Some departments opt to give employees a pre-evaluation form several weeks prior to their formal evaluation (Appendix G). **Pre-evaluation** is a procedure that allows those being evaluated to have input by completing a form outlining their accomplishments. The Redondo Beach Evaluation Manual (p.17) notes:

> The prime factor in obtaining the best results of the performance evaluation is the supervisor's fair, impartial and sincere desire to help the employee grow and advance. *The performance evaluation process can either be the key link in the supervisor-employee relationship or a periodic source of irritation, depending on the way it is used.* Periodic performance evaluation and counseling is the very best method available in improving relationships with employees and helping them to fulfill their needs for satisfactory recognition and growth.

Information for Performance Appraisals

Law enforcement managers responsible for evaluation must record all information as soon as possible after an incident is observed. A form for each officer the manager rates should be maintained. It is impossible to remember such information over long periods. A simple form and notation are all that is required. When it is time to complete the formal evaluation form, all the information will be available. This lessens the tendency for information gathered closer to the time of the formal evaluation to overshadow information gathered months before. The information may be about specific incidents such as a high-speed chase, a shooting by an officer or a public-relations-type incident. Enter such information immediately after the occurrence while facts are remembered.

Common Types of Performance Evaluations

Numerous types of performance evaluations are available to managers.

 Among the performance evaluations are the following:

- Ratings by individual traits or behaviorally anchored rating scales (BARS)
- Critical incident ratings
- Group or composite ratings
- Narrative, essay or description
- Overall comparison ratings
- Self-evaluation

Opinions vary on the value of each type of evaluation. Any of the preceding common types of performance evaluations can be used to evaluate subordinates.

Ratings by Individual Traits Behaviorally anchored rating scales (BARS) are individual trait ratings usually done by the manager immediately above the employee in rank. Various factors concerning individual employees and the job are rated on a scale of 1 to 5 or 1 to 10. For example, a factor such as dependability would be rated from 1 to 10, with 1 being poorest and 10 being outstanding or excellent. It is fairly easy to perform this type of rating. The Redondo Beach Evaluation Form in Appendix F is an example of this type of evaluation.

behaviorally anchored rating scales (BARS) • specific characteristics for a position are determined. Employees are then rated against these characteristics by on-the-job behaviors in each area.

Differences arise over how to do individual trait rating. Some think managers should rate the first item for all employees before proceeding to the second item. Others think all factors for one employee should be rated at once before going to the next employee rating.

Unless department policy dictates otherwise, raters should try both ways to decide which works better. The total score is the composite rating. Some think that poor and excellent ratings should be justified by performance evidence. Trait categories fall into those related to *performance* measured by quantity and quality, accuracy, efficiency and amount of supervision required; *personal qualities*, such as personality, attitude, character, loyalty and creativeness; and *ability*, which involves knowledge of job, mental and emotional stability, initiative and judgment. The traits must be job related.

Group or Composite Ratings Many departments are changing from individual to group ratings, in which traits are rated by a group instead of one manager. For example, rather than having a sergeant rate the patrol officers, a group of three or four people of different ranks in the department might evaluate the patrol officers. This might include one officer from the same level as the person rated, overcoming single-rater bias. Varied percentage weights may be applied to different raters according to rank. Or employees could be rated by all members in the organization of the same rank or a selection of first-line supervisor, a higher manager, their peers or other group members. Some departments use a member of the personnel department to interview those associated with the employee, and this interviewer makes the rating for the personnel file. This method involves more time.

Critical Incident Ratings Most managers keep *critical incident logs* that record all good and bad performances of employees. Although keeping such logs is time consuming, the information is of great value when it is time for the formal performance appraisal. If an officer did an excellent investigation or made an excellent arrest, this would be recorded. If the officer made a bad arrest or conducted a poor investigation, this would also be recorded. All incidents would be discussed with the employee.

Keeping track of how officers handle incidents can help a department reduce its risk of civil liability, identify situations where more officer training is warranted and keep track of outstanding officer performance so commendations can be awarded (Careless, 2005, p.10). Officers, and in some instances their direct supervisors, should update records whenever they are involved in incidents involving use of force, officer-involved shootings, vehicle pursuit, K-9 deployment, missed or tardy court appearances and civil and/or criminal actions (Careless, p.10).

Narrative, Essay or Description In this method, raters use a written description of what they observed rather than a rating scale. It is also possible to combine numerical and narrative in the same form, with words replacing numbers.

Overall Comparison Ratings Managers review all their subordinates and then rate which one is top and which bottom. They then arrange the others on a comparative scale.

Self-Evaluation Self-evaluation is becoming more popular. Self-evaluation forms allow subordinates to rate themselves. There is value in people comparing how they perceive themselves with how others perceive them. Self-evaluation assists in getting employees to accept other types of evaluations. In some instances, individuals are more self-critical than external raters, simply because they know things about themselves others do not. These ratings have substantial value if no other evaluation exists.

Evaluation of Managers and Supervisors by Subordinates

One form of performance evaluation allows subordinates to evaluate their supervisory and administrative personnel. This gives command personnel a new source of information and a reasonably accurate assessment of subordinates' perceptions.

Higher level managers and the chief or sheriff might also be evaluated by their subordinates using an instrument that includes management and leadership skills. Although subordinates evaluating managers is not common, it has value. Rating managers could help both managers and the organization, and the same rating method would be used for managers and subordinates. Subordinates should have as much right to rate their managers as managers have to rate their subordinates.

performance interviews •
private, one-on-one discussions of the performance appraisal by manager and subordinate.

Performance Interviews

Performance interviews are private, one-on-one discussions of the performance appraisal by manager and subordinate. The performance interview should be based on comprehensive, accurate records and should focus on employee performance and growth. The appraisal form is the basis for the performance interview. Although rating forms and managers vary, it usually takes two to three hours of preparation time for each person rated. Many managers mark the evaluation forms lightly in pencil in case the interview brings facts to light that change the rating.

Managers should allow 45 minutes to an hour for each performance interview. They should prepare in advance so as not to omit important items. Planning includes the time and place, preventing interruptions and topics to be discussed. A starting point is to review the evaluation form.

Performance interviews open with a statement of purpose and should seek to make the employee feel at ease. Personalize the interview so it does not appear "canned." After rapport has been established, the employee's accomplishments are usually discussed. The appraisal form can serve as the foundation for the discussion. Compare it with the last appraisal. The tone throughout the interview should be positive. Ask employees to indicate what they see as their strengths and weaknesses. Ask what you, as manager, can do to help improve the weaknesses. Encourage participation.

 The performance appraisal interview should help employees do their jobs better and therefore improve individual performance and productivity.

All employee performance interviews should be private. Employees are normally apprehensive about evaluation. They are concerned about the manager's perceptions and how these compare with their own. An interview is a chance for managers and employees to establish rapport. If the interview is conducted properly—inviting input from employees—it will decrease controversy. Emphasize strengths rather than weaknesses.

Interviews of this type may identify conditions; distractions; lack of resources, training or equipment to do the tasks required; or other obstacles, none of which may have been known to the manager before the interview.

A positive approach is likely to produce positive responses. A negative approach normally generates defensiveness and lack of cooperation. This does not mean everything needs to be "hearts and roses." Criticism is necessary for development, but it should be constructive.

Law enforcement managers are employee problem solvers. During performance appraisal interviews, employees will be concerned about any low ratings and individual problems. They should be encouraged to mention perceived problems. Explain precisely what makes performance unsatisfactory, and do not apologize for discussing the matter. As a supervisor or manager, correcting your subordinates is your responsibility. Ask whether the employee understands the problem and has any ideas on how to approach it. Offer help in resolving the problem. If the problem is resolved at the first meeting, follow up by further monitoring. Congratulate the employee if the problem is corrected.

If the employee's position is one you cannot immediately discuss further or resolve, tell the employee of your next step. Set a time and place to continue the discussion. Explain that in light of what you have been told, you will investigate further and will reach a decision as soon as possible. Follow through within a day or two.

In some extreme cases of intentional misbehavior, for instance, an officer who abuses alcohol or drugs, it may be necessary to suggest termination if immediate remedies are not available.

Agree on important issues discussed, set future expectations, discuss training opportunities available for personal improvement and summarize the entire meeting with a positive ending. If you agree to do certain things, follow through.

The Redondo Beach Evaluation Manual (pp.14–15) contains the following suggestions, based on experience and research:

- Plan the appraisal interview in advance. Define your objectives and outline the key points you want to cover.
- Plan and schedule the interview for a time and place that will give you and the employee privacy and allow your undivided attention to be devoted to the subject.
- Get right into the appraisal at the outset, but encourage the employee to speak his/her mind about any portion of the appraisal the employee thinks is incorrect or unfair.
- Listen to the employee during the interview—especially immediately after negative feedback has been given.

Your attitude and interest regarding the employee are more important than any counseling technique you might use. If employees see that your prime objective is to help them do a better job, the appraisal is on its way to a successful result. If you put yourself in the role of a judge and the employee is the defendant, the appraisal will in all likelihood be a waste of time.

The appraisal interview should not be the only time you talk with employees about performance. Appraisal, to be effective, must be continuous.

 The most common recommendation for frequency of performance appraisals is twice a year and more frequently for employees who perform below expectations.

When the interview is completed, managers should make appropriate meeting notes immediately. These should be part of the permanent personnel file. Another file should contain any agreements reached that must be performed before the next appraisal, along with the date of the next appraisal.

Generally, appeals regarding ratings can be made to the next higher manager and on up to the department head. There may even be provision for an appeals board. The decision of the appeals board is usually final. Appeals should be required within a specified time and hearings held as quickly as possible.

Guidelines for Conducting Performance Appraisals

The following guidelines are summarized from the Redondo Beach Police Department Evaluation Manual:

- Communicate your expectations in advance.
- Appraise performance for the entire period. Critical incident reports can highlight performance over the entire rating period.
- Keep the appraisal job related. Don't let your attitude toward individuals or their personal attitudes bias your evaluations.
- Employees should participate. During the appraisal interview, the supervisor may choose to alter his/her appraisal after the subordinate provides additional information and insights regarding performance.
- Avoid the halo effect.
- Use descriptive statements to support your evaluations. Describe the performance on which you base your evaluations.

Problems of Performance Appraisals

Every employee evaluation system has shortcomings. Some problems of performance appraisals are the following:

- Lack of faith in any appraisal system
- "Late-inning" results count most
- The halo or horn effect
- Inaccurate numerical or forced-choice methods
- Unfair percentage ratings
- Rating personality rather than performance
- Rater bias
- Rating at the extremes

Lack of Faith in Appraisal Systems Some managers have a defeatist attitude about performance rating. "It won't work." "Employees should not be compared with one another." "It all depends on the rater." "Managers are not trained to be evaluators." "Employees don't like it." "The seniority system is good enough for me."

A defeatist attitude can arise from excessively high expectations about performance evaluations. Perfection is not the goal; growth and development are. Sometimes choosing the best method is a problem. Any formal performance appraisal is better than no appraisal if it is **valid**, meaning it is well grounded, sound, the factors rated are job related and the raters are trained.

valid • appraisals that are well grounded and sound in which the factors rated are job related and the raters are trained.

Late-Inning Results Count Most When ratings are performed annually, the actions and performance in the final months of the rating period are often better remembered and given more weight. This works both ways. Employees may have a good first nine months and a bad last three months or vice versa.

The Halo and Horn Effects The **halo effect** is the tendency to allow an employee's performance in one area to unduly influence the ratings in other areas. Some evaluation experts use a narrower meaning of the halo effect, reserving that term for allowing highly positive attributes in one area to carry over into rating all characteristics positively. When the opposite happens and a highly negative attribute causes other attributes to be rated low, this is called the **horn effect**.

halo effect • tendency to rate one who performs above average in one area above average in all areas or vice versa.

horn effect • allowing one negative trait to influence the rater negatively on other traits as well.

Inaccurate Numerical or Forced-Choice Methods Numerical ratings do not provide the information needed for improving employee performance because they do not indicate specifics about individuals. Managers who do the ratings are not put to the test of really knowing their employees.

Unfair Percentage Ratings When raters must place a percentage of employees in the upper, middle and lower third of ratings scales, they tend to be unfair. The same unfairness exists when raters place all employees at or near the average or middle of the scale. Employees should be rated on the basis of their actual performance, regardless of how many are upper, middle or lower. Some managers do not have the courage or training to do such ratings. In other instances, managers have a problem of being either high, low or middle raters.

Rating Personality Rather Than Performance Some raters tend to use their personal prejudices to rate employees. Instead of looking at each task or criterion and considering it individually, raters use a personal opinion of the individual based on a single experience. They may also rate on prejudice based on education, race or other factors.

Rater Bias Closely related to rating personality is allowing one's personal biases to interfere with the evaluation, for example, preferring men over women or non-minorities over minorities.

Rating at the Extremes Some evaluators rate in extremes of too lenient or too strict. This is especially true with marginal employees. Rather than terminate an employee who is liked, managers give a higher rating than the employee deserves. The opposite is true if the rating supports termination because the employee is not a "yes" person but performs other tasks well.

Other rating problems arise when managers rate employees in higher-level positions higher than those in lower-level positions, especially when raters have no training in rating or when raters do not care about the process. Other problems arise when the instructions are unclear or the terms and standards are not clearly defined.

Benefits of Performance Evaluation

Performance evaluations benefit all levels of a police department. First, they benefit the *organization as a whole* by accurately assessing its human resources so informed decisions can be made about assignments. They provide a permanent written record of the strengths and weaknesses of the department, which can help determine salary changes, promotions, demotions, transfers, court evidence and so on.

Second, they benefit the departments' *supervisors and managers* by giving them a clear picture of their subordinates' abilities and allowing them input into officer development. Areas in which training is needed become more obvious.

Third, they benefit the department's *officers* by letting each know exactly what is expected and identifying areas needing improvement. Once employees come to recognize personal weaknesses, they should be stimulated to set goals for self-improvement. Perhaps most important is that they document officers' good work.

Evaluating the Team

Although it might be tempting to think that adding up all the individual performance ratings would be sufficient to evaluate the team as a whole, this is not the case. Periodically, managers and supervisors should formally assess the effectiveness of their teams. A form such as that in Figure 16.2 might be used.

Abilities to evaluate include how the group works together; effective use of individual skills; competence in addressing community issues; ability to engage the citizenry, other city departments and community groups in addressing local problems; adaptability to change; ability to function as part of the organization; ability to problem solve and reach a consensus on methods to define solutions; and the quality of solutions produced.

Evaluating the Entire Department

Evaluation must also consider the entire agency and how well it is accomplishing its mission. Again, this cannot be done simply by looking at the performance of individual officers or even of the teams making up the organization.

TEAMWORK ASSESSMENT

Listed below are characteristics of effective, productive work teams. This assessment seeks feedback about (1) how important you feel each characteristic is and (2) how well you feel your team exhibits the characteristic. Please use a rating scale of 1 to 10, with 1 indicating lowest rating and 10 highest rating.

Characteristic	*Importance*	*Performance Rating*
Officers work toward common goals, known and understood, that serve both individual officers and the agency.	_____	_____
Officers know their individual responsibilities as well as those of their team.	_____	_____
Officers have the skills and knowledge to accomplish the job.	_____	_____
Team morale is high. Officers are enthusiastic and upbeat.	_____	_____
Productivity is high. Officers work hard and perform to the best of their ability.	_____	_____
Officers have confidence and trust in their team members.	_____	_____
Officers cooperate rather than compete with one another.	_____	_____
Officers can disagree without being disagreeable.	_____	_____
Communication lines are open. Officers can openly discuss their ideas and feelings, and they also listen to their team members.	_____	_____
Officers are not threatened by change. They are eager to try new approaches to routine tasks.	_____	_____
Officers take pride in their team and its accomplishments.	_____	_____
The team frequently evaluates how well it is dong.	_____	_____

Figure 16.2   Team Evaluation

Law enforcement agencies generally measure their results in terms of crime statistics and response times and, from a managerial perspective, such outcome measures have important disadvantages (Stephens, 2003, p.60). Even if proper outcome measures are chosen, there is an enormous problem in measuring the police contribution to the results. First, outcome measures do not directly measure the value of the police. Second, clearance rates are notoriously unreliable and arrest data are also suspect (Stephens, p.61).

As managers evaluate the department as a whole, they should remember that people tend to use crime rates, number of arrests and case clearance rates to measure how the police are doing. Such measures have several problems:

- Low crime rates do not necessarily mean a police agency is efficient and effective.
- A high arrest rate does not necessarily show that the police are doing a good job.
- A high ratio of police officers to citizens does not necessarily mean high-quality police services.
- Responding quickly to calls for services does not necessarily indicate that a police agency is efficient.

Rather than looking at crime rates, number of arrests and response time, evaluation should assess whether the agency is effective in fulfilling its responsibilities to the community and the value it provides to the community.

Positive officer–citizen interaction is extremely important because when an officer interacts with a citizen, both may be informally evaluating each other.

Recognizing Value in Policing

Before looking at ways to measure the performance of the entire department, consider what valuable goals of policing are and measures associated with them:

- Reduce criminal victimization—reported crime rates; victimization rates.
- Call offenders to account—clearance rates; conviction rates.
- Reduce fear and enhance personal security—reported change in levels of fear; reported changes in self-defense measures.
- Guarantee safety in public spaces—traffic fatalities, injuries and damage; increased use of parks and other public spaces; increased property values.
- Use financial resources fairly, efficiently and effectively—cost per citizen; deployment efficiency/fairness; scheduling efficiency; budget compliance; overtime expenditures; civilianization.
- Use force and authority fairly, efficiently and effectively—citizen complaints; settlements in liability suits; police shootings.
- Satisfy customer demands/achieve legitimacy with those policed—satisfaction with police services; response times; citizen perceptions of fairness (Moore et al., 2002, p.132).

If important values are not measured, the police will pay less attention to them than is desirable (Moore et al., p.71):

> Citizens need high-quality measures of police performance to determine whether their police department is performing well. As "owners" of the police, they need to see the extent to which the police department is producing results that matter to them, and whether the organization is positioning itself for even better performance in the future.

At the moment police departments are being driven by performance measures that capture only a portion of the value they can contribute to their local communities. The systems can describe levels of reported crime, and efforts the police have made to respond to crimes with both arrests, and threats of arrest. They can describe the extent to which the police have been successful in calling offenders to account for their crimes.

Missing from these measures is the contribution the police make to many other important purposes. These include preventing crime through means other than arrest, reducing fear, enhancing safety and security in public spaces, and providing responsive, high-quality services to citizens. . . .

To improve the system [of assessing police performance], three conceptual steps must be taken.

First, we must recognize the wide variety of valuable contributions that police departments make to their communities, and treat all these valuable effects as important, interlocking components of the police mission.

Second, we must recognize that we are interested in economizing on the use of force and authority, as well as money, and that the police must be evaluated in terms of the quality of justice they produce as well as the amount of safety and security. . . .

Third, we must recognize our interest in helping police departments strengthen their capabilities for the future, as well as perform well in the present (p.171).

Using Internal Surveys to Evaluate an Agency

An internal survey can be used as a catalyst for improvement ("Internal and Community Surveys," 2005, p.197). An internal survey might ask the following questions of all employees for specific areas within the agency, including prosecution; salary, benefits and human resources support; patrol operations; communications; parking enforcement; bike patrol; animal control; investigations; clerical staff, computerization and other technology; and special programs:

- How effective are we?
- What, if anything, should we change?
- What challenges do we face *now*?
- What challenges will we face in the *future?*

Surveys might be used to determine how effective a department is in doing the following (on a scale of 1 to 5, with 1 being ineffective and 5 being very effective): responding to employee ideas and suggestions, communicating important information through appropriate channels, treating employees fairly and consistently, praising employees for work well done, providing constructive criticism for work not so well done, providing appropriate training, providing informative and helpful work evaluations, and involving employees in decisions that impact them, involving employees in research and planning ("Internal and Community Surveys," p.213).

An internal survey might solicit employees' opinions on the importance of various department goals such as the following: technology improvements; increase support staff; increase number of sworn officers; increase racial/ethnic/gender diversity, increase community partnerships, broaden and enhance current training offerings, improve the field training officer (FTO) program, solicit community input on police operations, improve personnel evaluations procedures, increase pay/benefits, work towards accreditation, provide crime prevention services, provide family services, provide youth services ("Internal and Community Surveys," p.214). Surveys might also assess how specific programs and innovations are perceived by employees.

Evaluating an Agency's Integrity Klockars et al. (2005) summarize research findings on police integrity and describe an assessment instrument that can measure integrity within an agency and pinpoint problems involving misconduct. The research is based on responses of 3,235 officers from 30 agencies across the country to questions about hypothetical scenarios related to misconduct.

Survey results suggested that, more than any other factor, officers refrained from reporting the misconduct of other officers out of concern for the welfare of their peers.

The researchers (p.6) identified two practices to enhance integrity. First, consistently address relatively minor offenses with the appropriate discipline. Second, disclose the disciplinary process and resulting discipline to public scrutiny.

Evaluating Training

 Evaluation may also be used to identify department-wide training needs and to assess the effectiveness of training.

Perhaps the most obvious evaluation occurs during the FTO program and the probationary period. Evaluation is continuous during this period. The performance of the FTOs should also be evaluated. The importance of ongoing training was a focus in Chapter 7.

It is important that training efforts also be evaluated. Evaluation expert Kirkpatrick identified four levels of evaluation in 1959 (Stoel, 2004, p.46):

- Level 1: Reaction—focuses on the participants' perceptions of the training. Surveys or questionnaires can assess whether participants felt the training was effective.
- Level 2: Learning—focuses on the knowledge or skill acquired, ideally through a pre/post test.
- Level 3: Behavior—looks at whether the knowledge or skill is actually applied on the job by observing the participants using what was learned.
- Level 4: Results—focuses on the department's increases in work output or quality.

Another renowned evaluator, Phillips, added a level to Kirkpatrick's four levels: return on investment (ROI). What was the cost effectiveness—that is, how much was spent per officer, per program, per type of services? Are there cost savings? Are there cost benefits—that is, how many benefits to society and the department resulted from the services, including intangibles such as reduction in fear and feelings of safety? Cost–benefit analysis (CBA) is a way to determine whether a program is worth doing (Roman, 2004, p.257).

 In addition to internal surveys, the department should also conduct a self-assessment, perhaps through a committee established for this purpose.

As with individual performance evaluations, the department evaluation should be a continuous cycle of evaluating performance, identifying areas to improve, making adjustments and evaluating the results.

In addition to the preceding ways to evaluate a department or agency, the decision might be made to seek an external evaluation of the department through the accreditation process.

Accreditation

Accreditation is a process by which an institution or agency demonstrates that it meets set standards. Schools, colleges and hospitals frequently seek accreditation as recognition of their high quality. Institutions that lack accreditation are often considered inferior.

accreditation • the process by which an institution or agency proves that it meets certain standards.

In 1979, four law enforcement agencies—the International Association of Chiefs of Police, the Police Executive Research Forum, the National Organization of Black Law Enforcement Executives and the National Sheriff's Association—established the Commission on Accreditation for Law Enforcement Agencies (CALEA). The purpose of CALEA was to set national standards against which agencies could evaluate themselves. The program is voluntary but involves a great amount of time and expense. Costs can range from $5,500 for small agencies to $22,000 for larger agencies. Currently CALEA has more than 500 agency members. Some states have also established standards and a process of accreditation, including California, Colorado, Idaho, Kentucky, New Hampshire, New York and Washington.

 Accreditation consists of meeting a set of standards established by professionals in the field authorized to do so. Currently, accreditation may be granted by the Commission on the Accreditation of Law Enforcement Agencies (CALEA) or by some state agencies.

Accreditation provides a number of tangible benefits, including controlled liability insurance costs, fewer lawsuits and citizen complaints, stricter accountability within the agency and recognition of a department's ability to meet established standards. Intangible benefits include pride, recognition of excellence and peer approval. Everyone involved in the process gains a broader perspective of the agency, which ultimately leads to improved management. Wilcox (2004, p.21) concludes: "[Accreditation] takes effort and money, but the benefits far outweigh the costs, monetary and otherwise." One of accreditation's main selling points is the lowering of liability insurance expenses, a claim that has been validated many times (Moore, 2004, p.114).

Accreditation is not without its critics, however. In addition to the expense, some think that local and regional differences in agencies make a national set of standards unrealistic. Many agencies think the number of standards is simply overwhelming. Smaller agencies must usually meet 500 to 700 standards; larger agencies must usually meet more than 700 standards. Other critics contend that accreditation is like having a "big brother" overseeing their activities. Further, most of the standards deal with departmental administration rather than with its mission.

Accreditation and Community Policing

Controversy exists regarding the compatibility of accreditation standards and efforts to implement community policing. Community policing, which is primarily operational, and accreditation, which is primarily administrative, are two

Table 16.1   Summary of Support for 14 Hypotheses about the Relationship between Community Policing and Accreditation

Hypotheses	Support
The Anti-COP Hypothesis: accreditation directly conflicts with COP	Little or no support
The Anti-POP Hypothesis: accreditation directly conflicts with POP	Little or no support
The Rigid Bureaucracy Hypothesis: accreditation creates formality which interferes with COP	Some support—mixed opinion
The Efficiency Hypothesis: accreditation's internal focus deflects attention from substantive problems in the community	Some support—mixed opinion
The Thin Blue Line Hypothesis: accreditation emphasizes accountability within the organization to the detriment of accountability to the community	Little support
The Style Over Substance Hypothesis: accreditation focuses attention on process rather rather than outcomes	Some support—mixed opinion
The Incident-Driven Hypothesis: accreditation takes an incident-oriented view to the detriment of the problem-oriented approach	Some support—mixed opinion
The Professional Model Hypothesis: accreditation implicitly favors the professional model over COP	Some support—mixed opinion
The Scare Resources Hypothesis: accreditation and COP compete for resources and attention	General support
The Police Politics Hypothesis: supporters of COP and accreditation compete for status and influence	Little support
The Support Hypothesis: accreditation directly supports COP/POP	Some support—mixed opinion
The Neutrality Hypothesis: accreditation is neutral toward COP/POP	Some support—mixed opinion
The Flexibility Hypothesis: accreditation does not interfere with COP/POP because of the flexibility of the standards	General support
The Null Hypothesis: no conflict because supporting one or the other (or both accreditation and COP) has no real impact	Some support—but not from chiefs or experts

Source: Gary W. Cordner and Gerald L. Williams. "Community Policing and Police Agency Accreditation." In *Policing Perspectives: An Anthology*, edited by Larry K. Gaines and Gary W. Cordner. Los Angeles: Roxbury Publishing Company, 1999, p.377.

significant initiatives of the late twentieth century. Whether these initiatives conflict or are compatible is often controversial. Table 16.1 summarizes the degree of support found for various hypotheses regarding the relationship between community policing and accreditation.

This research found that accreditation does not directly conflict with community-oriented policing (COP) or problem-oriented policing (POP). In addition accreditation does not emphasize accountability within the organization to the detriment of accountability to the community. It also found that supporters of COP and accreditation do not compete for status and influence and that accreditation does not interfere with COP/POP because of the flexibility of the standards. The one area in which the research shows accreditation and community policing to conflict was the scarce resources hypotheses, where accreditation and community policing were found to compete for resources and attention.

Although it is important to conduct performance assessments and to evaluate teams, training, programs and the entire agency, evaluation efforts are incomplete unless they also assess community satisfaction with the services provided by the agency.

Evaluating Citizen Satisfaction with Services

Citizens are the police department's customers: "By collecting and applying in-depth information about customer satisfaction (and dissatisfaction), police agencies can identify and build upon their strengths, and correct their deficiencies, improving the delivery of police service to their various customer groups" (Witte, 2004, p.21). Three of the most important customer groups are citizens as potential victims of crime, the community as stakeholders and taxpayers as investors in the police agency (Witte, p.21).

Most citizens want to live in safe, orderly neighborhoods. Recall from the discussion of productivity in Chapter 13 that police are considered effective when they produce the perception that crime is under control. Reduction of fear is a very important measure. A fear and disorder index allows police to measure citizens' concerns and also sends a message to citizens that the department is addressing their fear of crime and neighborhood disorder.

Citizen approval or disapproval is generally reflected in letters of criticism or commendation, support for proposed police programs, cooperation with incidents being investigated, letters to the editor, public reaction to a single police–citizen incident or responses to police-initiated surveys.

Citizen Surveys

One way to assess citizen approval or disapproval is through citizen surveys, which can measure trends and provide positive and negative feedback on the public's impression of law enforcement.

Community surveys are often a win-win situation—citizens are better served and officers receive positive feedback. Community surveys can also be key in establishing communication. One citizen survey developed by the Plainsboro Township (New Jersey) Police Department uses a closed-end form (answer yes or no), asking very specific questions to assess the performance of individual officers (see Figure 16.3).

Surveys can be conducted by mail or by phone. Mailed surveys are less expensive and reduce the biasing errors in phoned surveys caused by how the person doing the phoning comes across to the respondent. However, they require that the person receiving the survey be able to read, which might not be the case. The major problem with mailed surveys is their low response rate.

Phone surveys have a much higher response rate but are also much more expensive unless volunteers can be enlisted to make the calls. In addition, individuals who do not have a phone cannot be included.

No matter which form of survey is used, the expense is small relative to the continued positive police–community relations. Citizen surveys might also help set organizational goals and priorities, identify department strengths and weaknesses, identify areas in need of improvement and training, and motivate employees.

A study of patrol officers' attitudes toward a survey on citizens' satisfaction with their department's services found that 66 percent of the officers felt the survey was personally useful, more than 75 percent felt it was useful for the organization, and 82 percent believed the survey was good for the citizens (Wells et al., 2005, p.171). However, the study also found that citizen feedback did *not* alter officers' performance, attitudes toward the communities they served or activities that put them in close contact with these communities. The researchers (pp.197–198) suggest that theories of information processing in organizations, such as **cybernetics,** help interpret these findings. The core principles of cybernetics suggest that organizations regulate themselves by gathering and reacting to information about their performance. The cybernetic perspective holds that perception, decision making and action are conceptually and functionally discrete. This decision-making

cybernetics • suggest that organizations regulate themselves by gathering and reacting to information about their performance.

Call-for-Service Contact

We have started a Citizen Response Survey as part of our continuing effort to provide professional and efficient police service to the residents of Plainsboro Township and other individuals with whom our police officers come in contact. Your name has been selected at random from among those who have had recent contact with one of our officers.

Your response will be used internally to help us recognize potential deficiencies, acknowledge officers who continually perform in the manner expected and evaluate our procedures and methods. The feedback you provide will facilitate the improvement of future relations between the police and the public, aid in the evaluation of individual officers and provide an important means of acquiring additional citizen input into how we serve the community.

Please return the questionnaire in the enclosed envelope. It is the policy of this department to follow up unfavorable comments. However, if you do not wish to be contacted, please indicate in the space provided. Thank you.

Sincerely,

Clifford J. Mauler
Chief of Police

Citizen Response Questionnaire

1. Did the officer repond quickly to your call for service?   Y ____   N ____
   Appoximately how long did it take for the officer to respond
   after being called? _____
2. Was the officer courteous?   Y ____   N ____
3. Was the officer neatly attired?   Y ____   N ____
4. Did the officer identify himself by name?   Y ____   N ____
   If not, do you think he should have?   Y ____   N ____
5. Did the officer speak clearly? Were you able to understand him?   Y ____   N ____
6. Were you satisfied with the service provided by the officer?   Y ____   N ____
7. Did the officer appear knowledgeable?   Y ____   N ____
8. Did he obtain all information that would seem pertinent under the   Y ____   N ____
   circumstances of this contact?
9. If applicable, did you feel satisfied with the supplemental investigation   Y ____   N ____
   conducted by the officer?
10. Upon completion of this police contact, did you feel satisfied with the   Y ____   N ____
    general quality of the service rendered?
11. Additional comments:
   _____
   _____
   _____

Signature _____   Date _____

Figure 16.3   Cover Letter and Citizen Response Questionnaire

Source: Elizabeth Bondurant. "Citizen Response Questionnaire: A Valuable Evaluation Tool." *The Police Chief*, November 1991, p.75. Reprinted from *The Police Chief*, Vol. LVIII, No. 11, November 1991, p.75. Copyright held by the International Association of Chiefs of Police, Inc., 515 N. Washington St., Alexandria, VA 22314, USA. Further reproduction without express written permission from IACP is strictly prohibited.

perspective views systems, including organizations, as similar to organic brains, continually detecting, processing and reacting to information (Wells et al.).

In this context, citizen surveys are the preceptor element, providing information about how the organization is performing. The officers interpret the feedback and decide on the appropriate action. In this research, the response is no response. Wells et al. suggest that the response might be different if the information was routed through managers who decide on appropriate remedies and assign supervisors the job of ensuring that those remedies are carried out. They (p.201) conclude that methods for processing citizen feedback and using it to implement meaningful change need to be developed and tested.

Other Ways to Assess Community Perceptions

Another way to obtain community input is through focus groups, forums or roundtable discussions, which usually take about three hours and have three phases. First, citizens talk and management listens. Second, together they brainstorm ways to work together, using a 10/10 target (coming up with 10 creative ideas in 10 minutes). They then evaluate the ideas and select those with merit. Third, they focus on implementation, setting up teams or task forces to implement and track the ideas. Groups should be kept small—eight to twelve participants—and should exclude competitors and have a trained facilitator.

Evaluation and Research

This chapter has focused on evaluating individuals, teams and entire departments, training and integrity and citizen satisfaction. Sometimes, however, administration wants to evaluate specific problems. In such cases, research is needed. One approach is using the SARA problem-solving approach introduced in Chapter 5, identifying problems, analyzing current responses and available resources, exploring alternatives and assessing the results of implementing alternatives.

Two kinds of statistics are generally helpful in such research: descriptive statistics and inferential statistics. **Descriptive statistics** focus on simplifying, appraising, and summarizing data. **Inferential statistics** focus on making statistically educated guesses from a sample of data.

> **descriptive statistics** • focus on simplifying, appraising and summarizing data.
>
> **inferential statistics** • focus on making statistically educated guesses from a sample of data.

At other times administration wants to determine how well a specific program is working. In such instances administrators might want to familiarize themselves with the National Institute of Justice's (NIJ) "Research Partnerships in Policing." The NIJ partnership program in policing complements the basic premise of community policing: working as partners achieves more than working alone. Such research partnerships typically consist of a local police department or other law enforcement agency and a local university and make extensive and effective use of graduate students. A valuable resource for departments wanting to undertake research is the Justice Research and Statistics Association (JRSA), whose Web site is www.jrsa.org.

Another resource is the Police Executive Research Forum (PERF) Center for Survey Research (LECSR). The center can assist departments in conducting neighborhood/community surveys, officer surveys, homeland security assessments and organizational climate surveys ("The New PERF Center for Survey Research, 2005, p.5).

Cosner and Loftus (2005, p.62) sound a "wake-up call" to researchers: "Practical use and ability to apply solutions is what the police seek in research." Much of the results from research fail to help managers improve the performance of their subordinates. For example, research on characteristics of high-performing patrol officers may be of use in the selection process, but managers need to deal with incumbent officers. They would welcome research on how to develop these characteristics: "Police want concepts that they can put to use today, not theories that may explain events but offer no immediate practical value" (p.63).

Partnerships between police leaders and academic researchers are critical to discovering and implementing best policing practices: "Robust research projects performed within law enforcement agencies with the direct involvement of law enforcement leaders can lead to sound and substantive policy" (Cosner and Loftus, p.67).

As has been stated, evaluation results must be analyzed and acted upon to be useful. Surveys, evaluations and research results often call into question the ways things have traditionally been done. Law enforcement managers and leaders must be willing to challenge the status quo when this occurs.

Challenging the Status Quo

Sometimes traditional practices are no longer productive. Consider the story of the four monkeys and the cold shower:

> In a conditioning experiment, four monkeys were placed in a room. A tall pole stood in the center of the room, and a bunch of bananas hung suspended at the top of the pole. Upon noticing the fruit, one monkey quickly climbed up the pole and reached to grab the meal, at which time he was hit with a torrent of cold water from an overhead shower. The monkey quickly abandoned his quest and hurried down the pole. After the first monkey's failed attempt, the other three monkeys each climbed the pole in an effort to retrieve the bananas, and each received a cold shower before completing the mission. After repeated drenchings, the four monkeys gave up on the bananas.

> Next, one of the four original monkeys was replaced with a new monkey. When the new arrival discovered the bananas suspended overhead and tried to climb the pole, the three other monkeys quickly reached up and pulled the surprised monkey back down. After being prevented from climbing the pole several times but without ever having received the cold shower, the new monkey gave up trying to reach the bananas. One by one, each of the original monkeys was replaced, and each new monkey was taught the same lesson—don't climb the pole.

> None of the new monkeys ever made it to the top of the pole; none even got close enough to receive the cold shower awaiting them at the top. Not one monkey understood why pole climbing was prohibited, but they all respected the well-established precedent. Even when the shower was removed, no monkey tried to climb the pole. No one challenged the status quo.

What implications do this story and its lesson hold for managers? The realization that precedents, enacted into policy manuals, and training programs can far outlive the situational context that created them. Simply telling officers, "That's the way it's always been done" can do a great disservice to the organization as a whole. When officers don't know *what* they don't know and, worse yet, aren't even aware *that* they don't know, they are kept from empowerment, and problem-solving efforts are seriously compromised.

Encouraging officers to think creatively, tackle public safety issues through innovative problem solving and question the status quo if necessary are basic challenges facing law enforcement managers and certainly affect the future success of their agencies. This is the focus of the next chapter.

 SUMMARY

The basic purpose of evaluation is to determine how well an agency is accomplishing its mission and how to make improvements. The three usual forms of inspections are line inspections, spot inspections and staff inspections.

Managers who provide the most immediate direction of subordinates should do the evaluation. Purposes of evaluation include promoting common understanding of individual performance levels, needs, work objectives and standards; providing feedback and suggesting specific courses of action to take to improve, including training needs; and setting objectives for future performance. Evaluation may also help identify department-wide training needs and make decisions about promotions, reassignments, disciplinary actions and terminations. Ultimately, the purpose of performance evaluation is to improve employee performance.

Job standards make it easier for employees to meet requirements and for managers to determine whether they have been met. Standards may include areas such as physical energy to perform and emotional stability while performing law enforcement tasks; individual judgment, reliability, loyalty and ability to get along with the public, fellow employees and managers; creativity and innovation; attitude; knowledge of tasks; competence; and amount of management required. By-the-numbers evaluation makes evaluation more objective by using a numerical scale for each dimension.

Evaluation should have consequences. Those who rate highly might be considered for promotions, special assignments or pay raises. Those who rate below the acceptable range might be given counseling; training; a demotion; salary reduction; probation; or, in extreme cases, termination.

Among the types of performance evaluations available to managers are ratings by individual traits or behaviorally anchored rating scales (BARS); group or composite ratings; critical incident ratings; narrative, essay description; overall comparison ratings; composite ratings; and self-evaluation.

Performance interviews are private, one-on-one discussions of the performance appraisal by manager and subordinate. The performance appraisal interview should help employees do their jobs better and therefore improve individual performance and productivity. The most common recommendation for frequency of performance appraisals is twice a year and more frequently for employees performing below expectations.

Some problems of performance appraisals are lack of faith in appraisal systems, late-inning results count most, inaccurate numerical or forced-choice methods, unfair percentage ratings, rating personality rather than performance and rating at the extremes.

In addition to citizen ratings, the department should conduct a self-assessment, perhaps through a committee established for this purpose. It might also consider seeking accreditation, which consists of meeting a set of standards established by professionals in the field authorized to do so. Currently, accreditation may be granted by the Commission on Accreditation of Law Enforcement Agencies (CALEA) or by some state agencies.

CHALLENGE SIXTEEN

The Greenfield Police Department requires performance appraisals at the end of each year. The appraisals use a numerical scale to evaluate several broad areas of performance. Categories include knowledge of policies, dependability and productivity. The appraisal forms provide room for optional narratives to explain numeric scores. Supervisors conduct appraisal interviews with their officers before forwarding the appraisals to the appropriate manager.

Detective Sergeant Bilko supervises 10 detectives. His detectives consider him a nice guy and a hard worker who often assists them with their cases. Sergeant Bilko is a fishing buddy of several of his detectives.

Detective Quick is one of the most talented detectives in the entire county. He takes on the most difficult and complex cases with a remarkable success rate. He is well liked in the community and by fellow officers. He is a credit to the department. Detective Delay does not make nearly the contribution that Detective Quick makes. He spends a good deal of time in several local coffee shops, and his fellow officers often say he missed his calling as a talk show host. Detective Delay is popular and entertaining, but not a great detective. He is usually assigned simple cases and often needs prodding to turn his cases in on time.

Sergeant Bilko asks his detectives to complete their own performance appraisal forms before their appraisal interview. He reviews the forms with them during the interviews and seldom questions the ratings. Every year his detectives all receive nearly identical above-average scores. Detective Quick's performance appraisal score is indistinguishable from Detective Delay's.

1. Sergeant Bilko is obviously doing an ineffective job of evaluating his detectives' performance. Is this a disservice to his detectives?
2. Are performance appraisals inherently more difficult for line supervisors like Sergeant Bilko?
3. If Sergeant Bilko's evaluations of his detectives have all been nearly the same for several years, is someone else failing to do their job?
4. Does Detective Delay have a defense against any action the department may take against him for performance deficiencies?
5. Suggest some changes to improve the Greenfield Police Department's performance appraisal system.

DISCUSSION QUESTIONS

1. What are the advantages and disadvantages of informal evaluation? Formal evaluation?
2. What can law enforcement managers do to prepare for employee evaluation interviews?
3. What main change would you recommend for future performance evaluations?
4. Should performance evaluations be used for promotions? Transfers? New assignments? Pay increases?
5. Who should rate subordinates? One person or several?
6. What type rating do you like best?
7. What are some uses of performance evaluation?
8. Have you been formally evaluated? What was your opinion of the evaluation? Should such appraisals be retained?
9. What are the advantages and disadvantages of having subordinates evaluate their managers?
10. Do you favor or oppose national accreditation? State accreditation? Why?

REFERENCES

Careless, James. "Evals Protect Officers from Law Suits." *Law and Order,* December 2005, pp.10–12.

Collingwood, Thomas R.; Hoffman, Robert; and Smith, Jay. "Underlying Physical Fitness Factors for Performing Police Officer Physical Tasks." *The Police Chief,* March 2004, pp.32–37.

The Cooper Institute for Aerobics Research Web site: http://www.cooperinst.org/lawenf.asp. Accessed January 2, 2006.

Cosner, Thurston L. and Loftus, Greg M. "Law Enforcement-Driven Action Research." *The Police Chief,* October 2005, pp.62–68.

Fuller, John. "Staff Inspection: A Strong Administrative Tool." *The Police Chief,* December 2004, pp.66–72.

"Guidelines for Police Psychological Services." *The Police Chief,* September 2005, pp.68–86.

Hilgenfeldt, Keith. "Improved Performance Appraisals." *Law and Order,* October 2004, pp.90–92.

"Internal and Community Surveys." In *A Police Chief's Desk Reference.* Washington, DC: The International Association of Chiefs of Police and the Bureau of Justice Assistance, 2005, pp.197–226.

Klockars, Carl B.; Ivkovich, Sanja Kutnjak; and Haberfeld, Maria R. *Enhancing Police Integrity.* Washington, DC: NIJ Research for Practice, December 2005. (NCJ 209269)

Marcum, Curtis. "Inspections Are a Good Thing." *Law and Order,* July 2005, pp.120–121.

Moore, Carole. "Is Accreditation Right for Your Agency?" *Law Enforcement Technology,* February 2004, p.114.

Moore, Mark; Thacher, David; Dodge, Andrea; and Moore, Tobias. *Recognizing Value in Policing: The Challenge of Measuring Police Performance.* Washington, DC: Police Executive Research Forum, 2002.

Mulder, Armand. "Improve the Performance Evaluation Process." *Law and Order,* September 2004, pp.100–103.

"The New PERF Center for Survey Research." *Subject to Debate,* October 2005, p.5.

Roman, John. "Can Cost-Benefit Analysis Answer Criminal Justice Policy Questions, and If So, How?" *Journal of Contemporary Criminal Justice,* August 2004, pp.257–275.

Sharp, Arthur G. "Wellness: A New Trend in Fitness Standards." *Law and Order,* February 2003, pp.58–61.

Sharp, Arthur G. "A Quota by Any Other Name." *Law and Order,* December 2005, pp.14–20.

Stephens, Darrel W. "Organization and Management." In *Local Government Police Management,* 4th ed., edited by William A. Geller and Darrel W. Stephens. Washington, DC: International City/County Management Association, 2003, pp.27–65.

Stoel, Diederick. "The Evaluation Heavy Weight Match." *Training and Development,* January 2004, pp.46–61.

Wells, William; Horney, Julie; and Maguire, Edward R. "Patrol Officer Responses to Citizen Feedback: An Experimental Analysis." *Police Quarterly,* June 2005, pp.171–205.

Wilcox, William L. "A Small Police Department's Success." *FBI Law Enforcement Bulletin,* February 2004, pp.18–21.

Witte, Jeffrey. "Identifying Elements of Customer Satisfaction in the Delivery of Police Service." *The Police Chief,* May 2004, pp.18–21.

BOOK-SPECIFIC WEB SITE

Go to the Management and Supervision in Law Enforcement Web site at www.thomsonedu.com/criminaljustice/bennett for student and instructor resources, including Internet Assignments and Case Studies.

CHAPTER 17

Challenges in Managing for the Future

The best way to predict the future is to create it.

Peter Drucker

DO YOU KNOW?

■ What currently is most important in management skills?

■ How the public will change in the future?

■ What the major challenges facing law enforcement are?

■ What four obstacles face local and state law enforcement in fighting terrorism?

■ What role technology will play in law enforcement work?

■ What the three basic principles of futuristics are?

■ What the fundamental premises of futuristics are?

■ What the three primary goals of futuristics are?

■ What the boiled frog phenomenon is?

■ How change should be viewed?

CAN YOU DEFINE?

bifurcated society

boiled frog

   phenomenon

distributed

   intelligence

environmental

   scanning

fusion centers

futuristics

Introduction

In a word, this chapter is about *change*. W. Edwards Deming has said: "It is not necessary to change. Survival is not mandatory." John F. Kennedy expressed a less facetious view of the criticality of change when he stated: "Change is the law of life. And those who look only to the past or present are certain to miss the future." Indeed, change is one of the "constants" law enforcement managers must be prepared for if they are to effectively guide their departments toward fulfilling their mission.

Throughout this text, several changes in the law enforcement organization have been discussed. Among the most important changes likely to affect management in the future are the following:

■ Participative management, the manager as a leader

■ Flattening of the organizational hierarchy

■ The necessity to provide more services with fewer resources

■ Better-educated law enforcement officers who are less willing to accept orders unquestioningly

- A shift in incentives, with intrinsic rather than extrinsic rewards becoming more motivational
- Implementing community policing and problem-oriented policing, including being proactive rather than reactive
- Developing partnerships with other agencies as well as with the public
- An increasingly diverse public to be served
- Privatization of services

Many of these changes will be briefly revisited during this final chapter as part of the summary of challenges facing today's law enforcement managers.

This chapter begins by examining global changes, or megatrends, for it is within a global context that our society and law enforcement exist and function. The focus of the discussion then narrows to look at current and emerging workplace trends in the United States and their applicability to law enforcement. The chapter then briefly examines how the forces of change have impacted the people involved—the law enforcement professionals and the public they serve. Next the major challenges and issues facing law enforcement in the twenty-first century are covered, including the problems of illicit drugs, violence, gangs and homeland security. Then advances in technology are explored, followed by a discussion of futuristics as a way of looking at law enforcement in the years ahead. The chapter concludes with an explanation of the need for creativity and innovation and a revisiting of change and the various ways it might be viewed by progressive managers to positively shape the future of law enforcement.

Megatrends—Looking to the Future

Naisbitt and Aburdene's *Megatrends 2000* (1990) noted the following worldwide trends:

We are moving from an industrial society to an information society. Children are learning computer skills in school; adults will need special training to catch up to them.

We are moving from forced technology to high tech/high touch. Although technology is stressed, it will not replace the need for human interaction.

We are moving from a national economy to a world economy. To be successful is to be trilingual, that is, fluent in English, Spanish and computer-ese.

We are moving from a short-term orientation to a long-term orientation. We need to pay attention to future trends and engage in long-range planning.

We are moving from centralization to decentralization. More decisions, including major life decisions, are being made at the local level.

We are moving from institutional help to self-help.

We are moving from representative democracy to participatory democracy.

Today's leaders need to be facilitators rather than order givers.

We are moving from hierarchies to networks. The old power structure is disappearing, being replaced with teamwork, quality circles and participative decision making.

Timeline Prediction

2005
Most government services are delivered on the Internet.
Crime mapping and crime analysis information will be available to neighborhood groups.
Crime mapping and crime analysis information will be transmitted directly to patrol cars.
Police cars will be equipped with accident avoidance sensing devices.
Electrode Implantation will allow rats to conduct search and rescue missions.

2007
Non–U.S. citizens will be hired by many American law enforcement agencies.
Non-lethal options for subduing violent criminals will be available.

2010
Virtual nations such as al Qaida will be prominent. Private security will perform more police duties.
Autocratic management is abandoned in law enforcement.

2012
More DNA computer information will become available.

2015
World Population is 7.1 billion. Half the world's population is living in urban areas.
ID cards are replaced by biometric scanning. Wearable computers are standard equipment for the police. Emotion control chips are imbedded in criminals.

2020
More than 16% of population is over the age of 65 in the United States.
More than 38% of the U.S. population is minorities.
Ninety-five percent of the world's population is located in developing countries.
Data storage created with nanotechnology allows smaller and more portable computers for police use while on patrol.

2025
Cyc develops common sense and is able to communicate with humans.

2029
Computer passes the Turing test, proving it has human-level intelligence.

2030
Vehicles will drive themselves. Twenty percent of the U.S. population is age 65 or older.

2040
The world population is double that of 2002.

2050
A new generation welcomes change. The population age 85 is five times that of 1995.

Figure 17.1   Timeline Predictions Made in 2003
Source: Alan C. Youngs. "Law Enforcement in 2003 and Beyond." *Law and Order*, April 2003, p.98. Used by permission.

We are moving (physically) from the north to the south. Spanish is becoming more necessary.

We are moving from an either/or orientation to one of multiple options.

These global trends continue into the twenty-first century and have implications for our country, its citizens and those whose job it is to protect and police them. Figure 17.1 presents some timeline predictions made in 2003. Notice that the predictions for 2005 appear accurate.

Workplace Trends Affecting Law Enforcement

Managers, as they prepare for the future, should be aware of eight current and emerging workplace trends, derived from focus groups, more than 100 thought leaders, a review of more than 30 research studies and articles related to trends affecting the workplace and survey responses from more than 2,000 workplace learning and performance professionals (Colteryahn and Davis, 2004, pp.28–36). Although these trends apply to the workplace in general, their applicability to law enforcement is clear.

#1: Drastic Times, Drastic Measures

Uncertain economic conditions are causing organizations to rethink the future: "Uncertainty exists due to the war on terrorism, additional costs associated with higher levels of security and the impact terrorism is having on economic stability and financial markers" (p.30). The labor shortage is likely to be prolonged, resulting in a seller's market for talent. Organizations will be challenged to do more with less.

#2: Blurred Lines—Life or Work

Organizations seek ways to become more efficient: "Changes include streamlining structure and becoming more flexible, networked, flat, diverse, and virtual" (p.30). Many people are overworked and expected to be available almost 24/7. Outsourcing will become more common.

#3: Small World and Shrinking

Globalization will increase. Criminals and terrorists will become increasingly international, but so will law enforcement's collaborative efforts to stop them. "Global competition is making way for global cooperation" (p.31).

#4: New Faces, New Expectations

As the workforce becomes more diverse, new attitudes, lifestyles, values and motivations will need to be accommodated. The Hispanic population will increase by 11.2 percent between 2000 and 2025 to become our largest minority group. All other minority groups will increase by about 9 percent; the number of Caucasians will decrease by about 19 percent. The American workforce will age, with more retirees and gaps in available experienced workers. By 2015 almost one in five U.S. workers will be age 55 or older (p.31).

#5: Work Be Nimble, Work Be Quick

Change is happening exponentially faster, requiring workers to adapt more readily and organizations to become increasingly more flexible: "The rate of change is doubling every ten years. During this same period the speed of information processing has increased significantly" (p.31).

#6: Security Alert!

Security concerns will increase, creating a renewed focus on workplace security: "There's cynicism, pessimism and anxiety about the future. The threat of terrorism is worldwide" (p.32).

#7: Life and Work in the E-Lane

"Technological advances are transforming the way we work and live" (p.32). E-mail is faster and easier, and wireless technology allows people to share text, video pictures and conversations instantly. New technologies are affecting how we work and how, when and where we learn.

#8: A Higher Ethical Bar

Business scandals involving Enron, World Com, Tyco, the New York Stock Exchange, law enforcement agencies and others have eroded loyalty, trust and sense of security: "The integrity of management and leaders has come into question" (p.33).

Before looking at specific examples of how such workplace trends are impacting law enforcement, consider how change has impacted and altered, quite literally, the face of law enforcement.

Law Enforcement for the Future

One of the more omnipresent challenges facing any manager, in any field, concerns the human element. Managers in law enforcement must not only adapt to change themselves to stay effective in their positions but must also recognize how workplace trends impact their peers and subordinates and how more ubiquitous changes in today's society continually alter the demographics of the U.S. population, factors that necessitate a constant retooling of the way law enforcement services are delivered.

A Basic Change in Needed Management Skills

One reason changes have been so overwhelming in past decades and will continue to be in the decades ahead is that the required management skills have changed.

 Technical competence used to be most important. Now and in the years ahead, "people skills" are most important.

Woodward and Buchholz (1987, pp.13–14) explain it this way:

One way to visualize this tactical, people-oriented approach is with a bicycle. The two wheels of a bicycle have different purposes. The back wheel powers the bike; the front wheel steers it. Extending this analogy to an organization, "back-wheel" skills are the technical and organizational skills needed for the organization to function. "Front-wheel" skills are the interpersonal "people management" skills. Corporations tend to rely on their back-wheel, that is, their technical skills.

Typically, however, when change comes, the response of organizations is primarily back-wheel response—do what we know best. But the real need is for front-wheel skills, that is, helping people understand and adapt to the changing environment.

Winning coaches know that games are not won or lost in the fourth quarter or the ninth inning. The outcome of any game is determined by the amount of preparation. Law enforcement managers must possess a combination of technical skills and people skills to successfully guide their departments through the new millennium.

A Changing Law Enforcement Officer

Sanow (2003, p.4) notes: "The faces of law enforcement have changed and for the better: many more women are in law enforcement and there is much greater ethnic diversity." Weitzer and Tuch (2004, p.26) quote the U.S. Department of Justice as saying: "A diverse law enforcement agency can better develop relationships with the community it serves, promote trust in the fairness of law enforcement, and facilitate effective policing by encouraging citizen support and cooperation." In addition to hiring for more diversity, departments are hiring fewer officers with military backgrounds. They are also seeking recruits with better education and encourage employees to continue to seek more education.

A Changing Public to Be Served

One of the most significant changes for modern law enforcement is the increasing diversity of the U.S. population. Numerous social changes have affected law enforcement and will continue to affect it in the future.

 The public to be served will include more two-income families, more single-parent families, more senior citizens and more minorities. The educational and economic gap will increase, with those at the bottom becoming more disadvantaged and dissatisfied.

The necessity for two-income families has increased the need for daycare centers, some without security-checked personnel. This has produced problems of child sexual abuse, which have gained national attention. On the other hand, development of work-at-home programs has helped those who want added income but also want to remain at home to care for their children. Preset performance standards make this possible without regard for when or where the work is actually performed.

The high rate of divorce has changed family relationships. R. Morton Darrow, speaking at the National Press Club, stated: "With growing divorce and remarriage, the United States is moving from a nation in which parents had many children to one where children have many parents. This results in different needs and pressures in the family."

In addition, our population is aging. The baby boomers have turned 50, and by 2010 one fourth of all Americans will be at least 55 years old. More efforts will need to be spent on crime prevention and on support programs for older adults.

Another change is that the educational gap is increasing, with those at the bottom becoming even more disadvantaged. As the gap widens, economic opportunities dwindle and frustrations increase. The gap between the haves and the have-nots is widening significantly, with the likely result being social unrest. The United States is becoming a **bifurcated society,** with more wealth, more poverty and a shrinking middle class.

bifurcated society • a society in which the gap between the "haves" and the "have nots" is wide—that is, there are many poor people, many wealthy people and a shrinking middle class.

The smokestack America of the early 1900s has been battered by the most accelerated technological revolution in history. Computers, satellites, space travel, fiber optics, robots, biometrics, electronic data interchange and expert systems are only the most obvious manifestations. All this has been combined with globalization of the economy, rising competition and many social and cultural changes as well.

While the American public has grown increasingly diverse, they have also become vitally important as partners to law enforcement in the effort to attain peaceful and prosperous communities. Indeed, community policing and its emphasis on problem solving have taken hold in agencies across the country. A nationwide survey of 1,792 adults, including large samples of black and Hispanic respondents, found widespread support for community policing: 69 percent of whites, 73 percent of Hispanics, and 78 percent of blacks said that they wished the police practiced community policing in their neighborhood (Weitzer and Tuch, p.30).

The community is an invaluable resource to police managers seeking more effective ways to address the major challenges and issues facing law enforcement in the new millennium.

Major Challenges and Issues Facing Twenty-First Century Law Enforcement

Most of the significant trends and challenges seen within law enforcement have been alluded to throughout this text. This section presents a more concentrated look at those areas of concern identified by law enforcement professionals, both line personnel and management, as these challenges will continue to consume the majority of agencies' fiscal resources, time and personnel.

A nationwide survey that asked, "What do you consider law enforcement's critical issues of the future?" revealed several common management-specific concerns: Most frequently mentioned was officer training (76 percent), followed by funding (62 percent), properly equipping officers (60 percent), information sharing (56 percent) and recruiting officers/lack of manpower (56 percent). Also mentioned were domestic defense (45 percent), problem-oriented policing (26 percent) and managing finances (23 percent) ("Law Enforcement Today," 2005, p.22).

In examining the current legislative status of law enforcement funding, the second most commonly mentioned concern, it was found that funding for the Community Oriented Policing Services (COPS) program was cut by 20 percent in 2005 and that the Edward Byrne Memorial Justice Assistance Grant (JAG) program had decreased by 34 percent (Greene, 2006, p.5). Since 2002 these programs have declined "precipitously" from their $1.5 billion by nearly 64 percent. Likewise, funding for the State Homeland Security Grant (SHSG) program has decreased by 64 percent (Greene, p.5). Another example of the concern over decreased funding is seen in Indian Country, where special treatment jails have emerged and are showing promising results, but funding is lacking to further test and expand these facilities ("What's Hot in Law Enforcement," 2005, p.9).

The 2005 Critical Issues in Policing Forum (Ederheimer and Cronin, 2006, p.1) brought together 80 law enforcement leaders from across the country and around the world to discuss what they considered to be the most challenging issue for police executives—managing force and conflict. The conference focused on strategies for resolving conflict and minimizing the use of force in three areas: building community trust, interactions with people with mental illness and less-than-lethal weapons. The Police Executive Research Forum (PERF), in recognizing the seriousness of this challenge, has reasserted its commitment to making police use of force a top priority, including promising practices in the use of conducted energy devices (CEDs) (Wexler, 2006, p.2). The Bureau of Justice Assistance (BJA) is also seeking to support more strategic implementation of less-than-lethal technologies ("What's Hot in Law Enforcement," p.9).

A workshop hosted by the BJA identified the following "burning issues" facing law enforcement ("What's Hot in Law Enforcement," pp.8–9):

- Methamphetamine abuse and trafficking, including the need for technical assistance and training, more community mobilization and further exploration of drug courts to help attack addiction
- Street crime, gangs, guns and the nexus with terrorism

- The impact of the Internet and emerging technologies on extortion, witness intimidation and identity theft
- Sex offender registration and ways to help law enforcement verify sex offenders' whereabouts
- Sex offender reentry—preparing communities to accept a sex offender in their neighborhoods
- Problem-solving courts and reentry
- Interoperability of law enforcement agency voice and data systems
- Use of Uniform Crime Reporting (UCR) to measure performance; many issues affect the number, including the fact that much crime goes unreported
- Crime prevention through community partnerships, including with faith-based organizations and academia

In addition to the "burning issues" identified by law enforcement participants, the BJA's deputy director of policy added issues the BJS would like to address, including the following:

- Forensic investigations and clearing cold cases—the BJA is working with the National Forensic Academy and with academia to provide technical assistance to law enforcement in this area.
- Intelligence fusion centers—the Global Justice Information Sharing Advisory Committee is developing guidelines on minimum standards for fusion centers.
- Performance measures for law enforcement services—law enforcement leadership development well before individuals are in positions of authority and law enforcement safety.
- Gang and drug interdiction as a tool for counterterrorism—the latest gang assessment found gangs remain the primary distributors of drugs in the United States.

 In addition to the challenges of drugs, violence and gangs, law enforcement is heavily focused on homeland security.

The Drug Problem

The national and international drug problem has placed law enforcement officers on the front line, not only in enforcing drug laws but also in establishing drug undercover operations and participative community programs. The drug problem is of such magnitude that no single individual, segment of society or government can resolve the problem, which means that no segment can move ahead alone. An attack on one segment of society must be accepted as an attack on all.

In 1989 the drug problem was the largest single issue and concern in the nation. The public still expects law enforcement organizations to deal with this problem. Many federal resources will have to be devoted to it, and law enforcement entities must develop new approaches to meet the local challenge. Resolving the problem may involve reducing individual civil liberties in the interest of overall social well-being.

Suggested approaches to address the drug problem include crime control, punishment, rehabilitation, prevention and legalization, as summarized in Figure 17.2. These approaches should support the goals of the National Drug Control Strategy (2005): (1) stopping use before it starts: education and community action, (2) healing America's drug users: getting treatment resources where they are needed and (3) disrupting the market: attacking the economic basis of the drug trade.

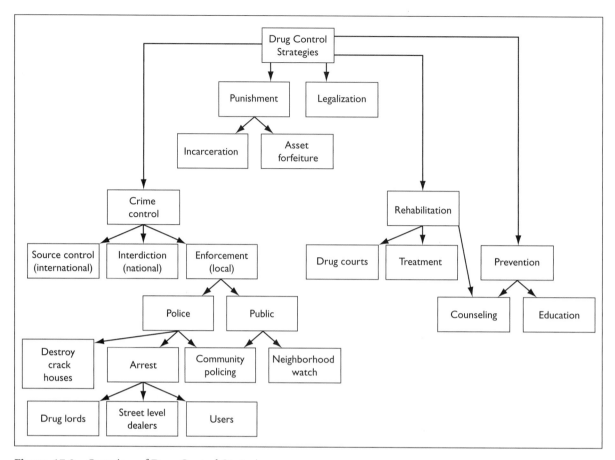

Figure 17.2   Overview of Drug-Control Strategies
Source: Henry M. Wrobleski and Kären M. Hess. *Introduction to Law Enforcement and Criminal Justice,* 8th ed. Belmont, CA: Thomson/Wadsworth, 2006, p.323.

A relatively new danger is that posed to children who are exposed to toxic methamphetamine lab operations: "Methamphetamine abuse and production have become major factors in the increase of child abuse and neglect cases" (Harris, 2004, p.8). Furthermore: "Estimates have indicated that children are found in approximately one-third of all seized meth labs. Of those children, about 35 percent test positive for toxic levels of chemicals in their bodies. In other areas, those numbers have proven even higher. More alarming, however, is the possibility that 90 percent of all meth labs go undetected, leaving many children to suffer needlessly" (Harris, p.8). Dealing with the methamphetamine problem is a high priority of law enforcement.

This is a war in which all willing and unwilling participants have been losers, either financially or in terms of human distress and suffering. Drastic measures will be necessary to bring about a resolution.

Shelden et al. (2004, p.123) state: "There is little question that drug usage and violent crime are closely related. What is still in doubt, however, is the relationship between drugs (both usage and sales) and gangs. Research on this issue has produced conflicting findings. . . . Gang members are about twice as likely as nongang members to use drugs and to use them more often." Violence and gangs are the next two challenges discussed.

Violence

One of the greatest challenges facing law enforcement is violence. *Domestic and family violence* are increasingly drawing the attention of law enforcement, including not only spousal abuse, but also child abuse and elder abuse. The Internet has complicated this challenge, with adults stalking other adults and children online.

Kingsnorth and Macintosh (2004, p.301) note: "During the last 25 years, social definitions of domestic violence have evolved from private wrongs to acts meriting an aggressive response from the criminal justice system. The change reflects the impact of the women's movement, civil liability lawsuits, changing criminal justice system ideology and academic research." Sherman ("Domestic Violence," p.1) speculates "family" violence is the most widespread form of violence in the country.

Women married to police officers face the additional difficulty of seeking help from their abuser's colleagues, some of whom may even be the batterer's close friends: "Research suggests violence may occur more frequently in police families than among the general public" (Gallo, 2004a, p.132). Gallo (2004b, p.60) contends: "Domestic violence in police families has always been one of the original 'don't ask, don't tell' issues—alternately ignored, hidden or denied, firmly protected by the blue wall of silence."

In addition, violence has taken its toll in our schools across the country, with mass shootings grabbing headlines. Between 1992 and 2001, the violent crime victimization rate at the nation's schools declined from 48 per 1,000 students to 28 (Rand, 2003). However: "School-associated violent deaths jumped to 43 during the 2003–2004 school year, exceeding the number of school deaths over the past two school years combined and totaling more than any other individual school years since before the Columbine shootings" (Garrett, 2004, p.6).

Workplace violence has also captured national headlines: "Incidents of workplace violence accounted for 14 percent of all work-related fatal occupational injuries in 2002, and according to the Department of Labor, violent acts continue to rank among the top three causes of workplace fatalities for all workers" (Rudewicz, 2004, p.41). According to the National Institute for Occupational Safety and Health Web site: "Each week, an average of 20 workers are murdered and 18,000 are assaulted while at work or on duty. Nonfatal assaults result in millions of lost workday's and cost workers millions of dollars in lost wages." A "Newspoll" conducted by *Security Director News* (2005, p.23) found that workplace violence was the number one security fear of security directors, as shown in Figure 17.3.

Gang violence is yet another challenge facing law enforcement now and in the future. On average, gang members commit about 373,000 of the 6.6 million violent victimizations. And from 1999 to 2003, gang members committed about 6 percent of violent crimes according to victims (Harrell, 2005). The gang problem is not restricted to metropolitan areas, as increasing numbers of rural jurisdictions are reporting the presence of and problems posed by gangs (Weisheit and Wells, 2004, p.2).

The National Alliance of Gang Investigators Association (NAGIA) Web site states: "The scourge of gangs is a clear and present danger to our internal national security and adversely impacts the quality of life within our communities with violence, drugs and associated criminal activities." Their *2005 National Gang Threat Assessment* found, however, that few gangs have been found to be associated with terrorist organizations. Gang affiliation or not, terrorism is also a challenge facing law enforcement.

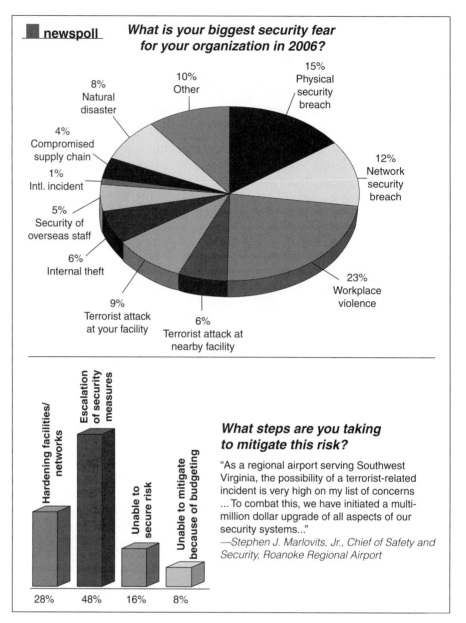

Figure 17.3   Biggest Security Fears for Organizations, 2006
Source: "Newspoll." *Security Director News,* December 2005, p.23. Reprinted by permission.

Terrorism and Homeland Security

Greene (p.6) contends: "In post-9/11 America, local law enforcement is increasingly being asked to assume a greater role in protecting our nation's homeland while continuing to perform its traditional crime-fighting responsibilities." "Homeland security is an integration project like no other," says Walker (2005, p.7), involving 180,000 government workers in 22 diverse federal agencies as well as 17,000 law enforcement agencies staffed by 700,000 sworn police officers, deputy sheriffs and criminal investigators. They are charged with securing more than 2.5 million square miles of land and the more than 280 million people making up the U.S. population. Doubtless, community policing efforts can and must

The need for homeland security was brought to the forefront by the events of September 11, 2001. A rescue helicopter surveys damages to the Pentagon Building as firefighters battle flames after terrorists crashed an airliner into the U.S. Military Headquarters outside Washington, DC.

play a large role in homeland security, with citizens serving as eyes and ears for local law enforcement.

Walker (p.7) stresses that homeland security requires a coordinated effort using realistic planning and multiple layers of security, including:

- A range of devices to detect weapons of mass destruction.
- Community exercises for preparedness.
- Secure networks to make sure information flows immediately to the right people.
- Warning systems and software that measure trends in disease symptoms.
- Monitoring systems to track pharmaceutical inventories.

Hoover (2002, p.1) notes: "State and local police agencies are facing a significant challenge in the wake of September 11. The federal government is asking for their substantive involvement in the homeland security effort." He outlines four broad categories of obstacles facing state and local law enforcement agencies in the terrorism intelligence effort.

 Four obstacles facing state and local law enforcement agencies in the terrorism intelligence effort are technological, logistical, political and ethical.

According to Hoover (p.1): "The *technological issue* that most challenges state and local participation in any national anti-terrorism intelligence effort can be summarized by one word—interoperability. The inability to exchange information on a regional and statewide level is overwhelmingly the primary issue." He suggests: "Some existing programs designed for drug trafficking information sharing might be able to serve concurrently as a homeland security database, hastening the implementation process." Fusion centers, as discussed momentarily, are one solution to the problem of isolated databases.

Hoover (p.4) asserts: "Data entry is the most problematic of the *logistical issues.* It is observed that if intelligence officers spend all day entering data, they are not doing very much intelligence analysis." Of the four obstacles, Hoover contends: "By far the most serious impediments to establishing a national interconnected antiterrorism database are *political.* There are several levels of political issues. . . . First and foremost among these is the issue of 'who pays for this.'" Other political issues include linkages to the Immigration and Naturalization Service (INS), relationship with the Federal Bureau of Investigation (FBI) and with state police, the need for confidentiality (viewed as secrecy by many local agencies) and the role of intelligence.

The final obstacle is *ethical,* including the possibility of racial profiling, the problem of open records legislation and new concerns about infringing on individuals' privacy and civil rights through new wiretapping laws.

In July 2002, the first *National Strategy for Homeland Security* was released, providing direction for steps that can be taken by local and state law enforcement agencies, private companies and organizations and individual Americans ("National Strategy for Homeland Security Released," 2002, p.7). The Strategy lists the strategic objectives of homeland security in order of priority as:

- Prevent terrorist attacks within the United States.
- Reduce America's vulnerability to terrorism.
- Minimize the damage and recover from attacks that do occur.

The threat of urban terrorism was vividly illustrated in the sniper-shooting spree in the fall of 2002 with 13 people shot, 10 of them fatally, over a three-week period on the nation's East Coast. Technology is being increasingly relied on as a powerful tool in the war on terrorism as well as in other facets of law enforcement.

Advances in Technology

Cowper and Jensen (2003, pp.124–125) contend: "Yesterday's science fiction is rapidly becoming a very real part of everyday life." They (p.125) suggest that using the current rate of technological change as a baseline, barring a global catastrophe, we could see 100 years of technological advancement in the first 10 years of the twenty-first century and 25,000 years of advancement before the twenty-second century. Futurist Ray Kurzwell also notes that technological change is occurring at an exponential rate and estimates that the first decades of the twenty-first century may produce the equivalent of several hundreds of years of technological growth (Cowper et al., 2003, p.125).

Law enforcement has grown increasingly reliant on technology and the many benefits it affords in terms of enhanced officer efficiency, effectiveness and safety. "Law Enforcement Today" (p.20) reports that 71 percent of departments have in-car computers, 59 percent have in-car video systems, 55 percent use electronic stun devices and 53 percent have wireless connectivity. However, only 27 percent use virtual training devices and only 10 percent have mobile AFIS devices.

Rapid availability and dissemination of restricted and confidential information assists investigators and results in increased apprehensions of criminals. At the same time, technology reduces the need for traditional reports and recordkeeping.

Officers spend less time completing official reports and have more time for field activities. Technology also allows administration to better know how time is actually being spent and how it should be spent. Tracking officer activities can be more immediate, but it should not be done to the point where officers lose their sense of reasonable freedom and control over decisions. Technology will continue to enhance law enforcement in communications, records, evaluation and investigation.

 Technology will expand in all phases of law enforcement and will greatly enhance efficiency. It will be increasingly imperative for most law enforcement personnel to be computer literate.

Global positioning systems (GPS) are an example of a technology being increasingly applied to law enforcement functions: "In the past two years, use of GPS technology has seen notable growth. . . . It may be used to track suspects, more efficiently monitor fleets or know the whereabouts of undercover surveillance officers, such as detectives or vice" (Rogers, 2003, p.74). Perhaps the single biggest benefit from GPS is enhanced officer safety (Rogers, p.78).

Wearable computers are now available and provide a head-mounted display on a pair of goggles or glasses, allowing officers to have the data they need without having to look away from their surroundings, improving their safety (Cowper, 2005, p.117). Development is underway on a retinal display that projects the information on the officer's retina. The "ultimate result" of this highly portable information technology is a mobile computing concept called Augmented Reality (AR): "AR technology overlays a comprehensive array of computer data and images directly onto the user's field of view in a way that dramatically improves individual performance and productivity by increasing his or her overall situational awareness" (Cowper, p.117). The yellow first-down lines used by the NFL and seen by television viewers are an example of AR technology.

Information technology (IT) is rapidly expanding the capabilities of public safety agencies at all levels to share information. Integrated justice information sharing, or "the ability to share critical information at key decision points throughout the justice enterprise," has become vitally important (Harris, 2005, pp.103–104). Integration, however, does not mean all agencies will be forced to use the same information, nor does it mean agencies must scrap their existing systems and buy new equipment. Tools, such as eXtensible Markup Language (XML), can be used to facilitate interoperability and information sharing among agencies and systems. XML involves data, text, documents, transmission protocols and standards. Harris (pp.109–110) explains: "XML is a structured language for describing information (such as an arrest/incident report) being sent electronically by one agency to another. XML sets a standard for electronic information exchange and describes the data contained in documents and electronic transmissions. XML is in a text format. It is license-free, platform-independent and well supported."

According to the National Criminal Justice Association (NCJA), the Missouri Office of the State Courts Administration (OSCA) has implemented the largest, most comprehensive data integration project ever successfully attempted. With 49 unique court case management systems, each with approximately 500 data fields and no standard to follow, conversion was tedious and expensive. But in 2005, the Department of Justice selected the Global Justice XML Data Model (GJXDM) as the first standard for creating the National Information Exchange Model (NIEM). The NCJA notes that the GJXDM allows more flexibility to deal with unique

Wireless technology is enhancing law enforcement's ability to share information instantly. Here a digital camera searches for a wireless network at a coffee shop in Rochester, New York, September 2005. Eastman Kodak Co. has begun shipping a groundbreaking digital camera that, within range of hotels, coffee shops, airport lounges, offices, homes and other wireless hot spots, can deliver high-quality pictures directly onto the Internet and into e-mail boxes around the globe.

agency requirements and changes. By using a common vocabulary that is understood system to system, GJXDM allows access from multiple sources and reuse in multiple applications. The GJXDM is being used by the Department of Justice, the Department of Homeland Security and the FBI. The NCJ notes that when the project is complete, Missouri citizens will have access to an "electronic courthouse," allowing them to obtain case information on the Internet and file documents electronically ("Missouri Leads Nation with Statewide GJXDM Conversion," 2006, pp.7–8).

fusion centers • serve multi-agency policing needs, providing information to patrol officers, detectives, management and others on specific criminals, criminal groups and criminal activities.

Fusion centers are also being implemented across the nation as a tool to facilitate information sharing among law enforcement agencies. These centers serve multiagency policing needs, providing information to patrol officers, detectives, management and others on specific criminals, criminal groups and trends in criminal activities. Fusion centers embody the core of collaboration, with the ultimate goal being to provide a mechanism through which law enforcement partners can come together with a common purpose and improve the ability to safeguard our homeland and prevent criminal activity (Modafferi and Bouche, 2005). Fusion centers are an emerging trend nationwide and at least a half-dozen states have established such centers (Ebbert, 2005).

Ebbert points out that what politicians regard as a vital technological defense against possible terrorist threats, civil libertarians view as an expensive new Big Brother. The American Civil Liberties Union (ACLU) has raised concerns about the potential for the center to use the new databases to gather and store information on private citizens.

Keeping abreast of innovations in technology can be a major challenge, especially for smaller departments. The IACP offers several resources and initiatives to help agencies select and use emerging technologies. Their publication *A Best Practices*

Guide: Acquisition of New Technology includes an acquisition plan, acquisition and delivery, and implementation and training recommendations. The guide is available on the Internet at www.iacptechnology.org

Cowper and Jensen (pp.125–127) note: "The critical component to effective policing in a rapidly changing world is the ability to think creatively about emerging technologies and how they can be used successfully within the constitutional limitations of a free society." It will be up to police managers and leaders to create police departments capable of obtaining and using powerful information systems to enhance public safety and at the same time preserve their commitment to the Constitution (Cowper, p.123).

How law enforcement will meet the special challenges ahead of it are addressed by futuristics.

Futuristics

As a profession, law enforcement has relied too heavily on experience and not enough on innovation. **Futuristics,** a new tool for managers and leaders, is the science of using data from the past to forecast alternatives for the future and to then select the most desirable alternatives.

People who study the future use environmental scanning; that is, they identify factors likely to "drive" the environment. **Environmental scanning** has been defined as "a process for systematically examining and evaluating various trends that may have future significance for an organization" (Cowper and Jensen, p.127). Three categories of change likely to affect the future criminal justice system Cowper and Jensen study are:

1. Social and economic conditions (size and age of the population, immigration patterns and nature of employment and lifestyle characteristics).
2. Shifts in the number and types of crimes and disorder challenges.
3. Developments in the criminal justice system itself, including community involvement in all aspects of the system.

Forecasting, a form of futuristics, is similar to the headlights on a car being driven in a snowstorm. The lights provide enough illumination to continue but not enough so the driver can proceed without caution. What lies ahead is still unknown. Futuristics is not something mystical or prophetic. It combines historical facts, scientific principles and departmental values with vision to imagine what could happen in the future. The Society of Police Futurists International (PFI) was founded in 1991 by Dr. William Tafoya. PFI is dedicated to futures research in policing and to stimulating new ideas on a variety of policing theories and practices.

Basic Principles of Futuristics

Futuristics rests on three basic principles or assumptions about the nature of the universe and our role in it (Tafoya, 1983, p.13).

The three basic principles of futuristics are:

1. The unity or interconnectedness of reality.
2. The significance of ideas.
3. The crucial importance of time.

futuristics • the science of using data from the past to forecast alternatives for the future and to then select those most desirable.

environmental scanning • identifying the factors that are likely to "drive" the environment, influencing the future. Includes social and economic conditions.

The *unity* or *interconnectedness of reality* suggests that we operate in a "holistic universe, a huge mega-system, the activities of whose systems, subsystems and components interface and interact in synergistic fashion" (Tafoya, p.13).

The *significance of ideas*, the second basic principle of futuristics, emphasizes the quest for new and better ways of doing things—exploring divergent new ways to deal with old problems and imagining new ways to anticipate potential problems.

The third basic principle, the *importance of time*, suggests a future focus. Rather than being absorbed with today's problems and holding on to traditions, futurists think five years ahead and beyond. Futuristics often uses the following time frames (Tafoya, p.15):

Immediate future	Present to 2 years
Short-range future	2 to 5 years
Mid-range future	5 to 10 years
Long-range future	10 to 20 years
Extended-range future	20 to 50 years
Distant future	50 years and beyond

Law enforcement managers tend to focus on the immediate future, dealing with problems that need resolution, trying to stay "on top of things" and "putting out fires." No wonder they do not notice a mere 2- to 4-percent annual increase in the crime rate. The crisis faced today is probably a minor one that was ignored yesterday. Time is significant. Do not let it be said of the future that it is "that time when you'll wish you'd done what you aren't doing now."

Fundamental Premises and Goals

Futurists also operate under three fundamental premises (Tafoya, p.15):

 Fundamental premises of futurists are the following:

- The future is not predictable.
- The future is not predetermined.
- Future outcomes can be influenced by individual choice.

The third premise is critical to managers because the choices made today will affect law enforcement in the future. As has been said, "The future is coming. Only you can decide where it's going." How can futuristics be used in law enforcement management? Tafoya suggests three primary priorities or goals (p.17):

 Goals of futuristics:

- Form perceptions of the future (the possible).
- Study likely alternatives (the probable).
- Make choices to bring about particular events (the preferable).

If people are to influence future outcomes, perceptions of the future must be formed. . . . Be alert to risks as well as opportunities. What is possible is what "could be"; this key role is characterized as *image-driven*. . . . What is required is breaking the fetters of one's imagination. It is the vital, creative goal of futuristics.

Once new images have been generated, likely alternatives must be studied. The probable path to the future must be analyzed; quantitatively as well as qualitatively. . . . What is probable is what "may be"; this aim is characterized as *analytically driven*. It is the detached, systematic and *scientific* goal of futuristics.

Having imagined the possible and analyzed the probable, it is necessary to make choices among alternatives. . . . What is preferred is what "should be"; this intent is characterized as *value-driven*. It is the *managerial, decision-making goal* of futuristics.

The Futures Working Group

An "extraordinary memorandum of understanding" has occurred between the PFI and the FBI in the shape of the Futures Working Group (FWG) (Myers, 2005, p.169). This group and PFI members prioritize community policing as one of the topics high on their agenda. This group found several challenges limiting broad and full implementation of community policing throughout the country:

- Lack of buy-in by personnel
- Insufficient training in COP/POP
- Lack of leadership and climates that do not support risk taking
- Fiscal constraints
- Challenges to defining "community" (Myers, p.170)

The group stresses that the post–September 11 era of policing has made the role of the first responder to disasters and crises a high priority of police departments and that the homeland security function may have even more profound effects on policing.

The group also identified several possible futures for community policing. It is possible that community policing may evolve into community-oriented government. It is also possible that public–private partnerships may evolve to the point where policing in wealthy neighborhoods will be provided by private police forces. Another possibility is that a department may have a *proactive,* or quality-of-life, division and a *reactive,* or crisis, division co-existing. It may be that in the future police responses to disturbances and violence are largely responded to by robotic devices because nearly all public places will be under video surveillance monitored by computers.

The working group also identified strategies for change that would bring about the best possible future for community policing. The first strategy is to assure that recruiting, selecting and training police officers must be grounded in the principles of COP/POP. Second, the organization hierarchies in law enforcement must be flattened. Third, the connection between academia and policing should be strengthened. Creativity and innovation are also needed.

The Need for Creativity and Innovation

Creativity and innovation in law enforcement must continue in the decades ahead. Considerable impetus for innovative projects was provided through past Law Enforcement Assistance Administration (LEAA)–funded programs. Much of this impetus has been retained mentally but slowed by decreased funding. Many improvements in law enforcement can be continued or developed within existing budgets and with existing personnel. These programs involve improvements in everyday activities.

One responsibility of managers is to examine and be creative about each task to be performed. Determine how each task can be done better and involve the task-doer in the process. Give subordinates input and control over what they do to increase a sense of contribution and well-being on the job and to reduce stress. Many law enforcement tasks generate a high degree of stress. Stress experts state that lack of control on the job is an additional stress producer. Getting the job done better and reducing stress at the same time is one key to future healthy officers.

Management should encourage creativity even at the cost of failures. Experimentation failures must be accepted as part of the process of growth and development. Officers who know that punishment will follow failure will not take the risks necessary for individual and departmental growth. Therefore, managers should encourage reasonable risk taking. They might encourage subordinates to think creatively and take risks by posting slogans such as the following in prominent places:

- Don't be afraid to go out on a limb. That's where the fruit is.
- Don't be afraid to take a big step if one is indicated. You can't cross a chasm in two small jumps.
- If you're made of the right material, a hard fall will result in a high bounce.

Those involved in research understand that failures are the stepping-stones to success. "Nothing ventured, nothing gained" remains true for the future and applies to law enforcement managers at all levels and to their subordinates.

Creativity and innovation do not automatically involve large amounts of money. Often they require only the present level of personnel and equipment to be used more efficiently. The future of law enforcement depends on federal financial and research assistance, supported by state and local willingness to support creativity and freedom on the job.

Creativity results from extending, searching into the unknown and trying the untried. It is risky. It may fail. In law enforcement, creativity means viewing a law enforcement problem in a new way, having a new idea.

Everyone can create, but few do. Studies indicate no relationship between high I.Q. and creativity. What is unique about creative people is that they keep trying. In the process they make mistakes but accept them and move on to the next idea. Creative people take time to dream.

Everyone reading this text can be creative. Have you ever said to yourself, "Why didn't I think of that before?" Creativity is nonconformity, not in the destructive sense of being difficult to get along with but in the useful, positive sense.

In police work, every task can be accomplished better. We need police who use their minds to create these better ways. Creativity means thinking of a better technique for handling domestics and, when successfully applied, thinking of an even better way. To give creativity a chance to work, try some of the following options:

- Take time out to research a specific subject.
- Delay a decision until you have time to think about it and perhaps sleep on it.
- When you feel mentally blocked, take a walk down the hall or outside the building.
- Expand your mental capabilities by going beyond what is known.
- Concentrate on a small part of the problem and deal with that.
- Consider different options and alternatives.

Thinking traps and mental locks described in Chapter 5 are relevant as a department strives for innovation. Other obstacles may exist in the form of politics, restrictions mandated by union contracts, local ordinances, special interest groups and so on.

McLagan (2003b, p.52) notes: "Successful organizations go beyond brawn and compliance requirements; they engage the hearts and minds of their people in a conscious and deliberate alliance for success." What is required for this to occur is distributed intelligence. **Distributed intelligence** occurs, says McLagan, "when everyone in an organization, regardless of role or level, proactively solves problems, makes decisions, and takes creative action as the need arises—without waiting to be told what to do" (p.52). McLagan (p. 54) gives as a "striking example" of people acting with distributed intelligence the passengers' behavior on ill-fated Flight 92 as they acted to thwart the 9/11 hijackers. McLagan notes that distributed intelligence is a key when an organization implements change: "Making change everybody's business is the responsibility of managers and individual workers" (p.54).

distributed intelligence • occurs when everyone in an organization, regardless of rank or role, proactively solves problems, makes decisions and takes creative action as the need arises—without waiting to be told what to do.

Change Revisited

Change occurs in several major areas directly affecting law enforcement. These include changes in the society itself, in technology, in the economy and in the environment, as well as political changes. Often, if things are going well for a department, it sees no reason to make a change. Recall the story of the monkeys, the banana and the cold shower told in the last chapter. Many managers believe, "if it ain't broke, don't fix it." However, managers who do not pay attention to the changes occurring around them do so at their own peril. Consider the boiled frog phenomenon.

The Boiled Frog Phenomenon

 The **boiled frog phenomenon** suggests that managers must pay attention to change in their environment and adapt—or perish.

boiled frog phenomenon • based on a classic experiment, suggests that managers must pay attention to change in their environment and adapt—or perish.

The boiled frog phenomenon rests on a classic experiment. A frog is dropped into a pan of boiling water and immediately jumps out, saving its life. Next, a frog is placed into a pan of room-temperature water that is gradually heated to the boiling point. Because the temperature rise is so gradual, the frog does not notice it and sits contentedly in the bottom of the pan. The gradually rising temperature initially makes the frog comfortable but eventually saps its energy.

As the water becomes too hot, the frog has no strength to jump out. It boils to death.

Resistance to Change

As discussed previously, resistance to change is natural. Consider the following statements:

"The horse is here to stay, but the automobile is only a novelty—a fad." Marshall Ferdinand Foch, 1911, a French military strategist.

"There is no reason for any individual to have a computer in his home." Ken Olsen, 1977, president of Digital Equipment.

Switzer (2003, pp.54–57) suggests five steps to overcome resistance and obtain commitment to change.

1. Identify whose commitment is needed.

Instructions: What is your level of commitment to try this new process that will help us provide better service to our citizens? Place an X next to the number that best reflects how you feel about this change.

☐ **5: Committed:** "I am committed to this new process. I will try to ensure that my actions reflect this commitment."

☐ **4: Genuine Compliance:** "This new process sounds like a good idea to me. Tell me what you want me to do and I'll do it."

☐ **3: Formal Compliance:** "You say this is part of my job I'll do it."

☐ **2: Grudging Compliance:** "I'll only do what's necessary to keep from losing my job."

☐ **1: Resistant:** "I don't like this idea. I won't do it. You can't make me do it. I'll show that this idea won't work."

Figure 17.4 Sample Commitment Ladder

Source: Reprinted from *The Police Chief*, Vol. LXX, No. 10, p.57, ©2003. Copyright held by the International Association of Chiefs of Police, 515 North Washington Street, Alexandria, VA 22314 USA. Further reproduction without express written permission from IACP is strictly prohibited.

2. Determine the level of commitment needed.
3. Estimate the critical mass.
4. Get the commitment of the critical mass.
5. Status check to monitor the level of commitment.

To accomplish the first step, consider who among those who would be affected by the change could help or derail the plan. Figure 17.4 shows a commitment ladder that could be used to begin the change process. The middle manager is an important player in making changes, for if they are not properly prepared, they will not provide supervisors with the rationale for organizational change (Charrier, 2004, p.60). It is the middle manager who must excite change in supervisors, who in turn can excite the first-line officers who are responsible for implementation.

To accomplish the second step, consider where those identified in the first step currently are. People usually fall into one of four categories: those who *resist* the change, those who *let* it happen, those who *help* it happen and those who *make* it happen. The first step identified where the key people currently are. The next step is to determine where they need to be to make the change happen. Figure 17.5 illustrates a commitment planning chart that can be used in this second step, with Xs indicating current level of commitment and Os indicating the level of commitment needed from each person.

Switzer (p.55) notes that there is no formula to determine the number of committed people needed to make the change happen, the critical mass (Step 2). A simple, uncontroversial change will need a lower critical mass than a complex, far-reaching change. The key to the fourth step is to determine what it will take for the

Key employee	Resist change	Let change happen	Help change happen	Make change happen
1.	X		O	
2.		X		O
3.		X	O	
4.				XO
5.			X	O
6.		XO		
7.	X	O		

Figure 17.5   Commitment Planning Chart

Source: Reprinted from *The Police Chief*, Vol. LXX, No. 10, p.55, ©2003. Copyright held by the International Association of Chiefs of Police, 515 North Washington Street, Alexandria, VA 22314 USA. Further reproduction without express written permission from IACP is strictly prohibited.

employees to buy into the change and take steps to meet those needs. Step 5 might return to the commitment ladder to determine progress in gaining commitment.

It often takes a catastrophe such as the attacks on America on September 11, 2001, to bring about change. Without such an impetus, initiating change may be difficult. Sparrow (1988, p.21) makes a classic analogy, comparing changes in policing to driving a 50-ton semi:

> The professional truck driver . . . avoids braking sharply. He treats corners with far greater respect. And he generally does not expect the same instant response from the trailer, with its load, that he enjoys in his car. The driver's failure to understand the implications and responsibilities of driving such a massive vehicle inevitably produces tragedy: if the driver tries to turn too sharply, the cab loses traction as the trailer's momentum overturns or jackknifes the vehicle.

Police organizations also have considerable momentum. Having a strong personal commitment to the values with which they have "grown up," police officers may find hints of proposed change in the police culture extremely threatening.

Often what is needed is change in the very culture of an agency. If the reality of an organization does not match its stated mission and goals, it is management's responsibility to change the organizational culture to meet the desired goals and expectations: "While the commitment to change is long-term, ordinary day-to-day decisions and actions must all be based upon making progress toward realizing the organization's vision" (Cresie, 2005, p.75). This can be accomplished by doing a little "management by walking around" (Cresie, p.78). Cresie (p.75) cautions that change takes time, that any significant change of culture requires at least five to seven years. It is what is done day by day that matters most.

The amount of time needed will vary from agency to agency, but managers should avoid becoming victims of the boiled frog phenomenon.

The Change-Capable Organization

Results of many surveys put change management at the top of the list of management concerns, and research has identified qualities of organizations that have an "inbuilt capacity for change" (McLagan, 2003a, p.50). These organizations link present and future, make learning a way of life, actively support and encourage day-to-day improvements and changes, ensure diverse teams, encourage mavericks, shelter breakthroughs, integrate technology, and build and deepen trust. McLagan (p.57) stresses: "Change isn't just something to manage when strategies shift or crises occur. It's an ongoing challenge and condition in organizational life. . . . It's time to admit that change is a way of life."

Acceptance of Change

Change is inevitable. No person or organization can stop it. Managers must accept that the only constant is change. Whether change is positive or negative is characterized by Enright (1984) this way:

> A branch floats peacefully down a river whose waters are high with the spring runoff. Although the branch is floating rapidly and occasionally bumps gently into a rock, it is almost effortlessly motionless in relation to the water it floats in.
>
> A similar branch has become wedged between some rocks and is thus resisting the swift flow of water around it. This branch is buffeted, whipped and battered by the water and debris floating past it, and will soon be broken by the pressures against it (unless it dislodges and "goes with the flow"). If branches could experience, the one wedged into the rocks would be experiencing change with intense pain and distress; the floating one would experience ease and, paradoxically, comfortable stability even in the midst of rapid motion.

 Change is inevitable. View it as opportunity.

Long-Term Change

A key to meaningful, long-term change is leadership sustainability: "Sustainable leadership systems provide intrinsic rewards and extrinsic incentives that attract and retain the best and brightest of the leadership pool" (Hargreaves and Fink, 2004, p.11). Research has found "inspiring examples of leaders who did more than just manage change; they pursued and modeled sustainable leadership" (p.12). Hargreaves and Fink (p.13) conclude: "If we want change to matter, to spread, and to last, then the systems in which leaders do their work must make sustainability a priority."

> The future is not a result of choices among alternative paths offered by the present but a place that is created—created first in mind and will, created next in activity. Ten two-letter words sum it up: *If it is to be, it is up to me.*
>
> We have trained [people] to think of the future as a promised land which favored heroes attain—not as something which everyone reaches at the same rate of 60 minutes an hour, whatever he does, whoever he is.—C. S. Lewis
>
> The future is not some place we are going to, but one we are creating. The paths are not to be found, but made, and the activity of making them changes both the maker and the destination.—John Schaar

The future never comes. It is like tomorrow. We can only function in today—but what we do today will influence all the todays to come. Managers and leaders must be forward looking, adapting as necessary to accomplish their mission.

SUMMARY

Technical competence used to be most important. Now and in the years ahead, people skills are most important. Several other changes have occurred in law enforcement. The public to be served will include more two-income families, more single-parent families, more senior citizens and more minorities. The educational and economic gaps will increase, with those at the bottom becoming more disadvantaged and dissatisfied. Many issues face law enforcement in the twenty-first century. In addition to the challenges of drugs, violence and gangs, law enforcement is facing the challenge of homeland security. Four broad categories of obstacles facing state and local law enforcement agencies in the terrorism intelligence effort are technological, logistical, political and ethical.

Technology will be increasingly used in all phases of law enforcement and will greatly enhance efficiency. It will be imperative for most law enforcement personnel to be computer literate. In planning to meet the challenges facing law enforcement, managers can benefit from futuristics. Futuristics is the science of using data from the past to forecast alternatives for the future and to then select the most desirable. The three basic principles of futuristics are (1) the unity or interconnectedness of reality, (2) the significance of ideas and (3) the crucial importance of time. Fundamental premises of futurists are that the future is not predictable, the future is not predetermined and future outcomes can be influenced by individual choice. Goals of futuristics include:

- Form perceptions of the future (the possible).
- Study likely alternatives (the probable).
- Make choices to bring about particular events (the preferable).

The boiled frog phenomenon suggests that managers must pay attention to change in their environment and adapt—or perish. Change is inevitable. View it as opportunity.

CHALLENGE SEVENTEEN

Your first year as the police chief of the Greenfield Police Department has been a resounding success. When you arrived the department was a traditional crime-fighting organization with a military command structure. Now the department is well on its way to implementing a community policing strategy and a participative management structure. You are confident the department's mission is in line with the current needs of the Greenfield community.

You cross your feet on your desk; clasp your hands behind your head; and take a deep, relaxing breath. You are proud of your leadership and the department's accomplishments. As you reach for a victory cigar, a troubling thought creeps into your head. What if community policing and participative management are outdated in 10 years? Will the next chief look back at you and wonder why you were entrenched in an antiquated paradigm of policing? Will you be the next generation's Chief Slaughter?

You want to be remembered as an innovator on the cutting edge of modern policing. You sit up in your chair, toss the cigar and pull out a note pad. You write across the top, "My 10 Year Plan."

1. Should police leaders plan to make major changes in policing strategies every 10 years?

2. Anticipate some major changes in the population that will affect American policing in the near future.

3. Will the Internet affect local law enforcement?

4. How will the trend toward private security affect policing?

5. The rapid pace of technology will continue to change the way we police. Can you recognize ways technology is currently changing American policing?

6. What traits come to mind when you envision a police leader of the future?

DISCUSSION QUESTIONS

1. What should be law enforcement's role in the drug problem? In the violence problem? The challenge of homeland security?

2. Do you think creativity can be learned? Why or why not?

3. What would be the advantages of "flattening" the hierarchy? Disadvantages?

4. What trends do you foresee in the future of policing?

5. What is the importance of innovation and creativity in a law enforcement organization?

6. What do you see for the future development of your law enforcement agency?

7. How would you meet the decline of law enforcement resources?

8. What changes do you think are needed in the selection of future officers?

9. What major changes have you experienced in the past year? The past five years? How well did you handle them?

10. How can you best prepare for the inevitability of change in your life and your career?

REFERENCES

Charrier, Kim. "The Role of the Strategic Manager." *The Police Chief*, June 2004, pp.60–64.

Colteryahn, Karen and Davis, Patty. "8 Trends You Need to Know Now." *Training and Development*, February 2004, pp.28–36.

Cowper, T.; Jensen, C; and Levine, B. "Let's Get with the Digital Age." *Law Enforcement Technology*, July 2003, pp.8–10.

Cowper, Thomas and Jensen, Carl. "Emerging Technology." *Law and Order*, June 2003, pp.124–127.

Cowper, Tom. "Emerging Technology." In *Issues in IT*, edited by Ronald W. Glensor and Gerard R. Murphy. Washington, DC: Police Executive Research Forum, February 2005, pp.113–125.

Cresie, John. "Changing the Culture of Your Organization." *Law and Order*, December 2005, pp.74–78.

Ebbert, Stephanie. "Fusion Center Takes Aim at Terror: But Secrecy Alarms Civil Libertarians." *Boston Globe*, September 26, 2005.

Ederheimer, Joshua A. and Cronin, Jim. "The 2005 Critical Issues in Policing Forum." *Subject to Debate*, January 2006, pp.1, 3.

Enright, John. "Change and Resilience." *The Leader Manager*. Eden Prairie, MN: Wilson Learning Corporation, 1984, pp.59–73.

Gallo, Gina. "Airing Law Enforcement's Dirty Laundry." *Law Enforcement Technology*, June 2004a, pp.132–137.

Gallo, Gina. "The National Police Family Violence Prevention Project Helps Departments Address Domestic Abuse in Police Families." *Law Enforcement Technology*, July 2004b, pp.60–64.

Garrett, Ronnie. "Keep an Eye on School Safety." *Law Enforcement Technology*, May 2004, p.6.

Greene, Kevin E. "Legislative Update." *Subject to Debate*, January 2006, pp.5–6

Hargreaves, Andy and Fink, Dean. "The Seven Principles of Sustained Leadership." *Educational Leadership*, April 2004, pp.8–13.

Harrell, Erika. *Violence by Gang Members, 1993–2004*. Washington, DC: Bureau of Justice Statistics Crime Data Brief, June 2005. (NCJ 208875)

Harris, Jerry. "Drug-Endangered Children." *FBI Law Enforcement Bulletin*, February 2004, pp.6–11.

Harris, Kelly J. "Information Sharing and Integrated Justice: What Law Enforcement Executives Need to Know." In *Issues in IT: A Reader for the Busy Police Chief Executive*. Washington, DC: Police Executive Research Forum, 2005, pp.103–111.

Hoover, Larry T. "The Challenges to Local Police Participation in the Homeland Security Effort." *Subject to Debate*, October 2002, pp.1–10.

Kingsnorth, Rodney F. and Macintosh, Randall C. "Domestic Violence: Predictors of Victim Support for Official Action." *Justice Quarterly*, June 2004, pp.301–328.

"Law Enforcement Today." *Law Enforcement Technology*, December 2005, pp.20–23.

McLagan, Patricia A. "Organizational Change." *Training and Development*, January 2003a, pp.50–71.

McLagan, Patricia A. "Distributed Intelligence." *Training and Development*, 2003b, pp.52–71.

"Missouri Leads Nation with Statewide GJXDM Conversion." *NCJA Justice Bulletin*, January 2006, pp.7–8.

Modafferi, Peter A. and Bouche, Kenneth A. "Intelligence Sharing: Efforts to Develop Fusion Center Intelligence Standards." *The Police Chief*, February 2005.

Myers, Richard. "What Future(s) Do We Want for Community Policing?" In *Issues in IT*, edited by Ronald W. Glensor and Gerard R. Murphy. Washington, DC: Police Executive Research Forum, February 2005, pp.169–182.

Naisbitt, John and Aburdene, Patricia. *Megatrends 2000: Ten New Directions for the 1990s*. New York: William Morrow & Co., 1990.

National Alliance of Gang Investigators Association Web site: http://www.nagia.org. Accessed January 3, 2006.

National Drug Control Strategy, Annual Report, February 2005. Washington, DC: Office of National Drug Control Policy, 2005, last updated December 6, 2005. Accessed January 2, 2006.

"National Strategy for Homeland Security Released." *NCJA Justice Bulletin*, July 2002, pp.7–10.

"Newspoll." *Security Director News*, December 2005, p.23.

Rand, Michael R. *Indicators of School Crime ands Safety: 2003*. Washington, DC: Bureau of Justice Statistics, October 2003. (NCJ 201257)

Rogers, Donna. "GPS Gains a Stronger Position." *Law Enforcement Technology*, September 2003, pp.74–78.

Rudewicz, Frank E. "The Road to Rage." *Security Management*, February 2004, pp.41–49.

Sanow, Ed. "No Changes in Policing." *Law and Order*, Fiftieth Anniversary Issue 1953–2003, p.4.

Shelden, Randall G.; Tracy, Sharon K.; and Brown, William B. *Youth Gangs in American Society*, 3rd ed. Belmont, CA: Wadsworth Publishing Company, 2004.

Sherman, Lawrence W. "Domestic Violence." In *Crime File Study Guide*, National Institute of Justice. Washington, DC: U.S. Government Printing Office, no date.

Sparrow, Malcolm K. "Implementing Community Policing." *Perspectives on Policing*, November 1988, pp.20–49.

Switzer, Merle. "Five Steps for Building Commitment for Change." *The Police Chief*, October 2003, pp.54–57.

Tafoya, William L. "Futuristics: New Tools for Criminal Justice Executives: Part I." Presentation at the 1983 annual meeting of the Academy of Criminal Justice Sciences, March 22–26, 1983, San Antonio, Texas.

2005 National Gang Threat Assessment, National Alliance of Gang Investigators Association, 2005.

Walker, Bruce. "Safeguarding America through Layered Defense Tactics." *Security Director News*, December 2005, p.7.

Weisheit, Ralph A. and Wells, L. Edward. "Youth Gangs in Rural America." *NIJ Journal*, July 2004, pp.2–5. (NCJ 204516)

Weitzer, Ronald and Tuch, Steven A. "Public Opinion on Reforms in Policing." *The Police Chief*, December 2004, pp.26–30.

Wexler, Chuck. "A Look Ahead to 2006." *Subject to Debate*, January 2006, p.2.

"What's Hot in Law Enforcement." *NCJA Justice Bulletin*, August 2005, pp.8–9.

Woodward, Harry and Buchholz, Steve. *Aftershock: Helping People through Corporate Change*. New York: John Wiley and Sons, 1987.

BOOK-SPECIFIC WEB SITE

Go to the Management and Supervision in Law Enforcement Web site at www.thomsonedu.com/criminaljustice/bennett for student and instructor resources, including Internet Assignments and Case Studies.

Offenses and Their Penalties— Progressive Discipline

Offense	Explanation	Penalties*		
		1st Offense	2nd Offense	3rd Offense
1. Failure to carry out assignment/insubordination				
a. Minor	Deliberate delay or failure to carry out assigned work or instructions in a reasonable period of time.	R	R to 5 days S	R to D
b. Major	Refusal to obey legitimate orders, disrespect, insolence and like behavior.	R to D	R to D	D
2. Absence without leave				
a. Minor	Unauthorized absence of 10 hours or less, repeated tardiness, leaving the job without permission.	R	R to 5 days S	R to D
b. Major	Unauthorized absence of more than 10 hours. (If misrepresentation is involved, see #8).	R to D	R to D	D
3. Neglect of duty				
a. Minor	Unauthorized participation in activities during duty hours that are outside of regularly assigned duties. The offense is usually considered minor when danger to safety of persons or property is not acute or injury or loss is not involved.	R	R to 5 days S	R to D
b. Major	The offense is usually considered major when danger to safety of persons or property is acute or injury or loss is involved.	R to D	D	
4. Careless workmanship or negligence				
a. Minor	When spoilage or waste of materials or delay in production is not of significant value.	R	R to 5 days S	R to D
b. Major	When spoilage or waste of materials or delay in production is extensive and costly; covering up or attempting to conceal defective work.	R to D	D	
5. Violation of safety practices and regulations				
a. Minor	Failure to observe safety practices and regulations and danger to safety of persons or property is not acute.	R	R to 5 days S	R to D
b. Major	Failure to observe safety practices and regulations and danger to safety of persons or property is acute.	R to D	D	
6. Loss of, damage to, unauthorized use or willful destruction of city property, records or information				
a. Minor	When loss or damage is of small value and such loss or damage is not knowingly perpetrated.	R	R to 5 days S	R to D
b. Major	When loss or damage is knowingly perpetrated.	R to D	D	
7. Theft, actual or attempted, in taking and carrying away city property or property of others	Penalty will be determined in part by value of property.	R to D	D	
8. False statements or misrepresentation				
a. Minor	When falsification, concealment or misrepresentation has occurred, but has not necessarily been done deliberately.	R to 10 days S	D	
b. Major	Deliberate misrepresentation, falsification, exaggeration or concealment of a material fact, especially in connection with matters under official investigation.	R to D	D	

*Note: R means reprimand, S means suspension and D means dismissal.

Continued

Offense	Explanation	Penalties* 1st Offense	Penalties* 2nd Offense	Penalties* 3rd Offense
9. Disorderly conduct				
a. Minor	Rude, boisterous play that adversely affects production, discipline or morale; use of disrespectful, abusive or offensive language; quarreling or inciting to quarrel.	R to 5 days S	R to D	D
b. Major	Fighting, threatening or inflicting bodily harm to another; physical resistance to competent authority; any violent act or language which adversely affects morale, production or maintenance of discipline; indecent or immoral conduct.	R to D	D	
10. Gambling				
a. Minor	Participation in gambling during working hours.	R	R to 5 days S	D
b. Major	Promotion of, or assisting in, operation of organized gambling.	R to D	R to D	D
11. Use of intoxicants				
a. Minor	Drinking or selling intoxicants or controlled substances on duty or on city premises.	R to D	D	
b. Major	Reporting for duty drunk, under the influence of controlled substances or intoxicated and unable to properly perform assigned duties or posing a hazard to self or others.	5 days S to D	D	
12. Misconduct off duty	Misconduct which adversely affects the reputation of the employee or reflects unfavorably on the city.	R to D	R to D	D
13. Failure to honor valid debts	Garnishment of an employee's wages by an appropriate court order.	R[†]	R	R to D
14. Discrimination				
a. Minor	Any action or failure to take action based on age, sex, race, color, religion or national origin of an employee, former employee or applicant which affects their rights, privileges, benefits, dignity and equality of economic opportunity.	R	R to 5 days S	R to D
b. Major	If the discriminatory practice was deliberate.	R to 20 days S	20 days S to D	S
15. Fiscal irregularity	Misappropriation of city funds which came into the employee's possession by reason of their official position; falsification of payroll records for personal gain.	D		
16. Political activity	Engaging in types of political activity prohibited by these personnel policies.	R to D	R to D	R to D
17. Violation of code of ethics	Acceptance of gifts or favors influencing discharge of duties; use of position to secure special privileges or exemptions; disclosure of information adversely affecting the affairs of the city; transaction of city business where personal financial interest is involved; deliberately thwarting execution of a city ordinance, rule or official program.	R to D	D	
18. Violation of the city charter or personnel or departmental personnel policies not already covered above				
a. Minor	Violation of a policy which has little adverse affect on production, employee morale, maintenance of discipline and/or the reputation of the city.	R	R to 20 days S	R to D
b. Major	Violation of a policy which adversely affects production, employee morale, maintenance of discipline and/or the reputation of the city in a direct way.	R to D	D	

Source: City of Boulder City, Nevada, Police Department. Reprinted with permission.

[†]The first offense requires more than one garnishment before applicable.

Sample Application Form

DEPARTMENT OF ADMINISTRATION
4801 West 50th Street • Edina, Minnesota 55424-1394
(612) 927-8861   TDD(612) 927-5461

DATE RECEIVED

OFFICE USE ONLY

Employment Application

THE CITY OF EDINA WELCOMES YOU as an applicant for employment. Your application will be considered with others in competition for the position in which you are interested. It is our policy to provide equal employment opportunities to all. Individuals are evaluated and selected solely on the basis of their qualifications.

Please furnish complete and accurate information so that the City of Edina can properly evaluate your application.

Be warned that the use of false or misleading information or the omission of important facts may be grounds for immediate dismissal. Also note that information you provide herein may be subject to later verification and/or testing.

You may attach to this application any additional information that helps explain your qualifications.

Please print clearly or type.

Personal Information

Name	Last	First	Middle	Previous
Present Address	Street	City	State	Zip Code
Permanent Address	Street	City	State	Zip Code
Telephone	Residence	Business	May we call you at work? Yes	No
Are you between the ages of 16 and 70?		Yes No	If "No", state date of birth:	
Do you have a Social Security Number?		Yes No		

Work Preferences

Position for which you are applying (or type of work in which you are interested):	Are you interested in . . . Full-Time Part-Time Seasonal Paid on call Volunteer Date available for work: _____

General Information

Have you previously been employed by the City of Edina?	If "Yes," Dates	Position
Yes No		

Do you have relatives or in-laws working for the City of Edina?   If "Yes," who:

Yes   No

How did you hear about a job at the City of Edina?

Came in on my own _____   Other (Specify) _____
City employee _____   Newspaper (Specify) _____
School (Specify) _____   Employment Agency _____
(Counselor) _____   (Specify) _____

Have you ever been convicted of a crime for which a jail sentence   Have you ever been convicted of a felony?
of more than 90 days could have been imposed?

Yes   No   Yes   No

You may answer "No" to these questions if the conviction or criminal records thereof have been annulled, expunged, sealed, set aside or purged, or if you have been pardoned pursuant to law. Before any applicant is rejected on the basis of a criminal conviction, he or she will be notified in writing and will be given any rights to processing of complaints or grievances afforded by Minnesota Statute Chapter 364. If the answer to this question is "Yes," please attach a separate sheet of paper giving full particulars.

If you are not a citizen of the United States, do you have a valid work permit?   Do you have a valid Drivers License?
Yes   No   Number _____   Yes   No
        State: _____   Class: _____

Are you subject to a child support or spousal maintenance order?   If "Yes," are you subject to withholding for child
Yes   No   support or spousal maintenance?
        Yes   No

Education

School Name and Location	Attendance Dates From To (mo/yr) (mo/yr)	Graduate	Type	Degree, Diploma or Certificate and Major/Minor	Academic Standing Grade Average, eg, (3.2/4.0)
High School last attended		Yes No			
Vocational, technical school		Yes No			
College or university		Yes No			
College or university		Yes No			
Other (skilled trade training, etc.)		Yes No			

Please list academic honors, scholarships, fellowships, memberships in professional and honorary societies, and any other extracurricular activities:

Clerical Skills	What is your present speed per minute?	Typewriter	Shorthand	Speedwriting	Can you operate	Dictating equipment Yes No	Computer/terminal Yes No
	Other office equipment you can operate (including word processing, database management, spreadsheet and other software):						
	Do you have experience in a skilled trade? If so, please describe the extent/nature of experience.						

Skilled Trade Skills, Licenses, Certifications	Have you completed an apprenticeship in a skilled craft? Yes No	If yes,	What craft?		Where did you complete it?
	List all machines and equipment you have operated:				
	List all current licenses and/or certifications together with an identification of the granting authority:				
	Do you have Advanced First Aid, EMS First Responder, Crash Injury Management (CIM) or EMT certification? Yes No				

Employment History

Please give accurate, complete and part-time employment record. *Start with present or most recent employer.*

Company Name	Telephone ( )
Address	Employed (State month and year) From To
Name of Supervisor	Salary Hourly Monthly Yearly $
State job title and list your duties/responsibilities beginning with the duty that consumed the greatest proportion of your time:	Reason for leaving

Company Name	Telephone ( )
Address	Employed (State month and year) From To
Name of Supervisor	Salary Hourly Monthly Yearly $
State job title and list your duties/responsibilities beginning with the duty that consumed the greatest proportion of your time:	Reason for leaving

Company Name	Telephone ( )
Address	Employed (State month and year) From To
Name of Supervisor	Salary Hourly Monthly Yearly $
State job title and list your duties/responsibilities beginning with the duty that consumed the greatest proportion of your time:	Reason for leaving

Company Name	Telephone ( )
Address	Employed (State month and year) From To
Name of Supervisor	Salary Hourly Monthly Yearly $
State job title and list your duties/responsibilities beginning with the duty that consumed the greatest proportion of your time:	Reason for leaving

If you need additional space, please continue on a separate sheet of paper. Be certain to complete both sides of this application.

Public Safety Applicants (Please Respond)

Date and location of POST licensing exam   Date:

Skills course attended

Date of graduation from skills course

Are you currently licensed?   Yes   No   If so, License Number

If you are currently licensed, status of license?   Active   Inactive   Part-time   Other_____

Additional Experience and/or Training

Describe any additional experience or training that qualifies you for this job.

Important facts concerning information on your application

MINNESOTA LAW AFFECTS YOU AS AN APPLICANT with the City of Edina. The following data is public information and is accessible to anyone: veteran's status, relevant test scores, rank on eligibility list, job history, education and training, and work availability. All other personally identifiable information is considered private, including, but not limited to, your name, home address and phone number.

If you are selected as a finalist for a position, your name will become public information. You become a finalist if you are selected to be interviewed by the City of Edina.

The information requested on the application is necessary, either to identify you or to assist in determining your suitability for the position for which you are applying. You may legally refuse, but refusal to supply the requested information will mean that your application for employment may not be considered.

If you are selected for employment with the City of Edina, the following additional information about you will be public: your name; actual gross salary and salary range; actual gross pension; the value and nature of your fringe benefits; the basis for and the amount of any added remuneration, such as expenses or mileage reimbursement, in addition to your salary; your job title; job description; training background; previous work experience; the dates of your first and last employment with the City of Edina; the status of any complaints or charges against you while at work; the final outcome of any disciplinary action taken against you, and all supporting documentation about your case; your badge number, if any; your city and county of residence; your work location and work telephone number; honors and awards; payroll timesheets and comparable data.

Anything not listed above which is placed in your application folder or your personnel file (such as medical information, letters of recommendation, resumes, etc.) is made private information by law. For further information, refer to Minnesota Statute, Chapter 13.

I understand that any false information on or omission of information from this application (including additional information required for Public Safety Applicants, if applicable), or failure to present the required proof, will be cause for rejection or dismissal if employed.

Public Safety Applicants Only: In consideration of being permitted to apply for the position herein, I voluntarily assume all risks in connection with my participating in any tests the City of Edina deems necessary to determine my fitness and eligibility, and I release and forever discharge the City of Edina, its officers and employees from any and all claims for any damage or injury that I might sustain.

Tennessen Warning. The purpose and intended use of the information requested on the application is to assist in determining your eligibility and suitability for the position for which you are applying. You may legally refuse to give the information. If you give the information, that information, or further investigation based on it, could cause your application to be denied. If you refuse to give the information, your application for employment may not be considered. Other persons or entities authorized to receive the information you supply are: Staff of Edina Police Department, Bureau of Criminal Apprehension, Hennepin County Warrant Office, Ramsey County Warrant Office, State of Minnesota, Driver's License Section, Hennepin County Auditor, and other governmental agencies necessary to process your application.

Applicant's Signature

Date

Sample Interview Rating Sheet

CITY OF ANYWHERE, U.S.A.
Oral Interview Board
Police Officer

Candidate's Name: _____

Total Score: _____

A. Interview Questions

Instructions: Do not permit candidates to give a "yes" or "no" answer to the following questions. Ask for justification or explanation of candidates' positions.

1. You and your partner have just stopped a driver for speeding. You observe the driver hand your partner some money and drive off. When your partner returns to your police vehicle, he offers you part of the money. What action would you take?
       6   7   8   9   10   _____

2. Give three good reasons why you have become a candidate for the position of police officer.
       6   7   8   9   10   _____

3. Do you think you could use deadly force, if necessary, to make an arrest? Justify your position.
       6   7   8   9   10   _____

4. What changes do you foresee having to make in your lifestyle to become a police officer?
       6   7   8   9   10   _____

5. What is the role of the police in crime prevention?
       6   7   8   9   10   _____

6. When did you decide to become a police officer? What preparations have you made toward that goal?
       6   7   8   9   10   _____

7. Is there anything else you would like to say about yourself with regard to this position?

NOTATIONS (FOR QUESTION 7 ONLY): _____

_____

_____

TOTAL SECTION "A": _____

B. Personal Characteristics

1. Appearance: Consider the candidate's personal appearance, bearing in mind the requirements of the position. Does the candidate give a satisfactory appearance as a representative of the local government?
   (Observe: dress, neatness, posture, sitting position, facial expressions, mannerisms)

   6   7   8   9   10   _____

2. Voice and ability to use the English language: Consider the quality of the candidate's voice in relation to the subject position. Does the candidate speak clearly and distinctly? Is his/her voice pleasant or harsh? Consider the candidate's choice of words, sentences, phrases, use of slang or needless technical jargon.
   (Observe: use of simple and correct English, logical presentation, coherence of thought)

   6   7   8   9   10   _____

3. Self-Confidence: Consider self-control. Is the candidate nervous or ill at ease? Is he/she poised and relaxed? Does he/she appear to be uncertain or hesitant about his/her ideas?
   (Observe: embarrassment, stammering, tension, poise, hesitation, confidence, timidness, over confidence)

   6   7   8   9   10   _____

4. Ability to get along with people: Consider the candidate's attitude toward the examiners. Does he/she seem over-sensitive? Is there antagonism, indifference, a cooperative attitude?

   6   7   8   9   10   _____

5. Suitability for this position: Consider whether the candidate will work out on the job. Does he/she reply readily to questions asked? Are his/her ideas original? Are statements convincing and appropriate? Is there evidence of leadership? Does he/she speak out voluntarily at proper times? Does he/she have a definite interest in this work?
   (Observe: alertness, responsiveness, tact, cooperation, enthusiasm)

   6   7   8   9   10   _____

TOTAL SECTION "B": _____

GRAND TOTAL: _____

REMARKS: _____

_____

_____

_____

_____

_____

SIGNATURE OF RATER _____

Accessibility Checklist for Complying with the ADA Regulations

Parking Lots

Designated parking spaces should be located near the building, and they should not be occupied by maintenance trucks, employee cars or the cars of able-bodied guests.

If parking spaces are not close to the building, valet service should be available at curbside.

Verify that access from the parking lot to the building is free and clear. (No gravel or loose impediments.)

The approach should be flat and smooth.

If the weather is bad, is access to the building covered?

Are curbs adjacent to designated parking spaces?

Are the angles on the curbs sharp?

Watch out for open stairs. Are handrails present?

The Building

The approach to the entrance should be a hard surface at least five feet wide.

There should be space for a wheelchair lift to be lowered flat to the ground (not on curb).

Is the doorsill raised?

How heavy is the door?

If there are revolving doors, are the side doors unlocked and easy to open?

A single-door entrance to the building must be at least 32 inches wide (a standard wheelchair is exactly 32 inches wide). The ideal width for a single-door entrance is 36 inches.

A double-door entrance must be at least 48 inches wide.

Once inside, is there signage? What is the height? Is it easily visible from a wheelchair?

The Front Desk

Most front desks are uncomfortably high. If inaccessible for wheelchair users, can registration be moved to the concierge table, or to another table to the side of the front desk, or can the guest use a clipboard to complete registration forms?

The Elevator

Are the control panels low enough to be accessible by wheelchair users?

Are the floor numbers in Braille for the sight-impaired?

Elevators must be a minimum of 48 inches deep and 22 feet square to permit the wheelchair user to turn around and face the door.

The door must be at least 32 inches wide.

The Guest Room

Door handles on the outside door and all inside doors should be levers.

Once inside the room, all doors and hallways must be a minimum of 32 inches wide.

---

*By January 1993, any major construction required for public accommodations must comply with ADA standards. Both tenants and owners of facilities are responsible for insuring that areas of public accommodation and where public services are offered are accessible. This is a comprehensive checklist for use in site inspections to make sure your site meets ADA standards.

*Note: Although developed for meeting sites, this checklist can be used for any public facility, including police departments.

Source: Cindy Alwood. "Checklist: Does Your Meeting Site Obey the ADA?" *Successful Meetings*, December 1992, pp. 131–132.

Reprinted with permission from the MPI Education Research Foundation Research Center's "Americans with Disabilities Act & Meeting Planning" research subject package.

Mirrors in a guest room should not be higher than 40 inches from the floor.

In rooms with two beds, there should be a space between the beds or along the outside.

Phones, remote controls and light switches should be located next to the accessible side of the bed.

Maneuverability is important in a guest room, so check for poorly placed furniture.

If the room has a thermostat, it should be no more than 40 inches from the floor.

If the temperature controls are on the heating/cooling unit itself, make sure furniture does not block the unit.

The closet bar should be 40 inches from the floor.

The peephole in the outside door and all locks should be low enough for a person in a wheelchair.

The Bathroom

There should be a cutaway under the sink to allow wheelchair users to roll up to the sink.

There should be space to maneuver along the bathtub.

The bathtub should be equipped with grip bars, ideally with both vertical and horizontal bars low to the tub.

Check for stability of grip bars. Poorly mounted grip bars might not withstand a strong pull.

Towels should be within reach of someone in a seated position.

Toilets should not be higher than 29 inches off the floor, urinals should not be higher than 17 inches.

Lounge

Is access to the restaurant/lounge a flat surface?

Are there stairs or a ramp?

Is there adequate space between tables for a wheelchair?

Check out table heights.

Is there access to the dance floor?

Are the restrooms accessible by wheelchair?

The upper edge of the drinking fountain should be no higher than 36 inches from the floor.

Phones should feature coin slots that are no more than 54 inches off the ground.

At least one phone should have hearing amplification in the handset.

A phone equipped with TDD (telecommunications device for the deaf) should be available.

Meeting Rooms

Aisles should be a minimum of 32 inches wide.

If you are using a riser, consider its accessibility: Risers require ramps with a slope of no more than 1 inch vertical to every 12 inches horizontal.

Noisy heating/cooling systems in older facilities can make hearing difficult.

Chandelier and fluorescent lighting are hard on the eyes.

If your meeting has recreation time built into it, recreation facilities—the pool, locker rooms, sundeck—should be accessible.

Staff

Staff should be sensitive to greeting and working with persons with disabilities.

In the event of emergencies:

Is there a sprinkler system?

Are fire alarms 40 inches from the floor?

Are there flashing lights to alert deaf or hearing-impaired guests?

Is there a voice alarm for guests who are blind or sight-impaired?

The door to the bathroom should open out. If the door does open out, make sure it does not block access to the outside door.

Sample Affirmative Action Questionnaire

The following information is necessary for the city of Anywhere to evaluate its recruiting and hiring practices and to prepare reports required by law for the state and federal governments. We ask your help in filling in the blanks that apply to you. The Civil Rights Act, Title VII, makes it unlawful to discriminate in employment on the basis of race, color, religion, sex or national origin. Federal and state laws prohibit discrimination in employment on the basis of disability or age. This form will be detached from your application and the information will not be used to make any employment decisions that affect you.

_____ American Indian or Alaskan Native (All persons having origins in any of the original peoples of North America.)

_____ Black (Not of Hispanic origin): All persons having origins in any of the Black racial groups.

_____ Asian/Pacific Islander (All persons having origins in any of the original peoples of the Far East, Southeast Asia, or the Pacific Islands. This area includes, for example, China, Japan, Korea, the Phillipine and Hawaiian Islands and Samoa.)

_____ Hispanic (All persons of Mexican, Puerto Rican, Cuban, Central or South American, or other Spanish culture or origin, regardless of race.)

_____ White (Not of Hispanic origin): All persons having origins in any of the original peoples of Europe, North Africa, the Middle East, or the Indian Subcontinent.

Birthdate: _____   Age: _____ yrs.   Sex: Male _____   Female _____

Do you have a physical, mental or addictive handicapping condition which substantially limits a major life activity?

Yes _____   No _____   If yes, explain: _____

Exact title of position for which you are applying: _____

DATE: _____   NAME: _____

Redondo Beach Sworn Personnel Evaluation Form

REDONDO BEACH POLICE DEPARTMENT
PEACE OFFICER PERFORMANCE EVALUATION

_____ _____ _____ _____

NAME (LAST, FIRST, INITIAL)   JOB CLASSIFICATION   SERIAL NUMBER
ASSIGNMENT/DIVISION
EVALUATION TYPE
( ) PROBATION   ( ) SEMI-ANNUAL   ( ) OTHER (SPECIFY)
_____

EVALUATION PERIOD: FROM: _____ TO: _____
RATING INSTRUCTIONS: Rate observed behavior with reference to the scale below by
using the numeric value definitions contained in the evaluation program guidelines. Specific
comments are required for all ratings of 3 or less or 7.

DIMENSIONS RATED   _GENERAL PERFORMANCE FACTOR_   _LEVELS OF PROFICIENCY_

JOB SKILLS

01. KNOWLEDGE OF LEGAL CODES AND PROCEDURES 1 2 3 4 5 6 7
02. NEATNESS OF WORK PRODUCT, SPELLING, GRAMMAR 1 2 3 4 5 6 7
03. ORAL EXPRESSION 1 2 3 4 5 6 7
04. PLANNING AND ORGANIZING WORK 1 2 3 4 5 6 7
05. PROBLEM SOLVING/DECISION MAKING 1 2 3 4 5 6 7
06. THOROUGHNESS AND ACCURACY 1 2 3 4 5 6 7
07. WRITTEN EXPRESSION 1 2 3 4 5 6 7

PRODUCTIVITY

08. ACCEPTANCE OF RESPONSIBILITY 1 2 3 4 5 6 7
09. INITIATIVE, RESOURCEFULNESS, AND OBSERVATION SKILLS 1 2 3 4 5 6 7
10. QUANTITY OF WORK 1 2 3 4 5 6 7
11. SEEKS TRAINING TO ENHANCE ABILITIES 1 2 3 4 5 6 7

WORK CONDUCT

12. ABILITY TO FOLLOW INSTRUCTIONS 1 2 3 4 5 6 7
13. ATTENDANCE 1 2 3 4 5 6 7
14. CARE OF EQUIPMENT 1 2 3 4 5 6 7
15. DEALING WITH CO-WORKERS 1 2 3 4 5 6 7
16. DEALING WITH THE PUBLIC 1 2 3 4 5 6 7
17. OBSERVANCE OF RULES, REGULATIONS, AND PROCEDURES 1 2 3 4 5 6 7
18. OFFICER SAFETY 1 2 3 4 5 6 7

ADAPTABILITY

19. PERFORMANCE IN NEW SITUATIONS/ACCEPTANCE TO CHANGE 1 2 3 4 5 6 7
20. PERFORMANCE UNDER PRESSURE 1 2 3 4 5 6 7
21. PERFORMANCE WITH MINIMUM INSTRUCTION 1 2 3 4 5 6 7

PERSONAL TRAITS

22. APPEARANCE 1 2 3 4 5 6 7
23. ATTITUDE TOWARD POLICE WORK 1 2 3 4 5 6 7

Continued

Redondo Beach Sworn Personnel Evaluation Form (continued)

SPECIFIC JOB CLASSIFICATION FACTORS

POLICE OFFICER/AGENT

24. DRIVING SKILL 1 2 3 4 5 6 7
25. FIREARMS 1 2 3 4 5 6 7
26. INTERVIEW TECHNIQUES 1 2 3 4 5 6 7
27. INVESTIGATIVE SKILL 1 2 3 4 5 6 7
28. RADIO PROCEDURES 1 2 3 4 5 6 7

SUPERVISION/MANAGEMENT (SUPERVISORY AND MANAGEMENT PERSONNEL ONLY)

29. APPROACHABILITY 1 2 3 4 5 6 7
30. BUDGETARY MANAGEMENT 1 2 3 4 5 6 7
31. DELEGATION 1 2 3 4 5 6 7
32. DISCIPLINARY CONTROL 1 2 3 4 5 6 7
33. EVALUATING EMPLOYEES' PERFORMANCE 1 2 3 4 5 6 7
34. FAIRNESS AND IMPARTIALITY 1 2 3 4 5 6 7
35. TRAINING AND INSTRUCTION 1 2 3 4 5 6 7
36. SUPPORTIVE OF POLICY AND PROCEDURE 1 2 3 4 5 6 7

TOTAL NUMERIC RATING: _____

NUMERIC AVERAGE: _____ *PROMOTABILITY/ASSIGNMENT FACTOR
(TO SECOND DECIMAL PLACE) (NUMERIC AVERAGE × 3.58)

*PROMOTABILITY FACTOR TO BE APPLIED AS 25% OF FINAL SELECTION PROCESS
SCORE FOR PROMOTION AND 50% OF THE OVERALL SCORE FOR ASSIGNMENT
SELECTION.

RBPD Form 345 11/87

Reprinted by permission.

Redondo Beach Pre-Evaluation Form

REDONDO BEACH POLICE DEPARTMENT
PERFORMANCE PRE-EVALUATION FORM

Name _____
Date _____

You are encouraged to complete this form to provide a more meaningful exchange of information during the performance evaluation.

If you wish, you may provide a completed copy to your supervisor prior to being evaluated on your performance.

1. Describe individual accomplishments, noteworthy achievements and/or projects that you feel should be considered. Also, discuss those situations you feel required special consideration or which involved extenuating circumstances.

2. What personal/professional growth has there been during this time period?
   (a) For yourself?

   (b) For your staff? (Supervisors/Managers ONLY)

3. What additional experiences or training would you like to obtain to enhance your professional development and job proficiency?

4. Do you have any ideas or suggestions that would enable you to function more efficiently/effectively?

RBPD Form 344 5/86

Reprinted by permission.

Number in parentheses is the chapter(s) in which the term is discussed.

Abilene Paradox—begins innocently, with everyone in a group agreeing that a particular problem exists. Later, when it comes time to discuss solutions, no one expresses a viewpoint that differs from what appears to be the group's consensus, even though many secretly disagree with it. Finally, after the solution has been implemented, group members complain privately about the plan and look for someone to blame for its development. (5)

abstract words—theoretical, not concrete, for example, tall rather than 6'10". (4)

accountability—makes people responsible for tasks assigned to them. (1)

accounting—the process by which financial information about an agency is recorded, classified, summarized and interpreted and then communicated to managers and other interested parties. (14)

accounting period—the time covered by the income statement and other financial statements that report operating results. (14)

accreditation—the process by which an institution or agency proves that it meets certain standards. (16)

active listening—includes concentration, full attention and thought. (4)

activity-based costing (ABC)—a modern version of the program budgeting system, except that rather than breaking costs down by program, the approach breaks down costs by activity. (14)

acute stress—severe, intense distress that lasts a limited time and then the person returns to normal. (12)

administrative decision—middle-management level decision. (5)

administrative services—supports those performing field services. Includes recruitment and training, records and communication, planning and research, and technical services. (1)

adverse impact—when the *rate* of selection is different for special classes than for the most selected class of applicants. The rule of thumb is that an adverse impact occurs when the selection rate, or percentage passing, of any special class of persons is less than 80 percent of the selection rate of the top scoring group. (15)

affirmative action program (AAP)—a written plan to ensure fair recruitment, hiring and promotion practices. (15)

afterburn—a stressful incident that greatly affects an officer's family and leaves damaging emotional scars. (12)

agenda—a plan, usually referring to a meeting outline or program; a list of things to be accomplished. (4)

aggressive patrol—proactive patrol, focuses on preventing and detecting crime by investigating suspicious activity. Also called *proactive patrol*. (13)

all-levels budgeting—everyone affected by the budget helps prepare it. (14)

andragogy—the art and science of helping adults learn. (7)

anticipatory benefit—criminals may be deterred even before the efforts are implemented. (4)

appeal—request for a decision to be reviewed by someone higher in the command structure. (10)

arbitration—turning a decision over to an individual or panel to make the final recommendation. (11)

assessment center—places participants in the position of actually performing tasks related to the anticipated position. Incorporates situational techniques in a simulated environment under standardized conditions. (9)

assets—items of value owned by an agency. (14)

asynchronous learning—learning in which interaction between teachers and students occurs intermittently with a time delay. Opposite of *synchronous learning*. (7)

audit trail—the chain of references that makes it possible to trace information about transactions through an accounting system. (14)

authority—the power to enforce laws, exact obedience and command. (1)

autocratic leadership—managers make decisions without participant input. Completely authoritative, showing little or no concern for subordinates. (2)

background check—investigating references listed on an application as well as credit, driving record, criminal conviction, academic background and any professional license required. (15)

balance of consequences analysis—a grid used to analyze problem behavior and the consequences that follow the behavior in an attempt to understand how the consequences might be altered to change the problem behavior. (10)

balance sheet—the financial statement that shows the financial position of an agency at a specific date by summarizing the agency's assets and liabilities. (14)

balanced performer managers—develop subordinates' and an organization's capabilities. (8)

balancing—unfairly stopping unoffending motorists to protect officers from the "statistical microscope" individually or collectively. (8)

behaviorally anchored rating scales (BARS)—specific characteristics for a position are determined. Employees are then rated against these characteristics by on-the-job behaviors in each area. (16)

bifurcated society—a society in which the gap between the "haves" and the "have nots" is wide—that is, there are many poor people, many wealthy people and a shrinking middle class. (1, 3, 17)

blind self—that part of you others can see but you do not know about. (8)

block grant—awarded to states or localities based on population and crime rate. Also called a *formula grant*. (14)

blue flame—the symbol of a law enforcement officer who wants to make a difference in the world. (12)

body language—messages conveyed by gestures, facial expressions, stance and physical appearance. (4)

boiled frog phenomenon—based on a classic experiment, suggests that managers must pay attention to change in their environment and adapt—or perish. (17)

bona fide occupational qualification (BFOQ)—a requirement reasonably necessary to perform the job. It may on the surface appear to be discrimination. (15)

bottom-line philosophy—allows shifting funds from one expense category to another as long as expenses do not exceed the total amount budgeted. (14)

brainstorming—a method of shared problem solving in which members of a group spontaneously contribute ideas, no matter how wild, without any criticism or critique. (5)

broken-window phenomenon—suggests that if it appears "no one cares," disorder and crime will thrive. (3)

budget—a plan or schedule adjusting expenses during a certain period to the estimated income for that period. (14)

burnout—occurs when someone is exhausted or made listless through overwork. It results from long-term, unmediated stress. Symptoms include lack of enthusiasm and interest; a drop in job performance; temper flare-ups; a loss of will, motivation or commitment. (12)

burst stress—to go from complete calm to high activity and pressure in one "burst." (12)

by-the-numbers evaluation—makes evaluations more objective by using a numerical scale for each characteristic or dimension rated. (16)

call management—calls are prioritized based on the department's judgment about the emergency nature of the call. (3)

call reduction—*see* **call management.** (3)

call stacking—a process performed by a computer-aided dispatch system in which nonemergency, lower priority calls are ranked and held or "stacked" so the higher priorities are continually dispatched first. (3)

capital budget—deals with "big ticket" items such as major equipment purchases and vehicles. (14)

certified public accountant (CPA)—an accountant licensed by a state to do public accounting work. (14)

chain of command—the order of authority; begins at the top of the pyramid and flows down to the base. (1)

channels of communication—how messages are conveyed; usually follows the chain of command. (1, 4)

chronic stress—less severe than acute stress, but continuous. (12)

circadian system—the body's complex biological timekeeping system. (12)

Civil Rights Act of 1964—prohibits discrimination based on race, color, religion, sex or national origin by private employers with 15 or more employees, governments, unions and employment agencies. (15)

civilianization—refers to hiring citizens to perform certain tasks for law enforcement agencies. (13)

closed shop—prohibits management from hiring nonunion workers. (15)

code of silence—encourages officers not to speak up when they see another officer doing something wrong. (8)

collective bargaining—the process whereby representatives of employees meet with representatives of management to establish a written contract setting forth working conditions for a specific time, usually one to three years. (15)

common costs—costs not directly traceable to a segment of an agency such as a department or division. They might include a municipality's insurance costs. (14)

communication—the complex process through which information is transferred from one person to another through common symbols. (4)

communication barriers—obstacles to clear to achieve effective communication, including time, volume of information, tendency to say what we think others want to hear, failure to select the best word, prejudices and strained relationships, judging, superiority, certainty, controlling, manipulation and indifference. (4)

communication enhancers—techniques for reducing or eliminating barriers to communication, including properly encoding messages, selecting the best channel, describing, equality, openness, problem orientation, positive intent and empathy. (4)

communication process—involves a message, a sender, a channel and a receiver; it may also include feedback. (4)

community era—(1980–present) characterized by police authority coming from community support, law and professionalism; provision of a broad range of services, including crime control; decentralized organization with greater authority given to patrol officers; an intimate relationship with the community; and the use of foot patrol and a problem-solving approach. (1)

community policing—decentralized model of policing in which individual officers exercise their own initiatives and citizens become actively involved in making their neighborhoods safer. This proactive approach usually includes increased emphasis on foot patrol. (3)

complainant—a person or group filing a complaint. (11)

complaint—a statement of a problem. (11)

comprehensive discipline—uses both positive and negative discipline to achieve individual and organizational goals. (10)

CompStat—a strategic crime-control technique centered around four principles: (1) accurate and timely intelligence, (2) effective tactics, (3) rapid deployment of personnel and resources and (4) relentless follow-up and assessment. (5, 13)

cone of resolution—narrowing in on the geographic locations of crime. (13)

conflict—a mental or physical fight. (11)

confrontation technique—insisting that two disputing people or groups meet face-to-face to resolve their differences. (11)

consideration structure—looks at establishing the relationship between the group and the leader. (2)

consultative leadership—employees' ideas and input are welcomed, but the manager makes the final decision. (2)

content validity—the direct relationship between tasks performed on the job, the curriculum or training and the test. (7)

contingency funds—money allocated for unforeseen emergencies. (14)

contingency theory—Morse and Lorsch's motivational theory that suggests fitting tasks, officers and agency goals so that officers can feel competent. (9)

convergent thinking—focused, evaluative thinking. Includes decision making, choosing, testing, judging, and rating. Opposite of *divergent thinking*. (5)

coordination—ensuring that all members of the department perform their assigned tasks and that, together, the department's mission is accomplished. (1)

creative procrastination—delaying decisions, allowing time for minor difficulties to work themselves out. (5)

crime triangle—a model illustrating how all three elements—motivated suspect, suitable victim and adequate location—are required for crime to occur. (13)

critical incident—an extremely traumatic event such as a mass disaster or a brutally murdered child. (12)

critical incident stress debriefing (CISD)—officers who experience a critical incident such as a mass disaster or crash with multiple deaths are brought together as a group for a psychological debriefing soon after the event. (12)

critical mass—in the context of community policing efforts, the smallest number of citizens/organizations needed to support and sustain the community policing initiative. (3)

cross flow—message stating a problem and asking other units if they have encountered the same thing and, if so, what they did about it. (5)

cross tell—one department alerts other departments about a mistake revealed during inspection. (5)

crunch—a major problem. (11)

cultural awareness—understanding the diversity of the United States, the dynamics of minority–majority relationships, the dynamics of sexism and racism, and the issues of nationalism and separatism. (8)

cumulative stress—less severe than acute stresss but continues and eventually becomes debilitating. Sometimes called *chronic stress.* (12)

cutback budgeting—providing the same or more services with less funding. Also called *budget reduction* or *reduced expenditure spending.* (14)

cybernetics—suggest that organizations regulate themselves by gathering and reacting to information about their performance. (16)

daily values—how people actually spend their time and energy. (8)

data mining—an automated tool that uses advanced computational techniques to explore and characterize large data sets. (5)

decentralization—encourages flattening of the organization and places decision-making authority and autonomy at the level where information is plentiful; in police organizations, this is usually at the level of the patrol officer. (1)

decode—decipher a message. (4)

deconfliction—avoiding conflict when working with other agencies during an investigation; deployed with declassified and confidential investigations. (4)

decoupling—discrepancies between an agency's formal policies and informal practices; occurs when an organization adopts a splashy new policy but then never really implements it to change how the work gets done. (10)

delaying tactics—stalling during negotiations. (15)

delegation—assigning tasks to others. (1)

Delphi technique—a way to have individual input; uses open-ended questionnaires completed by individuals. Answers are shared, and the questionnaires are again completed until consensus is achieved. (5)

democratic leadership—does not mean every decision is made by a vote, but rather that decisions are made only after discussion with and input of employees. (2)

demographics—the characteristics of the individuals who live in a community; includes a population's size; distribution; growth; density; employment rate; ethnic makeup; and vital statistics such as average age, education and income. (3)

demotion—places an employee in a position of lower responsibility and pay. Often a part of progressive discipline. (10)

depreciation—the process of allocating the cost of a long-term asset to operations during its expected useful life. For example, squad cars will depreciate as they are used. (14)

descriptive statistics—focus on simplifying, appraising and summarizing data. (16)

direct expenses—operating expenses that can be identified specifically with individual departments. This would include such things as salaries and benefits. (14)

discipline—training expected to produce a desired behavior—controlled behavior or administering punishment. Also a state of affairs or how employees act, in contrast to morale, which is how employees feel. (10)

discretionary budget—funds available to be used as the need arises. (14)

discretionary grant—awarded based on the judgment of the awarding state or federal agency. (14)

dismissal—termination of employment. Usually the final step in progressive discipline. (10)

dispersed leadership—the twenty-first century trend to not tie leadership to rank, but rather to instill leadership qualities through the department. (2)

distress—negative stress. (12)

distributed intelligence—occurs when everyone in an organization, regardless of rank or role, proactively solves problems, makes decisions, and takes creative action as the need arises—without waiting to be told what to do. (17)

diurnal—day-oriented. Humans are by nature diurnal in their activities. (12)

divergent thinking—free, uninhibited thinking. Includes imagining, fantasizing, free associating, and combining and juxtaposing dissimilar elements. Opposite of *convergent thinking*. (5)

dog shift—late night, early morning shift, typically from midnight to 0800 hours. (13)

downward communication—messages from managers and supervisors to subordinates. (4)

driving forces—forces that foster goal achievement. (5)

eclecticism—the blending of the best teaching approaches to meet students' needs. (7)

educating—generally refers to academic instruction that takes place in a college, university or seminar-type setting and deals with knowledge and mental skills. (7)

employee assistance program (EAP)—may be internally staffed or use outside referrals to offer help with stress, marital or chemical-dependency problems. (12)

empowered—given legal authority to act on their own discretion. (1)

encode—place a message into a form to be transmitted. (4)

environmental scanning—identifying the factors that are likely to "drive" the environment, influencing the future. Includes social and economic conditions. (17)

Equal Employment Opportunity Commission (EEOC)—enforces laws prohibiting job discrimination based on race, color, religion, sex, national origin, handicapping condition or age between 40 and 70. (15)

equilibrium—the problem in force-field analysis—the equilibrium is not where you want it to be. (5)

ethical behavior—that which is "moral" and "right." (8)

ethics—standards of fair and honest conduct. (8)

eustress—helpful stress, stress necessary to function and accomplish goals. (12)

evaluate—to determine the worth of, to find the amount or value of or to appraise. (16)

exonerated—a complaint or grievance in which the investigation determines that the matter did occur, but was proper and legal. (11)

expectancy theory—Vroom's motivational theory that employees will choose the level of effort that matches the performance opportunity for reward. (9)

external complaints—statements of a problem made by a person or group outside the law enforcement organization. (11)

external motivators—*see* **tangible rewards**. (9)

face time—time spent in the agency or department long after a shift ends and on weekends when not on duty to make sure you are seen putting in extra time by those with the power to promote you. (6)

facilitators—assist others in performing their duties to meet mutual goals and objectives. (2)

Fair Labor Standards Act (FLSA) of 1938—established the 40-hour week as the basis of compensation and set a minimum wage. (15)

feedback—the process by which the sender knows the receiver has understood the message. (4)

field services—directly help accomplish the department's goals using line personnel. Main division is uniformed patrol. Also includes investigations, narcotics, vice, juvenile and the like. (1)

field training—learning that occurs on the job, usually under the direction of a field training officer (FTO). (7)

field training officer (FTO)—an experienced officer who serves as a mentor for a rookie, providing on-the-job training. (7)

financial budget—*see* **budget.** (14)

financial statements—periodic reports that summarize the financial affairs of an agency. (14)

firefighter's rule—states that a person who negligently starts a fire is not liable to a firefighter injured while responding to the fire. (7)

fiscal year—the 12-month accounting period used by an agency. A calendar year runs from January 1 through December 31. This may or may not be the same as an agency's fiscal year. (14)

5P principle—proper planning prevents poor performance. (6)

fixed costs—expenses that do not vary in total during a period even though the amount of service provided may be more or less than anticipated, for example, rent and insurance. Also called *overhead.* (14)

flat organization—one with fewer lieutenants and captains, fewer staff departments, fewer staff assistants, more sergeants and more patrol officers. (1)

flexible budget—a projection that contains budgeted amounts at various levels of service. (14)

focus groups—usually consist of people from the educational community, the religious community, neighborhood watch groups and the like. (5)

force-field analysis (FFA)—identifies forces that impede and enhance goal attainment. A problem exists when the equilibrium is such that more forces are impeding goal attainment than enhancing it. (5)

formal organization—how a group of people is structured on paper, often in the form of an organizational chart. (1)

formula grant—awarded to states or localities based on population and crime rates. Also called a *block grant.* (14)

free-rein leadership—leaderless, laissez-faire management. (2)

fusion centers—serve multiagency policing needs, providing information to patrol officers, detectives, management and others on specific criminals, criminal groups and criminal activities. (17)

futuristics—the science of using data from the past to forecast alternatives for the future and to then select those most desirable. (17)

Garrity protection—a written notification that an officer is making his or her statement or report in an internal affairs investigation involuntarily. (11)

gender barrier—differences between men and women that can result in miscommunication. (4)

general orders—formalize a department policy on a particular issue and are a central mechanism to law enforcement leadership confronting recurring and potentially problematic enforcement issues. (10)

generalists—officers who perform most functions, including patrol, investigation, juvenile and vice. (1)

generally accepted accounting principles (GAAPs)—the rules of accounting used by agencies in reporting their financial activities. (14)

geographical diffusion of benefit—properties immediately adjacent to the intervention implemented also experienced a reduction in burglary. (4)

ghosting—falsifying patrol logs to make the numbers come out right to avoid charges of racial profiling. (8)

GIGO—computer acronym for "garbage in, garbage out." (5)

goals—broad, general, desired outcomes; visionary, projected achievements. What business calls *key result areas.* (1)

grapevine—informal channel of communication within the agency or department. Also called the *rumor mill.* (4)

gratuity—a favor or gift, usually in the form of money, given in return for service, for example, a tip given to a waiter in a restaurant. (8)

grievance—a formally registered complaint. A claim by an employee that a rule or policy has been misapplied or misinterpreted to the employee's detriment. (11)

grievant—the person or group filing a grievance. (11)

groupthink—the negative tendency for members of a group to submit to peer pressure and endorse the majority opinion even if it individually is unacceptable. (5)

guiding philosophy—the organization's mission statement and the basic values to be honored by the organization. (1)

gunnysack approach—occurs when managers or supervisors accumulate negative behaviors of a subordinate and then dump them all on the employee at the same time rather than correcting them as they occurred. (10)

halo effect—tendency of a person who performs above average in one area to be rated as above average in all areas or vice versa. (15, 16)

hands-on learning—learning by doing. (7)

Hawthorne Effect—workers are positively affected by receiving attention. This affects research efforts. (9)

healthy conflict—challenges the status quo and offers constructive alternatives. (11)

heterogeneous—a community in which individuals are of different ethnicities. (3)

hidden self—that which is secret and which you do not share with others. (8)

hierarchy—a group of people organized or classified by rank and authority. In law enforcement, typically pyramid shaped with a single "authority" at the top expanding down and out through the ranks to the broad base of "workers." (1)

hierarchy of needs—Maslow's motivational theory that people have certain needs that must be met in a specific order going from basic physiological needs to safety and security, social, esteem and self-actualization needs. (9)

highlighting—using a special pen to graphically mark important written information. Should be done after the initial reading of the information. (6)

holistic management/leadership—views personnel as total individuals who make up their team. (2)

holistic personal goals—includes all aspects of a person's life: career/job, financial, personal, family/relationships and spiritual/service. (8)

homogeneous—a community in which people are all of a similar ethnicity. (3)

horizontal (lateral) communication—messages sent between managers or supervisors on the same level of the hierarchy and between subordinates on the same level. (4)

horn effect—allowing one negative trait to influence the rater negatively on other traits as well. (16)

hot spots—specific locations with high crime rates. (13)

hygiene factors—tangible rewards that can cause dissatisfaction if lacking. (9)

impact evaluation—an assessment to determine whether a problem declined. (5)

incentive programs—programs designed to motivate. (9)

incident—an isolated event that requires a police response. (3)

incident command—an organizational structure designed to aid in managing resources during incidents. (1)

incivilities—signs of disorder. (3, 13)

indirect expenses—costs that cannot be easily assigned to a particular department when transactions occur and are recorded. Some indirect expenses, such as depreciation, have a meaningful relationship to individual departments and can be allocated based on this relationship. Other indirect expenses must be allocated on the most logical basis possible. (14)

inferential statistics—focus on making statistically educated guesses from a sample of data. (16)

informal organization—groups that operate without official sanction but influence department performance. (1)

initiating structure—looks at how leaders assign tasks. (2)

in-service training—in-house training. (7)

insubordination—failure to obey a lawful and direct order from a supervisor. (10)

intangible rewards—internal motivators such as goals, achievement, recognition, self-respect, opportunity for advancement or to make a contribution and belief in individual and department goals. (9)

integrated patrol—the end goal resulting from the combination of the two elements of community policing and aggressive enforcement. (3)

integrity—steadfast adherence to an ethical code. (8)

interactors—communicate with other groups and agencies: the press, other local government departments, the business community, schools, and numerous community committees and organizations. (2)

interdependent (stage of growth)—cooperate, care for, assist and support the team effort. (8)

interfacers—coordinate law enforcement agency's goals with those of other agencies within the jurisdiction. (2)

internal complaints—statements of problems made by officers or employees within a law enforcement agency. (11)

internal motivators—*see* **intangible rewards.** (9)

interoperability—the ability of public safety emergency responders to work seamlessly with other systems or products without special efforts. (4)

intersubjectivity approach—uses 3-by-5-inch cards as a means to get people in conflict to share their most important ideas about a problem and to come to a mutual understanding of and respect for each other's viewpoints. (11)

interval reinforcement—presenting information several times, with breaks between the repetition. (7)

jargon—nonsense or meaningless language, often called legalese, for example, party of the first part, hereafter referred to as . . . . Also, specialized language of a field, for example, perpetrator. (4)

job description—detailed, formally stated summaries of duties and responsibilities for a position. (8)

job enlargement—assigning additional responsibilities to an existing job. (9)

job enrichment—similar to job enlargement, except that in job enrichment the focus is on the quality of the new jobs assigned rather than on the quantity. Emphasizes adding variety, deeper personal interest and involvement, increased responsibility and greater autonomy. Appropriate for any highly routine job. (9)

job rotation—changing the job assignment or shift. (9)

Johari window—a model to illustrate how people can learn more about others and themselves. (8)

just cause—a reasonable, fair, honest reason. (15)

key result areas—the goals of an organization. (1, 8)

killer phrases—judgmental, critical statements that serve as put-downs and stifle others' creativity. (5)

KISS principle—axiom in communication: "Keep It Short and Simple." (4)

lag time—time elapsed between the occurrence of an incident and it being reported to the police. Often more important than response time. (13)

laissez-faire leadership—involves nonintervention; lets everything run itself without direction from the leader; there is little or no control. (2)

Landrum-Griffin Act of 1959—required regularly scheduled elections of union officers by secret ballot and regulated the handling of union funds. (15)

lateral (horizontal) communication—messages sent between managers or supervisors on the same level of the hierarchy and between subordinates on the same level. (4)

leadership—influencing, working with and through individuals and groups to accomplish a common goal. (2)

learning curve principle—states that grouping similar tasks together can reduce the amount of time each takes, sometimes by as much as 80 percent. (6)

left-brain thinking—primarily using language and logic. (5)

line items—specific expense categories, for example, personnel, maintenance, training. (14)

line personnel—those who actually perform most of the tasks outlined in the work plan. (1)

line-item budgeting—identifies specific categories (line items) and dollars allocated for each. Line-item budgets are usually based on the preceding year's budget and anticipated changes in the upcoming year. (14)

lines of communication—similar to channels of communication. May be downward, upward (vertical) or lateral (horizontal) and internal or external. (4)

magnet phenomenon—occurs when a phone number or address is associated with a crime simply because it was a convenient number or address to use. (5)

majority worldview—beliefs held by those representing more than 50 percent of a group. (8)

management—the process of combining resources to accomplish organizational goals. (2)

management by objectives (MBO)—involves managers and subordinates setting goals and objectives together and then tracking performance to ensure that the objectives are met. Term first used by Peter Drucker. (2)

management information systems (MIS)—software programs that organize data to assist in decision making. (5, 13)

marginal performer—employee who has demonstrated ability to perform but who does just enough to get by. (10)

mechanistic model—divides tasks into highly specialized jobs where job holders become experts in their fields, demonstrating the "one best way" to perform their cog in the wheel (Taylorism). The opposite of the *organic model.* (2)

mediation—bringing in a neutral third party to assist in negotiations. (11)

mental locks—thinking patterns that prevent innovative thinking. Also called *thinking traps.* (5)

mentor—a trusted teacher, counselor, role model, motivator, coach, resource person, supporter, advisor, talent developer, guide, demonstrator and protector. A more experienced person who helps a less experienced person develop his or her capabilities and maximize potential. (8)

minority worldview—beliefs held by those representing fewer than 50 percent of a group. (8)

mission—the reason an organization exists. (1)

mission statement—a written explanation of why an organization exists. (1)

modified Delphi technique—uses objective rather than open-ended questions. (5)

morale—a person or group's state of mind, level of enthusiasm and involvement with work and with life. How employees feel, in contrast to discipline, how employees act. (9)

motivation—an inner or outer drive or impetus to do something or to act in a specified manner. An inner or outer drive to meet a need or goal. (9)

motivator factors—intangible rewards that can cause satisfaction. (9)

narrow eye span—occurs when a reader focuses on one word at a time rather than taking in groups of words or phrases in one look. (6)

National Labor Relations Act of 1935 (Wagner Act)—legalized collective bargaining and required employers to bargain with the elected representatives of their employees. (15)

National Labor Relations Board (NLRB)—the principal enforcement agency for laws regulating relations between management and unions. (15)

negative conflict—disagreements that are destructive. (11)

negative discipline—punishment or reprimand in an effort to compel expected behavior. (10)

negative reinforcement—rewarding a given behavior by removing something negative. (9)

negligent hiring—failure to use an adequate selection process resulting in hiring personnel unqualified or unsuited for law enforcement work. Often includes failure to check for prior offenses of misconduct. (15)

negligent retention—failing to terminate an employee when justified. (10)

news media echo effect—occurs when a highly publicized criminal case results in a shift in processing for similarly charged but nonpublicized cases. (4)

911 policing—incident-oriented (reactive) policing. (3)

nominal group technique—an objective way to achieve consensus on the most effective alternatives by using an objective ranking of alternatives. (5)

nonactor liability—when an officer is present at a scene where use of force is in question and is obviously excessive and the nonactor officer did nothing to prevent it, that officer is also held liable by the courts. (10)

nonverbal communication—messages conveyed by body language as well as tone of voice. (4)

norms—the attitudes and beliefs held by a group of individuals. (8)

Norris-LaGuardia Act of 1932—regulated court injunctions against unions and made yellow-dog contracts illegal. (15)

objectives—specific, measurable ways to accomplish goals. They are more specific than goals and usually have a timeline. (1)

one-minute managing—Blanchard's approach to giving one-minute praises and reprimands. (10)

on-the-job training (OJT)—occurs during field training, in-house training sessions and roll call. (7)

open self—what you know about yourself and what you show to others. (8)

operating budget—a budget that contains projections for income statement items as well as expenses. (14)

operating expenses—costs that arise from the normal activities of the agency. (14)

operational decision—first-line supervisor level decision. (5)

organic model—a flexible, participatory, science-based structure that will accommodate change. Designed for effectiveness in serving the needs of citizens rather than the autocratic rationality of operation. The opposite of the *mechanistic model*. (2)

organization—an artificial structure created to coordinate people or groups and resources to achieve a mission or goal. (1)

organizational chart—visually depicts how personnel are organized within the department. Might also depict how the department fits into the community's political structure. (1)

overhead—*see* **fixed costs.** (14)

paradigm—a model, theory, or frame of reference. (1)

paradigm shift—a dramatic change in how some basic structure is viewed. (1)

Pareto Principle—20 percent of what a person does accounts for 80 percent of the results. (6)

Parkinson's Law—the principle that work expands to fill the time available for its completion. (6)

participative leadership—managers build a team and view themselves as a part of this team. (2)

participatory decision making (PDM)—employees have a say in the decision-making process. (5)

passive resistance—a form of civil disobedience reflecting a philosophy of nonviolence. Often used by protestors and demonstrators. (10)

pedagogy—the science of helping children learn. (7)

perception—how one views or interprets things. (9)

performance appraisal—formal evaluation of on-the-job functioning; usually conducted annually. (16)

performance budgeting—allocates dollars based on productivity. Budget defines the agency's objectives for the year, the specific activities or programs needed to achieve those objectives and the cost. Also called *planning-programming-budgeting system* or *PPBS*. (14)

performance interviews—private, one-on-one discussions of the performance appraisal by manager and subordinate. (16)

perks—tangible rewards. (9)

perp walk—suspects paraded before the news media. (4)

petty cash fund—a cash fund of a limited amount used to make small expenditures for which it is not practical to write checks. (14)

pinch—a minor problem. (11)

Pinch Model—illustrates the importance of communication in dealing with complaints and the consequences of not communicating effectively. A pinch, a minor problem, can turn into a crunch, a major problem. (11)

political era—(1840–1930) characterized by police authority coming from politicians and the law, a broad social service function, decentralized organization, an intimate relationship with the community and extensive use of foot patrol. (1)

positive conflict—*see* **healthy conflict.** (11)

positive discipline—uses training to foster compliance with rules and regulations and performance at peak efficiency. (10)

positive reinforcement—rewards following a desired behavior that tend to increase that behavior. (9)

posteriorities—tasks that do not have to be done, have a minimal payoff and have very limited negative consequences. (6)

posttraumatic stress disorder (PTSD)—a psychological ailment following a major catastrophe such as a shooting or dealing with victims of a natural disaster. Symptoms include diminished responsiveness to the environment; disinterest; pessimism; and sleep disturbances, including recurrent nightmares. (12)

pre-evaluation—a procedure to allow those being evaluated to have input by completing a form outlining their accomplishments. (16)

prerequisites—necessary background needed to master a given skill. (7)

PRICE method—Blanchard's five-step approach to employee performance problems: Pinpoint, Record, Involve, Coach, Evaluate. (10)

principled negotiation—pays attention to basic interests and mutually satisfying options. Avoids positional bargaining that tends to produce rushed agreements that can lead to damaged relationships. (11)

priorities—tasks that must be done, have a big payoff and prevent negative consequences. (6)

proactive—involves recognizing problems and seeking the underlying cause(s) of the problems. (3)

problem-oriented policing—management ascertains what problems exist and tries to solve them, redefining the role of law enforcement from incident driven and reactive to problem oriented and proactive. (3, 5)

process evaluation—an assessment to determine whether the response was implemented as planned. (5)

procrastination—putting things off. (6)

productivity—converting resources to results in the most efficient and effective way possible. In law enforcement, productivity is achieved through people and is measured by what types of services are provided and how well. (13)

professional model—crime control as the primary function, a centralized and efficient organization, a professional remoteness from the community and an emphasis on preventive motorized patrol and rapid response to crime. (1)

program budgeting—*see* **performance budgeting.** (14)

progressive discipline—uses disciplinary steps based on the severity of the offense and how often it is repeated. Steps usually are oral reprimand, written reprimand, suspension/demotion, dismissal. (10)

promotability/assignment factors—an attempt to make evaluation "count for something." (16)

proportionate assignment—area assignments are determined by requests for services, based on available data. (13)

psychological hardiness—the ability to successfully cope with stress. (12)

Pygmalian Effect—what managers and supervisors expect of their officers and how they treat them largely determine their performance and career progress. (9)

pyramid of authority—the shape of the typical law enforcement hierarchy, with the chief at the peak and having full authority, down through managers (captains and lieutenants) and supervisors (sergeants), to those who accomplish most of the tasks (officers). (1)

Q & A—question and answer method of teaching. (8)

qualitative data—examines the excellence (quality) of the response—that is, how satisfied were the officers and the citizens. This is most frequently determined by surveys, focus groups or tracking of complaints and compliments. (5)

quantitative data—examines the amount of change (quantity) as a result of the response. This is most frequently measured by pre/post data. (5)

quota—a specific number or proportional share that each officer is expected to contribute or receive. (13)

racial profiling—any police-initiated action that relies on the race, ethnicity or national origin rather than the behavior of an individual or information that leads the police to a particular individual who has been identified as being or having been engaged in criminal activity. (8)

random patrol—officers on patrol are unsystematically (randomly) assigned areas to cover. (13)

reactive—simply responding to calls for service. (3)

reform era—(1930–1980) characterized by police authority coming from the law and professionalism, crime control as the primary function, a centralized and efficient organization, a professional remoteness from the community and an emphasis on preventive motorized patrol and rapid response to crime. (1)

reframing—a conflict resolution skill; a psycholinguistic technique that shifts a person's perspective to recast conflict as a positive, rather than a negative, force. (11)

regression—tendency to look back over previously read material. (6)

reinforcement theory—B. F. Skinner's motivational theory that behavior can be modified by using positive and negative reinforcement. (9)

reprimand—formal criticism of behavior. May be oral or written. (10)

responsibility—answerable, liable, accountable for. (1)

restraining forces—forces that impede goal achievement. (5)

reverse discrimination—giving preferential treatment to women and minorities, to the detriment of white males, in hiring and promoting. (15)

rhetorical questions—those to which answers are not expected. The purpose is to get the listener thinking about a topic. (7)

right-brain thinking—primarily using images and emotions. (5)

right-to-work laws—make it illegal to require employees to join a union. Established by the Taft-Hartley Act of 1938. (15)

roll call—brief period before each shift when officers check in and receive their briefing prior to going on duty. (7)

rote learning—memorization, not necessarily with understanding. (7)

rumor mill—informal channels of communication within a department or agency. Also called the *grapevine*. (4)

scanning—reading material rapidly for specific information. (6)

scuttlebutt—one employee complaining to another, uninvolved employee who cannot remedy the situation about an adverse action taken by upper management. (1)

seagull management—manager hears something's wrong, flies in, makes a lot of noise, craps on everybody and flies away. (2)

self-actualization—refers to achievement, to meeting individual goals and fulfilling one's potential. It is fostered by the chance to be creative and innovative and by being given the opportunity to maximize skills and knowledge. (9)

self-discipline—self-imposed rules for self-control. (10)

self-fulfilling prophecy—the theory that people live up to expectations. If people believe they can do a job, they usually can. If people believe they cannot do a job, they usually cannot. (9)

self-motivation—acting in an expected way from personal choice. (9)

semi-variable costs—expenses that have characteristics of both fixed costs and variable costs. For example, utility expenses. (14)

sexual harassment—unwelcome sexual advances, requests for sexual favors, and other verbal or physical conduct of a sexual nature. A type of sex discrimination prohibited by Title VII in federal law, as well as by most state laws. Types include *quid pro quo harassment, hostile-environment harassment* and "indirect" or "third party" sexual harassment. (10)

shift—time span to which personnel are assigned. Most agencies have three 8-hour shifts. Some agencies call this time span a *watch*. (13)

simulation—imitation of a process. (7)

single handling—not picking up a piece of paper until you are ready to do something with it. Applies particularly to the daily stack of mail. (6)

situational leadership—leadership viewed as an interplay between the amount of direction (task behavior) a leader gives, combined with the amount of relationship behavior a leader provides and the maturity level that followers exhibit on a specific task the leader is attempting to accomplish through the individual or group (Hersey and Blanchard). (2)

skimming—reading information rapidly for the main ideas, usually the first and last paragraph, the first sentence of all other paragraphs and the captions of any charts or figures. (6)

SMART goals and objectives—objectives that are specific, measurable, attainable, relevant and trackable. (2)

social capital—a concept to describe the level or degree of social structure within a community and the extent to which individuals within the community feel bonded to each other. Exists at two levels (local and public), and can be measured in terms of *trustworthiness*, or citizens' trust of each other and their public institutions, and *obligations*, or the expectation that service to each other will be reciprocated. (3)

sound bite—good information stated briefly. Two essential elements are (1) that it contain good, solid nuggets of information, not speculation or opinion, and (2) that it is short. (4)

span of control—how many people one individual manages or supervises. (1)

special employment groups—groups included in affirmative action programs such as African Americans, Asians,

Eskimos, Hispanics, homosexuals, immigrants, individuals with AIDS, individuals with disabilities, Middle Easterners, Native Americans, religious group members, substance abusers, Vietnam veterans, whites (reverse discrimination), women and young and aging individuals. (15)

specialists—those who work in a specific area: investigators, juvenile officers, SWAT officers and the like. (1)

split-second syndrome—a condition that affects police decision making in crisis. Asserts that if a person has intentionally or unintentionally provoked or threatened a police officer, at that instant the provoker rather than the police should be viewed as the cause of any resulting injuries or damages. (12)

spoils system—motto, "To the victor go the spoils," resulted in political interference with policing. (1)

staff personnel—those who support line personnel. (1)

stakeholders—those affected by an organization and those in a position to affect it. (1)

standard English—language that follows the grammatical rules of American English. (4)

standards—targets to be met, including level of performance. (16)

strategic decision—executive-level decision involving long-range plans. (5)

strategic planning—long-term planning. (2)

stress—tension, anxiety or worry. Can be positive, eustress, or negative, distress. (12)

stroke approach—using positive strokes rather than negative, crooked or plastic strokes. (10)

subconscious self—that part of you neither you nor others have yet discovered. Also called *undiscovered self*. (8)

subvocalization—the contraction of the tongue and other speech-related organs made during learning to pronounce each letter of the alphabet. Becomes ingrained and can slow down adult readers. (6)

summary discipline—discretionary authority used when a supervisor feels an officer is not fit for duty or for any reason the supervisor feels a need for immediate action. Also called *summary punishment*. (10)

summary punishment—*see* **summary discipline**. (10)

sunk costs—historical costs that have already been incurred and are thus irrelevant for decision-making purposes. For example, the purchase of a K-9. Other costs associated with the dog, however, will continue. (14)

supernorms—overriding expectations of a given work group, for example, *do not volunteer* or *do not criticize*. (8)

supervision—overseeing the actual work being done. (2)

suspension—being barred from a position for a period of time. May be with or without pay. Often part of progressive discipline. (10)

sustained—complaint or grievance in which the investigative facts support the charge. (11)

synchronous learning—real-time, instructor-led online learning in which all participants are logged on at the same time and communicate directly with each other. Opposite of *asynchronous learning*. (7)

synergism—occurs when the whole is greater than the sum of its parts; the team achieves more than each could accomplish as individuals. (2)

synergy—where the whole is greater than the sum of its parts. (8)

tactical planning—short-term planning. (2)

Taft-Hartley Act of 1947—balanced the power of unions and management by prohibiting several unfair labor practices, including closed shops, which prohibited management from hiring nonunion workers. (15)

tangible rewards—external motivators such as salary, bonuses, insurance, retirement plans, favorable working conditions, paid vacation and holidays, titles and adequacy of equipment. (9)

termination—being fired from employment. Usually the final step in progressive discipline. (10)

thinking traps—habits people fall into without recognizing what they are doing, including either/or thinking, deciding too quickly, deciding based on personality rather than facts, being a victim of personal habits and prejudices and being unimaginative. Also called *mental locks*. (5)

tickler file system—a set of file folders, organized by year, month and day, into which lists of tasks to be accomplished are placed. (6)

time abusers—activities or tasks that waste time, for example, socializing, drop-in visitors and telephone tag. (6)

time log—a detailed list of how time is spent each day, usually broken into 10- to 15-minute segments. (6)

time management—dividing and organizing time to accomplish the most tasks in the most efficient way. (6)

tone—emotional effect of language, for example, an angry tone of voice. (4)

total quality management (TQM)—Deming's theory that managers should create constancy of purpose for improvement of product and service, adopt the new philosophy, improve constantly, institute modern methods of training on the job, institute modern methods of supervision, drive fear from the workplace, break down barriers between staff areas, eliminate numerical goals for the work force, remove barriers that rob people of pride of workmanship and institute a vigorous program of education and training. (2)

touchstone values—what people say is important to them. (8)

training—generally refers to vocational instruction that takes place on the job and deals with physical skills. (7)

trait theorists—those who research special characteristics that leaders possess. (2)

transformational leadership—treats employees as the organization's most valuable assets. Is employee centered and focuses on empowerment. (2)

traumatic stress—severe, extremely intense distress that lasts a limited time, and then the person returns to normal. Sometimes called *acute stress.* (12)

two-factor theory—Herzberg's motivational theory that employees' needs can be classified as hygiene factors and motivator factors. Hygiene factors are tangible rewards that cause dissatisfaction if lacking; motivator factors are intangible rewards that can cause satisfaction. (9)

type A personality—describes people who are aggressive, hyperactive "drivers" who tend to be workaholics. (12)

type B personality—describes people who are more laid back, relaxed and passive. (12)

unconditional backup—dictates that other officers must take action, get involved and back each other up ethically. (8)

undiscovered self—that part of you neither you nor others have yet discovered. Also called *subconscious self.* (8)

unfounded—complaint or grievance in which the act did not occur or the complaint/grievance was false. (11)

unified command—allows agencies with different legal, geographic, and functional authorities and responsibilities to work together effectively without affecting individual agency authority, responsibility or accountability. (1)

union—any group authorized to represent the members of an agency in negotiating such matters as wages, fringe benefits and other conditions of employment. (15)

union shop—must belong to or join the union to be hired. (15)

unity of command—means that every individual in the organization has only one immediate superior or supervisor. (1)

upward (vertical) communication—messages conveyed from subordinates to supervisors and managers or from supervisors to managers. (4)

valid—appraisals that are well grounded and sound in which the factors rated are job related and the raters are trained. (16)

values—the beliefs, principles or standards considered worthwhile or desirable. (1)

variable costs—expenses that vary in total directly with the amount of service provided. For example, personnel costs including overtime. (14)

variance analysis—comparing actual costs against what was budgeted and examining the differences. (14)

vertical (upward) communication—messages conveyed from subordinates to supervisors and managers or from supervisors to managers. (4)

vicarious liability—the legal responsibility one person has for the acts of another. Managers, the entire agency and even the jurisdiction served may be legally responsible for the actions of a single officer. (15)

videoconferencing—simultaneous, interactive audio and video communication. (7)

Wallenda Effect—the negative consequences of fear of failure. (2)

watch—*see* **shift.** (13)

whole-brain thinking—using both the logical left side and the emotional right side of the brain together for best results. (5)

work plans—the precise activities that contribute to accomplishing objectives. Detailed steps or tasks to be accomplished. (1)

working in "silos"—when local government agencies and departments work quite independently of each other. This lack of partnering with other city and county agencies hinders problem-solving success. (3)

workplace culture—the sum of the beliefs and values held in common by those within the organization that formally and informally communicate what is expected. (8)

yellow-dog contract—makes union membership illegal under the penalty of discharge. (15)

zero-based budgeting (ZBB)—begins with a clean slate, justifying each expenditure anew. All budget lines begin at zero base and are funded according to merit rather than the preceding year's funding level. (14)

zipper clause—clearly states that the contract is a complete, full agreement between the two parties and neither party is obligated to negotiate on other items during the term of the contract. (15)

Weber, Max, 10
whole-brain research, 135–136
whole-brain thinking, 136
Wickersham, George, 6
Wickersham Commission, 6
Wilson, O. W., 6–7, 68
win-lose situations, 345
win-win situations, 345
withholding information, 127–128
women officers
    affirmative action, 464
    language use, 110, 111
    quotas, 409, 482
    recruiting, 450
    stress and, 363
work plans, 13
working conditions, 267
working in "silos," 81
workplace culture
    changing, 226–227
    description, 223–224
    violence and, 513

workshop training, 212–213
worldviews, 237
written communication channels, 105–106
written examinations, 280–281, 452–453

X
XML. *See* eXtensible Markup Language (XML)

Y
yellow-dog contract, 465

Z
ZBB. *See* zero-based budgeting (ZBB)
zero-based budgeting (ZBB), 426
Ziglar, Zig, 179
zipper clause, 468